Career Counseling

A Holistic Approach

9th EDITION

Career Counseling

A Holistic Approach

Vernon G. Zunker

Southwest Texas State University (retired)

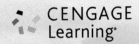
CENGAGE
Learning®

Australia • Brazil • Mexico • Singapore • United Kingdom • United States

CENGAGE
Learning®

Career Counseling: A Holistic Approach, 9th Edition
Vernon G. Zunker

Product Director: Jon-David Hague

Product Manager: Julie Martinez

Content Developer: Sean Cronin

Product Assistant: Nicole Richards

Media Developer: Sean Cronin

Marketing Manager: Shanna Shelton

Content Project Manager: Rita Jaramillo

Art Director: Vernon Boes

Manufacturing Planner: Judy Inouye

Production Service: Lynn Lustberg, MPS Limited

Text Researcher: Kavitha Balasundaram

Copy Editor: Martha Williams and Carolyn Acheson

Text/Cover Designer: Diane Beasley

Cover Image: Joseph C. Justice Jr./Getty Images

Compositor: MPS Limited

Library of Congress Control Number: 2014939785

Student Edition:
ISBN-13: 978-1-305-08728-6

Loose-leaf Edition:
ISBN-10: 978-1-305-40106-8

Cengage Learning
20 Channel Center Street
Boston, MA 02210
USA

Cengage Learning is a leading provider of customized learning solutions with office locations around the globe, including Singapore, the United Kingdom, Australia, Mexico, Brazil, and Japan. Locate your local office at: **www.cengage.com/global**

Cengage Learning products are represented in Canada by Nelson Education, Ltd.

To learn more about Cengage Learning Solutions, visit **www.cengage.com** Purchase any of our products at your local college store or at our preferred online store **www.cengagebrain.com**

Printed at Quad/Graphics, USA, 09-17

To my wife ROSALIE

Brief Contents

Detailed Contents

Chapter 3   Career Counseling Models 77

Chapter 6 Using Standardized Test and Self-Assessment Procedures in Career Counseling 161

PART TWO
Career Counseling for Special Populations 221

Chapter 9   Career Counseling for Multicultural Groups 222

PART THREE

Career Transitions and Adult Career Development Concerns 297

Chapter 13 Job Loss and Transitions 298

PART FOUR

Career Counseling in Educational Settings 345

Chapter 16 Career-Related Programs for Career Development in Middle School 369

Chapter 17 Career-Related Programs for Career Development in High School and Beyond 386

Preface

More than 33 years ago I wrote the first edition of this book. It was a rather small book, but within its red cover career counseling was highlighted as a viable counseling program for a diverse society. I have continued to support that premise! Much of what was emphasized in the first edition has been updated and continues to be a vital part of current career counseling programs. It soon became obvious, however, that what I had written was actually a work in progress. Over time my readers requested more information about the significance of changes in the nature of work. How to help clients choose a career among the many careers that were available only a few years ago was of the utmost importance to most counselors who read the early editions of this book.

The current major changes in the job market, however, have created new and different problems for clients who are in the process of choosing a career. Millions of Americans have lost their jobs in the last decade and currently are among the unemployed and underemployed. Many others have one or two part-time jobs. A significant number of college graduates are having difficulty finding a job in a career for which they have been trained. Thus, it is not unusual for some clients to ask what has happened to the good jobs, "How can I be sure that I will find a job if I chose this major?" These examples of client concerns support current needs of clients that are addressed in this edition.

In addition, career, work, and mental health have been, and continue to be, viable concerns that should be addressed in current career counseling programs. Recent research in neuroscience, genetics, and cognitive psychology has significantly influenced how one is to view human development. The biopsychosocial model of behavior highlighted in the previous edition has been endorsed by an increasing number of professionals in the social sciences and in abnormal and developmental psychology. Behavior in this context is driven by combinations of factors that interact, and in the process there is mutual giving and receiving. Sue and colleagues (2014) have labeled this process as a *multipath model*.

External and internal factors that can influence an individual's career development are currently a major part of the career counseling process. Career counselors, for example, focus on individual traits such as personality, interests, and values, as well as mental health issues. Career and personal concerns that interact and influence each other are relevant in determining individualized valid interventions in current career counseling approaches. In this 9th edition I continue to emphasize that career counseling is most viable in a society that has ever-changing needs and is becoming more diverse.

Each of the eight preceding editions of this book attempted to capture trends in the practice of career development. Over time, career development and counseling continue to evolve in an ever-changing society that includes the influence of globalization. Current social, economic trends and other factors have impacted the workforce and workplace. The challenges surrounding globalization have significantly affected the American worker, especially those involved in the manufacturing sector. The low cost of labor in other countries has prompted many corporations to outsource jobs to stay competitive. I address these concerns in several chapters in this text when discussing the challenges associated with globalization. I also address the loss of jobs experienced by millions of Americans during the federally declared economic recession in 2009 and its fallout. I focus on workers who continue to search for the kind of work for which they have been trained. This 9th edition clearly and overwhelmingly supports the position that counselors are to address both career and personal concerns in the career counseling process.

New to the Ninth Edition

In this 9th edition I have given added support to research results from positive psychology. Clearly, there needs to be a more balanced approach to addressing the needs of clients. More important, however, counselors are to recognize the value of supporting and enhancing each client's assets and strengths. Career counselors are to direct more attention to the concept of resiliency. In several chapters in this 9th edition, I focus on helping each client to become more resilient. Counselors are to embrace their clients' focus on positive assets when making career choices, as well as when they face adversity. Some additions and changes in each of the 17 chapters are summarized next.

In chapter 1, the basic issue of globalization and economic restructuring now includes more information about how low wages in other countries have led to job loss for millions of Americans. By 2010, for instance, 3 million jobs were outsourced to other countries. In chapters 2 and 3, the connection between career development theories and counseling models is highlighted in this edition. The career development theories in chapter 2 now be can be matched with the career counseling models in chapter 3 by a number assigned to each career counseling model. The reader is provided with the matching career counseling model number within the discussion of some of the career counseling theories.

In chapter 4, a Multipath Model takes the position that abnormal behavior includes biological, psychological, social, and sociocultural elements. This position supports the premise of the biopsychosocial model also discussed in this chapter. Chapter 5 has added a summary of factors promoting feelings of well-being in the workplace. The focus of well-being in this chapter supports a client's strengths and assets. Some of the standardized tests in chapter 6 have been updated in this edition.

The title for chapter 7 has been changed to "The Impact of New Technology on Work, Career Development, and Learning Platforms." This chapter has been restructured and now includes examples of new technology that is changing the workplace, how we live, and how technology-driven instruction can enhance career development. New examples of websites that offer career information are identified. Ethical concerns about computer-based assessments interpretations are discussed. Several questions that counselors can use to determine the validity of computer-based assessments interpretations also are provided. Chapter 8 adds a new case study entitled "The Witnessing of a Breach of Ethics". Also added in this chapter is a model for ethical decision making. To illustrate differences between cultures, in chapter 9 I present how the processes involved in negotiations differ in some nations. These differences are to be recognized as a result of the socialization process in one's culture. This message, as well as others in this chapter, should suggest that counselors be sensitive to cultural differences.

Chapter 10 adds a disussion of gender inequality in the workplace. Included are income differences between men and women, lack of promotion for women, explanations of income differences, workplace and family needs, and home-based work through new technology. Increased support of gay and lesbian rights is discussed in chapter 11. Gay and lesbians now can serve openly in the armed forces, for example. Other issues discussed are harassment of LGBT individuals, same-sex marriages, and workplace concerns.

In chapter 12, the ADA Amendment Act of 2008 has been added and reviewed. Featured is the expanded definition of disability, which allows more individuals to qualify for services. Chapter 13 has been restructured, and its title has been changed to "Job Loss and Transitions." Major changes include an explanation of the connection between globalization and job loss, causes of unemployment and underemployment, an example of outplacement counseling in organizations, job opening changes between 2008 and 2018, and social networking. The title for chapter 14 also has been changed to Career Development and Transitions of Working Adults. The focus of this chapter is on how globalization has affected career development, and a new case study entitled "A Stay at Home Mom Returns to the Workplace" has been added.

In chapter 15, the characteristics of effective schools has been added. In addition, the concept of resiliency is discussed and reinforced with a table presenting the protective factors of resilience. Also added is information on at-risk children. Chapter 16 emphasizes the importance of students' developing personal strengths and assets in middle school, supported with a recently developed model of becoming resilient. Chapter 17 has added case study entitled "A High School Student's Father Loses His Job." This case study challenges the reader to justify interventions that strengthen resilience. All chapters include updated refrence citations.

Organization of Content

Career Counseling is divided into four parts. Part One, "Foundations and Resources," covers historical developments, basic issues, career development theories, career counseling models, integrating career and personal concerns, intake interviews, use of assessment results, career information resources, technologically driven training programs, and ethical standards. Chapter 1 provides a perspective of career counseling's historical development and some basic issues of the 21st century. Chapter 2 is devoted to career development theories and their practical application. Chapter 3 covers five career counseling models using case illustrations. A holistic counseling approach is discussed in Chapter 4. Chapter 5 covers the intake interview with case examples. Chapter 6 addresses the use of standardized and nonstandardized test results. Chapter 7 focuses on interactive and information-oriented computer programs designed to enhance the career counseling process, including the appropriate use of Internet resources, and technological platforms for training. Chapter 8 introduces ethical boundaries and examples of violations.

Part Two, "Career Counseling for Special Populations," includes a discussion of innovative counseling models and career counseling programs for special populations. Chapter 9 focuses on multicultural groups to emphasize how counselors can apply culturally appropriate techniques and procedures. Gender and dual career issues and solutions are discussed in Chapter 10. Chapter 11 covers the issues and needs of sexual minority clients. Chapter 12 points out the unique needs of persons with disabilities and presents a variety of resources for helping individuals with various disabilities.

Part Three, "Adult Transitions and Career Development," addresses transitions in the workplace and changes in work requirements and workplace environments, as well as transitions in career development over the life span. Chapter 13 is devoted primarily to adult concerns associated with job loss and/or the threat of job loss. Interventions are designed to assist clients who have experienced job loss. Chapter 14 includes a discussion of issues associated with early, middle, and late career. The discussion of life roles is designed to create an awareness of the benefits associated with a balanced life style. In the final part of this chapter, a case study illustrates how life-course events can influence career development.

Part Four, "Career Counseling in Educational Settings," includes three chapters that identify issues and needs of elementary school, middle school, and high school students, as well as recently formulated career development programs, goals, and competencies. Chapter 15 suggests that support for career-related programs from teachers, administrators, and parents is essential in all schools, and especially for elementary school students. Counselors are to be aware of cognitive development of elementary school students, including information processing strategies and learning by observation. Family support and the use of community resources is a high priority for career-related programs in all educational institutions. In addition, all schools—elementary, middle, and high school—are provided with career development goals and competencies by the American School Counselors Association and the National Career Development Guidelines.

Chapter 16 identifies potential problems for middle school students including the impact of puberty, peer relationships, and identity issues. The development of information-processing skills during adolescence is highlighted. Using assessment results for career development is also described.

Chapter 17 covers career development in high school and beyond. This chapter discusses enhanced conceptual skills of high school students and the use of memory strategies they have developed over time. Programs are to be available to assist students who will seek employment following high school, as well as readiness programs for an increasing number of high school graduates who will continue their education. Included in this chapter are descriptions of special programs for low-income students who plan to attend college, tech-prep programs, career and technology education, and partnerships between high schools and community colleges that enhance students' ability to continue their education. Examples of career counseling programs in universities and colleges also are reviewed briefly.

MindTap

MindTap for Career Counseling engages and empowers students to produce their best work—consistently. By seamlessly integrating course material with videos, activities, apps, and much more, MindTap creates a unique learning path that fosters increased comprehension and efficiency.

For students:

- MindTap delivers real-world relevance with activities and assignments that help students build critical thinking and analytic skills that will transfer to other courses and their professional lives.
- MindTap helps students stay organized and efficient with a single destination that reflects what's important to the instructor, along with the tools students need to master the content.

- MindTap empowers and motivates students with information that shows where they stand at all times—both individually and compared to the highest performers in class.

Additionally, for instructors, MindTap allows you to:

- Control what content students see and when they see it with a learning path that can be used as-is or matched to your syllabus exactly.
- Create a unique learning path of relevant readings and multimedia and activities that move students up the learning taxonomy from basic knowledge and comprehension to analysis, application, and critical thinking.
- Integrate your own content into the MindTap Reader using your own documents or pulling from sources like RSS feeds, YouTube videos, websites, GoogleDocs, and more.
- Use powerful analytics and reports that provide a snapshot of class progress, time in course, engagement, and completion.

In addition to the benefits of the platform, MindTap for Counseling offers:

- Video clips tied to the learning outcomes and content of specific chapters.
- Activities to introduce and engage students with each chapter's key concepts.
- Interactive exercises and in-platform discussion questions to provide direct, hands-on experiences for students of various learning styles.
- Review and reflection activities to demonstrate growth and a mastering of skills as students progress through the course.

Supplements

A companion text, *Using Assessment Results in Career Development*, 9th Edition (Osborn & Zunker, 2015), has been developed as a supplement to this book. This ancillary text illustrates how assessment results can be used to increase self-awareness and rational choices. Readers will find that *Using Assessment Results* provides detailed information about applying knowledge of tests and measurements in counseling encounters and using assessment results in a wide variety of counseling situations. Also available is a website with additional study materials that includes learning activities to help students build an understanding of career development theories and quiz questions to help students assess knowledge and enrich their learning experience. Finally, a suite of instructor course preparation materials is available online including an electric test bank and an online instructor's manual.

Acknowledgements

I am most appreciative to the reviewers of this edition who have made this book a better one through their insightful suggestions. My thanks and appreciation to each and every one in alphabetical order by last name, as follows:

Mary Anderson   Western Michigan University
Walter Chung   Eastern University

Joelle France	Colorado Christian University
Gregory S. Garske	Bowling Green State
Thomas J. Hernandez	The College of Brockport
Tammy Jorgensen-Smith	University of South Florida
Robert Michael Orndorff	Penn State University Park
Charlotte Rinaldi	California Polytechnic State University
Michael Roadhouse	University of the Cumberlands
Alaric A. Williams	Angelo State University

I also want to thank Amelia Blevins for the detailed survey she conducted of both potential and previous users of past editions of this textbook. The information she compiled identified significant content for including in this edition. I appreciate the contributions of Sean Cronin, who was instrumental in developing the cover for the 9th edition and for preparing this edition for production. As usual, Rita Jaramillo was always available for advice as content project manager. Finally, I am grateful for the relevant information obtained from the Internet by Jonathan Reyes.

When this edition was ready for production, I requested that Lynn Lustberg of MPS Limited be coordinator of the production process. She is a superb leader, well organized and very capable! I also was pleased when Martha Williams once again was chosen as the copy editor. However, we were all saddened and shocked when she became seriously ill and passed away. Martha Williams was not only a skilled editor and an accomplished musician but also a wife, mother, and wonderful person who will be greatly missed by all those who knew her. Finally, I also want to recognize the thorough and excellent work of another talented copy editor, Carolyn Acheson. She was able to keep the editing process on schedule with her dedication and perseverance.

Dedication

The nine editions of this book would not have been written without the encouragement and support of my wife and best friend Rosalie. Her clever wit, keen perception, and great sense of humor have been most inspirational and enjoyable. All my accomplishments are hers as well and we continue on this exciting journey.

PART ONE
Foundations and Resources

1

Historical Development and Some Basic Issues

This book is about career counseling in an ever-changing world. Professional counselors assist individuals with career and personal concerns. This specialized content includes initial career choice, the connection between career and personal problems, adaptations to changes in the workplace, multiple career dilemmas, unemployment, and maintenance of a balanced lifestyle. The career counseling process does not separate career and personal concerns but integrates them to evaluate better how all life roles are interrelated. Understanding the whole person as a member of complex social systems is the cornerstone of effective career counseling. Counselors are to recognize the relationship between career issues and all other life roles and assist people and systems to discover healthier ways of living.

I begin with a chronology of the birth and growth of "career guidance." The term "career guidance" is used in a historical context to represent all components of services and activities in educational institutions, agencies, and other career-related educational programs. This book, however, includes both the career counseling role and components of career services but is primarily devoted to developing counseling skills for integrating career and personal concerns. One of the major purposes of the historical perspective in this opening chapter is to illustrate how the birth and growth of career counseling was influenced by a number of factors, including sociocultural changes, the Industrial Revolution, world wars, federal programs, advanced technology, and advances in the study of human development. The second section of this chapter is devoted to some basic issues in career counseling that provide a means of discovering some significant challenges that currently face the counseling profession. Using the historical development section as a backdrop, basic issues introduce some current and future challenges of a growing and ever-expanding career counseling movement. You will discover that counselors are very flexible and continually modify programs, methods, and procedures for solution-focused strength-based counseling approaches.

Historical Development

The career counseling movement is a product of our development as a nation. It is the story of human progress in a nation founded on the principle of human rights. Career counseling touches all aspects of human life for it has involved political, economic, educational, philosophical, and social progress and change. To think of the career counseling movement as merely another educational event is a gross misinterpretation of its broader significance for social progress. In fact, this movement has had and will have a tremendous impact on the working lives of many individuals. Understanding the historical perspectives of this movement will provide greater insight into the development of the career counselor's role in the 21st century.

Six Stages of Development from 1890

Pope (2000) has suggested that the development of career counseling in the United States has evolved in six stages starting in 1890 to the present time. These stages have been paraphrased as follows:

- Stage one (1890–1919) began the growth of placement services in urban areas to meet the needs of growing industrial organizations.
- Stage two (1920–1939) marked the growth of educational guidance in elementary and secondary schools.
- Stage three (1940–1959) was a time of significant growth of guidance needs in colleges and universities and in the training of counselors.
- Stage four (1960–1979) was highlighted by organizational career development. The nature of work became more appropriately viewed as a very pervasive life role.
- Stage five (1980–1989) was a period of significant transitions brought on by information technology and the beginning of career counseling private practice and outplacement services.
- Stage six (1990–present) is viewed as a time of changing demographics, the beginning of multicultural counseling, continued development of technology, and a focus on school-to-work transitions.

The historical stages by Pope (2000) represent significant developmental periods of career counseling that include vast changes in our society and especially in the work role of many Americans. Career counseling was created to meet the needs of a society during the shift from rural to urban living in the industrial age and has expanded its focus during other transitional periods of changes in how and where we work and live. Intertwined in this movement are significant databases of information that have enlightened our knowledge of human behavior and development, social issues, political events, and studies of career development and life roles. The growth of career counseling therefore has been influenced by a number of variables, factors, global issues, and events in a changing society.

Future stages of career counseling will more than likely be impacted by the September 11, 2001, terrorists' attack on the United States and years of military action and peacekeeping duties in Afghanistan and other nations. Thousands of men and women who were reserves in the armed forces had to leave their jobs when called to active duty. Thus their career development had to be put on hold for an extensive period of time. Their eventual return to the workforce may require counseling interventions that integrate career and personal concerns. A most significant related issue is the federally declared recession in 2009 that has led to job loss for a significant number of American workers as well as workers in many other countries. Job loss concerns and threats of job loss are discussed in several chapters including chapter 2.

In the next paragraphs I will briefly discuss some historical events while highlighting their influence on the career counseling movement. An inclusive chronology of the career counseling movement from the 1800s to current times can be found in appendix A. I begin our brief discussion of historical events with the rise of the industrial movement.

The Rise of Industrialism

The rise of industrialism in the 1800s dramatically changed work environments and living conditions. Urban areas expanded at tremendous rates largely through immigration. This rapid growth and centralization of industry attracted many workers from rural areas as well. It did not take long, however, for many to become disillusioned by harsh, crowded living conditions in tenement houses and impersonal industrial systems. Soon there developed a spirit of reform that included scientific studies of human behavior and abilities that could be used to address problems of living in the chaotic conditions of urban life and in work environments that were much less than desirable. The case for the individual had been carefully formulated. Within this context a leader emerged who would later be referred as the "father" of the career counseling movement—his name was Frank Parsons.

Frank Parsons's Early Contributions

The social reform movements and civic development of the late 1800s captured the interests of young Frank Parsons who had been educated as an engineer at Cornell University. He wrote several books on social reform movements and articles on such topics as women's suffrage, taxation, and education for all. He taught at public schools, passed the bar for a law license, and taught at Boston University law school and at Kansas State Agricultural College. His real interests, however, were social reform and helping others make occupational choices. These interests surfaced when Parsons went to Boston in the early 1900s. Parsons was named director of the Breadwinners Institute which was one of what were referred to as Civic House programs. Through Parsons's leadership the Vocational Bureau of Boston was established on January 13, 1908. Parsons's major work *Choosing a Vocation* was posthumously published in 1909.

Parsons is given credit for formulating the conceptual framework for helping a person choose a career as follows:

First, a clear understanding of yourself, aptitudes, abilities, resources, limitations, and other qualities.

Second, a knowledge of the requirements and conditions of success, advantages and disadvantages, compensation, opportunities, and prospects in different lines of work.

Third, true reasoning on the relations of these two groups of facts (Parsons, 1909, p. 5).

Parsons's three-point formulation greatly influenced the procedures used in career counseling over a significant period of time. Moreover, Parsons, conceptual framework ignited a national interest in career guidance. By 1910, 35 cities had some form of career guidance in their schools. The need for organizing a national effort to promote vocation guidance became an important agenda for public schools in the early 1900s.

First National Conference on Vocational Guidance

The first national conference of career guidance was held in Boston in 1910, the second in New York City in 1912, and the third in Grand Rapids, Michigan, in 1913 where the National Vocational Guidance Association was founded. That organization is currently known as the National Career Development Association (NCDA). The efforts to form a national organization to aid in the employment of working Americans also gained the support of the federal government, especially after World War I, the Great Depression, and World War II.

After World War I, federal acts were passed to assist veterans in returning to the workforce. Tests that were developed during World War I were used to assist veterans in making decisions about educational pursuits and/or in finding an optimal job. The Great Depression took place during the 1930s and beyond and was accompanied by endless lines of people who were unemployed and in search of food for their families. The federal government supported the creation of work projects throughout the country as the economy continued a downward trend. Many of the families during the 1930s and into the early 1940s struggled to survive. World War II followed in the 1940s during which women replaced men in the workplace. After World War II ended in 1945, the GI Bill of Rights was passed to encourage veterans to attend college. The passage of bills on the part of the federal government was designed to help veterans find employment and also encouraged the career guidance movement. Chapter 14 contains a case study that focuses on the influence of life course events experienced by an individual who was in the armed services. Programs to train career counselors were also funded by the federal government. During the 1950s several important theories of career development were published—many of these theories are still in vogue today.

As you will observe in the chronology of the career counseling movement in appendix A, the government has continually sponsored programs that directly or indirectly supported the career guidance movement. The career education concepts of the 1970s was another government-sponsored program that was designed to address career development, attitudes, and values in public schools. Career development goals were established for all grade levels and for adults. What was missing however was up-to-date career information systems that are easily accessible.

The National Occupational Information Coordinating Committee (NOICC)

In 1976, the National Occupational Information Coordinating committee was established by an act of Congress to (1) develop occupational information systems for each state; (2) assist in the organization of state committees; (3) assist all users of occupational information to share information; and (4) provide labor market information for the needs of youth. This committee was also charged with the creation of national career counseling and development guidelines. In 1992, NOICC developed the National Career Development Training Institute to train personnel to assist students and adults to acquire career planning skills. The practice of career development is now found in Canada, Australia, and many countries in Europe and the Far East.

A Glance into the Past and a Look into the Future

In the beginning of this discussion, I referred to events and social conditions that determined the course of the career counseling movement. The chronology of the career counseling movement reflects the continuous influence of social, political, economic, and other changes in our nation. In the political arena, the career counseling movement has found support in federal legislation that has provided funds for career-related service programs and counselor training programs.

This field has been influenced by foresight, dedication, and pioneering efforts of many individuals. Those who came forth with conceptualizations of career counseling that have endured for many decades provided the guidelines for contemporary practices. Other individuals concentrating on basic research in human development also contributed immeasurably to the career counseling movement. The leaders in related branches of applied psychology and contributors to technological advancements all played a part in developing what has become the mainstream of this movement. What I have reported thus far is not much more than an outline of significant events and contributions of many individuals. In appendix A one can find detailed information about the career counseling movement.

The basic issues that follow are examples of career counseling perspectives that reflect some current issues in career counseling and suggest future needs that are ingrained in our development as a nation. As in the past, events, conditions, and situations will greatly determine the needs of our society. In our early development the focus on career services was driven primarily by conditions within our geographical boundaries. The immediate future, however, is inextricably intertwined with a global economy. Market forces and workplace changes driven by globalization have created vast changes in how work is structured and how it will be accomplished. I will address both personal and career issues in the pages that follow.

Some Basic Issues

I now turn to identifying some basic issues in career counseling that provide a means of discovering some of the significant challenges that currently face the counseling profession. These issues are discussed in a straightforward manner in an attempt to transcend the clutter usually associated with controversy. I have attempted to go after the jugular instead of the capillaries and briefly make direct and simple statements about each issue. The reader is encouraged to learn more about basic issues from references and the chapters that follow.

Be aware that I do not suggest that our list of basic issues is complete. I have, however, included those issues that are thought to introduce some of the challenges associated with learning to become an effective career counselor. The basic issues selected, not necessarily in order of importance, are as follows: the case for the individual, career life perspective, career choice, working in the 21st century, lifelong learning, counseling in a culturally diverse society, globalization and economic restructuring, effective use of career information, and integrating career and personal counseling. Some terms used in career counseling are identified in Box 1.1.

BOX 1.1

Some Terms Defined

Many terms will be introduced and defined throughout this book. Some of the terminology that is briefly described in this chapter to clarify the basic issues discussed will be explained in greater detail in succeeding chapters, within the context of program descriptions and practical illustrations.

The definition of **career** has been developed by the National Career Development Association and cited by Reardon, Lenz, Sampson, and Peterson (2000) as follows: "**Career:** Time extended working out of a purposeful life pattern through work undertaken by the person" (p. 6). Here, career refers to the activities and positions involved in vocations, occupations, and jobs as well as to related activities associated with an individual's lifetime of work.

Hall and Mirvas (1996) suggest an updated definition of **career** that reflects a more current role of flexibility required of contemporary workers. They submit the term "protean career" that "encompasses any kind of flexible, idiosyncratic career course, with peaks and valleys, left turns, moves from one line of work to another, and so forth. Rather than focusing outward on some ideal generalized career path, the protean career is unique to each person—a sort of career fingerprint" (p. 21). Thus, this perception of future work environments realistically points out that some workers in the 21st century, especially those who work for industrial organizations, will make multiple career choices.

As Feldman (2002) points out, many poor and blue-collar workers may view their environments as very constrained, with limited potential for finding work. Therefore, practically any work may be viewed as a necessity to provide for family; **career** is at best a vague term with little or no meaning. Counselors are to provide a more enlightened and encouraging perspective of self-development through learning new skills in trades and basic skills for advancement. Keys to solutions of current problems and methods to take advantage of opportunities that may occur should be fostered.

Career development as defined by the American Counseling Association "is the total constellation of psychological, sociological, educational, physical, economic, and chance factors that combine to influence the nature and significance of work in the total life span of any given individual" (Engels, 1994, p. 2). Specifically, the term reflects individually developed needs and goals associated with stages of life and with tasks that affect career choices and subsequent fulfillment of purpose.

Career counseling includes all counseling activities associated with career choice over a life span. In the career counseling process, all aspects of individual needs (including family, work, personal concerns, and leisure) are recognized as integral parts of career decision making and planning. Career counseling also includes counseling activities associated with work maladjustment, stress reduction, mental health concerns, and developmental programs that enhance work skills, interpersonal relationships, adaptability, flexibility, and other developmental programs that lead to self-agency.

Career guidance encompasses all components of services and activities in educational institutions, agencies, and other organizations that offer counseling and career-related programs. It is a counselor-coordinated effort designed to facilitate career development through a variety of professional services that foster each client's ability and desire to manage their own career development.

Practice in career development is used internationally by researchers and counselors in some countries to replace the terms "career guidance" and "counseling" (Herr, 2001). It appears that this is an effort to remove the confusion of terms that are often used interchangeably and are not clearly defined. For example, the use of career

(Continued)

BOX 1.1 (*CONTINUED*)

information can be accomplished through a career guidance curriculum module, but it also can be described verbally in an individual counseling session. Practice in career development therefore suggests a wide range of career services that are to be specifically identified by content and context.

According to Reardon et al. (2000), "***work*** is an activity that produces something of value for oneself or others" (p. 7). This description of work points out that work is a broad term that not only includes work for which one is paid a salary, but also unpaid work such as a volunteer who participates in a fund-raising event for a community project. Thus, work can mean many different things to those who do it. In career counseling, we tend to use this broader perspective of work to communicate to clients that work role is very pervasive in one's life and is interrelated to all life roles.

The term ***career intervention*** has become more prominent in career-related literature. It is defined by Spokane (1991) as follows: "Any activity (treatment of effort) designed to enhance a person's career development or to enable that person to make more effective career decisions" (p. 22). Thus, a career intervention may include an interpretation of measured interests for career decision making or a group counseling component designed to enhance one's interpersonal skills.

The Case for the Individual

Career counseling was founded on the principle of individual differences in assets and strengths. Measures of individual traits were the primary focus of early career counseling. The major goal was to match an individual's assets and strengths with job requirements (Picchioni & Bonk, 1983). From these early beginnings, career counselors gradually and carefully expanded the scope of human traits used in the career choice process. In the meantime, researchers built career development theories and subsequent counseling procedures that are currently being addressed in the career counseling process. The eventual shift from vocational to career counseling reflected a need to include the individual's purposeful life pattern through work.

Current career counseling practices include a concerted effort to build an understanding of an individual's traits, aspirations, motives, preferred lifestyle, and career and personal concerns. With the mindset that accompanies a holistic counseling approach, counselors evaluate how individual problems and subsequent challenges are interrelated. The uniqueness of each individual is used to build tailored individualized intervention strategies. Each strategy may require a variety of techniques and materials, so not everyone takes the same test or uses the same career information resources.

Individual concerns also determine the content and purpose of intervention strategies. Solution-based interventions can take many different paths. Small groups may share family life problems and solutions. A large group may share information about certain training programs. Yet another individual may receive personal counseling and career counseling simultaneously to solve major problems that are interfering with making a career choice. Still another may learn effective communication skills.

The emphasis on individual differences strongly suggests that we address all issues of diversity in the counseling process; for example, counselors focus on gender differences, culture differences, sexual orientation, physical or cognitive disabilities, and differences within groups. Special attention is given to individuals who have experienced discrimination and oppression. Each individual is viewed as a product of their heritage shaped by a variety of experiences and circumstances in a unique environment. Individuals differ, for example, in their values, family structure, and motivation as well as in their worldviews. Career choice, for instance, may be influenced by the lack of family resources rather than what an individual desires. More information about factors that influence career choice can be found in several chapters that follow, including chapters 9–11 that are devoted to special populations.

Counselors must ask the question: Who is this person who sits before me? One thing we do know is that this person is human and we both participate in human existence. But, there are many facets about this person we do not know. What are this person's motives, drives, and aspirations? How much depth of psychological insight does this person have? The client will also seek the answers to such questions as, How do I choose a career? How can I improve? Which job is best for me? These questions and others will to a large extent determine the course of action that will lead to self-discovery, enlightenment, and empowerment in a counseling relationship.

The case for the individual is a straightforward concept that helps counselors maintain a focus on the uniqueness of each client. An effective counseling approach maintains that each client is indeed a unique individual. This position discourages stereotyping, especially in a society that is culturally diverse. The basic issue here is that clients who come to us with critical unmet concerns must be viewed as unique individuals with unique backgrounds and traits.

Career Life Perspective

The career life perspective is a good example of how career counseling has developed a more inclusive role. The term "career life" or, as some prefer, *life/career*, illuminates the interconnection between all life roles. Donald Super (1984) developed a conceptual model that illustrates the interaction of life roles over the life span that is discussed in chapter 2. He suggests that because people are involved in several life roles simultaneously, success in one role facilitates success in another and all roles affect one another over the life span. This conceptual model is a prime example of integrating career and life development as well as a need to focus on the interrelationships of all life roles. It also suggests that career life perspective is a basic issue that should be addressed in career counseling.

Following this logic, the career life perspective introduces some key factors that may influence career choice. More specifically, how much does one value time for family and leisure, for instance, and the social status associated with a job, place of residence, and financial opportunities? These questions are examples of discussion topics that may have otherwise been ignored or overlooked.

One approach to incorporating the career life perspective is to clarify the client's lifestyle orientation. The individual's commitment to work, leisure, volunteer activities, home, and family are relevant topics. In addition, attention could be directed to individual aspirations for social status, a particular work climate, education and training, mobility, and financial security. These factors add depth, direction, and diversity to the counseling process. They provide stimulus for discussion groups and assist individuals in clarifying their individual needs for both career and life roles.

The career life perspective opens the door for counselors to introduce concepts that add meaning and clarity to how work and life are intertwined. From this perspective, the work role is viewed as a major determiner of each individual's life story. On the other hand, the interrelationship of life roles suggests that the joys and frustrations one experiences in life are balanced through an assortment of activities and different roles. Although work occupies a large part of our lives, it is not the only life role in which one can express their individuality. In this context, a balanced lifestyle takes on a more significant meaning.

In the process of clarifying career and life roles, an important perspective emerges from which to evaluate potential careers and their interrelationships. The strength of lifestyle orientations for self-improvement through education, leadership roles in work, financial independence, and participation in community activities and services are specific examples of discussion topics. In addition, a comparison of lifestyle factors with skills, interests, and personality, for example, can point out congruence or striking differences. An ever-expanding role of career counseling will certainly include the comprehensive nature of the career life perspective.

Career Choice

Career counselors traditionally have focused on a number of significant factors that influence career choice. Values, interests, abilities, skills, and work-life experiences are viable factors that are discussed and clarified. There are, however, many other interacting factors and contextual issues that are a significant part of the career choice process. An ever-changing workforce and the uncertainties associated with a global economy exacerbate the confusion inherent in future work role projections. In the 1990s a significant number of jobs were outsourced to other nations. Changes in economic conditions can also create significant job loss; millions of jobs were lost during the recession in 2009. Thus the chances are that one may have multiple careers over the life span.

It is no surprise that career choice is considered tentative from the standpoint that practically every choice involves some doubt about the credibility of the chosen career and the possibility that workplace changes may make it obsolete. The individual's uncertainty is compounded by the career possibilities that have disappeared because of economic conditions, and the career uncertainties forecast by imminent technology changes. Moreover, career choice is a process in which one not only chooses but also eliminates—and consequently stifles—some interests and talents. Parts of us are left to lie fallow when a career choice is made. Career choice is also clouded by the search all of us experience for self-identity and meaning in a world society that is drawing closer together.

Career choice is a complex process that cannot be explained in a few paragraphs. In chapter 2, some theories of career choice are discussed. In chapter 3, five career counseling models suggest step-by-step procedures that counselors use to assist an individual make an optimal career choice. Finally, you will learn that there is an almost endless number of factors that can influence career choice. The recent growing movement to integrate career and personal counseling will justifiably introduce many more variables into the career choice process. The recognition that career and personal concerns are not inseparable suggests that counselors address the interrelationship of personal and career problems. In essence, career choice is a process that encompasses a concerted effort by both counselor and client. Skills learned by the client in the initial choice process can be used in future decisions.

Working in the 21st Century

Work for most Americans is the focus of their attention for much of their adult life. One's career is a major factor of each individual's life story. To a large extent, work determines the joys and frustrations of daily life. One's work provides the means through which an individual expresses personal identity and accumulates financial resources (Newman & Newman, 2009).

Peter Drucker (2002) suggested that the next society will be dominated by knowledge workers. Their career development is characterized by finely tuned skills that are built around a solid knowledge base that continually needs updating. Medical doctors, dentists, and psychologists are examples of traditional established knowledge workers. The new breed of knowledge worker, however, has emerged from advances in technology, for example, a hi-tech information technologist and/or one who has the knowledge and skills to build secure websites. Future knowledge workers will replace some of the current ones as technology continues to change the workplace with the introduction of advanced products. Currently, technology has significantly changed the workplace and has become a very powerful tool for training programs.

The work environment has increasingly experienced changes in how work tasks are accomplished. We have witnessed or read about new diagnostic devices currently used in the health care industry. Automobile mechanics are now trained to use computerized diagnostic equipment to determine if our vehicle is operating properly. Large distribution organizations can determine their inventory almost immediately through personalized software programs. Plumbers use advanced technology to locate leaks in underground pipelines. Even the amount of wax in your left ear can be determined by a small camera whose image is enlarged and viewed on a screen. Cameras can be used to supervise workers without their knowledge. We do not know, however, how future advances in technology will change the way we work and live, but they are sure to come. New technology should continue to offer significant innovations for the future workplace. (See chapters 7 and 13 for more information on technology.)

We have also witnessed changes from established work patterns of the past. We now have an abundance of independent contractors, self-employed individuals, freelance workers, and consultants. The contingent workforce, for instance, is part of a growing trend of new work arrangements. Originally, contingent workers filled in for an absent employee; however, the emerging contingent worker of today is one who agrees to work for a specified time in an organization. Under these conditions, there is no guarantee of future employment.

The rapid growth of temp agencies and professional employment organizations is the result of organizational restructuring and the act of "outsourcing" its employees. More and more organizations have opted to contract with temp agencies or employment organizations for a workforce. They keep a core of employees that devote most of their time to planning and developing strategies for increasing their productivity. The rationale is that organizations are relieved of the increasing amount of "red tape" involved with large groups of employees and are not required to offer certain benefits. They do not make lifetime commitments to employees.

Yet another change for the worker in the 21st century is the practice of contracting for services and/or special personnel. A business group may opt to contract with an organization or with individuals to take over payroll and accounting services. A health care facility may contract with another organization to furnish registered nurses. These two examples suggest that some workers will work at the same site for a considerable time whereas other workers will shift sites on a regular basis.

Individuals who work for temp agencies, professional organizations, and contract organizations are promoted strictly for their specialized knowledge and their ability to perform. The highest paid jobs are very competitive and take considerable dedication to updating knowledge and skills. The duties of the knowledge worker can be done equally well by both sexes and by individuals of different cultures and/or race or sexual orientation.

The changes we have discussed will affect some workers more than others. What has and will change is how we work. Some knowledge workers, for example, will learn to make use of the results of new technological tools. One knowledge worker will gather information for another knowledge worker—thus, it is the new technology that will determine how the work is accomplished. According to Drucker (2002), we will depend heavily on knowledge workers in the next society.

Lifelong Learning

Working in the 21st century and the concept of lifelong learning have much in common. The forecast of a changing workplace underscores the need for developing a commitment to lifelong learning. Patton and McMahon (1999) suggest the term "life career development learning" to emphasize the interrelationship of lifelong learning and career development. The basic assumption is that new knowledge will bridge changes in work and life in the 21st century.

At first glance, lifelong learning may appear to be a concept we can take for granted. We cannot assume, however, that all our clients have conceptualized the significant relationship between lifelong learning and career development. To some the connection between lifelong learning and living more fully is at best a vague concept. Counselors may be required to offer concrete examples of the interrelationships between education and work in an effort to correct faulty thinking.

In 1994, the School-to-Work Opportunities Act was passed to help high school students receive more experience and coursework that relate directly to the kinds of work they may enter. Follow-up studies of students in these programs suggested that those students who were irregular in school attendance were also irregular in attendance in the workplace (Fouad, 1997). Many of these students continued to need support from counselors, mentors, and supervisors at work. Most important, students need to accumulate positive job experiences before they understand the value of future planning (Gelso & Fretz, 2001).

One of the major counseling goals of lifelong learning is to provide each client with a knowledge base and skills that can be used for current and future concerns and needs. Decision making and communication skills, for instance, are good examples of skills that can be nurtured and used over the life span. Survival skills and networking techniques may be essential during periods of low employment and job loss experienced by many workers as a result of the recession in 2009. Information resources that can be accessed for a variety of client interests can be used to locate career projections or leisure and recreational needs. Finally, clients should periodically evaluate their own career development in an effort to determine their individualized learning needs. These suggestions are representative of an almost endless number of potential learning opportunities that can assist clients now and in the future. Counselors will find some challenging situations when promoting lifelong learning that include becoming an advocate for learning and/or training programs in a client's community.

Counseling in a Culturally Diverse Society

An introduction to multicultural counseling usually begins with a definition of culture such as the one by Ogbu (1990) who suggests that, "Culture is an understanding that a people have of their universe—social, physical, or both—as well as their understanding of the behavior in that universe. The cultural model of a population serves its members as a guide in their interpretations of events and elements within the universe; it also serves as a guide to their expectations and actions in their universe or environment" (p. 523). A learned system of meaning and behavior implied in this definition of culture suggests that each individual is indeed shaped by a unique environment of experiences in his or her culture. Two important concepts emerge from this definition. First, individuals develop worldviews shaped in their cultural ethnic groups and second, there are individual differences within ethnic groups. These concepts provide the foundation on which to build multicultural counseling competencies.

In the last two decades an abundance of information on the subject of multicultural counseling has been published. Much of it has been directed at developing new and modified counseling procedures to meet the needs of a growing culturally diverse society. Critics have pointed out that the assumptions of Western thought and psychology of human development need to be modified into a broader, more integrated knowledge base. The point to consider in this context is that individuals from different cultures develop their own set of values and work needs that were shaped in their unique environment. Values that differ from those of the dominant white culture are to be recognized and appreciated.

Career choice, for example, may be driven by goals of family as opposed to individual aspirations. In the individualistic cultures of Europe and North America, great value is placed on individual accomplishment. In the collectivistic cultures of Africa, Asia, and Latin America, the individual focuses on the welfare of the group and their collective survival (Matsumoto & Juang, 2013; Ridley, 2005).

We do not, however, assume that all individuals of a particular culture have maintained the value structure of their parents. Some cultural values do break down as younger generations assimilate the values of the dominant culture. The term "acculturation" refers to the degree a client has assumed beliefs, values, and behaviors of the dominant culture. Differences in worldviews are frequently found in views about family, cooperation versus competition, communication styles, and locus of control (Gelso & Fretz, 2001).

The special needs of multicultural groups are addressed in all chapters of this text. This emphasis signifies the importance of meeting the counseling needs of a culturally diverse society. Counselor training programs for the most part continue to focus on updating competencies for career counselors. Counselors are to be alert to hard copy and online professional association guidelines for effective multicultural counseling.

The following counseling competencies are introduced here and are followed by a more complete explanation in chapter 9. Counselor competence begins with counselor self-understanding. Counselors are to increase their awareness of their own culture in order to change their racist behaviors. This process leads to an understanding of biases, stereotypes, and unintentional behaviors. Second, counselors acquire knowledge of each client's culture by focusing on culture-specific behavioral patterns, life experiences, and value systems. Finally, the concept of differences within groups suggests that we view each client as a unique individual.

In sum, counselors will be challenged to meet the needs of an increasingly culturally diverse society. Counselors modify their procedures, techniques, and tools and learn culturally appropriate ones. Assessment instruments, for example, have to be carefully scrutinized to determine if they are culturally appropriate. The call is for career counselors to not be culture bound. The role and scope of career counseling should include techniques and tools that are more sensitive to different cultural values and concerns.

Globalization and Economic Restructuring

There now exists what many have labeled as a global economy which is the driving force of economic restructuring. The term "globalization" represents many international interactions including global exchange of goods and services through multinational and global corporations that are also referred to as transnational corporations. International interactions are not a new phenomenon; trade agreements and attempts to build international relationships have a long history. Increased economic, political, and social interactions, however, have escalated in a world in which borders and boundaries are vanishing (Ferrante, 2013). What is suggested here is that social and financial activities, for example, transcend national borders. Markets have opened around the globe resulting in more trade and nations have increasingly become more interdependent. Wages in some nations, however, are significantly lower than those paid in this country. U.S. industries simply cannot compete but have attempted to balance the competition with significant changes in work itself and in the workplace. These changes have had a very disturbing impact on the lives of many workers and their families. Market changes in the 1990s have affected both white-collar and blue-collar jobs. By 1995, millions of jobs were eliminated in the United States, and the casualties at that time were white-collar jobs (Uchitelle & Kleinfield, 1996). In the early 2000s, the American workforce had the smallest proportion of factory workers in all of the developed countries (Drucker, 2002). According to Wessel (2011), between 2000 and 2010, 3 million jobs were outsourced to other countries where the cost of labor is much cheaper. In addition, many of the U.S.-owned factories in Mexico were moved to China and Vietnam (Brinkerhoff, Weitz, & Ortega, 2014). In other situations, organizations downsized their workforce to cut costs. Workers lost many guarantees that had previously existed in the workplace and with it, lower wages and the loss of job security.

The interconnectedness of globalization suggests that when there are disruptive economic events in one nation, other nations will be affected as well. Thus the recession in 2009 has not only resulted in the loss of millions of jobs and subsequent financial problems in the United States, but also in other nations. I am not suggesting that globalization was the primary cause of the 2009 recession, but there is sufficient evidence to support the conclusion that the shift away from production of goods has created significant job loss for many Americans. In the meantime, globalization has intensified through digital technologies, the Internet, and mobile phones (Ferrante, 2013). A number of American industries have opened places of business in countries around the world. China and several nations in Europe and elsewhere now have a local McDonald's or designer clothes from different countries as well as other commodities. Again, this is not a new phenomenon. The U.S. automotive industry has a long history of competition with other nations. Thus the process of globalization is not new but has definitely intensified. Andersen and Taylor (2013) focus on worldwide social changes that are primarily the result of globalization as follows: "The causes of social changes are many including cultural diffusion, inequality, changes in population, war, technology innovation, and mobilization of people through social movements" (p. 405).

What sociologists see as troubling is the ever-expanding influence of multinational organizations and the potential of more job losses for Americans. Globalization and social changes are indeed relevant for a fuller understanding of human behavior in the American workforce as well as how individuals view their lifestyle and the future. In the chapters that follow there will be case examples of job loss and severe personal and family concerns that are usually associated with it. I will also present a case study that involves personal concerns associated with job insecurity. In the meantime, the transformation of economic, political, and social changes that are predicted for the United States will more than likely be accompanied by work and workplace changes that will surely occupy the interests of career counselors in the future.

Effective Use of Career Information

In the not too distant past, career information consisted of a collection of unappealing, drab files and books containing technical-oriented descriptions of work tasks. In the last three decades there has been an explosion of published career information materials in the form of colorful books, files, audiovisual resources, and computer-based programs. In addition, we now have computer-generated career information and a vast array of Internet resources. It is not unusual to find sections in the local newspaper that are devoted to job openings, a list of online sources of job information, and the usual want ads. The point here is that we now have at our disposal a variety of current career information resources. The significant challenge, however, is how can we most effectively use career information.

Spokane (1991) reviewed the rather meager research on how clients filter and process career information into the career decision process. He focused on information-seeking behavior, the cognitive process involved in assimilating career information, and the social restraints that restrict some individuals in the career search process. All these elements suggest that more attention and research need to be directed to the effective use of career information in the career counseling process. To underscore this point researchers have suggested that effective career information processing skills, for example, are key requirements in the decision process (Sampson, Reardon, Peterson, & Lenz, 2004).

Rounds and Tracey (1990) and Sampson and colleagues (2004) suggest that information processing skills are essential for making optimal career decisions. They recommended that counselors evaluate client skills in processing information during the career decision process. They also suggest that the timing of intervention strategies is essential to maintaining productive effective information-seeking behaviors. Their methods for assessing levels of information processing skills are summarized and illustrated in chapter 3.

Sharf (2013) lists a number of specific sources on career information that he recommends. He believes that counselors have the responsibility to know certain types of occupational information and specific sources of information. According to Sharf, counselors are to provide occupational descriptions including salary ranges, outlook, educational requirements, and where more information can be found about an occupation a client selects.

Reardon and colleagues (2000) firmly believe that instead of an individual asking for specific information, such as where is the best paying job, the client should begin career counseling by focusing on self-knowledge. They suggest that clients should focus on past experiences, connect and relate life experiences, and recognize that all life experiences contribute to self-understanding. Self-knowledge is also illuminated through clarification of values, interests, and knowledge of personal skills. Finally, they suggest that career information is more effective in timing and content when a client has gone through a period of readiness that is prompted by an empowerment to evaluate and comprehend self.

Readiness for career information suggests that clients have realistic expectations, are free of faulty beliefs that interfere with rational decision making, have learned how to effectively process career information, and have a fairly accurate perception of self. In other words, clients are capable of projecting self into requirements of work environments found in career exploration and are subsequently able to make appropriate decisions as to their fit. Be aware that the ability of clients to analyze data is of the utmost importance in career decision making. Young adults can be overwhelmed by the number of career possibilities and find themselves with information overload (Feldman, 2002). The lesson here is to prepare clients for effectively evaluating career information. Finally, uncovering underlying constraints that limit client career options is a most worthy objective.

Clients are to begin career exploration by evaluating both negative and positive reactions to all careers. They continue their search by focusing on information obtained from discussions with workers, parents, and other important adults. Productive exploration can come from shadowing workers on the job and participating in work-based education programs, internships, and apprenticeships. Finally, the counselor collaborates with the client on each phase of career information processing.

Integrating Career and Personal Counseling

Traditionally, career counseling has been viewed as a counseling process that has focused on career choice and career development over the life span. Historically, career counselors placed clients by matching measured human traits with requirements of jobs. Gradually, a broader approach to career choice and placement included additional variables such as personality, values, lifestyle preferences, and the significance of person-in-environment interactions. This movement was supported by a solid database of research developed during the last century that has provided career counselors with a greater insight into career development theory and effective career-related interventions. The need to integrate career and personal concerns in the practice of career development has emerged as the next challenge in the ever-expanding role of career counseling (Zunker, 2008).

Current practice places a strong emphasis on the connection between career development and mental health. A growing awareness of evidence suggests that mental health concerns that inhibit systematic, logical thinking, for example, can interfere with the career choice process as well as career development (Gelso & Fretz, 2001, Zunker, 2008). Personality disorders, for instance, may make it difficult for some clients to function in a work environment (Sue, Sue, Sue, & Sue, 2014). Faulty cognitions that result in dysfunctional thinking can adversely affect one's ability to make career choices as well as interfere with one's career development. Work dysfunctions of poor performance, absence from work, and other maladaptive reactions to the work environment may be the result of complex interactions of personal characteristics and the workplace (Aamodt, 2013). These examples and more that are discussed throughout this text will underscore the rationale of integrating career and personal concerns in the practice of career development.

The implications of blending career and personal concerns are very pervasive for both client and counselor. Clients who present concerns that are considered potential mental health problems will best be served by counseling professionals skilled in the integration of services. Obviously, not all clients will present severe personal concerns that require therapy. Some clients, however, may require personal counseling before career counseling and some can be provided with career and personal counseling simultaneously. The important implication here is that career and personal concerns can be interconnected and so tightly woven together that progress in one domain affects the progress in another domain. Thus in some cases clients can best be served by a holistic or whole person counseling approach that addresses all client concerns illustrated in the next paragraphs.

Counselors focus on sets of client concerns. Some concerns will involve career-related problems and others may represent personal ones that are interrelated to multiple life roles, including the work role. Within this framework, counselors focus on a multiple spectrum of domains of the "whole person" as in a holistic approach to counseling. Career and personal concerns are considered as inseparable and interrelated. I use the example of a depressed client to illustrate the interrelatedness of personal and career concerns in Case 1.1, The Depressed Worker.

Case 1.1   **The Depressed Worker**

Alma, a worker in her late thirties, told her career counselor that she wanted to change jobs. Alma was currently doing secretarial work in a large firm, a job she had held for two years. Her reasons for seeking a change were somewhat vague. She stated, "I just don't like it there anymore." And, she added, "I'm very depressed."

Depression can come from a variety of sources, and it can be work related, nonwork related, or both. As Durand and Barlow (2013) point out, however, depression can both lower work performance and affect nonwork factors. In Alma's case, work seems to be at the center of her problem.

Many aspects of work have been found to influence depression, such as problems with supervision, overly demanding work, ambiguity of authority, lack of social support, and corporate instability (Harrington, 2013; Lowman, 1993; Zunker, 2008). The career counselor was able to determine that Alma's depression was related to a poor relationship with her immediate supervisor. Alma also perceived that her work was demanding and that she received little feedback support.

When clients present concerns of depression, there are many questions to be answered, for instance, What are possible sources of stress in the workplace and in the home? Is this client predisposed to depression? How do we decrease depression and/or anxiety?

Such cases may follow several pathways. If the counselor determines that the client is suffering from work-related depression, the counselor and client focus on concerns the client has about the work environment and other life roles. When job change is the best choice, the client must reevaluate goals, changing values and developed abilities. Client and counselor seek solutions to the current concerns with the work environment and requirements to determine a future work role.

The choice to change the person could involve stress reduction exercises, cognitive-behavioral therapy, addiction treatment, medication, physical activity programs, interpersonal skills training, and logotherapy, among others. Combinations of such programs are often used. More than likely, Alma's counselor would suggest programs of stress reduction to accompany the process of choosing a different occupation.

In this brief review of a case study, several counseling skills were suggested and implied, for example, skills in diagnosing symptoms of depression, skills of interviewing, skills in anxiety-reduction programs, and skills in career decision-making procedures. A more holistic approach in the practice of career development recognizes that an individual's total development includes a broad spectrum of domains; helpers are not just career counselors; helpers counsel individuals. Chapter 4 among other chapters is devoted to a broader explanation of integrating career and personal concerns.

In sum, basic issues represent both the historical development of career counseling and its exciting future. More information is provided about basic issues in the chapters that follow. At this point you have hopefully gained a greater perspective of the role and scope of career counseling. It is a very inclusive counseling role that is centered around the meaning of work in each person's life. Career counseling is an approach that involves the "whole person." Career counselors focus on each client's life course perspectives and balancing all life roles in an ever changing world.

Summary

1. The career counseling movement was embedded in changes in our society, especially in the work role. Career counseling was created to meet the needs of society during transitional periods of change. Its growth was influenced by a number of variables, factors, and events. Some key influences include the rise of industrialism, needs of war veterans and their families, social reform movements, studies of human development, growth of urban areas, the measurement movement, federal acts and initiatives, studies of career development, changing demographics, growth of technology, and global market forces.
2. Frank Parsons, known as the father of the career guidance movement, established a career guidance program in the early part of the 19th century in Boston.
3. The first national conference on career guidance took place in Boston in 1910. The National Vocational Guidance Association was created in 1913.
4. Some basic issues in career counseling include the case for the individual, career life perspective, career choice, working in the 21st century, lifelong learning, counseling in a culturally diverse society, globalization and economic restructuring, effective use of information, and integrating career and personal counseling.

Supplementary Learning Exercises

1. Should all career counseling focus on individual needs? Elaborate and cite examples.
2. Give at least five reasons the federal government has supported the career counseling and guidance movement.
3. Give at least five examples of how changes in the workplace will influence career choice.

4. Identify what is meant by the term "knowledge worker"? How are they different from other workers?
5. Why is so much importance attributed to the lifelong learning concept? Illustrate your answer with examples.
6. Explain why one should become a culturally competent counselor.
7. Explain the significance of effective use of career information in career counseling.
8. Why should counselors integrate multiple life roles in the counseling process?
9. Rank the basic issues discussed in this chapter in order of importance. Support your top three choices in a debate with a classmate.
10. Add at least three additional basic issues that you consider to be essential for effective career counseling in the 21st century.

2

Theories of Career Development

CHAPTER HIGHLIGHTS

- Trait-oriented theories

- Developmental theories

- Social learning and cognitive theories

- Person-in-environment perspective

- How career development theories influence career counseling

---

The career development theories discussed in this chapter have been most instrumental in providing the foundation for research in vocational behavior. To comprehend these theories is to understand the priorities in career counseling today. The conceptual shifts in career counseling, test format, work satisfaction studies, and classification systems of occupations have evolved primarily from theories. Understandably, the study of career counseling should begin with some sources of its foundation.

I begin with a brief discussion of how career development theories emerged, what constitutes a theory, and, finally, general information about theories. Next, I review nine theories, grouped according to Gelso and Fretz (2001) as follows: trait-oriented theories, social learning and cognitive theories, developmental theories, and person-in-environment theories.

Vocational counseling's initial focus was primarily on the use of assessment techniques for job placement. Beginning in the early 1950s, vocational counseling started to expand its boundaries by including a broader range of factors in the career choice process, such as self-concept, self-knowledge, and an array of developmental issues. The career development theories that followed in the 1970s and beyond have contributed to an even broader and growing perspective of the career development process. The theories discussed here will include basic assumptions, key terms, outcomes, and practical applications. Be aware that there will be references associated with the unfolding of some theories that go back to 1909. Hence, some theories have historical value in the early studies of vocational psychology and as such have significantly influenced current career counseling practices. The overarching objective here, however, is to discover how theories influenced the development of counseling procedures, and the components of theories that are most relevant for building an understanding of and a basic foundation for career counseling. Keep in mind that the purpose of this chapter is to introduce the basic elements of career development theories. More in-depth and extensive information can be found in Brown and Associates (2002), Brown and Brooks (1996), Osipow and Fitzgerald (1996), Sharf (2013), and Swanson & Fouad (2010). Other theorists who contributed to career development theory such as Ginzberg, Ginsberg, Axelrad, and Herma (1951), Roe (1956), Tiedeman and O'Hara (1963) are mentioned in appendix A.

Career development theories have been criticized by both students and practitioners as being vague about how findings and conclusions can be used and are thought to be "out of touch" with what counselors really want and need—a more direct link between theory and practice. The most compelling and enduring questions have focused on what purpose career development theories serve and, more importantly, how they contribute to career counseling practice. To answer the first question, one must understand the nature of theories. A career development theory is a set of concepts, propositions, and ideas that provides us with insights into what is believed to be true about the process of career development. A theory presents some clues about what is most important to study, how it should be studied, and how results will address counseling concerns (Shaffer, 2002; Sigelman & Rider, 2009). A career development theory is not step-by-step, how-to-do career counseling; however, what is learned from the results of concepts and propositions of theories does provide the guidelines for counseling procedures and interventions discussed in the next chapter's career counseling models. Some theories discussed do offer suggestions for how to do career counseling, and some provide diagnostic measures, workbooks, and other counseling materials. Generally, career development theories present different views of what is most important in the career development process and provide the basis for future research.

One fact known for certain from career development theories is that the career development process can take many different pathways. It is often difficult, therefore, to filter out what each theory has contributed to counseling practice and how one theory differs from another. My major objective in this chapter is to bring theories to life and illustrate how the study of career development has influenced the methods used in counseling all clients who come to human service providers with sets of concerns. Near the end of the chapter, a fictitious client will be introduced to briefly illustrate how a client can be helped by a counselor using the outcomes of career development research. A summary of four groups of theories' significant findings and recommendations for counseling offers some practical solutions that can be used to help address a client's problems. Be aware that only some of the career development theory positions are discussed in the summaries. The point here is that research efforts on career development have led to a significant number of counseling procedures and interventions that are currently used. Only some have been selected as examples to illustrate helpful links to client concerns.

Trait-Oriented Theories

This first group of theories evolved from the measurement movement in the early part of the 20th century. They are embedded in Parsons's (1909) vocational counseling paradigm of matching individual traits with requirements of occupations. From this rather straightforward approach emerged the study of work adjustment and job satisfaction variables. A key finding was potential sets of reinforcers in the work environment that enhance job satisfaction. The position that individuals are attracted to an occupational environment that meets their personal needs and provides them with satisfaction became the driving force behind one of the most popular career counseling approaches. In this section I introduce trait-and-factor theory, person-environment-correspondence counseling, and John Holland's typology. (Holland is recognized worldwide as a most prolific leader in career counseling.)

Trait-and-Factor Theory

Among the earliest theorists on vocational counseling, Parsons (1909) maintained that vocational guidance is accomplished first by *studying the individual*, second by *surveying occupations*, and finally by *matching* the individual with the occupation. This process, called trait-and-factor theory, became the foundation of many vocational counseling programs in the early part of the 20th century, including those used by the Veterans Administration, YMCA, Jewish vocational services, and colleges and universities.

The trait-and-factor approach has been the most durable of all career counseling theories. Simply stated, it means matching the individual's traits with requirements of a specific occupation, subsequently solving the career search problem. The trait-and-factor theory evolved from early studies of individual differences and developed closely with the psychometric movement. This theory greatly influenced the study of job descriptions and job requirements as theorists attempted to predict future job success by measuring job-related traits. The key characteristic of this theory is the assumption that individuals have unique patterns of ability and/or traits that can be measured objectively and correlated with the requirements of various types of jobs.

The development of assessment instruments and the refinement of occupational information are closely associated with the trait-and-factor theory. The study of aptitudes in relation to job success has been an ongoing process. Occupational interests occupy a major part of the research literature on career development. The importance of individual values in the career decision-making process has also been highlighted by the trait-and-factor theory.

Through the efforts of Parsons (1909) and Williamson (1939, 1965), components of the trait-and-factor theory were developed into step-by-step procedures designed to help clients make wise career decisions. Parsons's three-step procedure—studying the individual, surveying occupations, and using "true reasoning" to match the individual with an occupation—may at first glance be judged to be completely dominated by test results. But, on the contrary, it has been argued that Parsons's first step suggests that evaluating each individual's background is an important part of his counseling paradigm and does not necessarily include psychometric data.

Williamson (1939, 1949) was a prominent advocate of trait-and-factor counseling. Williamson's counseling procedures maintained the early impetus of the trait-and-factor approach that evolved from Parsons's work. This straightforward approach to counseling contained six sequential steps: analysis, synthesis, diagnosis, prognosis, counseling, and follow-up. When integrated into other theories of career counseling, the trait-and-factor approach played a vital role in the development of assessment techniques whose results are used with other data to reveal congruence between individual and work environment. Thus, a major criticism of this theory has been a dependence on and an overuse of test results.

Brown, Brooks, and Associates (1990), however, argued that trait-and-factor theory has never been fully understood. They suggested that advocates of trait-and-factor approaches never approved of excessive use of testing in career counseling. For example, Williamson (1939) suggested that test results are but one means of evaluating individual differences. Other data, such as work experience and general background, are as important as test results in the career counseling process.

Recently, Sharf (2010) summarized the advantages and disadvantages of trait-and-factor theory and suggested that it is a static theory rather than a developmental one. Furthermore, it focuses on identifying individual traits and factors but does not account for how interests, values, aptitudes, achievement, and personalities grow and change.

The major point here is that clients can benefit from dialogue that is directed toward continually evolving personal traits and how changes affect career decision making.

The following assumptions of the trait-and-factor approach also raise concerns about this theory: (1) There is a single career goal for everyone and (2) career decisions are based primarily on measured abilities (Herr, Cramer, & Niles, 2004). These assumptions severely restrict the range of factors that can be considered in the career development process. In essence, it suggests that the trait-and-factor approach is too narrow in scope to be considered a major theory of career development. One should recognize, however, that standardized assessment and occupational analysis procedures stressed in trait-and-factor approaches are useful in career counseling. In fact, assessment instruments designed primarily to assist in career decision making continue to be developed and refined. The same may be said about occupational information, as growing numbers of research projects have focused on optimal use of job descriptions and requirements, work environments, and job satisfaction studies. Finally, bridging the gap between assessment scores and work environments is a huge challenge for career counselors now, as in the past (Prediger, 1995).

Will trait-and-factor theory be revitalized for the 21st century? Prediger (1995) suggests that person-environment fit theory has indeed enhanced the potential for a closer relationship between assessment and career counseling; assessment information can provide the basis for developing career possibilities into realities. For example, assessment results, along with other information, can provide a pathway for growth and propose how that growth can be accomplished. Prediger suggested a *similarity model,* designed not to predict success or to find the "ideal career," but to provide a means of evaluating occupations that "are similar to you in important ways" (Prediger, 1995, p. 2).

Using the similarity model to provide client focus when exploring careers may revitalize the role of trait-and-factor in current career counseling models (Rounds & Tracey, 1990; Zytowski, 1994). The relevant message here is that trait-and-factor theory has an important role in future career development theory and in career counseling practice.

Summary of Practical Applications

1. One of the major career counseling roles of early trait-and-factor approaches was that of diagnosis. In this context, assessment was the process of analyzing data collected through a variety of tests. Individual strengths and weaknesses were evaluated, with the primary purpose of finding a job that matched measured abilities and achievements. Assessment data were used primarily to predict job satisfaction and success.

2. Contemporary career counseling practices are expanding the use of test data. One example is the study of the relationship between human factors and work environment variables. The results of this research are used to find congruence between individual human factors and reinforcers that exist in work environments. In Holland's (1996) typology approach, one major objective is to find work environments that are congruent with a client's personality traits.

3. Instead of predicting the possibility of success in a particular career on the basis of actuarial information, the counselor interprets test data and informs the client of observed similarities to current workers in a career field. For example, a client who has a similar interest pattern to current workers in a particular field of work may find that work to be satisfying. Clients use this information, along with other data, in the career decision process. Finally, assessment data are considered to be one source of information that can be most effectively used in conjunction with other data.

Person-Environment-Correspondence (PEC) Counseling

This theory has a long history, and, as late as the early 1990s, it was referred to as the theory of work adjustment (TWA). In 1991, it was revised once again to include descriptions of the differences between personality structure and personality style and between personality style and adjustment style. The theory at that point had become more inclusive, embracing how individuals interact in their everyday lives as well as how they interact in a work environment. The broader label of person-environment-correspondence (PEC) was added in 1991 (Dawis, 2002; Lofquist & Dawis, 1991).

PEC theory has always emphasized that work is more than step-by-step task-oriented procedures. Work includes human interaction and sources of satisfaction, dissatisfaction, rewards, stress, and many other psychological variables. The basic assumption is that individuals seek to achieve and maintain a positive relationship with their work environments. According to Dawis and Lofquist, individuals bring their requirements to a work environment, and the work environment makes its requirements of individuals. To survive, the individual and the work environment must achieve some degree of *congruence* (correspondence).

To achieve this consonance, or agreement, the individual must successfully meet the job requirements, and the work environment must fulfill the individual's requirements. Stability on the job, which can lead to tenure, is a function of correspondence between the individual and the work environment. The process of achieving and maintaining correspondence with a work environment is referred to as *work adjustment*.

Four key points of Dawis's and Lofquist's theory are summarized as follows: (1) Work personality and work environment should be amenable, (2) individual needs are most important in determining an individual's fit into the work environment, (3) individual needs and the reinforcer system that characterizes the work setting are important aspects of stability and tenure, and (4) job placement is best accomplished through a match of worker traits with the requirements of a work environment.

Dawis and Lofquist (1984) and Dawis (2002) have identified *occupational reinforcers* found in the work environment that are vital to an individual's work adjustment. They evaluated work settings to derive potential reinforcers of individual behavior. In the career counseling process, individual needs are matched with occupational reinforcers to determine an individual's fit into a work environment. Some examples of occupational reinforcers are achievement, advancement, authority, coworkers, activity, security, social service, social status, and variety.

Lofquist and Dawis (1984) and Dawis (2002) continue to stress the significance between the relationship of job satisfaction and work adjustment. Job satisfaction has been evaluated from outcomes (results or consequences) of work experience, such as tenure, job involvement, productivity, work alienation, and morale. A significant but not surprising conclusion suggests that satisfaction is negatively related to job turnover, withdrawal behavior (such as absenteeism and lateness), and worker alienation. But perhaps more importantly, job satisfaction was found to be positively related to job involvement, morale, and overall life situations or nonwork satisfaction.

This theory assumes that job satisfaction is a significant indicator of work adjustment. For example, job satisfaction is an indicator of the individual's perception of work and the work environment and is highly related to tenure in a work situation.

The theory of work adjustment, therefore, has the following implications for career counselors:

1. Job satisfaction should be evaluated according to several factors, including satisfaction with coworkers and supervisors, type of work, autonomy, responsibility, and opportunities for self-expression of ability and for serving others.
2. Job satisfaction is an important career counseling concern but does not alone measure work adjustment. Work adjustment includes other variables, such as the individual's ability to perform tasks required of work.
3. Job satisfaction is an important predictor of job tenure, and the factors associated with job satisfaction should be recognized in career counseling. An individual's abilities and how they relate to work requirements are not the only career counseling components of work adjustment.
4. Individual needs and values are significant components of job satisfaction. These factors should be delineated in career counseling programs designed to enhance work adjustment.
5. Individuals differ significantly in specific reinforcers of career satisfaction. Therefore, career counseling must be individualized when exploring interests, values, and needs.
6. Career counselors should consider the reinforcers available in work environments and compare them with the individual needs of clients.

What does all this mean for the career counselor? First, it should not be surprising that career counselors should consider clients' job satisfaction needs to help them find amenable work environments. Keep in mind that job satisfaction is a significant variable in determining productivity, job involvement, and career tenure. Second, career counselors should use occupational information to assist clients in matching individual needs, interests, and abilities with patterns and levels of different reinforcers in the work environment. For example, the reinforcer of "achievement" is related to experiences of accomplishment in the work situation. Social service is related to the opportunities that a work situation offers for performing tasks that will help people. In the following paragraphs some core elements of this theory are briefly reviewed. They include work reinforcers, personality traits, abilities and values, environmental structure and work adjustment, and future perspectives.

Work Reinforcers. Some significant problems with identifying work reinforcers in the 21st century are constant changes in work requirements in workplaces and how and by whom success will be evaluated. Lofquist and Dawis warned that career counselors may have difficulty identifying occupational reinforcers because of the lack of relevant research, the vast variety of jobs in the current labor force, and emerging jobs. Meanwhile, the theory of work adjustment has focused more attention on the importance of worker satisfaction. In the future, however, workers may have to adjust to finding satisfaction in a variety of jobs in a work environment that makes use of their individual skills. Workers in the 21st century may work in teams and use sets of skills to meet work requirements.

Personality Traits, Ability, and Values. A core element of PEC is the identification of personality traits, ability, and values. Dawis (1996, 2002) identified personality structure as stable characteristics of personality that consist primarily of abilities and values. *Personality style* is seen as "typical temporal characteristics" of an individual's interaction with the environment. In other words, do the worker's behavior and actions fit well in the work environment or are there indications of conflicts? As in other trait-and-factor theories, *ability dimensions* are used to estimate the individual's probable levels of work skills or abilities. *Values* are viewed as work needs and are identified primarily through the *Minnesota Importance Questionnaire* (University of Minnesota, 1984), discussed in the next chapter. Work needs resemble a client's "ordinary psychological needs," which develop outside the work environment but also apply to the work setting, such as recognition and need for achievement. Most important, this theory emphasizes that both abilities (work skills) and values (work needs) are important components of optimal career selection.

Environmental Structure and Work Adjustment. Two other key elements are *environmental structure* and *work adjustment.* Environmental structure is identified as the characteristic abilities and values of individuals who inhabit the work environment. The basic assumption here is that clients who have abilities and values similar to individuals already on the job will make it less difficult for an individual to adjust to a work environment. This assumption is an example of "matching" and is one of the core elements of trait-and-factor counseling.

Work adjustment is ideal when person and environment have matching work needs and work skills; however, changes in either can lead to worker dissatisfaction. A worker's attempt to improve his or her fit within the work environment can be viewed as actions designed to achieve work adjustment. Adjustments usually follow one of two modes: active and reactive. In the active mode, the worker attempts to change the work environment, whereas in the reactive mode, the worker attempts to correspond better with the work environment.

Important to the career counselor here is that work adjustment is closely related to personality style, although they are considered to be distinct concepts. Because of changing work conditions, counselors can expect to find more clients with work adjustment problems, thus, work adjustment counseling is one of the areas that should increase in the 21st century. PEC counseling suggests that adjustment behavior includes degrees of flexibility, one's ability to react positively to changes, perseverance, and personality style or style of interaction within the environment. Herein lies a major contribution of this theory—work adjustment counseling. This is a relatively unaddressed issue and should garner more attention in the near future as we witness more violence in the workplace as a result of worker dissatisfaction.

The Future. Some counselors may find that their services may be needed as consultants to organizations. There is a growing awareness among organizations that employees who learn to balance their lifestyle are more satisfied in the workplace, which in turn leads to improved productivity and less absenteeism. Worker satisfaction among employees has long been the goal of organizations. Counselors are to recognize that antisocial behavior in the workplace is a complex phenomenon that often parallels violence in other life roles (Baron, Hoffman, & Merrill, 2000).

Empirical Support for the Person-Environment-Correspondence Theory

For PEC, see Holland (1992), Spokane (1985), and Gelso and Fretz (2001). For prediction of satisfactoriness, see Hunter and Hunter (1984). For prediction of satisfaction, that is, worker satisfaction from need-reinforcer correspondence, see Dawis (1991). For other studies that offer information about various propositions of the theory, see Rounds (1990), Bretz and Judge (1994), and Dawis (2002).

Summary of Practical Applications

1. The person-environment-correspondence theory depends heavily on client assessment because its major objective is to identify groups of occupations that hold the greatest potential for a client's satisfaction in a work environment and, conversely, those that will be less likely to meet the criteria for satisfaction. Of major concern are a client's abilities (work skills) and values (work needs).

2. The *U.S. Employment Service's General Aptitude Test Battery* (U.S. Department of Labor, 1970a) is recommended for measuring abilities, whereas the *Minnesota Importance Questionnaire* (MIQ) (University of Minnesota, 1984) is used to assess values. Personality style is to be evaluated by the counselor in an interview.

3. The *Minnesota Occupational Classification System III* (Dawis, Dohm, Lofquist, Chartrand, & Due, 1987) provides an index for level and patterns of abilities and reinforcers that different occupations provide. This index is used for matching work skills to requirements of occupations and as a means of determining reinforcers available by occupation. Clearly however, reinforcers are becoming more difficult to identify in the current workplace.

4. Presentation of assessment information should be tailored to the client's abilities, values, and style. The point here is that the counselor should present information in the most meaningful way for clients.

5. Career planning should be conceptualized to be most meaningful to the client by determining whether the client is more achievement oriented (satisfactoriness) or more self-fulfilled oriented (satisfaction). The rationale here is that the counselor should ascertain client orientation to determine which prediction system to emphasize in the career planning process.

Work adjustment counseling is an important counseling goal that is emphasized by this theory; however, many clients are faced with constantly changing work environments. Thus helping clients learn new skills and develop appropriate work habits that match the needs of changing work environments are relevant counseling strategies for the 21st century (Dawis, 1996). As we have already noted, the nature of work will change along with the workplace in the 21st century. The general themes of work adjustment, work environment, and job satisfaction derived from this theory should continue to be recognized as viable factors in career counseling.

John Holland's Typology

According to John Holland (1992), individuals are attracted to a given career because of their particular personalities and numerous variables that constitute their backgrounds. First, career choice is an expression of, or an extension of, personality into the world of work, followed by subsequent identification with specific occupational stereotypes. Congruence of one's view of self with an occupational preference establishes what Holland refers to as the *modal personal style*. Central to Holland's theory is the concept that one chooses a career to satisfy one's preferred modal personal orientation. If the individual has developed a strong dominant orientation, satisfaction is probable in a corresponding occupational environment. If, however, the orientation is one of indecision, the likelihood of satisfaction diminishes. The strength or dominance of the developed modal personal orientation as compared with career environments will be critical to the individual's selection of a preferred lifestyle. Again, the key concept behind Holland's environmental models and environmental influences is that individuals are attracted to a particular role demand of an occupational environment that meets their personal needs and provides them with satisfaction.

A socially oriented individual, for example, prefers to work in an environment that provides interaction with others, such as a teaching position. On the other hand, a mechanically inclined individual would seek out an environment where his or her trade could be quietly practiced and where socializing is minimal. Occupational homogeneity, therefore, provides the best route to self-fulfillment and a consistent career pattern. Thus individuals who do not experience occupational homogeneity will have inconsistent and divergent career patterns. Holland therefore stressed the *importance of self-knowledge* in the search for vocational satisfaction and stability. From this frame of reference, Holland proposed six kinds of modal occupational environments and six matching modal personal orientations. These are summarized in Table 2.1, which also offers representative examples of occupations and themes associated with each personal style.

Table 2.1	**Holland's Modal Personal Styles and Occupational Environments**	
Personal styles	**Themes**	**Occupational environments**
May lack social skills; prefers concrete vs. abstract work tasks; may seem frank, materialistic, and inflexible; usually has mechanical abilities	Realistic	Skilled trades such as plumber, electrician, and machine operator; technician skills such as airplane mechanic, photographer, draftsperson, and some service occupations
Very task-oriented; is interested in math and science; may be described as independent, analytical, and intellectual; may be reserved and defers leadership to others	Investigative	Scientific such as chemist, physicist, and mathematician; technician such as laboratory technician, computer programmer, and electronics worker
Prefers self-expression through the arts; may be described as imaginative, introspective, and independent; values aesthetics and creation of art forms	Artistic	Artistic such as sculptor, artist, and designer; musical such as music teacher, orchestra leader, and musician; literary such as editor, writer, and critic
Prefers social interaction and has good communication skills; is concerned with social problems, and is community service oriented; has interest in educational activities	Social	Educational such as teacher, educational administrator, and college professor; social welfare such as social worker, sociologist, rehabilitation counselor, and professional nurse
Prefers leadership roles; may be described as domineering, ambitious, and persuasive; makes use of good verbal skills	Enterprising	Managerial such as personnel, production, and sales manager; various sales positions, such as life insurance, real estate, and car salesperson
May be described as practical, well-controlled, sociable, and rather conservative; prefers structured tasks such as systematizing and manipulation of data and word processing	Conventional	Office and clerical worker such as timekeeper, file clerk, teller, accountant, keypunch operator, secretary, bookkeeper, receptionist, and credit manager

SOURCE: Adapted from Holland (1985a,b, 1992, 1996).

FIGURE 2.1

Holland's model of personality types and occupational environments

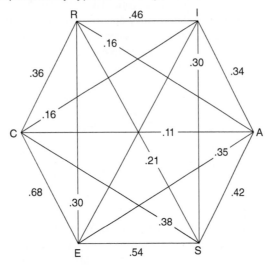

SOURCE: From "An Empirical Occupational Classification Derived from a Theory of Personality and Intended for Practice and Research," by J.L. Holland, D.R. Whitney, N.S. Cole, and J.M. Richards, Jr., ACT Research Report No. 29, The American College Testing Program, 1969.

Holland proposed that personality types can be arranged in a coded system (RIASEC theory) following his modal-personal-orientation themes such as R (realistic occupation); I (investigative); A (artistic); S (social); E (enterprising); and C (conventional). In this way, personality types can be arranged according to dominant combinations. For example, a code of CRI would mean that an individual is very much like people in conventional occupations, and somewhat like those in realistic and investigative occupations. Counselors and clients can use Holland's Occupational Classification (HOC) system to identify corresponding Dictionary of Occupational Titles (DOT) numbers for cross-reference purposes. The four basic assumptions underlying Holland's (1992) theory are as follows:

1. In our culture, most persons can be categorized as one of six types: realistic, investigative, artistic, social, enterprising, or conventional. (p. 2)
2. There are six kinds of environments: realistic, investigative, artistic, social, enterprising, or conventional. (p. 3)
3. People search for environments that will let them exercise their skills and abilities, express their attitudes and values, and take on agreeable problems and roles. (p. 4)
4. A person's behavior is determined by an interaction between his personality and the characteristics of his environment. (p. 4)

The relationships between Holland's personality types are illustrated in Figure 2.1. The hexagonal model provides a visual presentation of the inner relationship of personality styles and occupational environment coefficients of correlation. For example, adjacent categories on the hexagon (e.g., realistic and investigative) are most alike, whereas opposites (e.g., artistic and conventional) are most unlike. Those of intermediate distance (e.g., realistic and enterprising) are somewhat unlike.

Holland's hexagonal model introduces five key concepts. The first, *consistency*, relates to personality as well as to environment. He suggests that some personality and environmental types share some common elements; for instance, artistic and social types have more in common than do investigative and enterprising types. What he is suggesting is that the closer the types are on the hexagon, the more consistent the individual will be. Therefore, high consistency is seen when an individual expresses a preference for adjoining codes such as ESA or RIC. Less consistency would be indicated by codes RAE or CAS.

The second concept is *differentiation*. Individuals who fit a pure personality type will express little resemblance to other types. Conversely, those individuals who fit several personality types have poorly defined personality styles and are considered undifferentiated or poorly defined.

Identity, the third concept, describes those individuals who have a clear and stable picture of their goals, interests, and talents. In the case of environments, identity refers to the degree to which a workplace has clarity, stability, and integration of goals, tasks, and rewards. Thus individuals who have many occupational goals have low identity.

The fourth concept, *congruence*, occurs when an individual's personality type matches the environment. Social personality types, for example, prefer environments that provide social interaction, concerns with social problems, and interest in educational activities. In reviewing the major studies investigating this concept, Spokane (1985) and Dumenci (1995) concluded that research did support the theory that congruence is highly related to academic performance and persistence, job satisfaction, and stability of choice.

Finally, Holland's model provides a *calculus* (the fifth concept) for his theory. Holland proposed that the theoretical relationships between types of occupational environments lend themselves to empirical research techniques. In essence, further research will provide counselors and clients with a better understanding of Holland's theory as changes in work environments occur.

Holland emphasized the importance of self-knowledge as well as occupational knowledge because he believed critical career judgments are drawn partially from an individual's occupational information. The importance of identification with an occupational environment underscores the significance of occupational knowledge in the career choice process. Knowledge of both occupational environment and corresponding modal personal orientations is, according to Holland, critical to appropriate career decision making.

In the process of career decision making, Holland postulated that the hierarchy or level of attainment in a career is determined primarily by individual self-evaluations. Intelligence is considered less important than personality and interest. Furthermore, the factor of intelligence is subsumed in the classification of personality types; for example, individuals who resemble the investigative type of modal personal orientation are generally intelligent and naturally have skills such as analytical and abstract reasoning.

According to Holland, the stability of career choice depends primarily on the dominance of personal orientation. Putting it another way, individuals are products of an environment that greatly influences their personal orientations and eventual career choices. Personality development, however, is a primary consideration in Holland's career typology theory of vocational behavior.

Holland's theory is primarily descriptive, with little emphasis on explaining the causes and the timing of the development of hierarchies of the personal modal styles.

He concentrated on the factors that influence career choice rather than on the developmental process that leads to career choice. Holland's early theory was developed from observations made on a population of National Merit Scholarship finalists. He later expanded the database to include a wider sample of the general population. His research has been extensive and longitudinal. Holland (1987a) compared his theories with developmental positions:

> I find experience for a learning theory perspective to be more persuasive [than developmental views]. In my scheme, different types are the outcomes of different learning histories. Stability of type is a common occurrence because careers [types] tend to snowball over the life course. The reciprocal interaction of person and successive jobs usually leads to a series of success and satisfaction cycles. (p. 26)

The RIASEC model has been tested with a wide range of ethnically diverse individuals, including those from different socioeconomic backgrounds, and with international groups. The results are mixed, that is, some studies support Holland's theory and others indicate less support (Rounds & Tracey, 1996; Ryan, Tracey, & Rounds, 1996). There does appear to be enough positive evidence, however, to use instruments that are based on Holland's codes with caution when testing culturally diverse populations (Gelso & Fretz, 2001).

Holland's theory emphasizes the accuracy of self-knowledge and the career information necessary for career decision making. The theory has had a tremendous impact on interest assessment and career counseling procedures; a number of contemporary interest inventories present results using the Holland classification format. Its implications for counseling are apparent; a major counseling objective would be to develop strategies to enhance knowledge of self, occupational requirements, and differing occupational environments. According to Hartung and Niles (2000), Holland's "practical experiences have influenced his emphasis of applying abstract concepts to counseling practice" (p. 7).

In sum, Holland's theory has proved to be of more practical usefulness than any of the other theories discussed in this text. In addition, most of his propositions have been clearly defined, and they lend themselves to empirical evaluations. The impact of his scholarly approach to RIASEC theory has had and will continue to exert tremendous influence on career development research and procedures (Spokane, Luchetta, & Richwine, 2002).

Empirical Support for Holland's Theory

Extensive testing of Holland's theory suggests that his constructs are valid, and in fact the body of evidence is extremely large—almost overwhelming. Reviews of research are by Spokane (1996), Osipow and Fitzgerald (1996), Holland, Fritzsche, and Powell (1994), Holland, Powell, and Fritzsche (1994), and Weinrach and Srebalus (1990). Examples of other research topics include the interplay between personality and interests by Gottfredson, Jones, and Holland (1993) and Carson and Mowesian (1993); the studies of the hexagon by Rounds and Tracey (1993); and person-environment congruence and interaction by Spokane (1985) and Meir, Esformes, and Friedland (1994). The best current statements about exploring careers with a typology are by Holland (1996) and, comparing the NEO five-factor model with Holland's typology, by Hogan and Blake (1999). According to Reardon and associates (2000), there are more than 500 studies on Holland's typology. The original documents should be read for more details of current research projects. An update and discussion of Holland's theory can be found in Spokane, Luchetta, and Richwine (2002).

Summary of Practical Applications

Applying Holland's theory in career counseling requires a working knowledge of several inventories and diagnostic measures. Some of these instruments will only be introduced here, as more information is given about them in chapter 6.

1. The *Vocational Preference Inventory* (Holland, 1985b) has undergone several revisions.
2. *My Vocational Situation* (Holland, Daiger, & Power, 1980) and *Vocational Identity Scale* (Holland, Johnston, & Asama, 1993) provide information about goals, interests, and talents.
3. *The Position Classification Inventory* (Gottfredson & Holland, 1991) is a job analysis measure of RIASEC environmental codes.
4. The *Career Attitudes and Strategies Inventory* (Gottfredson & Holland, 1994) measures work environment variables.
5. The *Self-Directed Search* (SDS) (Form R) (Holland, 1994a) is one of the most widely used interest inventories; it has more than 20 foreign language versions, can be administered by a computer that includes computer-based reports, and is available on the Internet. It has gone through several revisions and is continually studied for effectiveness. Accompanying the assessment booklet are several companion materials: *The Occupations Finder* (Rosen, Holmberg, & Holland, 1994b); the *Dictionary of Educational Opportunities* (Rosen, Holmberg, & Holland, 1994a); the *You and Your Career Booklet* (Holland, 1994b); a *Leisure Activities Finder* (Holmberg, Rosen, & Holland, 1990); and a *Dictionary of Holland Occupational Codes* (Gottfredson & Holland, 1989). The *Self-Directed Search and Related Holland Materials: A Practitioner's Guide* by Reardon and Lenz (1998) is a most helpful tool when using the SDS.

Figure 2.2 presents the steps for using the SDS assessment booklet and The Occupations Finder.

FIGURE 2.2

Steps in using the SDS

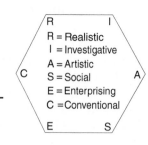

Step 1
Using the assessment booklet, a person:

– lists occupational aspirations

– indicates preferred activities in the six areas

– reports competencies in the six areas

– indicates occupational preferences in the six areas

– rates abilities in the six areas

– scores the responses he/she has given and calculates six summary scores

– obtains a three-letter summary code from the three highest summary scores

R = Realistic
I = Investigative
A = Artistic
S = Social
E = Enterprising
C = Conventional

Step 2
Using the occupations finder, a person locates among the 1335 occupations those with codes that resemble his/her summary code.

Step 3
The person compares the code for his/her current vocational aspiration with the summary code to determine the degree of agreement.

Step 4
The person is encouraged to take "Some Next Steps" to enhance the quality of his/her career decision making.

Source: Adapted from John Hollands SDS report, PAR, Inc.

Summary Comments Concerning Trait-Oriented Theories

Trait-oriented theories emphasize how standardized tests are used and the importance of choosing appropriate testing tools. Human traits such as aptitudes, interests, and personality, for example, can be matched with certain work environments as a means of evaluating potential work sites. An individual's work needs can be compared with components of job satisfaction found in certain occupational environments. Self-knowledge in terms of understanding the level and depth of one's traits and characteristics is an essential element for evaluating career information: Traits of aptitude, interests, and personality type are projected into potential work environments to find congruence and fit.

A significant development in trait-oriented approaches is the position that one observes work environments from several perspectives, including work requirements, personal-environment-fit, and potential reinforcers of one's personal needs. For example, a socially oriented individual prefers to work in an environment that provides interactions with people whereas a mechanically inclined individual would seek out an environment where her trade could be practiced quietly. This very logical approach to career choice suggests that one should consider a number of occupations that match their personal needs and abilities found in particular work environments rather than just focus on one specific occupation. Holland's typology approach is a logical and refreshing method to identify certain individual salient characteristics by type such as life goals and values, among other characteristics. Trait-oriented theories have clearly identified and expanded individual characteristics and traits used in the career counseling process. See career counseling model I in the next chapter.

Finally, more attention needs to be given to work adjustment, job satisfaction, and problems faced by individuals in career transition. It is expected that many individuals in the 21st century will change jobs several times over their life span. The job market will more than likely continue to fluctuate between up and down times. With all the unknowns, workers will be required to adapt quickly to new and different work environments. Workers in the 21st century will be challenged with new procedures, tools, requirements, and culturally diverse coworkers and associates. Keep in mind that many have entered a career with the expectation of a continuous, challenging, intrinsically rewarding work environment only to experience something quite different. For these individuals and others, work adjustment counseling can be very relevant. Although reinforcers may be more difficult to identify in the work world of the 21st century, counselors have been alerted to address sources of work satisfaction variables in career choice and maintenance.

Social Learning and Cognitive Theories

The theories in this section focus on a wide range of variables that affect career choice and career maintenance over the life span. In general, social conditioning, social position, and life events are thought to significantly influence career choice. More specifically, individuals are thought to be influenced by many factors including genetic endowments and special abilities, contextual experiences, learning experiences, and skills learned in managing tasks. Key elements in the career choice process are problem-solving and decision-making skills. Career choice also involves the interaction of cognitive and affective processes. Individuals must be able to process information effectively and think rationally.

Individuals who resort to personal agency or assume total responsibility for their future model an attitude others should emulate. In addition, individuals are encouraged to develop strategies to overcome barriers that interfere with choice implementation. Learning is a key element in this group of theories; for example, learning experiences can expand and increase the range of occupations one considers exploring. Keep in mind that indecision may be related to a limited educational background. Finally, this group of theories addresses faulty thinking that can obscure rational decision making. Discovering and unlearning faulty beliefs about career choice and multiple life roles are major objectives of these theories. I begin with a learning theory, proceed to a cognitive information-processing theory, and, finally, explore a social cognitive perspective.

Krumboltz's Learning Theory of Career Counseling

A social-learning-theory approach to career decision making was first proposed by Krumboltz, Mitchell, and Gelatt (1975), followed several years later by Mitchell and Krumboltz (1990). More recently, Mitchell and Krumboltz (1996) have extended the earlier social-learning-theory approach to include Krumboltz's learning theory of career counseling, and they now suggest that the entire theory be referred to as learning theory of career counseling (LTCC). I review the theory's two parts: Part one explains the origins of career choice, and part two addresses the important question of what career counselors can do to help solve career-related problems.

The theory is an attempt to simplify the process of career selection and is based primarily on life events that are influential in determining career selection. In LTCC, the process of career development involves four factors: (1) genetic endowments and special abilities, (2) environmental conditions and events, (3) learning experiences, and (4) task approach skills.

Genetic endowments and *special abilities* include inherited qualities that may set limits on the individual's career opportunities. The authors do not attempt to explain the interaction of the genetic characteristics and special abilities but emphasize that these factors should be recognized as influences in the career decision-making process.

Environmental conditions and *events* are factors of influence that are often beyond the individual's control. What is emphasized here is that certain events and circumstances in the individual's environment influence skills development, activities, and career preferences. For example, government policies regulating certain occupations and the availability of certain natural resources in the individual's environment may largely determine the opportunities and experiences available. Natural disasters, such as droughts and floods that affect economic conditions, are further examples of influences beyond the control of the individuals affected.

The third factor, *learning experiences,* includes instrumental learning experiences and associative learning experiences. Instrumental learning experiences are those the individual learns through reactions to consequences, through direct observable results of actions, and through the reactions of others. The consequences of learning activities and their later influence on career planning and development are primarily determined by the activity's reinforcement or nonreinforcement, by the individual's genetic endowment, special abilities, and skills, and by a task itself.

Associative learning experiences include negative and positive reactions to pairs of previously neutral situations. For example, the statements "all politicians are dishonest" and "all bankers are rich" influence the individual's perceptions of these occupations. These associations can also be learned through observations, written materials, and films.

The fourth factor, *task approach skills,* includes the sets of skills the individual has developed, such as problem-solving skills, work habits, mental sets, emotional responses, and cognitive responses. These sets of developed skills largely determine the outcome of problems and tasks the individual faces.

Task approach skills are often modified as a result of desirable or undesirable experiences. For example, Sue, a high school senior, occasionally takes and studies class notes. Although she was able to make good grades in high school, she may find that this same practice in college results in failure, thus causing her to modify note-taking practices and study habits.

Krumboltz and associates emphatically stress that each individual's unique learning experiences over the life span develop the primary influences that lead to career choice. These influences include (1) generalization of self derived from experiences and performance in relation to learned standards, (2) sets of developed skills used in coping with the environment, and (3) career-entry behavior such as applying for a job or selecting an educational or training institution. Clearly this social learning model emphasizes the importance of learning experiences and their effect on occupational selection. In the scheme of things, genetic endowment (especially one's intellectual functioning) is considered primarily as a factor that can limit learning experiences and subsequent career choice. What is also emphasized is that career decision making is considered to be an important skill that can be used over one's life span.

The factors that influence individual preferences in this social learning model are composed of numerous cognitive processes, interactions in the environment, and inherited personal characteristics and traits. For example, educational and occupational preferences are a direct, observable result of actions (referred to as self-observation generalizations) and of learning experiences involved with career tasks. If an individual has been positively reinforced while engaging in the activities of a course of study or occupation, the individual is more likely to express a preference for that course of study or field of work. In this way, the consequence of each learning experience, in school or on a job, increases the probability that the individual will have a similar learning experience in the future. Proficiency in a field of work, however, does not ensure that an individual will remain in that field of work. An economic crisis or even negative feedback may initiate a change of career direction.

Genetic and environmental factors are also involved in the development of preferences. For example, a basketball coach might reinforce his players for their skills, but the coach will more likely reinforce tall players more than those smaller in stature. Other positive factors influencing preferences are valued models who advocate engaging in a field of work or an educational course, or who are observed doing so. Finally, positive words and images, such as describing an occupation in glamorous terms, will more than likely lead to positive reactions to that occupation.

In sum, social learning theory suggests that learning takes place through observations as well as through direct experiences. The determination of an individual's problematic beliefs and generalizations is very important in this social learning model (Mitchell & Krumboltz, 1996). For example, identifying content from which certain beliefs and generalizations have evolved is a key ingredient for developing counseling strategies for individuals who have problems making career decisions. The counselor's role is to probe assumptions and presuppositions of expressed beliefs and use this information to explore alternative beliefs and courses of action. Assisting individuals to understand fully the validity of their beliefs is a major component of the social learning model. Specifically, the counselor should address the following problems (Krumboltz, 1983):

- Persons may fail to recognize that a remediable problem exists (individuals assume that most problems are a normal part of life and cannot be altered).
- Persons may fail to exert the effort needed to make a decision or solve a problem (individuals exert little effort to explore alternatives; they take the familiar way out).
- Persons may eliminate a potentially satisfying alternative for inappropriate reasons (individuals overgeneralize from false assumptions and overlook potentially worthwhile alternatives).
- Persons may choose poor alternatives for inappropriate reasons (individuals are unable to realistically evaluate potential careers because of false beliefs and unrealistic expectations).
- Persons may suffer anguish and anxiety over perceived inability to achieve goals (individual goals may be unrealistic or in conflict with other goals).

LTCC is both descriptive and explanatory: The process of career choice is described and examples of factors that influence choice are given. Although the authors have attempted to simplify the process of career development and career choice, the many variables introduced in this theory make the process of validation extremely complex. Meanwhile, the authors should be commended for specifying counseling objectives based on this theory and for providing strategies designed to accomplish these objectives. They also provided several observations for career counseling (Krumboltz et al., 1975, pp. 11–13):

1. Career decision making is a learned skill.
2. Persons who claim to have made a career choice need help, too (career choice may have been made from inaccurate information and faulty alternatives).
3. Success is measured by students' demonstrated skill in decision making (evaluations of decision-making skills are needed).
4. Clients come from a wide array of groups.
5. Clients need not feel guilty if they are not sure of a career to enter.
6. No one occupation is seen as the best for any one individual.

Empirical Support for Krumboltz's Learning Theory

The learning theory of career counseling has yet to be fully tested. The original theory, social learning theory of career decision making, claimed validity from the development of educational and occupational preferences, the development of task approach skills and factors that cause people to take action, and from an extensive database on general social learning theory of behavior. Sharf (2013) has suggested that LTCC is an outstanding example of the relationship between social learning approaches and the human learning process. Gelso and Fretz (2001), however, complain that many of the propositions of this theory have not been researched, especially studies of the use of this theory with culturally diverse groups. More information about the validity of this theory can be obtained from Mitchell and Krumboltz (1996).

Happenstance Approach Theory

In the late 1990s, Mitchell, Levin, and Krumboltz (1999) developed happenstance approach theory for career counseling. The primary premise suggests that chance events over one's life span can have both positive and negative consequences. An individual may learn about an interesting job from an acquaintance, for example, or lose a job as a result of outsourcing only to find a better one. Unpredictable social factors, environmental conditions, and chance events over the life span are to be recognized as important influences in clients' lives.

In LTCC, the client is viewed as one who is exploring and experimenting and should be empowered to take actions that help to create a satisfying life. Challenges that involve educational opportunities and available work options, for instance, should be approached with a positive attitude that promotes positive outcomes. Happenstance approach, therefore, suggests that counselors are to assist clients respond to conditions and events in a positive manner. In short, clients are to learn to deal with unplanned events, especially in the give-and-take of life in the 21st-century workforce.

Five critical client skills—curiosity, persistence, flexibility, optimism, and risk taking—are identified by Mitchell and associates (1999) and are paraphrased as follows:

> Curiosity suggests that one explore learning opportunities and take advantage of options offered by chance events. Persistence is emphasized as a way of dealing with obstacles that may be the result of chance events. Flexibility is used in this context to describe how one learns to address a variety of circumstances and events by adapting and adjusting as events unfold. Optimism implies a positive attitude when pursuing new opportunities. Thus, positive actions can be productive in a changing workplace when one seeks a new or different career. Risk taking in this context may be necessary during unexpected and new events. Clients, for instance, are to learn that risk taking can result in positive outcomes for career development such as finding a more secure job.

Happenstance approach should be an integral part of the counseling interview. As counselors elaborate on person-in-environment experiences, chance events become focus points for conceptualizing counseling interventions. In this respect, happenstance-related questions can reveal how a client has learned to deal with certain situations in the past. From this position the counselor can enable the client to transform these past experiences into opportunities for learning and exploration.

Counselors can also expect to find that some clients have developed barriers to actions resulting from chance events. In essence, they have difficulty in taking positive actions and are reluctant to address difficult issues. Consequently, attending to a client's belief system is reinforced as a major counseling goal in happenstance theory. The overarching desirable outcome here is to empower and prepare each client for positive actions that take advantage of unexpected events and to help them cope with negative consequences in the future (Mitchell et al., 1999).

Happenstance theory suggests that clients learn to approach the future with a positive attitude and the curiosity and optimism that produce positive results. Foster an attitude that takes advantage of unplanned events: Clients are to look for solutions to their circumstances and develop strengths based on their past experiences in life and work. The workplace of the 21st century will present unexpected events and consequences for many workers. Some examples are presented in a number of chapters that follow.

Summary of Practical Applications

According to Mitchell and Krumboltz (1996), when people in modern society make career choices, they must cope with four fundamental trends. Counselors are to recognize trends and changes and more importantly be prepared to help.

1. Clients need to expand their capabilities and interests, not base decisions on existing characteristics only. This first trend centers around the use of interest inventories. Because many individuals have limited experiences with most activities that interest inventories measure, clients may become indifferent to many activities they have not had the chance to experience personally. The point here is that career counselors should assist individuals in exploring new activities, rather than routinely directing them to base career decisions on measured interests that reflect limited past experiences.

2. Clients need to prepare for changing work tasks, not assume that occupations will remain stable. The changing role of job requirements and workplace environments in our current society suggests that career counselors must be prepared to help individuals learn new skills and attitudes so they can meet the demands of international competition. The radical restructuring of the workforce and the disruptions of expectations can be very stressful. Therefore, career counselors should also be prepared to help individuals cope with stress as they learn to develop new skills on an ongoing basis.

3. Clients need to be empowered to take action, not merely be given a diagnosis. Many issues about career decisions are often overlooked, including a lack of information about working per se, families' reaction to a member's taking a particular job, and how to go about getting a job. These issues and others, such as restructuring the workplace, could cause fear of the decision-making process itself, referred to as zeteophobia, or cause procrastination about making a decision. Career counselors are directed to help individuals find answers to these questions and others while providing effective support during the exploration process.

4. Career counselors need to play a major role in dealing with all career problems, not just with occupational selection. Krumboltz (1993), Gelso and Fretz (2001), Richardson (1993), and Zunker (2008), among others, have suggested that career and personal counseling should be integrated. Such issues as burnout, career change, peer affiliate relationships, obstacles to career development, and the work role and its effect on other life roles are examples of potential problems that call for interventions by the career counselor.

Other suggestions:

1. The role of career counselors and the goals of career counseling need to be reevaluated. Counselors need to continue to promote client learning, but perhaps in a different way. Counselors may have to become coaches and mentors to help individuals meet the changes in workforce requirements.

2. Learning experiences should be used to increase the range of opportunities that can be considered in career exploration. Counselors should attempt to discover both positive and negative experiences of their clients and offer efficient learning solutions.

3. Assessment results can be used to create new learning experiences. For instance, aptitude test results can be used to focus on new learning. Key interests identified through interest inventories need to be developed. In essence, assessment results can be starting points for establishing new learning experiences.

4. Intervention strategies suggested by Mitchell and Krumboltz include the use of job clubs in which individuals can offer support to each other during the job search process. A wide range of media should be made available to clients, and local employers should offer high school students structured work-based learning experiences.

5. Career counselors should become adept at using cognitive restructuring. For the youngster who is to report to work with fear of doing a poor job, the counselor can suggest another perspective. Cognitive restructuring suggests to such a client that he or she should view the new job as a chance to impress the boss and fellow workers with his or her enthusiasm. "Reframing" the perspective for this client should be helpful in making the first day on a job a satisfactory one.

6. Career counselors should also use behavioral counseling techniques, including role playing or trying new behaviors, desensitization when dealing with phobias, and paradoxical intention. The latter technique suggests that a client engage in the types of behavior that have created a problem (Mitchell & Krumboltz, 1996). See counseling model III in the next chapter.

Career Development from a Cognitive Information Processing Perspective

Our next career development theory is based on cognitive information processing (CIP) theory and was developed by Peterson, Sampson, and Reardon (1991). CIP theory is applied to career development in terms of how individuals make a career decision and use information in career problem solving and decision making. CIP is based on the 10 assumptions shown in Table 2.2. Using these assumptions as a focal point, the major strategy of career intervention is to provide learning events that will develop the individual's processing abilities. In this way, clients develop capabilities as career problem solvers to meet immediate as well as future problems.

The stages of processing information begin with screening, translating, and encoding input in short-term memory, then storing it in long-term memory, and later activating, retrieving, and transforming the input into working memory to arrive at a solution. The counselor's principal function in CIP theory is to identify a client's needs and develop interventions to help clients acquire the knowledge and skills to address those needs.

Peterson and colleagues (1991) and Sampson and colleagues (2004) stress that career problem solving is primarily a cognitive process that can be improved through a sequential procedure known as CASVE, which includes the following generic processing skills: communication (receiving, encoding, and sending out queries); analysis (identifying and placing problems in a conceptual framework); synthesis (formulating courses of action); valuing (judging each action as to its likelihood of success and failure and its impact on others); and execution (implementing strategies to carry out plans). Table 2.3 describes the CASVE cycle using career information and media.

This model emphasizes the notion that career information counseling is a learning event. This is consistent with other theories that make this same assumption. One major difference between CIP theory and other theories discussed in this chapter, however, is the role of cognition as a mediating force that leads individuals to greater power and control in determining their own destinies. Take, for example, a client who expresses a need to make a career decision. This client is viewed as one who has a career problem or, as expressed in this theory, a gap exists between the client's current situation and a future career situation. Counselors are to seek out the problems and

Table 2.2	**Assumptions Underlying the Cognitive Information Processing (CIP) Perspective of Career Development**

Assumption	Explanation
1. Career choice results from an interaction of cognitive and affective processes.	CIP emphasizes the cognitive domain in career decision making; but it also acknowledges the presence of an affective source of information in the process (Heppner & Krauskopf, 1987; Zajonc, 1980). Ultimately, commitment to a career goal involves an interaction between affective and cognitive processes.
2. Making career choices is a problem-solving activity.	Individuals can learn to solve career problems (that is, to choose careers) just as they can learn to solve math, physics, or chemistry problems. The major differences between career problems and math or science problems lie in the complexity and ambiguity of the stimulus and the greater uncertainty as to the correctness of the solution.
3. The capabilities of career problem solvers depend on the availability of cognitive operations as well as knowledge.	One's capability as a career problem solver depends on one's self-knowledge and on one's knowledge of occupations. It also depends on the cognitive operations one can draw on to derive relationships between these two domains.
4. Career problem solving is a high-memory-load task.	The realm of self-knowledge is complex; so is the world of work. The drawing of relationships between these two domains entails attending to both domains simultaneously. Such a task may easily overload the working memory store.
5. Motivation.	The motivation to become a better career problem solver stems from the desire to make satisfying career choices through a better understanding of oneself and the occupational world.
6. Career development involves continual growth and change in knowledge structures.	Self-knowledge and occupational knowledge consist of sets of organized memory structures called *schemata* that evolve over the person's life span. Both the occupational world and we ourselves are ever changing. Thus, the need to develop and integrate these domains never ceases.
7. Career identity depends on self-knowledge.	In CIP terms, career identity is defined as the level of development of self-knowledge memory structures. Career identity is a function of the complexity, integration, and stability of the schemata constituting the self-knowledge domain.
8. Career maturity depends on one's ability to solve career problems.	From a CIP perspective, career maturity is defined as the ability to make independent and responsible career decisions based on the thoughtful integration of the best information available about oneself and the occupational world.
9. The ultimate goal of career counseling is achieved by facilitating the growth of information-processing skills.	From a CIP perspective, the goal of career counseling is therefore to provide the conditions of learning that facilitate the growth of memory structures and cognitive skills so as to improve the client's capacity for processing information.
10. The ultimate aim of career counseling is to enhance the client's capabilities as a career problem solver and a decision maker.	From a CIP perspective, the goal of career counseling is to enhance the client's career decision-making capabilities through the development of information-processing skills.

SOURCE: From *Career Development and Services: A Cognitive Approach*, by G. Peterson, J. Sampson, and R. Reardon, pp. 7–9. Copyright © 1991. Reprinted with permission of Brooks/Cole, a part of The Thomson Corporation.

Table 2.3	**Career Information and the CASVE Cycle**
Phase of the CASVE cycle	**Example of career information and media**
Communication (identifying a need)	A description of the personal and family issues that women typically face in returning to work (information) in a videotaped interview of currently employed women (medium)
Analysis (interrelating problem components)	Explanations of the basic education requirements for degree programs (information) in community college catalogues (medium)
Synthesis (creating likely alternatives)	A presentation of emerging nontraditional career options for women (information) at a seminar on career development for women (medium)
Valuing (prioritizing alternatives)	An exploration of how the roles of parent, spouse, citizen, "leisurite," and homemaker would be affected by the assumption of the worker role (information) in an adult version of a computer-assisted career guidance system (medium)
Execution (forming means-ends strategies)	A description of a functional résumé emphasizing transferable skills, followed by the creation of a résumé (information) presented on a computer-assisted employability skills system (medium)

SOURCE: From *Career Development and Services: A Cognitive Approach*, by G. Peterson, J. Sampson, and R. Reardon, p. 200. Copyright © 1991. Reprinted with permission of Brooks/Cole, a part of The Thomson Corporation.

factors involved in this gap. One problem, for example, could be a family situation that has restricted and limited the client's possible career choices. Another could be the current work environment. Yet another could involve a child care problem. The point here is that career problems can result from a variety of factors that may involve internal domains such as faulty thinking and/or external domains of various personal and social factors. Once the problems are identified, the counselor develops problem-solving interventions. Problem solving and decision making are valuable skills that can be used throughout one's life span.

In this theory, problem solving is considered to be a series of thought processes that eventually lead to solutions of problems and remove the gap between a current situation and a preferred one. The accomplishment of this goal involves information-processing domains such as self-knowledge, occupational knowledge, and decision-making skills. In the decision-making process, the individual uses self-talk, concentrates on increasing self-awareness, and develops the ability to monitor and control information processing by recognizing when the next step in the decision process would be beneficial. The strength of this theory is in its practical application to solving career problems. As we learn more about CIP theory, the CASVE approach will be further delineated for the counseling profession.

Empirical Support for the CIP Perspective

For a discussion of metacognitions or executive processing domain, see Helwig (1992). For information about the Career Thoughts Inventory, see Peterson and colleagues (1991), Sampson, Peterson, Lenz, Reardon, and Saunders (1996a), and Sampson and

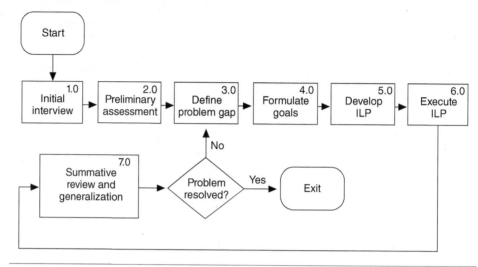

FIGURE 2.3

A career counseling sequence for individuals

SOURCE: From *Career Development and Services: A Cognitive Approach*, by G. Peterson, J. Sampson, and R. Reardon, p. 231. Copyright © 1991. Reprinted with permission of Brooks/Cole, a part of The Thomson Corporation.

colleagues (2004). Major strengths of theory are covered in Krumboltz (1992) and Gelso and Fretz (2001).

Summary of Practical Applications

Peterson, Sampson, Reardon, and Lenz (1996), and Sampson and colleagues (2004), the developers of this theory, have also proposed a seven-step sequence for career delivery service, as shown in Figure 2.3. This sequence can be used as a delivery option for both problem solving and decision making, and it can be used for individual, group, self-directed, and curricular programs. Group counseling requires that the counselor do prescreening in steps 1 and 2. In the next chapter, these steps are explained in some detail in a career counseling model referred to as the cognitive information processing approach. I strongly encourage you to read the original source for a more complete understanding of this theory. See counseling model IV in the next chapter.

Career Development from a Social Cognitive Perspective

The study of cognitive variables and processes has become a popular topic for researchers, who apply what is often referred to as the "cognitive revolution" to the study of career development. This theory has indeed followed such a script by offering a *social cognitive career theory* (SCCT) to complement existing theories and to build connecting bridges to other theories of career development.

According to Lent, Brown, and Hackett (1996, 2002), the theory's authors, there are three ways to translate and share knowledge between existing theories and emerging ones. The first is to agree on a common meaning for conceptually related concepts, such as self-concept and self-efficacy. Betz (1992b) defines career self-efficacy as "the possibility that low expectations of efficacy with respect to some aspect of career behavior may serve as a detriment to optimal career choice and the development of the individual" (p. 24). Further delineation of this theory involves Betz's reference to career-choice content (content domains such as math, science, or writing) and career-choice process (behavioral domains that enhance career implementation). From this frame of reference, an individual might avoid areas of course work associated with a career because of low self-efficacy. Likewise, self-efficacy deficits can lead to procrastination in or avoidance of a career decision.

Hackett and Betz (1981) suggest that social beliefs and expectations are the mechanisms through which self-efficacy deficits are developed, particularly for women. Hackett and Betz cite a restricted range of options and underutilization of abilities as important factors hindering women's career development. Using this logic, women's vocational behavior can at least be partially explained.

The second way to translate and share knowledge about existing theories and emerging ones is to fully describe and define common outcomes, such as satisfaction and stability, found in a number of theories. Finally, a third way is to fully explain the relationships among such diverse constructs as interests, self-efficacy, abilities, and needs. Clearly, the challenge is to find a common ground for communicating a conceptual order to the vast number of variables found in career-related literature.

The underlying assumptions and constructs of this theory are embedded in general social cognitive theory (Bandura, 1986), which blends cognitive, self-regulatory, and motivational processes into a lifelong phenomenon. More specifically, SCCT's major goals are to find methods of defining specific mediators from which learning experiences shape and subsequently influence career behavior. Furthermore, the aim is to explain how variables such as interests, abilities, and values interrelate and, most important, how all variables influence individual growth and the contextual factors (environmental influences) that lead to career outcomes. Also emphasized is the term "personal agency," which reflects how and why individuals exert power to either achieve a solution, such as a career outcome, or adapt to career changes. To identify and conceptualize the causal influences interacting between individuals and their environment, SCCT subscribes to Bandura's (1986) model of causality known as the triadic reciprocal. Within this bidirectional model, there are three variables: (1) personal and physical attributes, (2) external environmental factors, and (3) overt behavior. All three interact to the point of affecting one another as causal influences of an individual's development. Using this logic, SCCT conceptualizes the interacting influences among individuals, their behavior, and their environments to describe how individuals influence situations that ultimately affect their own thoughts and behavior.

What we have here is a complex, interacting system that is bidirectional and within which behavior, as one factor, and situations in the environment, as another, act as co-determinants in shaping personal thoughts and behaviors and external environmental factors. In essence, this is a person-behavior-situation interaction.

Key Theoretical Constructs

The personal determinants of career development have been conceptualized as *self-efficacy, outcome expectations,* and *personal goals.* The "big three" are considered to be building blocks within the triadic causal system that determine the course of career development and its outcome. Self-efficacy is not viewed as a unitary or fixed trait but, rather, as a set of beliefs about a specific performance domain. Self-efficacy is developed through four types of learning experiences (Lent, Brown, &

Hackett, 1996): "(1) personal performance accomplishments, (2) vicarious learning, (3) social persuasion, and (4) physiological states and reactions" (p. 380). Self-efficacy is strengthened when success is experienced within a performance domain, whereas it is weakened when there are repeated failures.

Outcome expectations are also regarded as personal beliefs about expectations or consequences of behavioral activities. Some individuals may be motivated by extrinsic reinforcement, such as receiving an award; others by self-directed activities, such as pride in oneself; and yet others by the actual process of performing an activity. Outcome expectations are shaped by learning activities similar to those of self-efficacy.

One of most important reasons for personal goals in this theory is that they are considered to be guides that sustain behavior. While processing personal goals, individuals generate personal agency that interacts with the three building blocks, which in effect shapes self-directed behavior.

Interest Developmental Model

Individuals develop interests through activities in which they view themselves as competent and generally expect valued outcomes. Interests fail to develop when weak and negative outcomes are expected from an activity. Activities that produce valued outcomes and that have been developed as personal interests are sustained by individuals through goals that ensure their involvement in those activities. Following this logic, activity practice tends to solidify interests and reshape and reinforce self-efficacy.

Attitudes and Values

Within the framework of SCCT, values are subsumed in the concept of outcome expectation. In effect, values are preferences for particular reinforcers, such as money, status, or autonomy. This theory stresses that outcome expectations are influenced by value systems that are positively reinforced when involved with a particular activity.

Gender and Race/Ethnicity

In this theory, we must focus on how career development was influenced from personal reactions to the social and cultural environment. Thus, the individual's socially constructed world, not inherited biological traits, is the focus of gender and race in the SCCT. It therefore is not surprising that this theory focuses on the social, cultural, and economic conditions that shaped learning opportunities to which individuals were exposed, interpersonal reactions experienced for performing certain activities, and the future outcomes that have been generated. In sum, the effects of gender and ethnicity on career interests, choice, and performance are associated primarily with differential learning experiences that influenced and subsequently shaped self-efficacy and outcome expectations.

Choice Model

The choice model is divided into three components: (1) establishing a goal; (2) taking action (by enrolling in a training or school program) to implement a choice; and (3) attaining a level of performance (successes or failures) that determines the direction of future career behavior. One's personal agency is seen as a most important variable in determining the degree of progression in the choice process. The pathways to career choice in SCCT are as follows: (1) Self-efficacy and outcome expectations promote career-related interests; (2) interests in turn influence goals; (3) goal-related actions lead to performance experiences; (4) the outcome determines future paths (determined by whether self-efficacy is strengthened or weakened); and (5) finally, one establishes a career decision or redirects goals.

One major hurdle for the individual in the choice model has to do with contextual or environmental influences. The rationale is based on opportunity structure experienced in the environment. For instance, individuals who experience support and other beneficial environmental conditions readily put their goals into actions more so than do those who experience the opposite from their environment.

Performance Model

The SCCT contains a performance model that appears to be a summary description of this theory. Its purpose is twofold: (1) It illustrates concern for the level and quality of an individual's accomplishments and for the personal agency involvement in career-related pursuits; and (2) it points out the interplay of ability, self-efficacy, outcome expectations, and the establishment of goals for judging performance. This model can also serve as a method of determining points of reference for implementing effective intervention strategies.

Empirical Support for Career Self-Efficacy

Selected references on career self-efficacy include Hackett (1995), Hackett and Lent (1992), Betz and Hackett (1986), Zimmerman (1995), and Schunk (1995). For relevant findings to SCCT's major hypotheses, see Coon-Carty (1995), Gelso and Fretz (2001), Multon, Brown, and Lent (1991), Sadri and Robertson (1993), Smith and Fouad (1999), Niles and Hartung (2000), and Sharf (2010).

Summary of Practical Applications

1. Suggestions for expanding interests and facilitating choice in SCCT include educational programs in schools that concentrate on developing interests, values, and talents and also focus on the cognitive basis for linking with these variables.

2. In the SCCT approach, individuals who are experiencing great difficulty with career choice or change should be presented with an array of occupations that correspond with their abilities and values, but not necessarily with their interests. This theory's authors argue that individuals will not consider some occupations because of false impressions of their abilities and, subsequently, will respond indifferently to such occupations on interest inventories. For example, the individual who does not indicate an interest in nursing may have been told that "you will have to take a lot of science courses." Because he views his ability to pass science courses as poor, he reacts negatively to nursing when in fact his past performance and ability scores indicate he has a better than average chance of being successful in a nursing program.

3. A strategy used in SCCT to combat perceived weaknesses includes using occupational card sorts. The individual is asked to sort occupational titles into categories of "might choose," "in question," and "would not choose." The client is then asked to further sort cards from "in question" and "would not choose" into subcategories by self-efficacy beliefs ("if I had the skills I might choose"); outcome expectations ("might choose if they matched my values"); definite lack of interest ("not considered a possible choice"); and others. Clearly, the purpose of this procedure is to assist the client in fully understanding the interacting forces that determine self-appraisals in the career decision process. Individuals who

have developed false notions about their abilities and values can indeed become indifferent toward certain occupations.

4. Overcoming barriers to choice and success is a significant goal for career counseling in SCCT. The rationale here is that individuals who perceive insurmountable barriers to career entry will be unwilling to pursue occupational interests in the career choice process. A decisional balance sheet is used to assist clients in evaluating perceived barriers. Each client is asked to generate a list of both positive and negative consequences for each career alternative he or she has selected. Each individual is then asked to develop strategies designed to overcome barriers that interfere with choice implementation.

5. School-to-work initiatives suggested by SCCT include designing skill programs that provide for self-efficacy enhancement, realistic outcome expectations, and goal-setting skills (Lent, Brown, & Hackett, 1996).

Summary Comments Concerning Social Learning and Cognitive Theories

The social learning and cognitive theories strongly suggest an emphasis on self-knowledge as the foundation for making a career decision. Information-processing skills, therefore, are considered to be of major importance. These theories also stress the importance of human traits such as ability, personality, and values, but, more importantly, they suggest research be directed to how these variables interrelate to influence growth and development. Other important factors that influence the depth and breadth of self-knowledge are social, cultural, and economic conditions. Hence, counselors are urged to unearth contextual interactions and relationship events and experiences of each client.

Self-efficacy or low expectations of what can be accomplished careerwise are thought to be the result of several factors, including environmental and economic conditions. Hence, career beliefs of a client are considered to be a core element to evaluate in the career counseling process. In all three theories in this group, faulty beliefs are aggressively addressed.

Learning programs are most important for increasing the range of career choices. Learning takes place in many ways, such as observations, reactions to others, situational conditions, and direct experiences. Following this logic, counselors are to have clients observe work activities and attempt to learn certain work tasks. Standardized tests are used primarily to determine educational and cognitive deficits. Individualized learning program goals and activities designed to debunk faulty thinking are developed from the results of test scores and intake interviews.

Finally, learning to process information effectively is a major goal of these theories. The rationale here is that skills learned in an initial career choice process can be used in the future. In this respect, clients also can prepare for future changes in work tasks and working conditions. The learning approach emphasized in these theories suggests that learning to adapt and adjust to multiple life roles in an ever-changing society is a lifelong endeavor. See career counseling models III and IV in the next chapter.

Developmental Theories

Career development is viewed as a lifelong process that is very inclusive. One major concept of developmental theories suggests that individuals make changes during developmental stages and adapt to changing life roles. Self-concept is a critical core element in developmental theories. Individuals should project self into work environments during the exploration stage and, ideally, implement a realistic self-concept into the work world. A system of developmental tasks over the life span provides key points for counseling interventions. Counselors are to evaluate the many unique developmental needs of each client when establishing counseling goals.

Adult developmental stages such as establishment and maintenance (Super, 1990) have received greater attention during the last three decades. Some workers have been "outsourced," many have experienced job loss, others opt to change careers, and some become involved in part-time work. Super's life-role approach suggests that work is very pervasive, to the point that one life role may affect others, explaining the current interest in multiple life roles. Super's position points out a weakness of other career development theories; he believes they have not addressed adult concerns and have focused primarily on initial career choice.

Counselors also learn from developmental theories that individuals circumscribe or narrow career choice through self-awareness that is determined by one's social class, level of interests, and experiences with sex typing. A primary counseling role is to assist clients to understand how their unique development influences perceptions of life roles, including the work role. In this section, we introduce a life-span, life-space approach to careers, and circumscription and compromise: a developmental theory of occupational aspirations.

Life-Span, Life-Space Approach to Careers

Donald Super (1972) thought that he had often been mislabeled as a theorist. In fact, Super did not believe that he had developed a theory that could be labeled specifically at that time. On the contrary, he viewed his work as the development of segments of possible future theories. He indicated that if he was to carry a label, it should be broad, such as differential-developmental-social-phenomenological psychologist. His multisided approach to career development was reflected first in his interest in differential psychology, or the trait-and-factor theory, as a medium through which testing instruments and subsequent norms for assessment are developed. Differential psychology suggested by Super is of utmost importance in the continuing attempt to furnish data on occupational differences related to personality, aptitude, and interests. This he viewed as an ongoing process as we learn more about the world of work and the changes that will surely come in work requirements.

As early as the 1940s, Super was promoting the idea that career development is a process that unfolds gradually over the life span. The real impact of this position was a change from the overwhelming emphasis on initial career choice to counseling programs that extended counseling to include work adjustment and multiple life roles. In essence, career development was viewed as a continuous process that involved multiple life roles. Counselors are therefore to be prepared to address client concerns over a lifetime of development during which individuals encounter situational and personal changes. In the 21st century, for example, it is forecast that a large number of individuals will change jobs several times over their life span (Drucker, 2002). The new buzz words are "multiple jobs" in "multiple places."

Self-Concept

Self-concept theory is the centerpiece of Super's approach to vocational behavior. Research projects generated as early as the 1960s aimed at determining how self-concept is implemented in vocational behavior. The significance of self-concept in the career development process was an ongoing research effort by Super and his colleagues over a span of some 50 years. Their conclusions generally indicated that vocational self-concept develops through physical and mental growth, observations of work, identification with working adults, general environment, and general experiences. Ultimately, differences and similarities between self and others are assimilated. As experiences become broader in relation to awareness of the world of work, a more sophisticated vocational self-concept is formed. Although the vocational self-concept is only part of the total self-concept, it is the driving force that establishes career patterns one will follow throughout life. The major practical application here is that individuals implement their self-concepts into careers as a means of self-expression. Second, the self-concept developmental process is multidimensional. Both internal factors (e.g., aptitude, values, and personality) and external situational conditions (e.g., contextual interactions) are major determinants of self-concept development.

In contemporary counseling, self-concept, self-awareness, self-esteem and self-knowledge are considered to be very important concepts to evaluate in the counseling process. These concepts are embedded in Roger's (1942) client-centered therapy. It appears that Super was also influenced by this seminal work as he informed those who counsel that it is imperative to understand that clients have a better chance of making optimal decisions when they are most aware of the work world and themselves. Within this position, the principle of "know thyself" becomes a prerequisite for optimal career choice. Herein we find the roots of the career education movement of the 1970s and beyond. Super suggested that students gain career maturity by learning how to plan for the future and understand the benefits of planning. School curriculums that offer opportunities for students to make connections between classroom activities and future work roles were a most important outcome recommendation. Super also emphasized the importance of enhancing one's self-knowledge. He suggested that individuals who learn more about self will also learn to expand their career considerations or at least to be more confident of their initial choices. The above contributions to career counseling have inspired computer-assisted career guidance programs as well as other resources that provide career information.

Developmental Stages and Tasks

In this section, we quickly review Super's initial developmental stages and tasks. These stages and tasks are core elements of Super's developmental approach to career development.

1. Growth (birth to age 14 or 15), characterized by development of capacity, attitudes, interests, and needs associated with self-concepts.
2. Exploratory (ages 15–24), characterized by a tentative phase in which choices are narrowed but not finalized.
3. Establishment (ages 25–44), characterized by trial and stabilization through work experiences.
4. Maintenance (ages 45–64), characterized by a continual adjustment process to improve working position and situation.
5. Decline (ages 65+), characterized by preretirement considerations, reduced work output, and eventual retirement (Issacson, 1985, pp. 51–53).

These stages of vocational development provide the framework for observing vocational behavior and attitudes, which are evidenced through five activities known as vocational developmental tasks. These five developmental tasks, shown in Table 2.4, are delineated by typical age ranges (tasks can occur at other age levels) and by their general characteristics.

Table 2.4	**Super's Vocational Developmental Tasks**	
Vocational Developmental tasks	Ages	General characteristics
Crystallization	14–18	A cognitive process period of formulating a general vocational goal through awareness of resources, contingencies, interests, values, and planning for the preferred occupations.
Specifications	18–21	A period of moving from tentative vocational preferences toward a specific vocational preference.
Implementation	21–24	A period of competing for vocational preference and entering employment.
Stabilization	24–35	A period of confirming a preferred career by actual work experience and use of talents to demonstrate career choice as an appropriate one.
Consolidation	35+	A period of establishment in a career by advancement status and seniority

SOURCE: From "A Life-Span Approach in Career Development," by D. E. Super in *Career Choice and Development: Applying Contemporary Theories in Practice*, 2nd ed., by D. Brown and Associates, p. 206. Copyright 1990 by Jossey-Bass, Inc. Reprinted with permission.

The crystallization task begins with the forming of a preferred career plan and the considerations involved in how it might be implemented. Pertinent information is studied with the goal of becoming more aware of preferred choice and if indeed it is a wise one. The specification task follows, in which the individual feels the need to specify the career plan through more specific resources and explicit awareness of cogent variables of preferred choice. The implementation task is accomplished by the completion of training and entry into a career. The stabilization task is reached when the individual is firmly established in a career and develops a feeling of security in the career position. Finally, the consolidation task follows with advancement and seniority in a career (Super, Starishesky, Matlin, & Jordaan, 1963).

Super (1990) modified developmental tasks through the life span, as shown in Table 2.5. He uses the terms "cycling" and "recycling" through developmental tasks. This formulation clarifies Super's position, which might have been misunderstood in the past; in essence, he views ages and transitions as very flexible and as not occurring in a well-ordered sequence. A person can recycle through one or more stages, which Super refers to as a minicycle. For example, an individual who experiences disestablishment in a particular job may undergo new growth and become ready to change occupations. In this instance, the individual has reached the point of maintenance but now recycles through exploration in search of a new and different position.

Career Maturity

One of Super's bestknown studies, launched in 1951, followed the vocational development of ninth-grade boys in Middletown, New York (Super & Overstreet, 1960).

Table 2.5	**The Cycling and Recycling of Developmental Tasks Through the Life Span**			
Life stage	Adolescence 14–25	Early adulthood 25–45	Middle adulthood 45–65	Late adulthood over 65
Decline	Less attention to leisure activities	Less activity in sports	More attention to essential activities	Decreasing time for work role
Maintenance	More focus on career decisions	Affirmation of career goals	Stabilized occupational competence	Maintaining a balance of work and leisure
Establishment	Focusing on new work requirements	Establish a permanent position	Improve one's work performance	Focus on personal goals
Exploration	Focus on more work opportunities	Explore opportunities in current work environment	Be alert to problems that need solutions	Begin search for retirement location
Growth	Build an understanding of self-concept development	Focus on improving relationships with others	Learn to recognize your limitations and strengths	Find activities that satisfy all life roles

SOURCE: From "A Life-Span, Life-Stage Approach in Career Development," by D. E. Super, in *Career Choice and Development: Applying Contemporary Theories in Practice*, 2nd ed., by D. Brown, L. Brooks, and Associates, p. 206. Copyright © 1990 by Jossey-Bass, Inc. Reprinted with permission.

One emphasis of this study was to identify and validate the vocational developmental tasks relevant to each stage of development. Super thought that the completion of the appropriate tasks at each level was an indication of what he termed "vocational maturity," now referred to as career maturity. The findings suggest that the ninth-grade boys in this study had not reached a level of understanding of the world of work or of themselves sufficient enough to make adequate career decisions. Career maturity seemed to be related more to intelligence than to age. Be aware that when Super conducted these studies he primarily studied the career maturity of white males; however, later studies of vocational maturity included ethnic groups and females.

Various traits of career maturity (such as planning, accepting responsibility, and awareness of various aspects of a preferred vocation) proved to be irregular and unstable during a three-year period in high school. However, those individuals who were seen as vocationally mature in the ninth grade (based on their knowledge of an occupation, planning, and interest) were significantly more successful as young adults. This finding suggests that there is a relationship between career maturity and adolescent achievement of a significant degree of self-awareness, knowledge of occupations, and developed planning capability. Thus, ninth-grade vocational behavior does have some predictive validity for the future. In other words, boys who successfully accomplish developmental tasks at periodic stages tend to achieve greater maturity later in life.

The career maturity concepts developed by Super have far-reaching implications for career education and career counseling programs. The critical phases of career maturity development provide points of reference from which the desired attitudes and competencies related to effective career growth can be identified and subsequently assessed. Moreover, the delineation of desired attitudes and competencies within each stage affords the specification of objectives for instructional and counseling projects designed to foster career maturity development. Super (1974, p. 13) identified six dimensions that he thought were relevant and appropriate for adolescents:

1. Orientation to vocational choice, an attitudinal dimension determining whether the individual is concerned with the eventual vocational choice to be made
2. Information and planning, a competence dimension concerning specificity of information individuals had concerning future career decisions and past planning accomplished
3. Consistency of vocational preferences, an individual's consistencies of preferences
4. Crystallization of traits, an individual's progress toward forming a self-concept
5. Vocational independence, such as independence of work experience
6. Wisdom of vocational preferences, a dimension concerned with an individual's ability to make realistic preferences consistent with personal tasks

Super's concept of career maturity should also be considered a major contribution to career developmental theories. An updated version of a standardized measure of career maturity variables by Crites and Savickas (1995) is evidence that this concept remains viable. Conceptually, career maturity is acquired through successfully accomplishing developmental tasks within a continuous series of life stages. Career maturity on this continuum is described in attitudinal and competence dimensions. Points of reference from this continuum provide relevant information for career counseling and career education objectives and strategies.

The concept of career maturity provides some important guidelines for career choice. Some clients simply are not prepared to make an optimal career choice. This may become clear in the intake interview and/or from the results of career maturity inventories and other assessment instruments. Thus counselors may need to assume the role of teacher or coach and provide learning and exploration activities designed to enhance self-knowledge, improve problem-solving skills, and increase the client's knowledge of work per se.

Life-Stage Model

About four years before Super's death, he developed a life-stage model by using a "life rainbow" as shown in Figure 2.4 (Super, 1990). This two-dimensional graphic schema presents a longitudinal dimension of life span, referred to as a "maxicycle," and corresponding major life stages, labeled "minicycles." A second dimension is "life space," or the roles played by individuals as they progress through developmental stages, such as child, student, "leisurite," citizen, worker, spouse, homemaker, parent, and pensioner. People experience these roles in the following theaters: home, community, school (college and university), and workplace. This conceptual model leads to some interesting observations: (1) Because people are involved in several roles simultaneously within several theaters, success in one role facilitates success in another; and (2) all roles affect one another in the various theaters.

In these early years of the 21st century, there appears to be an increased interest in the interrelationships of life roles. How pervasive, for example, is the work-role in our lives? Do problems observed in the work-role affect the family role or is the source of problems from family-role conflicts? Such questions suggest that we use a more holistic approach in solving the concerns that clients bring to counseling. Super's early work on life roles and their interrelationships should provide the impetus for more research on multiple life roles for career and personal counseling.

F I G U R E   2 . 4

The life-career rainbow: Six life roles in schematic life space

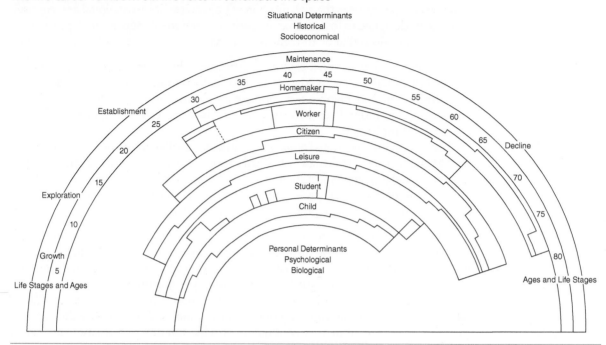

SOURCE: From "A Life-Span, Life-Space Approach to Career Development," by D. E. Super in *Career Choice and Development, Applying Contemporary Theories to Practice*, 2nd ed., edited by D. Brown, L. Brooks, and Associates, p. 212. Copyright © 1990 by Jossey-Bass, Inc. This material is used by permission of John Wiley & Sons, Inc.

Archway Model

In the early 1990s, Super also created an "archway model" to delineate the changing diversity of life roles experienced by individuals over the life span. This model is used to clarify how biographical, psychological, and socioeconomic determinants influence career development. Figure 2.5 illustrates the archway model. One base stone in the arch supports the person and his or her psychological characteristics, and the other base stone supports societal aspects such as economic resources, community, school, family, and so on. The point is that societal factors interact with the person's biological and psychological characteristics as he or she functions and grows.

The column that extends from the biological base encompasses the person's needs, intelligence, values, aptitudes, and interests—those factors that constitute personality variables and lead to achievement. The column rising from the geographical base stone includes environmental influences such as family, school, peer group, and labor markets that affect social policy and employment practices. The arch joining the columns is made up of conceptual components, including developmental stages from childhood to adulthood and developed role self-concepts. The keystone of the archway is the self or person who has experienced the personal and social forces that are major determinants of self-concept formation and active life roles in society.

In essence, interactive learning is the fundamental concept that forms the keystone (self) of the archway as the individual encounters people, ideas, facts, and objects in personal development. The relationship of the model's segments highlights the profound

FIGURE 2.5

A segmental model for career development

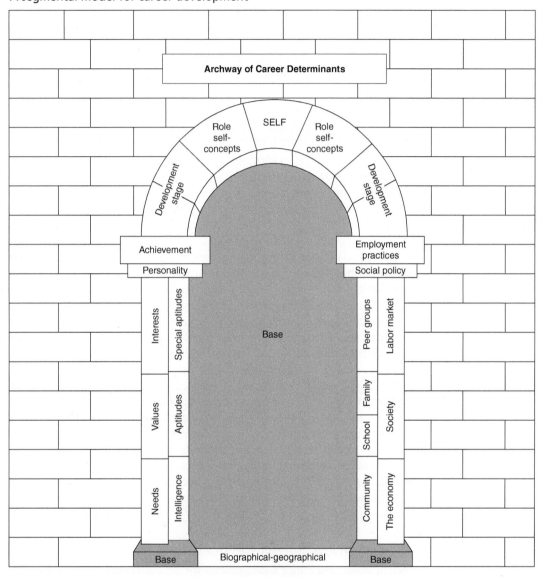

Archway of Career Determinants

SELF

Role self-concepts

Role self-concepts

Development stage

Development stage

Achievement

Employment practices

Personality

Social policy

Interests

Special aptitudes

Base

Peer groups

Labor market

Values

Aptitudes

Family

Society

School

Needs

Intelligence

Community

The economy

Base

Biographical-geographical

Base

SOURCE: Based on "A Life-Span, Life-Space Approach to Career Development" by D. E. Super in *Career Choice and Development: Applying Contemporary Theories to Practice,* 2nd ed., by D. Brown, L. Brooks, and Associates, pp. 206–208. Copyright © 1990 by Jossey-Bass, Inc., Publishers. Reprinted by permission.

interaction of influences in the career development process. The integration of life activities and developmental stages is a prime example of perceiving career development as a pervasive part of life. Career guidance programs that incorporate developmental concepts must address a broad range of counseling techniques and intervention strategies. This seems to be the message that Super promoted for several decades.

In a publication after Super's death in 1994, his theory was labeled "the life-span, life-space approach to careers" (Super, Savickas, & Super, 1996). Because this theory evolved during 60 years of research, it is no wonder that it stands out as one of the most comprehensive vocational development models in the career counseling profession. Over this 60-year period, Super's theory was constantly refined and updated, once being labeled "career development theory" and later "developmental self-concept theory." The recent name change reflects contemporary issues related to life-span needs and Super's most recent research of life roles. In this broad-based approach, gender and cultural differences are also addressed; the needs of cultural and ethnic minorities are considered important variables in the career counseling process.

Empirical Evaluations of Super's Theory

Evaluations of Super's theory have been predominantly positive, although empirical research has been difficult to accomplish because of the theory's broad scope (Brown, Brooks, & Associates, 1990). Swanson (1992) has suggested that more segments of the theory be evaluated empirically, especially the life space of adolescents and young adults and the life-span research of adults.

In a very provocative article that traces the development of Super's theory, Salomone (1996) suggested that Super had not offered testable hypotheses for various propositions of his theory. Salomone argued that Super failed to consistently define hypothetical constructs that are operational and that lend themselves to quantitative measures that support his statements. In Salomone's opinion, such constructs as work satisfaction, career maturity, and vocational development are not readily measurable, either because they are rather vague in concept or instruments at a given point in time were not available to measure them. Perhaps Salomone's criticism of Super's concepts can best be explained with the example of Super's definition of career. Salomone contended that Super expanded the concept of career (child, leisurite, and citizen) to be too inclusive for "three ingredients of good definitions—clarity, specificity, and exclusivity"; thus, when concepts are vague and nonspecific, they lose their usefulness. In this respect, Super's theory is very elusive; the relationship between theoretical propositions and empirical findings is not clearly delineated. Despite the limitations of Super's theory as outlined in his article, however, Salomone did recognize that Super has had a monumental impact on career development.

Finally, several outstanding researchers offered support to Super's theory in general, and specifically as one that describes the process of vocational development and one that will provide the mainstream of research for developmental psychology in the future (Hackett, Lent, & Greenhaus, 1991; Osipow & Fitzgerald, 1996).

Summary of Practical Applications

When observing Super's suggestions for practical applications, we must remember that he remained dedicated to the roles of developmental stages within three major segments of his theory—life space, life span, and self-concepts. He and his colleagues developed numerous assessment instruments designed to measure developmental tasks over the life span that are currently used in the career counseling process. Following are summaries of the counseling steps:

1. *Assessment.* A career development assessment and counseling model (C-DAC) was developed to measure constructs from the basic life-span, life-space theory in four phases: (1) life structure and work-role salience; (2) career development status and resources; (3) vocational identity with its work values, occupational interests, and vocational abilities; and (4) occupational self-concepts and life themes. Sharf (2013) reports that C-DAC assessment programs were expanded recently to include more culturally oriented interventions in the practice of career

development. Counselors begin with an intake interview, encouraging the client to express career concerns. Background information is gathered from school records and other sources. After comparing background information with the client's career concerns in the first interview, the counselor begins a four-step procedure to complete the assessment component.

a. The first step focuses on the client's life structure (social elements that constitute an individual's life) and work-role salience. If the client considers the work role to be important, further assessment will be more meaningful. If not, career orientation programs are recommended. The *Salience Inventory* (Nevill & Super, 1986) is used to determine the client's life space (participation and commitment to five life roles for school, work, family, community, and leisure). Scores for the client's life structure are also obtained from the constellation of 15 scores from the inventory, and they provide clues to the pattern of the client's activity in—and hope for—five major life roles.

b. The second assessment phase measures the client's perception of the work role, referred to as the client's career stage (vocational developmental tasks that concern the client) and career concerns (the amount of concern the client has with exploration, establishment, maintenance, and disengagement). The *Adult Career Concerns Inventory* (ACCI) (Super, Thompson, & Lindeman, 1988) measures career stage and career concerns, or they can be obtained through an interview.

In addition, assessment within this step includes a measure of the client's resources for choosing or coping with tasks when making decisions. The *Career Development Inventory* (Savickas, 1990; Thompson, Lindeman, Super, Jordaan, & Myers, 1984) is used to measure the variables of career planning, career exploration, information about work, and knowledge of occupations. Finally, an assessment is made of the client's resources of adapting through use of the *Career Mastery Inventory* (Crites & Savickas, 1995).

c. The third phase includes measures of abilities, interests, and values. Interest inventories that provide estimates of realistic, investigative, artistic, social, enterprising, and conventional (RIASEC) types as defined in Table 2.1 (Holland, 1992) are recommended. The *Differential Aptitude Test* (Bennett, Seashore, & Wesman, 1991) is recommended to measure aptitudes, and the *Values Inventory* (Nevill & Super, 1986) or the *Work Value Inventory* (Super, 1970) are recommended to measure values.

d. The fourth phase includes assessment of self-concepts and life themes by using adjective checklists, card sorts, or a repertory grid technique to assess the client's self-schema in world space.

2. *Data integration and narrative interpretation.* After assessment has been accomplished, the counselor interprets the data to the client. The interpretation process is referred to as integrative interpretation, in which the client's life story unfolds.

3. *Counseling goals.* In the process of setting goals, the counselor attempts to assist the client to develop an accurate picture of his or her self and life roles. Choices are to be based on implementing the self-concept into the work world in a realistic manner.

4. *Procedures.* Career development counseling procedures pertinent to career development tasks such as exploration, establishment, maintenance, and disengagement are recommended. A variety of techniques may be used that incorporate life stages and developmental tasks.

5. *Processes*. Counseling to promote career development may use coaching, educating, mentoring, modifying, or restructuring during an interview. Super also recommends cyclical counseling, in which the counseling interviews are sometimes directive but nondirective at other times. For example, directive approaches can be used to provide confrontations with reality, whereas nondirective approaches assist the client with interpreting the meanings associated with confrontations.

Life-span, life-space theory is indeed a comprehensive framework from which career development counseling has emerged. The counseling procedures developed from this theory are designed to foster maximal development (Super et al., 1996). See career counseling model II in the next chapter.

Circumscription, Compromise, and Self-Creation: A Developmental Theory of Occupational Aspirations

The development of occupational aspirations is the main theme of Gottfredson's (1981) theory. Incorporating a biosocial developmental approach, her theory describes how people become attracted to certain occupations. Self-concept in vocational development is a key factor to career selection, according to Gottfredson, because people want jobs that are compatible with their self-images. Yet self-concept development in terms of vocational choice theory needs further definition, argued Gottfredson: Key determinants of self-concept development are one's social class, level of intelligence, and experiences with sex typing. According to Gottfredson, individual development progresses through four stages:

1. Orientation to size and power (ages 3–5): Thought process is concrete; children develop some sense through sex roles of what it means to be an adult.
2. Orientation to sex roles (ages 6–8): Self-concept is influenced by gender development.
3. Orientation to social valuation (ages 9–13): Development of concepts of social class contributes to the awareness of self-in-situation. Preferences for level of work develop.
4. Orientation to the internal, unique self (beginning at age 14): Introspective thinking promotes greater self-awareness and perceptions of others. Individual achieves greater perception of vocational aspirations in the context of self, sex role, and social class.

In this model of development, occupational preferences emerge within the complexities that accompany physical and mental growth. A major determinant of occupational preferences is the progressive circumscription of aspirations during self-concept development, that is, from the child's rather simplistic and concrete view of life to the more comprehensive, complex, abstract thinking of the adolescent and adult. For example, in stage 1, the child has a positive view of occupations based on concrete thinking. In stage 2, the child makes more critical assessments of preferences, some of which are based on sex typing. In stage 3, the child adds more criteria to evaluate preferences. In stage 4, the adolescent develops greater awareness of self, sex typing, and social class, all of which are used with other criteria in evaluating occupational preferences.

Gottfredson suggested that socioeconomic background and intellectual level greatly influence individuals' self-concept in the dominant society. As people project into the work world, they choose occupations that are appropriate to their "social space," intellectual level, and sex typing. In the Gottfredson model, social class and intelligence are incorporated in the self-concept theory of vocational choice.

Another unique factor in this theory is the concept of compromise in decision making. According to Gottfredson, compromises are based primarily on generalizations formed about occupations or "cognitive maps" of occupations. Although each person develops a unique map, each uses common methods of evaluating similarities and differences, namely through sex-typing, level of work, and field of work. In this way, individuals create boundaries or tolerable limits of acceptable jobs. Gottfredson suggested that people compromise their occupational choices because of the accessibility of an occupation or even give up vocational interests to take a job that has an appropriate level of prestige and is an appropriate sextype. In general, individuals are less willing to compromise job level and sextype because these factors are more closely associated with self-concept and social identity.

In its early stages, this theory had a strong sociological perspective. The external barriers that limit individual goals and opportunities concern Gottfredson, and her theory differed from other theories in four major ways. First, in career development, there is an attempt to implement the social self and, secondarily, the psychological self. Gottfredson places much more emphasis on the idea that individuals establish social identities through work. Second, how cognitions of self and occupations develop from early childhood is a major focus of the theory. Third, the theory's premise is that career choice is a process of eliminating options, thus narrowing one's choices. Fourth, the theory attempts to answer how individuals compromise their goals as they try to implement their aspirations. In Gottfredson's view, career choice proceeds by eliminating the negative rather than by selecting the most positive.

Although these differences make this theory distinctive, the theory also shares some fundamental assumptions with other theories. For example, career choice is a developmental process from early childhood. Second, individuals attempt to implement their self-concepts into career choice selections. Finally, satisfaction of career choice is determined largely by a "good fit" between the choice and the self-concept.

Major Concepts of Gottfredson's Theory

Self-Concept. Following Super and colleagues (1963), Gottfredson defines self-concept as one's view of self that has many elements, such as one's appearance, abilities, personality, gender, values, and place in society.

Images of Occupations. Images of occupations refer to occupational stereotypes (Holland, 1992) that include personalities of people in different occupations, the work that is done, and the appropriateness of that work for different types of people.

Cognitive Maps of Occupations. These cognitive maps constitute how adolescents and adults distinguish occupations into major dimensions, specifically, masculinity/femininity, occupational prestige level, and field of work. A two-dimensional map of sex type (Holland's term) and prestige level has been constructed to portray certain occupations by these two dimensions, and Holland's typology is used to indicate field of work. For example, an accountant (field of work) has above-average prestige level, and sex type is rated as more masculine than female. This map is primarily used to locate "areas" of society that different occupations offer. Individuals use images of themselves to assess their compatibility with different occupations. Some refer to this process as congruence, or person-environment fit. If the core elements of self-concept conflict with an occupation, that occupation is rejected in Gottfredson's scheme.

Social Space. This term refers to the zone of acceptable alternatives in each person's cognitive map of occupations, or each person's view of where he or she fits or would want to fit into society. Gottfredson suggests that career decision making should center around points of reference as "territories," either measured or contemplated, rather than around specific points of reference to a single occupation.

Circumscription. Circumscription reflects the process by which an individual narrows his or her territory when making a decision about social space or acceptable alternatives. The stages of circumscription were outlined earlier.

Compromise. This is a very significant process in Gottfredson's theory. As she puts it, "individuals often discover, when the time comes that they will be unable to implement their most preferred choices" (Gottfredson, 1996, p. 187). Within this process, individuals will settle for a "good" choice, but not the best possible one. Compromise is the process of adjusting aspirations to accommodate external reality, such as local availability of educational programs and employment, hiring practices, and family obligations. According to Gottfredson, individuals will not compromise their field of interest by prestige or sex type when there are small discrepancies. When there are moderate trade-offs within the process of compromise, people avoid abandoning prestige rather than sex type. In major trade-offs, people will sacrifice interests rather than prestige or sex type (Gottfredson, 1996).

The scope of this theory has been greatly expanded by Gottfredson (2002), primarily through a biosocial perspective of career counseling. She stresses that career development is to be viewed as a nature–nurture partnership. She was greatly influenced by Eysenck's (1998) findings from genetically sensitive family studies over several decades that suggest both genes and environment drive human experiences, which in turn consolidate individual traits. In other words, genetically distinct individuals create different environments and each individual's genetic uniqueness shapes their experiences. This position differs from socialization theory, which suggests we are passive learners from our environmental experiences and supports the view that we are active participants in creating self-directed experiences. Not only are one's experiences self-directed, but also how one perceives and interprets them is unique for each individual. Eysenck suggested that both genes and environment contribute to one's unique development.

What stands out as a different perspective here is the genetic influence on one's behavior. It seems that genetic propensities drive our evaluations of experiences and as such are precursors of individual uniqueness. The nature–nurture partnership approach therefore adheres to an inner compass from which one may circumscribe and compromise life choices. Gottfredson's theory is distinguished from others by her emphasis on inherited genetic propensities that shape individual traits. Following this logic, individuals "seek and create environments that reinforce their genetic proclivities" (Gottfredson, 2002, p. 115).

The implications for career counseling include a perspective on individual differences that focuses on the influence of genetic individuality. Studies of genetic intelligence support the principle that genetic influence on intelligence is clearly evident (Shaffer, 2002). As early as the late 1920s, Spearman (1927) suggested that a general mental ability exists called the "g" factor that contributes to the ability to perform specific tasks such as numerical reasoning and word memory (Sigelman & Rider, 2009). In addition, there appear to be genetic influences on the development of personality traits in that many personality traits are considered to be moderately heritable (Shaffer, 2002). Most important to recognize here is the interplay of genetic and environmental factors that contribute to behavior. As Gottfredson suggests, individuals and their environments are involved in a continuous state of dynamic interaction that leads to change and modification of both. Thus, counselors are to respect the individuality of all clients and make no assumptions about a client's vocational interests, attitudes, and abilities. More applications of her theory follow.

Empirical Support

Lapan and Jingeleski (1992) found some agreement with the concept of social space in that individuals did assess compatibility with regard to zones of alternatives within the broad scope of the occupational world. Sastre and Mullet (1992) confirmed that gender, social class, and intelligence are related to work field and level of occupational aspirations. Leung, Conoley, and Scheel (1994) studied 149 immigrant and native-born Asian American college students to determine whether the boundaries of social space are set by age 13 (stage 3). They concluded that social space increased in size from age 8 through 17, disconfirming the theory's predictions. Although this one study should not negate Gottfredson's individual development through four stages, there remains the possibility that some students widen their range of career exploration during high school. Also see Armstrong and Crombie (2000), Gottfredson (1997), and McLennan and Arthur (1999).

Summary of Practical Applications

Gottfredson directs career counselors to what she refers to as underappreciated problems and possibilities in career development. Counselors should encourage clients to be as realistic as possible when exploring potential occupational goals. She concludes that reality is either ignored, or the client fails to deal effectively with it. She recommends five developmental criteria to aid the counselee in dealing with reality.

1. The counselee is able to name one or more occupational alternatives. If not, then the counselor is to determine whether indecision reflects the inability to choose among high-quality alternatives or whether there is an unwillingness to attempt to choose. Some questions to be answered are the following: Is there a lack of self-confidence? Are there internal or external conflicts in goals? Is there impaired judgment?
2. The counselee's interests and abilities are adequate for occupations chosen. If not, is this the result of misperceptions about self? Are there external pressures from parents or other important adults?
3. The counselee is satisfied with the alternatives he or she has identified. If dissatisfied, does the counselee consider the selected alternatives as an unacceptable compromise of interests, sex type, prestige or family concerns, or other concerns? Attempt to determine internal or external constraints.
4. The counselee has not unnecessarily restricted his or her alternatives. Did the counselee consider suitable and accessible alternatives? Has there been a lack of exposure to compatible alternatives? Does the counselee have an adequate knowledge of his or her own abilities?

5. The counselee is aware of opportunities and is not realistic about obstacles for implementing the chosen occupation. What are the reasons the counselee has not been realistic about obstacles? Is there wishful thinking or a lack of information or planning? Information to seek during the counseling interview includes why certain options seem to be rejected and why some compromises are more acceptable than others. Use the following questions: What is the preferred self, in both sociability and personality type? Are the perceptions of boundaries in social space adequate? Who are the primary reference groups, and what family circumstances influence the counselee?

Finally, Gottfredson suggests that information that provides compatibility and accessibility is essential. One may do this through exploration of social space that includes aptitude requirements of occupations, arrays of occupational clusters, and the counselee's perceptions of sex type and prestige. Occupational clusters depicted on a map are to be used to focus attention on compatible clusters. As the counselee selects more specific occupations, the characteristics of the occupation and the availability of training should be discussed. Eventually, as the client reaches the realm of constructive realism, a subset of best choices can be selected realistically and, subsequently, one best choice made, with a list of alternatives.

Gottfredson adds a biosocial perspective to the career development of the very young. She strongly suggests that more attention be given to the development of individuals in their young years. Of her key concepts, circumscription and compromise are the most dynamic and need further research to determine how to minimize their limiting effects on career choice. Her theory has been criticized because it is limited to children and leaves much to be said about adult development (Gelso & Fretz, 2001).

Summary Comments Concerning Developmental Theories

Developmental theories give a perspective of career development that is continuous and discontinuous and is indeed multidimensional. The concept of vocational maturity illuminates the proposition that some clients simply are not prepared to make an optimal career decision. Counselors are to assess a client's orientation to work, planning skills, and reality of occupational preferences to determine readiness for career choice. There are developmental tasks and stages in career development that provide windows of opportunity for counseling interventions. Self-concept is the driving force that establishes a career pattern. One of the major goals of developmental theory is to assist each client develop an accurate picture of self in multiple life roles. The assumption that clients are involved in several life roles simultaneously, and success in one life role facilitates success in another, underscores the important perspective of life-span development. Super has called special attention to adult concerns in the scheme of career development that will be most relevant in the 21st century. See career counseling model IV in the next chapter.

Gottfredson's research underscores a well-known position that career education should begin with the very young. Counselors need to make every effort to empower children to learn more about the work world and promote the proposition that each child should feel free to choose any career. Counselors need to be aware of how parental status influences children and social restraints of circumscription limit their career development.

Finally, each client's unique development should be the focus of the intake interview. Developmental theories point out that each individual's development is unique, multifaceted, and multidimensional. Counselors must recognize that client concerns can emerge from internal and external factors or a combination of both. In the next section we expand the developmental process to include contextual interactions.

Person-in-Environment Perspective

The person-in-environment perspective focuses attention on contextual interaction over the life span. Clients are viewed as products of an environment that is very inclusive, but also unique. One's career development is thought to be *influenced and constructed* within several environmental systems such as family, church or synagogue, neighborhood, school, neighbors, friends, workplace, community agencies, culture, and customs of the larger environment. Major tenets of these theories emphatically support the position that concerns of clients do not exist totally within the person.

Counselors are to look not only for internal pathology, but also for causes of client concerns that may have developed through a variety of experiences, relationships, and situations. This position is not necessarily a new one in that a number of theorists have stressed the need to unearth background variables of clients. The major differences here, however, are the inclusive nature of influence variables that are viewed as systems, constructs, and the proposition that there is a reciprocity affect, that is, individuals influence and are influenced as they interact within their environment. Therefore, effective counseling procedures need to unearth both internal and external variables that contribute to career development.

Person-in-environment and ecological systems are often used interchangeably (Cormier, Nurius, & Osborn, 2013), but an ecological system is not in itself a career development theory. An ecological system is one of the most inclusive methods of understanding human development. It is, as the name implies, a study of the relationship between person and environment. An ecological system theory provides a detailed analysis of ongoing environmental influences over the life span. The developing person is viewed as "being at the center of and embedded in several environmental systems that interact with one another" (Shaffer, 2002, p. 59).

Bronfenbrenner (1979) suggested that there are four systems that make up an environment. The first is the microsystem or the person; second is the mesosystem of family, peer group, and schoolmates, among others; third is the exosystem of friends of family, extended family, neighbors, workplaces, media, and others; and, finally, the macrosystem is the sum of broad ideologies expressed and modeled by the sociocultural group. These systems are illustrated in Figure 2.6.

This human development theory posits that people develop in changing historical contexts and in sociocultural interactions and relationships. Such a perspective makes an important point for counselors to contemplate by suggesting that not all client problems are "within" the client, but on the contrary, many concerns are embedded within person-in-environment experiences. Within this view of human development that is both continuous and discontinuous, individuals are also involved in ongoing systems that change. Uniqueness emerges from individualized and shared experiences, and one's unique interpretation of those experiences: Each individual life story unfolds within changing ecological systems.

The ecological systems perspective provides the counselor with the opportunity to view all aspects of a person as a whole. It is a "who" and "where" approach to counseling that offers a balanced view of human development (Cormier et al., 2013). The lesson here is that counselors search for causes of client concerns and constructs that have developed from a wide range of interactions in his or her environment. Core assumptions, for instance, may well be embedded in learning experiences within ecological systems. For example, are Joy's mood swings the result of faulty perceptions of environmental events or from poor environmental fit? Is Jim's problem in school

FIGURE 2.6

Ecological systems map

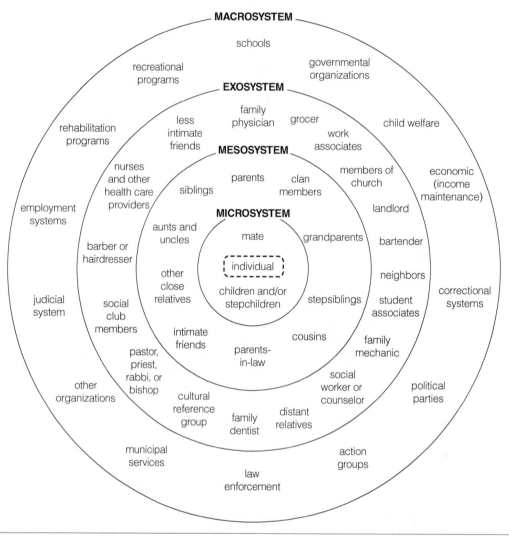

a learning disability or the result of current marital conflicts between his parents? Is poor self-esteem and lack of assertiveness the reason Jessica has not been promoted or is it because she has a controlling and demanding family? Or both? Dan thinks he is too stupid to get accepted to college. Is this a self-concept problem or the result of underfunded and inadequate schools, or both?

These examples illustrate the significance of unearthing one's life story from environmental factors that may contribute to a client's faulty thinking or inappropriate behavior and the internal conflicts a client brings to counseling. One's life story can also be a valuable source of information that can be fostered in the career counseling process. In sum, an ecological system includes a broad perspective of potential influences that can affect learning, thinking, reasoning, decision making, and subsequent behavior. More importantly, it suggests that human behavior can be understood only in the context in which it occurs. The person-in-environment approach to counseling is touted as a more inclusive and balanced approach to the practice of career development. A greater understanding of person-in-environment perspectives includes an introduction to constructivism in the next paragraphs.

Constructivism

Since the early 1980s, the psychological approach of constructivism to career development has emerged from the philosophical position of postmodernism that suggested there is no fixed truth. This position is a reaction to traditional modernist thinking of logical positivism, from which theories with logical proofs were directed to gather empirical data to either approve or disapprove them. The logical positivism approach served the physical sciences well, but some social scientists turned to alternative paradigms of constructivism to better understand human behavior. The constructivist's viewpoint of career development is quite a departure from other theories that rely on logical proofs supported by empirical data. Constructivists support the belief that individuals define themselves as they participate in events and relationships in their environment. In order to make sense of environmental interactions and events, each individual develops personal constructs in which his or her views of the world differ from others. For example, different worldviews develop from different cultures and within cultures. These sets of personal constructs continue to be modified over the life span. In this context, the client is an active participant in her or his career development and each client is considered as a unique individual who has developed personal constructs from her or his perceptions of unique events and interactions. What is suggested here is that counselors concentrate on assisting individual clients to identify and understand their unique personal constructs as a precursor for intervention strategies. The life history of each client provides them with a means for understanding their own career story and the direction of their vocational behavior (Savickas, 2002). Gelso and Fretz (2001) suggest that Brown, Brooks, and Associates (1996) have captured the essence of the emergence of constructivism in the following propositions:

- All aspects of the universe are interconnected; it is impossible to separate figure from ground, subject from object, people from environments.
- There are no absolutes; thus, human functioning cannot be reduced to laws or principles, and cause and effect cannot be inferred.
- Human behavior can be understood only in the context in which it occurs.
- The subjective frame of reference of human beings is the only legitimate source of knowledge. Events occur outside human beings. As individuals understand their environments and participate in events, they define themselves and their environments (p. 10).

Following this logic, individual careers are constructed through unique learning experiences in an ecological system. Personal constructs therefore are developed by individuals through the way they interpret and view their lives (Kelly, 1955). Life-role clarity and meaning of life, for example, are expressed in one's career (Sharf, 2010). Thus, counselors emphasize person–work-environment fit from two perspectives—how the person fits into the work role and how the work role fits into the person's lifestyle. Keep in mind that individual sets of constructs are modified continually over a life span, suggesting that individuals are best served by learning to manage their own career development. Clients who learn to understand that the direction of their vocational behavior may change over time are best prepared to make careful and meaningful life and career decisions. The focus of this viewpoint is on individual behavior rather than on the behavior of groups of individuals that may provide a norm from which one judges their own career development. Such norms can be used as guidelines, however, as individuals process and comprehend their own personal agenda. Two career development theories are reviewed, career construction and a developmental theory of vocational behavior, followed by a contextual explanation of career.

Career Construction: A Developmental Theory of Vocational Behavior

Using our brief introduction to constructivism as a backdrop, we review some of the highlights of a career construction theory by Savickas (2002). Using Super's theory of vocational development, Savickas expands and extends this theory by using the psychological approach of constructivism, which suggests that individuals construct their own reality or truth. Second, he suggests that careers are to be viewed from a developmental contextual viewpoint that focuses on one's adaptation to an environment through the development of inner structures. Savickas carefully states 16 propositions of career construction theory that include (1) developmental contextualism, such as the core roles developed through an individual's life structure, preferences of life roles, and an individual's career pattern; (2) development of vocational self-concepts that include individual differences, vocational characteristics, occupational requirements, work satisfaction, how self-concepts develop and are implemented in work roles, and continuity of self-concepts; and (3) vocational developmental tasks experienced as social expectations, the growth experienced during career transitions, vocational maturity as a psychosocial construct, career adaptability as a psychological construct, and how career construction is fostered. Some of these propositions will be discussed in the following paragraphs, but readers are encouraged to read the original text for more complete information.

Developmental contextualism that is used to designate how individual constructs are developed appears to be built around the concepts of Bronfenbrenner's (1979) ecological system discussed earlier. As one develops in a social context, personal constructs evolve from one's perception of events and interactions within a social ecology system. It is the context of reciprocal development in a social ecology that gives meaning to the personal constructs that influence life-role development. For instance, gender differences in work roles may be fostered. Occupational choice could be restrained or embellished as individuals interact within contextual opportunities. The point to remember here is that individuals participate in their own development that leads to perceptions of core roles, so counselors can assist clients to consciously influence the direction of future life roles.

As core roles emerge in the constructivist's view, there is an increasing sense of personal awareness and integration of constructs. As more personal constructs are developed, one becomes increasingly aware of individual differences and dichotomous constructs. Gradually, one integrates constructs into a system that gives clarity to purpose and role. Life in an ever-changing society provides for an ongoing process of individual construct development that influences adaptations and modification of life roles. Within this context, Savickas (2002) makes the point that each person's core roles interact to reciprocally shape each other. Therefore, to understand an individual's career choice and commitment, for instance, is to understand and appreciate the inner constructs that give meaning to that individual's life roles.

Following Super's lead, Savickas illuminates the importance of self-concept development. He describes the forming of self-concept in early childhood "as a collection of percepts that is neither integrated nor particularly coherent." In early adolescence a more unified and coherent self-concept permits individuals to form some abstract self-descriptions. Finally, the more organized self-concept becomes a filter through which one forms self-perceptions that guide and control behavior. As one experiences the give-and-take of life, new and different percepts lead to self-concept revision. Thus, in this context, the process of career development is never complete.

There are also dimensions of self-concept that are worthy of mention. The vocational self-concept is viewed as an individual's perception of her or his personal attributes that are considered relevant to certain work roles. Examples of self-concept dimensions of attributes that were suggested by Super include assertiveness and gregariousness, whereas examples of self-concept metadimensions include consistency and stability (Savickas, 2002). This distinction is particularly important in career choice counseling. In Savickas's career construction theory, the self-concept dimensions direct the content of alternative choices whereas the metadimensions of self-esteem, realism, and clarity, for example, direct the process of making a choice. Thus, one individual may project the vocational self-concept into a certain work environment of interest but withdraw from it because of poor self-esteem. This situation illustrates that contradictory self-percepts make it difficult to find occupational fit and provide the counselor with clues for developing tailored interventions. I now turn to a brief explanation of career construction theory.

Career Construction: Developmental Tasks Within Vocational Development Stages

Career construction theory endorses Super's (1990) basic principles of developmental tasks. The basic principles of tasks and stages, for instance, suggest that successful passage from one stage to another is considered as individual progress over the life span. Second, the degree to which one successfully adapts to each task and meshes this progress with career concerns indicates one's level of career maturity. It is therefore important that clients and counselors recognize the relevance of completing the goals of the developmental stages of growth, exploration, establishment, maintenance, and disengagement. In the following paragraphs, the developmental tasks within each developmental stage will be briefly discussed, primarily from a constructivist's point of view. A major point here is that each individual's experiences in processing developmental tasks form the foundation for a greater self-understanding and vocational identity.

Growth, the first developmental stage, is characterized by Super as development of capacity, attitudes, interests, and needs associated with self-concepts. It is a lifespan developmental process as outlined in Table 2.5 earlier in this chapter. Savickas (2002) emphasizes developmental factors associated with children. He suggests that there are four major tasks that society has imposed upon children as follows:

1. Become *concerned* about one's future as a worker.
2. Increase personal *control* over one's vocational activities.
3. Form *conceptions* about how to make educational and vocational choices.
4. Acquire the *confidence* to make and implement these career choices (p. 168).

In sum, the concerned child is influenced by numerous interactive relationships. Among the most significant are interactions between parents and children. Children who have secure attachments to caregivers are more likely to feel positive about themselves and other people. Conversely, those who have insecure attachments develop poor self-perceptions and view others with distrust. Because children experience and learn from numerous relational activities in early childhood, positive relationships are to be fostered (Tiedeman & O'Hara, 1963). *Career control* refers to self-determination (Blustein & Flum, 1999) and the development of personal agency. The individual gains control of her or his future by fostering her or his own independent actions and intentional behavior that reinforces actions of decisiveness and self-competence. The forming of *career conceptions* involves consideration and reconsideration of possible courses of action. Curiosity about the future prompts some individuals to project into tentative goals and form some tentative results. Thus, distorted career perceptions during this period can hamper future career choices. Sources of one's *career confidence* in this scheme are numerous and most important. Some sources include daily interactions with peers and significant experiences such as learning to solve problems. One outstanding source of career confidence is success in school activities that help build positive attitudes, beliefs, and competencies.

The exploration stage is characterized by Super as a tentative phase in which choices are narrowed, but not finalized. One learns more about occupational opportunities and self-in-situation. In the process of constructing a career, the individual searches for congruent work environments in which to express vocational identity. There is a continued assessment of alternatives; some are discarded but may be reconsidered in other tasks. During this stage, individuals are searching for a clearer definition of self in order to establish a sense of vocational identity (Savickas, 2002).

There are three tasks associated with the exploration stage: crystallization, specification, and actualization. During the crystallization process, there is a continued assessment of alternatives. Goals become more definite and formed but are not irreversible. One major goal of the crystallization process is for individuals to stabilize and integrate self-percepts into a stable structure. Those who lag behind and fail to gain clarity of self and role are often classified as being indecisive. Thus, it is not surprising that disharmony significantly interferes with career development. In general, Savickas takes the position that in a structural model of career development, competencies derive from knowledge about one's self and occupations, as in other career theories, and are inextricably intertwined with development of skills needed for problem solving, matching, and life planning.

Specification tasks direct individuals toward specifying an occupational choice. The individual becomes involved in carefully reviewing tentative preferences in an in-depth exploration of reality testing. There is a focus on the particular behaviors that are necessary to meet one's chosen goal. At first glance this task may appear rather simplistic, but it is indeed a relevant step in the career choice process. One who makes a declaration of intent suggests that the crystallization process is complete. Thus, in specifying an occupation the individual declares how he views himself in relation to the world and implies a unity and wholeness of purpose that has prompted a significant commitment.

Actualization is a period that is highlighted by one's focus on career identification. It may include trial jobs in the chosen occupational group. During this period, the individual searches for fit in a work environment. One may experiment with a series of related jobs before finding a congruent one. There are internal and external barriers that may delay actualization. Poor attitudes, inappropriate behavior patterns, and beliefs are internal factors that disrupt progress. External barriers can come in many forms, such as outsourcing of jobs and lack of opportunity to advance. Individuals should therefore be prepared to face a work world where there is little in the way of promises for a lifetime job. In sum, actualization tasks are ongoing, as one may experience multiple jobs over the life span.

The third career stage of establishment infers a settling-down process in a permanent job. One begins the implementation of self-concept in an occupational role. Individuals are to refine their occupational role and consolidate their position. This stage is also characterized by greater self-understanding and identification with the total system of a career field. Developing a perspective of positive growth orientation is to be fostered. Individuals must distinguish between real barriers (no growth, slow growth, and organizational decline) and perceived barriers (role confusion, poor career identity, nebulous perceptions of career success and direction) that affect their ability to reach personal goals.

The fourth career stage is maintenance or management. Here individuals become more aware of life stages in terms of time spans and begin to view career in terms of implementing future opportunities. Savickas suggests that this stage is a time for a renewal of vocational development. It involves refinding the self and maintaining and preserving one's self-concept. Workers in this stage avoid stagnation by updating their skills and knowledge. They become innovative in developing new and different strategies. They become lifelong learners. In spite of these actions, changes in how and for whom one works makes it apparent to workers who have reached the maintenance stage that they must be resilient and willing to start over in a different career path. Counselors can suggest a recycling through one or more of the career-stage maxicycles.

Finally, career stage five, disengagement, is characterized by preretirement considerations. The individual prepares to "let go" of responsibilities and pass them on to others. One major adjustment during late career is learning to accept a reduced work role and changing focus away from a highly involved work identity. It is, as the name implies, a disengagement of vocational self-concept and a recycling to retirement living. One has to organize a new and different lifestyle. One would suspect that the sequence of events for retired workers in the 21st century will be quite different from those of their predecessors in the last century. The new social corporate culture that is being driven by global market forces should drastically change the work history of many citizens.

Empirical Support for Career Construction Theory

Much more research is needed on various aspects of career construction theory; however, empirical research on the theory by Hackett and Lent (1992) and Osipow and Fitzgerald (1996) suggests the following:

1. The data generally support the model.
2. The development segment is well documented.
3. Data relative to the self-concept generally agree with the theory (Savickas, 2002, p. 183).

Summary of Practical Applications

Career construction theory stresses the development and implementation of self-concept into society. Clients are to learn how to construct a career path that fosters individual progress to discovering and experiencing a meaningful life. In order to foster self-concept development and implementation, constructivist career counseling begins with the discovery of career concerns.

Assessment of Career Construction Theory

The intake interview focuses on career concerns that can be identified by the *Adult Career Concerns Inventory* (Super, Thompson, & Lindeman, 1988). This inventory measures concerns with the developmental stages of exploration, establishment, management, and disengagement. Thus, the assessment phase is very inclusive but does focus on life space, career adaptability, vocational self-concept and career themes, and vocational identity.

The counselor begins by identifying concerns in life space and, more specifically, the work role. Uncovering a client's level of commitment to work role is a major goal of this first phase. Counselors are also to determine the cultural context in which concerns originate. When it is found that a client has a strong commitment to the work role, adaptability, vocational self-concept, and vocational identity become focus points. A major objective is to find out if vocational identity is accurate. If the work role is not a major concern of the client, the counselor shifts to identifying the relative importance of other life roles.

Assessing Career Adaptability. Inventories that are used include the following: *Career Maturity Inventory* (Crites & Savickas, 1996) for high school students and *Career Development Inventory* (Savickas & Hartung, 1996) for college students. These inventories are generally used to evaluate competencies for making educational and vocational decisions. They focus on (1) the choice process of crystallizing, specifying, and actualizing, and (2) the implementing process of stabilizing, consolidating, and advancing. The interview may also be used to obtain this information. See Dix and Savickas (1995) and Savickas (2002).

Assessing Vocational Self-Concept and Career Themes. This step in client assessment attempts to uncover a cross-sectional view of self-concept and a longitudinal view of career themes. Self-concepts may be measured by adjective checklists (Johansson, 1975), card sorts (Hartung, 1999), or a repertory grid technique (Neimeyer, 1989). Career theme assessment usually includes an autobiography, but it can be attained through a career-theme interview (Savickas, 1989).

Assessing Vocational Identity. To obtain an objective picture of an individual's vocational identity, the counselor is instructed to use measures of interests such as the *Self-Directed Search* (Holland, 1994a) or *Strong Interest Inventory* (Harmon, Hansen, Borgen, & Hammer, 1994). The major purpose of measures of objective interests is to identify how a client resembles workers employed in different occupations. Objective measures of interests that indicate some congruence with certain occupations are compared with vocational self-concepts and career themes to determine their fit.

Finally, Savickas suggests that test results are presented most effectively in an integrated and narrative format. The narrative serves as the client's life story; it includes the importance of life roles and the emerging career experiences. The narrative should include the client's concerns and illuminate the client's character in the context of a client's life space. The client's concerns are to be conceptualized by the counselor as the current predicament and are linked to career themes that encourage speculation about the future. Clients are to connect with alternative choices that make sense out of the work world. One of the key counseling methods used in constructivist career counseling is autobiographical reasoning.

Finally, career narratives consist of career stories that assist clients in relating vocational self-concepts to work roles. Narratives are designed to foster self-concept clarification as a most important connection with self-fulfillment. In sum, constructivist approaches to career development recognize that individuals develop their own constructs and views of what is real for them; thus, the career narrative provides an effective tool to connect career themes with one's vocational identity. See Savickas (1993) for more information and Sharf (2010) for a detailed and straightforward account of narrative counseling. In the next section, I discuss a contextural explanation of a career.

A Contextual Explanation of Career

The contextualism method establishes a contextual action explanation of career research and career counseling. Contextualism is based on the philosophical position known as constructivism (Brown, Brooks, & Associates, 1996). According to Sharf (2010), the constructivist position suggests "that individuals construct their own way of organizing information and that truth or reality is a matter of perception" (p. 425). Understanding how clients construct personal meanings from present actions and subsequent experiences is the core of this theory (Savickas, 2002).

The contextual model for human development is an ever-changing, ongoing interplay of forces. The major focus is on the relationship between person and environment because they are considered to be inseparable and are regarded as a unit. As people and the environment interact, development can proceed along many different pathways, depending on how one influences the other (Shaffer, 2002).

Young, Valach, and Collin (1996, 2002) propose that one way to understand a contextualist explanation of career counseling is by action theory. Action, in this sense, focuses on the whole in the context in which action is taken. For example, a career counselor, a client, and a worker in the field the client is currently interested in have a discussion about the work, peer affiliates, and work environment. The total action of all three people is the context in which this particular counseling took place, and their actions form the basis for constructing personal meaning. To break the process into parts would be similar to unraveling an event into meaningless fragments. Thus, the wholeness of an event and the succession of changes that result from interaction with others and their contexts is the contextualist's perspective. In essence, contextualists support the idea that events take shape as people engage in them, and only then is an analysis of actions and events practical. Thus, their focus is on "human intention, processes, and change in context rather than on context as a setting (environment) for action" (Young et al., 2002, p. 207).

The study of actions is the major focus of the contextual viewpoint. Actions are conceptualized as being cognitively and socially directed and as reflecting everyday experiences; actions are social processes and, as such, reflect each individual's social and cultural world. Actions are viewed from three perspectives: They *manifest behavior,* for example, taking notes of a lecture; they are *internal processes,* such as feeling nervous about an examination; and they have *social meaning,* such as being successful in a career.

Action systems are composed of joint and individual actions and two terms, project and career. Joint action simply means that many career-related actions occur among people. According to the contextualist point of view, career values, interests, identity, and behaviors are constructed largely through language in conversation with others. Instead of evaluating the discussions individually between client and counselor, the contextualist conceptualizes joint action as a unit between client and counselor. The major focus here is on the action of the dyad. In other words, each person influences the other and their conclusions may direct some changes in each participant's behavior or cause them to modify their thinking about the subject discussed. Their subsequent actions may result in positive or negative consequences in the future.

Project refers to an agreement of actions between two or more people. For example, a single parent and adolescent child form an agreement of household responsibilities so that both can work. Because of changing work conditions and working hours, parent and child renegotiate responsibilities. In this example, individual and joint actions—including manifest actions—internal processes, and social meaning contribute to the project. The parent's and the child's behavior can be interpreted individually and jointly by this project.

The term "career," as used in this theory, is similar to the term "project." It can also be used to construct connections among actions and to evaluate plans, goals, emotions, and internal cognitions. The major difference between project and career is that career extends over a longer period of time and subsequently involves more actions. The actions can become complex and include greater social meaning. In this way, career approximates the idea of vocation.

The authors of this theory have developed an aspects-of-action theory to illustrate action systems, perspectives on action, and levels of action organization. Levels of action organization include elements, functional steps, and goals. Elements refer to physical and verbal behavior, such as words, movements, and environmental structures. Functional steps refer to higher level actions than elements—for example, pleading and reminding can be used to convey a desired action. Goals, the highest level of action, usually represent the general intention of the individual or group.

The major purpose of defining actions in this manner is to organize the interpretation of human actions. Interpretation within this script offers a systematic method of evaluating and interpreting actions and the context in which they happen—what the counselor and client are doing together.

Much more research is needed on how a person affects the environment and how the environment affects that person. As we learn more about the ecology within which significant interactions occur, we may discover some dimensions that are relevant to career development. A good description of how both individuals and the world interact is by Vondracek, Lerner, and Schulenberg (1986), who see "levels of being" as multiple dimensions of interdependent forces that are developing and changing over time. This is a very complex person-context model that will take time to delineate in research.

In the meantime, the effects of salient contextual interactions have some very important implications for career counseling. Our perception of the individual in context can be somewhat conceptualized if we consider individual and environment as a circular interaction, as in Figure 2.6. Within this process an individual brings unique characteristics to an environment and is influenced by the characteristics of others and situational conditions in the environment. One individual might be greatly influenced to limit career choice according to the mores of his or her environment, whereas another might not vocally express a lack of agreement but will adapt his or her behavior to find some fit in the environment.

One very important outcome from our discussion of contextual influences is that development is shaped by the historical and cultural context of one's environment. Perhaps Sigelman and Rider (2009) offer the most clearly stated perspective of person-in-environment as follows:

> (1) humans are inherently neither good or bad; (2) nature and nurture, interacting continually, make us what we are; (3) people are active in their own development; (4) development probably involves some continuity and some discontinuity, some stagelike changes and some gradual ones; and (5) although some aspects of

development may be universal, development also varies widely from individual to individual and can change directions depending on experience. (p. 51)

Empirical Support for Action Theory

For more on action theory, see Polkinghorne (1990) and von Cranach and Harre (1982). For discussions on context and environment, see Holland (1992) and Krumboltz and Nichols (1990). For more on this theory in general, see Valach (1990), Young and Valach (1996), Shotter (1993), Richardson (1993), Hermans (1992), Sigelman and Rider (2003), and Shaffer (2002).

Summary of Practical Applications

Narrative counseling represents a practical approach for the practice of career development. Counselors are to ask clients to tell their life story. In this context, the major purpose of a life-story narrative is to discover how clients intentionally interact within segments of their environment. Counselors focus on career as a story to derive meaning from what the client views as important and unimportant. Client and counselor derive meaning from the chronology of events as well as the implied meaning of those events.

Two other goals of narrative counseling are (1) to establish a sense of client identity by how the story is told and constructed, and (2) to gain insight into a client's future goals. Counselors are to focus especially on client conceptualizations, concepts, and constructs. Counselors assist clients in developing awareness of self from joint interpretation of narratives that brings meaning to the past and direction for the future (Savickas, 2002; Sharf, 2010).

Summary Comments Concerning Person-in-Environment Perspective

The person-in-environment perspective is indeed an inclusive view of career development. The major focus on initial career choice, for instance, should be expanded to account for interactive influences over the life span. There is to be a greater emphasis on the recognition that initial good fit between person and career may *not* continue to be a good fit over the life span; career development is therefore both continuous and discontinuous. Individuals and work environments change and these changes are bidirectional: In contextual career theory, individuals influence environments and a broad array of factors in the environment influence the individual. From a contextual development viewpoint, we are active in our own development. Clients therefore are to assume responsibility for their development in all life roles. A self-directed approach to satisfying changing needs should be fostered. The recognition of reciprocal influence calls for more attention to the interrelationships of continuous changes in work environments and within individuals.

To become effective helpers, counselors also must focus on understanding the dynamics of changes in individual development and the salient messages individuals receive from their environment. Counselors not only address environmental influences in the initial choice, but also the relatively fast-moving changes in restructured work environments and the significant demographic changes forecast for the 21st century. What is suggested here is that counselors help clients explore the meaning and origins of core assumptions to more fully understand self, self-in-situation, and self in multiple life roles. Finally, counselors are to empower clients to challenge the core assumptions that limit career options. A case study follows.

Case 2.1   Career Development Theories Influence Career Counseling

The following case study illustrates how career development theories have influenced career counseling procedures and development of counseling materials. Counseling methods and procedures suggested by trait-oriented, social learning and cognitive, developmental, and person-in-environment theories have been selected as examples of counseling practice. In addition, client-centered and Gestalt techniques are included to represent a more holistic counseling approach. Maurice's case illustrates initial counseling responses to sets of concerns. As in many other counseling encounters, additional problems surface during interventions and require further evaluations to establish counseling goals. The purpose of this case, however, is to provide an example of how some client *career concerns* can be addressed from the results of career development theory research. *Personal client concerns* are addressed by counseling interventions from the affective and cognitive-behavioral theoretical domains.

Maurice, a very shy and soft-spoken 19-year-old male, presented the following concerns: He wanted help to find a job because he had failed in school and had little work experience. The counselor spent considerable time to establish rapport, primarily by offering support and encouragement before interviewing him.

In the intake interview, through probing questions of the presenting concerns, it became clear to the counselor that Maurice was greatly influenced by his family's social status and level of employment of family members. He was convinced that certain kinds of work were "off limits" for him and in fact should not even be considered. His self-concept was judged as poor because of self-deprecating comments he made. He had little knowledge of the work world and, likewise, had little in the way of skills in making appropriate decisions. There were indications of faulty thinking, to the point that he was confused as to what the future held in store for him. He had assumed that his "place in life would be like his family and something would just happen to show the way." After further discussion the counselor *tentatively* conceptualized Maurice's concerns as follows:

1. Lacks self-knowledge concerning skills, interests, personality traits, and aptitudes.
2. Is confused as to how to find a sense of direction.
3. Restricts career options, probably because of limited exposure to work roles and his family's social status.
4. Lacks basic information about the work world.
5. Has a very poor educational background and left high school before graduating.
6. Needs assistance in restructuring faulty perceptions and subsequently in how to rationally solve problems.
7. There appears to be an affective domain problem involving self-identity, self-concept, and feelings of helplessness.

Many concepts and propositions of several career development theories can be used to address Maurice's concerns. Person-in-environment perspectives and developmental theories focus on the relevance of an individual's unique development according to stages and tasks, contextual interactions, and learning experiences. Thus, information about Maurice's background and life story should reveal how he interprets events, situations, and experiences. This information should provide insights into the development of personal constructs and his vocational identity. The goal here is to attempt to gain a perspective of how Maurice constructs meaning from his experiences and relationships and help him to understand the consequences of his unique development. The counselor especially focused on Maurice's development in a social context. The major purpose for this intervention was to help Maurice recognize that his current social expectations may cause him to limit career options.

From a developmental perspective, it appeared that Maurice was not prepared to make a career decision, that is, he lacked career maturity. The problem of self-knowledge, which cuts across several theories, can first be addressed by a similarity model when discussing test results of academic achievement, interests, and personality traits, as suggested in trait-oriented theories. An inventory that measures vocational identity, need for information, and perceived barriers to choice will be administered from Holland's typology approach. All assessment results will be discussed and used as a planning tool for counseling interventions with Maurice's approval. Counseling will be focused on developing a greater sense of self through structured exercises and concrete experiences.

A learning plan stressed in social learning and cognitive theories is designed to improve Maurice's skills and educational development. The development of basic skills will be emphasized. Education is viewed as a key factor to broaden the scope of occupations Maurice will consider. He will learn more about the world of work by using a computerized-assisted career guidance system. Maurice will also visit job sites and shadow some workers. What is emphasized here is one of the major principles of social learning theory which suggests learning takes place through observations as well as through direct experiences.

Maurice will be taught how to use positive self-talk effectively in order to debunk stereotypes and restrictive career aspirations. His ability to sort out and resolve problems will be carefully monitored. He will be given examples of problem-solving exercises for current and future use. Cognitive behavioral interventions will be employed to help him unlearn faulty cognitions gleaned from an inventory that measures one's beliefs about careers (Mitchell & Krumboltz, 1996). Career development learning theory approaches suggest that some individuals overgeneralize from false assumptions and overlook worthwhile alternatives. Thus, in the case of Maurice, he may choose alternatives for inappropriate reasons.

Client-centered therapy and/or Gestalt techniques will focus on building positive self-concepts and help Maurice understand the sources of his feelings of helplessness. Active listening, empathy, and positive regard will be stressed. Coaching designed to reframe his thinking will also be emphasized. Incorporated within interventions are references to self in work role, planning skills, and reality of occupational aspirations.

In Maurice's case, it is clear that counselors should fuse career and personal concerns. A "whole person" holistic approach to Maurice's concerns will place both counselor and client in a better position to judge when an optimal career decision is possible. An integrated counseling approach makes use of strategies that are derived from several career development theories and combines them with client-centered and Gestalt techniques. The counseling suggestions in this case point out both differences and similarities of career development theory approaches, and so, counselors select technical tools from several theoretical frameworks that can best address a client's concerns. Maurice's case suggests that some client concerns may best be addressed from a holistic point of view that fosters the use of the most appropriate interventions that address unique individual needs. Be aware that not all the interventions suggested may be used. Interrelationships found between concerns suggest that some concerns can be addressed simultaneously. More information about holistic counseling is discussed in chapter 4 among others. Summaries of career development theories are presented in appendix B as described in Box 2.1.

Implications for Career Counseling

Career development theories are conceptual systems designed to delineate apparent relationships between a concomitance of events that lead to causes and effects. Although the theories described in this chapter have a variety of labels, all emphasize the relationships between the unique traits of individuals and the characteristics of society in which development occurs. The major difference among the theories is the nature of the influential factors involved in the career decision process, but all the theories have common implications for career guidance.

1. Career development takes place in stages that are somewhat related to age but are influenced by many factors in the sociocultural milieu. Because career

BOX 2.1

Summary of Career Development Theories

The career theories in this chapter and in other chapters are summarized by major assumptions, key terms, and outcomes in appendix B. Included are the following:

Trait-Oriented Theories
    Trait-and-Factor
    Person-Environment-Correspondence
    John Holland's Typology

Social Learning and Cognitive Theories
    Learning Theory of Career Counseling
    Cognitive Information Processing
    Social Cognitive Perspective

Developmental Theories
    Life-Span, Life-Space Approach
    Circumscription and Compromise: A Developmental Theory of Occupational Aspiration

Person-in-Environment
    Career Construction: A Developmental Theory of Vocational Behavior
    A Contextual Exploration of Career

Other Theories
    Ann Roe: A Needs Approach

development is a lifelong process, career-related programs must be designed to meet the needs of individuals over their life spans.

2. The tasks associated with stages of career development involve transitions requiring individuals to cope with each stage of life. Helping individuals cope with transitions is a key concept to remember while promoting development.

3. Career maturity is acquired through successfully accomplishing developmental tasks within a continuous series of life stages. Points of reference from this continuum provide relevant information for the practice of career development.

4. Each person should be considered unique. This uniqueness is a product of many sources, including sociocultural background, genetic endowment and other biological influences, personal and educational experiences, family relationships, and community resources. In this context, values, interests, abilities, personal constructs, and behavioral tendencies are important in shaping career development.

5. Self-concept affects career decisions. Self-concept is not a static phenomenon, but rather is an ongoing process that can gradually or abruptly change as people and situations change. Accurate self-concepts contribute to career maturity.

6. The stability of career choice depends primarily on the strength and dominance of one's personal orientation of personality characteristics, preferences, abilities, and traits. Work environments that match personal orientations provide appropriate outlets for personal and work satisfaction. Finding congruence between personality traits and work environments is a key objective of career development.

7. Individual characteristics and traits can be assessed through standardized assessment instruments. Identified traits are used to predict future outcomes of probable adjustments. Matching job requirements with personal characteristics might not dominate career-counseling strategies but remains a viable part of some programs.

8. Social learning emphasizes the importance of learning experiences and their effect on occupational selection. Learning takes place through observations as well as through direct experiences. Identifying the content of individual beliefs and generalizations is a key ingredient in developing counseling strategies.

9. Introducing occupational information resources and developing skills for their proper use are relevant goals for all educational institutions. Moreover, this need persists over the life span.

10. Career development involves a lifelong series of choices. Counselors help clients make appropriate choices by teaching decision-making and problem-solving skills. Understanding the individual processes involved in choices enables counselors to better assist during the decision-making process.

11. The concept of human freedom is implied in all career development theories. This concept implies that career counselors should provide avenues of freedom that allow individuals to explore options within the social, political, and economic milieu. The limits of personal freedom are often external (e.g., economic conditions, discrimination, and environmental conditions), but freedom can also be constrained by such internal sources as fear, lack of confidence, faulty attitudes, poor self-concept development, and behavioral deficits. Within this context, the career counselor should be concerned not only with career development, but also with all facets of human development. Counseling strategies must be designed to meet a wide range of needs. (See Box 2.1.)

12. The importance of cognitive development and its relationship to self-concept and subsequent occupational aspirations are receiving greater attention. This focus is concerned primarily with the role of cognitive development in terms of appropriate gender roles, occupational roles, and other generalizations that directly affect career development. This fine-tuning of relationships between human and career development implies that counselors must develop a greater sensitivity to both.

Summary

1. Trait-oriented theories include trait and factor approach, person-environment-correspondence counseling, and John Holland's typology approach.

2. Social learning and cognitive theories include Krumboltz's learning theory of career counseling, career development from a cognitive information processing perspective, and career development in a social cognitive perspective.

3. Developmental theories include life-span, life-space approach to careers and circumscription, compromise, and creation: a developmental theory of occupational aspirations.

4. Person-in-environment approaches include a career construction theory and contextual explanation of career.

5. A case example is used to illustrate how to apply strategies from career development theories.

Supplementary Learning Exercises

1. Explain why the trait-and-factor approach is considered the most durable theory. Give examples of the use of the trait-and-factor theory in current career counseling programs.
2. Defend the statement: Career development is a continuous process. Explain how it is a discontinuous process.
3. Write your own definition of career development and career counseling. Identify theories you agree and disagree with in summary form.
4. What are some of the implications of learning theories? How do these theories affect career development?
5. Compare Holland's approach to career development with person-in-environment theories. Summarize some similarities and differences.
6. Using the following reference, explain the principles behind Holland's theory of vocational choice. Defend or criticize his thesis that vocational interests are not independent of personality. J. L. Holland (1992). *Making Vocational Choices* (2nd ed.). Odessa, FL: Psychological Assessment Resources.
7. Why do some clients limit their career choices? Explain with examples.
8. Outline the factor that you consider most important in the career development of an adult you know or one you interview.
9. Defend and criticize the position of integrating theories in career counseling.
10. Develop your own theory of career development. Identify the components of theories you agree with and why you agree with them.

3

Career Counseling Models

CHAPTER HIGHLIGHTS

- Trait-and-factor and person-environment-fit model

- Developmental model

- Learning theory model

- Cognitive information-processing approach model

- Multicultural career counseling model for ethnic women

- Model summary of counseling goals, intake interview techniques, use of assessment, diagnosis, and counseling process

In this chapter we shift from the theoretical foundations of career development theories to the practical application of theoretical concepts. Five career counseling models are introduced, discussed, and illustrated with case studies. Four of the career counseling models in this chapter have been developed over time to reflect what has been learned from career development theories discussed in the previous chapter. The background for the fifth career counseling model that addresses the special needs of multicultural groups is covered in chapter 9. It is most important to recognize that the career counseling models that follow are not career development theories but do represent an attempt to apply theoretical concepts in the form of interventions and counseling procedures. The step-by-step procedures illustrated in the five career counseling models provide the reader with a sequential overview of effective interventions.

It is most important to recognize that the career development research introduced in the preceding chapter has successfully produced guidelines for career counseling practice. The career counseling models discussed here present suggestions for building a repertoire of practical applications that can serve as a foundation for career counseling models of the future. First, I briefly discuss some basic issues and concepts that have emerged from model development. Next, five career counseling models are outlined and described. The major parameters of the five models are briefly discussed in the final section.

Some Issues and Concepts Emerging from Model Development

During the early development of career counseling models, the trait-and-factor approach received the most attention and has survived as a viable part of current trait-oriented models. In fact, trait-oriented models continue to be a most popular part of contemporary models. The assumption that clients have unique traits that can be matched with requirements of occupations has endured. One may also find that trait-oriented approaches are referred to as an actuarial method of predicting success in an occupation from the client's measured trait characteristics. Trait-oriented approaches are often characterized as objective data (valid standardized test scores), rather than as subjective information clients reveal about themselves and perceptions of their environment, usually in an interview. The terms "actuarial," "objective," and "subjective data" are viable parts of current career counseling models.

Diagnosis of client problems, at times referred to as appraisal or simply as problem identification, has involved some interesting criteria. Several decades ago Crites (1981) suggested three types of diagnosis—differential, dynamic, and decisional. Differential diagnosis is based on individual psychology that is, how individuals differ from norms, and identifies the client's problems in such categories as undecided or indecisive. The focus of the diagnosis is on describing the client's problems and most importantly, the reasons why a client has problems. Irrational beliefs, anxiety, or lack of information, for example, suggest that the client's decision-making style, especially the process, should be addressed.

Three client labels that have been used extensively are *decided, undecided,* or *indecisive.* Decided clients are those who have made a career decision. These clients might profit from counseling that is designed to formulate other steps in decision making and to determine if their choice was inappropriately made.

Undecided clients have not made a career decision but might *not* view their current status as a problem; they prefer to delay making a commitment. The prevalent developmental view of this client is of an uninformed, immature person who generally lacks self-knowledge, information about occupations, or both. Yet, from another perspective, undecided clients could be described as multipotential individuals; they have the competencies to pursue several different types of careers.

The indecisive client is characterized as one who has a high level of anxiety accompanied by dysfunctional thinking. This client type is often labeled as not having cognitive clarity or as having irrational beliefs. For instance, the indecisive client could have problems embedded in a personality disorder that might be accompanied by depression. In general, clients with this label lack self-confidence, tolerance for ambiguity, and a sense of identity. These clients often need psychotherapy or personal counseling before they can benefit from career counseling. In some cases, both personal and career counseling can be introduced simultaneously (Meara, 1996; Zunker, 2008). In sum, contemporary models employ a combination of diagnostic criteria for specifying tailored interventions to meet specific client needs.

Five Career Counseling Models

Five career counseling models represent a broad spectrum of career counseling strategies that are directed toward a common goal of assisting clients make a career decision. Each of the following models is introduced with some brief comments about its origins: trait-and-factor and person-environment-fit (PEF); developmental; learning theory; cognitive information-processing (CIP) approach; and multicultural career counseling model for ethnic women. Model I, trait-and-factor and

PEF, includes two different career development theories. Model II, the developmental model, was primarily drawn from Super's (1957, 1980) work. Model III, the learning theory model, was structured from Mitchell and Krumboltz (1996), and Model IV, the CIP approach, from Peterson, Sampson, and Reardon (1991). The background information for Model V, a multicultural career counseling model, is contained in several chapters that follow. All the models are flexible enough to include occupational classification systems such as Holland's classification system, assessment instruments discussed in chapter 6, and a variety of occupational information resources, including written materials, computer-generated materials, and multimedia aids.

The point here is that the career counseling models described in the following pages can use the very popular Holland typology approach and materials, some of which were described in chapter 2. All the models discussed endorse an individualized approach to career counseling. Individual needs, therefore, dictate the kind and type of assessment instruments used and the materials and procedures used in the counseling process.

Because occupational information is an important part of intervention strategies in the five counseling models described in this section, some suggestions for its effective use are summarized. The following recommendations for the effective acquisition of occupational information have been compiled from several sources:

1. When exploring occupations, counselors should urge clients to record both negative and positive reactions to each occupation. Both disconfirming and confirming reactions can suggest personal constructs that need further evaluation.
2. Counselors should have clients complete a list of occupations that are most congruent with their interests and abilities and those occupations that are rated as acceptable. Clients should begin with a broad-based exploration and follow it with a more focused, complete study. This process is considered most effective in confirming congruency.
3. Sources of occupational information can be information from parents or friends and job sites. Counselors should indeed prepare clients to focus their research efforts on more in-depth study of occupations from which more accurate information can be obtained.
4. Career exploration involves both behavioral and cognitive processes; however, a framework for processing information, such as a form that requires clients to record relevant information, allows clients to derive the most benefits. Counselors can most effectively present sources of information when clients indicate readiness and express an interest in the information (Reardon et al., 2000; Spokane, 1991).

Trait-and-Factor and Person-Environment-Fit

The brief discussion of the historical development of trait-and-factor theory in chapter 2 points out its controversial development. Trait-and-factor theory is viewed by some as promoting a very simplistic counseling process that is characterized by Crites (1981, p. 49) as "three interviews and a cloud of dust." Others, however, have argued successfully that the applied concepts of the theory represent a misinterpretation of what was intended by early counseling programs of the 1930s. What appears to have been a theory that met society's needs in the

1930s, within the role and scope of counseling practices at that time, was eventually viewed as a counselor dominated, very inflexible, simplistic, and extremely test-oriented method. Over time trait-and-factor has remained a viable method for obtaining client information that is invaluable in the career decision process. In fact, the basic assumptions of trait-and-factor theory can easily be translated into practice and, with some modifications designed to meet contemporary societal needs, represent a viable philosophical basis for use within current career counseling models.

Model I Trait-and-Factor and Person-Environment-Fit (PEF) Converge

During the last decade we have seen a gradual convergence of trait-and-factor methods and procedures with person-environment-fit constructs—also referred to as person-environment-correspondence in its early development. In general terms, some trait-and-factor methods have been adapted to determine person-environment-fit, but significant changes have also occurred: (1) Both cognitive and affective processes are now involved; (2) clinical information and qualitative data are included in the appraisal process; and (3) the counselor's role has shifted from a directive approach to one in which counselor and client negotiate and collaborate (Swanson & Fouad, 2010).

The following summary statements include some major counseling guidelines that can serve as a connection between theory and practice:

- Job satisfaction is a significant variable in determining productivity and career tenure.
- Measured abilities, interests, and values can facilitate the individual's match to a work environment.
- Ideally, achievement needs can be satisfied in one's work environment.
- Client problems are often the result of lack of fit between an individual and her or his work environment.
- Counselors are to focus on the individuality of their clients; individuals differ in their abilities, needs, values, and interests.

The following model includes seven stages (Dawis 1996; Swanson & Fouad, 2010; Walsh, 1990) which will be briefly described:

Stage 1. Intake Interview

    a. Establish client–counselor collaboration relationship
    b. Gather background information
    c. Assess emotional status and cognitive clarity
    d. Observe personality style

Stage 2. Identify Developmental Variables

    a. Perception of self and environment
    b. Environmental variables
    c. Contextual interactions
    d. Gender variables
    e. Minority group status

Stage 3. Assessment

    a. Ability patterns
    b. Values

    c. Reinforcer requirements
    d. Interests
    e. Information-processing skills

Stage 4. Identify and Solve Problems

    a. Affective status
    b. Self-knowledge needs
    c. Level of information-processing skills

Stage 5. Generate PEF (Person-Environment-Fit) Analysis

    a. Cognitive schema
    b. Criteria on which to base choice
    c. Optimal prediction system

Stage 6. Confirm, Explore, and Decide

    a. Counselor and client confirm PEF analysis
    b. Client explores potential work environments
    c. Client makes a decision

Stage 7. Follow-Up

    a. Evaluate progress
    b. Recycle if necessary

The major goal of PEF is the enhancement of self-knowledge. It is most important to recognize that clients who have developed an adequate self-identity are better equipped to self-assess potential satisfaction and congruence with work environments. Therefore, the focus on self-knowledge emphasized in the PEF process is a major contribution to the career choice process and effective optimal career selection (Dawis, 1996). It can indeed be a tedious and most comprehensive step-by-step process. Within this model of career counseling, counselor and client form a partnership that endures numerous challenges and doubts on the pathway to an optimal career choice.

Stage 1, the Intake Interview, begins with the client and counselor forming a compatible working relationship. Counselors do not assume an authority-expert role; rather, they build a relationship in which they will share responsibility and negotiate options in a collaborative manner.

Background information includes a biographical history that can be obtained from a questionnaire and through discussion. Information about the client's environmental influences is a high priority. During the interview, the counselor evaluates the emotional status of the client and the client's cognitive clarity. Personality style and personality characteristics are also observed. The information obtained in the intake interview is used throughout the counseling process. For example, background variables are used to evaluate personality structure and style. Any problems that surfaced are further evaluated in the stages that follow.

Stage 2, Identify Developmental Variables, includes the information obtained in the intake interview that is reviewed to account for important elements that are involved in PEF counseling, such as perception. Perception in this context refers to perception of self, such as one's identity, self-concept or self-image, and, in addition, perception of one's environment or work environment including its requirements, reinforcers, and demands. What is suggested here is that counselors are to assist clients in observing the environment in which they work and the contextual interactions within it in order to evaluate and determine opportunities, relevant experiences, and limitations. Of particular interest are restrictions of developmental opportunities from environmental variables for women and minority groups.

Assessment, stage 3, involves a comprehensive evaluation of the client's cognitive abilities, values, and interests. These measured traits are used with other variables to determine a client's reinforcement needs found in occupational environments. Thus, the major purpose of this information is to match client needs with occupations or groups of occupations that are predicted to result in satisfaction (self-fulfillment) and satisfactoriness (achievement).

Information-processing skills are important for clients to appropriately process information presented to them in PEF counseling. Those clients who need assistance for processing information are assigned intervention strategies designed to improve these skills before PEF counseling continues. More details about information-processing skills can be found in stage 4.

In stage 4, Identify and Solve Problems, information gathered in the first three stages is used to identify any affective concerns, self-knowledge needs, and the client's level of information processing. Clients who are identified as having serious emotional problems or dysfunctional thinking are referred for psychotherapy or for a complete psychological evaluation. Clients who have unrealistic or faulty beliefs about self-perceptions or perceptions of work environments or both are provided with tailored intervention strategies designed to assist them.

A most important point made here is that counselors are to evaluate each client's ability to process information for optimal career decision making. Rounds and Tracey (1990) suggest that there are three types of knowledge bases: working (active, conscious thought), declarative (knowledge of facts), and procedural (processing the relationship between different pieces of knowledge). Beginners using a trial-and-error procedure tend to use declarative knowledge, whereas experts use procedural knowledge, that is, experts are able to process the relationship of different knowledge and information in decision making. This process in turn involves four steps of information processing: encoding (sorting out the information's meaning), goal setting, plan development and pattern matching, and finally action. Each step is briefly described in Box 3.1.

In stage 5, Generate PEF Analysis, the counselor and client develop a cognitive schema or a conceptual framework to direct the search for PEF. In this context each client's ability patterns are used to predict satisfactoriness in different occupations. Values and personality style are used to predict satisfaction with certain occupations and also to describe the client's reinforcer requirements. An occupational classification system is used to locate occupations for abilities required and the reinforcers that are provided. The next step is to list occupations that correspond to the client's satisfaction and satisfactoriness needs. Within this procedure, clients find congruent occupations and choose one that is the optimal fit. The prediction system is more accurate when the client's dominant orientation (satisfactoriness or satisfaction) is known. An illustration of PEF analysis is given in Case 3.1.

Stage 6, Confirm, Explore, and Decide, begins when counselor and client review test data and the prediction analysis to determine if the client is comfortable with the results. If the client does not agree with work environments that are predicted to be congruent, recycling in the model may be recommended. Clients who do agree should be directed to explore potential work environments that are predicted to be congruent. Finally, a decision is reached.

BOX 3.1

Assessing Level of Information Processing

a. *Encoding* involves the client's perception and interpretation of information. For example, client can recognize relevant advantages and limitations of an occupation.

b. *Goal setting* is best accomplished by concrete, realistic steps in an organized sequential process. For example, recognizing procedural requirements to reach goals.

c. *Effective plan development and pattern matching* involves establishing alternative solutions, several means of reaching goals, and considering the consequences of actions taken.

d. In the *action* step, the client selects an appropriate behavior to solve problems exposed in previous steps.

Rounds and Tracey (1990) also point out that effective information processing includes active and conscious deliberation, which is referred to as central processing rather than peripheral processing. The counselor's rapport with a client and the counselor's behavior in presenting information can negatively influence the client's motivation to process information and is referred to as peripheral processing. Thus, if clients appear not to be motivated, the counselor should focus on persuasion cues that are related to counselor behavior of projecting warmth, trustworthiness, and competence.

In sum, treatment interventions are a function of the following:

1. Level of client information processing
2. Client motivation
3. "Relative progress in the counseling process." (Rounds & Tracey, 1990, p. 30)

Client levels of information processing are rated as very high, high, medium, and low. Very high levels of information processing indicate clients who have demonstrated competence in the four stages (encoding, goal setting, pattern matching, and action selection) as described earlier. Clients at this level need little treatment and consideration; computer-assisted career guidance programs and self-help procedures are recommended.

Those with high levels of information processing generally lack pattern-matching knowledge but have mastered other steps. They should benefit from instruction on career decision-making skills. The focus should be on integrating information for a decision.

Clients *rated* as having medium-level information-processing skills usually have difficulty with encoding. They exhibit little insightful knowledge about the role and scope of an occupation or an academic major. The treatment should focus on encoding information and depth of insight through individual counseling or by taking a career course. In addition, a thorough analysis of coping and problem-solving skills is recommended.

Clients with low-level skills in information processing are characterized as having significant deficits in problem solving, that is, they are only able to encode and process a little of the information presented to them. These clients may require the counselor to assume a teaching role that directly provides needed skills in a step-by-step fashion. The counselor also assumes a very active role in guiding the client in the decision process.

Stage 7, Follow-Up, involves an evaluation of the client's progress and the procedures used to assist clients in finding a work environment in which they experience satisfaction. Counselors also assist clients in their job searches.

In sum, this model emphasizes fit-of-person with an optimal career. Standard assessment instruments are used to determine the client's abilities, values, and interests. Subjective data (cognitive clarity, emotional status evaluations, and problem-solving processes) are used with assessment data in the counseling process. A significant part of this model involves the identification of information-processing skills. Intervention strategies that are matched to specific identified deficits in information processing are a major focus of the career counseling process. The basic assumption of person-environment-fit is that individuals seek to achieve and maintain a positive relationship with their work environments. Thus, counselors assist clients in finding some degree of congruence between themselves and work environments in the career decision process.

Generating a PEF Analysis

Figure 3.1 represents the PEF analysis schematic that is used for optimal career choice. Following the steps from left to right, the client is administered an abilities test and a values questionnaire. In the second step, ability and value patterns of occupations are compared with the client's ability and values. This comparison is used to predict satisfactoriness, or the probability that the worker will satisfy the work requirements in a work environment and whether the worker will find satisfaction performing the work that is required. These predictions are based on comparing the individual's abilities and values with the work environment requirements and reinforcers that are available. Finally, the individual selects specific occupations of interest and researches each one until an optimal choice is made. A PEF analysis stresses that career choice should be based on one's fit with the requirements of a job and the satisfaction and feeling of well-being one receives for a job well done.

FIGURE 3.1

Use of the theory of work adjustment in career choice

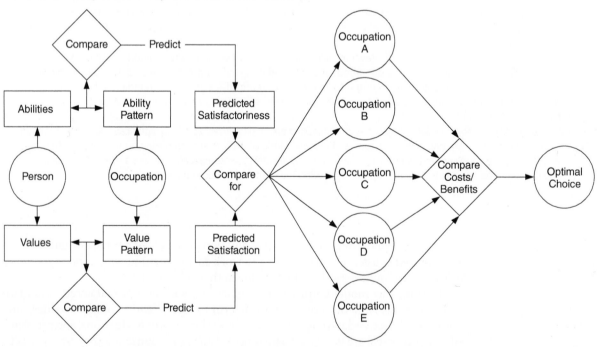

SOURCE: From "The Theory of Work Adjustment and Person-Environment-Correspondence Counseling," by R. V. Dawis, in *Career Choice and Development*, 3rd ed., pp. 75–121, by D. Brown, L. Brooks, and Associates, Copyright © 1996 by Jossey-Bass, Inc. This material is used by permission of John Wiley & Sons, Inc.

Case 3.1 The Undecided College Student

This is a counselor's summary of the case of a 19-year-old female who was undecided about a career goal.

Lee presented a background from a stable home environment, and there were no indications of irrational thinking or faulty beliefs. She appeared to be stable and expressed a positive self-concept. There was no evidence that she felt she must limit her career options because she is female. She felt free to explore any career of interest and was fully aware that some careers are stereotyped as male and female. Lee mentioned that her mother was a Chinese American born in this country and that her father was also American, of Irish and German descent. She identified with the dominant society. She finished high school in the top 20% and was in her first semester of college. She was found to have a very high level of skills in information processing. The counselor concluded that Lee was now serious about making a career decision. During the assessment stage, Lee and the counselor collaborated on the tests that could be helpful.

COUNSELOR: Lee, earlier I explained the idea of career counseling based on PEF. Do you have any questions at this time?

LEE: Not really, but I believe you mentioned that ability and values are used to help people like me find the right kind of job or as you said fit between person and work requirements.

COUNSELOR: Very good! I'll review the procedure once more. First, we will measure your abilities, and values. Second, we will both assess work environments by not only observing work requirements, but also by whether you feel a particular occupation would be satisfying for you. We will do this by matching your traits with work reinforcers found in work environments. When we find a match, we refer to this as personal-environment-fit, or simply PEF.

The following tests were chosen after an introduction of the purpose and use of each test. The *General Aptitude Test Battery* (GATB) (U.S. Department of Labor, 1970b) was chosen to measure nine specific abilities as shown in Lee's score results. The *Minnesota Importance Questionnaire*

(MIQ) (University of Minnesota, 1984) was chosen as a measure of needs based on values. Although these two instruments were developed decades ago, they have been periodically updated.

Test score results for Lee were grouped by high, moderate, or low for nine abilities and six values as follows:

FIGURE 3.2

Test score results for Lee

	High	Moderate	Low
GATB	Intelligence	Motor coordination	Finger dexterity
	Numerical aptitude	Spatial aptitude	
	Verbal aptitude	Clerical perception	
	Form perception	Manual dexterity	
	Achievement	Status	
MIQ	Comfort	Altruism	
		Safety	
		Autonomy	

The counselor presented assessment results to Lee by carefully explaining the meaning of each ability and value score. Counselor and client observed assessment scores in the order suggested in Figure 3.2. The ability scores as measured by the GATB present scores as high, moderate, and low. Lee was asked to react to the ability measures first. The counselor asked Lee to define the meaning of the subscale scores of each ability. Lee's ability to express herself was outstanding and she also provided evidence of someone who is very interested in finding an optimal career.

COUNSELOR: Lee, do you recall the meaning of verbal aptitude from our earlier discussion?

LEE: Well, I think it is a measure of my ability to express myself and communicate with others.

COUNSELOR: That's right! It was a vocabulary test that required you to identify words that have the same meaning or opposite meaning.

LEE: Yes, that was a tough one!

COUNSELOR: You're right—some people have a difficult time with it. But more importantly, how does this score link with finding a career?

LEE: I was told by one of my high school teachers that a good vocabulary is important for so many things—like meeting people, making a speech, and even studying. It is also important in work—I will need to be able to communicate with other people, like a boss or a customer.

The counselor was impressed with Lee's answers and continued explaining and discussing each of the ability measures. In each case counselor and client linked score results with career choice; the focus was on the decision process. The counselor also emphasized that occupations require a combination of abilities and skills that are listed in available references that describe job requirements for a variety of occupations.

After defining each value measured by the Minnesota Importance Questionnaire (MIQ), the counselor turned to the MIQ report. See Figure 3.3. The individual's responses on the MIQ that measures six values and 20 needs are compared with *occupational reinforcer patterns* (ORPs) for 90 representative

---

FIGURE 3.3

Values, need scales, and statements from the Minnesota Importance Questionnaire

Value	Need Scale	Statement
Achievement	Ability utilization	I could do something that makes use of my abilities.
	Achievement	The job could give me a feeling of accomplishment.
Comfort	Activity	I could be busy all the time.
	Independence	I could work alone on the job.
	Variety	I could do something different every day.
	Compensation	My pay would compare well with that of other workers.
	Security	The job would provide for steady employment.
	Working conditions	The job would have good working conditions.
Status	Advancement	The job would provide an opportunity for advancement.
	Recognition	I could get recognition for the work I do.
	Authority	I could tell people what to do.
	Social status	I could be "somebody" in the community.
Altruism	Co-workers	My co-workers would be easy to make friends with.
	Moral values	I could do the work without feeling it is morally wrong.
	Social service	I could do things for other people.
Safety	Company policies and practices	The company would administer its policies fairly.
	Supervision–human relations	My boss would back up the workers (with top management).
	Supervision-technical	My boss would train the workers well.
Autonomy	Creativity	I could try out some of my ideas.
	Responsibility	I could make decisions on my own.

SOURCE: From *A Psychological Theory of Work Adjustment*, by R.V. Dawis and L. H. Lofquist, p. 29. Copyright 1984 University of Minnesota Press. Reprinted by permission.

occupations. Individual needs are matched with occupational reinforcers to determine an individual's fit into a work environment. Some examples of occupational reinforcers are achievement, advancement, authority, coworkers, activity, security, social service, social status, and variety. ORPs and occupational ability patterns are given for more than 1700 careers in the *Minnesota Occupational Classification System* (Rounds, Henly, Dawis, Lofquist, & Weiss, 1981).

The counselor spent considerable time explaining how one is to interpret the MIQ report form and scores. On this report form a C value indicates the strength or importance of a need. For example, if a C value is greater than .49, then the occupation is considered satisfying or of value to you. If the C value is between .10 and .49, there is likely to be job satisfaction, but, if the C value is less than .10, it is likely that there would be no job satisfaction. See Figure 3.4.

LEE: That's interesting. Let me see—I have a high value for achievement and autonomy. What does that mean?

COUNSELOR: Good point! Let's look at the definition of each value we discussed earlier. After

reading the description of the two values, Lee was able to summarize how they could be linked to a work environment.

LEE: This means I would like a job that would give me the opportunity to use my skills and be creative. But how will I know if I have the ability to be a lawyer or an architect?

COUNSELOR: Good question, Lee! After you have developed a list of occupations that interest you, we can compare your ability scores with the requirements of each occupation. As you evaluate each occupation, we will discuss what you have found and I will refer you to individuals who work in some of the professions.

During the course of the semester, Lee was very diligent in pursuing some specific interests. She visited the university's prelaw advisor and a local attorney. She also had a conference with a representative from the school of business and an accountant. Shortly before her sophomore year in college, Lee declared an accounting major. Her overall goal was to attend law school and become a tax attorney.

FIGURE 3.4

Correspondence report for SAMPLE REPORT 06/04/93

The MIQ profile is compared with Occupational Reinforcer Patterns (ORPs) for 90 representative occupations. Correspondence is indicated by the C index. A prediction of *Satisfied (S)* results from C values greater than .49, *Likely Satisfied (L)* for C values between .10 and .49, and *Not Satisfied (N)* for C values less than .10. Occupations are clustered by similarity of Occupational Reinforcer Patterns.

	C Index	Pred. Sat.		C Index	Pred. Sat.
CLUSTER A (ACH-AUT-Alt)	.17	L	CLUSTER E (Com)	.47	L
Architect	.11	L	Assembler, Production	.35	L
Dentist	.11	L	Baker	.56	S
Family Practitioner (M.D.)	.27	L	Bookbinder	.58	S
Interior Designer/Decorator	.24	L	Bookkeeper I	.55	S
Lawyer	.27	L	Bus Driver	.23	L
Minister	.11	L	Key-Punch Operator	.49	L
Nurse, Occupational Health	.06	N	Meat Cutter	.49	L
Occupational Therapist	.15	L	Post Office Clerk	.43	L
Optometrist	.33	L	Production Helper (Food)	.47	L
Psychologist, Counseling	.08	N	Punch-Press Operator	.44	L
Recreation Leader	.02	N	Sales, General (Department Store)	.33	L

FIGURE 3.4 (*CONTINUED*)

	C Index	Pred. Sat.		C Index	Pred. Sat.
Speech Pathologist	.11	L	Sewing-Machine Operator (Automatic)	.29	L
Teacher, Elementary School	.20	L			
Teacher, Secondary School	.25	L	Solderer (Production Line)	.45	L
Vocational Evaluator	.06	N	Telephone Operator	.42	L
CLUSTER C (ACH-Aut-Com)	.48	L	Teller (Banking)	.38	L
Alteration Tailor	.46	L	CLUSTER B (ACN-Com)	.36	L
Automobile Mechanic	.43	L	Bricklayer	.29	L
Barber	.31	L	Carpenter	.44	L
Beauty Operator	.23	L	Cement Mason	−.03	N
Caseworker	.31	L	Elevator Repairer	.74	S
Claim Adjuster	.47	L	Heavy Equipment Operator	.37	L
Commercial Artist, Illustrator	.51	S	Landscape Gardener	.07	N
Electronics Mechanic	.57	S	Lather	.11	L
Locksmith	.45	L	Millwright	.29	L
Maintenance Repairer, Factory	.49	L	Painter/Paperhanger	.41	L
Mechanical-Engineering Technician	.28	L	Patternmaker, Metal	.43	L
			Pipefitter	.58	S
Office-Machine Servicer	.69	S	Plasterer	.07	N
Photoengraver (Stripper)	.54	S	Plumber	.40	L
Sales Agent, Real Estate	.18	L	Roofer	.01	N
Salesperson, General Hardware	.35	L	Salesperson, Automobile	.51	S
CLUSTER D (ACH-STA-Com)	.64	S	CLUSTER F (Alt-Com)	.33	L
Accountant, Certified Public	.51	S	Airplane Flight Attendant	.09	N
Airplane Co-Pilot, Commercial	.60	S	Clerk, General Office, Civil Service	.32	L
Cook (Hotel-Restaurant)	.57	S			
Department Head, Supermarket	.42	L	Dietitian	.21	L
Drafter, Architectural	.48	L	Fire Fighter	.33	L
Electrician	.66	S	Librarian	.21	L
Engineer, Civil	.35	L	Medical Technologist	.39	L
Engineer, Time Study	.29	L	Nurse, Professional	.13	L
Farm-Equipment Mechanic I	.73	S	Orderly	−.01	N
Line-Installer-Repairer (Telephone)	.50	S	Physical Therapist	.24	L
Machinist	.67	S	Police Officer	.23	L
Programmer (Business, Engineering Science)	.55	S	Receptionist, Civil Service	.27	L
			Secretary (General Office)	.30	L
Sheet Metal Worker	.63	S	Taxi Driver	−.02	N
Statistical-Machine Servicer	.72	S	Telephone Installer	.44	L
Writer, Technical Publication	.55	S	Waiter-Waitress	.26	L

SOURCE: *Minnesota Importance Questionnaire.* Copyright 1984 Vocational Psychology Research, Department of Psychology, University of Minnesota. Reprinted with permission.

In Lee's case the client's needs and values became the central focus of discussion, which led to a better understanding of how these factors affect job satisfaction and adjustment. In PEF, job satisfaction is considered a significant variable in determining job involvement and career tenure. In sum, the PEF analysis stresses the use of occupational information to assist clients in matching needs and abilities with patterns and levels of different reinforcers in the work environment. As work environments change in the future, more research will be needed to maintain the effectiveness of the MIQ.

For more information on PEF counseling and the MIQ, see Dawis (1996, 2002), Osborn and Zunker (2012), Swanson and Fouad (2010), and Sharf (2013).

Model II Development Model

This developmental model has been built from the position that career development is a lifelong process and the career development needs of unique individuals must be met during all stages of life (Healy, 1982; Gelso & Fretz, 2001; Swanson & Fouad, 2010; Sharf, 2013). Goals, learning strategies, and timing of interventions in this model are guided by what was labeled as Super's (1957, 1990) vocational developmental tasks and stages. Counselors are to focus on all barriers that may diminish one's development of career maturity and self-concept. Ideally, clients should focus on the development of all life roles for a balanced lifestyle; an individual's unique needs are emphasized. As you learned from chapter 2, Super's career development theory is very extensive and inclusive. The following summary statements include some major counseling concerns that can serve as a connection between theory and practice:

- Career development is a lifelong process; individuals change during developmental stages as they adapt to changing life roles.
- There are five life stages—growth, exploration, establishment, maintenance, and disengagement. Each stage has a series of developmental tasks.
- Readiness (career maturity) is essential for optimal career decision making.
- Counselors focus on developmental tasks as key points for appropriate interventions.
- Unique individual needs are most important as guidelines for establishing counseling goals.
- Clients must be prepared to project self into the work world; a realistic self-concept is essential.
- The importance of adult concerns is highlighted; what happens in one life role affects other life roles.
- Clients are to not to restrict career alternatives; self-knowledge and exposure to compatible alternative career paths are essential.

The following counseling model includes five stages as follows:

1. Intake Interview
   a. Establish client individuality.
   b. Uncover barriers to career choice.
   c. Evaluate affective concerns such as poor self-concept and self-awareness.
   d. Establish level of occupational knowledge.
   e. Identify work experiences.
2. Career Development Assessment and Counseling (CDAC)
   a. Life structure and work salience.
   b. Career development status and resources.
   c. Abilities, interests, and values.
   d. Occupational self-concept and life themes.

3. Data Integration and Narrative Interpretation
   a. Explanation of accumulated data.
4. Establish Counseling Goals
   a. Develop an accurate portrait of self.
   b. Project self-concept into work world.
5. Counseling Procedures and Process
   a. Emphasize career development tasks.
   b. Counseling process includes coaching and mentoring and, if necessary, recycling previous steps.

In the first stage of this model, as in most of the other models, the counseling relationship between counselor and client is of the utmost importance. The counselor makes tentative appraisals of the client that are to be verified or debunked during the assessment phases and discussions that follow. A good example is the tentative conclusion that a client is of average intelligence or more specifically able to learn more about occupations and self-concept through learning programs. The verification and specification of this tentative conclusion will be determined by ability tests and further discussions. The counselor employs interview skills that encourage clients to verbalize their past experiences as well as future goals and lifestyle issues.

The second stage of this model, known as career development assessment and counseling (CDAC), is very extensive and inclusive. There are four very important steps in this stage and each will be explained separately. During the first step in this stage, the client's social development and role salience are assessed. The emphasis of assessment is on the client's relative importance of life roles that involve education, work, family, community, and leisure.

The second step consists of an evaluation of the client's perception of the work role, such as his or her current career status, as well as career concerns that are associated with growth, exploration, establishment, maintenance, and disengagement. In addition assessment includes measures of the client's knowledge and attitudes about career choice, especially when one is involved in career planning and career exploration and gathering information about work and occupations. The client's adaptability (making mature career decisions) and perception of current job market trends are also of utmost importance.

The third step includes the often used measures of abilities, interests, and values. A variety of instruments that measure these characteristics are available as described in chapter 6. In the developmental model, interest inventories that present results as estimates of realistic, investigative, artistic, social, enterprising, and conventional (RIASEC) types are preferred. Thus counselors would use the very popular and effective Holland (1992) typology as described in chapter 2. The overarching goal here is to present the client with valuable information concerning the relationship and connection of her or his abilities, interest, and values in the choice process.

The fourth and final step focuses on self-concepts and life themes. The procedures in this step are often referred to as subjective evaluations of the client's view of self and dominant lifestyles and life themes expressed by clients in conversations or in an autobiography. Counselors guide and encourage clients to discuss their work and other life-role experiences, including how one has made decisions in the past and negotiated transitions. Another method is to ask clients to write about their life experiences and future projections. Salience of life-role indicators includes, the amount and quality of participation in different roles, the commitment one makes to life roles, and the opportunities provided by life roles for meeting numerous value needs. This concludes the assessment steps in stage two of this counseling model.

The third stage in this model is primarily devoted to an explanation and interpretation of the key measurement instruments and the counselor's subjective information that was garnered from the interview and other discussions of life roles. Counselors often use profiles of score reports as a visual aid when discussing the significance of client scores. One advantage of using test data to get to know your client better is through score reports that usually encourage clients to self-assess and express agreement and disagreement with scores. Counselors have the opportunity to encourage clients to draw conclusions about their future from score results.

In this model's fourth stage, counselor and client in a working consensus relationship are to establish future counseling goals. Counselors are to assist clients in conceptualizing an accurate self-concept. According to Super (Super, Starishesky, & Matlin, Jordan, 1963), self-concept development includes one's ability to self-differentiate, role play, explore, and test reality. Over time other explanations of how self-concepts are developed and expressed have been suggested. In some of the following chapters I will discuss the importance and relationships of self-efficacy and self-concept. In the developmental model, self-concept is a most important factor in the choice process—one is to project one's self-concept into the work world to find an optimal fit.

The fifth and final stage of this model emphasizes that counselors should include a careful analysis of the client's progress in career development and maintenance of career. Counselors are encouraged to challenge clients to be aware of developmental tasks such as those for early adulthood: Strive to make your work position secure and a permanent position, but also find more opportunities for your work of choice. Such tasks are especially relevant when the economy is in recession and job loss does indeed happen. What is also suggested here is that workers may have to make multiple career choices over time.

Super (1990) suggests that counselors may need to use a variety of helping procedures in the career counseling process. Counselors may function as mentors, coaches, and teachers. Career coaching has received increasing attention; one is to offer task and advice giving as well as help clients develop solutions to their problems. In sum this model is designed to help clients "(1) develop and accept an integrated and adequate picture of themselves and their life roles, (2) test the concept against reality, and (3) convert it into reality by making choices that implement the self-concept and lead to job success and satisfaction as well as benefit society" (Super, Savickas, & Super, 1996, pp. 158–159).

Excerpts from the following case study are examples of how a counselor can assist a client after a job loss because of a weak economy. The counselor uses Super's CDAC model to introduce procedures for learning more about one's self-concept, the world of work, and one's current career development status.

Case 3.2   **The Case of Job Loss and Family Concerns**

Larry, a 26-year-old Caucasian male, has been married for six years and has fathered two children ages 2 and 4. He is currently a construction carpenter specializing in framing buildings. He and his wife both have a high school education. The counselor was impressed with Larry's ability to express himself. He appeared to be very happy with his marriage and as he put it, "I married my high school sweetheart." His wife is employed as a bank teller. His parents are in their mid-60s and his father is a licensed electrician. He has three siblings. His parents have both been very supportive and encouraged Larry to work hard to support his family.

Larry grew up in a small town near a large city. He has commuted to different job sites in the nearby city. Currently there has been a downturn in the construction industry because of a severe recession. Many of his fellow workers have not been able to find work and he is very concerned about being laid off and in addition is worried that his wife may also lose her job. As Larry put it, "We may lose everything we have worked for including our home! Somehow I will need to find other work to support my family."

In the discussions that followed Larry informed the counselor that he became a carpenter because the pay was good and the work was steady. He added that he liked to work with his hands and had never considered going to college. He admitted that considering other jobs that required a higher education was not a part of what he had learned while growing up. As he said, "Most of my family and friends became workers like plumbers, carpenters, and electricians. I always thought I would end up in the building trades."

Not surprisingly, the counselor realized that Larry's knowledge of occupations was very limited and now might be the time to introduce skill development programs and technological advances that could offer Larry some opportunities for employment. The counselor concluded that Larry was sincere and highly motivated to learn more about occupations that could offer stability and security. It was also obvious that Larry was anxious about finding solutions to his current financial problems. In addition, Larry grew up with a strong family background in which the welfare of the family as a group was of utmost importance—thus the counselor was not surprised when Larry reacted very positively to the possibility of pursuing educational programs to improve his chances of getting a job. Larry agreed that a battery of tests could be used to learn more about his abilities, interests, and values as well as learning more about different kinds of work.

COUNSELOR: What other kind of work have you considered?

LARRY: The only kind of work that my wife and I have thought about is the building trades and that's why I came to see you for help. This recession could get worse and new building projects have already shut down. The trouble is I don't know a lot about other kinds of work. But I sure want to find something to support my family.

The counselor continued by asking Larry about his past education especially about his grades in school and if there was any particular subject he liked best.

LARRY: I made good grades in mathematics courses and I liked that subject better than English or history, but I never failed a course. My folks encouraged me to study for all my courses but never pushed us to go to college.

The counselor took this opportunity to point out that the job market today and in the future will require more education and skill development. She made a most relevant point that future workers will need to adopt the position that one must be willing to be a lifelong learner in order to stay employed.

LARRY: This recession has taught me a lot of lessons and one of them is that I need to improve my skills in order to find more permanent work. I am ready to do just that if I can find something interesting that offers me future opportunities.

The counselor cautioned that there are very few guarantees of a lifetime job in the current job market, but there is no question that if one improves their skills and develops multiskills the chances are better of finding and keeping a job.

LARRY: That makes sense to me, but where do we go from here?

The counselor used this opportunity to explain the purpose of tests and inventories used in the CDAC model. In a working consensus counseling relationship, every test that Larry was to take was explained in terms that he could understand, especially its purpose and, more importantly, how it could be helpful. Larry was to agree to take each test. Examples of how the counselor summarized the order of assessment in the CDAC model are contained in the next paragraph.

In the first phase of testing, the counselor emphasized the importance of the work role and its relationship to other life roles. The point was made that what happens in one life role can affect other roles; anger and unhappiness resulting from work dissatisfaction can spill over to family life. Thus the purpose for evaluating one's commitment and participation in all life roles has a definite connection to future goals. In the second, assessment phase the purpose is to measure one's career concerns and how they are related to career development tasks. Lack of occupational information, for instance, may be related to a lack of exploration skills needed to locate and process career information. Interests, values, and abilities will be measured in the third assessment phase in order to develop a better understanding of the kind of work one is interested in, values highly, and has the necessary ability to accomplish required tasks. In the final assessment phase, Larry was informed that discussions will focus on how he currently views himself and the world around him. Finally, Larry was told: "We will put all these data together and come up with some goals and plans for the future." What follows is more information about the four assessment phases in the CDAC model.

Assessment of Life Roles and Work-Role Salience

The *Salience Inventory* (Nevill & Super, 1986) measures the relative importance of five life roles; Student, Worker, Homemaker, Leisurite, and Citizen. What we have here are measures of one's involvement in educational activities such as studying, taking a course or developing skills, one's work experiences and commitment, one's role as a parent or family member, participation in leisure activities, and involvement in community activities and civic affairs. The indicators of salience of work roles are the quality and content of one's participation, strength of commitment, and knowledge through experience, observation, and study. The rationale here is that individual development is a process that is multidimensional and multifaceted. Clients are to consider the position that one learns from life experiences while participating in different life roles. Thus there are opportunities to fulfill individual needs by one's participation and commitment in a variety of activities. What is not to be overlooked is the suggestion that one is to participate, commit, and become involved for maximum benefits of a balanced lifestyle. Larry's score on the Salience Inventory indicated high scores in Working, Home and Family, and Leisure and will be included in the data integration narrative stage.

Assessment of Career Development Status and Resources

The *Adult Career Concerns Inventory* (Super, Thompson, & Lindeman, 1988) measures one's current career stage and current concerns with career developmental tasks. In Super's approach to career decision making and maintenance, one should have good exploration skills in which one can crystallize or clarify what it is one wants to do in the future. One is able to specify desired work roles and develop the savvy to implement their plans. Or one may be struggling with establishing a career, especially getting started with one. Another may be attempting to consolidate their position and is looking forward to preparing for advancement. Yet another person is ready for retirement planning. By identifying one's current career status, counselors are able to offer assistance with developmental tasks. Larry's most pressing concerns were in exploration, followed by maintenance and establishment.

Another instrument used in this assessment phase is the *Career Development Inventory* (Super et al., 1971) which is designed to measure Larry's resources (how to do career planning and exploration) and his procedures for making decisions. For example, the counselor wanted to know more about how Larry would go about career planning and obtain information about work and occupations. The results of the inventory indicate that Larry has serious concerns about career planning and exploration, knowledge of the world of work, and is also very concerned about decision-making skills. A subjective appraisal of Larry's adaptability (career maturity), such as making mature decisions when exploring potential careers, was obtained in the interview and by listening carefully to discussions concerning initial and secondary appraisals of information. Both the score results and the interview indicate a general weakness in career planning, decision making, and exploration and knowledge of the work world. More about the meaning of these scores will be discussed in data integration.

Assessing Abilities, Interests, and Values

In chapter 6 there are a number of ability tests listed that can be used to match one's abilities with job requirements. In the same chapter one can also find a number of interests and value inventories. In Larry's case the following test and inventories have been selected: the *Differential Aptitude Test* (Bennett, Seashore, & Wesman, 1991), the *Strong Interest Inventory* (Strong, Hansen, & Campbell,

1994) and the *Values Scale* (Nevill & Super, 1989). On the aptitude test Larry scored highest in mechanical reasoning, numerical ability, and verbal reasoning. The interest inventory results indicated that Larry's highest scores were in the realistic occupational environment. The Holland typology codes in order of preference were REC (Realistic, Enterprising, and Conventional). Larry's highest scores on the Values Scales were Achievement, Lifestyle, Ability Utilization, and Autonomy.

Assessing Self-Concepts and Life Themes

Each person's perception of self is indeed a most relevant concern for helpers, especially those who are assisting clients in making important life decisions such as career choice. One's ability to project into a work environment and do a reality check concerning their ability to meet work requirements is certainly a complex process that is very inclusive. One of the important factors involved in the choice process is self-efficacy. Self-efficacious thinking suggests that one has expectations to succeed through their own initiative, skills, and knowledge. More than likely, clients who have experienced previous success and job satisfaction have developed confidence so they can succeed in other work roles. Counselors, therefore, are to be alert as to how clients approach making choices that may be primarily influenced by past experiences. One way to uncover self-efficacious thinking is through dialogue that encourages clients to express reasons why they feel comfortable with some work requirements and environments and why they dismiss considering others. One could also use card sorts to observe how clients react to work environments.

There are a variety of card sorts that are used in counseling, but for our purpose we select cards that have the occupational titles and Holland code titles on one side of the card and the occupational description on the other. Clients are instructed to sort the cards into three stacks: "Would Choose," "Undecided," and "Would Not Choose." As clients respond verbally to their choices, the astute counselor listens carefully for clues that are related to self-concept development and self-efficacious thinking as well as clues to negative cognitions that may be the driving force behind one's view of the

world as well as the future. Larry responded "undecided" and "would not choose" to certain occupations because he knew very little about them. This reaction could be typical of individuals who have little exposure to occupational requirements and have focused only on those that are related to past experiences. Clearly Larry can benefit by increasing his knowledge of occupations through effective exploration. In addition, Larry's future can be enhanced through his efforts to develop a more balanced lifestyle.

Data Integration and Goal development

The counselor began the data integration stage by asking Larry to state the reasons given for coming to counseling. The counselor's goal was to have Larry participate from the very beginning. After repeating his need for help in finding a job, Larry stated that he began to realize that even though finding work was now a necessity, he soon recognized he should have gone through this process long ago.

LARRY: I guess I just took the easy way out and thought things would work out, but now I have to admit I have been hoping for something better for quite some time.

COUNSELOR: Keep that observation in mind as you continue to learn more about accessing occupational information.

The counselor outlined the steps for assessment and made the point that discussions of score results should help develop some plans and goals for the future. A synopsis of score reports can be found in Box 3.2.

COUNSELOR: The results of the Salience Inventory indicate that you consider work to be the most important life role. You scores also indicates that home, family, and leisure roles are also important. Do you think this rank order of life roles is a correct one?

LARRY: That's right! I grew up with the idea that work is one of the most important things a person can do. And yes, I want to have a happy family and enjoy the downtime. I couldn't agree more with the results.

BOX 3.2

Larry's Score Report

Salience Inventory	High scores (relative importance of roles)
	Work role
	Home and family role
	Leisure
Adult Career Concerns Inventory	High Self-Rated Concerns
	Tasks involved in exploration
	Maintenance
	Establishment
Career Development Inventory	Low scores
	Planning orientation
	Readiness for exploration
	Information about Decision Making
Differential Aptitude Test	High scores
	Numerical Ability
	Mechanical Reasoning
	Verbal Reasoning
Strong Interest Inventory	High scores
	REC (Realistic, Enterprising, Conventional)
Values Scales	High scores
	Achievement
	Lifestyle
	Ability
	Utilization
	Autonomy

A discussion followed about how one life role affects other life roles. The spillover effect from one life role to other life roles was emphasized as well as benefits of a balance between life roles.

LARRY: Right now I think about my work and family roles most of the time—the recession has me worried. But even before the recession I often thought about finding a different job. It seems that I was not committed enough to do something about it.

The counselor asked Larry to explain the strategies he would now use in finding a "different job." Larry explained that he has never had to look for work because his friends and family told him about the kind of work available. "I didn't give much thought to other kinds of work, but yet I knew I didn't want to do framing work the rest of my life."

COUNSELOR: We can help you develop effective exploration skills, but we also need to find out what kind of skills you have and the kind of work you are interested in and value. When you learn more about other occupational requirements, you should be in a better position to expand your opportunities.

The next set of score results is from the *Career Development Inventory* (Super et al., 1971) that measures one's ability to do career planning and the skills needed to learn more about occupations. It is also a measure of one's decision-making skills. Not surprisingly Larry's score report indicated low scores in career planning, exploration techniques, decision making, and knowledge of the world of work. Larry and the counselor both agreed that he would need to vastly improve his skills in all the areas measured by this inventory. The counselor offered support by informing Larry that not all his score results are negative and in fact he has some strong characteristics he can build on. She reminded him that these inventories are used to identify ways in which one can be helped.

The *Adult Career Concerns Inventory* (Super et al., 1988) is an instrument that can be used to identify one's career concerns in terms of developmental tasks. Test takers are instructed to self-rate their concerns with developmental tasks. Score results include concerns with the developmental tasks associated with growth, exploration, establishment, maintenance, and decline. According to the score report, Larry's greatest concerns were with the tasks of exploration, maintenance, and establishment.

Larry once again explained that he is very concerned about learning more about the world of work but admits he is not sure about the best way to do this. He added he is most interested in maintaining an occupational position so that he could have the possibility of advancing in a career. The counselor took this opportunity to once again make the point that lifelong learning is a good philosophy to adopt. She then informed Larry that one of his future goals can be to learn how to effectively access occupational information and to discuss ways in which one can make an occupational position secure.

The counselor then informed Larry that there were some positive signs in the next set of test scores, especially on the aptitude test. The overall results suggest that Larry is certainly capable of learning complicated tasks that are required in some occupations. He has good numerical and verbal reasoning skills and also has a high score in mechanical reasoning. In addition, he values achievement which suggests that he sets high standards and makes every attempt to utilize his abilities in a constructive way. Also, Larry prefers to make his own decisions about work procedures and planning lifestyle activities. He informed the counselor that his boss often praised some of his decisions he made concerning tasks in the workplace. It appears that Larry feels he can improve his decision-making abilities, but he has also been encouraged by accurate decisions he previously made at work. Thus, there are good indications of self-efficacy. The interest inventory score results of REC (Holland's typology codes) suggest that Larry prefers skilled trades, and leadership roles and is rather conservative and practical.

Larry's reaction: I have always attempted to do my best at work and I guess my independent feelings come from my parents who taught me to listen to all opinions about a subject and then make up my own mind.

This statement by Larry is a good example of someone who has developed a sense of self that is strong enough to make decisions based on both positive and negative information. This sense of self also suggests that Larry's confidence is based on self-efficacious thinking. He gives the impression that he has confidence in his beliefs but also recognizes his deficiencies. His life theme suggests that he has a strong background of beliefs, especially of family values and community service. His strong career convictions suggest that he is willing to use alternative strategies when making decisions and he is most willing to negotiate transitions in the future.

Both Larry and the counselor recognized that the job market is very limited at this time because of a severe recession. They reached a consensus of opinion that Larry would select the best local job option available. Larry wanted to keep his home and remain in the community he and family enjoyed. Fortunately, there was an initiative program being developed in the nearby city that was designed to help people locate and train for jobs available. A foundation had given a grant to pay individuals a small amount per hour while in training. A company that was a part of the initiative program was offering an eight-week training program for learning the skills to build customized doors and other milled products. Larry entered the training program with the idea that he would do his best but would also continue to learn more about exploration skills and decision-making techniques; he would keep his options open for the future. In sum his goals included: (1) developing effective methods of processing career information, (2) enhancing efforts to develop a balanced lifestyle, (3) developing career planning skills and decision-making techniques, and (4) engaging in planning for a secure future which would include lifelong learning.

Larry's career counseling was to continue to involve his career development needs over the life span. Larry expects to experience a series of up-and-down times in the future economy but vowed that he would be better prepared to face the challenges he may encounter. As he put it, "I want to be what you referred to as flexible and be able to adapt to changes that might occur." In the meantime, he plans to make the best of the opportunity to learn how to work with milled products and will engage in exploring the possibility of learning new skills and more about the future trends in the job market. To no one's surprise Larry will continue his strong commitment to family and home and his involvement in community affairs. In short Larry learned that career development is indeed a lifelong process.

Model III A Learning Theory of Career Counseling (LTCC)

A most comprehensive approach to career decision making has been carefully delineated by Krumboltz, Mitchell, and Gelatt (1975); Krumboltz and Hamel (1977); Krumboltz and Nichols (1990); Mitchell and Krumboltz (1990, 1996); and Krumboltz (1996). These authors emphasize that each individual's unique learning experiences over the life span are most influential in the career choice process. Therefore, learning is a key ingredient in career counseling and career guidance, suggesting that a career counselor's major task is to enhance learning opportunities for clients by using a wide array of effective methods that begin in childhood and endure throughout a lifetime.

The scope of the career counselor's role is viewed as very complex and inclusive—suggesting a number of skills, knowledge, and methods to deal with all career and personal problems that act as barriers to goal attainment. Career counselors may take the role of mentor, coach, or educator and should be prepared to solve unique beliefs that hinder personal development. As Krumboltz (1996) sees it, the counselor as educator provides the environment for clients to develop interests, skills, values, work habits, and many other personal qualities. From this learning perspective, clients can be empowered to take actions that promote the creation of satisfying lives now and in the future. For future reference, counselors help clients identify elements of a satisfying life that could change over time and especially how to adapt to changing circumstances and constantly changing work environments.

In this model, the client is viewed as one who is exploring and experimenting with possibilities and tentative decisions. A client should not be condemned for abandoning a goal in the exploratory process of learning about self, workplaces, and careers. In fact, Krumboltz (1996) strongly suggests that clients do not need to make a career decision for the sake of deciding but, rather, should be encouraged to explore, eliminate, and make tentative tryouts in a learning process that makes progress toward accomplishing their personal goals. Within this perspective, indecision is viewed as what is expected from clients who seek assistance; indecision should not be viewed as a negative diagnosis, but as an existing condition of a client who is open to learning and exploration.

In sum, the following practical applications for counselors are paraphrased as follows: (1) Assessment instruments are used to stimulate new learning by identifying needed new skills, cultivating new interests, and developing interpersonal competencies; (2) educational interventions should be increased to provide more opportunities of learning about one's abilities to meet career demands, the demands of the workplace, changing work habits, changing beliefs, and values; (3) success criteria should be based on learning outcomes and not solely on whether a client has made a career decision—the focus is on new behaviors, attempts to learn, and revised thoughts; and (4) counselors should integrate career and personal counseling; learning should focus on personal as well as career issues (Krumboltz, 1996).

The following career counseling model relies heavily on a decision-making model developed by Krumboltz and Sorenson (1974) and has been updated by more recent publications as noted in the beginning of this discussion and by Walsh (1990) and Savickas and Walsh (1996):

Stage 1. Interview

    a. Establish client–counselor relationship.
    b. Have client commit to time needed for counseling.
    c. Reinforce insightful and positive client responses.

d. Focus on all career problems, family life, environmental influences, emotional instability, career beliefs and obstacles, and traditional career domains of skills, interests, values, and personality.

e. Help clients formulate tentative goals.

Stage 2. Assessment

a. Objective assessment instruments are used as a means of providing links to learning interventions.

b. Subjective assessment attempts to attain the accuracy and coherence of the client's information system, identify client's core goals, and faulty or unrealistic strategies to reach goals.

c. Beliefs and behaviors that typically cause problems are evaluated by using an inventory designed for this purpose.

Stage 3. Generate Activities

a. Clients are directed to individualized projects such as taking another assessment instrument, reviewing audiovisual materials, computer programs, or studying occupational literature.

b. Some clients may be directed to counseling programs that address personal problems and/or lack of cognitive clarity.

Stage 4. Collect Information

a. Intervention strategies are reviewed.

b. Individual goals, including newly developed ones, are discussed.

c. A format for previewing an occupation is presented.

d. Clients commit to information gathering by job-site visit or using job-experience kits.

Stage 5. Share Information and Estimate Consequences

a. Client and counselor discuss information gathered about occupations and together estimate the consequences of choosing each occupation.

b. Counselor evaluates client's difficulty in processing information.

c. Counselor evaluates client's faulty strategies in decision processing.

d. Counselor develops remedial interventions.

e. Clients can be directed to collect more information or recycle within the counseling model before moving to the next step.

Stage 6. Reevaluate, Decide Tentatively, or Recycle

a. Client and counselor discuss the possibilities of success in specific kinds of occupations.

b. Counselor provides the stimulus for firming up a decision for further exploration of a career, or changing direction and going back to previous steps in making a decision.

Stage 7. Job Search Strategies

a. Client intervention strategies can include using study materials, learning to do an interview or write a résumé, joining a job club, role playing, or doing simulation exercises designed to teach clients the consequences of making life decisions. Client and counselor reintroduce the concepts of career–life planning and, specifically, how the procedures of learning to make a career decision can be used with other major decisions in life.

The following paragraphs summarize and highlight additional information to make this model more user friendly.

In stage 1, Interview, client–counselor relationships are established and maintained throughout the counseling process. The client must be allotted the status of collaborator and allowed the freedom and given the encouragement to learn, explore, and experiment. A working partnership may best characterize an appropriate relationship.

Some techniques of interviewing discussed and illustrated in the next two chapters, can be used as examples for at least partially fulfilling the requirements of an intake interview. Counselors obtain more specific information of client learning experiences and environmental conditions that have significantly influenced the development of task approach skills.

In stage 2, Assessment, results are used in two ways: (1) to suggest to clients how their preferences and skills match requirements found in educational and occupational environments and (2) to develop new learning experiences for the client (Krumboltz, 1996).

Using test results as a method of identifying what a client may want to learn for the future, for example, encourages clients to identify learning intervention strategies that are needed for occupations of interest. In this context, career development is considered as a temporary state that can be improved to enhance a client's potential for career exploration. One may also want to use criterion-referenced tests that evaluate what a client can or cannot do rather than norm-referenced tests that reveal what percentage of the population the client exceeds.

Assessments designed to measure interests, values, personality, and career beliefs are also used as points of reference for developing learning interventions. In essence, using assessment results for identifying learning needs to improve career decision making suggests that (1) clients should not only base their decisions on existing capabilities and interests but also expand them and (2) occupational requirements are not expected to remain stable—thus, clients need to prepare for changing work tasks and work environments. Tailored and remedial intervention strategies designed to meet each client's unique needs are most effective (Krumboltz, 1996).

Tentative goals formulated during the intake interview are further evaluated during stage 3, Generate Activities. Client and counselor determine steps necessary to reach goals. Some clients might want to confirm their goals by taking an interest inventory. Another client might want to evaluate abilities. Yet another client might be best served by personal problem counseling before making a goal commitment. Before completing this stage, clients select two or more occupations to explore.

The major objectives of stage 4, Collect Information, are to introduce clients to career information resources, their purpose, and use. Client and counselor also develop a format for evaluating occupations. Included in the format are opportunities for advancement, pay scales, worker associates, preparation time for certain occupations, and skills that are required. Clients are assigned individual projects involving career exploration and may be required to job shadow or use job-experience kits.

Client and counselor discuss the information gathered for each occupation evaluated in stage 5, Share Information and Estimate Consequences. Counselors assist clients in estimating their chances of success in a chosen occupation. During this process, the client is directed to state tentative conclusions, reasons for conclusions, and ideas for further exploration. Some clients may be directed to collect more information before conclusions can be reached.

In stage 6, Reevaluate, Decide Tentatively, or Recycle, client and counselor establish a firmer commitment to career direction. Some clients continue to the next step of job search whereas others recycle for more information or a change in direction. Counselors maintain the position that clients should not be judged harshly for changing their minds during this process of discovery. Some clients require more time and information before deciding tentatively. Counselors should support clients who make reasonable and realistic requests during this stage.

In the final stage, Job Search Strategies, clients become involved in the usual programs of interview training, preparing a résumé, or joining a job club. A unique feature of this model, however, is the emphasis on teaching clients the consequences of making a career decision. Client and counselor reintroduce the concepts of career life planning and, specifically, how the procedures of learning to make a career decision can be used with other major decisions in life.

In an attempt to understand how clients arrive at decisions, counselors view core goals as driving forces underlying an individual's motivation toward certain activities and, as such, goals function as a fundamental sense of self. For example, one who has a core goal "to be in charge" might not be motivated to evaluate certain work environments and to complete an agreed-on activity. In this case, the counselor assists the client in clarifying core goals as underlying reasons for a lack of interest in pursuing certain activities. Counselors are to assist clients in resolving issues associated with core goals, especially those that influence decision making. This step in the career counseling process is considered a key role of the career counselor (Krumboltz & Nichols, 1990).

Two major goals of this model are to build an understanding of what motivates human behavior and how thought processes and actions influence career development and subsequent career decisions. According to the living systems framework (LSF) developed by Ford (1987) and Ford and Ford (1987) as discussed in Krumboltz and Nichols (1990, p. 175), the primary and most direct influences on decision making are (a) one's accumulated knowledge about the world and about one's self (information processing and storage); (b) one's entire set of desired and undesired outcomes (directive cognitions); (c) evaluative thought processes that determine what one can or should try to accomplish right now (regulatory evaluations); and (d) thought processes that determine strategies for how to accomplish current objectives and coordinate action (control processes).

Krumboltz and Nichols's explanation of decision making underscores the magnitude of extremely complex systems from cognitive science that are used as guidelines to understand what motivates human behavior and how information about self and environment is processed when one makes a career decision. See Case 3.3 for a case involving a reluctant decision maker.

In sum, learning is the key to enhancing self-knowledge. A key focus is to develop a greater sensitivity to the advantages and limitations of environmental experiences that influence career decision making. Using learning intervention strategies to develop skills, interests, and abilities to expand a client's outcome potential is a unique feature of this model. Finally, one must recognize that cognitive functions provide clients with a model of the world and their relationship to it. As clients evaluate changing work environments, they also evaluate their skills, abilities, and other personal qualities to meet their perceptions of what is demanded. In this context, appropriate and realistic information processing is essential.

Case 3.3	**The Case of the Reluctant Decision Maker**

Joe was accompanied to a community counseling center by a friend who was also a career counseling client. Joe needed a great deal of support and encouragement before he agreed to make an appointment. He reluctantly asked for help to find a better job.

Joe dropped out of high school when he was in the 10th grade to work in a fast-food establishment. He recently completed a high school equivalency course and received a diploma. Now 22, he continues to live with his parents. His father is a factory worker, his mother is a homemaker, and he has four siblings.

The counselor immediately recognized that Joe was very uncomfortable asking for help. He appeared to be very nervous and restless; the counselor attempted to help Joe feel more comfortable.

COUNSELOR: Joe, I am pleased to know you (shaking hands). Your buddy here has been telling me about what a nice guy you are and what a good friend you have been.

JOE: Well, ah, thank you. He is a good friend too.

COUNSELOR: It's great to have good friends, Joe. This reminds me of when a friend of mine helped me get started in college a few years ago.

The counselor continued to make small talk to help Joe feel more at ease. When it appeared that Joe was more relaxed, the counselor outlined his role as counselor and what is expected of a client during the career counseling process. Joe was receptive to suggestions and agreed to keep his appointments and complete work away from the counseling center that might be assigned during the course of counseling.

During the intake interview the counselor discovered that Joe had taken part in career counseling while in a high school equivalency program.

JOE: Yes, I took several tests before I finished training.

COUNSELOR: Do you recall the kind of tests?

JOE: One was for interests and I believe the other was an aptitude test.

COUNSELOR: Good! What did you decide after going over the results?

JOE: Well, I decided to think about two or three different jobs, but I didn't get anywhere.

COUNSELOR: Explain more fully.

JOE: I thought the counselor was supposed to tell me more about what I should do and what I'm qualified for.

As Joe and the counselor continued their discussion, it became very apparent that Joe had some faulty beliefs about career decision making. He evidently thought that someone would decide for him or provide a recipe for choosing a job with little effort on his part. In addition, the counselor suspected that there were some underlying reasons Joe was not taking appropriate actions to solve his problems, but this would have to be confirmed by additional data and observation.

JOE: I just was not able to decide, and I really needed some help.

COUNSELOR: Could you tell me about the kind of help you need?

JOE: I don't exactly know, but I just couldn't see myself in those jobs. I just don't know about all those jobs. My family makes fun of me when I talk about more school.

COUNSELOR: Tell me more about your family and what they said.

JOE: They all work hard. They have labor-type jobs and don't make much money. They want me to do the same kind of thing—just live from one paycheck to another and somehow get by. You know, sometimes I think they are right! Maybe I'm not cut out to do any other kind of work.

After further discussion, the counselor was greatly concerned that Joe would not progress very far in the career decision-making process with faulty beliefs such as those he had expressed. The counselor jotted the following notes of a thinking pattern that could inhibit Joe's career development:

- Apparent anxiety about career planning
- Lack of flexibility in decision making
- Lack of willingness to consider a variety of occupations
- Faulty beliefs about career decision making and occupational environments
- Lack of family support
- Limited career choices from salient messages in the environment

COUNSELOR: Joe, we can help you make a career decision, but first we both should learn more about your career beliefs. Would you be interested in taking an inventory that would help us understand more about your beliefs and your assumptions about careers?

JOE: Sure, I guess so, but I don't understand how it will help me.

COUNSELOR: Let me explain how we will use the results. We can find out about some of the factors that influence your decisions, what may be necessary to make you feel happy about your future, and changes you are willing to make. Discussing these subjects should help in clarifying your role and my role in the career decision-making process.

The results of the *Career Beliefs Inventory* (CBI) (Krumboltz, 1988) described in chapter 6, not surprisingly, indicated low scores on several scales, especially on acceptance of uncertainty and openness. Low scores on these scales indicate that excessive anxiety can lead to viewing career decision making as overwhelming, and Joe's scores also suggested that he had fears about the reactions of others. The counselor felt more certain about his tentative conclusions from the intake interview. In the next session with Joe, and following a review of the purposes of the inventory and its scores, the counselor and Joe discussed the results.

The counselor asked Joe to tell him the reasons why he was uncertain about his future and career plans. The counselor was not surprised when Joe told him that his family had never supported any plans for him to continue his education. As Joe put it, his entire family did not agree that a college education was worth the effort. The lack of support and the ridicule he received from family members had convinced Joe that he was not capable of meeting the demands of college courses.

The counselor took this opportunity to focus on Joe's experience with academic courses he took when pursuing a high school equivalency. Joe replied that he received a C or better in every course and also received two As. The following exchange took place:

COUNSELOR: What does this tell you about your ability to do academic work?

JOE: OK, I guess I was successful then, but that does not mean I could do the same in college.

COUNSELOR: You are absolutely right. There are no guarantees, but we have known for a long time that past academic performance is a good indicator of future performance in school.

JOE: But my brother and mom keep telling me that we aren't the kind to go to college.

COUNSELOR: If I provide you with information about your chances of making a C or better in community college, would you be willing to talk with your family about options you are considering for the future?

JOE: Okay, but I don't believe it will help.

Each of the scales with low scores from the results of the CBI was discussed in a similar manner, that is, faulty beliefs were identified, followed by specific plans of actions. The counselor continued to confront Joe with facts about individuals who were the first in their family to complete a college degree and stressed that he must arrive at a decision based on his own desires and potential.

The counselor and Joe agreed that he should take an achievement test to determine his academic deficiencies. Their plan was to have Joe improve his skills as a means of improving his chances of being a successful college student. In the next four months Joe spent a considerable part of his spare time in studying and being tutored to improve basic academic skills. He also gained a great deal of confidence by being involved in such a project. A follow-up test boosted Joe's confidence when he discovered that he had shown significant academic progress.

The counselor and Joe met on a regular basis to discuss his interests and to change his faulty beliefs. The counselor met with less resistance from Joe as he became more comfortable in the college environment. Finally, Joe convinced his parents to visit with the counselor about his future plans. To everyone's surprise, especially Joe's, they agreed to let Joe "give it a try for a semester."

Joe and the counselor agreed that they would delay making a firm career commitment at this time.

They both felt that Joe should be open to look at several options as he progressed in college.

In this case, the CBI provided the stimulus for discussing relevant career problems that inhibited Joe from making choices in his best interests. Learning theory counseling makes it quite clear that faulty beliefs are to be challenged throughout the counseling process. Clients are to be empowered to discover their abilities and improve them as well as to explore various options before making a firm career commitment. In this case learning to improve his skills gave Joe confidence in his ability to perform at a college level.

SOURCE: Adapted from Zunker and Osborn (2002).

Model IV Cognitive Information-Processing (CIP) Model

Peterson and colleagues (1996) have proposed a seven-step sequence for career delivery service as shown in chapter 2, Figure 2.3. This sequence can be used as a delivery option for both problem solving and decision making and can be used for individual, group, self-directed, and curricular programs.

This model is an extension of a career development theory, a cognitive information-processing approach to career problem solving and decision making, developed by the same authors and introduced in chapter 2. This unusual approach of illustrating and carefully describing how a theory can be applied to career counseling should be placed on the practitioner's list of events to celebrate.

A CIP approach to career development and its application to career counseling require an in-depth understanding of cognitive information process theory. I strongly encourage you to read the original source for more information. This brief introduction to evaluating career information problems within a cognitive processing model should be considered a starting point only for understanding this theory's application to an individual career counseling model.

Information processing for career decision making is conceptualized within this model as a hierarchical system from a base of Knowledge Domains (self-knowledge and occupational knowledge) to a Decision Skills Domain, and finally to an Executive Processing Domain, as shown in Figure 3.5.

In the Knowledge Domain, self-knowledge is related to one's interests, abilities, and values whereas occupational knowledge consists of an individual's view of individual occupations and structural relations between occupations.

The Decision Skills Domain consists of five stages referred to as the CASVE cycle. The acronym CASVE consists of Communication (problem perceived as a gap); Analysis (problem is reduced to components); Synthesis (problem is restructured by creating alternatives); Valuing (problem solutions are evaluated by valuing alternatives); and Execution (problem solutions are accomplished by formulating strategies).

The Executive Processing Domain consists of skills of initiating, coordinating, storing, and retrieving information. These skills are considered to be metacognitions

FIGURE 3.5

Pyramid of information-processing domains

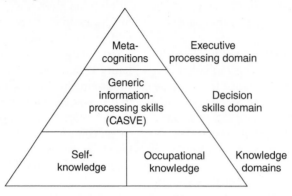

SOURCE: From *Career Development and Services: A Cognitive Approach*, p. 28, by G. Peterson, J. Sampson, and E. Reardon, Copyright © 1991. Reprinted with permission of Brooks/Cole Publishing Company, a part of The Thomson Corporation.

that are used in problem solving and by self-talk, increased self-awareness, and control. Briefly, self-talk ("I think I can be a good engineer") creates expectations and reinforces behavior. Self-awareness influences decision making, in this context, by serving as a balance between individual goals and the goals of important others. Control refers to one's ability to control impulsive actions in the career decision process. The following summary statements include some major counseling concerns that can serve as connection between theory and practice:

- Career choice should be approached as a problem-solving activity.
- Information processing is a key skill in career exploration.
- Self-knowledge and occupational knowledge are essential elements in the career choice process.
- Career information processing is a leaning event; thus individual learning plans provide a sequence of activities that are jointly planned by counselor and client.

Combining this very brief introduction to cognitive information processing with the material presented in chapter 2, a career counseling model in a seven-step sequence follows in a paraphrased format (Peterson et al., 1996, pp. 450–457).

Step 1: Initial Interview. The major purpose of the interview is twofold. The counselor seeks information about the client's career problems and establishes a trusting relationship. More specifically, the counselor attends to both the emotional and cognitive components of the client's problems. The counselor recognizes that an effective relationship enhances client self-efficacy and fosters learning.

Step 2: Preliminary Assessment. To determine the client's readiness for problem solving and decision making, the Career Thoughts Inventory (Sampson et al., 1996a) is administered. This inventory is used both as a screening assessment and as a needs assessment; as such, it will identify clients who could experience difficulty in the career choice process as a result of dysfunctional thinking.

Step 3: Define Problem and Analyze Causes. In this step, the counselor and the client agree on a preliminary understanding of the client's problem(s). For example, the problem may be defined as a "gap" between the state of the client's indecision and the ideal state of "career decidedness." A word of caution: The client's problem should be explained and stated in neutral, rather than in judgmental terms.

Step 4: Formulate Goals. Formulating goals is a collaborative effort between counselor and client. Goals are put in writing in an individual learning plan (ILP), as shown in Figure 3.6.

Step 5: Develop an Individual Learning Plan. Again, the counselor and the client collaborate when developing the ILP, which provides a sequence of resources and

---

FIGURE 3.6

Individual learning plan

Individual Learning Plan

Career Resource Center
Central Community College—110 Social Science Building

Goal(s)
1. Understand personal barriers to decision making.
2. Clarify self-knowledge and occupational knowledge.
3. Improve decision-making skills.
4.

Goal	Priority	Activity	Purpose/Outcome
1, 2 & 3	1	Individual Counseling	Clarify issues and obtain information
1	2	Modules EP∅ and EP2 and cognitive exercise	Explore Self-Talk
1	3	Monitor thoughts related to a real decision	Monitor Self-Talk
3	4	Module IP∅	Clarify decision-making knowledge
2	5	OCC-U-SORT & Module SK∅	Self knowledge and generate options
2	6	SDS:CV	" "
2	7	Written Summary of Self-Knowledge	" "
2	8	Career Key & module OK∅	Identify resources & obtain occ. info.
2	9	CHOICES	Narrow options
2	10	Video tapes, information interviews and shadowing	" "
2	11	Print Materials	" "

Joe Williams — Client   Marilyn Abbey — Career Counselor   3/12/90 — Date

---

SOURCE: From *Career Development and Services: A Cognitive Approach*, p. 28, by G. Peterson, J. Sampson, and E. Reardon, Copyright © 1991. Reprinted with permission of Brooks/Cole, a part of The Thomson Corporation.

activities that will assist the client in meeting goals established earlier. These goals and resources are very evident in the example of an ILP. The ILP also serves as a contract between client and counselor.

Step 6: Execute Individual Learning Plan. This step requires that the client take the initiative in proceeding with the agreed-on plan. The counselor encourages and directs the progress and may provide more information, clarification, or reinforcement of the client's progress and also offer planning for future experiences. With dysfunctional clients, a workbook is used as a supplement to learning about the results of the Career Thoughts Inventory administered in step 2. This workbook, entitled *Improving Your Career Thoughts: A Workbook for the Career Thoughts Inventory* (Sampson, Petersen, Lenz, Reardon, & Saunders, 1996b), is used for cognitive restructuring, within which the client uses a four-step procedure (identify, challenge, alter, and take action).

Selected strategies for enhancing career problem solving and decision making are summarized as follows. For discovering self, trace the development of your interests, write an autobiography, and prepare a vocational history; for life experiences, write a description in the third person and analyze emergent themes; for linking measured interests to past experiences, take an interest inventory and relate the results to real-life events.

Step 7: Summative Review and Generalization. Progress in solving the gap that might have motivated the client to seek counseling is perceived in this last step. A determination is also made about how effective the progress has been in following through with the ILP. The focus through all steps is on the client's career decision-making status. Finally, the lessons learned within the preceding six steps are generalized as skills learned to solve future career and personal problems.

In the initial interview, the counselor's goal is to analyze the characteristics of each client's problem according to a gap, ambiguous cues, interacting courses of action, unpredictability of courses of action, and new problems. Gap is used here to describe a career problem of dissonance between what actually exists and what the client feels should exist. For example, a low-paying job with minimal responsibilities is quite different from the client's mental image of an ideal situation of higher pay, higher status, and independence. Recognizing a gap in this manner provides viable information for problem identification and subsequent goal development.

Ambiguous cues are clues the counselor and client can use to understand sources of problems or the underlying reasons for certain behavior patterns. For instance, a client might be experiencing extreme anxiety when faced with a situation in which competing cues are difficult to resolve. A client who might be searching for a stable job that is secure could also be struggling with a desire to be in a position of risk that provides the opportunity of becoming wealthy. In such situations, personal desires and motives or internal drives that are in conflict can be sources of anxiety. Sources of anxiety can also emerge from situational conditions or external factors. Identifying sources of anxiety is a major step toward resolving conflicting ambiguous cues.

Interacting courses of action and uncertainty of outcome also affect decision making and problem solving. For instance, a client might decide to pursue a nursing career and identify requirements, but while doing so might also explore an unrelated career. In this case, this client might lack the confidence to proceed on her own and could need more information about personal traits and career information. Counselors assist clients in identifying actions and elements of actions that provide clues to solving problems. Moreover, the uncertainty of outcome is a major barrier for clients who lack self-confidence to advance on their own. Some issues might be external, such as the lack of financial means for higher education. Another client might be directed toward self-talk or be given support and reinforced by discussing unique assets. Cognitive problems that are identified as dysfunctional are directed toward interventions that replace dualistic thinking with relative thinking, methods of developing self-control strategies, and acquiring effective methods of problem solving.

In addition to uncertainty of outcome, new problems arise during the course of decision making, and they are viewed as sets of subordinate problems. For example, should a decided client seek a low entry position or go through training for a higher level job? Another client might be searching for which university provides the best program that is affordable. The point here is that subordinate problems can tend to discourage clients who foresee insurmountable barriers to reaching their goals. The uncertainty of outcome and new problems are critical issues at critical stages in a counseling model; the counselor must be prepared to support the client and offer solutions that are discovered in a collaborative relationship between counselor and client.

The next step in the outline, preliminary assessment, is basically a screening and needs assessment procedure. An inventory that can be used for problem identification in the screening process is *My Vocational Situation* (Holland, Daiger, & Power, 1980). This instrument provides scores for vocational identity, need for information, and perceived barriers to occupational choice. Other instruments that measure career maturity, indecision, career beliefs, career decision-making style, and occupational certainty also can be used in the preliminary assessment step.

Defining problems and analyzing causes (step 3) requires counselor and client to identify probable causes of gaps and subsequent problems. For example, a client who cannot make a decision between two plausible choices might need individual counseling to clarify life roles or other important unique issues. Collaborative inter-action between client and counselor is an important relationship that fosters problem identification and, by this process, provides for client agreement and understanding of probable causes.

The formulation of goals (step 4) follows with continued collaboration for careful detailing of each goal. An active client role reduces the likelihood of misunderstand-ings and confusion about the sequence of the counseling process.

Client and counselor develop an ILP (step 5) for each counseling goal, followed by an intervention activity. Learning activities included in the ILP can also be instruc-tional modules that contain objectives, self-administered diagnostic tests, alternative learning activities, and a self-administered summary assessment.

In step 6, execute an ILP, several practical suggestions are given in the outline, including self-talk. Self-talk comments are viewed as self-efficacy beliefs (Bandura, 1989); thus, both negative and positive statements made by clients are discussed with each client. Positive statements are used to reinforce client's actions, and negative statements are considered self-deprecating and should be fully evaluated.

Finally, step 7, summative review and generalizations, focuses on learned skills that can be used in problem solving and career-making decisions in the future. A review of all steps reinforces client progress and enhances learned experiences.

This model and its theory attempt to answer some important questions about problem solving and the career decision-making process. This career counseling model is basically a learning model built around CIP theory. In applying this theory to a career counseling model, the authors have developed a sound system of steps that are clearly delineated for the practitioner. An ILP is a unique element of this model, which also has a variety of intervention modules. A career counseling case that illus-trates some elements of this model is presented in Case 3.4.

Case 3.4   The Case of a Lot of Bravado

(This case was recorded by a counselor in the first person. Excerpts from the case are used as an example of one of the important stages in the CIP model.)

When Pat walked in the counseling center he impressed the secretary as someone who has to be very important. Pat had a swagger in his walk that gave the impression of one who is most confident, considers himself attractive, and has got the world by the tail. He didn't ask for a counselor; he wanted to see the director or the "person who is in charge." The secretary did not question Pat's motives but meekly showed him the way to my office.

He quickly made his entry and almost cracked my knuckles while shaking hands. I am sure they could hear him clearly in the adjoining rooms as his first comments went something like this, "Howdy!! My name is Pat. I came to see you today for a little help."

As Pat and I got to know more about each other during our early conversations, he stated that he wanted help in "picking out a good job" and agreed to proceed with career counseling as it was outlined. Pat grew up on a ranch in west Texas that his father managed for a wealthy oil man. In the area where Pat grew up there were extremely large ranches, and many of them contained significant oil and gas deposits. As Pat put it, the people there were "friendly and down home." Pat felt his parents were very supportive of him and it was understood that he would attend college. He had two younger siblings. Pat was now a first-semester freshman. His grades in high school were slightly above average. But he explained that he had to ride the school bus for considerable periods of time because his home was 30 miles from the school. When he got home he had to help his father, which left little time for studying.

After further discussion that was not very productive because of Pat's bravado and guarded comments, we agreed that he should write an autobiography of his life and include his perception of a career goal, his experiences at home, school, and work, and hobbies and interests.

COUNSELOR: I have learned a great deal about your background from our discussion, but I believe it would benefit both of us if you would be willing to write about some events in your life.

PAT: Yes, sir, that might help to get everything down 'cause you see that I like to talk a lot and skip around.

COUNSELOR: I do enjoy hearing about your experiences on such a large ranch. We don't have a lot of students who come in here with a similar background. But we are meeting to help you, and this might be a way to get started.

Pat dropped off his autobiography at the designated time of five days. As I read the autobiography I could not help observing that this was a different Pat than I had met only a few days ago. There seemed to be a private Pat who is reflected in his autobiography and a public Pat who you get when you meet face-to-face. Of course I realized we all have our public and private self-concepts, but Pat's behavior appeared to be overcompensating for some reason. The Pat who wrote expressed himself as an individual who is in search of a future that was realistic. He expressed interest in jobs that he evidently observed in his environment, such as geologist, petroleum engineer, and businessman. Yet he admitted he was uncertain about a career choice. Conversely, when he spoke about possible occupations in the counseling center, he mentioned professor so he could drive a Mercedes and stockbroker so he could be rich. Besides being unrealistic about a professor's salary, his statements reflected a naïveté about occupations per se.

The gap between perceived income and actual income had to be resolved before Pat could make appropriate career decisions. In essence, Pat needed to learn more about occupations and options. But what seemed to be the most pressing matter was to discover the sources of anxiety that Pat was currently experiencing.

During the next counseling session when discussing the autobiography, Pat appeared to be very anxious. It appeared that he was experiencing ambiguous cues such as wanting a lot of money regardless of risk but also wanting a secure job that would give him "time to take care of the livestock."

COUNSELOR: I have an inventory that might help us clarify your needs and help you make some decisions. It only takes a few minutes.

PAT: That sounds good to me—let's get started.

COUNSELOR: The inventory is the *Career Thoughts Inventory* (CTI) (Sampson, Peterson, Lenz, Reardon, & Saunders, 1996a). It will give us scores about decision-making problems, anxiety, and conflicts you may have.

Pat scored high on the scale that measures commitment anxiety, and the counselor explained his score as follows:

COUNSELOR: Your high score on this scale may mean that you are having difficulty committing to a career option because you may be afraid of what might happen when you do make a decision.

PAT: I'll have to think about that but it might just be true. To tell the truth I don't really know what I want to do. I suppose that if I decide now it might be wrong and I would be wasting my time and my parents' money.

I informed Pat that many students are undecided about their future and that is understandable, but it is most important to put forth the effort to create some options during the first year in college. This was the first time I met the private Pat face-to-face—he was actually a down-to-earth person struggling to determine an optimal career.

COUNSELOR: Pat, I have met with many students over the years who have struggled to find a career choice. We can help you do that, and I must add that you have made a sincere effort to help yourself and that is most important!

PAT: Thank you. I can really use some help.

Pat and the counselor negotiated an ILP similar to the one displayed in Figure 3.3. Pat was to filter out barriers to decision making and to learn more about lifestyle factors and occupations. He was to improve his decision-making skills. This plan involved individual counseling that focused on self-talk to improve his self-esteem and debunk negative thoughts. He was to identify resources for occupational information and use a computer program to narrow his career options. He would be offered training in information interviews that are designed to assist clients in learning about workplaces, and he would be able to do job shadowing to learn more about the give-and-take of specific occupations.

Pat continued to visit with me while reporting his progress with the ILP. We discussed options and the feasibility of choices. Pat's sophistication in career exploration improved significantly as we were able to tease out the sources of his anxiety and point out his assets. Pat's self-talk continued to be monitored to make certain that he concentrated on positive thoughts. It was noticed that he began to walk with that "peacock swagger" again, but this time it was a different Pat—he had a realistic reason for being proud of his progress in college and in the career choice process.

Pat kept in touch after he graduated from college. He married a woman from another state and moved close to the Canadian border where they also have large ranches. He once wrote that he continues to use his business major and information he learned from animal husbandry courses on a ranch that will "all be mine someday where I can take care of the livestock."

In sum, the counselor assisted Pat in closing the gap between reality and what he perceived about some professions that was incorrect. Most important, Pat learned to know more about himself and the anxiety he had experienced from a lack of confidence that he attempted to mask and deny. A carefully thought-out ILP focused on how to assist Pat make appropriate career decisions and solve personal problems.

Model V A Multicultural Career Counseling Model for Ethnic Women

An introduction to steps or stages in a multicultural model for ethnic women by Bingham and Ward (1996) provides a means of comparing techniques designed to identify specific needs of a special group of clients and the methods and materials used in the counseling process. This model focuses on contextual elements of influence and recognizes that salient racial factors were not a part of theoretical conceptualizations of most of the career development theories discussed in the two preceding chapters. Theories, however, cannot directly guide specific counseling processes at a microlevel that are necessary to meet the unique needs of special groups. Counselors should, however, remain alert and open to learning more about the needs of minorities and especially the context of their worldview.

This model is presented with the recognition that background issues in multicultural counseling have not been discussed. Chapter 9 is devoted to multicultural counseling and should be considered an introduction to a vast amount of published material on this subject. However, Bingham's and Ward's model emphasizes contextual factors that limit career choice and stereotypes that hinder career development and introduces counselors to racial identity as a significant variable in client–counselor relationships. These unique features and others are not emphasized in the career counseling models that were developed from career development theories described in previous chapters.

The following are the steps in the multicultural career counseling model for ethnic women developed by Bingham and Ward (1996)*:

Step 1. Establish Rapport and Culturally Appropriate Relationships

Step 2. Identify Career Issues

Step 3. Assess Impact of Cultural Variables

Step 4. Set Counseling Goals

Step 5. Make Culturally Appropriate Counseling Interventions

Step 6. Make Decision

Step 7. Implement and Follow-Up

Bingham and Ward strongly suggest that counselors are to prepare for clients by using a self-administered *Multicultural Career Counseling Checklist* (MCCC) (Ward & Bingham, 1993) as displayed in appendix C. The first section of this instrument assesses the counselor's preparation for counseling a culturally different client by identifying both counselor's and client's racial/ethnic backgrounds. The other sections of this instrument concern the counseling process of exploration and assessment and establishing a negotiating and working consensus.

Also in the precounseling phase, the client is administered a *Career Counseling Checklist* (CCC) (Ward & Tate, 1990) displayed in appendix D. This instrument contains 42 statements that measure such factors as knowledge of the world of work, gender issues, role of family in the decision process, and client's concerns about choosing an occupation.

A *Decision Tree* (Ward & Bingham, 1993) is a schematic, as displayed in appendix E, that provides counseling decision points and pathways. One major decision point determines if the client is to be referred for psychological or personal counseling before obtaining career counseling.

A brief explanation of each step in the career counseling model follows.

Step 1: Establish Rapport and Culturally Appropriate Relationships

Client–counselor relationships are considered to be most important in all career counseling models, but especially in this model. Trust and collaboration are key components in counseling relationships, particularly when client and counselor are from different ethnic backgrounds. One should welcome a discussion of different worldviews by acknowledging racial differences between counselor and client and invite the client to discuss his or her feelings about racial differences (Paniagua, 2005).

Counselors must be aware of various specific cultural cues such as the client's nonverbal actions and reactions. Some clients, for example, may not consider it appropriate to maintain eye contact during counseling; the counselor's reciprocal behavior will enhance the relationship. Counselors should use as much time as necessary to establish a collaborative relationship, especially with clients who have been socialized in a cultural context that is different from that of the counselor. Respect and appreciation of differences on the part of the counselor and client are most desirable in establishing rapport.

Ivey, Ivey, and Zalaquett (2014) suggest that a counseling relationship should be built on trust that can take the entire initial counseling session to develop. The developers of this model suggest that listening and observing are two ways to determine how the counselor should respond to their client; one learns how to establish the context of the working relationship. Also suggested is that counselors should ask clients to clarify some of their comments to demonstrate interest in their thoughts and gain a more adequate understanding of their constructs. What is most important here are the recognition and appreciation of the cultural context the client has experienced.

Step 2: Identify Career Issues

In step 2, the effective counselor focuses on cultural variables that influenced career development. Clients are not to be stereotyped, but observed as unique individuals. One attempts to identify any barriers that could impede career decision making. Ethnic minority clients who have experienced discrimination, for example, might feel they cannot overcome the barriers that have conditioned them to limit career choice. Counselors should realize that cultural groups often share a common set of experiences of oppression that can collectively limit their perspectives of future opportunities.

Although ethnic minority clients can experience a sense of responsibility for career identification, they must also be guided to realize that past and present internal and external barriers have in some way influenced their career decision process. It is also likely that socioeconomic limitations diminish a client's perspective of a future lifestyle. Thus ethnic minority clients may have limited experiences with other ethnic social groups and view others as being unreceptive to them.

One major goal of this step, therefore, is to assist clients in identifying those experiences that limit career choices. If your client suggests that her gender has limited future opportunities, she could be reflecting the social mores of her ethnicity in which women are restricted from working outside the home. Yet another client who is looking for a job is focused on taking care of immediate financial needs rather than searching for a career; career development over the life span may at best be a vague concept. Another client's perception of career development is that it has nothing to do with self-determination, but more to do with luck and who you know.

It should not surprise anyone that salient messages received by clients from contextual interaction can cause some ethnic minorities to circumscribe choices for what is considered an appropriate job. It is very likely that some clients limit their choices without being fully aware of it. Moreover, ethnic minority groups that have developed worldviews that limit their career choices suggest that counselors must be prepared to address both career and personal needs. More on this subject is discussed in chapter 9.

Step 3: Assess Impact of Cultural Variables

In this step, counselors identify cultural variables that have the most limiting influence on career choices. This process can be very time consuming, yet productive, when clients recognize the importance of understanding how their family environment, religion, and cultural history, for example, have shaped their prospects for the future. Counselors need to isolate unique cultural variables that need further delineation in culturally appropriate intervention strategies.

A good example to illustrate the problems associated with this stage in career counseling is the influence of one's extended family. If you ask a Native American how her family is doing, she might respond by telling you how the entire village is attempting to solve their problems. Family for Native Americans is an extended family, which among some tribes means an entire village (Ivey et al., 2014). For other ethnic groups, the extended family can include parents, siblings, grandparents, aunts and uncles, and even godfather. Thus, the influence from family among ethnic minorities, especially first-generation ones, can be very extensive and inclusive. Clients are often in conflict when attempting to decide between what they want to pursue and what their families see as appropriate.

Another related issue is how decisions are made in some ethnic groups. In this country, the rugged individual takes charge of his own destiny and independently determines its course. We as a society have endorsed the individualistic perspective of behavior in which one focuses on individual goals; the individual is empowered to make decisions. In many ethnic minority groups, the opposite is true; collective decision making among family members is considered more appropriate. A friend who grew up in Puerto Rico explained that he consulted his father in all major decisions by telephone from wherever he lived, which included several countries in South America. He had been conditioned that this was the proper way to make a decision. Thus, counselors who include the family in the decision-making process recognize the collectivist's view of the future. More about collectivism is discussed in chapter 9.

Step 4: Set Counseling Goals

Goal setting is to be a collaborative negotiation between client and counselor. This process encourages clients to be more active in pursuing satisfactory outcomes. A collaborative counseling relationship is especially important for ethnic minority clients. Some ethnic minority clients, for example, assume that they are to be passive participants, leaving all decisions to the counselor. In this context, clients are reluctant to share their true feelings and experiences and are uncomfortable being actively involved in the entire career counseling process. Thus, counselors should inform clients that it is proper and acceptable to negotiate activities throughout the entire counseling process. One begins in the very beginning of counseling by asking clients to participate whenever possible and asking for their agreement on procedures or options.

Leong (1993) suggests that pragmatic goals are more appropriate for ethnic minority groups than are goals based on self-actualization. The point here seems to be that clients who are more *collective* oriented, that is, placing family before self, might be more concerned about how a career benefits the family. Also, clients might need immediate placement in a job to support their needs and plan to consider long-term goals in the future. Even though circumstances may determine goal direction, counselors and clients who confer on outcome goals within a relationship that has established trust and respect for each other have the better chance of agreeing on appropriate goals.

Step 5: Make Culturally Appropriate Interventions

Although individual needs typically determine appropriate interventions, for some ethnic minorities, however, family approval and involvement in developing and delivering intervention strategies are recommended. It should not be considered unusual for some minorities to seek family approval. Counselors will find that it is very productive to fully investigate which members of the family are empowered to make major decisions.

Group interventions are also considered as very productive for some cultural groups. Clients who are struggling to learn English, for example, may be served best by group interventions that use the client's native language; interpreters may also be used to facilitate groups. It is generally believed that group counseling is more effective when composed of the same racial group, biracial group, ethnic gender group, and community members.

Bingham and Ward point out counseling interventions may require several sessions because many ethnic minority groups take considerable time to complete an agenda. Finally, if an inventory is used during the course of an intervention strategy, it must be appropriate for the client's racial/ethnic group. (See chapter 6.)

Step 6: Make Decision

Monitoring the decision-making process is most important in all career counseling cases, but especially when clients are faced with multiple barriers that inhibit ethnic minorities. No doubt some barriers can be difficult to overcome for someone who speaks a different language and is living in a country with different customs and traditions. As a result some clients will make a decision mainly to please the counselor. In these cases, client's can be invited to recycle in this model without a sense of embarrassment; in fact, a review of the model steps can suggest to the client that it is a legitimate request to continue counseling.

Step 7: Implement and Follow-Up

Implementation suggests that clients are referred to information resources, individual contacts, or agencies for assistance. Counselors are to closely monitor each client's progress and invite them to return for counseling in the future.

The following recommendations for the multicultural career counseling process as suggested by Bingham and Ward (1996) follow.

1. The counselor should be aware of a variety of worldviews.
2. The counselor's preparation for multicultural counseling should be directed by recommendations of Sue, Arredondo, and McDavis (1992).
3. The counselor should fully understand his or her racial identity.
4. The counselor–client relationship should be a collaborative one, that is, a negotiating and working consensus relationship.
5. The role of the family in the decision-making and counseling process should be emphasized.
6. Worldview, history of client, local sociopolitical issues, and stereotypes should be fully discussed.

7. The influence of racial/ethnic factors that limit career choices should be discussed.
8. Nontraditional interventions such as conversing in groups in the client's native language, using interpreters, and involving community members who can offer insight and direction should be used. Encourage clients to join a biracial network.
9. Client–counselor process should be evaluated continually during counseling and after counseling is terminated.
10. An extensive follow-up should be done and the client should be invited to recycle if necessary.

Case 3.5 illustrates the use of the Career Counseling Checklist with a Hispanic senior high school student who currently resides in a small town in Texas. Experiencing conflicts between his former culture and the dominant culture, he asks for help from a career counselor. This case illustrates a few examples of the problems faced by individuals from a different culture who want to become working American citizens.

Case 3.5   The Case of Questionable Future Status

Carlos wanted to go to college but was unsure of his future status as a citizen. He came from the interior of Mexico at age 8 to join his mother, who had left him for one year with his grandmother while she found a place for them to live in the United States. She married a U.S. citizen and has now established a home. For the first two years of school, Carlos was placed in a bilingual program. Once he learned the English language, he was able to make very good progress in school. He graduated from high school in the top quarter of his class and had made mainly As and Bs on most subjects. His favorite subject was precalculus and his least favorite was economics. He belonged to French and Spanish clubs as well as to a high school spirit club.

Carlos reported that both Spanish and English are spoken in his home. He prefers English and uses it more than his mother does. He and his family belong to the Catholic Church. Carlos does not care to go to Mexico because, as he put it, "of the corruption there." The family celebrates the traditional holidays but relate more to respecting their ancestors on Halloween than is the custom here.

Carlos is now 18 years of age and is working full-time at a company that specializes in mailing services. He claims to identify more as an American than as a Mexican and plans to make his home permanently in this country. Carlos spoke excellent English and expressed himself very well. It was apparent that he had assimilated many of the dominant culture's social values, but he had also retained many values from his own culture.

Carlos had asked for career counseling because he was not sure about his dream career and needed more information about it and wanted to know which nearby university offered degrees in photography or in how to produce and direct films. He told the counselor that he was interested in photography and the film-making industry because he had worked on some productions at his high school. He would very much like to become a film editor or a producer. The counselor told Carlos that he could be of help but wanted to begin counseling with a Career Counseling Checklist.

After Carlos completed the checklist, a discussion followed. Different worldviews and specific items as a way of establishing rapport (step 1) were covered. A collaborative working relationship was established.

Carlos checked several items on the checklist that were thoroughly discussed in step 2, Identify Career Issues.

COUNSELOR: I noticed that you checked item 14. "My ethnicity may influence my career choice." Could you tell me more about this item?

Carlos stated that he was unsure that most people would think that he is capable of being successful in some of the jobs he would like to choose. He explained further that he was aware that many Americans do not think Hispanics can do certain jobs. He explained that conclusion by stating that most Hispanic men do simple labor jobs or work that does not require one to be smart. Furthermore he stated that it's okay for Hispanics to mow the yard but not work as an engineer or an accountant. Carlos also stated that all he wants is a chance to prove he is capable to meet the challenges of higher level jobs that require rigorous training.

The counselor wisely realized that he could not convince Carlos to change his views by simply having discussions about race relations, but he felt he could encourage Carlos to follow through with his goals with evidence that Hispanics and other minorities are successfully getting professional jobs by completing a college degree.

COUNSELOR: To an extent, that is a realistic appraisal of what could happen. But on a more positive note, more and more minorities are moving into other than labor-type jobs. I would rather you think of it as a golden opportunity right now to choose the job that you are interested in and pursue it using your best abilities.

CARLOS: That is what I want to do and if I am given the chance, I am confident I'll be successful.

COUNSELOR: Good, but let us move on by removing the negative feelings you still have about getting an equal opportunity in the future.

Counselor and client continued their discussion, and during the next session Carlos revealed that part of his worry about the future was that he must try to remain close to his mother. He was afraid that he would be required to move to another location for an education and much farther away from her later to fulfill his dream of being in the film industry.

As they continued their discussion, the counselor identified several career issues, including the following:

- Fear of being stereotyped as an individual who was only capable of doing menial jobs, thus not given consideration for jobs involving creativity and responsibility.
- Fear that family responsibilities would limit his career ambitions.
- Fear that his immigration status would not be taken care of appropriately, or that he might have problems becoming a citizen.

The counselor concluded that Carlos had evaluated his current situation in a fairly realistic manner. However, it was obvious that he needed more support from his family to fulfill his ambitions. For example, it was clear that his mother did not want him to move far from her, and as a result there was evidence of serious conflicts before he even launched his career journey. Even though Carlos expressed confidence, he was also doubtful about his future that included taking a calculated risk in an environment that has not always been affirmative and friendly to minorities and pursuing a career that was unknown to the family. Carlos stated that he also wanted to remain near his family for consultation on major decisions in the future.

The counselor and Carlos negotiated three goals for the time being: Carlos would (1) gather information about university programs, admission requirements, and financial aid; (2) gather information about related careers in film editing, production, and photography and probable locations of opportunities; and (3) arrange a meeting with his parents and counselor to discuss the information he had gathered.

The counselor made certain that both parents could speak and understand English. The first meeting was a difficult one. It was clear that Carlos's parents were not sure they could trust another "Gringo," but the counselor was prepared to make them as comfortable as possible by introducing a friend who was a highly respected individual in the Mexican American community. The friend put in a good word for the counselor and made his exit. This ally helped tremendously to get the first session going with some sense of trust.

Another ally was used in the second session to explain that her daughter was now attending a university in another state and she was most proud of her. Some of the conversations were in Spanish. As expected, Carlos's parents delayed a decision about his future until they could consider all the information that was discussed. Carlos was to continue working to earn money for college and was encouraged to be tutored by a volunteer from the community who had attended a university.

In this case example, the counselor first made certain that he had developed a trusting relationship with Carlos. It was apparent that Carlos felt free to discuss personal and family problems with the counselor. The counselor recognized that Carlos's mother had experienced a great deal of stress in her lifetime and was very protective of her son. Carlos also recognized his mother's reluctance to agree with a plan that might require him to move to another state. There was a genuine concern that Carlos would not be given the opportunity to prove himself because of his race. Goals were set to include parents in the decision process and allies were brought in to encourage trust and an open mind about their son's future. Finally, Carlos and his family compromised by agreeing to let him apply at two universities nearby. What we have here are special needs of minority clients that must be addressed in the career counseling process; in many of the chapters that follow one's cultural background is a key factor for identifying concerns.

Major Parameters of Five Models

In this section, five career counseling models are summarized by describing each according to its counseling goals, intake interview techniques, using assessment, diagnosis, and counseling process. The process of career counseling usually begins with an intake interview, moves to assessment, on to diagnosis and problem identification, followed by a counseling process that maintains a client-collaborative relationship, then intervention strategies, and ends with an evaluation of outcomes and future plans. Individual needs may dictate different paths for some individuals. I begin with counseling goals.

Counseling Goals

Counseling goals provide the reader with goals specific to the model's purpose and procedures that are described in each parameter. For example, the trait-and-factor and PEF model emphasizes optimal fit of clients with an occupation; the developmental model stresses strategies that delineate clients' individual traits to promote career development over the life span; learning theory model suggests interventions to enhance and expand the client's current status; CIP model uses a variety of individual learning plans to improve cognitive processing; and the multicultural model for ethnic women explores avenues of removing salient cultural variables that inhibit and restrict career choice. Within these frameworks, client–counselor relationships are critical. The counselor might simultaneously be a teacher, a mentor, an overseer, and, in most cases, a collaborator who establishes a working consensus relationship.

Intake Interview

The intake interview has many purposes, including building the foundations from which client–counselor relationships are established, and plays a major role by assessing client problems. Ivey and colleagues (2014) make a distinction between interviewing and counseling, even though they are often used interchangeably. However, interviewing is often considered the be a key process that is used for information gathering and solving problems whereas counseling is a more intensive and personal process. In the parameter descriptions that follow, the intake interview is used for information gathering, building client–counselor relationships, assessing problems, assessing client readiness for career counseling, and establishing the process of counseling.

A preliminary *assessment* of the client's personal and career problems are obtained through background information and observation in the trait-and-factor and PEF model. This information is used with valid test results to form a subjective and objective appraisal of the client. The client's social networks, support system, and unique beliefs are the subjects of an intensive interview in the developmental model. This information is used with standardized measures to form a picture of the client's career development. In the learning theory model, the interview identifies both personal and career problems and obstacles such as career beliefs that could block optimal career decisions. The major emphasis is identifying learning opportunities for each client. Both emotional and cognitive problems are emphasized in the CIP model. Furthermore, this model considers a trusting relationship that enhances self-efficacy and fosters learning to be most important. In the multicultural model for ethnic women, culturally appropriate relationships are established. A structural interview is used to determine client needs and to discuss client worldviews.

Use of Assessment

In this parameter, assessment refers to both standardized and nonstandardized methods used in the five models. This broader use of assessment is found in all career models as a part of client problem identification and is used in ongoing career counseling to identify appropriate intervention strategies. Within this framework, counselors not only have to understand the technical aspects of standardized tests that determine their appropriate use but must also sharpen their skills in applying nonstandardized measures. Assessment use is determined through a consensus between client and counselor that generally leads to a client's increased self-knowledge. All models make the point that testing is not the dominant force in making career choices but, rather, can be used effectively as a counseling tool.

The trait-and-factor and PEF model uses assessment to provide valid and reliable information of interests, values, and cognitive abilities. Emotional stability, cognitive clarity, and skills in information processing are also evaluated. The developmental model requires assessment of the client's uniqueness in a variety of trait characteristics including career development status, self-concept, and life themes. This information *informs* clients of their personal characteristics that are used to determine learning strategies. The learning theory model uses assessment to determine learning experiences and to determine personal beliefs. Two stages of assessment are used in the CIP model. The first stage is used to measure dysfunctional thinking and the client's readiness for problem solving. The second stage is used to measure cognitive processing domains and to develop individual learning plans. The major use of assessment in the multicultural model for ethnic women is to assess salient racial factors from interview results and the results of inventories specifically designed for this purpose.

Diagnosis

Identifying client problems is a major focus of the diagnosis parameter—not only for providing a client label but, more importantly, as a starting point from which goals can be set to resolve client problems. The diagnostic parameter is also used to identify client mental health problems that require further psychological evaluation or treatment. In all five models, diagnosis of irrational or dysfunctional thinking is determined by appraisal systems involving subjective or objective evaluation and, in most cases, both. In sum, diagnosis primarily serves as a means of identifying the client's level of knowledge, information-processing skills, readiness, and motivation to engage in intervention strategies that lead to problem solving and career decision making.

Client deficiencies in information processing are an important function of diagnosis in the trait-and-factor and PEF model. The client's optimal person-environment-fit is determined by valid relationships. Extensive diagnostic procedures are used in the developmental model to determine intervention strategies. Counseling goals evolve from data integration. In the learning theory model, faulty beliefs that interfere with goal achievement are identified in the interview and with an inventory designed for this purpose. The status of client skills and their personal qualities are used to determine learning interventions. The effectiveness of cognitive processing is an important element in the CIP model. The causes of gaps between what the client desires in the future and reality provide guidelines for intervention. A decision tree schematic is used as a diagnosis procedure for determining the direction counseling may take in the multicultural model for ethnic women. In this process, clients receive career-style counseling or psychological counseling. Those on the career-style counseling path will be further diagnosed for the impact of cultural variables that influence career choice.

Counseling Process

The career counseling process in all five models involves a multitude of skills; although the following summary is not meant to be an all-inclusive list, it does include the major focus by most models. First, the counselor must be prepared for each counseling encounter that will involve a unique individual whose uniqueness must be accurately delineated. Client and counselors need to form a bond that will endure throughout the entire counseling process. The counselor must be an effective interviewer. The client–counselor relationship is very inclusive, as the counselor may function as a teacher, mentor, coach, advisor, confidante, and overseer, but mainly as a collaborator who involves the client in the ongoing counseling process. Counselors must be knowledgeable of a variety of standardized and nonstandardized assessment instruments. Identifying client problems is a major counseling function. Effectively using intervention strategies including occupational information is an important component of the counseling process within all models. The effective use of decision making is also a major model focus. Finally, clients need to be prepared to recycle in the future.

Counselors introduce clients to the person-environment-fit process and assist them in matching their self-knowledge with congruent work environments in the trait-and-factor and PEF model. This process may follow interventions designed to improve the client's ability to process information. Counselors discuss individual and unique traits with clients in the *developmental* model. Goals are established as the client is able to project self-concept into potential work environments. Learning strategies are developed in collaborative client–counselor relationships. In the learning theory model, counselors assist clients in identifying career beliefs that could interfere with progress in decision making. Counselors try to motivate clients to participate in a learning process that will improve their skills and abilities to function in changing work environments. Clients are to visualize a life span of occupational decisions and learning opportunities. In a CIP model, dysfunctional thinking and cognitive processing problems are a major concern in the opening stages of counseling. Counselors clarify problems and goals and match them with intervention strategies that are developed by consensus between client and counselor. Counselors offer assistance in decision making through cognitive restructuring. The counselor must be prepared to establish and maintain a collaborative, negotiating client–counselor relationship in a multicultural model for ethnic women. An open discussion of worldviews and salient cultural variables that are unique to the client's experience is fundamental in an effective counseling process. Counselors need to respond appropriately to culturally related cues and develop culturally appropriate intervention strategies.

In sum, the parameters of the five counseling models discussed in this chapter provide a wide range of techniques as well as a number of similar procedures. These models were developed during the last two decades of the 20th century and may serve as a foundation for building *new* models or minitheories to meet clients' unique needs in the future. There seems to be a consensus among model developers that information gathering is the first step, followed by discovery of unique client needs through subjective and objective data. Standardized assessment does not dominate the counseling process. The locus of control has shifted from counselor dominant to counselor collaborator; client involvement throughout the counseling process is prevalent. The final step in all models is the client learning effective decision-making skills and the counselor extending an open invitation for future counseling.

Summary

1. Career development research has produced a solid database that answers questions about theories. Practitioners need research that focuses on effective counseling procedures and materials. Career development theory research, however, has influenced the development of counseling models.
2. Trait-and-factor is the most popular theory in practical application. Predicting success in occupations from traits measured by objective data is an actuarial method that is widely used.
3. Three types of diagnosis are differential, dynamic, and decisional. Clients can be classified as decided, undecided, or indecisive.
4. The five career counseling models discussed represent a broad spectrum of techniques. The trait-and-factor theory converged with the person-environment-fit theory and emphasizes optimal fit of client with an occupation. The developmental model stresses promoting career development over the life span. The learning theory model uses learning interventions to improve each client's skills and other personal characteristics. The cognitive-approach model stresses individual learning plans and cognitive restructuring. Finally, the multicultural model for ethnic women emphasizes recognizing salient cultural variables that inhibit career choice.
5. The five counseling models use a wide range of techniques, but the steps in each model are very similar. A consensus of model procedures includes information gathering, assessment, diagnosis, intervention strategies, and decision making. Standardized assessment does not dominate career counseling, and the locus of control has shifted to give the client equal responsibility in counseling decisions.

Supplementary Learning Exercises

1. Design intervention strategies that you would use for each of the following clients: decided, undecided, and indecisive. Which model would you choose for each?

2. Give an example of the type of intake interview you would use to answer the question of why a client has a particular cultural problem. Explain your choice.

3. Describe the techniques you would use to discover a client's career identity and relevant environmental information about a client to help clarify the client's goal or problem. Identify models you would use.

4. Explain the influence of interacting contextual variables on career choice. What are good references for understanding more about this topic?

5. Give reasons why contemporary career counseling models employ collaborative counselor–client relationships.

6. Debate the following: Trait-and-factor counseling techniques were misinterpreted by users.

7. Which of the five models described in this chapter most often subscribes to and emphasizes the concept of learning over the life span? Give your opinion and reasons.

8. How would you characterize the use of assessment in the five models described in this chapter? Which of the models are considered to be most assessment oriented?

9. Explain under what conditions racial identity of the counselor and client are most significant.

10. Give concrete examples of how salient cultural variables limit career choice of ethnic groups.

4

Integrating Career and Personal Counseling

CHAPTER HIGHLIGHTS

- The call to integrate career and personal counseling

- The biopsychosocial model of interacting influences

- Biological, psychological, and social/cultural forces that drive behavior

- Development of a personality disorder

- Observing symptoms of a personality disorder

- Career work connection to anxiety

My focus in this chapter is on a counseling approach that addresses both personal and career concerns. The point was made in chapter 1 that the role and scope of career counseling have been and continue to be influenced by an ever-changing society in which the workforce and workplace have also experienced significant changes. How to effectively address career-related concerns in a world that is rapidly changing has been the subject of numerous research projects and debates over several decades. In the meantime, the more sophisticated career development approaches and counseling interventions developed since the latter part of the last century have dramatically expanded the role and scope of career counseling in contemporary society. As pointed out in chapters 2 and 3, career development theorists currently address a wide range of client concerns, including multiple life roles, learning deficiencies, cognitive difficulties, emotional problems, multicultural issues, and social restraints.

Historically, career and personal domains were viewed as separate entities and, as a result, studies of career development were approached as a distinct domain (Spokane, 1991). Following this perspective, counselor training programs also considered career and personal concerns as separate domains. The relationship and interplay of personal and career concerns, however, have focused more attention on strategies that integrate them. Some may complain that the counseling profession has been too cautious in addressing the position of integrating career and personal concerns. In the 1970s, for example, Osipow (1979) put forward the idea of blending vocational development with mental health when working with adults in the workplace. He labeled this effort occupational mental health. Counselors were to address work maladjustment, work-related stress, depression, and other concerns that might involve an interplay between work, personal concerns, and all life roles.

Keep these suggestions in mind as I address the rationale for a holistic approach in career counseling next.

The Rationale for a Holistic Approach

In the 1990s, there was considerable dialogue as to whether career counseling should devote more attention to the interrelationships of personal and career problems and how they affect multiple life roles. This debate is not new to the counseling profession. Some researchers have suggested that career and personal concerns should be dealt with separately (Crites, 1981), whereas others, believing that career and personal concerns are intertwined, have promoted a more holistic counseling approach (Betz & Corning, 1993; Krumboltz, 1993). Moreover, Richardson (1996) prudently suggests that the pervasive nature of work in each person's life needs to be researched by several academic disciplines to clarify its position and role in the counseling process. What we have here is a reinforcement of the position that work is a core element of an individual's everyday existence. It gives meaning to many facets of each person's life and as such should be addressed more aggressively in the counseling profession. Conversely, this position also suggests that a client's personal concerns can significantly affect work roles and career development over the life span. Thus, personal concerns that evolve from different life roles and interfere with career development should not be ignored in career-related programs and in counseling interventions. The important question here for the practice of career development is how to effectively integrate an individual's career and personal concerns.

What is being suggested is a *holistic counseling approach* that is much more inclusive when addressing client concerns. This stance is underscored by the ever-expanding role of career counseling, from its early focus on career choice and placement of young adults to today's greater emphasis on the concerns of adults in multiple life roles. The interrelationship of personal and career problems has become more apparent in the lives of adults as they experience changes in work environments and difficulties associated with other life roles. Work maladjustment, career transitions, job loss, work stress, changing work requirements, concerns of older adults, and changing values and interests are examples of career-related problems that can affect all life roles. In more inclusive counseling models, however, counselors are also to address the concerns of some clients who, for example, present symptoms of depression, dysfunctional thinking, behavioral problems, a lack of cognitive clarity, and affective domain concerns of inner conflicts that restrict or interfere with career choice and development.

The Call to Integrate Career and Personal Counseling

The call for the counseling profession to integrate career and personal counseling was heightened in the 1990s, underscored by a profusion of articles in professional journals. In 1993, the *Career Development Quarterly* (Vol. 42, pp. 129–173) contained articles that supported the integration of career and personal counseling. Different points of view were expressed, including those predisposed toward a need to integrate career and personal counseling by expanding the role of counseling to address problems of a personal nature that are incurred in multiple life roles over the life span (Gelso & Fretz, 2001).

Super (1993) suggested that "there are two kinds of counseling, situational and personal, and they are not dichotomous but rather a continuum" (p. 132). Counselor and client are to work together to develop the client's self and situational knowledge as shaped in person-in-environment interactions. Clients who are aware of their own needs are empowered to effectively begin an independent exploration that leads to decision making. In this process, career and personal concerns are integrated and not dichotomized.

Krumboltz (1993) strongly advocates integrating career and personal counseling. He suggests that the terms "career counseling" and "personal counseling" convey the impression of a dichotomy that has been reinforced by different training courses and certification. His major point is that personal problems cannot be separated from career problems as they are inextricably intertwined. He illustrates his point with some case examples, such as, "Linda is depressed because she has lost her job and doesn't think she can ever find another one. Is this a career problem? Or a depression problem?" (p. 144). According to Krumboltz (1993), compartmentalizing client concerns limits our ability as counselors to help them understand, for example, how belief systems and interests are interrelated in the career counseling process.

Davidson and Gilbert (1993) approach career counseling as a highly personal matter that includes the multidimensional self and its relationship to life and work. Counselors, therefore, are to acknowledge and recognize the personal and contextual realities that clients bring to counseling. Career is seen as a personal identity and as such is interrelated with multiple life roles over the life span, including dual-career roles. Finally, these authors conclude that career and personal counseling are the same.

Career issues that engage aspects of the total person are the theme of a research project by Haverkamp and Moore (1993). Their conclusions suggest that the supposed dichotomy of personal and career counseling was exaggerated by career counseling's narrow focus on career choice with young adults. They also argue that more attention should be paid to work adjustment and personal aspects of the whole person. Finally, they conclude that there is little question that career and personal issues are intertwined in adult development.

Betz and Corning (1993) viewed career and personal counseling as inseparable and recommended a "whole person," holistic philosophy of counseling, a belief apparently shared by an increasing number of counselors (Farmer, 2009; Gelso & Fretz, 2001; Schultheiss, 2000; Zunker, 2008). The overwhelming rationale is that career and personal issues are inseparable and intertwined. The most effective mind-set when using a holistic approach is one that views each client from a total person perspective. In a collaborative relationship, client and counselor uncover all problems—not just career ones, nor just personal ones, but both—and more importantly, how they interrelate.

The call to integrate career and personal counseling underscored a need for an effective counseling model that could address all client concerns that interfere with career choice and development. An extension of career counseling suggests an increased focus on addressing such personal concerns as severe anxiety and apprehension, mood disorders of depression, faulty cognitions, and a host of psychological disorders. What we have here is the recognition that mental health concerns present potential problems for clients who are engaged in the initial career choice process and choices that follow as well personal interactions in the workplace and the ability to perform appropriately. Clearly what are needed are comprehensive methods for identifying factors that influence behavior and development. What is suggested is that counselors are to view behavior as being influenced by multidimensional forces as suggested by a biopsychosocial model of development (Durand & Barlow, 2013; Kail & Cavanaugh, 2014; Sue et al., 2014).

Biopsychosocial Model

Over time the study of factors that influence behavior has emerged as an ongoing process that will continue to unlock multidimensional influences that affect human development. The contributions of cognitive science and neuroscience have underscored the position that the interplay of biological, psychological, and social/cultural influences are recognized as major forces that drive behavior. Behavior is no longer to be viewed as one dimensional but as multidimensional and multifaceted. Durand and Barlow (2013) clearly state this position as follows: "Behavior both normal and abnormal is the product of a continual interaction of biological, psychological, and social influences" (p. 26). This conclusion has led to what is referred to as a scientific method of determining influences that drive behavior and is labeled an integrative approach. What is suggested here is that what individuals think and do does not occur in isolation; on the contrary, there is an interaction of influences involved in career decision making, in one's perceptions of a work role and other life roles, and in the development of cognitions and emotions that could lead to a psychological disorder. What is also suggested is that client concerns can affect all life roles including the work role. An integrative approach suggests that mental disorders are the product of a very complex interacting process involving three dimensions, biological, psychological, and social/cultural, as depicted in Figure 4.1.

To illustrate an interactive process, I use a stressful life event that triggers a number of biological reactions including an activation of neurons that transmits messages through neurotransmitters to the central nervous system and brain. Thus, a stressful life event can cause physiological responses including cardiovascular system reactions such as increased heart rate and high blood pressure. Psychological reactions include learned conditioned responses such as negative cognitions, self-defeating thinking, and excessive emotional responses. In the social/cultural dimension unique social and cultural experiences influence each person's reaction to stressful life events. This is a process that involves the interaction of three dimensions that could result in an anxiety response followed by a panic reaction. Anxiety and panic, which are closely related, are often considered precursors for development of a psychological disorder. As one would suspect, a psychological disorder involving anxiety and panic can have long-term effects on one's ability to function in all life roles. Counselors are to be aware of multiple influences involved in the development of behavior that can lead to pathology as well as the complexity of the process itself. Behavior is not the product of one dimension, but a combination of interacting influences; there is reciprocity. The following paragraphs contain brief summaries of three dimensions in the integrative model. For more information, see Ashford and Lecroy (2013); Durand and Barlow (2013); Goldstein (2011); Kail and Cavanaugh (2014); Sue and colleagues (2014); and Zunker (2008) among others.

The assumption that behavior is the product of multiple interactive influences suggests that counselors are to focus on multipath models of development in the process of building an understanding of a client's interrelated concerns. Furthermore, the complexity of mental health concerns suggests the involvement of more than one dimension in an integrative model. Multiple interactive influences are most likely to

FIGURE 4.1

An integrated approach of influences on behavior

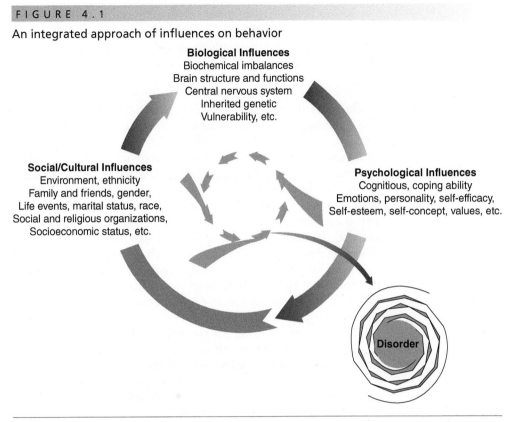

SOURCE: From *Abnormal Psychology: An Integrative Approach,* 5th ed., p. 32, by D. Barlow, and V. Durand, Copyright. 2009. Reprinted with permission from Wadsworth Cengage Learning, Belmont, CA.

contribute to the development of a mental health concern or concerns, but this does not imply that all dimensions have contributed equally to a disorder. Finally, one must be reminded that individuals react differently when exposed to identical events and stressors (Sue et al., 2014). Biological, psychological, and social/cultural influences that drive behavior are discussed next.

Biological. Biological vulnerability is very complex as well as inclusive. Biological explanations of human behavior have focused on brain functions as well as functions of the central nervous system. The brain, for example, contains billions of interconnected cells called neurons that communicate with each other (Goldstein, 2011). Complex processes involving functions of the brain emphasize that there is much about behavior that we do not know. What we do know is that psychological interventions can alter brain functions but so can stressful life situations. Biological vulnerability also includes genetically inherited predispositions to develop psychological disorders. There are indeed higher rates of depression found in relatives of individuals who have experienced mood disorders. Some relatives, however, may not suffer from depression (Zunker, 2008). Keep in mind that inherited predispositions, sometime referred to as tendencies, are not certainties or one's destiny (Schultz & Schultz, 2013) but are part of the equation that has many interconnections. Yet there are also biochemical imbalances that are a part of the interaction process; for example, the neurotransmitter serotonin is believed to influence behavior; thus drug therapy is used to either increase or decrease serotonin levels. Obviously, there is much more to be learned about biological functions and their influences on human behavior. Counselors should remain alert to the results of continuing research.

Psychological. Psychological vulnerability is also a very broad-based force that "includes all internal perceptual, cognitive, emotional, and personality factors that affect development" (Kail & Cavanaugh, 2010, p. 6). What is implied in the previous description of psychological vulnerability is a strong endorsement for evaluating each person as a unique individual. An individual client's psychological vulnerability could be heightened, for example, by a severe emotional reaction to a stressful life event. The counselor may view this client as being very fragile, as having a poor self-concept, and as one who tends to fall apart when faced with stressful conditions. In this case the client is likely to have difficulty functioning in a work role, especially one that is stressful. This client would more than likely experience problems in all life roles. Also observed in this case is the interconnection to biological and social vulnerability. Distorted beliefs and poor self-concept, chemical imbalances, and perceptions of isolation from peers are interacting forces that are very problematic. Clients who have tendencies to react emotionally may find their problem to be exacerbated by chemical imbalances and poor interpersonal skills. High serotonin levels, for instance, can influence the development of distorted beliefs that interfere with all life roles. Vulnerable psychological characteristics and traits can be reinforced by biological factors and social contexts. What is emphasized here is the often mentioned interaction between dimensions that influence behavior; one's emotions and faulty cognitions are either reinforced or diminished in the interaction processes that drive behavior (Durand & Barlow, 2013; Kail & Cavanaugh, 2014; Sue et al., 2014).

Social/Cultural. In the social/cultural dimension counselors should recognize that much of what one learns is through social contexts that include cultural beliefs, values, and worldviews. Social contributions to the development of anxiety, for example, can include social pressure to succeed, a lack of social support, and prior experiences in social interactions. Poverty, social inequality, discrimination, and oppression can diminish one's sense of control; one's self-concept and self-esteem can be adversely affected. Social vulnerability also includes experiences of being rejected by authority figures and diminished feelings of well-being when one does not have social support. On the other hand, social support is a most important weapon in combating a number of psychological problems including depression. Recently more attention has been directed to the importance and relevance of one's environmental experiences in the search for solutions to both career and personal concerns and their interrelationships. Self in situation is indeed an important factor in research of influences that drive behavior. Life-course events are one of the influential driving forces of human development (Kail & Cavanaugh, 2014).

The point was made very early in this discussion that behavior is the product of multiple influences that are very pervasive. The function and structure of the brain, the nervous system, and genetic endowments are but a part of biological influences involved in this very complex process that defies our desire for simplicity. Researchers continue to uncover more information concerning the complexity of biological functions, for example when studying the effects of genetic inheritance. Nobel Prize winner Eric Kandel (1983) concludes that environmental influences can diminish the effects of genetic tendencies. He observes that in the process of learning there is a change in the genetic structure of cells, suggesting that situational experiences may indeed modify the influence of genetic endowments (Durand & Barlow, 2013). More recently, researchers strongly suggest that there appears to be a social connectivity to the re-engineering of new cells, suggesting that social experiences can become a part of one's biology (Rutter, 2010).

What is most important for counselors to learn here is that environmental influences can alter brain functions (Kolb, Gibb, & Robinson, 2003). This position calls attention to the impact of social/cultural influences on both biological and psychological factors. Counselors should also be aware that positive thinking and subsequent behavior can increase the effectiveness of the immune system (Durand & Barlow, 2013). These examples can serve to solidify the position that behavior is influenced by the interaction of multidimensional forces that are interconnected. Furthermore, Sue and colleagues (2014) suggest that one-dimensional perspectives of observing behavior are overly simplistic. Counselors are to recognize the important contribution of reciprocal influences in the development of mental disorders. I will continue to explore interrelationships by observing the potential development of such traits as irresponsibility, impulsiveness, deceitfulness, and disregard for the rights of others.

Development of Dysfunctional Personality Dimensions

I have selected some personality factors to illustrate their development by biological, psychological, and social/cultural influences as shown in Figure 4.2. The interactions of influences in this illustration suggest that the development of one's personality typically begins in early childhood. The chronic nature of development is characteristic of most personality disorders. The significance of this observation suggests to

FIGURE 4.2

Development of personality dimensions

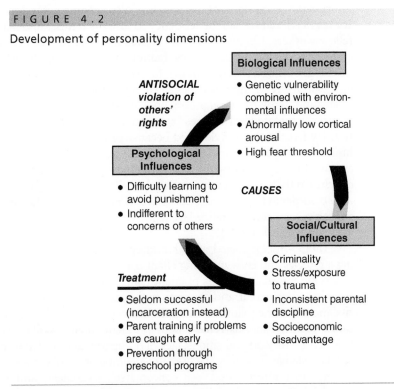

SOURCE: From *Abnormal Psychology: An Integrative Approach*, 5th ed., by D. H. Barlow and V. M. Durand, 2009. Reprinted with permission of Wadsworth Cengage Learning, Belmont, CA.

counselors that early detection of the influences that could lead to the development of a psychological disorder is of the utmost importance. There is little evidence at this time of success in moderating behavior associated with personality problems that have developed over time. Typical behavior patterns of an individual who is considered severely antisocial, for example, suggest a lack of respect for the concerns of others and one who is likely to be involved in overt criminal acts. Extreme aggressiveness and little or no concern for the violation of the rights of others can be the driving forces that lead to vandalism, stealing, and chronic criminal behavior. Poor emotional control and a nonconformity attitude present serious problems for interpersonal relations in all life roles, especially in the work role. In the next section we examine a case of poor emotional control. I will introduce a model for career counselors that consists of four domains, one of which is the career domain. Keep in mind that we have discussed a multipath model for understanding the development of behavior. We now focus on how we can use that information in the career counseling process. The goal is to integrate personal and career concerns and their interrelationships.

Conceptualizing Concerns in Four Domains

What follows is a good example of interacting influences that have led to a serious disorder that has long-term consequences. All life roles are adversely affected by personality factors that could lead to psychological disorders; the interrelationships of career and personal concern are quite obvious. There are clients, however, who will present symptoms that are considered antisocial but do not meet the criteria for a full-blown psychological disorder. Such is the case of Irv, a 17-year-old Caucasian male, who informs the counselor that he "has difficulty keeping a job." Further explanations by Irv revealed that he has the tendency to lose his temper and get into arguments with fellow workers. On two occasions he was fired because of his inability to control his emotions. During the interviews that followed the counselor learned that Irv grew up in a neighborhood that was known for its high crime rate. His father was a day laborer and as Irv put it, there was never enough money to sustain the family. He admits to stealing items from neighbors on several occasions, but he was never charged or arrested. He stated he becomes "stressed out" when thinking about future opportunities; Irv felt that he was doomed because of his background. Irv was able to express himself very well and it was noted that his achievement test scores were very close to average for his age group even though he dropped out of high school. The counselor concluded that Irv does not meet all the criteria necessary for a diagnosis of a personality disorder at this time but does have some symptoms that are most troubling. Irv's concerns were conceptualized by using the representing strategies and four domains as described in Table 4.1.

Table 4.1 is modeled after Hackney and Cormier (2001) and contains counseling strategies and corresponding client concerns. This perspective provides a means of observing interrelationships of client concerns from four domains: Career, Affective, Cognitive-Behavioral, and Cultural. In the career domain, client concerns are very inclusive including the following examples: career decision making, inadequate basic skills, career identity, indecisiveness, poor problem-solving skills, work-related stress, job loss, school-to-work transitions, lack of occupational knowledge, poor self-concept, and self-knowledge. The affective domain encompasses problems—frequently emotionally driven—that affect mood, self-concept, self-awareness, and feelings of inferiority, impulsivity, and helplessness among others. The cognitive-behavioral domain focuses on cognitions and cognitive schemas that influence behavioral reactions. The rationale

Table 4.1	**Representative Strategies and Client Concerns in Four Domains**

CAREER

Strategies

Trait-oriented counseling, developmental counseling, social learning and cognitive counseling, person-in-environment counseling

Assessment of traits, clarifying interests, self-concept development, vocational identity development, awareness of developmental stages and tasks, rational decision making, self-directed career maintenance, interpersonal skills development, sources of job satisfaction, work adjustment variables, coping with job loss, and preparing for retirement.

Concerns

Indecisive, deficiencies in basic skills, career maturity issues, poor work identity, work impairment, work maladjustment, adjusting to career transitions, balancing life roles, job loss, stress, violence in the workplace, relational problems, failure to adapt to changing work requirements, loss of work identity, and adjustment to retirement.

AFFECTIVE

Strategies

Cognitive-behavioral interventions, client-centered therapy, existential therapy, psychodynamic therapies

Empathy, active listening, awareness techniques, dignity and worth of individual, ventilation and catharsis, self-regulation, wholeness of individual, insight and awareness, meaning in life, positive regard, and internal frame of reference.

Concerns

Emotional instability, sad, anxious, angry, panic attacks, impulsivity, poor self-esteem, feelings of inferiority and helplessness, depressed mood, lethargy, fatigue, and poor personal relationships.

COGNITIVE-BEHAVIORAL

Strategies

Behavioral counseling, cognitive restructuring, rational-emotive therapy, reality therapy, Beck's cognitive therapy

Counterconditioning, bibliotherapy, reframing, A_B_C_D_E analysis, systematic desensitization, modeling, contingency management, homework assignments, assertiveness training, problem-solving techniques, contracting, and social skills training.

Concerns

Faulty thinking, inappropriate behavior, self-destructive behavior, cognitive distortions, maladaptive behavior, faulty beliefs, overgeneralizations of negative experiences, poor information-processing skills, and problems in decision making.

CULTURE

Strategies

Culturally based interventions, multicultural counseling

Focus on level of acculturation and worldview, cultural identity, cultural orientation, work-related values, culturally appropriate assessment techniques and resources, adjustment techniques to new socioeconomic system. Use indigenous helpers, alternative counseling procedures, and expanded repertoire of helping responses.

Concerns

Deficiencies in the use of English language and basic skills, poor adjustment to the dominant cultural values, collectivist worldview, cultural shock, lack of job skills, difficulty with assimilating new lifestyle, restrictive emotions, level of cultural identity, effects of discrimination and oppression, and relating to others.

is that faulty cognitions can lead to inappropriate behavior. In the cultural domain the client's level of acculturation is assessed; worldview is weighed, especially the constructs of individualism versus collectivism. The cultural context of a client's development is considered an important factor in the counseling process. The use of this model is illustrated by the conceptualization of Irv's concern in four domains as follows:

Career: Irv has given little attention to finding an optimal career. His focus has primarily been on survival and he has resorted to criminal acts of stealing. His decision-making skills are practically nonexistent and his ability to accurately process career information is very questionable. His career development needs are many, including identification of his abilities, interests, and values through appropriate standardized assessment instruments. In addition how to locate and process career information, learn career decision-making techniques, and find the means and motivation to complete high school are essential. Career development should be accompanied by addressing the interrelationships of a multitude of personal needs. The rationale here is that progress in the career domain will enhance progress designed to moderate personal problems and vice versa.

Affective: Irv needs help in learning to control his emotions. He is emotionally unstable, impulsive and resorts to criminal acts with little thought given to the consequences of his actions. Some of his emotional responses are driven by an attitude of nonconformity. His poor emotional control also adversely affects his ability to focus on future needs, including career information and decision making. His focus appears to be only on short-term interests in that planning for the future is at best a vague concept. The evidence of poor emotional control and accompanying underlying anxiety suggests that interventions should focus on the interrelationship of concerns. This recommendation is based on the premise that what happens in one life role affects other life roles; there is a spillover effect.

Cognitive-Behavioral: Irv's view of the world has been colored by inconsistent parental discipline, a lack of social support, and other negative environmental experiences. He appears to believe that the way one gets ahead is to be very aggressive regardless of the effect one's actions have on others. His aggressive behavior is driven by immediate rewards with little thought given to future consequences. Cognitive restructuring should focus on faulty cognitions involving negative self-talk and negative cognitions that reflect self-concept and self-efficacy deficits. To help Irv with interpersonal relationships, assertiveness training and behavioral rehearsal should focus on the differences between aggressiveness and assertiveness. Behavioral rehearsal should target interpersonal relationships, especially one's lack of concern for others. Irv should participate in several selected roles which will be followed with discussions of real-life experiences and their consequences. A major emphasis will be placed on addressing cognitive schemas and their influence on behavior. Dysfunctional thinking will be assessed by the *Career Thoughts Inventory* (Sampson et al., 1996a) and *My Vocational Situation* (Holland et al., 1980) (see chapter 6). Homework assignments will focus on preparing for taking the test for a GED and learning and practicing relaxation techniques.

Cultural: Irv was born into a white working-class home. Although he was exposed to the individualistic view which champions individual accomplishment, an appropriate role model in the home was definitely missing. The environment in which he was raised did not provide a model of consistency; on the contrary, there were constant mixed messages which left Irv confused. In fact his development appears to include negative perceptions of all life roles accompanied by socioeconomic status disadvantages. Irv's situational conditions are a good example of how one's expectations of the future can be quite limited as a result of contextual experiences. Irv is in need of exposure to more positive life roles and the benefits of a balanced lifestyle; self-awareness will be stressed in interventions designed to enhance self-knowledge.

The counselor was very aware that Irv needed immediate attention in order to moderate symptoms that, left unchecked, could develop into a psychological disorder. Although his symptoms were very troubling, there were indications that he was sincere in addressing them. Clients of this ilk, however, can be deceitful and are effective con artists. The road ahead could be perilous, but well worth the effort. The tightly woven connection between career and personal concerns suggests that interventions should address concerns simultaneously. Thus, interests, values, and aptitudes will be evaluated and addressed as well as career decisions techniques. In a working consensus counseling relationship, counselor and client agree on the purpose of all interventions in order for the client to be an active participant in setting goals and selecting the content of interventions. Irv has many needs and among them is the need to learn that structure and consistency can be achieved through his own efforts that are supported by others. Other interventions to restructure his thinking process are to be accomplished through the above planned use of cognitive-behavioral techniques. Hopefully Irv will recognize that future perspectives can be positive and filled with opportunities. What is important to recognize here is that addressing interrelationships of concerns can enhance the meaning of counseling interventions. Another case example is used next to illustrate significant interrelationships of concerns.

The Career-Work Connection to Anxiety

Susie, a 28-year-old Hispanic female, stated, "I want to find a different job—something that's easier for me to do." She explained that her current job as an appliance salesperson was not what she liked and she felt incompetent. Susie was appropriately dressed and expressed herself well. Susie has never been married and lives with her elderly parents. She has three older married sisters who are living nearby but has little personal contact with them. Susie was considered to be a good student in high school, but a loner. After she graduated from high school, she stayed home to help her parents. Eventually her parents convinced Susie to seek work and she reluctantly applied for a job at a local department store. She was put through a training program to prepare her for dealing directly with customers. Susie, however, seemed to worry about every aspect of her job. She explained that her worries were about making mistakes and if she could meet all the demands of the job. The counselor realized that many workers focus on meeting the demands of a job, but in Susie's case the concerns seemed excessive. Susie's expressions indicated a great deal of underlying anxiety that will need to be addressed. There also appeared to be a spillover effect in that Susie not only worries about her work but also worries about other activities and life events. She constantly worries about relationships with her older sisters. As an example, she stated, "They don't like me. I'm not one of them." In addition, the counselor learned that Susie has few friends, and when she rarely dated, she worried intensely about being an appropriate and adequate date. Susie's world was filled with anxiety including what the future would hold in store for her. The counselor realized that some of Susie's worries were shared by others her age, but the difference in Susie's case was the intensity of the anxiety she experienced. The examples of constant worrying illustrate how anxiety can consume an individual and more importantly destroy one's ability to function in all life roles. Susie's concerns are conceptualized in the following four domains.

Conceptualizing Concerns in Four Domains

The counselor recognized that there was much more to learn about Susie, but at this point it was clear that personal concerns of anxiety need to be addressed first. Anxiety and tension can often result in confusion and increase one's vulnerability to develop a psychological disorder. Susie's negative self-talk and faulty cognitions can interfere with her ability to make appropriate decisions about future needs. Readiness for career counseling will be determined later. In the meantime the counselor will investigate the focus of Susie's anxiety in order to determine the purpose and goals of intervention strategies. There appeared to be a general sense of uncontrollability in response to stress that triggers inherited and/or conditioned tendencies to overreact to life events and circumstances. The focus of interventions will address faulty perceptions and negative cognitive schemas. Difficulties with interpersonal relations will need to be moderated and more social support from family members is to be encouraged. What was known about Susie's concerns at this time was conceptualized as follows:

Career: Susie's ability to make optimal career choice decisions at this time is very questionable. There seems to be sufficient evidence that she has given little thought to establishing a work identity. Self-knowledge, career information, and the ability to process information are among important goals for interventions. Career readiness will be evaluated by the following standard assessment instruments: *Career Maturity Inventory—Revised* (CMI-R) (Crites & Savickas, 1995) and *My Vocational Situation* (Holland et al., 1980) (see chapter 6). In the meantime interventions will focus on interpersonal relations in the workplace.

Affective: The anxiety Susie is currently experiencing can result in severe emotional reactions and panic attacks. In addition, the overwhelming and constant worry she experiences leave little time for other considerations such as establishing a work role and becoming involved in social activities. Susie's feelings of helplessness and poor self-esteem are important factors to be addressed in counseling interventions. In short, excessive emotionally driven behavior needs to be moderated.

Cognitive-Behavioral: Susie's feelings of anxiety associated with fear of the future can make rational decision making difficult. She tends to overgeneralize negative thoughts in all life situations including the work role. Cognitive distortions associated with high levels of anxiety will be addressed through cognitive restructuring as well as negative self-talk. It appears that Susie's poor self-concept is reinforced by cognitive distortions and poor self-esteem. In addition, demeaning self-talk will be addressed by interventions that are designed to generate self-enhancing thoughts.

Cultural: Susie is a second-generation Hispanic. She self identifies as a Mexican American and embraces many traditional values. Although she is family and community oriented, her relationships with her three older sisters are estranged. In collectivist-oriented Hispanic families, it is most important for each family member to embrace the welfare of the family group rather than one's individual goals. Family support and approval are sought by all its members. The lack of social support from family members can contribute to the anxiety Susie is currently experiencing. Thus, another major goal for the counselor is to unite the family in offering support of Susie's efforts to overcome anxiety.

Susie's case is a good example that illustrates the connection of career and personal concerns. Counselors may find that career counseling is best delayed with some clients until some or most personal problems are moderated. This is a call that counselors must often make, but there are also situations when career and personal concerns can be effectively dealt with simultaneously. In the case of Susie, the decision to delay career counseling was determined by the severity and pervasive nature of an anxiety disorder. Interventions can include discussions of interactions in the workplace; successful experiences in the work environment can be very therapeutic. An example of an intervention in Susie's case is described as follows:

Addressing an Anxiety Disorder with Systematic Desensitization

Systematic desensitization is a progressive muscle relaxation technique. One reduces anxiety through muscle relaxation while visualizing anxiety-provoking events; a relaxed state of mind inhibits severe reaction to stress. The client is encouraged to construct a hierarchy of events, arranged in order of least to most intense, that heighten anxiety reactions. Susie's hierarchy included the following events involving a work day and her work environment:

1. Take a bus to work
2. Check in
3. Discuss day with work associates
4. Enter meeting room
5. Leader calls meeting to order
6. Discussion of current sale priorities
7. Report to work area
8. Meet with first customer

Clients begin by imagining that they are in the first situation twice without increasing muscle tension. They are to stop when they are unable to visualize a situation without becoming tense. Clients recycle through the hierarchy until they are able to move forward without tension. This exercise is usually followed with homework assignments such as practicing muscle relaxation.

Susie will also participate in practicing methods of enhancing self-thoughts and moderating self-talk that is demeaning. Drug therapy may be used in conjunction with other interventions. Social support provided by her family and other members of the community such as church groups should help Susie prepare for the future through effective career counseling. Establishing a work identity will require Susie to view the future in a much more positive manner. The counselor will attempt to remove all barriers to career choice by addressing both career and personal concerns. Early detection of anxiety and panic provides the counselor with opportunities to address those concerns in an effort to halt the development of a full-blown psychological disorder. Susie will be given the opportunity to select a career with an increased knowledge of her interests, abilities, and values, and more importantly, the ability to adequately process career information.

In both of the case examples, counselors are to select career counseling models that provide opportunities for systematic and consistent plans and actions. Integration of career and personal concerns suggests (1) that technical eclecticism involving valid techniques from different approaches to address personal concerns would be used with (2) career counseling techniques from career development theories that provide consistency of procedures. In these two cases, cognitive-behavioral approaches were used to address personal concerns; similar techniques and supportive assessments instruments are used in social learning and cognitive career development theories discussed earlier. In the chapters that follow, more case examples will illustrate the integration of career and personal concerns.

Summary

1. The pervasive nature of work should be the subject of research by several academic disciplines to clarify its position in counseling programs.
2. Career development theorists address a wide range of client concerns including cognitive difficulties, emotional problems, and social restraints.
3. Historically, career and personal domains were viewed as separate entities.
4. The call to integrate career and personal counseling was heightened in the 1990s.
5. The biopsychosocial model suggests an interactive process that includes the interplay of biological, psychological, and social/cultural forces that influence behavior. Biological influences include inherited genetic vulnerability, immune system responses, central nervous system responses, and biochemical imbalances. Psychological influences include emotional, cognitive, and behavioral responses. Social/cultural influences include events and situational influences, lack of social support, oppression, discrimination, and poverty.
6. The chronic nature of development is typical of most personality disorders. Symptoms that present the lack of respect and concerns for others and overt criminal acts require effective cognitive-behavioral interventions.
7. The client Irv illustrates behavioral patterns that are similar to behaviors of someone who has been diagnosed as having severe personality problems. Interventions addressed faulty cognitions and career concerns simultaneously.
8. Career work connection to anxiety required the counselor to determine that readiness for career counseling would be evaluated later. In the meantime interventions focused on negative self-talk and negative cognitions, poor self-esteem, and feelings of helplessness. Fear of the future associated with anxiety can make rational decision making difficult.

Supplementary Learning Questions and Two Case Studies

1. Describe how you would inform a client about how a personal problem of anxiety is interfering with career choice.
2. The career counseling profession has been criticized for devoting most attention to initial choice for young adults. Do you agree or disagree? Justify your conclusions.
3. What do you see as the major obstacles to managing a holistic counseling approach?
4. Defend or criticize the position that career and personal needs are to receive equal attention.
5. Do you think counselor training programs should include a broader perspective of counseling needs?

Case 4.1   The Case of Indecision

Jim, a 19-year-old Caucasian male, told the counselor that he is looking for "the kind of work in which I can do my job without any hassle." When asked what kind of work he was referring to, he replied, "something I can do on my own." These and similar statements made it very clear that Jim preferred working alone. The counselor learned that Jim's previous job had been on an assembly line at a local cannery. He was required to coordinate his responsibilities with a small group of fellow workers. It appeared that Jim was able to meet the demands of his work role but disliked required meetings. Everyone was encouraged to participate by making recommendations to solve problems that had been encountered in the workplace. Jim rarely said a word but when he was challenged by the group to at least express an opinion, he never returned to the work site—he received a notice in the mail that his job had been terminated.

Not only did his fellow workers have difficulty in getting Jim to respond, but so did the counselor. Jim is very shy and makes little eye contact, noted the counselor, and answers questions with a short, abrupt response or usually yes or no. She also noted that when he is pressed to respond he appears confused and very anxious.

Jim grew up in small town and moved to a large city in which he now lives when he finished high school. His father is a plumber and he has one older brother whom he rarely sees. He lives alone and claims he has few friends. He has not dated since moving to the city. His hobbies are listening to musical records and going to an occasional movie or sporting event. He reported average grades in high school. He was unable to identify a preferred occupation but once again made it clear he preferred to work alone.

QUESTIONS AND EXERCISES FOR DISCUSSION

1. How would you conceptualize Jim's career concerns?
2. What are your conclusions concerning Jim's reactions to group meetings?
3. What is the significance of Jim's desire to work alone?
4. How would you describe Jim's major problems in the cultural/social domain?
5. Conceptualize interrelationships of career and personal concerns in the case of Jim.

Case 4.2   The Case of the Confused Decision Maker

Kris, a 19-year-old high school graduate, asked for help in choosing a college major. She reported to the counselor's office with one of her older brothers. Kris was neatly dressed and well groomed. Her speech was fluent and she tended to speak very softly. When questioned about work experience, she informed the counselor she was "let go" from a retail sales job in a local clothing store. The counselor noticed that Kris seemed to be somewhat anxious when questioned directly and she constantly looked to her brother for approval.

In the top 10% of her class, Kris had a record of being a very capable student. She had good rapport with teachers as well as with her peer group. She strongly identified with several girls her age at the high school. Kris has five brothers, and her father was a meat inspector in a local plant. He worked hard to maintain the family. Her mother has never worked outside the home.

When the counselor asked Kris to come into his office, she seemed to be very uncomfortable and asked if her brother could attend the session with her. The counselor reassured her that they would have ample time to talk with her brother later. She reluctantly agreed to begin the interview.

From the description Kris gave of her home environment, the counselor assumed it was very traditional. Moreover, the chores assigned to the children typically were based on what the parents considered appropriate work for boys and for girls. There seemed to be strict stereotypical roles embedded in Kris's perception of traditional work roles for women. She appeared to be very passive and gave the impression that she expected someone else to make decisions for her.

When discussing future objectives, Kris seemed quite confused when the counselor suggested she consider all careers, including nontraditional ones. At one time she had expressed an interest in architecture but considered it to be only for men and therefore decided against it as a possible choice.

Kris's behavior pattern reflected little confidence in her abilities and she deferred to others for decision making. She constantly referred to her brothers as giving her good advice and reassuring her of what was best for her.

QUESTIONS AND EXERCISES FOR DISCUSSION

1. How would you characterize Kris's emotional state?
2. How would you address Kris's dependence on others?
3. How would you explain to Kris that her personal and career concerns are interrelated?
4. What does self-efficacy have to do with Kris's current status?
5. Which, if any, assessment instruments would be most helpful?

5

Career Counseling Intake Interview

CHAPTER HIGHLIGHTS

- Rationale for career counseling intake interviews

- Suggested sequence for an interview

- Suggestions for interviewing multicultural groups

- Identifying strengths and assets

- Identifying career development constraints

- Identifying some psychological and personality disorders

- Key standardized assessment instruments

The call for integrating career counseling to include personal concerns clients bring to counseling suggested a more comprehensive and inclusive role for the intake interview. Focusing on both career and personal concerns and their interrelationship is the key factor in current career counseling programs. This is not a new position. As you may recall some of the counseling models discussed in chapter 3 included suggestions for addressing personal concerns that interfere with the career choice process. A client's dysfunctional thinking, for example, is a most legitimate concern as discussed in the previous chapter. In the whole person approach to career counseling, I emphasized that one is to address both career and personal concerns aggressively and how the interrelationships of concerns can affect the career choice process as well as career development. What was suggested is that counselors are not only to focus on a client's measures of ability, assets, and interests for instance, but also on symptoms of psychological disorders that could present barriers to making an optimal career choice. The position that behavior is the product of multidimensional influences suggested that not only are abilities, assets, values, and interests involved in the career choice process, but also so are many other important factors including socioeconomic and mental health issues. All information obtained in an intake interview is used with other data to develop the content of interventions that address both personal and career concerns.

Identifying Strengths and Assets

We begin the interview with an informal evaluation of the client's strengths and assets. The counselor is to focus on identifying positive traits as well as negative ones. A balanced view of human functioning includes subjectively measured feelings of well-being that could include a discussion of a client's relationship with others, a sense of meaning and purpose in life, job satisfaction, happiness, contentment, hope, self-determination, and optimism for the future (Compton & Hoffman, 2013). The position of using positive traits in the career choice process can be traced back to Parsons's (1909) very perceptive conceptual framework for helping a person choose a career. He focused on a client's resources including aptitude and ability as a first step in the career choice process. The emphasis was on identifying positive individual traits. Currently, the strength-based approach to career counseling supports and underscores the important focus on exploring one's existing resources. A most important goal in positive psychology is to identify and enhance an individual's strength and resilience (Seligman, 2011). Wellness concepts are to be recognized and serve as a major roles in the career counseling process. What is clearly suggested here is that career counselors are to balance their counseling approach by spending sufficient time focusing on individual positive characteristics (Harrington, 2013). The emphasis on individual strengths does not cancel the need to identify and address client concerns that are problematic. One could emphasize that a stable sense of well-being, however, could serve as a barrier to halt the influence of negative emotions. In essence, the counselor uses the client's positive assets to counteract feelings of anxiety, worry, and fear (Shmotkin, 2005). The results of numerous research projects suggest that optimal human functioning includes such qualities as happiness, optimism, resilience, hope, courage, ability to cope with stress, self-actualization, and self-determination (Sue et al., 2014). Client and counselor greatly benefit by addressing the interrelationship of positive traits as well as negative concerns in the counseling process.

Later in this chapter I briefly review a well-known standardized personality inventory, the *NEO-PI-3* (McCrae & Costa, 1997), also known as the big five-factor model. The results of this personality inventory are straightforward and provide useful information for use in the career counseling process as well as measures of a client's subjective feeling of well-being. Ten determinants of well-being in the workplace are introduced next.

Determinants of Well-Being in the Workplace

Ten determinants of well-being in the workplace that have been paraphrased from Warr (1987, 2005) are contained in Box 5.1. Counselors who are aware of work environments that can determine one's feeling of well-being and fit are in a better position to foster discussions about the give-and-take associated with one's workplace. It should not be surprising to find that many workers seek security, interpersonal contact, and a valued social position that can be job related. In addition, one usually desires to be challenged with tasks that can be mastered in order to experience competence and the satisfaction of a job well done. Variety of tasks, supportive supervision, and environmental clarity are other examples of important subjects one can discuss and clarify in the counseling process. I continue with a discussion of the intake interview.

BOX 5.1

Well-Being in the Work Environment

1. Opportunity for control. Work environments that promote opportunities for workers to control some work tasks enhance mental health and feelings of well-being. This logical conclusion suggests that when individuals are able to make decisions concerning their work procedures, they are in a better position to predict the consequences of their actions.
2. Opportunity for skill use. The ability to make use of one's skills promotes and provides opportunities for growth and self-satisfaction. Successful use of skills enhances one's feeling of competence.
3. Externally generated goals. Organizational goals should be clearly stated with obtainable objectives that are reasonable. Sufficient resources are to be available for meeting the requirements of job demands. Individual workers should be able to experience the satisfaction of a job well done.
4. Environmental variety. The challenge of learning new skills creates an interesting environmental variety of tasks and reduces boredom. The opportunity to successfully learn different and effective work procedures promotes personal growth.
5. Environmental clarity. Clarifying role assignments for each worker should also include opportunities for feedback of job performance. The worker's feelings of well-being are greatly enhanced by the certainty of the future for a job well done.
6. Availability of money. Job satisfaction is to some extent measured by one's level of pay. Workers who can provide sufficient funds for the welfare of their families are likely to experience satisfaction and self-esteem. In addition, satisfaction with one's income is often related to a comparison of what others make who do the same job.
7. Physical security. Pleasant and safe working conditions enhance feelings of well-being. Workers who experience healthy work environments and safety on the job can experience positive reinforcement in the workplace.
8. Supportive supervision. Workers especially respond positively to effective leadership, support, and encouragement. Managers who provide support and offer constructive advice create work environments that offer workers the opportunity to fulfill work goals and experience the feeling of well-being.
9. Opportunity for interpersonal contact. An important aspect of job satisfaction is the opportunity of interpersonal contact with fellow workers. Workers usually respond positively to the opportunity for social support in the workplace. The opportunity to socialize with others reduces feelings of loneliness. Mutual goals that are shared with others provide the potential for forming relationships.
10. Valued social position. Work has a long history of being valued in our society. When a worker feels that his job is appreciated by others, there is indeed a sense of life purpose, a belief that his or her job makes a difference, and a feeling of accomplishment (Compton & Hoffman, 2013; Harrington, 2013; Warr, 1987, 2005; Zunker, 2008).

An Intake Interview for Career and Personal Concerns

Be aware that I make the assumption that users of this text have been thoroughly trained in interview techniques. Thus, the purpose of this chapter is to present a suggested sequence for an interview that addresses the interrelationships of career and personal concerns. You will recognize that this outline contains the same or similar components that are used in other sequences for an interview. What is different here, however, is a focus on interrelationships of concerns and their effects on all life roles—not just career concerns, but personal ones as well. Counselors are to uncover barriers to career choice including personal concerns that can interfere with the choice process. A very inclusive interview also addresses behaviors that can lead to work maladjustment and in addition the potential of a spillover effect to other life roles. One is to focus on dysfunctional thinking and its effect on all life roles. The whole person approach to helping is very inclusive; career and personal concerns are viewed as sets of needs that are interrelated. In sum, the purpose of the interview is to learn as much as we can about an individual and use this information to unravel the tightly bound connection between career and personal concerns. The intake interview outlined next was adapted from a number of sources including Brems (2001); Cormier, Nurius, and Osborn (2013); Ivey and colleagues (2014); and Sue and colleagues (2014).

I. Identifying Information
   Name, address, age, gender, marital status, occupation, university, school or training facility, and work history can be taken orally or by written response on a preinterview form. Direct questioning has the important advantage of being able to observe behavior and emotional responses. Therefore, even if a written self-report is used, a discussion of this information could be included in the interview.

II. Presenting Problem
   Reason client has come to counseling

III. Current Status Information
   Affect, mood, attitude

IV. Health and Medical Information
   Including substance abuse

V. Family Information
   Current status and past history

VI. Social/Cultural issues
   Cultural identification

VII. Some Career Choice and Career Development Constraints
   Contextual experiences
   Changing nature of work
   Negative cognitions
   Psychological disorders
   Contextual experiences

VIII. Clarifying Problems
   Counselor and client collaborate
   State problems clearly and concretely

IX. Strength and Wellness

X. Identify Client Goals
   Determine feasibility of goals
   Establish subgoals
   Assess commitment to goals

Most human service providers typically provide client information forms in which the information in Parts I through VI is self-reported with the exception of current status information and social/cultural issues. As suggested previously, the discussion of self-reported information may provide important observations of the client's current status. One may also want to clarify the reasons clients have given for coming to counseling. In addition, discussions of self-reported information can be used to establish rapport with one's clients. Before continuing our discussion of the remaining parts of the intake interview, I will offer some suggestions for interviewing multicultural groups next.

Suggestions for Interviewing Multicultural Groups

Developing a greater sensitivity to culturally diverse clients has become increasingly important for career counselors; one must foster specific counseling techniques to accommodate the human diversity that exists in our society. The core dimension of interviewing is effective communication between clients and counselors, especially with multicultural groups. Also, during the interview, counselors form opinions and assumptions about clients from both verbal and nonverbal communications. Because of cultural and ethnic differences between counselor and client, the counselor must be alert to a wide spectrum of ethnic and cultural characteristics that influence behavior. Some cultural groups conceptualize their problems differently from those of the dominant culture and seek solutions based on these assumptions. For instance, a client who believes he is being ostracized because of race might be much more interested in finding immediate employment than in pursuing a program for identifying a long-term career goal. Another client might be reluctant to share her personal problems with someone outside the family circle and, in fact, might interpret direct questioning as an infringement of her privacy (Paniagua, 2005; Sue et al., 2014).

Although it is difficult to generalize techniques suggested for different cultural groups, it seems feasible to first determine the level of acculturation including the following: socioeconomic status, language preference, place of birth, generation level, preferred ethnic identity, and ethnic group social contacts (other measures of acculturation will follow) (Matsumoto & Juang, 2013). Questions must be carefully selected and presented to avoid offending clients who may be quite sensitive to the questioning process. Directness, for example, may be judged as demanding, intrusive, or abrupt by some cultural groups. Furthermore, an "open" person may be seen by some cultures as weak, untrustworthy, and incapable of appropriate restraint. Some other factors to remember when interviewing people from other cultures are offered by Cormier and colleagues (2013), Ivey and colleagues (2014), and Ponterotto, Casas, Suzuiki, and Alexander (2010) and are paraphrased as follows:

- General appearance can be quite distinctive for some subcultures and should be accepted on that basis.
- Attitude and behavior are considered difficult to ascertain. Major belief themes of certain cultures influence members' attitudes about themselves and others. Their perceptions of the world may be quite different from those of the counselor.
- Affect and mood are also related to cultural beliefs and to what is considered appropriate within a culture. The meaning given to gestures often differs by culture. Work experience may be quite limited because of lack of opportunity. Also, in some cultures, it is considered immodest to speak highly of yourself and the skills you have mastered.
- Life roles, and particularly relationships, are unique to cultural socialization. In some cultures, females are considered equal to males, whereas in others, females are expected to be subservient.

These examples of cultural differences are given here to underscore the necessity of building an extensive body of resources for interviewing ethnic minorities. Other general recommendations include (1) using straightforward, slang-free language, (2) becoming familiar with cultural life-role models, (3) identifying a consultant who can provide helpful information, and (4) becoming familiar with support networks for different cultural groups (Matsumoto & Juang, 2013; Ridley, 2005).

Most important to remember is that cultural groups are not to be stereotyped as homogeneous. Thus, with our focus on the uniqueness of individuals, one should begin by establishing a collaborative working relationship with each client: A trusting relationship is essential for productive interviewing. The multicultural career counseling model for ethnic women (Bingham & Ward, 1996) discussed in chapter 3 suggests that a *Multicultural Career Counseling Checklist* that is counselor self-administered (Ward & Bingham, 1993) and a *Career Counseling Checklist* (Ward & Tate, 1990) for clients are to be administered as an aid in establishing rapport. Selected items from the client's checklist can be used as an entry to discuss problems that are related to cultural diversity.

The acculturation level of the client should be assessed to help determine the client's cultural transition and adaptation to life in a different culture. In chapter 6, I discuss achieving equity in assessment that includes a list of contextual assessment areas that should help assess a client's cultural transition, adaption, and acculturation. Please refer to the section of chapter 6 that discusses achieving equity in assessment for more information about this very important subject.

The information one receives from an assessment of acculturation may be used to determine the individual's level of assimilation in the transformation process of balancing values, beliefs, and traditions brought from the country of birth with new ideas of lifestyle and traditions of the host country. The stage of identity development should also be evaluated. Additional focus should include the following:

- Neighborhood contextual experiences
- Quality of housing
- Experiences with racism
- Religious beliefs

Interviewing culturally different individuals requires a variety of techniques and skills. Ivey and colleagues (2014) among others have developed a list of suggestions. Each technique has been listed with an explanation, an illustration, or both; this is an outstanding resource for interviewing culturally diverse clients. The following suggestions for managing an interview with a culturally diverse individual should be used in conjunction with the previously suggested sequence for an interview.

Eye Contact. In Native American and Latino/a cultural groups, direct eye contact, especially by the young, is considered disrespectful. Okun, Fried, and Okun (1999) note that in many cultures individuals are forbidden to look directly at others who have more power. It is inappropriate in Muslim cultures for women to make direct eye contact with a nonfamily male. Obviously, direct eye contact is interpreted differently among cultures; some cultures consider it to be an invitation to a sexual liaison, whereas others consider it an invitation to conflict (Paniagua, 2005; Sue et al., 2014).

Touch. Guidelines for touching across gender lines are clearly defined in some cultures. For instance, in many societies, especially in the Middle East and among Asian groups, women do not touch or shake hands with unrelated men. The counselor should let the client initiate the greeting and ending of a counseling session.

Probing Questions. In some cultures, especially among some Asian groups, asking for more in-depth information is considered to be very rude and intrusive. Being aware of this potential problem, counselors restructure their questions to focus on the topic the client has initiated, as shown in the following samples:

COUNSELOR: How do you think you could best help the situation with your brother?

COUNSELOR: What can you tell me about the relationship?

The counselor has a delicate balancing problem with Asian groups that respect individuals who demonstrate proficiency in their profession but resent those who appear to be too intrusive.

Space and Distance: Be alert to cultural differences in what is considered to be an appropriate distance from another individual when interviewing. Remember that the British prefer more distance than do North Americans (more than an arm's length), Latino/a people like being closer, and those from the Middle East prefer to be "right in your face."

Verbal Style: "I" is not a word in Vietnamese; individuals are defined by their relationships: Son (I) asks Father (you) for permission, Mother speaks to children (them).

Restrictive Emotions: Many cultural groups are taught to mask their emotional feelings. Thus, they might appear to be disinterested and preoccupied. This is particularly true of Native Americans who consider masking emotional responses a sign of maturity. In most cases you can expect African Americans and Latino/a people to openly express emotions.

Confrontation Issues: Ivey and colleagues (2014) suggest that one must be very sensitive to the cultural orientation of each client if confrontation is used in the interview. What is suggested is that extreme confrontational statements may not be helpful with certain groups, especially in the opening stages of interviewing. Counselors must remember that personal and family honor are almost sacred among some cultural groups, especially in Asian cultures. Thus, direct confrontation may be perceived as being ill-mannered by some groups. Counselors are to be very careful and most flexible when they construct questions, such as, "Tell me more about your feelings when that event took place," or "What is your son's typical story of that behavior?" In short, use the principles of supportive, empathic confrontation to construct questions. Skilled counselors have learned that at times silence can be very helpful in that it provides the client time to struggle with a problem.

Self-Disclosure: This technique is quite paradoxical in that it is most essential when establishing rapport for a trusting client–counselor relationship and can be most damaging to the counseling relationship if the counselor is perceived as being immature. For instance, self-disclosure at the initiation of the interview can be helpful for building trust: "I grew up in the South and I'm white and you are an African American. Do you think we can work together?" However, counselors who focus too much time on their own personal lives and intimacies can lose face with their clients (Matsumoto & Juang, 2013; Paniagua, 2005). Again, a delicate balance must be maintained.

Focus on Self-in-Relation and Self-in-Context

The point has been made that in North America we tend to focus on the "I." In many other cultures, the focus is on family or solidarity of groups. In making career decisions, the focus can be directed to include the family. The individual perceives himself or herself as a self-in-relationship and makes decisions that meet the needs and approval of the family. Family honor and loyalty may be the driving forces that the counselor must recognize (Matsumoto & Juang, 2013; Ponterotto et al., 2010).

In sum, what one is expected to remember about the differences between cultures and what are considered to be acceptable and culturally appropriate verbal and non-verbal techniques can be overwhelming. This points out, however, the necessity of preparation for counseling and interviewing encounters, especially with individuals from culturally diverse groups. Counselors must also remember that they are interviewing unique individuals who share some cultural values with others but who have also been shaped by nonshared experiences. The techniques we have just reviewed are generalized suggestions that might not apply to all members of a particular culture. Nevertheless, the career counseling profession must prepare itself for diversity to be effective in the 21st century. I continue our discussion of the intake interview beginning with step VII in the interview sequence.

Step VII Some Career Choice and Career Development Constraints

The focus on constraints and/or barriers to career choice and development in step VII has been the centerpiece of research for a number of decades. Career choice and development share many common barriers; a client's negative cognitions, for example, would more than likely affect initial career choice and those that follow as well as one's development. I will make some distinctions between career choice and development in the discussions that follow, but my primary focus will be on the connection between career and personal concerns. Be aware that the constraints listed are not all inclusive but provide the counselor with examples of specific barriers that can hinder one's ability to make an optimal career choice as well as constraining one's career development. Contextual experiences have had an important role in both career and personal counseling. One's values and core beliefs influenced by environmental experiences and life-course events are the driving forces behind significant life decisions. We are in many respects a product of our environment; people are active information processors. Recall that life events can trigger anxiety reactions that could foster the development of a full-blown anxiety disorder for example. I am suggesting that contextual experiences are very important influences on the development of one's worldview, the development of cognitive schemas, and subsequent behavior. Influences on behavior that emerge from contextual experiences are a major focus of the interview. What I am discussing here is a socialization process involving situational influences from which one absorbs their culture, develops a basis for identity, and establishes a personality. Socialization takes place in ecological systems which are very inclusive; people learn without reinforcement (Bandura, 1986). Uniqueness emerges from individualized and shared experiences. What counselors should take from these statements is that contextual experiences greatly influence how each individual views the world; people internalize values, beliefs, and expectations of the future (Sue et al., 2014; Zunker, 2008). A representative list of career barriers that may be the result of contextual experiences follows:

Discrimination against and oppression of career ideals

Lack of educational and occupational opportunities

Lack of quality educational experiences

Lack of openness to career selection

Poor role models

Socioeconomic disadvantages

Unstable familial experiences

The lack of access to educational and occupational opportunities may force some clients to search for the best job opportunity currently available rather than engage in counseling to find a work environment that is considered to be the best fit. Clients with a poor educational background are most likely to view the future quite differently than someone who has experienced enriched educational experiences and plans to attend a university. Counselors may find that some clients have been conditioned to believe that they are destined to take jobs that do not require a strong educational background; it is their fate to work in lower level jobs. Socioeconomic disadvantages can limit one's ability to obtain a college education and/or attend a professional school. Although there are many examples of individuals who have succeeded in moving from working class to middle-class status, research tell us that most people remain in the social class of their origin (Andersen & Taylor, 2013). Poor role models and unstable familial experiences that can be found in most class status groups can negatively affect an individual's self-esteem as well as future expectations. What is most important for the counselor here is the recognition of how contextual experiences can influence one's view of the future. Self-perceptions are particularly significant for discovering pathways to form a career identity.

Changing Nature of Work

Establishing a work identity and having a job that sustains one's family have been and remain part of the American dream. The changing nature of work in America has been ongoing and will continue to present new opportunities for the American worker. Many in the workforce today are known as knowledge workers who maintain their position by staying up to date in their field of work (Drucker, 2002). More workers are now required to manage their own career development and are encouraged to become lifelong learners. Current workers and individuals who are in the process of making an initial career choice currently experience the challenges that are created by a diminishing number of jobs and workplaces. In current economic times many workers have lost the guarantee of a lifetime job. In many work environments job security is threatened. Not only do current workers have concerns about their future long-term interests but so also do those who are making an initial career choice (Feldman, 2002). There appears to be a growing distrust among some workers of those who employ them and in the strength of our economy in general. These feelings have been exacerbated by the loss of millions of jobs during the recession in 2009 and the outsourcing of jobs in the 1990s. Counselors can expect to find that many of their clients will experience serious career and personal concerns when their source of income has disappeared. I will discuss more about work and the workplace in chapters 7, 13, and 14.

Negative Cognitions

Faulty beliefs and assumptions have been a primary target of human service practitioners over time. Practitioners have come to recognize the pervasive nature of negative cognitions. Negative views of the future, about self, and about the world of work, for example, suggest that a client has low self-esteem as well as self-concept and self-efficacy deficits. Negative cognitions usually increase the level of demeaning self-talk that can lead to indecision and negative overgeneralizations; one's view of life can be almost completely negative. It should surprise no one that faulty beliefs and assumptions can lead to an identity crisis that could affect a person's ability to function in all life roles (Cormier et al., 2013; Zunker, 2008). Negative beliefs and assumptions can also lead to severe anxiety, fear, and panic attacks. One may become so overwhelmed with worry that they are unable to accomplish even daily tasks. Indeed negative cognitions have the potential to severely diminish ones' ability to make appropriate life decisions that have long-term consequences (Durand & Barlow, 2013). Thus, interviewers should be alert to any indications of dysfunctional thinking when involved in dialogue with their clients. Finally, early detection of negative cognitions is essential. Assessment instruments that can provide an objective appraisal of dysfunctional thinking will follow in the discussion of psychological and personality disorders.

Psychological Disorders

At this point it should be clear to the reader that psychological disorders can affect all life roles including the work role. Someone with an anxiety or a mood disorder or both, for example, will have difficulty in choosing a career and maintaining employment as well as functioning in other roles. Human service practitioners address a variety of client problems including concerns that are identified by symptoms of psychological disorders. Examples of groups of psychological disorders include: anxiety disorders, development disorders, mood disorders, personality disorders, schizophrenia and other psychotic disorders, somatoform and dissociative disorders, substance-related and impulsive control disorders, and many others. Symptoms of psychological disorders are contained in the *Diagnostic and Statistical Manual of Mental Disorders* (5th ed. text revision) (American Psychiatric Association, 2013).

The point was made earlier that helpers are to detect early symptoms of disorders in an attempt to prevent the development of psychopathology. What is suggested here is that counselors are to sharpen their skills for detecting symptoms of disorders during the interview and learn more about assessment instruments that could assist them in the identification process. Let me be clear. The counselor is more interested in determining symptoms of psychological disorders for the purpose of developing interventions to moderate their severity rather than for labeling a client with a particular disorder or disorders. In the case of a mood disorder of depression for example, typical symptoms include the observation that the client appears to be lethargic, sad, and anxious and displays feelings of helplessness. One can expect depressed clients to be indecisive and have serious relational problems. They tend to be slow to respond to questions and have trouble recalling past events. One can also expect to find work impairment and poor work identity. There can be strong indications of emotional instability and most often clients with symptoms of depression are consumed with negative self-evaluations (Durand & Barlow, 2013; Sue et al., 2014). What is clear is that clients with symptoms of depression will need interventions designed to modify negative cognitions as well as relaxation exercises. In addition, self-talk will have to be modified and closely monitored. Some clients with these symptoms are able to participate in personal and career counseling simultaneously. This decision, as you would expect, is based on the severity of the client's condition. In the following paragraphs, a career counselor and a mental health counselor are involved in an intake interview with their respective clients.

Using good listening and observation skills, a career counselor detects symptoms of depression. Although the severity of depression is unknown, the client's demeanor could be described as someone who is rather sad and emotionally unstable. The counselor wanted to verify her tentative conclusions of mild depression. Most helpers will want to use effective standardized assessment instruments to confirm their observations during the intake interview. Helpers are particularly interested in measuring the severity of symptoms. The career counselor in this case had dealt with a limited number of clients who had similar symptoms and she wanted objective data to confirm her observations. She chose the *Beck Depression Inventory* (BDI-II) (Beck, Street, & Brown, 1996) that measures the severity of symptoms of depression.

In another counseling situation, a mental health counselor also detected symptoms of depression in a client she interviewed. This particular mental health counselor had considerable experience with clients who had symptoms of depression and she also chose to use the results of the BDI-II. In addition, the mental health counselor was also most interested in becoming more familiar with standard measures of interest to assist her client in the career choice process. She chose the *Self Directed Search* (SDS) (Holland, 1994a) as an interest measure and *My Vocational Situation* (Holland et al., 1980) in order to observe possible causes of vocational difficulties including lack of vocational identity, lack of information or training, and environmental or personal barriers. It is likely that both helpers would use all three inventories. In addition, more information on dysfunctional thinking could assist both counselors in addressing negative cognitions so prevalent in cases of depression. One of the instruments that could be used for this purpose is the *Career Thoughts Inventory* (CTI) (Sampson et al., 1996a), which is designed to measure negative thinking. The CTI provides scores for three scales, Decision-Making Confusion, Commitment Anxiety, and External Conflict plus a total score. Both the career and the mental health counselor chose specific assessment inventories to confirm their observations in order to prepare for problem identification in the next step of the interview process. In both counseling cases, the focus was on identifying the interrelationship of career and personal concerns. In the next section of this chapter, I will provide a brief description of some selected psychological disorders, including anxiety, mood, somatoform, and personality disorders. Much more information on the psychological disorders discussed in this chapter and other psychological disorders not discussed here can be found in abnormal psychology textbooks including Durand and Barlow (2013) and Sue and colleagues (2014).

Identifying Symptoms of Psychological Disorders

The brief review of some psychological disorders that follows will hopefully be used as a quick reference for identifying potential client problems in the intake interview. Keep in mind that there are many other psychological disorders that are not discussed here. Counselors who are alert to symptoms of psychological disorders will be in a much better position to identify potential barriers that can constrain one's career choice and interfere with one's career development as well. More importantly, problem identification provides a pathway to effective interventions. Counselors focus on symptoms of disorders when engaging clients in discussions involving goal selection. When a clinical assessment is necessary, counselors are to refer clients to determine if presenting problems meet the criteria for a specific psychological disorder (Durand & Barlow, 2013). I begin with anxiety disorders.

Anxiety disorders

Apprehension, worry, fear, and panic characterize anxiety disorders. In most of the disorders that follow, anxiety is usually persistent and intense and accompanied by fearfulness and even terror that can impair normal functioning. Currently there are seven anxiety disorders:

Panic disorder consists of episodes of panic attacks with and without agoraphobia (fear of leaving one's house). Individuals with a panic disorder are focused on avoidance of situations that are considered unsafe.

Agoraphobia is fear of places such a mall or theatre and/or avoidance of feared situations and people. In extreme cases people will not leave their home.

Specific phobia is a fear of specific objects such as a spider or some or most animals. In addition, there is extreme fear of closed spaces such as a cave, tunnel, or even a closed room and also heights.

Social phobia is a fear of being judged harshly by others when performing or making a speech or even when interacting with others. Fear of being watched by others may result in a panic reaction.

Generalized anxiety disorder is characterized as excessive worry that persists for at least six months. In this disorder, anxiety is focused on minor everyday events. One is consumed with worry and anxiety.

Obsessive-compulsive disorder is characterized by recurrent obsessions (persistent or uncontrollable thoughts) or compulsions (an overwhelming need to repeatedly wash one's hands, for example). One can be so involved in rituals that all life roles are affected.

Post-traumatic stress disorder is characterized by re-experiencing an extremely traumatic event. One focuses on avoiding images or thoughts about a traumatic experience. Some war veterans, for example, experience daily stress for years after they have retired from the service (Sue et al., 2014).

Like most other psychological disorders, anxiety and panic attacks are very pervasive in the lives of those who are afflicted with these disorders. Anxiety is considered one of the building blocks that can lead to disorders that are very debilitating (Durand & Barlow, 2013). An individual's reaction to excessive anxiety can be overwhelming and take an enormous toll on one's lifestyle.

Somatoform Disorders

This group of disorders is characterized by concerns with the physical body and its functions. Imagined illnesses and physical complaints that have no medical bases are good examples of this disorder. One may fear they have a terminal illness that will come forth at anytime. Others constantly complain about numerous physical conditions that are undocumented. In extreme cases an individual can actually become paralyzed without a medical basis. Yet another individual believes that he has a physical condition that is so horrible that everyone who sees it is appalled. There are four disorders in this group (Durand & Barlow, 2013; Sue et al., 2014) as follows:

Hypochondriasis is characterized by anxiety about a preoccupation with an imagined illness or serious physical condition that is nonexistent. A hypochondriac is certain that he or she has a serious physical condition even though a physician may conclude there is no evidence of one.

Somatization disorders are characterized by persistent complaints of multiple physical conditions that have no medical basis. An individual can be convinced that they are afflicted by serious multiple physical problems and are not able to focus on anything else.

A *conversion disorder* has somewhat of a different twist. In this case the client actually has a serious physical problem such as blindness or paralysis, but there is no apparent physical cause. The distinct difference here is that one actually is experiencing a physical problem yet no medical basis for the problem can be found.

Body dysmorphic disorder is a diagnosis used to identify individuals who falsely believe that he or she has a physical defect that is apparent to everyone. In addition, the individual is convinced that the imagined defect is hideous and disgusts everyone who sees it.

Somatoform disorders are good examples of how distorted thinking can adversely influence one's existence. These disorders develop over time and are considered chronic in nature. Counselors who are able to detect early symptoms of dysfunctional thinking that is so common among somatoform disorders should help their clients learn how to cope with stressful events with the use of cognitive-behavioral techniques. In most cases of somatoform disorders, support groups are used to provide reassurance whereas counseling emphasizes methods to resolve conflicts and reduce stress (Durand & Barlow, 2013).

Mood Disorders

Emotional states are usually associated with mood disorders in that there are types of depression that are defined by "high" or "low" states of emotion. Mood can also change rapidly in that there are mood "swings" that alternate between depression and mania. To fully understand the significance of mood disorders, one must become familiar with two types of mood disorders labeled depression and bipolar.

Depression disorders consist of major depressive episodes that are most severe, can come about very suddenly, and can last for months and even years. Over time one can experience repeated episodes and may develop long-lasting symptoms. On the other hand, symptoms of mild depression that are also long lasting are known as *dysthymia*. One can also be diagnosed as having *double depression* when one experiences alternating periods of severe depression and dysthmia (Durand & Barlow, 2013).

Bipolar disorders, as the name implies, include a depressive phase and a manic phase. This diagnosis is characterized as a roller coaster ride of ups and downs. In the depressive phase, one is unable to enjoy pleasurable experiences, is often described as having difficulty in concentrating, and appears to be experiencing significant loss of self-esteem. In the manic phase, to no one's surprise, there are elation, joy from every activity, self-assurance, and grandiose plans for the future. There appears to be no in-between, but there are serious functional problems for individuals in both the depressive state and the manic state. In the depressive state, one may experience even suicidal thoughts and in the manic state exaggerated feelings of euphoria and excitement can lead to poor decision making that has long-term consequences. There are three types of bipolar disorders:

Bipolar I—major depression and full mania

Bipolar II—major depression and mild mania

Cyclothymia—mild depression with mild mania that is chronic and long term (Durand & Barlow, 2013)

Helpers recognize that a mood disorder such as depression can negatively impact all life roles, including the work role. People with depression have difficulty processing information and the meaning associated with life events that are critically important in the decision-making process. Negative self-appraisals so common in depression can disrupt job performance and career development. There are certainly personal concerns as well such as inappropriate behavior, feelings of helplessness, and overgeneralization of negative experiences. Long-term interests can be grossly affected by decisions influenced by reckless behavior during a manic phase of a bipolar disorder (Sue et al., 2014).

Personality Disorders

In chapter 4, a case example was used to illustrate how symptoms of a personality disorder can interfere with one's career development as well as one's ability to function in all life roles. Counselors who discover symptoms of a personality disorder are challenged to develop intervention goals to aggressively address a client's concerns. Research informs us that personality disorders develop over time; thus, the chronic nature of their development presents tremendous challenges to counselors. As I briefly discuss symptoms of personality disorders in general terms, one should remember that a client's perceptions of multiple influences and experiences over time are an individual matter. What is suggested here is that the severity and the length of time symptoms dominate one's behavior are most significant. I will briefly review symptoms that can dominate one's behavior and corresponding work role projections in Table 5.1. In the brief discussions that follow, the focus will be on six personality disorder types from the *Diagnostic and Statistical Manual 5* (DSM-5) (American Psychiatric Association, 2013; Sue et al., 2014). It is most important for all counselors to recognize that the diagnostic process involved in identifying a personality disorder requires rigorous training and professional supervision. I repeat, counselors are to refer their clients to a qualified clinician if necessary.

Clients with an antisocial personality disorder are characterized as having a pervasive disregard of the rights of others. There is usually repeated involvement in illegal behavior and a substantial record of unlawful acts. All life roles are affected, particularly the work role.

Clients with an avoidant personality disorder tend to avoid occupational activities that require interpersonal contact. They live with fear of being rejected. There is low self-esteem and avoidance of situations in which they are subjected to criticism. There is a tendency to be very dependent upon others.

Instability and impulsive behavior characterize the borderline personality disorder. Emotional instability is accompanied by brief, but intense, episodes of depression and anxiety. Individuals with this disorder have a deep sense of abandonment.

A sense of self-importance is the major characteristic of clients who have been diagnosed with a narcissistic personality disorder. Some clients may consider themselves as ultraspecial and extremely unique. As a result, they constantly seek excessive

Table 5.1	**Personality Type Disorders—Symptoms and Work-Role Projections**	
Symptoms	Disorders	Work-Role Projections
	Avoidant	
Clients who lack social skills and are socially isolated—sit alone, eat alone, and prefer isolation. Nonresponsive and aloof, flat affect.		Clients with these symptoms are usually very indecisive, vague about future, and very aloof. Prefer solitary activities; may work well in an environment that provides social isolation. There is a tendency to not seek out close relationships—group work is difficult.
	Schizotypal	
Clients who are viewed as eccentric and have bizarre ways of dressing. Believe they are the center of all events—odd thoughts and unusual actions.		Clients with these symptoms are usually very suspicious of others, have very poor interpersonal relationship skills. They are likely to be shunned by work associates due to bizarre behavior and dress.
	Antisocial	
Clients who are antisocial fail to conform to social norms and are guilty of aggressive acts against others. They harbor a disregard for the rights of others.		Clients with these symptoms tend to behave inconsistently, especially in the work role. There is typical nonconformity to social norms, poor emotional control, and extreme aggressiveness that may result in truancy and stealing. Clients are likely to have difficulty in sustaining productive work.
	Borderline	
Clients who have poor control over their emotions and show definite signs of instability. Severe mood swings interfere with consistent patterns of behavior.		Expect clients with these symptoms to have a poor self-concept, difficulty with career choice, career maintenance, and establishing long-term goals. Impulsive behavior can interfere with work-role functioning and other life-role commitments. It is not unusual for clients with these symptoms to experience significant problems with relationships including those with work associates.

Table 5.1	**(Continued)**	
Symptoms	**Disorders**	**Work Role Projections**
	Narcissistic	
Clients who have a strong desire and need for admiration especially from someone they view as important. They consider themselves to be ultraspecial and and extremely unique.		Clients with these symptoms will likely attempt to exploit others, expect favorable treatment, and possess excessive feeling of self-importance. Be aware of unrealistic goals and and the exploitation of others.
	Obsessive-Compulsive	
Clients who are obsessive-compulsive desire complete control of everyone and everything; they are perfectionist and desire order.		The avoidance of decision making is often associated with these symptoms. Clients are often subject to stress due to indecisiveness and a strong need to work within highly structured and organized tasks. Clients with these symptoms are preoccupied with trivial details and seek perfection to the point that task completion is constantly delayed. On the other hand, they are able to function well in work roles that require highly organized activities.

SOURCE: Durand and Barlow (2013) and Sue, Sue, Sue, and Sue (2014).

admiration, especially from others they view as "high-status" individuals. In addition, they have little regard for others and, if given the opportunity, will exploit anyone who stands in their way of grandiose plans.

An obsessive-compulsive personality pattern is characterized as one in which there is preoccupation with rules and details to make certain that every activity is done correctly. Perfectionism and overly strict standards interfere with task completion. There is a need to control all aspects of most situations and there is a tendency to focus on fears associated with failing to do the right thing.

Individuals with schizotypal personality disorder have odd beliefs and peculiar ideation; for example, they may believe in clairvoyance and magical thinking. It should surprise no one that clients with a schizotypal personality disorder are often viewed as very eccentric. More information on personality disorders can be obtained from abnormal psychology textbooks including references in this chapter.

I continue our discussion of personality by reviewing a measure of personality labeled the NEO-PI-3 (Costa & McCare, 1992), also known as the big five-factor model. This instrument is used to measure dimensions of personality that can be used to build rapport, understand the client's worldview and insight, and provide measures of positive and negative characteristics. Although it was not designed to measure symptoms of personality disorders, the authors of this instrument make the point that personality traits are very relevant factors in determining personality disorders. The five-factor model includes the following dimensions of personality and facets for each factor:

Neuroticism	A measure of psychological distress and emotional stability
Facets	anxiety, hostility, depression, self-consciousness, impulsiveness, vulnerability
Extraversion	A measure of the tendency to be sociable and feel happy and optimistic
Facets	warmth, assertiveness, active, excitement seeking, positive emotions
Openness to Experience	A measure of the degree of openness to experience and emotional expressiveness
Facets	fantasy, aesthetics, feelings, actions, ideas, values
Agreeableness	A measure of the degree of compassion and hostility to others
Facets	trust, straightforwardness, altruism, compliance, modesty
Conscientiousness	A measure of self-control and the ability to plan and commit to personal goals
Facets	Competence, order, dutifulness, achievement striving, self-discipline, deliberation

The NEO-PI-3 reports interpretations of both low and high scores of these personality dimensions. Thus, a client who presents emotional instability can be further evaluated to learn the degree or severity of instability. In addition, the counselor is now in the position to evaluate five personality dimensions that describe measures of such variables as depression, impulsiveness, assertiveness, positive emotions, compliance, and achievement striving among others. Schultz and Schultz (2013) present the highlights of their research of the six factors of personality as follows:

Neuroticism, extraversion, openness, and conscientiousness have a strong heredity component.

The factor of agreeableness has a strong environmental component.

All five factors have been found in diverse cultures.

Most factors remain stable over the life span.

Women report higher levels of neuroticism, extraversion, agreeableness, and conscientiousness than men.

We tend to see others as being more conscientious and less neurotic than ourselves (p. 231).

In addition, Schultz and Schultz (2013) found that individuals who score high in extraversion tend to be high in emotional stability, are successful in coping with stress, and do exceptionally well in college. High scores in conscientiousness suggests that one is realistic, efficient, and punctual, gets better grades, is well organized, creates friendships, and sets high personal goals.

Engler (2014) suggests that many of the personality traits measured by the five-factor model are related to positive achievement in work. She also suggests that the personality traits measured by the five-factor model are associated with other work-related behaviors. For example, an individual who has a high score in openness to experience will tend to seek work in which one is to assume responsibility, find meaning, autonomy, and responsibility. The individual high in neuroticism will likely stress the importance of a good salary and care less about other job satisfaction factors. Engler strongly endorses well-structured personality questionnaires that do not discriminate against people with disabilities, women, the elderly, and minority groups.

Harrington (2013) suggests that the five-factor model can also be used as a measure of resilience. The factor Extraversion is a measure of good feelings, happiness, positive affect, and subjective well-being whereas the factor Neuroticism is negatively associated with subjective well-being. Other factors associated positively with subjective well-being are Conscientiousness (responsible, hardworking, self-disciplined), Openness, and Agreeableness.

Counselors are to use objective standardized assessment instruments to confirm their observations of clients they are interviewing. This step may be necessary to distinguish between clients who present some symptoms of a personality disorder with no previous history of abnormal behavior. Counselors are likely to find that healthy, functional individuals may be somewhat suspicious of others, lack self-esteem, and be somewhat dependent (Zunker, 2008). Establishing the level of severity and the length of time a client has symptoms of one or more personality disorders can be essential information for both career and personal counseling. In the next section, I briefly review screening instruments for substance abuse and standardized checklists that focus on a client's self-report of as many as 90 symptoms of disorders.

Standardized Instruments for Substance Abuse Screening

Alcoholism and drug abuse in the workplace have not only been a hot topics of discussion over several decades but also continue to be major foci of concern by personnel offices worldwide. Industrial and civic organizations have invested considerable funds for substance abuse programs that are designed to prevent one from using alcohol and drugs and also for those who are in need of help to kick a habit. There appears to be significant evidence that workers continue to lose their jobs because of substance abuse whereas for others there are job impairment and excessive absenteeism (Aamodt, 2013; Muchinsky, 2003). The results of a drug and alcohol abuse survey indicated that 8.2 % or more than 9 million working adults reported using illicit drugs in the past month of when the survey was taken and more than 8.8% or 10 million reported heavy use of alcohol in the past month. In addition, 18.6% of unemployed adults used illicit drugs within the past month and 13.6% of unemployed adults admitted to heavy use of alcohol (Substance Abuse and Mental Health Administration, 2007). The point here is that most human resource practitioners are certainly aware of the significant substance abuse problem in this country as well as the professional training needed to qualify as a substance abuse counselor. What I am suggesting here is that career and personal counselors can screen their clients for substance abuse and refer them to qualified substance abuse counselors.

The following are two examples of standardized assessment instruments for assessing substance abuse:

Substance Abuse Subtle Screening Inventory-3 (SASSI-3) (Miller, 1997)

Adolescent *Substance Abuse Subtle Screening Inventory-A2* (SASSI-A2) (Miller, 2001)

Although there are a number of other standardized screening instruments for substance abuse on the market, these instruments are good examples of what is available. The important point here is that substance abuse screening inventories are available to help counselors during the interview to identify and confirm their client's problems with substance abuse. Client information obtained from screening instruments can help prevent the counselor from addressing issues that are a result of the client's substance abuse (Whiston, 2013). Being arrested for unlawful behavior, for example, may or may not be connected to one or more personality disorders, but more related to one's abuse of alcohol and/or drugs. Substance abuse is a very pervasive factor in one's life as described by Wilson (2003) as follows: When a person begins to use a drug, that drug use is sporadic and voluntary. But after an addiction develops, the addicted individual is compelled to seek out the drug and consume it. This compulsive drug use is the hallmark of addiction. Addicts lose control of their drug intake. They have a difficult time thinking of anything else but acquiring the drug, and they forsake all kinds of social obligations (including family and work) in order to obtain and use the drug. We still do not know how an addiction develops, but research in this area has given us some clues (p. 402). For more information on substance abuse, use the following website: Substance Abuse and Mental Health Services Administration (SAMHSA)

(http://guide.helpingasmericasyouth.gov/)

Standardized Checklists for Client Symptoms of Disorders

In the final section of this chapter, I discuss standardized checklists on which clients report their current symptoms. Two instruments that stand out among many others are *The Symptoms Checklist-90-Revised* (SCI-90-R) (Derogates, 1994) and the *Brief Symptoms Inventory* (BSI) (Derogates, 1993). On the SCI-90-R there are 90 symptoms listed and on the BSI there are 53. On both of the instruments, clients are to respond to a list of symptoms by using a 5-point scale of distress ranging from 0 (not at all) to 4 (extremely). Both inventories can each be completed in 15 minutes or less. These instruments provide measures of nine scales as follows: Somatization, Obsessive-Compulsive, Interpersonal Sensitivity, Depression, Anxiety, Hostility, Phobic Anxiety, Paranoid Ideation, and Psychoticism. In addition, there are three composite scores: global severity index, positive symptom total, and positive symptom distress index. The composite scores can be compared to nonpatient adults, nonpatient adolescents, psychiatric outpatients, and psychiatric inpatients (Whiston, 2013). Clearly, counselors can use the results of these two checklists to determine interventions for their clients or to refer them for further evaluation and treatment. Counselors can also scan the results of the checklists to determine the most distressing symptoms the client has checked. Finally, counselors are to become familiar with the myths and reality of the mentally disturbed as explained in Box 5.2.

Over the years there have been mergers of publishing companies including those that publish standardized testing instruments. Counselors are advised to contact their professional association for an updated list of test publishers. One fact is clear, however: Updated versions of older tests and inventories plus the development of new ones will continue to occupy the attention of most test publishing companies. In the meantime computer-assisted and online career counseling programs and testing will continue to update programs, interventions, and supply the most recent information concerning the job market. Professional associations have issued guidelines and more will surely follow. The increased use of advances in technology will likely provide more

BOX 5.2

Stereotypes About People Who Are Mentally Disturbed

MYTHS VERSUS REALITY

Myth: People who are mentally disturbed can always be recognized by their abnormal behavior.

Reality: People who are mentally disturbed are not always distinguishable from others on the basis of consistently unusual behavior. First, no sharp dividing line usually exists between normal and abnormal behavior. Second, even when people have some form of emotional disturbance, their difficulties may not always be detectable in their behavior.

Myth: People who are mentally disturbed have inherited their disorders. If one member of a family has an emotional breakdown, other members will probably suffer a similar fate.

Reality: The belief that insanity runs in certain families has caused misery and undue anxiety for many people. Heredity does play a role in some mental disorders, such as schizophrenia and mood disorders. However, even though heredity may predispose an individual to certain disorders, mental problems are the result of an interaction of biological, psychological, social, and cultural factors.

Myth: Mentally disturbed people can never be cured and will never be able to function normally or hold jobs in the community.

Reality: This is an erroneous belief. Nearly three fourths of people who are hospitalized with severe mental disorders will improve and go on to lead productive lives.

Myths: People become mentally disturbed because they are weak willed. To avoid emotional disorders or cure oneself of them, one need only exercise will power.

Reality: Needing help to resolve difficulties does not indicate a lack of willpower. In fact, recognizing one's own need for help is a sign of strength rather than a sign of weakness. Many problems stem from situations not under the individual's control, such as the death of a loved one or loss of a job. Other problems stem from lifelong learning patterns of faulty learning; it is naive to expect that a single exercise of will can override years of experience.

Myth: Mental illness is always a deficit, and a person who has it can never contribute anything of worth until "cured."

Reality: Many people with mental illness were never "cured," but they nevertheless made great contributions to humanity. Ernest Hemingway, one of the great writers of the 20th century and winner of the Nobel Prize for Literature, experienced lifelong depression, alcoholism, and frequent hospitalizations. The famous Dutch painter Vincent van Gogh produced great works of art despite the fact that he was severely disturbed. Others, such as Pablo Picasso and Edgar Allan Poe, contributed major artistic and literary works while seriously disturbed.

SOURCE: From *Essentials of Understanding Abnormal Psychology*, 2nd ed., p. 11, by D. Sue, D. W. Sue, D. Sue, and S. Sue. Copyright 2014. Reprinted by permission from Wadsworth Cengage Learning.

valid information for counselors to use when addressing the interrelationships of personal and career concerns. More information that could be accessed by counselors concerning the identification of psychological and personality disorder symptoms would be most helpful. More valid positive and negative information about each client could insure a greater balance in the counseling process. I provide some suggestions for problem identification next.

Clarifying Problems

A most important stage in the career counseling process is client problem identification. You will recall that all five career counseling models in chapter 3 emphasized methods and procedures that identify problems and concerns clients bring to counseling. Counselors are to clarify client concerns and needs into a format that is straightforward and concrete. This step often requires in-depth probing. A client's presenting problems, for example, may be the client's way of "testing the waters" before a trusting relationship is established. Counselors, therefore, use their interviewing skills to uncover the "real problems." The following questions adapted from Brems (2001) and Cormier and colleagues (2013) are examples that can be used:

In what circumstances does this problem arise?

How intense is this problem and how often does it occur?

When and where does this problem arise?

Could you please describe some of the things that disturb you?

Whiston (2009) suggests that the counselor is to "(1) explore the problem from multiple perspectives, (2) gather specific information on each problem, (3) assess problem intensity, (4) assess degree to which client believes the problem is changeable, and (5) identify methods the client has used to solve the problem previously" (p. 119).

Thus, the importance of clarifying problems is obvious in that it suggests criteria from which one selects counseling goals and effective interventions. In order to be most effective, problems are clarified into concrete statements that clearly state specific examples of the client's environmental influences, emotions, thinking, and behavior. Keep in mind that problems are usually multidimensional. Some examples for clarifying problems follow.

Kent's presenting problem was "difficulty in getting along with the people I work with." Instead of labeling the problem as one of "poor interpersonal relationships," the counselor wisely probed for more specific information. Kent's private beliefs included the feeling that "no one really cares for me." His expressed self-criticism indicates that he tends to reject people first so that they will not have the chance to reject him. Kent also revealed that early interactions with his family were very unpleasant and stressful, which resulted in poor self-regard and feeling that he was misunderstood. He seemed convinced that his chances of getting hurt would be less in the future if he ignored others.

Instead of developing interventions from the vague presenting problem, the counselor was now in the position to use specifically stated real problems and subsequent behaviors. The counselor zeroed in on the client's perceptions, feelings, and actions and developed a collaborative relationship in which they agreed jointly on strategies. In this case *underlying reasons* for poor personal interrelationships were addressed as well as strategies in how to effectively relate to others. Client and counselor explored how problems of this type are very pervasive and can affect all life roles. As discussed in chapter 4, career and personal concerns are often inseparable and intertwined.

Carla was referred as an anxious client who was unable to make a career decision. Considerable time was spent with Carla to establish rapport and trust. Eventually, after a number of probing questions, Carla identified her overriding problem as conflicts with her family over career choice. She wanted a career in engineering, but her family wanted her to work in a local factory. She was torn between her loyalty to family and what may be best for them and her own individual goals. Carla was raised by a family that expected each member to do what is best for their collective survival as a group. The real problem in this case was a conflict between the influences of an American individualistic view versus another culture's collectivist view. This case points out that some client concerns involve *culturally shaped relationships* that may be different than the dominant society's. The major problem for Carla was embedded within cultural contexts of her environment.

In sum, counselors use *all the information* gathered in the intake interview to determine counseling strategies. The rule of thumb is to not overlook the smallest detail that at times may be expressed by the client in a rather cavalier manner. A health problem, for example, may be the clue to an underlying emotional situation. As we discovered in the previous examples, presenting problems do not always tell the whole story. Counselors must have the skills to ask probing questions in a manner that will encourage clients to reveal the real problems that have been held back. Finally, counselor and client are to clarify problems in specific concrete terms and agree on intervention strategies that will meet the client's needs and concerns.

Summary

1. The sequence for an interview includes an informal assessment of well-being, assets, and strengths, identifying information, presenting problems, current status, health and medical information, family life, social/development history, life roles, problems that interfere with career choice, problems that interfere with career development, clarifying problems, and identifying goals.
2. An informal evaluation of the client's feeling of well-being focuses on the identification of a client's assets and strengths. The client is to recognize that positive as well as negative factors are to be unearthed in the interview. Clients are to recognize the importance of resilience in the career choice process; a discussion of both positive and negative factors provides a more balanced counseling approach.
3. Counselors must develop a greater sensitivity to culturally diverse clients when conducting an interview. Technique issues include eye contact, touch, probing questions, space and distance, verbal style, restrictive emotions, confrontation, self-disclosure, and focus on self-in-relation and self-in-context.
4. Career choice and career development constraints include contextual experiences, changing nature of work, negative cognitions, and psychological and personality disorders.
5. Examples of standardized assessment instruments for substance abuse screening are listed.
6. Standardized checklists for symptoms of disorders are discussed and listed.

Supplementary Learning Exercises

1. Why is it a good procedure to have a client verbalize their presenting problem? Give an example of a presenting problem and why you would want this client to verbalize their problem.
2. Explain the necessity of having a client clarify their problems before goal selection.
3. How could one's socioeconomic status affect career choice?
4. When and why is it a good idea to administer a substance abuse screening inventory?
5. List as many reasons that you can think of for using a checklist of symptoms that could indicate a psychological disorder.

Case 5.1   A Divorced Mother Who Frequently Changes Jobs

The following are excerpts of what a client told a counselor in an intake interview.

My name is Inez and I am a divorced mother with three children whose ages are 23, 17, and 16. I am currently employed by a grocery chain that specializes in health foods. Currently I oversee the coffee, tea, and chocolate section in the store. I like my work, but I haven't always been happy in a working situation. In the past I have gone from one job to another including the following jobs: working in a cleaning business, wreath making, waitress, nurse's aide, cook, teacher's aide, truck driver, and health care assistant for disabled individuals. As you can observe I have difficulty sticking to a job and I tend to procrastinate. I seem to be searching for something I can't find or really identify. Sometimes I feel that I could identify what I want to do in the future but I am afraid to try for fear of failure once more. It is hard for me to generate the confidence and energy to get started on a project.

My main problems have been depression, feelings of anger, helplessness, and fear of leaving my home. There are times when I feel happy and enthusiastic and other times I feel very depressed. It is during the feelings of depression that I cannot focus and function well. Often, I cannot complete even simple tasks. On the other hand, when I feel well, I can relate to other people, but I resist becoming involved in close relationships.

I am now 44 years old. My father was in the armed services and we moved quite often. I have lived in Colorado, Virginia, Louisiana, Texas, Germany, and Italy. I have two younger brothers. My parents divorced soon after I graduated

from high school. My marriage also failed and my children have become quite discouraged with my mental health problems. One of my major goals is to give them a better home environment.

When I have been able to work, I have had hope for the future. I am currently seeing a therapist and taking antidepressants. I have never had any career counseling even when I was enrolled in college, but work has been very important to me. I feel much better when I can function well on a job, and this feeling of well-being has fostered my lifestyle and other life roles. I still have a secret ambition of owning my own business. I would welcome the opportunity to explore some options. I know from past experience that my personal problems will hinder my progress toward upgrading my vocational skills, but I am willing to try to find a pathway to a more fulfilling work role.

QUESTIONS AND EXERCISES FOR DISCUSSION

1. What do you consider to be the major career problems for Inez?
2. How does Inez's emotional instability affect both career and personal concerns?
3. What is the significance of the statement, " I can relate to other people but I resist becoming involved in close relationships"?
4. Conceptualize the interrelationships of career and personal concerns.
5. What are your counseling recommendations for Inez including the use of assessment instruments?

Case 5.2   Cal's Faulty Reasoning

Cal's career counseling took place in a community mental health agency. A brief summary of his intake interview provides some significant background information. Cal reported for his appointment on time. He was very neatly dressed, in freshly pressed

clothes that were well coordinated and his shoes looked as though they had just been polished. Cal was very verbal and expressed himself well. He was overly precise with his answers, adding much more information than was asked for. He reported no significant physical health problems. Eye contact was appropriate.

Cal grew up in a small town in which his father had owned a hardware store. He has no siblings. He is now 36 years old. Cal described his father as being very strict and his mother as too judgmental. Cal was divorced after three years of marriage. He has no children and remarked that he felt incapable of being a good parent. He further explained this comment by stating that it was difficult to raise children properly today. Cal's wife asked for a divorce because they had "different beliefs and lifestyle." He explained that his wife stated she could not live up to his expectations and there was always tension between them. Cal lost his job as a bank clerk when the regional office was shut down. He currently lives with his parents.

Cal's stated reason for coming for help was to find a job and to solve some "personal problems." He had worked for his father for several years and then obtained a bank clerk's job, which he held for three years, after his father's store was closed. He was not always pleased with his bank job; as he put it, "I make too many mistakes." Cal viewed his personal problem as a failed marriage. Cal claimed that he tried to be a good husband, but his wife complained that he tried to control her every move. Cal reported periodic episodes of depression, for instance, "I felt helpless and slept a lot." He appeared to be fearful of leaving his parents' house for help, but they insisted that he find a job. Currently, his demeanor suggests a very poor self-concept. He admits feeling guilty about his failures and is confused about his future.

The counselor made several notations as follows:

Poor self-confidence and self-image
Difficulty in making decisions
Negative expectations of others
Attempts to control important others
Perfectionist attitude
Exhibited dependency needs
Faulty reasoning

QUESTIONS AND EXERCISES FOR DISCUSSION

1. How would you conceptualize Cal's career concerns?
2. How would you characterize Cal's emotional demeanor?
3. What are your tentative conclusions?
4. Conceptualize interrelationships of career and personal concerns.
5. Which type of assessment instruments would you chose in Cal's case?

6

Using Standardized Tests and Self-Assessment Procedures in Career Counseling

CHAPTER HIGHLIGHTS

- Problems associated with selecting standardized assessment instruments

- Achieving equity in assessment

- Identifying career beliefs

- Identifying skills, proficiencies, and abilities

- Identifying academic achievement

- Identifying and confirming interest levels

- Discovering personality variables

- Determining values

- Exploring career maturity variables

- Using computer-assisted career guidance assessment

- Using self-estimates of traits

The development of standardized tests and assessment inventories has been closely associated with the career counseling movement. As early as 1883, the U.S. Civil Service Commission used competitive examinations for job placement (Kavruck, 1956). Multiple aptitude-test batteries developed during the mid-1940s have been widely used in educational and vocational counseling. Scholastic aptitude tests used as admission criteria for educational institutions were implemented through the Educational Testing Service (ETS) established in 1947 and the American College Testing Program (ACT) established in 1959.

During the last three decades more emphasis has been placed on skills identification through informal techniques (Bolles, 2009; Holland, 1992; Osborn & Zunker, 2012). The growing popularity of informal methods of identifying skills strongly suggests that some assessment of individual aptitudes, skills, and other individual characteristics is vitally important in the career decision process despite the controversy surrounding standardized aptitude tests and job success predictions. Human service practitioners have long suggested that encouraging clients to develop self-assessment skills is an effective way of focusing more fully on career options.

The major issue seems to be how assessment results can be used most effectively in career counseling. A good approach considers assessment results as only one facet of individuality to be evaluated in the career decision process. More specifically, career decision making is seen as a continuous counseling process within which all aspects of individuality receive consideration. Skills, aptitudes, interests, values, achievements, personality characteristics, dysfunctional thinking, maturity, contextual interactions, and salient cultural variables are among the more important aspects that can be evaluated by assessment measures. Thus, assessment results constitute counseling information that can provide the individual with an awareness of increased options and alternatives while encouraging greater individual exploration in the career decision process.

The career counseling models discussed in chapter 3 suggest that all relevant information be included in the career decision process to encourage greater individual participation and consideration of a wider range of career options. Furthermore, the more knowledge counselor and client have of individual characteristics, the greater is the assurance of a balance of considerations in career decision making. Career counseling programs that are designed to incorporate all relevant information should lessen the chances that career decision making could be dominated by any one factor.

Recognizing the increasingly diverse groups in our society for whom tests were not developed, standardized, or validated, the Association for Assessment in Counseling (AAC) issued a document in 1993 entitled *Multicultural Assessment Standards: A Compilation for Counselors* (Prediger, 1994). The revised second edition of *Standards for Multicultural Assessment,* an improved updated version, was issued in 2003 (Association for Assessment in Counseling, 2003). These documents contain vital information for selecting assessment instruments, administration and scoring, and interpreting assessment results. As far back as 1988, a joint committee on testing practices sponsored by the American Psychological Association (APA) published a document entitled *Code of Fair Testing Practices in Education* that was undated by a joint committee on testing practices in 2003. In 2005, the American Counseling Association issued their Code of Ethics which details the responsibilities of test users and test developers. All these publications clearly point out the necessity for counselors to select and use assessment instruments that are appropriate for each client.

In this chapter I will include some suggestions for the appropriate use of standardized assessment results. The first section briefly discusses some psychometric procedures used for standardizing tests; validity and reliability are briefly reviewed. These concepts are assumed to be covered in other courses; thus, the emphasis here will be directed to assessment use in career counseling. In the next section, we will discuss some issues associated with achieving equity in the use of assessment. Finally, goals of assessment are introduced with example assessment instruments.

Psychometric Concepts for Selecting Assessment Instruments

The career counseling models discussed in chapter 3 suggest a variety of uses of assessment in career counseling. Although testing does not dominate counseling procedures in all counseling models, assessment usually has an important role in information gathering, accurate client self-assessment, problem identification, interventions, and outcome evaluations. The unique characteristics and identified traits of each client provide the direction for identifying options and guide the structure of intervention strategies that are tailored to meet individual and special needs. There are many other uses of assessment in career counseling, but these examples underscore the importance of selecting appropriate instruments that will result in valid and reliable results for all groups, including diverse groups. Counselors are to be knowledgeable about psychometric concepts that are necessary in selecting and using assessment instruments (Kaplan & Saccuzzo, 2013).

Reliability

The coefficient correlation of reliability is the degree to which a test score is dependable and consistent; repeated trials will yield approximately the same results. Clearly, the consistency and dependability of a test score determine its role in the counseling process. Although measurement errors can reduce reliability, the intended use of assessment results should be the determining factor for a final judgment of test reliability. For instance, when test scores are used in high-stakes decisions, such as placement in a special program, each test should be scrutinized carefully according to its purpose, content, appropriate use, and validity and reliability; valid and reliable test results are critically important. For the individual exploring several occupational options suggested by an interest inventory, a more moderate reliability coefficient may be acceptable. Keep in mind that the test developer is responsible for providing evidence that reliability is sufficient for its intended use.

Finally, reliability coefficients are obtained by test-retest (same test is given twice with certain time intervals); alternate forms (equivalent tests are administered within certain time intervals); and internal consistency (results of one test are divided into parts referred to as split-half). The stability of a test is determined by coefficients of correlation that remain high over long intervals. Factors that affect stability are summarized by Peterson et al. (1991, pp. 127–128) as follows:

1. the stability of the human trait itself; for example, daily moods have low stability, whereas verbal aptitude has high stability
2. group differences, such as gender or ethnic background
3. individual differences within groups, such as genetic endowment, age, and learning
4. the nature of performance; for example, whether it is a maximum effort, as in an achievement test, compared with rating what is generally true, as in an interest inventory
5. the internal consistency of the test itself

Validity

According to the American Psychological Association standards for educational and psychological testing, validity refers to the meaningfulness and usefulness of certain inferences based on a test score derived from a test in question. Counselors need to answer whether a test measures what it purports to measure. For instance, does a nationally administered aptitude test measure success for the freshman year in a particular college when predicting that the chances are "good" that one's client will make a grade of "C" or better? This question and more should be asked about validity—more specifically, content validity, criterion validity, and construct validity.

Content validity involves opinions of experts about whether the items of a test or inventory represent the content domain of characteristics being measured. For instance, do test questions adequately sample measures of skills, abilities, values, interests, or personality? Measures of human traits such as personality, values, and interests require considerable understanding of traits that are to be measured and considerable skill in developing questions that successfully tap the universal content domain of such human traits.

Criterion validity is determined by the degree to which test scores predict success for outcome criteria. In predicting success in college, as cited earlier, aptitude test scores are related to the behavior (earned grades) during the first semester in college. Criterion-based interest inventories relate an individual's score with a normative group, such as geologists and ministers who are satisfied and stable in their occupations. The rationale is that individuals who have similar scores will experience satisfaction in those occupations.

Constructs developed from theory and research, such as cognitive ability and anxiety states, are related to test scores that are derived from tests or inventories developed to measure the defined construct. The result, the construct validity coefficient of correlation, provides the evidence that the interpretation of scores is associated with the theoretical implications of the construct label. For example, the construct of intelligence may include one's ability to build colored block designs within time intervals. This part of an intelligence test contributes to an overall score from which the IQ is derived. The point here is that counselors should evaluate carefully the focus of the construct and the items that are used to measure it.

In sum, selecting assessment instruments requires an understanding of psychometric concepts used in the development of standardized tests. As client and counselor collaborate on selecting tests, counselors should be able to explain the purpose of a test, what the test is designed to measure, why a certain test could be useful, how and why a test is considered a valid and reliable instrument, and how the results can be used to assist the client. Finally, the counselor must be certain that the test administration is appropriate for the client and the results fully account for the client's background and diversity.

Issues in Achieving Equity in Assessment

Changing demographic trends since the last quarter of the 20th century have transformed American society into a more diverse culture. More members of our society speak a second language other than English in their homes. We can expect to find that a significant number of children enter school without English language skills. Bernstein (2007), cited in Whiston (2009), points out that almost one in every 10 counties in the United States currently has a population that is 50% minority. We can expect to see periodic updates on these data, but clearly, the clientele of career counselors is changing and will continue to change as the national workforce grows more diverse (Higginbotham & Andersen, 2012).

Standardized tests must be used with caution or not used at all when assessment techniques, content, and norms are not applicable "because of an individual's gender, age, race ethnicity, national origin, religion, sexual orientation, disability, language, or socioeconomic status" (APA, 1992, p. 1601). It is not entirely clear at this time how test publishers will deal with the issues of diversity, but it should be clear to test users that each test must be chosen carefully for each client. Some helpful suggestions for counselors are briefly reviewed in the next sections.

Evaluating Adaptations and Translations of Assessment Instruments

Read the test manual carefully to determine if the client is a member of a group that has been included in the normative sample used for validity and reliability analysis. This information is often included in a separate publication from the test administration manual and is usually referred to as a technical information manual. Specifically, evaluate the test-taking sample and make notes about its composition.

Counselors should also obtain relevant background information about their clients, including if English is their dominant language, socioeconomic status, ethnicity, gender, and other variables. If there are language differences, counselors are to determine if a test version in the client's dominant language is available. One may have to contact test publishers for this information and it is also the counselor's responsibility to determine if a translated version is appropriate.

A translated version of a standardized assessment instrument is usually accomplished by translating the instrument from the original language to the target language, and this is followed by a "back translation": A second translator translates the version of the target language back to the original version. The extent to which they are comparable can best be assessed during this process; significant differences in word meanings can change the nature of a test and make it invalid. Keep in mind that cultural differences among individuals who grew up in different language environments can lead to different interpretations of what test questions are intended to evaluate (Geisinger, 1998; Whiston, 2013).

Adapted and accommodated versions of a test can also provide information that is helpful to the counselor, although there are numerous problems that must be solved. Adapting or accommodating an assessment instrument usually refers to changes made in the test administration, scoring, or norms to accommodate special groups. It is obviously important that the nature of the test or inventory should not be changed by an adaptation. Changes in the administration of a measuring instrument are also very relevant; for example, when a typical paper-and-pencil test is given verbally or by audiotape or the test time has been increased, one must evaluate its effect on the test results.

A second most important step is to determine the usefulness of the score report. Counselors are to determine if a significant proportion of members from the client's ethnic group were represented in the norm sample. It is most helpful if special population norms are available for the purpose of comparing assessment scores taken by Hispanics, for instance, with national norms. The major purpose here is to make test results as equitable as possible for all groups. One should be cautious, however, when interpreting scores from a sample of Hispanics or any other ethnic racial group. Be aware that ethnic racial groups such as Hispanics may share some cultural values and environmental influences, but they are not necessarily a homogenous group.

In sum, counselors should be skilled in evaluating assessment instruments and, more importantly, have resources available for this purpose. Most test-publishing companies now have 800 numbers, e-mail, and Internet access. Published materials can also be helpful, and a list is provided near the end of this chapter. Counselors should also be skilled in evaluating the unique characteristics of each client's environmental background. All clients have been shaped by cultures that are organized according to unique roles, rules, cultural values, behavior patterns, expectations, and interpersonal history (Cormier, Nurius, & Osborn, 2013; Matsumoto & Juang, 2013). Understanding how clients construct personal meanings from past experiences provides counselors with vital information for establishing accurate interpretations of test data. In the next section I continue our discussion about contextual issues that should be considered when using standardized assessments.

Evaluating Acculturation Contextual Issues

Finally, there is an important central concept, acculturation, that counselors should use in selecting and using assessment. This term refers to the adoption of beliefs, values, and practices of the host culture (Matsumoto and Juang, 2013; Ponterotto et al., 2010; Ridley, 2005). I will discuss this concept more in chapter 9, but in this context, acculturation contains contextual developmental issues that should be considered in assessment.

Table 6.1 displays a list of contextual assessment areas that should help assess a client's cultural transition, adaptation, and acculturation. An evaluation process of contextual areas is referred to as an ethnocultural assessment (Comas-Diaz & Grenier, 1998). Information is collected about a client's maternal and paternal cultures of origin, including countries of origin, religions, social class, languages, gender roles, sociopolitical factors, family roles, and biological factors, such as genetic predisposition to certain health problems. Recall that multidimensional forces influence the development of behavior (Durand & Barlow, 2013; Sue et al., 2014). Thus, a practical tool such as ethnocultural assessment should prove invaluable for establishing an assessment plan as well as a guide for appropriate interpretation of assessment results. What is suggested here is that counselors who are interpreting assessment results to multicultural groups should have a comprehensive knowledge of the client's culture (Matsumoto & Juang, 2013).

Table 6.1	**Contextual Assessment Areas**

1. Ethnocultural heritage
2. Racial and ethnocultural identities
3. Gender and sexual orientation
4. Socioeconomic status
5. Physical appearance, ability or disability
6. Religion when being raised and what now practicing, spiritual beliefs
7. Biological factors (genetic predisposition to certain illness, etc.)
8. Historical era, age cohort
9. Marital status, sexual history
10. History of (im)migration and generations from (im)migrations
11. Acculturation and transculturation levels
12. Family of origin and multigenerational history
13. Family scripts (roles of women and men, prescriptions for success or failure, etc.)
14. Individual and family life-cycle development and stages
15. Client's languages and those spoken by family of origin
16. History of individual abuse and trauma (physical; emotional; sexual; political including torture, oppression, and repression)
17. History of collective trauma (slavery, colonization, Holocaust)
18. Gender-specific issues such as battered wife syndrome
19. Recreations and hobbies, avocations, and special social roles
20. Historical and geopolitical reality of ethnic group and relationship with dominant group (including wars and political conflict)

SOURCE: From "Cultural Considerations in Diagnosis," pp. 159–160, by L. Comas-Diaz, in F. W. Kaslow (Ed.), *Handbook on Relational Diagnosis and Dysfunctional Family Patterns*. Copyright © 1996 by John Wiley & Sons, Inc. This material is used by permission of John Wiley & Sons, Inc.

Assessment Goals in Career Counseling

In this section, assessment goals will be followed by examples of assessment instruments on the current market. These examples should not be considered as endorsements of instruments for use with all clients. With advancing technology, we can expect continuous changes in how we use assessment (Kaplan & Saccuzzo, 2013). No doubt, many of the well-known and highly used instruments will continue to be popular and will be updated for use with all clients. Counselors should remain alert to new tests that have proved to be valid and reliable. More detailed information on the selection and use of career-related inventories can be found in the references in this text.

Assessment can be a part of the intake interview or follow it during which, among other goals, a collaborative client–counselor relationship is established. The role and implications of assessment should be delineated; counselors should make it clear that clients will be actively involved in the selection of each test and/or inventory. The standardized assessment instruments that follow are to be considered as examples of what may be available for meeting nine established goals.

Goal 1: Identifying Career Beliefs

The inventories and questionnaires used for this purpose reveal some of the client's beliefs about careers, dysfunctional thinking, decision-making styles, identity issues, maladaptive behaviors, degrees of anxiety, fear of failure, and reasons why people are undecided. Some of the inventories used are the following:

Career Beliefs Inventory
Consulting Psychologists Press
1055 Joaquin R., Suite 200
Mountain View, CA 94043
800-624-1765
Fax 650-969-8608
www.cpp-db.com

This inventory is used as a counseling tool to help clients identify career beliefs that can inhibit their abilities to make career decisions that are in their best interests. The results are computed for 25 scales under the following five headings: My Current Career Situation, What Seems Necessary for My Happiness, Factors That Influence My Decisions, Changes I Am Willing to Make, and Effort I Am Willing to Initiate. Norms are available for junior high school students, and separate norms are available for male and female employed adults. Scores can be interpreted in percentile ranks for each scale.

Career Thoughts Inventory
Psychological Assessment Resources, Inc.
16204 Florida Avenue
Lutz, FL 33549
800-331-8378
Fax 800-727-9329
www.parinc.com

This inventory is designed to measure the degree of a person's dysfunctional thinking and how that can affect the career decision-making process. The inventory consists of 48 items and 3 scales: Decision-Making Confusion, Commitment Anxiety, and External Conflict. The total score is an indicator of an individual's overall dysfunctional thinking.

This inventory can be used for high school and college students and adult clients. The reading level is sixth grade, and the inventory takes about 7 to 15 minutes to complete.

My Vocational Situation
Psychological Assessment Resources, Inc.
16204 N. Florida Avenue
Lutz, FL 33549
800-331-8378
Fax 800-727-9329
www.parinc.com

This inventory consists of three scales—Lack of Vocational Identity, Lack of Information or Training, and Emotional or Personal Barriers (that can cause problems). It can be completed in less than 10 minutes.

Identifying problems by assessment plays a major role in establishing rapport and determining intervention strategies during the first phase of counseling. Counselors who detect depression or anxiety will probably want to determine the level of severity by the use of assessment instruments. Scores on selected assessment instruments are used with other data to determine the content of intervention strategies.

Goal 2: Identifying Skills, Proficiencies, and Abilities

Aptitude tests primarily measure specific skills and proficiencies or the ability to acquire certain proficiencies. More specifically, aptitude test scores provide an index of measured skills that are intended to predict how well an individual may perform on a job or in an educational or training program. In addition, aptitude test scores indicate an individual's cognitive strengths and weaknesses, that is, differential abilities that provide an index to specific skills. For example, a measure of scholastic aptitude tells us the probability of success in educational programs. A clerical aptitude test score provides an index of ability to perform clerical duties. In the former example, we are informed of combinations of aptitudes that predict scholastic success, whereas in the latter we are provided with more specific measures of skills needed to perform well on a specific job.

Aptitude tests may be purchased as batteries measuring a number of aptitudes and skills or as single tests measuring specific aptitudes. Combinations of battery scores provide prediction indexes for certain educational or training criteria, as well as performance criteria on certain occupations that require combinations of skills. An example of an aptitude battery is the *General Aptitude Test Battery* (GATB) published by the U.S. Department of Labor (1970b). This test was originally developed by the U.S. Employment Service for state employment counselors. The GATB measures the following nine aptitudes: intelligence, verbal, numerical, spatial, form perception, clerical perception, motor coordination, finger dexterity, and manual dexterity.

Other aptitude tests published as single-test booklets measure a wide range of specific skills, including dexterity, mechanical comprehension, occupational attitude, clerical aptitude, design judgment, art aptitude, and musical talent.

Although aptitude tests primarily provide a basis for predicting success in an occupation or in training programs, they can also be used as counseling tools for career exploration. In this approach, measured individual traits provide a good frame of reference for evaluating learning needs. The following sample cases illustrate the use of aptitude test batteries:

• Susan is a senior in high school and does not plan to attend college. She is interested in obtaining work after graduation from high school. Her academic record indicates she is an average student with no particular strengths evidenced by academic grades. Her interests have not crystallized to the point at which she would be able to specify a particular occupational interest. Several assessment inventories were administered, including a complete battery of aptitude tests. These scores were used to discover areas of specific strengths and weaknesses for inclusion in Susan's career exploration program. Identification of specific aptitudes was seen as a stimulus for discovering potential career considerations.

- Ron is returning to the workforce after a serious head injury received in a car accident. During several months of recovery, his previous job in construction work was terminated. He is now interested in "looking for other kinds of work." An aptitude battery was administered to determine possible deficits resulting from the head injury. As the counselor suspected, the test scores indicated poor finger and manual dexterity. Jobs requiring fine visual–motor coordination were to be eliminated from consideration in career exploration.

In Susan's case, aptitude scores provided the stimulus for the discussion of measured aptitudes along with other materials used in career counseling. Susan was provided with a specific focus in career exploration. Ron's deficiencies were found and considerable time in career exploration was saved. Following are representative examples of multiple aptitude test batteries available on the market today:

The Differential Aptitude Test (DAT)
Pearson Assessment
800-328-5999
EACustomerService@Pearson.com
http://www.pearsonassessments.com/

This test consists of eight subtests: Verbal Reasoning, Numerical Ability, Abstract Reasoning, Spatial Relations, Mechanical Reasoning, Clerical Speed and Accuracy, Spelling, and Language Usage. The entire battery takes more than three hours to administer. This battery was designed primarily for use with high school and college students. When verbal and numerical scores are combined, a scholastic aptitude score is created. Other subtests are used for vocational and educational planning.

The General Aptitude Test Battery (GATB)
U.S. Employment Service
Washington, DC 20210
(Call your regional employment agencies)

This battery is composed of eight paper-and-pencil tests and four apparatus tests. Nine abilities are measured by the 12 tests: intelligence, verbal aptitude, numerical aptitude, spatial aptitude, form perception, clerical perception, motor coordination, finger dexterity, and manual dexterity. This test is administered to senior high school students and adults. Testing time is two and a half hours. Test results may be used for vocational and educational counseling and placement. This test is available to the public through nonprofit agencies, such as Rehabilitation Offices, and in schools.

Flanagan Aptitude Classification Tests (FACT)
J. C. Flanagan
Pearson Reid London House
3361 Rouse Road
Suite 225

Orlando, FL 32617
800-922-7343

This test consists of 16 subtests: Inspection, Coding, Memory, Precision, Assembly, Scales, Coordination, Judgment/Comprehension, Arithmetic, Patterns, Components, Tables, Mechanics, Expression, Reasoning, and Ingenuity. Each test measures behaviors considered critical to job performance. Selected groups of tests may be administered. The entire battery takes several hours. This test is designed primarily for use with high school students and adults.

Armed Services Vocational Aptitude Battery (ASVAB)
ASVAB Career Exploration Program
Defense Manpower Data Center
400 Gigling Road
Seaside, CA 93955
831-583-2400
www.asvabprogram.com

The ASVAB 19 consists of 10 short tests: Coding Speed, Word Knowledge, Paragraph Comprehension, Arithmetic Reasoning, Mathematics Knowledge, Electronic Information, Mechanical Comprehension, Auto and Shop Information, Electronics Information, and General Science. The test yields scores on each subtest and a composite score for academic ability, verbal ability, and mathematical ability. A workbook provides information for interpreting scores. A computer-adapted version will shorten the time needed to take the test.

Goal 3: Identifying Academic Achievement

Achievement tests are designed primarily to assess present levels of developed abilities. Current functioning and basic academic skills, such as arithmetic, reading, and language usage, are relevant to planning for educational intervention strategies. Academic proficiency has long been a key factor in career planning for individuals considering higher education; however, basic academic competencies are also major determinants in qualifying for certain occupations. For example, identified academic competencies and deficiencies are major considerations for placement of training of school dropouts. Achievement test results provide important information to be included in programs for adults who are entering, returning to, or recycling through the workforce. Changing technology and economic conditions will force many workers to enter programs to upgrade their skills or to train for completely different positions. Assessment of present levels of abilities will be needed to determine the possible scope of career exploration for these individuals.

For our use in career counseling programs, consider achievement tests in three categories: (1) general survey battery; (2) single-subject tests; and (3) diagnostic batteries. The general survey battery measures knowledge of most subjects taught in school and is standardized on the same population. The single-subject test, as the name implies, measures knowledge of only one subject/content area. Diagnostic batteries measure knowledge of specific proficiencies such as reading, spelling, and arithmetic achievement.

The use of achievement tests in career counseling is illustrated in the two cases that follow. In the first example, achievement test results are used to assist a student in determining a college major. In the second example, a diagnostic battery is used to assist a woman who is returning to the workforce after several years of being a homemaker.

- Juan is a senior in high school who is considering college, but he cannot decide between biology and chemistry as a major. All other factors being equal as far as career opportunities are concerned, the decision is made to determine in which one of the science courses Juan has excelled. The counselor and Juan selected single-subject tests in biology and chemistry, as these tests are relatively more thorough and precise than the general survey battery and the diagnostic battery. Thus, single-subject achievement tests provide a more thorough evaluation of specific subject abilities for Juan's consideration.

- Betty quit school when she was in the sixth grade. After several years of marriage, she was deserted by her husband and is now seeking employment. Previous test data reveal that she is of at least average intelligence. After careful review of alternatives by counselor and client, a diagnostic battery was selected for the specific purpose of determining basic arithmetic skills and reading and spelling levels. Both client and counselor were especially interested in determining academic deficiencies for educational planning; that is, consideration should be given to upgrading basic skills for eventual training for a high school equivalency. This information was seen as essential for both educational and career planning.

Because of the wide range of achievement tests on the market today, individual tests will not be listed here. Instead, the following are representative major publishers of achievement tests:

CTB-Macmillan-McGraw-Hill
20 Ryan Ranch Road
Monterey, CA 93940
800-538-9547
Fax 800-383-0366
www.ctb.com

Educational Testing Service
P.O. Box 6736
Princeton, NJ 08540
609-406-5050
www.ets.org

Houghton Mifflin Company
222 Berkeley Street
Boston, MA 02116
800-225-3362
www.hmco.com

Harcourt Assessment
19500 Bulverde Road
San Antonio, TX 78259
800-211-8378
Fax 800-232-1223
www.harcourtassessment.com

Riverside Publishing Company
425 Spring Lake Drive

Itasca, IL 60143-2079
800-323-9540
Fax 630-467-7192
www.riverpub.com

Goal 4: Identifying and Confirming Interest Levels

A considerable body of literature has been published on the subject of gender bias and unfairness in career interest measurement. The National Institute of Education (NIE) published guidelines as early as 1975 that identified gender bias as "any factor that might influence a person to limit—or might cause others to limit—his or her consideration of a career solely on the basis of gender" (Diamond, 1975, p. xxiii).

According to Diamond (1975; Whiston, 2013), the guidelines have led to some progress in reducing gender bias in interest inventories by calling for fairness in the construction of item pools as follows:

Items such as statements, questions, and names of occupations used in the inventory should be designed so as not to limit the consideration of a career solely on the basis of gender.

[Fairness in the presentation of technical information.]

Technical information should include evidence that the inventory provides career options for both males and females.

[Fairness in interpretive procedures.]

Interpretive procedures should provide methods of equal treatment of results for both sexes (p. xxiii)

Generally, the guidelines were designed to encourage both sexes to consider all career and educational opportunities and eliminate sex-role stereotyping by those using interest inventory results in the career counseling process. Moreover, counselors are not to assume that there is fairness in interest inventory item pools. Thus, the debate about sex bias in interest inventories has focused on the question of whether men and women have different interests. What is most important here, however, is that men and women may differ in the way they respond, react, or endorse interest inventory items (Swanson & Fouad, 2010; Whiston, 2013).

What is being suggested here is that interest inventory results might not reflect actual differences between men and women for occupational groups or specific occupations. What is being called for is an evaluation of interest inventory items to determine if they appropriately represent interests of both genders. Most important to this argument is that interest inventory items should not be based only on male perspectives. We can expect further research on the imbalance of attention given to men over women in the study of interest development.

In the meantime, interest inventories have long been associated with career counseling. Two of the most widely used were the *Strong Interest Inventory (SII)*, originally developed by E. K. Strong (1983), and the Kuder interest inventories, developed by G. F. Kuder (1963). Currently, Holland's (1992) approach to interest identification (as discussed in chapter 2) has received considerable attention. For example, a number of interest inventories—including the SII, the *American College Testing Program Interest Inventory,* and the *Self-Directed Search* (Holland, 1987a)—are constructed to correspond with Holland's personality types and corresponding work environments. In most inventories, interests are primarily designated by responses to compiled lists of occupations and lists of activities associated with occupations. The rationale is that individuals having interest patterns similar to those found in an occupational group would probably find satisfaction in that particular occupational group.

Following are some representative examples of interest inventories:

Kuder Occupational Interest Survey
National Career Assessment Services, Inc.
210 N 10th St.
P.O. Box 277
Adel, IA 50003
515-993-3005
Fax 515-993-5422
www.kuder.com

This survey is computer scored and consists of 109 occupational scales, 40 college-major scales, and 8 experimental scales. Recommended uses of the inventory include selection, placement, and career exploration. The survey is untimed, usually taking 30 to 40 minutes. Norms are based on samples of data from college seniors.

Self-Directed Search (SDS)
Psychological Assessment Resources, Inc.
16204 N. Florida Avenue
Lutz, FL 33549
800-331-8378
Fax 800-727-9329
www.parinc.com

This interest inventory is based on Holland's (1992) theory of career development. It is self-administered and self-scored, as well as self-interpreted, and takes approximately 30 to 40 minutes to complete. The scores are organized to reveal an occupational code or a summary code of three letters representing the personality types and environmental models from Holland's typology: Realistic, Investigative, Artistic, Social, Enterprising, and Conventional. This inventory is used with high school and college students and with adults.

The Strong Instrument
Consulting Psychologists Press
1055 Joaquin R., Suite 200
Mountain View, CA 94043
800-624-1765
Fax 650-969-8608
www.cpp-db.com

This inventory combines the male and female versions of the *Strong Vocational Interest Blank* into one survey. The interpretation of scores is based on Holland's typology. The interpretation format includes 6 general occupational themes, 23 basic interest scales, and 124 occupational scales. Administrative indexes include an academic-orientation index and an introversion-extroversion index. The time to complete is about 30 to 40 minutes. Both male and female occupational scale scores are available.

Career Assessment Inventory (CAI)
Pearson Assessments
P.O. Box 1416
Minneapolis, MN 55440
800-627-7271
Fax 800-632-9011
www.pearsonassessments.com

This computer-scored inventory can be administered in approximately 45 minutes. It is designed for eighth-grade students through adults. General occupational theme scales, basic interest scales, and occupational scales are reported. This inventory is primarily used with noncollege-bound individuals.

Wide Range Interest and Opinion Test
Wide Range
P.O. Box 3410
Wilmington, DE 19804
800-221-9728
Fax 302-652-1644
www.widerange.com

This test consists of 150 sets of three pictures from which the individual is asked to indicate likes and dislikes. The pictures depict activities ranging from unskilled labor to the highest levels of technical, managerial, and professional training. The test evaluates educational and vocational interests of a wide range of individuals, including the educationally disadvantaged and the developmentally disabled.

The Campbell Interest and Skill Survey (CISS)
Pearson Assessments
P.O. Box 1416
Minneapolis, MN 55440
800-627-7271
Fax 800-632-9011
www.pearsonassessments.com

This instrument is part of a new integrated battery of psychological surveys that currently includes the CISS, an attitude-satisfaction survey, and a measure of leadership characteristics. Two other instruments, a team development survey and a community survey, are being developed and will complete this integrated battery. The CISS, developed for individuals 15 years and older with a sixth-grade reading level, has 200 interest and 120 skill items on a 6-point response scale. The results yield parallel interest and skill scores: orientation scales (e.g., influencing, organizing, helping, creating, analyzing, producing, and adventuring); basic scales (e.g., leadership, supervision, counseling, and international activities); occupational scales (e.g., financial planner, translator/interpreter, and landscape architect). Special scales measure academic comfort and extroversion.

Goal 5: Discovering Personality Variables

Major career theorists have emphasized personality development as a major factor to be considered in career development. For example, Roe (1956) long ago postulated that early personality development associated with family interactions influences vocational direction. Super (1990) devoted considerable attention to self-concept development. Tiedeman and O'Hara (1963) considered total cognitive development in decision making. Holland's (1992) system of career selection is directly related to personality types and styles. The case for the use of personality inventories in career counseling programs seems well established.

The development of the *Sixteen Personality Factor Questionnaire* (16 PF) by Cattell et al. (1970) led the way for integrating personality inventories into career counseling programs. Vocational personality patterns and occupational fitness are considered major components of this questionnaire. The 16 factors measured by the 16 PF are "source" traits or factors, which are derived from early studies of distinct combinations of an individual's personality traits (Cattell et al.). These traits are compared with occupational profiles and provide vocational observations and occupational fitness projections. Vocational observations include information concerning the individual's potential for leadership and interpersonal skills and potential benefits from academic training. Occupational fitness projections rank how the individual compares with specific occupational profiles from extremely high to extremely low. Specific source traits are recorded for each occupational profile available, providing a comparison of characteristic traits common to individuals employed in certain occupations. The 16 PF is singled out because a major portion of the inventory development was devoted to vocational personality patterns and occupational fitness projections. Throughout this text, references are made to the importance of satisfying individual needs associated with work, family, and leisure. Within this frame of reference, individual personality patterns greatly assist in identifying and clarifying each individual's needs. Personality inventories provide valuable information for identifying needs and providing a stimulus for career exploration. The following examples demonstrate the use of personality inventories in career counseling:

- Ahmed reports that he is quite frustrated in his present working environment and is considering changing jobs. His unhappiness has caused family problems and social problems in general. His performance ratings by his superiors were high until the last two years, when they dropped to average. Assessment results indicate that he is interested in his current job as accountant and a personality inventory indicated a strong need for achievement. In consultation with his counselor, Ahmed stated that he was still interested in the field of accounting, but in his current position, he was not able to meet his needs to achieve and he was frustrated with the repetitive work in his current position. Earlier, these needs were apparently met from positive reinforcement received from high ratings by his superiors. At this point in his life, however, Ahmed was searching for something more than "just doing a good job of bookkeeping." Recognizing his source of frustration, he decided to stay in accounting but moved to another division in the firm.

- Shayna had definitely decided that she was interested in an occupation that would provide her with an opportunity to help people. A personality inventory indicated that she was very reserved, and nonassertive, and deferred to others. She agreed with the results of the personality inventory and further agreed that these characteristics would make it difficult for her to accomplish her occupational goal. Shayna became convinced that she would have to modify these personality characteristics through a variety of programs, including self-discovery groups, assertiveness training, and cognitive restructuring.

In these two example cases, personality inventory results provided the impetus and stimulation for action to meet individual career needs. In the first example, Ahmed recognized a motivational drive that he had repressed for years as the major source of his frustrations. Fortunately, he was able to meet his needs to achieve in another division of the firm in which he was employed. In the second example, Shayna chose to keep her career goal but increased her chances of success with further training. These examples provide only two illustrations of the use of personality inventories in career counseling but clearly establish their potential usefulness. Personality inventories provide important information that can be incorporated into group or individual counseling programs to assist individuals with career-related problems.

Representative examples of personality inventories follow.

California Test of Personality
CTB-Macmillan-McGraw-Hill
20 Ryan Ranch Road
Monterey, CA 93940
800-538-9547
Fax 800-282-0266
www.ctb.com

Five levels of the test are available: primary, elementary, intermediate, secondary, and adult. The test assesses personal and social adjustment. Subscale scores are provided for the two major categories. The test is used primarily in career counseling to assess measures of personal worth and of family and school relations.

Minnesota Counseling Inventory
Harcourt Assessments
19500 Bulverde Rd.
San Antonio, TX 78259
800-211-8378
Fax 800-232-1223
www.harcourt assessments.com

This inventory was designed to measure adjustment of boys and girls in grades 9 through 12. Scores yield criterion-related scales as follows: family relationship, social relationship, emotional stability, conformity, adjustment to reality, mood, and leadership. Scales are normed separately for boys and girls. These scores provide indexes to important relationships and personal characteristics to be considered in career counseling programs.

NEO Personality Inventory-3
Psychological Assessment Resources
16204 N. Florida Avenue
Lutz, FL 33549
800-331-8378
Fax 800-727-9329
www, parinc.com

The NEO-PI-R is also known as the Big Five Personality Inventory. The results of this inventory include five structures or domains of personality: Neuroticism, Extraversion, Openness, Agreeableness, and Conscientiousness. The meaning of each of the domains is further delineated by facets or subscale scores. A bipolar profile presents the meaning one can derive from elevated and/or low scores for each domain. One focuses on combinations of five big factor scores and their subscales. There is some evidence to support the claim that these five personality factors are universal.

Sixteen Personality Factor (16 PF)
Institute for Personality and Ability Testing Inc.
1801 Woodfield Drive
Savoy, IL 61874
800-225-4728

Fax 217-352-9647
www.ipat.com

This instrument measures 16 personality factors of individuals 16 years or older. A major part of this questionnaire has been devoted to identifying personality patterns related to occupational fitness projections. These projections provide a comparison of the individual's profile with samples of occupational profiles. The instrument is hand scored or computer scored. Four forms have an average adult vocabulary; two forms are available for low-literacy groups.

Temperament and Values Inventory
Pearson Assessments
P.O. Box 1416
Minneapolis, MN 55440
800-627-7271
Fax 800-632-9011
www.pearsonassessments.com

This inventory has two parts: (1) temperament dimensions of personality related to career choice, and (2) values related to work rewards. The inventory has an eighth-grade reading level and is not recommended for use below the ninth grade. The inventory is untimed and computer scored. Scores help determine congruence or incongruence with an individual's career aspirations.

Myers-Briggs Type Indicator
Consulting Psychologists Press, Inc.
1055 Joaquin R. Suite 200
Mountain View, CA 94043
800-624-1765
Fax 650-969-8608
www.cpp-db.com

This inventory measures individual preferences by personality types: extroversion or introversion; sensing or intuition; thinking or feeling; and judging or perceiving. Scores are determined according to the four categories. The publisher's manual provides descriptions of the 16 possible types (combinations). Occupations that are attractive to each type are presented in the appendixes. This inventory provides direct references to occupational considerations based on one's personality type.

Goal 6: Determining Values

During the last three decades, much has been written about beliefs and values. One of the major career counseling goals is to help others find congruence with the inseparables—work and life. Thus, one is to emphasize the relevance of a balanced lifestyle with the use of value inventory results. Career counselors may want to classify values inventories into two types: (1) inventories that primarily measure work values, and (2) inventories that measure values associated with broader aspects of lifestyle. Work value inventories, as the name implies, are designed to measure values associated with job success and satisfaction (achievement, prestige, security, and creativity).

Other measured values found to be high priorities for some clients provide another dimension of information that can be used in career exploration. Thus, both types of inventories provide information that can be especially helpful for clarifying individual needs associated with work, home, family, and leisure. Following are representative examples of work values inventories:

Work Environment Preference Schedule

Harcourt Assessments
19500 Bulverde Rd.
San Antonio, TX 78259
800-211-8378
Fax 800-232-1223
www.harcourtassessments.com

This inventory measures an individual's adaptability to a bureaucratic organization. It is untimed and self-administered. A total score reflects the individual's commitment to the sets of attitudes, values, and behaviors found in bureaucratic organizations. Separate norms by sex are available for high school, college, and Army ROTC students.

Work Values Inventory (WVI)

Houghton Mifflin Company
222 Berkeley Street
Boston, MA 02116
800-225-3362
www.hmco.com

This inventory measures the sources of satisfaction individuals seek from their work environments. Scores yield measures of altruism, aesthetics, creativity, intellectual stimulation, independence, prestige, management, economic returns, security, surroundings, supervisory relations, value of relationship with associates, way of life, and variety. Norms are provided by grade and sex for students in grades 7 through 12. The scores provide dimensions of work values that can be combined with other considerations in career counseling.

Following are representative examples of other value inventories:

Study of Values

Houghton Mifflin Company
222 Berkeley Street
Boston, MA 02116
800-225-3362
www.hmco.com

This self-administered inventory measures individual values in six categories: theoretical, economic, aesthetic, social, political, and religious. Norms are provided by sex for high school, college, and various occupational groups. The measured strength of values (indicated as high, average, or low) provides points of reference for individual and group counseling programs.

Survey of Personal Values

Pearson Reid London House
3363 Rouse Rd., Suite 225
Orlando, FL 32817
800-992-7343
www.pearsonreidlondonhouse.com

This inventory measures values that influence how individuals cope with daily problems. Scores yield measures of practical mindedness, achievement, variety, decisiveness, orderliness, and goal orientation. The inventory is self-administered. National percentile norms are available for college students, and regional norms are available for high school students.

The Values Scale
Consulting Psychologists Press, Inc.
1055 Joaquin Rd., Suite 200
Mountain View, CA 94043
800-624-1765
Fax 650-969-8608
www.cpp-db.com

This scale measures 21 values: ability utilization, achievement, advancement, aesthetics, altruism, authority, autonomy, creativity, economic rewards, lifestyle, personal development, physical activity, prestige, risk, social interaction, social relations, variety, working conditions, cultural identity, physical prowess, and economic security. The measures are designed to help individuals understand values in relation to life roles and evaluate the importance of the work role with other life roles. Scores are interpreted by using percentile equivalents. Norms are available for high school and university students and adults.

Goal 7: Exploring Career Maturity Variables

Career maturity inventories—also referred to as career development inventories—measure vocational development as specified dimensions from which one is judged to be vocationally mature. The dimensions of career maturity are derived from career development concepts. That is, vocational maturity, like career choice, is a continuous development process that can be segmented into a series of stages and tasks (Crites, 1973; Savickas, 2002; Super, 1957). Super views the process of career choice on a continuum with "exploration" and "decline" as endpoints. Career maturity or adaptability is considered the degree of vocational development measurable within this continuum. Super also measured career maturity within several dimensions: orientation toward work (attitudinal dimension); planning (competency dimension); consistency of vocational preferences (consistency dimension); and wisdom of vocational preferences (realistic dimension). These dimensions identify progressive steps of career development and determine the degree of development relative to normative age levels.

Following is a list of representative career maturity inventories:

Career Development Inventory
Consulting Psychologists Press, Inc.
1055 Joaquin RD., Suite 200
Mountain View, CA 94043
800-624-1765
Fax 650-969-8608
www.cpp-db.com

This inventory is a diagnostic tool for developing individual or group counseling procedures; it can also be used to evaluate career development programs. Scores yield measures of planning orientation, readiness for exploration, information, and decision making. The reading level is sixth grade, and the inventory applies to both sexes. Both cognitive and attitudinal scales are provided.

Career Maturity Inventory (CMI)
Psychological Assessment Resources, Inc.
16204 North Florida Avenue

Lutz, FL 33549
800-331-8378
Fax 800-727-9329
www.parinc.com

The 1995 edition of the CMI yields three scores: Attitude Scale, Competence Test, and Overall Career Maturity. The test can be both hand-scored and machine-scored. The CMI is designed to be used with students from grades 6 through 12 and with adults.

Cognitive Vocational Maturity Test (CVMT)
Center for Occupational Education
North Carolina State University
Raleigh, NC 27607
www.store.ets.org

This test is primarily a cognitive measure of an individual's knowledge of occupational information. Scores yield measures of knowledge of fields of work available, job selection procedures, work conditions, educational requirements, specific requirements for a wide range of occupations, and actual duties performed in a variety of occupations. This inventory provides important information about career choice abilities and can be used as a diagnostic tool for curricula and guidance needs.

Adult Career Concerns Inventory
Consulting Psychologists Press, Inc.
1055 Joaquin Rd., Suite 200
Mountain View, CA 94043
800-624-1765
Fax 650-969-8608
www.cpp-db.com

Three major purposes are listed for this inventory: career counseling and planning; needs analysis; and measuring relationships between adult capability, and previous and concurrent socioeconomic and psychological characteristics. Scores are related to career development tasks at various life stages as follows: exploration, establishment, maintenance, disengagement, retirement planning, and retirement living. Norms are available by age, starting at 25, by combined sexes, and by age groups and sex.

The Salience Inventory
Consulting Psychologists Press, Inc.
1055 Joaquin Rd., Suite 20
Mountain View, CA 94043
800-624-1765
Fax 650-969-8608
www.cpp-db.com

This instrument is designed to measure the importance one assigns to five major life roles: student, worker, homemaker, leisurite, and citizen. Inventory results provide counselors with an evaluation of an individual's orientation to life roles and the readiness for career decisions and exposure to work and occupations.

Goal 8: Using Computer-Based Assessment: Computer-Based Guidance Systems (CACG) and Online Systems

During the last three decades, the use of computer-based assessment has steadily increased. One primary reason for the growth is that results are immediately available to clients. Computer-based assessment programs also interpret results to clients by occupational fit with lists of career options. However, some concerns about the validity of instruments in computer-based assessment have been expressed by independent researchers (Sampson, 1994; Sampson & Pyle, 1983; Whiston, 2013) and by professional organizations such as the American Psychological Association. Significant problems associated with computer-based assessment include various forms of instrument validity, scoring, search, and interpretative functions. Be aware that validity of any assessment system should meet the same set of standards used for other psychometric measures. The validity of scoring standardized instruments, for example, includes weighting items into scales and ensuring error-free scoring. However, errors in these two processes are difficult to identify in computer-based assessment. Thus, career service providers might not be aware of potential errors and subsequent misleading results (Whiston, 2013).

Finally, interpretative statements generated by computer-based testing systems should be evaluated carefully for their validity; one must ask for some proof that they are indeed valid results that clients can understand fully and apply to their search processes. As computer-based assessment continues to grow, career service providers must insist that system developers and independent researchers meet the testing standards that have been clearly defined by the American Psychological Association. Evidence of valid testing standards should be clearly delineated in promotional materials, as well as in professional manuals. For more information on computer-based assessment, see chapter 7.

The primary purpose of using standardized assessments instruments in career counseling has been to empower clients to make rational decisions. I have also made it quite clear that standardized assessment instruments may not be appropriate for all members of a diverse society. Alternative methods of fostering self-knowledge can be accomplished through self-estimates of traits. One is to recognize that self-assessment is a means of learning more about oneself through self-observation of current and previous learning experiences and/or through nontraditional measuring instruments and exercises. Self-assessment of traits should be focused in order to increase one's self-awareness and to provide direction for expanding growth. Counselors should inform clients of the purpose and techniques used in the self-assessment process. The outcome of this process should enable clients to have greater control and direction of the career counseling process. See *Using Assessment Results for Career Development* (9th ed.) by Osborn and Zunker (2012) for more information.

Self-Assessment Procedures for Career Counseling

This section will provide some examples for encouraging and stimulating self-assessment. Counselors should use these methods as examples from which they can develop their own procedures to meet the unique needs of each client. Clients who can conceptualize the purpose of self-assessment should be more willing to participate in the process. Counselor and client agree to the purpose of, and need for, each procedure in counseling; therefore clients also collaborate in the selection process of nontraditional assessment measures. Some examples follow.

Autobiography

Counselors may find that an autobiography helps complement the intake interview. The autobiography is usually written but can be given orally. Counselors instruct clients to simply "write an autobiography of your life" with no further instructions. The unstructured autobiography has the advantage of leaving the subjects of the response up to the client. The disadvantage is that clients may choose to avoid subjects that could be significant. Thus, one may also suggest a structured outline to follow in composing the autobiography, or write a work autobiography.

Focused Questions to Uncover Specific Variables

Counselors may develop specific questions that can be used to tap subjects of importance revealed in the interview or from other background information. Counselors can introduce clients to such questions by pointing out the value of discussing significant influences from contextual variables. Some examples follow.

How did you become who you are?

What does your family want you to do?

Father? Mother? Siblings? Uncle and aunt? Others?

Who has been the most influential person in your life? How?

What do you predict will be your career (job) (work) in the future?

What have others (friends, family, teachers, etc.) told you your career should be?

In outline format, trace the development of your interests and abilities.

What were some major events in your life?

Make a list of your likes and dislikes and relate them to your experiences.

Compose a list of your most significant problems. Circle those that are most troublesome.

Such probing questions and exercises were designed to focus attention on relevant contextual interactions and the messages the client received from them. Clients self-assess the major influences and relate them to interests, skills, personality, and vocational identity for further evaluation.

Interest Identification

Goodman (1993) presents an intriguing method of assessing interests.* Clients are presented activities she has devised to stimulate their desire to know more about their interests.

Clients are instructed to write down 20 things they like to do. They can list activities done at work; leisure activities, such as movies, parties, and reading; or taking classes. The following code is assigned to each interest listed:

1. Put a T next to the activities that you would enjoy with additional training.
2. Put an R next to each item that involves risk—physical, emotional, or intellectual.
3. Put a PL beside those items that require planning.
4. Indicate with an A or a P or an A/P whether you prefer to do the activity *alone, with people,* or *both.*
5. Next to each activity, put the date when you last engaged in it.
6. Star your five favorite activities.

---

*From "Using Nonstandardized Appraisal Tools and Techniques," presentation to Michigan Career Development Association Annual Conference. April 29, 1993, Kalamazoo, MI. Reprinted by permission of J. Goodman.

Each activity provides the counselor and client with relevant subjects for discussion and evaluation of their significance. Clients are encouraged to draw conclusions from each statement through self-assessment and relate it to interests. Other examples of techniques used to encourage clients to self-assess interests include the following:

1. Develop a list of at least 10 role models. Explain why you selected each model and relate your choices to interests.
2. List five occupations you like and five you do not like.
3. List the types of activities you enjoy.
4. List the school subjects you like most and least.
5. List your favorite TV programs, magazines, and books.

In sum, interests can be identified through a variety of questions and exercises that require clients to be active participants. Many of the suggested exercises can be done in groups and have the advantage of group interactions; however, some clients may be more comfortable when relating environmental contextual interactions to counselors who have established a trusting relationship with them.

Card Sorts

Card sorts are another method of determining interests. Clients sort cards that have the name and description of an occupation on them into three categories: "Would Not Choose," "Would Choose," and "No Opinion." Counselor and client discuss all categories and identify common themes that emerge. Clients relate interests and common themes to their backgrounds.

Counselors should be aware that card sorts are also available for identifying values, hobbies, skills, and personality characteristics.

Lifeline—A Career Life Planning Experience

This exercise requires the client to draw a line from birth to death and indicate on it key life experiences and present position. The major purpose of this exercise is to actively involve clients in concentrating on future tasks and life planning. The following exercise was used at Colorado State University to prompt self-awareness and the recognition that each individual has certain responsibilities in developing his or her future:

Exercise	Purpose
Lifeline	To identify past and current situations in life
Identifying and stripping of roles	To become free of all previous roles by temporarily discarding them
Fantasy time	To develop more self-awareness when free of identified roles
Typical day and a special day in the future	To further crystallize self-awareness and individual need for the future when free of identified roles
Life inventory	To identify specific needs and goals with emphasis on identifying each individual's positive characteristics
News release	To further clarify specific interests and future accomplishments desired

Resume goals	To clarify or reformulate goals while reassuming originally identified roles
Goal setting	To set realistic short-term and long-term goals

This exercise has been recommended for use with groups primarily for the purpose of group interaction.

Guided Fantasy—An Exercise to Increase Self-Awareness

Brown and Brooks (1991) point out that guided fantasy should not be used with all clients; some may be unwilling to participate for a variety of reasons. In a literature review, however, Skovholt, Morgan, and Negron-Cunningham (1989), as cited in Brown and Brooks (1991), report that guided fantasy has been used successfully for more than 60 years with clients of different age levels, sexes, and cultural groups.

One major purpose of guided fantasy is to uncover subconscious material that can be used in career decision making (Cormier et al., 2013; Skovholt et al., 1989). Spokane (1991) suggests that mental imagery does increase self-awareness and encourages expressions of aspirations that could go undetected. The purpose and procedure for this exercise suggest that clients will express their needs and desires openly when they are free of perceived restraints. The procedures for guided imagery include the following:

1. Induce relaxation through Jacobson's relaxation techniques.
2. Establish the fantasy itself, such as a day on the job or my workplace in the future.
3. Discuss the reactions to the fantasy.

Skills Identification

Skills identification through self-assessment techniques has received renewed attention (Bolles, 2000; Brown & Brooks, 1991; Holland, 1992). The focus is on identifying skills from previous experiences in a number of activities including work, hobbies, and volunteer work. The rationale for this objective is that clients may fail to recognize skills they have developed through experiences and also do not know how to relate them to occupational requirements (Bolles, 2009).

The Self-Directed Search (Holland, 1992) includes a section in which clients evaluate themselves on 12 different traits based on previous experience. In addition, Brown and Brooks (1991) suggest several methods involving self-assessment of skills. Specific skills identification encourages clients to consider skills developed from a variety of experiences as important factors in career exploration. Most intervention strategies stress skill identification from the individual's total lifestyle experiences.

Some computerized career counseling programs are designed to identify client skills by having clients self-rate their abilities according to well-constructed scales such as top 10% as high, upper 25% as above average, middle 50% as average, and bottom 10% as low. Thus, users rate a variety of skills according to this scale. Be aware that clients who have limited opportunities to use skills could have some difficulty in ranking themselves. In these cases, counselors can provide opportunities for clients to try out and improve their existing skills and to learn new ones.

In sum, counselors may personalize numerous nontraditional methods of self-assessment to meet the unique needs of their clients. These procedures provide an alternative assessment process when standardized assessment is not appropriate.

Nontraditional methods can also be used as an initial assessment to assist clients in recognizing additional evaluation needs. Finally, self-assessment results should help clients recognize the relevance of self-knowledge and career awareness. In the final section of this chapter, selected references are listed to assist counselors in evaluating standard assessment instruments.

Information About Assessment Instruments

Numerous publications can help you gather information about career assessment instruments, including the following:

> *Mental Measurements Yearbook*
> Buros Institute of Mental Measurements
> University of Nebraska Press
> 135 Bancroft Hall
> Lincoln, NE 68588-0348
> www.unl.edu/buros

> *Test in Print*
> Buros Institute of Mental Measurements
> University of Nebraska Press
> 135 Bancroft Hall
> Lincoln, NE 68588-0348

> *Tests*
> Psychological Assessment Online
> nww.wso.net/assessment
> ERIC Clearinghouse of Assessment and Evaluation
> http://ericae.net/testcol.htm

Summary

1. Standardized tests and assessment inventories have been closely associated with career counseling. Skills, aptitudes, interests, values, achievements, personality characteristics, and vocational maturity are among the assessment objectives of career counseling.
2. The use of standardized assessment procedures in career counseling provides the client with increased options and alternatives, subsequently encouraging greater individual involvement in the career decision process. In career counseling programs, assessment scores are used with other materials to stimulate and enhance career exploration.
3. There is a growing concern about the appropriate use of assessment results for diverse groups that were not included in a test's standardization and validation. Professional groups have issued guidelines to assist test users and developers.
4. Reliability and validity are two psychometric concepts that counselors must evaluate when selecting assessment instruments.

5. Issues involved in achieving equity in assessment include a wide range of variables that must be considered in test selection and use for diverse groups. Test manuals containing technical information should be reviewed carefully to make certain all assessment information is appropriate for each client.

6. The goals of assessment include evaluating traits for career exploration and career decision making. It is most important to establish a client–counselor relationship of collaboration to select tests and set goals for using them. Inventories that measure career beliefs are used as measures of dysfunctional thinking.

7. Aptitude tests primarily measure specific skills and proficiencies or the ability to acquire certain proficiencies. Measured aptitudes provide a good frame of reference for evaluating potential careers.

8. Achievement tests primarily assess present levels of developed abilities. The level of basic academic skills such as arithmetic, reading, and language usage is relevant information that should be included in planning for educational or training programs.

9. Interest inventories are relevant counseling tools because individuals having interest patterns similar to those of people in certain occupations will probably find satisfaction in those occupations. Interest inventories can effectively stimulate career exploration.

10. Personality development is a major factor in career development because the individuality of each counselee must be considered. Personality patterns are integral in identifying and clarifying the needs of each individual.

11. Assessment and clarification of beliefs and values are important components of career counseling. Two types of values inventories are (a) inventories that primarily measure work values and (b) inventories that measure dimensions of values associated with broader aspects of lifestyles.

12. Career maturity inventories measure the dimensions from which one is judged to be vocationally mature. Super identified dimensions of career maturity as orientation toward work, planning, consistency of vocational preferences, and wisdom of vocational preferences. Career maturity inventories have two basic purposes: (a) to measure an individual's career development and (b) to evaluate the effectiveness of career education programs.

13. Computer-assisted career guidance assessment has steadily increased. Validity of instruments and the proper reporting of meeting usual testing standards have been and remain a chief concern of researchers and professional organizations.

14. Self-estimates of one's traits can be used to stimulate career exploration.

Supplementary Learning Exercises

1. Visit a state rehabilitation office to determine the assessment programs used for rehabilitation programs. Summarize the purpose of assessment in this context.

2. Administer and interpret one or more of the tests and inventories discussed in this chapter. Summarize the results and discuss strategies for using the results in career counseling.

3. Interview a personnel director of an industrial company and discuss the company's assessment program for placement counseling. Identify the rationale for each assessment instrument used.

4. Review AAC's Multicultural Assessment Standards: A Compilation for Counselors. Present your review to the class.

5. Interview a high school or a college counselor concerning his or her assessment programs for career counseling. Identify the counseling strategies underlying the use of assessment instruments.

6. Request permission from a university counseling center to take (or self-administer and interpret) some of their tests and inventories used in career counseling. Summarize the results.

7. Evaluate two or more of the following: an aptitude test; an achievement test; and the interest, value, personality, or career maturity inventory in the *Mental Measurements Yearbook*.

8. Write an essay defending this statement: Assessment results can be used effectively in career counseling programs for diverse groups.

9. Choose one or more of the following situations and develop an assessment battery that can be incorporated in career exploration programs:
    a. Middle school in a socioeconomically deprived neighborhood
    b. Senior high school from which 70 percent of the graduates enter college
    c. Community college in a large city
    d. Small four-year college
    e. Large university
    f. Community agency providing career counseling for adults
    g. Rehabilitation agency
    h. Private practice in career counseling

10. List the reasons one would use self-assessments in career counseling. Compare them with a classmate.

7

The Impact of New Technology on Work, Career Development, and Learning Platforms

CHAPTER HIGHLIGHTS

- Impact of new technology in the workplace
- Steps in using computer-assisted career guidance programs
- Suggestions for using the Internet
- How career information can provide support for career counseling
- Technology-driven instruction
- Learning platforms for training workers

New technology has indeed transformed the way we live and work. In many workplaces the ongoing changes in the nature of work have been unprecedented. Current work procedures include some very key changes in the workplace. One example is the use of portable computers that clerks use to obtain an inventory of goods on hand. One clerk I observed used a handheld computer to read bar graphs on shelved merchandise. He quickly compiled the inventory on a number of products to determine if replacements were needed. In addition the clerk was able to get a count of the number of recent sales of each product on a daily, weekly, and monthly basis. He also used the handheld computer to order products stored in the local warehouse and was able to determine the amount of goods that were available in the regional warehouses. One clerk who used a handheld computer was able to do an inventory in a very short time period that would have taken several clerks considerably more time.

Other examples of workplace changes include the use of telecommuting which has provided some workers with the option of working at home part or full time. In some factories robots are designed to perform certain tasks on an assembly line. Robots, also referred to as porters, carry heavy luggage in some of Japan's airports. More manufacturing jobs now require workers to use highly sophisticated new technology in producing medical devices and supplies and equipment for the aerospace and energy industries, for example. Word processors have replaced some typists and secretaries. One can also find self-check-out aisles in a variety of stores. E-commerce is the term used to signify the buying and selling of goods on the Internet (Mooney, Knox, & Schacht, 2013). It now represents almost half of all retail sales in the United States (U.S. Bureau of the Census, 2011).

In the near future one can expect to witness more significant changes in the retail marketplace. Somerville (2014), for example, suggests that a number of big-name retailers are in the process of experimenting with virtual reality as a means of improving access to store layouts for prospective customers. Virtual reality is a computer-simulated 3D environment that can be viewed on a computer screen, tablet, and/or smart phone. When sound and images are added to computer-simulated 3D environments, it is referred to as augmented reality. Using this new technology, shoppers will be able to try on virtual clothes without going to a dressing room. Grocery shoppers will be able to locate desired products in a large grocery store more easily. Using a smart phone or tablet, one will be able to locate sugar-free and/or gluten-free foods, for example. Furniture shoppers will be able to view a 3D rendering of their house and add objects to each room. How soon virtual and augmented reality will be available as described is not certain. We can expect, however, that new technology will be used in the near future to make the shopping experience more effective, personalized, and enjoyable. Near the end of this chapter I provide more information about the use of virtual reality as a method of training students and workers.

Finally, even the used-car salesman can make use of new technology. There is now a device called a disabler that can be used to prevent cars from starting. If a borrower defaults on a loan, the disabler is activated (Mooney et al., 2013). Clearly, the advantages of new technology in the workplace are speed and accuracy. There are good and bad outcomes. Employers have been able to reduce expenses with fewer employees. The downside is that this also means that some employees will not be needed in a job market that is becoming increasingly competitive.

New technology also has some other downsides. Rosen (2000) surveyed 1,000 corporations and found that two-thirds of them collected personal data on their employees. One of the major issues here is that an employee's personal activities, such as one's affiliation in civic, political, and/or religious organizations, may prejudice a supervisor's evaluation of an employee. In the workplace, video technology is used to observe and evaluate job performance, sometimes without the employee's knowledge of when it takes place. In the current workplace there is more supervision without a supervisor present. Workers can be more vulnerable to stress reactions in a workplace they may view as a threat to their job security.

Clearly, some jobs have been replaced by the use of technology; however, new technology has created the need for highly trained workers to use and maintain an increasing number of new devices that can be used effectively in future workplaces that appear to be ever changing. What is also clear, however, is that many tasks that can be accomplished through new technology can save time and are more than likely to be accurate. Current and future workers are to be informed of the increased use of technology in the workplace as well as its use as a tool to supervise workers on many job sites (Brinkerhoff et al., 2014). More on new technology is discussed in chapter 13.

In the meantime, there has been an explosion of career information in printed materials, computerized career information programs, and an abundance of career information systems on the Internet. Counselors are now faced with an overwhelming amount of career information that must be organized to be useful—always requiring an enormous time commitment. In addition, career counseling has broadened in scope to include personal problems, and more emphasis is now placed on multiple choices over the life span. Hence, the traditional primary role of the occupational information provider is now only a part, albeit a most important tool, in comprehensive career counseling programs. By necessity, the time once allocated to organizing, editing, and classifying occupational information has been reduced by the increasing demand for broad-scope career-related programs. Nevertheless, the effective career counselor must focus on how to provide each client with *useful information* that includes resources reflecting the ever-changing labor market. Today's sophisticated clientele demands up-to-date projections about the workforce and then uses this information as a major factor in making career decisions and transitions. Current job search strategies must include labor market projections as well as current job descriptions. Therefore, keeping abreast of changing occupational trends remains a very important part of career counseling. It should not be surprising that counseling professionals have for the most part emphatically endorsed the development of computer-assisted career guidance systems as well as online career counseling programs and job information. The fast-paced development of both hardware and software systems has created very attractively designed programs for different populations and for different purposes. The easily accessible, up-to-date career information on computer-based and online programs is a very powerful tool to help meet the needs of many clients. Other developments such as online assessment and interactive career guidance software systems have added greatly to the flexibility of programming. Clearly, counselors periodically need easily accessible information to help clients anticipate future developments.

Technology has also provided the tools for innovative learning delivery systems that provide current workers with the opportunity to develop skills and increase general and industry-specific knowledge. The worker who assumes a self-directed, career-managed program will seek out learning programs that are accessible and individualized. New technology and prototype learning systems are being refined and fine-tuned to meet the learning needs of the 21st century workforce. Counselors who provide relevant information about new learning technologies available to most clients will be in a good position to help clients maintain a lifelong learning position.

Computer-Assisted Career Guidance (CACG) and Online Systems

As discussed in the previous chapter and repeated here for emphasis, counselors should be aware that CAGG and online systems should meet the same standards used to evaluate traditional psychometric measures. Validity and reliability must be established for the instruments' use within career guidance systems. In particular, scrutiny should be given to the possibility of scoring errors and subsequent weighting of psychometric scales that can lead to misleading results. Most important, the counselor must have substantial evidence that the interpretative statements generated by computer-based testing are valid. Finally, counselors should be certain that each client fully understands the implications of computer-generated interpretative statements when applying them to the career search process (Osborn & Zunker, 2012; Welfel, 2013). I will continue our discussion of computer-generated materials later in this chapter.

Another fear among some career counseling professionals is that computerized systems will become the sole source of career guidance programming. Professional associations stress that the use of CAGG and online guidance systems should supplement, but not replace, the counselor. Although software programs are becoming more user friendly, the career counselor should structure the career counseling process and sustain the client throughout the career guidance sequence, especially in choosing career-related programs on the Internet (Whiston & Oliver, 2005). Computers do allow for independent and individualized courses of action but do not remove the counselor's responsibility for direction and structure. Finally, the counselor must address the problem of user anxiety. Inadequately prepared users can easily become discouraged with computerized systems. Personnel must be available to instruct users during the initial stages and assist users through various phases of the system and follow-up that includes user satisfaction and future needs.

Advantages of Online and CACG Systems

The advantages of computer-based guidance systems is most obvious to the general public as people of almost all ages have become more computer literate with an ever-increasing use of the Internet. Counselors, however, have witnessed most of the following advantages: 1. The interactive capability of computerized systems allows users to become more actively involved in the career guidance process; users seek more information about the process itself. 2. User motivation is sustained through the unique use of immediate feedback. 3. The opportunity to individualize the career exploration process provides opportunities to personalize career search strategies. 4. Computer-based guidance systems provide systematic career exploration and career decision programs that may be accessed at any given time. 5. Access to large databases of up-to-date information for local, state, national, and international locations is immediately available. The availability of service to remote locations, cost-effectiveness, and rapid turnaround for assessment results have distinct advantages.

Most computer-based programs contain career information systems and guidance systems. Information systems provide users with direct access to large databases on such subject areas as occupational characteristics (work tasks, required abilities, work settings, salary) and lists of occupations, educational and training institutions, military information, and financial aid.

Guidance systems are typically becoming broader in scope. They contain a variety of available modules, such as instruction in the career decision process, assessment, prediction of future success, assistance with planning, and development of strategies for future plans. Many systems are directed toward certain populations, such as students in junior high school, high school, and college; some systems are for people who work in organizations; and some address the needs of the elderly and retirees.

The following components are found in most systems:

- Occupational information
- Armed services information
- Information about postsecondary institutions of higher learning
- Information on technical and specialized schools
- Financial aid information
- Interest inventories
- Decision-making skills

Other common components include the following:

- Local job information files
- Ability measures
- Value inventories

- Methods of predicting academic success in college
- Job search strategies
- Résumé preparation information
- Information on job interviews
- Components for adults

An example of a CACG system is presented next.

System of Interactive Guidance and Information (SIGI) and SIGI PLUS

One of the early major computerized systems is the System of Interactive Guidance and Information (SIGI) and SIGI PLUS, developed by Katz (1975, 1993) and published by the Educational Testing Service (1996). There are five SIGI subsystems: Values, Locate, Compare, Planning, and Strategy. These subsystems were developed to assist college students by clarifying values, locating and identifying occupational options, comparing choices, learning planning skills, and developing rational career decision-making skills.

SIGI PLUS contains the following components:

Introduction

Self-Assessment

Search, Information

Skills

Preparing

Coping

Deciding

Next Steps

This system was developed to include adults in general and those who are seeking information about organizations. Katz (1993) suggests that individual needs determine the level of motivation in the career search and, as such, are considered domains of self-understanding. Thus, needs are centered around values, interests, temperament, and attitudes that should be assessed as important variables in the search process. One outstanding feature of this program is the special needs of adults in transition; it is designed to assist adults who may be changing occupations, moving into new occupations, or reentering the labor force. Reardon and colleagues (1992) found that students liked both SIGI and SIGI PLUS but preferred the latter because of its greater flexibility. Evidently, students opted for more control of a system that is user friendly to their individual needs. For more information, see www.ets.org.

Examples of other CACG systems include:

XAP (www.bridges.com)

Career Information Delivery Systems

Career Finder Plus

Career Leader (www.careerdiscovery.com)

The Career Key (www.careerkey.org)

Career Scope (www.vri.org)

Career Visions Plus

Career WAYS

Embark.com (www.embark.com)

Steps in Assisting Users of CACG and Online Systems

Throughout this chapter, several direct references have been made about the use of computer-based programs. The primary purpose of this discussion has been to emphasize the computer's role in meeting the career exploration needs of individuals and groups. Structured procedures that use components of computerized programs as a career counseling assistant are a major advantage. Computer-assisted career guidance programs can also be a major component of a total career guidance program. As such, they are coordinated with other components, materials, and procedures; they are not the sole delivery system. Individual needs may dictate the use of several components including computerized systems, or in some cases, computerized systems alone may meet client needs. Within this framework, I suggest the following steps for using computer-assisted career guidance programs:

1. *Assessment of needs.* Individualized needs of each student should determine the direction of program use and the components accessed. For example, one student might need information on financial aid programs only. A client moving to a distant state could be seeking information on two-year and four-year colleges within driving distance of his or her future residence.
2. *Orientation.* Each client or group of clients should be given a thorough orientation to the purpose, goals, and demonstrated use of computerized systems.
3. Individualized programs. Each individual should follow a preconceived plan based on needs. This plan can be modified as needed; the flexibility of computerized programs can be a distinct advantage when plans change.
4. *Counselor intervention.* The individualized plan should provide for counselor intervention. For example, it may be appropriate to discuss the results of one of the inventories. Providing sources of additional occupational information and discussing tentative occupational choices are good strategies in the career exploration process. The point is that individuals should not be "turned over to the computer" without any planned intervention from a counselor.
5. *Online assistance.* Provisions should be made to assist individuals in various stages of career exploration. How to return to the main menu or how to access various components can be frustrating experiences for the computer novice. The following questions can be anticipated: "How can I print this?" "I need to stop now and go to class—what should I do?" "I hit the wrong key, can you help me?"
6. *Follow-up.* As in all phases of career exploration, individual progress should be monitored. Career counselors should help individuals sustain their motivation and evaluate their progress and the effectiveness of programs.

In sum, many computer-based modules are designed primarily to develop the individual's decision-making skills. The counselor should assist clients at various stages, however, including help accessing different functions of a system. Most important, the counselor demonstrates how computer-based programs can be helpful in the practice of career development.

Using the Internet

The Internet is a significant resource that is actively used by both counselors and clients. The future use of the Internet will continue to be an important subject for professional counseling associations as well as practicing counselors. The Internet may be described as a proverbial sleeping giant that has enormous potential for the career counseling profession. We are beginning to tap the resources that are available now, but the future use of the Internet will be an important subject of the career counseling profession in the generations to come. Currently, one can search bulletin boards and gopher sites that list available jobs, and submit a résumé. One may also take part in job fairs online where one can present their résumé and find job openings. These examples suggest that the Internet is and will remain a vital and relevant part of career counseling. By early 2000, however, many professionals have gone on record requesting new credentials for certifying online counselors (Boer, 2001).

Harris-Bowlsbey, Dikel, and Sampson (2002) have developed a guide for using the Internet in career planning. This guide contains sample websites for assessment and databases containing education and training opportunities, financial aid, internship opportunities, job openings, career information, education and training information, military information, and career counseling programs. In sum, websites can assist individuals with self-assessment of such traits as interests, skills, abilities, values, intelligence, and personality. Websites also provide information for (a) exploring occupations, (b) educational institutions, (c) scholarships, (d) financial aid opportunities, and (e) job openings. Some websites provide free information, whereas others charge a fee. Still other websites provide information resources that link occupations, educational institutions, and other opportunities with trade journals, government agencies, professional organizations, and so on. You can also locate chat rooms and support groups, or post a résumé for job placement. Many other networking possibilities can be used to meet individual needs.

The growth of web resources and their use by both counselors and clients are indications of their value. Counselors should be aware of the counseling competencies of Internet providers, especially their training experiences (Barak & English, 2002). In chapter 6, the necessity of using valid and reliable assessment instruments is clearly stated. But the problem does not stop there; one must also interpret the results according to the prescribed use of the instrument. Invalid interpretation of results can lead to invalid conclusions and subsequently to invalid decisions. Most important is the readiness of the client for decision making in terms of his or her focus on unique individual concerns that may require individual counseling. This precaution is directed not just to clients who may need psychotherapy, but also to those individuals who require counselor direction to overcome barriers that prohibit appropriate career-decision techniques. A major point here is the availability of user support when needed (Harris-Bowlsbey et al., 2002).

An illustration of an appropriate use of the Internet in career planning and in the decision-making process includes six steps that are driven by an inclusive database as follows:

1. Become aware of your need to make a choice.
2. Take a snapshot of yourself.
3. Identify occupational alternatives.
4. Get information about identified alternatives.
5. Choose among alternatives.
6. Get the required education and training.
7. Get a job (Harris-Bowlsbey et al., 2002, p. 2).

In the first step, individuals realize a need to decide by learning about and/or reevaluating self. Step 2 suggests that clients be alert to their personal attributes and limitations. In step 3, occupational information is presented in a manner "that facilitates the transition of self-information into occupational alternatives" (Harris-Bowlsbey et al., 2002, p. 2). The next three steps are used to refine the identified alternatives into possible tentative choices by using the vast database of information that is continually updated on the Internet. Finally, the individual decides to seek more information and eventually selects the new alternative.

Examples of Web Locations

To assist counselors in providing services appropriately through Internet-based career resources and services, the National Career Development Association (NCDA) and the National Board for Certified Counselors (NBCC) have published guidelines. (See appendix I for NCDA websites that list guidelines.) The following book is a valuable resource for Internet use by counselors:

The Internet: A Tool for Career Planning
National Career Development Association
4700 Reed Road, Suite M
Columbus, OH 43220
888-326-1750
Fax 614-326-1760

Following are some examples of current programs:

America's Job Bank
www.ajb.org

Currently one of the most widely used sites, this is a computerized network that links 2,000 state employment offices and contains a national pool of active job opportunities. Labor market information and training resources for federal and state employment can also be obtained here. In addition, the replacement for the *Dictionary of Occupational Titles* (DOT), O'NET, can be accessed at www.onetcenter.org.

The *Occupational Outlook Handbook* of career information and labor market projections is another important government publication that is in printed form and available on CD-ROM. It can also be obtained online at www.bls.gov/oco/.

This brief introduction to the Internet suggests that computerized career-related programming has only begun to surface. We can expect to see a growing list of innovative ideas that will build to a comprehensive linked system in the future. The unique career-related programs developed at this time should serve as the foundation for the continuing evolution of computerized career-related programming. The list of gopher sites which are designed to assist job hunters include the following websites:

Career.com

Careerbuilder.com

Careermag.com

Careermosiac.com

Dice.com

Jobs.com

Monster.com

Nationjob.com

Using CACG and Online Assessment Results

I begin this section of the chapter with an emphasis on ethics. The focus will be on the use of assessment results from online career counseling programs and CACG systems. What is being emphasized here is the responsible use of test interpretation services from computer-generated testing known as computer-based interpretations (CBIs). Welfel (2013) suggests that the use of computer-based scoring services avoids human errors and as a result is certainly ethical. The use of computer-based interpretations, however, has to be ethically justified. First and foremost, counselors are to make certain that computerized interpretations of test scores are based on criteria that can be validated; there must be scientific evidence that is documented.

Counselors are to be alert to the possibilities that combinations of scores could produce a second or third interpretation. There could be different validity, for instance, for multicultural groups. Counselors should be very cautious when using CBIs in the diagnosis process. Counselors are proceeding ethically when CBIs are used as an aid to accurate interpretations of assessment results. Do not overrely on CBIs!

Valid Computer-Based Interpretations. Counselors should use the following questions by Whiston (2013, p. 354) to assist in the evaluation of computer-based interpretations:

1. What is the basis for the programming of the report?
2. Who was involved in the writing of the computer programs and what are their professional credentials?
3. Were the individuals knowledgeable about the instrument, and did they have extensive experience in interpreting results?
4. Is the interpretation based on sound research and validation information?
5. Is there evidence that the technology-generated reports are comparable to clinician-generated reports?
6. Is the interpretative information in the report helpful and appropriate for the client with whom the counselor is working?
7. Is the cost of the technology-generated report (e.g., software, hardware) worth the information produced by the report?
8. Are supplemental resources, such as hotline number, available for questions?

Technology-assisted assessment is expected to significantly increase in the future. Counselors and clients are to take advantage of the ease and speed of administration, scoring accuracy, and valid interpretation of results. Counselors are also expected to access a variety of assessment instruments that can be found through search engines online. Resources on the Internet currently include the Buros Institute database that contains more than 25,00 tests. Counselors can also locate most websites of test publishers for purchasing or reviewing tests. Reviews of tests can also be obtained from the *Mental Measurement Yearbooks*. Translations of tests are also available from a number of test publishers. In addition, the counselor can obtain the necessary professional qualifications to administer and interpret assessment instruments. In the future, expect more sophisticated assessment instruments that hopefully can accurately predict client behavior (Trull & Prinstein, 2013; Whiston, 2013).

Organizing Career Information

An often overlooked role of the career counselor is that of organizing career information that has exceedingly become more complex with an abundance of printed material, video, audio, and microform media. Not only does one want to provide career information that is attractive and accessible for clients, but one must also have a designated area that is also attractive and accessible. Today we can usually find career resource centers in colleges, universities, and schools that satisfy the above criteria. The systems used to arrange career information within the career resource centers can vary, but many offer assistance for locating material for clients by paraprofessionals who have been thoroughly trained for this purpose.

One way to arrange noninteractive career information materials is by the use of the Holland code letters, RIASEC, that can be color coded to help make information easier to find and also to return it to its proper location. This arrangement is usually accompanied by a large display chart that describes the Holland typologies. The chart can also be used to translate job families from other computer-based programs to the same color categories (Andersen & Vandehey, 2012). As you may recall, in the Holland system one is directed to a grouping of jobs or job families from which the client can find a specific occupation. In this process clients are also exposed to other possibilities that could be of interest. What is being suggested here is that this system may work well for beginning university students who may be seriously considering career choice for the first time (Andersen & Vandehey, 2012). This does not rule out the benefits of the Holland system, however, for other clients including adults who may be changing their career goals. The Holland system has been a very popular and straightforward one.

There are reasons and benefits for having a more extensive and inclusive system such as the one developed for the Florida State University Career Resource Center. What stands out in this system is the ability to organize a broad and diverse group of career-related materials. The center is able to incorporate noninteractive career information media, some of which was described earlier, with interactive career information media as displayed in Table 7.1. One of the major reasons for combining career-related materials was to provide the counselor with an organized set of materials to address readiness for career choice; decidedness (one who is undecided needs more counselor attention); motivation (poorly motivated clients need more attention); verbal aptitude (lower verbal aptitude clients need more assistance); and decision-making style and balance of presentation (clients need both positive and negative information about choices). The organization of career information is a vital part of the career information processing (CIP) model discussed in chapters 2 and 3. Counselors can focus on individual needs, such as assigning a client to proceed with an individual learning plan in which the client can work on his or her own in the career library. In some cases, however, clients who are found to lack motivation and/ or skills for processing information are likely to have needs that require them to work more closely with a paraprofessional. The client's ability to process career information should be carefully monitored and is of the utmost importance in the CIP career developmental theory as well as in all other theories.

As stated in the introduction of this section, there is an increasing amount of career information that seems to be ever changing. Counselors who are confident of

Table 7.1	**Interactive Career Information Media**
Medium	**Examples**
Internet websites	Employer, job bank, occupational, or educational information websites
Computer-assisted career guidance systems	Personal computer-based or Internet-based guidance systems
Computer-assisted instruction	Instruction and assistance in résumé preparation
CD-ROM or DVD	Reference or descriptive information on various employers
Card sorts	Self- or counselor-guided assessment of values, interests, skills, and employment preferences
Programmed instruction	Job experience that provides the opportunity to perform actual job tasks
Structured interview	Interviewing a currently employed worker at the job site or a career day or career fair
Role playing or games	Classroom or guidance activities that allow students to try out career and life options
Instruction	Classroom activities that allow individuals to try out various work behaviors (accounting, welding)
Synthetic work environments	A flight simulator for pilots
Direct observation	Shadowing a worker for a day to observe typical work tasks, or taking field trips to places of employment
Direct exploration	Volunteer work, cooperative education, internships, work-study programs, or part-time employment
Social interaction	Conversations with parents, relatives, peers, school personnel, and acquaintances about various career opportunities

SOURCE: From *Career Counseling and Services: A Cognitive Information Processing Approach,* by J. Sampson, R. Reardon, G. Peterson, and J. Lenz, p. 126. Copyright © 2004. Reprinted with permission of Brooks/Cole Publishing Company, a part of the Thomson Corporation.

the availability of career information and its presentation are more likely to make use of it in counseling interventions. The following five categories of career information were selected for the comprehensive career library at Florida State University:

I. Career and Life Planning

A. Education and Training
B. Employer Information Resources
C. Job Hunting
D. Occupations
E. Work Experience

Examples of Keys. Accessing information from the library is made easier by what is referred to as the Career Key: A Tool for Finding and Managing Career Resources. Two examples of the Career Key are as follows:

II. Occupations

   A. Multiple occupations (resources with information on a lot of different occupations)
   B. Specific occupations (used with an occupational code)
   C. Occupations by program of study (used with major code)

V. Job Hunting

   A. Résumé Writing
   B. Interviewing
   C. Letter Writing
   D. Job Hunting Methods

The career-key approach provides easy access to a vast amount of diverse career information and, most importantly, clients are offered assistance in learning how to locate it (Sampson et al., 2004). Both systems used in the two career resource centers discussed here can easily be updated—a task that is by necessity often repeated. Both systems employ paraprofessionals to assist clients. I have not personally visited either one of the career resource centers, but from descriptions I have read they appear to be very user friendly. In the final section of this chapter, I use the experience of a young mother who wants to work out of her home to help support the family. Her story represents how some moms have been able to become a dual-earner through the use of new technology. The major focus in the next section is on how technology-driven instruction is a most efficient learning tool for lifelong learning.

Technology-Driven Instruction (TDI)

I begin this section with a story about a young mother who had decided to stay at home and be a housewife and mom. Shortly before Lisa's first child was born, she resigned from a secretarial job in a local firm. At that time she and her husband decided they could meet the family's needs with only one paycheck. Two years later, however, the manufacturing company where her husband was working outsourced their jobs to an overseas site. After weeks of searching for another job, her husband obtained a part-time job at a local restaurant. Like so many other families during the fallout from the 2009 recession, it became necessary for both parents to find work in order to maintain the family. Lisa decided to search for a job that would allow her to work at home.

Lisa was able to find a company that was impressed with her previous work experience and agreed to allow her to work out of her home. After several meetings with her future supervisor, Lisa was trained for her new position in her home by using a training program that is usually identified as distance learning (Aamodt, 2013). Her training included printed materials, DVDs, videos, and web-based programs. Lisa was able to complete a series of learning programs during time periods that were most convenient for her and at her own pace. In addition, Lisa was given access to an instructor she could consult with through e-mail and chat rooms.

Lisa eventually learned to interact with the general office through telecommuting (phone, computer, and fax machine). Over time while working from her home,

Lisa experienced less family conflict, less stress, and more importantly she was able to continue with her role as a mom. In this case, technology-driven instruction made it much easier for Lisa to be properly trained for her new job. Technology also gave her the tools to work out of her home. Research by Gajendran and Harrison (2007) suggests that most workers who are able to work out of their home, as Lisa is doing, experience increased job satisfaction.

The need for lifelong learning supports an ongoing relationship between client and counselor that is continuous and discontinuous. There are indeed periods of time when clients need to upgrade their skills in order to remain viable in the current job market. The outsourcing of jobs beginning in the 1990s and the recession in 2009 are valid reminders of difficult times for the American worker. As I write these pages, the unemployment and underemployment rates remain high; many American workers are searching for training opportunities to upgrade their skills or to learn new ones. In the meantime, organizations are also most interested in providing opportunities to upgrade their current workforce. In a number of states there is a growing need for more skill training and/or tech programs in public education. Counselors should be prepared to help clients discover job opportunities from ongoing training programs that can provide pathways to finding a career identity and a job. Training and development activities result in benefits for both the client and organization (Aguinis & Kraiger, 2009). In the following paragraphs I will briefly review some methods of training employees by a variety of organizations.

Methods of Training in Organizations

Training programs generally have multiple goals and objectives and as a result there are a variety of methods used in training at most organizations. Methods of training can be divided into three major categories: classroom setting, distance learning, and on-the-job learning (Aamodt, 2013).

Classroom Setting. The most familiar setting for most clients is classroom learning that includes lectures, role playing, case studies, and behavior modeling. Within this group of training activities, one may also be trained by simulation. More specifically, trainees practice learned skills they have observed of actual job conditions and activities. Videos and DVDs are also used to present certain tasks and requirements of actual job demands. Advances in virtual reality technology, discussed later in this chapter, are expected to greatly enhance simulation exercises in training programs (Zielinski, 2010).

Distance Learning. An example of distance learning was covered in the case of Lisa who found a job with an organization that allowed her to work out of her home. Other methods of distance learning include Webinars and Webcasts. A web seminar (Webinar) is transmitted over the Internet and is designed to be interactive. The Webcast is not interactive. Organizations may also use Blog (a collection of web pages on a subject being addressed); Wiki (another collection of web pages that the reader can edit); and Listerv (distributes e-mail messages for study) (Aamodt, 2013).

On-the-job Training. The third group of training procedures have been used by organizations over time and remain effective. Job rotation, apprentice training, coaching, and mentoring are popular methods of on-the-job training programs. In these training procedures the trainee is given the opportunity to observe work tasks, do the tasks, and receive feedback in the form of mentoring and/or coaching (Aamodt, 2013; DeRouin, Parrish, & Salas, 2005).

Counselors assume an important role in helping clients build an understanding of why career management is best driven by activities that are self-directed. Those who take full responsibility for their career development recognize the necessity of lifelong learning and how skill development influences their career direction. When there is a fit between the individual (interests, abilities, skill acquisition) and occupation, there is a greater likelihood of job satisfaction and tenure (Ostroff, Shin, & Feinberg, 2002). Hence, counselors provide *reasons* for self-directed skill acquisition activities as well as information about delivery systems of learning.

Career development theorists have pointed out numerous variables that determine career progression leading to initial career choice and multiple choices over the life span. Abilities, interests, values, and personality are often mentioned as personal characteristics that influence individual choice. Of this group of variables, interest patterns have been emphasized, especially in the research of Holland's typology, that is, congruence between one's interests and occupational types makes for a good fit (Holland, 1985b). The importance of this research has been underscored by individuals who discover careers that fit their interests and remain in those occupations (Feldman, 2002). In addition, emphasis on skill development in the current job market suggests that counselors give this variable equal attention. Keep in mind that it was Mitchell and Krumboltz (1996), among others, who emphasized skill development through learning programs as a key ingredient in one's career development. Drucker (2002), who suggests that the next society will be dominated by knowledge workers, clearly endorses educational and training programs that develop skills and increase knowledge.

In assessing the dynamics among interests, abilities, skill acquisition and fit, Ostroff and colleagues (2002) suggest that initial choice of career goals is indeed influenced by interest patterns but, as workers are exposed to work requirements and on-the-job experiences over time, they gravitate to occupations that are commensurate with their abilities. What we have here is a relationship that develops largely through demands, requirements, and activities different occupations make. Career interests and abilities crystallize at various times during career development (Worthington & Juntunen, 1997); thus, workers experience congruence with requirements of certain work activities and develop skills accordingly. Those who are forced or choose to learn new skills may also be required to change their career goals, suggesting that initial career choice may not result in a longtime commitment for everyone. Skill development, therefore, is a continuous lifelong learning commitment that can significantly influence one's career transitions. In the next paragraphs I present more information on skill development by the use of technology-driven instruction.

Web-Based Instruction

Of all training programs, web-based instruction is probably the most flexible in that users can access programs at any time through widely available web browsers. Web training is easily updated and is enhanced by hyperlinks to additional training material, exercises, and feedback, allowing users to determine the level and depth of information needed. There appear to be endless possibilities for learning opportunities through linking to other Internet sites or corporate intranet sites (sites within an organization, for instance). Users can also share information and ideas and discuss problems with an expert and/or other trainees. Brown, Milner, and Ford (1998) have suggested that web-based instruction include a guidance component. Guidance would usually include information about the purpose of learning and how to learn the material effectively. Thus, such guidance programs can help learners make more effective decisions about what to learn and how to learn it effectively (Aguinis & Kraiger, 2009). We can expect many more innovations that should be of interest to all counselors who offer career-related counseling.

Intelligent Tutoring Systems (ITS)

Intelligent Tutoring Systems (ITS) is a computer-based (learning) program that is highly individualized and is considered to be an improved tech version of programmed instruction (Steele-Johnson & Hyde, 1997). This system is designed to diagnose a user's level of understanding, performance, and types of errors made in performing a task. Using the data collected from each user, the system provides guidelines for more appropriate procedures and learning activities. The individualized approach of ITS makes it most attractive and feasible simply because training interventions are developed from an assessment of the individual's needs. More specifically, a writing process tutor component that focuses on developing writing process skills identifies errors and presents solutions. Likewise, a scientific inquiry component of an individual's data analysis skills presents errors and suggestions for improving ones' accuracy. Interactive systems have the distinct advantage of allowing users to ask questions about particular tasks. Feedback may first come in the form of hints about correct procedures but, eventually, direct analogies are given, followed by explicit instructions. The downside of this system is the high cost of developing programs. The following extract is a good example of this system's current use and suggests the potential of the future use of ITS:

> Thus, these high end systems respond adaptively to both learning level and learning style, making judgments about student knowledge and learning needs. For example, NASA employed ITS to train flight dynamics officers how to deploy satellites in space that indeed is a complex task that requires performing the correct sequence of activities (Steele-Johnson & Hyde, 1997). Learners are also presented with deployment problems that include information based on the types of errors committed in performing the task for further study and analysis. The trainees can also engage in dialog with the system by querying the system with help messages. The success of the trainee in navigating these sequences of activities affects the type of feedback and tutoring the trainee receives. (Goldstein & Ford, 2002, p. 262)

Cognitive Tutor. More recently one can find an ITS known as a cognitive tutor that is being used in over 2,000 school systems in a number of states. This system is designed to aid students in solving problems in algebra, geometry, computer programming, languages, and other subjects. A most important part of the cognitive tutor program is its ability to give users both positive and negative feedback. Impressive learning gains have been reported in experimental and classroom settings (Graesser, Conley, & Olney, 2012).

Intelligent Essay Assessor. The Intelligence Essay Assessor is another popular ITS program that can grade essays in science, history, and other subjects. Research reports indicate that grades resulting from the intelligence essay assessor assessment are as reliable as experts in English composition (Landauer, 2007).

Auto Tutor. Another example of ITS is the Auto Tutor. This tutoring program is designed to help college students with computer literacy, physics, and critical thinking skills. This program is designed to engage students in conversation during which the system analyzes language and discourse (Jurafsky & Martin, 2008).

At this time, counselors should be aware of ITS and consider it to be an example of training programs for skill development. Although most of the ITS programs are currently being used in universities and schools, organizations have similar needs for training key employees. It appears that the high cost of building ITS programs has limited their use at the present time. Counselors should be aware of ITS and consider it to be an example of what the near future may bring in terms of tutoring programs for skill development. This observation also holds true for virtual reality training.

Virtual Reality (VR) Training

The virtual reality (VR) learning system is a hi-tech version of work simulations through virtual reality. Work simulation in this case, however, is viewed in a three-dimensional (3D) world that workers will encounter. It purports to be a captivating experience that takes advantage of visual learning and experiential engagement that is highly motivating. It is a very flexible system that permits control of time in its simulations in that it can move faster, slow down, reverse, or halt. It is designed to present different levels of detail. Learning modules can be updated and/or integrated with other modules.

In the late 1990s, an animated person named Steve was placed in a 3D mock-up of a work environment (Rickel & Johnston, 1999). Users can ask Steve to demonstrate how to perform tasks and provide assistance while they are practicing certain tasks. One advantage of VR training systems is clear: They are flexible enough to demonstrate a variety of workplace interactions within different work environments. Groups of virtual people can be used to simulate work environments in order to observe significant interactions between workers. VR will more than likely become available on the Internet and will expand its programs to include a variety of work environments full of virtual people (Gunther-Mohr, 1997).

Goldstein and Ford (2002) have compiled applications of VR systems and some are summarized here. The military has been quite involved in virtual reality training; for instance, the U.S. Air Force trained aircrews in how to use emergency parachutes by simulating different conditions they might encounter. Using virtual reality, they created different weather conditions, hostile locations, day and night-time environments, and examples of different wind conditions. The U.S. Army, HOPE, and the Center for Advanced Technologies developed VR training for traditional skill trades (HOPE in Focus, 2000). In the private sector, Motorola has offered VR training in how to use machines on the manufacturing line in several of its locations. Again, VR training is individualized in that learners can stop and start machines they will use and become actively involved in solving problems that may occur. Finally, VR systems are being developed at Penn State to train surgeons to perform a very delicate microsurgical procedure of joining two blood vessels. In sum, VR is used in a variety of training programs ranging from learning how to parachute in emergencies, develop skills for traditional skill trades, operate machinery on manufacturing lines, and perform microsurgical procedures. In all cases, simulated conditions in 3D were created to represent real problems that may be encountered in performing certain tasks. Learners have the advantage of setting their own pace and are able to ask for help and directions whenever needed.

Advances in virtual reality technology hold tremendous promise for trainers (Zielinski, 2010).

In conclusion, it is not certain at this time which of the current training delivery systems will emerge as the leader. It is also not certain what kind of new and different technologies will emerge that may prove to be even more effective than the ones currently are being developed. More than likely we will experience a mixture or blend of systems that prove to be effective with certain training goals and modules. The focus of future training models could be on integrated learning systems that are designed to meet specified requirements and needs of the workforce in the 21st century (Goldstein & Ford, 2002). Finally, skill development should be available for all clients. There appears to be an increasing number of programs that focus on developing basic skills. The message here is that counselors are to recognize that in a knowledge society continuous career development requires one to effectively read, write, and do basic math. On the other end of the knowledge spectrum, continuous development requires the fine-tuning of developed skills through a variety of training programs. For all clients, technology may offer opportunities to learn and develop skills determined by each individual's needs and interests.

Summary

1. The impact of new technology has transformed the nature of work in many current workplaces. Portable computers, robots, virtual reality, telecommuting, and more worker supervision are examples of changing workplaces.
2. Easily accessible career information has helped clients anticipate future development.
3. The rationale for computerized career counseling stems from the need for up-to-date information and the unique capabilities of the computer to satisfy this need. A number of computerized counseling systems with different combinations of computer hardware and software and different sets of objectives have been developed.
4. Career guidance systems and online guidance systems provide independent and individualized courses of action but do not replace the counselor.
5. SIGI and SIGI PLUS for colleges and adults are examples of systems that include online assessment programs, job descriptions, and educational information, all of which are easily accessible.
6. A seven-step implementation model should be followed when implementing a computer-based program.
7. The Internet has tremendous potential for the career counselor. Currently, information on the Internet includes self-assessment programs, search databases, and career development resources.
8. Computer-based interpretation of assessment results should be used as an aid to accurately interpret assessment results.
9. Organizing career information provides counselors with support for all phases of the career choice process. Career information should be made very accessible and user friendly.
10. Technology-developed instruction provides training programs for developing skills needed in the current workplace.
11. Methods of training by organizations include classroom settings, distance learning, and on-the-job training.

12. Skill development is an important factor in determining occupational fit. Innovative learning systems include simulated training, intelligent tutoring systems, and virtual reality training.

Supplementary Learning Exercises

1. Visit a school, college, or agency that has a computer-based and/or an online career information system. Develop a written report about its use and effectiveness.
2. Outline and discuss the advantages of having a computer-assisted career guidance system in one or more of the following: a high school, a community college, a four-year college, and a community agency providing career counseling to adults.
3. Form two groups and debate the issues relating to the following statement: Computer-assisted career guidance systems and online guidance systems will replace the career counselor.
4. Develop a local visit file (individuals in selected occupations who agree to visits by students) that could be included as a component in a computer-assisted career guidance system. Describe the advantages of a visit file.
5. Interview a career counselor who has substantial experience in using computer-assisted career guidance and online systems. Write a report on the systems used and summarize the counselor's evaluation of the systems.
6. Describe the advantages of having a statewide occupational information data bank of job openings and labor forecasts. How could you incorporate this information in career counseling programs in high schools, community colleges, four-year colleges or universities, and community programs for adults?
7. List disadvantages and advantages of using a web-based interpretation report of a personality inventory.
8. Explain your conception of the future role of the Internet as a counseling tool. Focus on the advantages and limitations.
9. Describe why skill development is so important in the current work environment. How would you help clients access learning and developmental programs?
10. What is meant by the term "virtual reality"? Explain how and why virtual reality could be an effective training approach.

8

On Being an Ethical Career Counselor

CHAPTER HIGHLIGHTS

- Practice within the boundaries of confidentiality

- Disclosure of information

- The client's right to privacy

- The use of peer counselors

- A model for ethical practice

Leaders of professional helping organizations have prudently spent considerable effort and time developing ethical standards for their members. In this chapter, I examine some ethical issues, principles, and standards that were developed by the National Career Development Association (NCDA) (1997). Because career counselors may be members of two or more professional associations, our discussions often include examples of ethical codes from other professional associations. In counseling encounters, counselors are often faced with crucial decisions concerning the welfare of their clients and so may ask the following questions: Is this in the best interest of my client? Which test should I use in this case? Is this intervention strategy appropriate? Is the information on this website accurate? Should I get the client's consent to confer with others? Do I have the necessary training to handle this case? These questions illustrate the nature of concerns among counselors for appropriate materials, techniques, and counseling competencies. There are, however, many more ethical issues that have surfaced in the last three decades that underscore the need for counselors to fully comprehend the boundaries implied in ethical standards (Welfel, 2013).

Ethical standards and codes of ethics are designed to be very inclusive. They address moral dimensions of counselor relationships and behavior as well as competency requirements, confidentiality, informed consent, misconduct, and violations of trust and care. As with most other laws and rules, ethical guidelines cannot possibly include each and every circumstance and situation that involve ethical behavior. Thus, ethical standards offer solutions for counselors in a wide range of categories in which the *intent* of standards is to be followed. More important, however, is the position that counselors are to establish patterns of action that help them respond appropriately to all client needs. In the diverse society of the 21st century, client concerns and needs can be quite complex. In this chapter, I present some examples of major ethical issues for counselors regarding competence, confidentiality, informed consent, measurement and evaluation, Internet user issues, and use of peer counselors. Examples of violations do not include sensational cases such as sexual exploitation. This chapter introduces readers to examples of subtle situations and consequences that can lead to misconduct.

Some Boundaries of Ethical Competence

I begin our discussion of competence by emphasizing the importance of the client's welfare. Client welfare should be the counselor's ultimate concern, suggesting that professional counselors practice within the boundaries of their competence. Counselors' competence is usually determined by an evaluation of their education, training, supervised experience, credentials, and appropriate professional experiences. Every counselor should be able to present evidence of qualifications for the counseling position they occupy or the position they seek. What matters are principles of integrity, professional and social responsibility, and respect for individuals' rights and dignity. Counselors, therefore, are to strive to maintain the highest standards of competence in their work. In essence, counselors have a moral and professional responsibility to ensure that each client receives appropriate guidance.

Two general guidelines from the National Career Development Association (NCDA) (2003) underscore the competency issue as follows:

> 6. NCDA members seek only those positions in the delivery of professional services for which they are professionally qualified.
>
> 7. NCDA members recognize their limitations and provide services or only use techniques for which they are qualified by training and/or experience. Career counselors recognize the need, and seek continuing education, to ensure competent services. (p. 2)

Within these boundaries there are many important considerations. For example, a counselor encounters a new, highly touted standardized measurement instrument that he or she has not used. It turns out that this is a very complex instrument that measures personality variables that are indicative of levels of career maturity and career choice indicators. Even after reading the technical manual carefully, the counselor is not certain of this instrument's appropriateness and the most effective method for interpreting the results. In this case the counselor correctly decides to not use this instrument until more information about its use is received and supervised training is available.

Another counselor uncovers a severe thinking disorder in a client who has a history of impulsively acting out, with little thought given to the consequences of his actions. His ability to function on a job has been impaired by his impulsive and hostile actions. Although good rapport has been established, the counselor decides treatment will require a long-term commitment and counseling skills that she is only beginning to develop. The counselor decides to refer this client for treatment of a potential thinking disorder and will delay career counseling until it is more appropriate. Counselors will find that decisions of this kind are ongoing ones that challenge professionals to continue their training and upgrade their competence.

The American Counseling Association (ACA) (1995) also clearly points out that new specialty areas require education, training, and supervised experience. In Section E: Evaluation, Assessment, and Interpretation, E.2 is stated as follows:

> a. Limits of Competence. Counselors recognize the limits of their competence and perform only those testing and assessment services for which they have been trained. They are familiar with reliability, validity, related standardization, error of measurement, and proper application of any technique utilized. Counselors using computerized-based test interpretations are trained in the construct being measured and the specific instrument being used prior to using this type of computer

application. Counselors take reasonable measures to ensure the proper use of psychological assessment techniques for persons under their supervision. (p. 7)

Example of a Violation

Counselor A accepts a position in a mental health agency to provide career-related counseling to a client population that is primarily from Asian families. Counselor A has no previous experience in counseling or assessing Asian clients. The issue of competence here addresses the need for supervised training with the particular client population being seen by the mental health agency, as stated by the American Psychological Association (1992):

> 1.08. Human Differences: Where differences of age, gender, race, ethnicity, national origin, religion, sexual orientation, disability, language, or socioeconomic status significantly affect psychologists' work concerning particular individuals or groups, psychologists obtain the training, experience, consultation, or supervision necessary to ensure the competence of their service, or they make appropriate referrals. (p. 4)

The NCDA (2003) ethical standards addresses this situation within the major heading of B. Counseling Relationships, Number 13, stated as follows:

> NCDA members who counsel clients from cultures different from their own must gain knowledge, personal awareness, and sensitivity pertinent to the client populations served and must incorporate culturally relevant techniques into their practice. (p. 5)

Other professional associations usually address this issue of competence in more general terms, stating that counselors are to offer only those counseling services for which they are qualified. In our example, Counselor A could accept such a position if arrangements were made for him to receive supervision that could be completed during training (Gelso & Fretz, 2001).

Example of a Violation

Counselor B, who has specialized in career counseling of adults, has been in private practice for several years. One of her most lucrative referral sources, a local business organization, requested that she administer a specific individual intelligence test to one of its employees. She was told that the results were to be used in a high-stakes decision concerning the promotion of the client to an important position in the organization. Counselor B informed the organization that she has not given an individual intelligence test for several years and did not take a graduate course in individual testing. The organizational representative sent back word that the results were needed immediately and she was to do her best. Realizing that she might lose a most important referral source, she agreed to administer the test.

The violations of competence are quite clear in this case. Counselor B violated ethical codes by performing functions in which she had not received appropriate training. Second, she did not address the issue of promotion based on results from a single standardized test of intelligence. The following codes of ethics from two professional groups apply.

NCDA (2003) ethical standards in Section C, Measurement and Evaluation, number 4, states: "Because many types of assessment techniques exist, NCDA members must recognize the limits of their competence and perform only those functions for which they have received appropriate training" (p. 6).

Likewise, the ACA (1995) code of ethical standards, Section C: Professional Responsibility, C 2 states: "a. Counselors practice only within the boundaries of their competence, based on their education, training, supervised experience, state and national professional credentials, and appropriate professional experience" (p. 4).

Counselor B could have approached this situation by offering assistance in developing valid criteria that can be used in the promotion process. She could also be prepared to offer alternate testing for which she had been trained. Counselors who accept referrals must also be in a position to inform clients of rights to information about the purpose and anticipated courses of action in the use of any and all assessment results.

Some Boundaries of Confidentiality

The principle of the client's rights to privacy is a key element in a counseling relationship, thus counselors usually begin counseling with a reinforcement of the privacy principle. The rationale is that clients expect that discussions of private events and thoughts revealed to counselors will not be shared with others without their consent. All professional counseling associations stress the importance of the client's right to privacy. In NCDA (2003) ethical standards, Section B, Counseling Relationship, it is clearly stated that

> . . . the counseling relationship and information resulting from it remains confidential, consistent with legal obligations of the NCDA member. In a group counseling setting, the career counselor sets a norm of confidentiality regarding all group participants' disclosures. (p. 7)

Example of a Violation

Counselor C shows a client's personality inventory profile to a student worker in the high school counseling center and remarks that this case is going to be difficult. This obvious violation is serious—one that could be damaging to the client even though the counselor in this case did not intend harm and considered his actions as "small talk."

Ethical standards for school counselors were developed by the American School Counselors Association (ASCA) (2003) and clearly identify ethical codes relating to confidentiality as follows:

> A. 2. Confidentiality
>   The professional school counselor:
>   b. Keeps information confidential unless disclosure is required to prevent clear and imminent danger to the counselee or others or when legal requirements demand that confidential information be revealed. Counselors will consult with other professionals when in doubt as to the validity of an exception. (p. 1)

Counselor C's remark is a good example of how casual conversation about clients can result in ethical misconduct. In a counseling center where there is good rapport between staff and professional counselors, one may be tempted to share some bits of confidential information about a client that could lead to damaging results. Information about an individual's personality profile, for example, can be grossly misconstrued by an untrained staff member who then shares this information with someone who makes further misinterpretations and shares his or her own conclusion with yet another person. The end result can be quite damaging to a client who has asked for help.

Example of a Violation

In a large community college, Counselor D is very busy overseeing and providing career counseling services to a steady stream of students. The large number of students using career services attracted the attention of a university professor, who asked for permission to use student files to gather data that were to be used in a research project. The counselor was thrilled to work with the well-known professor and offered to provide access to student records. The data were promptly collected by student workers from open files without the consent of the students who had used career services.

NCDA (2003) ethical standards, Section D, Research and Publication, 9 states: NCDA members who supply data, aid in the research of another person, report research results, or make original data available must take due care to disguise the identity of respective subjects in the absence of specific authorization from the subject to do otherwise.

The implications of this ethical standard are very clear in directing counselors and researchers to the importance of keeping client records confidential. In this case the counselor should only make data available with the student's permission or by providing essential data in a manner that would disguise the identity of each student. Likewise, researchers should make certain that the identity of all subjects studied in research projects is protected and their privacy is maintained. Research projects are most important in the search for answers to improve career counseling effectiveness but should not be accomplished in a way that would not intrude on the individual client's rights of confidentiality and informed consent.

The Code of Ethics of the American Mental Health Counselors Association (AMHCA) (2000) Principle 3 on Confidentiality states:

> Mental Health counselors have a primary obligation to safeguard information about individuals obtained in the course of practice, teaching or research. Personal information is communicated to others only with the person's written consent or in those circumstances where there is clear and imminent danger to the client, to others or to society. Disclosure of counseling information is restricted to what is necessary, relevant and verifiable. (p. 3)

The client's rights to privacy have far-reaching implications for counseling practice. First, the client must be assured that confidentiality will be maintained. Second, effective counseling practices have focused on gaining client rapport and trust in order to freely exchange information. The legal implications of a client's rights to privacy, however, are much more complex and inclusive. It is therefore in the best interest of every professional counselor to review the many issues involved in the confidentiality code of ethics of their professional associations carefully, particularly the boundaries of informed consent.

Example of a Violation

Because of a client's serious personal problems, Counselor D decides to refer this client to another professional located in a nearby mental health agency. Thus, the counselor received written permission to give another professional information gathered in the interview and subsequent counseling sessions. Some contents of the confidential information sent to the mental health agency were leaked to a relative of the client by a part-time clerk. An investigation of the agency revealed that security for confidential information was meager at best and there were no clearly defined policies on maintaining confidential records. In fact, information about clients could be accessed by a number of workers at the agency.

In addition to the violation committed at the mental health agency, the referring counselor violated client confidentiality by not making certain that defined policies were in place that effectively ensured the confidentiality of client information in the agency to which the client had been referred. The lesson here is that you do not assume client confidentiality when you refer clients but in fact have an obligation to the client to see that confidentiality will be maintained.

The ACA Code of Ethics (2005) also addresses confidentiality of records as follows:

Section B. Consultation, b. Cooperating Agencies

Before sharing information counselors make every effort to ensure that there are defined policies in other agencies serving the counselor's client that effectively protect the confidentiality of information, confidentiality of any counseling records they create, maintain, transfer, or destroy, whether the records are written, taped, computerized, or stored in the other medium. (p. 4)

Some Boundaries of Informed Consent

Informed consent involves disclosure by the counselor of important information the client needs in making the decision as to whether she or he is to start counseling. *Free consent* is when a client agrees to engage in counseling without coercion (Welfel, 2013). In informed consent the counselor informs the client of the purpose, goals, and procedures of engaging in a counseling relationship. The counselor and counselee roles should be defined clearly enough so the client is empowered to make informed decisions during the counseling process. In other words, the client is not to be coerced into a counseling relationship but, on the contrary, will have the freedom to choose to participate in certain counseling activities. Free consent also implies that clients have the right to refuse to engage in certain counseling activities; it is imperative therefore that a collaborative counseling partnership be established and effectively maintained. In this kind of counseling relationship, clients and counselors *both* agree on goals and counseling interventions and jointly share in the selection of materials and procedures.

The APA (1992) code of ethical standards, Section 4.01, is one of the most inclusive examples of how to build a counseling relationship (Welfel, 2013).

Section 4.01 Structuring the Relationship

(a) Psychologists discuss with clients or patients as early as is feasible in the therapeutic relationship appropriate issues such as the nature and anticipated course of therapy, fees, and confidentiality.

(b) When the psychologist's work with clients or patients will be supervised, the above discussion includes that fact and the name of the supervisor, when the supervisor has legal responsibility for the case.

(c) When the therapist is a student intern, the client or patient is informed of that fact.

(d) Psychologists make reasonable efforts to answer patients' questions and to avoid apparent misunderstandings about therapy. Whenever possible, psychologists provide oral and/or written materials, using language that is reasonably understandable to the patient or client. (p. 9)

In the process of establishing and structuring a counseling relationship, the counselor communicates basic information concerning the parameters of informed consent. Welfel (2013) has compiled the following list of information that is recommended and should be communicated when applicable:

Goals, techniques, procedures, limitations, risks, and benefits of counseling

Ways in which diagnoses, tests, and written reports will be used

Billing and fees

Confidentiality rights and limitations

Involvement of supervisors or additional mental health professionals

Counselor's training status

Client's access to records

Client's right to choose the counselor and to be active in treatment planning

Client's right to refuse counseling, and the implications of that refusal

Client's right to ask additional questions about counseling and to have questions answered in comprehensible language. (p. 109)

Although this list appears to be very inclusive, there are many more situations in which informed consent is necessary. For example, the use of experimental counseling techniques and electronically recording or observing counseling sessions should be added to the list of information communicated. In sum, what we have here is the *intent* of providing clients with all information about what is to take place in counseling, the materials used, other professionals who may assist or observe, alternative programs, and goals of the counseling process itself. Finally, counselors are to be alert to the methods of obtaining informed consent with special populations such as minors, clients with diminished capacity, and court-mandated counseling (Welfel, 2013).

Finally, we mention that there is increasing concern among professionals of violations of informed consent that are related to telecommunication in psychological practice. Counselors may not be able to verify ages and the mental capacity of individuals who access a counselor's home page and submit e-mail questions. Consequently, there is no adequate way at this time to verify that the recipient of personal advice is a responsible adult and understands the parameters of informed consent.

Some Boundaries of Measurement and Evaluation

Career counselors frequently use standard assessment instruments to measure traits such as interests, personality, and ability, among many others. Computer-generated assessment has also been a popular means of measuring traits that are integral to the counseling process. It should not be surprising that the NCDA has developed ethical codes that foster the use of assessment results. In Section C: Measurement and Evaluation of the NCDA Ethical Standards (2003), there are 15 statements concerning topics such as selection, use, limitation, and interpretation of assessment instruments. They begin by stating the ethical importance of informing the client of the purpose and explicit use of test results. Some other ethical standards include the recommendations that counselors are to recognize the limits of their competence with assessment instruments and all assessment instruments used must meet the standards of validity, reliability, and appropriateness. The administration of tests should follow directions in the test manual and one is not to use tests that contain obsolete data. The following selected ethical standards are quoted in full for emphasis; they contain references to the release of test data and the use of computer-generated assessment:

> 8. An examinee's welfare, explicit prior understanding, and agreement are the factors used when determining who receives the test results. NCDA members must see that appropriate interpretation accompanies any release of individual or group test data (e.g., limitations of instrument and norms).
>
> 9. NCDA members must ensure that computer-generated assessment administration and scoring programs function properly, thereby providing clients with accurate assessment results. (pp. 6–7)

Example of a Violation

Groups of community college students are invited to the career center for help in choosing a major. During the course of the discussions, students are invited to take an interest inventory to help them decide on a college major. They are told to drop by the counseling center to pick up the results the next day. Those who want more advice at that time can make an appointment to see a counselor or join a group for more information.

All test results, including interest inventories, should be "placed in proper perspective with other relevant factors" in the career counseling process (NCDA, 2003). The release of test data to clients without the benefit of interpretation of the results and the meaning and proper perspective of those results is a serious violation of ethics. Assessment results are used most effectively when their purpose is clearly established through a review of their applications for the individual, their limitations, and how the results will specifically assist in goal attainment.

Example of a Violation

A student in a university psychology class obtains an appointment with a career counselor. He tells the counselor that after reading about personality disorders in his textbook, he thinks that he has a personality disorder that has "bothered me for a long time." Although he has made a definite career decision, he has doubts about his ability to accomplish his goal since "I might have a personality disorder." The counselor explains that verifying a personality disorder will require extensive testing and interview time. He suggests to the client that he should return after semester break for an appointment, but if there is an emergency he should find a professional near his home. The counselor also offered to help find a qualified person. The student was insistent, however, about finding some other way of checking out his problem before he returns. Because the semester was over and he was on his way home, the counselor suggested that he take a personality inventory on the Internet and bring the results for interpretation when he returned from semester break.

The APA (1992) on ethical principles, Section 2.08: Test Scoring and Interpretation Services, states:

> (b) Psychologists select scoring and interpretation services (including automated services) on the basis of evidence of the validity of the program and procedures as well as other appropriate considerations.

(c) Psychologists retain appropriate responsibility for the appropriate application, interpretation, and use of assessment instruments, whether they score and interpret such test themselves or use automated or other services. (p. 7)

Several ethical principles were violated by the counselor in our example. The exact number of sites on the Internet that offer psychological and career assessment is unknown, but there is evidence that the number has increased significantly (Sampson & Lumsden, 2000). Counselors are to use only test administration and interpretation services for which there is sufficient evidence of their validity and reliability and evidence of appropriate application and interpretation. Many unanswered questions remain about the marketing and availability of psychological testing on the web. Counselors are advised to exercise extreme caution with such services at the present time. In the case of a suspected personality disorder, the counselor had insufficient information about the client's problems. He was in no position to suggest any standardized testing, much less a personality test administered on the Internet in which the client was to interpret his results.

Some NCDA Guidelines for Using the Internet

The use of the Internet for the delivery of career-related services has been carefully scrutinized by the NCDA (1997) and other professional organizations. It is quite evident that the capabilities of Internet delivery services will expand rapidly with the onset of sound and video. We can expect that the NCDA will monitor online career-related services very carefully in the future; more ethical standards and codes should follow. In the meantime we review guidelines approved by the NCDA in October 1997.

Some distinctions are made between career planning and career counseling services when clients are using the Internet. When clients are involved in specific planning needs such as identification of occupations based on interests, skills, and experiences, or support for job seeking, they are engaging in career planning. Even though these same services are a part of career counseling, this term implies a more in-depth procedure in a counseling relationship. Client Y, for example, is majoring in accounting and is looking in a specific location for a future job. Client Y is considered to be a career planner, although if client Y becomes discouraged and considers a career change, he or she will take part in a systematic career counseling process. Thus, there are multiple needs of clients that may involve the use of the Internet. In all cases, however, the counselor has a significant ethical responsibility.

Here are some general suggestions based on NCDA (1997) guidelines for the use of the Internet for provision of career information and planning services as paraphrased:

1. Counselors are to evaluate websites and other services to make certain they have been prepared by professional career counselors; the developer's credentials and qualifications should be carefully evaluated.
2. Counselors are to have knowledge of free public access points to ensure that all clients have the advantage of Internet career-related services.
3. The appropriateness of the content on the website should be carefully scrutinized. Each website should state the kinds of client concerns its programs can address.
4. Counselors should screen each client's career counseling needs and determine if those needs can be addressed appropriately on the Internet.

5. Counselors are to monitor each client's progress periodically and be prepared to offer referrals in the client's geographical location. A review of client progress should be thorough and, if there is doubt about the client's progress, a referral to face-to-face services should be made.

6. The provider of Internet services should present credentials to the user; develop individual counseling goals for each user; inform the user of costs; how to report unethical behavior; security measures used; information about electronically stored data, how privacy is maintained; and provide easily accessed pathways to career, educational, and employment information.

7. The website should also include information and services available through linkage with other websites.

8. The use of assessment guidelines includes (a) the need to assure that psychometric properties of assessment instruments on the Internet are the same as printed forms, (b) the ethical standards of administering and interpreting the printed form of a test used must be maintained, (c) assessment results are to be confidential, (d) clients who do not fully understand the meaning of assessment results should be referred to a qualified counselor, and (e) all measurement instruments used that require interpretation by the user must be validated as self-help instruments.

Finally, unacceptable counselor behavior on the Internet was identified by NCDA (1997) as follows:

1. Use of false e-mail identity when interacting with clients and/or other professionals. When acting in a professional capacity on the Internet, a counselor has a duty to honestly identify him/herself.

2. Accepting a client who will not identify him/herself and be willing to arrange for phone conversation as well as online interchange.

3. "Sharking" or monitoring chat rooms and bulletin board services, and offering career planning and related services when no request has been made for services. This includes sending out mass unsolicited e-mails. Counselors may advertise their services but must do so observing proper "netiquette" and standards of professional conduct. (p. 5)

Concerns about Internet counseling relationships have also been expressed by the National Board for Certified Counselors, Inc. and Center for Credentialing and Education, Inc. (2001). Some concerns are difficulty in identifying Internet clients, need for parental/guardian consent of a minor, confidentiality of Internet counseling, identification of local assistance in case of emergencies, and lack of visual cues during the counseling process. These and other concerns should occupy the research efforts of many professionals in the future. Clearly, there is much to be learned about the use of the Internet for career-related assessment and counseling. Also see Ethical Standards for Internet On-Line Counseling approved by the ACA governing council in October 1999.

Some Ethical Implications of Using Peer Helpers

In the 1960s, Zunker and Brown (1966) published a study involving the use of trained peer counselors to deliver academic adjustment guidance to entering college freshmen students. The purpose of the student-to-student counseling program was to assist students in adjusting to the changes in academic demands and requirements from high school to college. In small groups of three to five students, trained peers, usually juniors and seniors, presented a very carefully structured program that included examples of how to plan a class schedule, take class notes, choose a college major, and improve study habits. Discussions focused on the give-and-take of college life and the discipline and skills necessary to be a successful student. The program was successful both in terms of student survival after one semester in college and in that many peer counselors became interested in counseling as a result of their peer counseling experiences.

When this study's results were reported in several presentations at professional association conventions, ethical concerns regarding peer helping programs surfaced. There was a general concern, and rightly so, that peer helping programs could pose some potential ethical risks such as confidentiality concerns, the client's rights of privacy, and competency issues of peer helpers. Over the years, peer counseling programs have grown and expanded to include such issues as suicide, drug and alcohol abuse, and depression. It is not unusual to find peer helpers or facilitators in high school counseling centers as well as universities and in community mental health programs. In career counseling programs, peer counselors are used in a variety of helping positions such as discussion leaders, career information facilitators, and in outreach programs. Lenz (2000) has published an outstanding review of the use of paraprofessionals in career services.

Welfel (2002) suggests that in career counseling programs that use peer counselors, clients are to be informed of issues of confidentiality. More specifically, clients should be informed that peer counselors have been thoroughly informed of ethical standards of confidentiality. Secondly, clients are also to be informed of the responsibility and oversight of professional directors of peer counseling programs on all issues of confidentiality. The implications of a well-informed peer helper suggests to clients that they are well trained for their helping roles and are regularly supervised. Peer counselors who are well trained are also aware of their limitations as a helper and therefore have explicit instructions on how and where to refer students who may express personal concerns that require professional help. The roles and limitations of peer helpers should be thoroughly defined. The dedication of a professionally trained and certified counselor to the administration and supervision of peer counseling programs is an essential part of what makes peer counselors effective and ethical.

A Model for Ethical Practice

At this point the reader may ask the question: What am I to do if I witness a breach of ethical standards? Or how can I decide if what I witnessed was unethical behavior that needs to be reported? One way of solving these difficult questions is to go through the steps of an ethical decision model. The following 10-step model of ethical decision making has been developed by Welfel (2013, p. 30):

Develop ethical sensitivity

Clarify facts, stakeholders, and the sociocultural context of the case

Define the central issues and the available options

Refer to professional standards and relevant laws/regulations

Search out ethics scholarship

Apply ethical principles to the situation

Consult with supervisor and respected colleagues

Deliberate and decide

Inform supervisor, implement and document decision-making process and actions

Reflect on the experience

This straightforward model strongly suggests that unethical conduct has many very important consequences. Wise counselors will do their ethical homework that prepares them not only for what they may witness, but also, perhaps even more importantly, for their own protection. Ethical codes and guidelines are to be kept up to date and periodically reviewed. One is to become most sensitive to the moral dimensions of practice. If one is in doubt about a situation, attempt to identify the facts and central issues in order to make a decision about options. Using this information, one is to consult ethical standards, laws, and regulations. In this process one is to respect confidentiality. At this point a trusted colleague should be contacted for assistance and consultation. It is also recommended that independent deliberation take place in order to make a decision. At this point it is most important that appropriate people are to be informed. Finally, one is to reflect on their actions in order to gain the full benefit of the action taken (Welfel, 2013).

On Becoming Ethical

In this brief review of ethical standards that included some ethical codes from several professional associations, I find that there are reminders of conduct that is considered ethically correct but which constitutes a violation of professional ethics. Be aware that only a small number of ethical violations have been discussed. Counselors should also remain alert to changes in the code of ethics of their professional organizations. There are general themes, however, that permeate the ethical position of most counseling associations. One theme suggests that counselors must be dedicated to the welfare of their clients. This dedication includes not only the development of counseling knowledge and skills to address presenting problems from clients, but also the desire and knowledge of how to appropriately accomplish counseling goals in an ethical manner. What is suggested here is that counselors not only expand and sharpen their skills to meet a variety of client needs, but also increase their knowledge of ethical codes and standards.

The intent of the counselor to do what is ethically appropriate in a counseling relationship is an essential part of a moral obligation of most professional counseling associations. Counselors are to fully understand that there are severe legal ramifications of misconduct. As with most standards, codes, rules, and laws, ignorance of the law does not excuse anyone from committing a violation. Counselors are to recognize that in the 21st century it is most important to learn the general principles of ethical standards and codes that have been developed by their professional associations. In addition, counselors should find a source or sources that are easily accessible for advice and consultation concerning appropriate ethical practice.

In sum, I have introduced only some principles of ethical codes and standards. My purpose was to inform readers of the importance of ethics in counseling practice. Second, there are indications that counselors can expect to find that the appropriateness of their methods, procedures, and counseling materials will be carefully scrutinized. All professional counselors must therefore be prepared to show evidence of their training and credentials as well as continued training to update their skills to use new and different procedures and materials. An increased sensitivity to potential ethical problems that could arise from certain counseling encounters should be fostered through workshops and by reviewing the details of ethical codes and standards of your professional associations. Finally, ethical complaints by NCDA members can be filed by any individual or group of individuals to this address:

ACA Ethics Committee
Executive Director
American Counseling Association
5999 Stevenson Avenue
Alexandria, VA 22304

Summary

1. Ethical standards and codes address moral dimensions of counseling relationships.
2. Counselors are to practice within the boundaries of their competence.
3. Counselors should only seek positions for which they are qualified.
4. Counselors are to recognize their limits of competence.
5. Information associated with a counseling relationship is to remain confidential.
6. Disclosure of information to another professional requires a signed written consent.
7. The client's rights to privacy must be upheld.
8. Free consent suggests that a client agrees to engage in a counseling relationship without coercion.
9. Informed consent suggests that clients are informed of the purpose and goals of counseling.
10. Clients are also to be informed of the purpose and explicit use of assessment instruments.
11. Counselors are to select scoring and interpretation services, including automated services, only on the basis of information of their validity.
12. The use of the Internet in career counseling requires a careful and thorough evaluation that is very inclusive.
13. Peer counselors must be thoroughly trained in the ethics of counseling, especially regarding issues of confidentiality and competency.
14. Counselors should evaluate ethical practices through an ethical decision-making model.

Supplementary Learning Exercises

1. Under what conditions could a counselor accept a position for which he or she is not qualified? Defend your answer.
2. Investigate professional associations to determine what is considered to be appropriate training for you to incorporate a newly developed counseling technique or assessment instrument in your practice. Share with classmates.
3. List and discuss the conditions under which you could disclose information about a client without his or her consent.
4. Discuss the importance of a client's rights to privacy in a counseling relationship.

5. Under what conditions can counselors be assured that peer counselors are following appropriate ethical standards? What do you consider to be the greatest ethical risk with the use of peer counselors?

Case 8.1   Witnessing a Breach of Ethics

Jan, a middle-school counselor, could feel the tension among students who were scheduled to take standardized achievement tests. It was also a very busy day for Jan as she assisted in distributing tests to each classroom. After all tests were in their proper place and as Jan was strolling down the hallway she was stunned when she witnessed a teacher giving students the correct answers to several test questions. When the teacher spotted Jan, she told her she was finished with instructions and closed the door. Jan, almost in shock, quickly returned to her office. Jan was certain that what she had witnessed was an obvious breach of ethics by a teacher she had worked with for several years.

Using the model for ethical decision making, reply to the following statements and questions.

1. Clarify facts and stakeholders involved in this case.
2. Define the central issue and available options.
3. List some of the professional standards and relevant regulations you could use that apply to this case.
4. How would you document what you witnessed?
5. With whom would you confer in this case?
6. What do you believe should be the optimal outcome in this case?

Option 1. Compare your answers with classmates.

Option 2. Divide into groups and compare your conclusions.

PART TWO
Career Counseling for Special Populations

9

Career Counseling for Multicultural Groups

CHAPTER HIGHLIGHTS

- Culture as a complex concept

- Cultural differences in work-related activities

- Five major culture groups

- Skills for cultural competence

- Strategies for dealing with multicultural influences

- Mental health issues of cultural groups

The need to develop career counseling strategies for multicultural groups will increase throughout this century. By the middle of the 21st century, the United States will no longer be a predominately White society. A more appropriate reference could be "a global society," in which half of all Americans will be from four ethnic groups: Asian Americans, African Americans, Hispanic Americans, and Native Americans. These projected demographics containing the potential of an increasingly diverse society will present significant challenges to all the human service practitioners. As more multicultural groups gain access to opportunities for education and higher status jobs, the career counseling profession should be prepared to assist them.

Career counselors are intent on developing career counseling objectives and strategies that will assist individuals of various ethnic groups to overcome a multitude of barriers including prejudice, socioeconomic status, language differences, cultural isolation, and culture-related differences. Because this group is composed of persons from a wide variety of ethnic backgrounds, counselors are being challenged to become culturally aware, evaluate their personal views, and understand that other people's perspectives may be as legitimate as their own (Brammer, 2012; Diller, 2011; Ponterotto et al., 2010; Ridley, 2005).

I begin this chapter with an introduction to the meaning of culture as it relates to career counseling. Second, cultural variability and worldviews are examined followed by culturally related work values and cultural differences in negotiations in the third section. In the fourth section, the challenge of becoming culturally competent is presented. Five major cultural groups are discussed in the fifth section. Mental health issues of cultural groups are reviewed in the sixth section. In the seventh section, I discuss issues when working with men and women of different cultures.

What Is Culture?

Cultural diversity is an important topic for all counselors, especially for the career counselor. In many respects, we have not addressed the issue of culture in the counseling profession. For example, researchers are in the early stages of studies to determine appropriate intervention strategies and assessment instruments for specific ethnic groups (Paniagua, 2005; Ponterotto et al., 2010) which are among the many issues and questions to be resolved. Because of the variety of ethnic groups found in the United States today, we may find the answer to these issues and questions to be very evasive and quite complex. To deal with this subject in greater depth, readers are provided with several relevant references in this chapter. In the meantime, the career counselor must give high priority to cultural variables that influence career development.

Returning to the question of identifying culture, perhaps each of us could offer an explanation of what culture means. We would be able to illustrate our definitions with examples of cultural aspects, variables, customs, and perceptions of different individuals from a variety of "cultures." We could describe activities associated with a culture, we could refer to the heritage and traditions of cultures, we could describe rules and norms associated with cultures, we could describe behavioral approaches associated with cultures, and we could describe the origin of cultures. These are examples of different meanings associated with the definition of culture and the different interpretations one can use to identify people of different cultures. Thus, culture is a complex concept that can refer to many aspects of life and living. In addition to the definition of culture by Ogbu in chapter 1, Matsumoto and Juang (2013) offer the following definition:

> Culture is a dynamic system of rules, explicit, and implicit, established by groups in order to ensure their survival, involving attitudes, values, beliefs, norms, and behaviors, shared by a group but harbored differently by each specific unit within the group, communicated across generations, relatively stable but potential to change across time. (p. 119)

This definition, although leaving a lot to be said about culture, provides a good fit for the career counselor's use of the word. For example, sharing implies the degree to which an individual holds the values, attitudes, beliefs, norms, or behaviors of a particular group. Furthermore, the emphasis is on cognitive processes of psychological sharing of a particular attribute among members of a culture. Although culture can be conceptualized in different ways, there appears to be agreement that language, family structure, environment (social context), and traditions are most influential in determining group differences (Higginbotham & Andersen, 2012; Sue et al., 2014). The lesson to be learned is that even within cultures, each individual should be treated as such rather than from a stereotypical viewpoint that one has about a particular culture. There is cultural diversity among members of any ethnic group; for instance, Wehrly (1995) points out that 56 ethnic groups identify with their own culture and have their own language in Mexico. The point is that one should not assume that any ethnic group is homogenous.

Culture is a learned behavior. Therefore, two people from the same race may share some values, attitudes, and so on but might also have very different cultural make-ups. How much has been acculturated from racial heritage through socialization varies even within the dominant cultural group of a country (Matsumoto & Juang, 2013; Ponterotto et al., 2010). Therefore, we must not make assumptions from cultural stereotypes—all clients are to be treated as individuals who have their own distinct characteristics and traits. In the next section, I will briefly review two important issues—cultural variability and worldviews.

Cultural Variability and Worldviews

In general terms, worldview refers to the individual's perception and understandings of the world. Several researchers including Matsumoto and Juang (2013) point out that worldviews include, among other variables, perceptions of basic human nature, the roles of families, relationships with others, locus of control, orientation of time, work values, and activities. Worldviews, in this context, are developed both through individual experiences that are nonshared and through shared experiences and events. Nonshared experiences account for much of the variability within cultures, whereas shared experiences reflect worldviews that are common among members of a specific culture. Individualism and collectivism are often used to explain cultural differences. In individualistic cultures, such as those in Europe and North America, a great amount of value is placed on individual accomplishment. The individual strives for self-actualization. The rugged individualist is revered for his or her autonomy and independence; individuals are empowered to achieve and become individually responsible.

In collectivist cultures, such as those in Africa, Asia, and Latin America, the individual's major function is focused on the welfare of the group for their collective survival. Individuals strive to build group solidarity. In these societies, individual uniqueness is not rejected, but more emphasis is placed on being identified with one's social group. The needs of the group take precedence over self-interest. What is important here are sharing, cooperation, and social responsibility. An individual may conceptualize a career choice, for example, from the perception of what is best for the family group rather than from an individualistic perspective. In many collectivist cultures, family is more important than the individual (Brammer, 2012).

When counseling individuals from different ethnic groups, counselors should evaluate the degree and nature of acculturation by how it has affected the client's worldview. One is to evaluate if some cultural values break down as the younger generations assimilate the values of the dominant White culture. In this context, acculturation refers to the extent to which a client has assumed the beliefs, values, and behaviors of the dominant White society. It is not unusual for some clients to make an attempt to adjust to local environments whereas others live biculturally or multiculturally: One can expect to find that some clients adopt behaviors of the White dominant culture but retain values from their own culture and the cultures of others they have come to know. Many experience conflicts, especially between generations, when older members of a family want to retain cultural rules, scripts, and roles, while the younger generation adopts those of the dominant White society. The collectivist view of family honor conditions one to never oppose family decisions, but members of the younger generation may prefer a shift of locus of control from a collectivist to an individualist position. Clients in this position share a growing desire to express themselves independently and make decisions based on their individual needs and self-interest (Matsumoto & Juang, 2013).

Among some cultures, differences in time orientation from the dominant society can present barriers to effective career planning and other time commitments that are normally assumed in career counseling. In traditional career counseling, the client is expected to be on time for appointments and abide by a set of deadlines to complete certain counseling interventions. In many collectivist cultures, individuals are not as obsessed with being on time and maintaining a strict time commitment. A Navajo Indian woman asked me if the next meeting would be "Indian time" or "American time." She explained that "Indian time" is "whenever we get together that is convenient." Being on time for most counselors is viewed as a positive value, and lateness is often misunderstood as a symptom of indifference or a lack of basic work skills. In this case, I learned firsthand that time orientation has different meanings for different cultural groups.

Another worldview perspective, how different groups view human nature, is an important concept for counselors to understand when working with multicultural groups. African Americans and European Americans consider human nature as both good and bad. In African American cultures, good and bad behavior is determined by their benefits to the community. European Americans judge good and bad as a part of each individual; good and bad are two sides of human nature that are in opposition and conflict (Diller, 2011).

The belief that human nature is basically good and that human beings can be trusted to have positive motives is shared by Asian, Native, and Latino/a American cultures. Following this logic has subjected these groups to being judged by the dominant society as naive and gullible in the workplace. The perception is that individuals who follow such logic need to "wise up" to reality. Counselors should help individuals from different cultures to be aware of and alert to workplace associations, which might require them to modify their conceptualizations of human nature.

Finally, personal space and privacy are also considered to be culturally oriented. Individuals from different cultures tend to invade each other's personal space without being aware of it. Triandis (1994), known for his cross-culture studies, suggests that you invade personal space by walking into it, staring into it, and even through smell by wearing a strong perfume. This invasion is culturally determined; for instance, North American and Arabic cultures expect others to look them in the eye when talking, whereas Asians consider direct eye contact to be insulting.

Conversational distances are also determined by language and culture; for example, Latino/as usually stand closer to each other than European Americans do when conversing. Arabs expect to stand very close to each other when engaged in serious conservation (Ivey et al., 2014). Counselors need to be alert to any signals of discomfort with regard to space and adjust distances accordingly.

In sum, individuals are socialized and shaped by their societies and contextual interactions within their environments. Thus, it is not surprising that one cultural group may generally view a behavior as being appropriate, but members of a different culture may view that same behavior as gross or insulting. The point here is that counselors must attempt to understand clients in terms of their origins, assimilation, and acculturation; one should learn to appreciate differences that exist in the way others think and behave. Stereotyping clients by their culture is to be avoided. Counselors are to recognize that there are different worldviews within cultural groups; each client must be approached as an individual. Worldviews are developed within cultural contexts and they are indeed unique for each individual. Finally, worldviews can be modified through experiences with other cultures (Ponterotto et al., 2010). In the next section, I discuss the findings of a well-known study concerning cultural differences in work-related activities.

Cultural Differences in Work-Related Activities

Many clients have different work values, including people from different cultural backgrounds. It should surprise no one that value orientations to work can be sources of serious conflict and misunderstanding in the workplace. One of the most provocative studies of work-related values was done by Hofstede (2001) in the 1980s and continues to be quoted in much of the literature concerning culture and work behavior. His study included 50 different countries in 20 different languages and 7 different occupational levels (Matsumoto & Juang, 2013). His aim was to determine dimensions of cultural differences of work-related values. His findings are paraphrased as follows:

1. *Power distance.* This dimension attempts to answer the basic hierarchical relationship between immediate boss and subordinate. In some countries, such as the Philippines, Mexico, Venezuela, and India, individuals tended to maintain strong status differences. In countries such as New Zealand, Denmark, Israel, and Austria, status and power differentials were minimized. In the United States, there was some degree of minimizing power differences.

2. *Uncertainty avoidance.* This term is used to describe how different cultures and societies deal with anxiety and stress. On a questionnaire designed for this study, countries that had low uncertainty avoidance indexes differed significantly from countries that had high scores. Workers with low scores had lower job stress, less resistance to change, greater readiness to live for the day, and stronger ambition for advancement. Workers with high uncertainty avoidance scores tended to fear failure, were less involved in risk taking, had higher levels of job stress, experienced more worry about the future, and tended to have higher anxiety. The countries with the highest scores on this dimension were Greece, Portugal, Belgium, and Japan. Countries with lowest scores were Sweden, Denmark, and Singapore.

3. *Individualism/collectivism.* This dimension attempted to answer the question about which cultures foster individual tendencies rather than group or collectivist tendencies. The results of this study suggested that the United States, Great Britain, Australia, and Canada had the highest scores for individualism. Peru, Colombia, and Venezuela were most collectivistic. People in highly individualistic countries were characterized as placing more importance on employees' personal lifestyle, were emotionally independent from the company, found small companies attractive, and placed more importance on freedom and challenge in jobs. People in countries with low individualism were emotionally dependent on companies, frowned on individual initiative, considered group decisions better than individual ones, and aspired to conformity and orderliness in managerial positions.

4. *Masculinity.* This dimension is thought to be an indicator of which cultures would maintain and foster differences between sexes in the workplace. However, most employees who answered the questionnaire were men, so the conclusions drawn here should be considered tentative. People in countries that had high scores on this variable were characterized as believing in independent decision making, having stronger achievement motivation, and aspiring for recognition. People in countries that had low scores on this variable were characterized as believing in group decisions, seeing security as more important, preferring shorter working hours, and having lower job stress. Countries with high scores on this dimension were Japan, Austria, Venezuela, and Italy. Countries with low scores were Denmark, the Netherlands, Norway, and Sweden.

These results appear to suggest that culture does have an important role in work-related values. Moreover, we can conclude that employees' perceptions of work roles—as well as of other life roles—are influenced by culture-related values. Differences between cultures help in understanding employee attitudes, values, behaviors, and interpersonal dynamics. Nevertheless, one must be reminded that differences between countries, as outlined in this study, need not necessarily correspond with similar differences on the individual level. The cultural differences found in this study suggest that we use them as general guidelines as follows: to understand how cultural differences can influence work-related values, lead to conflicts in the workplace, provide an awareness of legitimate cultural differences, and challenge all to recognize that individual differences exist within cultures (Diller, 2011; Pedersen, Lonner, Draguns, & Trimble, 2008).

Cultural Differences in Negotiations

One would also expect to find additional differences between cultural groups in their approach to negotiations with other countries and in the process itself. The delicate process of negotiations between two different cultures underscores the need to understand the impact of cultural values and customs. Kimmel (1994) points out that in the United States most negotiators approach others with a firm commitment to established assumptions that are rooted in American culture and values. Pragmatism, independence, and competition, for instance, are characteristic of an American's business person's approach to negotiating with others. The major goal is to get the best deal as quickly as possible. In America, for example, one focuses on getting the job done quickly with little attention paid to social activities or building relationships.

What is implied here is that American negotiators tend to give little consideration to what is expected in the process of negotiations by some cultures. People of many other cultures, for example, place a great deal of emphasis on the role of socializing as a most important part of the negotiation process. There is an expectation to engage in such social activities as having dinner together, playing golf, and/or just hanging out. The differences of expectations and basic beliefs on how to reach agreements are quite clear. To the American negotiator this is business only: get the job done, meet the deadline, and make sure bottom-line objectives have been accomplished. In contrast, the basic beliefs and values of many other cultures are that negotiations are built from human relationships that are fostered by social activities. The goal in this case is to build long-term relationships. In addition, when both parties benefit from negotiations, it is considered a success (Matsumoto & Juang, 2013).

Counselors are to be prepared to assist clients build an understanding of intercultural issues in the workplace. The United States currently has an abundance of multinational and international corporations and more are expected in the future. Globalization will bring the challenges that accompany interactions of workers with vastly different views and lifestyles. An understanding and respect of the beliefs and values of other cultures should certainly contribute to harmony in the working world.

The Challenge of Becoming Culturally Competent

During the last three decades, an increasing number of publications have addressed the need for counselors to become culturally competent, that is, to develop the ability to provide appropriate services cross-culturally. In the early 1990s, Sue and colleagues (1992) developed nine competence areas as basic for a culturally skilled counselor.

The three overarching dimensions were (1) understanding one's assumptions, values, and biases; (2) understanding the worldview of the culturally different client; and (3) developing appropriate intervention strategies and techniques. The three dimensions are broken down into subgroups of beliefs and attitudes, knowledge, and skills, and each of the subgroups is delineated in self-explanatory statements. Information about competencies can be obtained from the American Counseling Association website listed in appendix I.

In an earlier publication, Cross, Bazron, Dennis, and Isaacs (1989) developed individual cultural competence skills. They suggested five skill areas that have some overlap with the nine competence areas reported by Sue and colleagues. Growth in each of the five skill areas can be measured separately, but growth in one area tends to support growth in the others. They include (1) awareness and acceptance of differences, (2) self-awareness, (3) dynamics of difference, (4) knowledge of the client's culture, and (5) adaptation of skills. Each skill area will be discussed next.

The first skill area, awareness and acceptance of differences, is essential for counselors to begin the process of becoming culturally competent. In addition to recognizing individual and unique differences with every client, counselors are to become more aware of cultural differences that exist in the worldviews and work-related activities that were discussed earlier. This first step is essential for developing an appreciation of cultural diversity.

When discussing awareness of differences, Diller (2011) suggested that Western-oriented mental health practices cannot be applied universally to culturally different populations without recognition of significant cultural differences. These groups of researchers implied that counselors who are unaware of different worldviews (psychological orientation, manners of thinking, ways of behaving and interpreting events) are essentially ineffective; counselors must learn to be more aware of the worldviews of others. The following characteristics are thought to be essential for one to be a culturally effective counselor (Sue & Sue, 1990, p. 451):

1. An ability to recognize which values and assumptions the counselor holds regarding the desirability or undesirability of human behavior
2. Awareness of the generic characteristics of counseling that cut across many schools of counseling theory
3. Understanding of the sociopolitical forces (oppression and racism) that have influenced the identity and perspective of the culturally different
4. An ability to share the worldview of his or her clients without negating its legitimacy
5. True eclecticism in his or her counseling.

Clearly counselors are to use their entire repertoire of counseling skills as long as they accept different views and are cognizant of the experiences and lifestyle of the culturally different. These researchers emphasized that counselors must be alert to the influences of different views and environmental factors that were developed in one's cultural context. Finally, counselors must be cautious not to impose their values on others.

The second skill area, self-awareness, requires the counselor to recognize any prejudice that would make it difficult to empathize with people of color. Counselors are to view the role of culture in their own lives as a backdrop for appreciating how and why others may be different. The recommended outcome is for an appreciation of how a variety of cultural variables shape human behavior. To develop this skill area, one is required to develop sufficient self-knowledge of culture-specific factors

that influence behavior and a personal awareness of one's own cultural background
In short, counselors must recognize their limitations when counseling someone of
different culture. An evaluation of racial attitudes, beliefs, and feelings may well
assessed by a White racial identity developmental model such as the one built arc
the work of Carter (1995b) and Helms (1990). Their conceptualization of an id
model that represents that of a White member of the dominant society cont
stages:

1. Contact stage: Is unaware of any biases associated with his or her rac
   identity.
2. Disintegration stage: Acknowledges a White identity that often re
   sion and conflict.
3. Reintegration stage: Devalues other races and idealizes whitene
4. Pseudo-independent stage: Intellectualizes the understanding
   other races and is somewhat tolerant.
5. Autonomy stage: Becomes nonracist and internalizes a mult

This model enlightens counselors to the behavioral cha
various stages of identity development for both the counselo
cess should not be conceived as a linear progression, but
cyclical, involving interactions with individuals from di
adaptive changes. Counselors should continually evaluate
as racial and cultural beings.

The third skill area, the dynamics of difference
This skill is seen as a counselor's knowledge of su
in the way they interact and communicate. Eye c
meanings; some cultures avoid eye contact and oth
Counselors can communicate an awareness of di
ing appropriate cultural counseling techniques.

The fourth skill area, knowledge of the c
are to prepare for counseling by familiarizing
entation. Suggested topics include country
language, religion, family role, gender r
behavior, cultural values and ideologies
ships, work roles, customs, and traditio
relevant in the counseling process, espe
laborative relationships between client
counseling outcomes.

The adaptation of skills, the fifth
grams and intervention strategies
counselors must be familiar with t
ents from collectivistic cultures m
sions, and counselors who ignore
need to evaluate the counseling
ods, procedures, and materials
appropriate.

Counselors who become f
trism" will fully appreciate th
procedures. The term "etic
The basic assumption, for
by universal cultural norm

of all cultures; one's perspective is to judge behavior on what a counselor considers to be universal standards of behavior. The term "emic" considers truths as culture specific. In this case the basic assumption is that we should judge an individual's behavior by the values, beliefs, and social mores of his or her particular culture. The emic perspective involves behavioral norms within the client's culture (Paniagua, 2005; Wehrly, 1995). When counselors insist on using their own background of biases, values, and beliefs to interpret culturally different actions and behaviors, they are suggesting that their race is superior, and that is known as ethnocentricism (Ivey et al., 2014).

l Identity

There has been a long association in career counseling with the term "identity." Career counselors focus on how individuals understand self and form a personal identity that is recognized by others. There are, however, numerous forms of identity, but the focus here is on personal, collective, and relational identities.

Personal identity makes one unique and has been a key issue in the career choice ocess for all clients, especially for those who come from different cultural groups. lective identities are created as members of social groups and networks, for exam- religious, cultural, occupational, and other social groups. Relational identities are d through group affiliation and interactions. People strive to build meaningful ting relationships. Interactions within groups teach social norms.

at is most important for counselors to recognize is that identities are fluid; hange over time. Multicultural identities may provide the possibility of ychocultural influences suggesting that both individualistic and collectiv- ws influence the formation of self-identity. Immigrant groups, however, in their original identity as a positive factor when facing uncertainties ment (Matsumoto & Juang, 2013).

ll and competency development are most important in meeting the ming culturally competent. Counselors, however, must also evalu- imptions about career counseling, that is, can contemporary theory the needs of an increasingly diverse population? What is implied s not only need to build skills for cultural competency, but must rlying principles of current theories and practices. In the next ive major cultural groups.

e grouped individuals by culture for a variety of reasons, l census. One of the most recent groupings is as follows: ften used), Asian, Southeast Asian, Asian Indian, and o/a is often used), Native Americans (First Nations (Anglo-Saxon and European American is often used). entages of our total population by race from 1990 and at almost 50% of the population in the United States (U.S. Department of Commerce, 1996). More spe- increase from 12% to 15% in African Americans; s; from 3% to 10% in Asian and Pacific Islanders; ecrease from 76% to 52% in White Americans.

FIGURE 9.1

Percentage of population by race

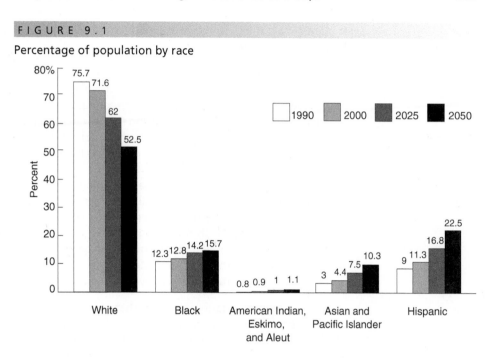

These data indicate that we must continue to rethink our counseling theories, models, and materials to meet the needs of this increasingly diverse population. Even though there appears to be justification for the construct of human universal issues common to all people, we must also remember that each individual is shaped by unique contextual experiences. This message has been repeated often throughout this text.

African Americans

The second largest racial minority group in this country is African Americans. Most African Americans live in urban areas and for the most part, they have been wage earners rather than being self-employed. Almost half of all African Americans own their home and a significant number are employed as business executives, managers, and professionals. African American men have achieved greater career mobility than African American women have. Some of both sexes have achieved upward mobility to professional occupations as the overall success of African Americans' upward movement increases. Those who have attained middle-class status are also in position to take advantage of educational opportunities and career mobility. Others, particularly those classified as underclass—primarily from three generations of families on welfare—are without job skills and experience both internal and external resistance to changing their status.

The loss of jobs in the manufacturing sector has reduced job opportunities for many minority workers, including African Americans. Many of these jobs were filled by unskilled and semiskilled workers. It is therefore critical to connect minority groups with training and educational opportunities. Counseling interventions that encourage skill development to compete for the more attractive jobs in the workplace are most desirable; however, occupations that are available to African Americans continue to be relatively constricted.

Paniagua (2005) suggests some relevant counseling procedures for African Americans as follows:

1. Discuss racial differences.

   One is to ask how the client feels about working with a White counselor. The obvious purpose of the discussion is to convince the client of the counselor's sensitivity to racism and oppression and that all clients have unique experiences that are considered in the counseling process. African American counselors are not to assume that they have a guarantee of success because of their ethnic background.

2. Assess the client's level of acculturation.

3. Avoid offering causal explanations of problems.

   One is to avoid linking mental health problems to members of the family.

4. Include the client's church in the counseling process.

5. Recognize and define the roles of those who accompany the client.

   Involvement of family in interventions can be very effective.

6. Emphasize strengths rather than deficits.

7. Avoid giving the impression that you as a counselor are a protector of the race.

These recommendations suggest that counseling someone of a different cultural background will require preparation designed to understand culture-specific variables in order to appropriately address their needs. In the case of African Americans, counselors can build an understanding of their needs by becoming familiar with their unique history, and the impact of contemporary racism and oppression.

Asian and Pacific Americans

In the 2000 census, four major groups emerged as a means of identifying the incredibly diverse Asian population that now resides in the United States: Asians, Southeast Asians, Asian Indians, and other Asians. These groups are further divided as follows:

Asian Americans	Chinese, Japanese, Filipino, Korean
Southeast Asians	Cambodian, Hmong, Vietnamese, Laotian, Thai, Malaysian, Singaporean
Asian Indians	Bengalese, Bharat, Dravidian, East Indian, Goanese
Other Asians	Bangladeshi, Burmese, Indonesian, Pakistani, Sri Lankan

It is not surprising that among these groups there are vast differences in ethnicity, language, religion, and cultural values. Each group has a distinct history and there are also within-group differences. It is therefore most important to view each Asian client as a unique individual whose status, characteristics, and traits have been shaped in a unique cultural context. Counselors may need to call on other helpers or individuals known to be familiar with certain populations of Asians.

We should also expect to find significant differences in educational achievement, occupation, wages earned, and standards of living among Asian Americans. Ridley (2005) suggests that there is a myth about Asians being a "model minority group." There is no doubt that some Asians have excelled in educational achievement, earn high wages, and are employed in prestigious jobs and professions, but there are also Asians Americans who are undereducated, receive public assistance, live in crowded urban areas, are unemployed, and are involved in juvenile delinquency. Similar to other culturally diverse groups, there are indeed within-group differences.

We do know, however, that many Asian American groups place high value on education. There seems to be general agreement that Asian Americans perceive education as a means of upward mobility and are highly motivated to remove barriers that could limit them. However, there appears to be substantial evidence that Asian Americans are often victimized by discriminatory employment practices (Slattery, 2004). Like many other minority groups, Asian Americans are hindered in the job market because of poor communication skills. There is little doubt that Asian Americans have been successful in the fields of engineering, computer science, business, and economics.

In evaluating counseling processes as a source of conflict for Chinese Americans, Sue and Sue (1990) and more recently Brammer (2012) and Ponterotto et al. (2010) have made several pertinent observations: (1) Chinese American students inhibit emotional expression and do not actively participate in the counseling process; (2) Chinese Americans are discouraged from revealing emotional problems by their cultural conditioning; and (3) Chinese American students react more favorably to well-structured counseling models. These conclusions emphasize the importance of understanding cultural influences when counseling Chinese Americans and other Asians.

The following special needs and problems associated with Asian Americans in counseling are summarized from suggestions by Pedersen and colleagues (2008); Ridley (2005); and Sue and Sue (2003):

1. Asian Americans are very sensitive about verbalizing psychological problems, especially in group encounters.
2. Asian Americans tend to be inexpressive when asked to discuss personal achievements and limitations.
3. Asian Americans tend to misinterpret the role of counseling in general and the benefits that may be derived from it.
4. Asian Americans can be perceived as very passive and nonassertive with authority figures, but in reality they are reacting to cultural inhibitions that discourage them from being perceived as aggressive.
5. Asian Americans may strongly resist suggestions to modify behavior that is unassuming and nonassertive.

As a group, Asian Americans are known to have a strong work ethic. In general, Asian Americans are very industrious workers, seem to value education, and have taken advantage of higher education to enhance their career development. They are also known to do well in business administration, engineering, and sciences. However, the stereotype of the Asian Americans as being good in sciences but lacking in verbal skills could limit their access to careers that require communication skills. Even though the most recent immigrants from Asia are employed mainly in service occupations, many Asian Pacific Americans can be found as workers in the professions, in office and clerical jobs, and as service workers.

Finally, among traditional Asian cultures, offering what is considered to be desirable help includes giving advice and suggestions, but avoiding confrontation and direct interpretation of motives and actions. When discussing personal issues for instance, it is more appropriate to be indirect, and counselors should do most of the initial verbalization with a rather formal interactive approach (Paniagua, 2005; Sue, 1994). Be aware that Asian Americans may resist help from a counselor or mental health worker because they often rely on a "natural healing" process (Leung & Cheung, 2001). According to Fong (2003, p. 270), Asian Americans may not seek help because they

1. do not recognize or acknowledge there is a mental health problem.
2. are afraid of being stigmatized if they seek help.
3. do not want to address negative comments about their traditional healing practices.
4. do not have access to bilingual bicultural services.
5. assume the provider will not be culturally competent.

Hispanic (Latinos/Latinas) Americans

The Hispanic population has grown much faster than predicted and as a result is currently the largest minority group in this country. Cohn and Fears (2001) point out that the largest subgroup of Hispanics is of Mexican ancestry. Other significant subgroups are from Central and South America, Puerto Rico, and Cuba. According to Ivey et al. (2014), some groups of Hispanic Americans prefer to be recognized as Mexican American, Cuban American, and Puerto Rican American, for example.

There appears to be solid evidence that Hispanics underuse counseling services in both mental health and academic settings (Ponterotto et al., 2010). Counselors need to encourage the use of services and advocate that there is good evidence that they could benefit from services, especially when intervention strategies are designed to meet their special needs. Interventions with academically and economically disadvantaged Puerto Rican women produced positive results by raising their levels of career maturity (adaptability) and developing beliefs that they can control their own destinies.

Social factors such as social-class membership, environment of the home and school, and the community in which many Hispanics reside have significantly influenced their career perspectives and attitudes toward work (Cormier et al., 2013; Diller, 2011; Ponterotto et al., 2010). What is emphasized here is that socioeconomic status and lack of opportunity have restricted Hispanics from access to higher education and subsequently in their occupational aspirations. Hispanics, however, are not a homogeneous group; there are important differences between subgroups and between Hispanics from different socioeconomic backgrounds. One is to recognize that many Hispanics are acculturated and fit into the mainstream of society; expect to find diverse value systems among Hispanics. There are, however, some Hispanics who cling to their traditional heritages and, consequently, may have difficulty in adjusting to an Anglo-dominant culture. Caught between conflicting cultures, the adolescent Hispanic, for example, seeks the support of peers who are experiencing similar conflicts. This reaction is not uncommon in most cultural groups, but when there is less interaction with other groups of students, school can become a low priority.

The Mexican American family, in particular, has been characterized as a closely knit group that greatly influences the values of its members (Paniagua, 2005). Spanish-speaking children are generally taught to value and respect family, church, and school as well as masculinity and honor. Families are primarily patriarchal (as far as the center of authority is concerned) with a distinct division of duties; that is, the father is the breadwinner, and the mother is the homemaker. Spanish is the primary language spoken in the home and in the barrio. However, it appears that traditions, including family solidarity, are breaking down among younger Hispanics (Ridley, 2005).

Fouad & Bingham (1995) recommends several career intervention strategies for Hispanics. Researchers are encouraged to assess these recommendations and to aim their research efforts toward examining the career behavior of Hispanics. The following career counseling recommendations have been paraphrased from Fouad (1997, pp. 186–187):

1. Consider the cultural context of all clients, including Hispanics. Some Hispanics have retained traditional value systems, whereas others may not be traditional. When we are not certain about the client's cultural background, we need to be creative, that is, adopt what is referred to as "creative uncertainty." Using this approach, one is to direct counseling efforts toward the client's willingness to inform us of how culture has influenced his or her life.
2. Be flexible in the career counseling process, especially when we incorporate familial and environmental factors in decision making.
3. Choose assessment instruments with care relative to what is appropriate for Hispanic cultures.
4. Use immediate intervention to retain Hispanic students in school. Career information should include reasons for taking math and science courses.
5. Develop strategies to include self-efficacy as a key to future career success.
6. Provide Hispanic females with a wide variety of career information, including information on nontraditional careers.

The following suggestions for developing effective interventions for Hispanic Americans are adapted from Zuniga (2003, pp. 257–258):

- Respond to cultural preferences of client rather than imposing your own.
- Include natural support networks.
- Address stress-related immigration issues.
- Attend to survival issues and personal needs of client and client's family.
- Use techniques to assist clients make adaptations to new and different living conditions.
- Utilize client's religion or belief system in strategy planning.
- Use narrative therapy, metaphor, and family system approaches.
- Act as an advocate for client's needs.

Native Americans

Over time, several terms have been used for identifying native groups such as Native Americans, Native Indigenous, and First Nations People. In our discussion I will continue to use the general term Native Americans as there is no consensus as to which better describes or identifies native people. We do know, however, that Native Americans are quite diverse. Within the United States, there are more than 500 distinct Native American nations that differ significantly in language, religious beliefs, and social characteristics among other aspects of their cultures. Many Native Americans have lived in urban areas for training, college, or employment. Keeping close contact with their families and friends who live on reservations is a high priority (Tischler, 2014). Of those Native Americans who live outside the reservation, the largest concentrations are in Los Angeles, San Francisco, and Chicago, but Minneapolis, Denver, Tulsa, Phoenix, and Milwaukee also contain significant numbers. The states with the highest numbers of Native Americans are Oklahoma, California, Arizona, New Mexico, Alaska, Washington, North Carolina, Texas, New York, and Michigan. The latest census taken indicates there are 5.2 million Native Americans (U.S. Bureau of the Census, 2012).

On the reservations, many are involved in farming, ranching, fishing, and lumber production. Off the reservations, Native Americans work in factories, on farms, and as skilled craft persons. Some tribes engage in various enterprises, such as motel management; others offer bingo and lottery games to the general public. Gambling casinos on reservations have also emerged.

An important variable in the career development of Native Americans is the degree to which they adhere to cultural customs, language, and traditions. The degree of cultural heritage is described on a continuum by Ryan and Ryan (1982, cited in LaFromboise, Trimble, & Mohatt, 1990) as follows:

1. Traditional: Speak only native language and observe traditions.
2. Transitional: Speak both native language and English and may question traditions of the past.
3. Marginal: Speak of themselves as Indian but identify with roles in dominant society.
4. Assimilated: Have generally embraced the dominant society.
5. Bicultural: Are accepted by dominant society but also identify with tribal traditions and culture.

As with other ethnic groups, one should not stereotype Native Americans, but rather focus on the degree to which each client adheres to cultural customs, language, and traditions. Significant differences between individuals within cultural groups must be addressed in the career counseling process. But one should also remember that old traditions should be respected, and some may be used to foster career development; the use of role models and experientially related activities are recommended (Chandler, Lalonde, Sokol, & Hallett, 2003).

Many Native Americans have a strong desire to retain the symbolic aspects of their heritage, much of which is different from the dominant culture. The challenge for counselors is to assist Native Americans in preserving the positive aspects of their heritage while encouraging them to modify some behaviors. For example, the ability to enjoy the present should be combined with planning skills, the ability to share with others, and assertive behavior. The value orientation of Native Americans is a sensitive issue for career counselors. Ritual and ceremony continue to be used to help the ill (Gurung, 2014). One's tribe and family are more important than the individual and one is determined to help others. Interpersonal harmony is of the utmost importance (Diller, 2011).

Native American resistance to counseling in general is exemplified by the underuse of existing mental health services. According to Weaver (2003), Native Americans are the most neglected group in the mental health field. Native Americans would take advantage of counseling relationships if appropriate counseling strategies were used. Trimble and LaFromboise (1985, p.131) summarized Miller's strategies that remain on target in current times as follows:

1. Personal ethnic identity in itself is hardly sufficient for understanding the influence of culture on the client.
2. The client's history contains a number of strengths that can promote and facilitate the counseling process.
3. The counselor should be aware of his or her own biases about cultural pluralism—they might interfere with the counseling relationship.
4. The counselor should encourage the client to become more active in identifying and learning the various elements associated with positive growth and development.
5. Most important are empathy, caring, and a sense of the importance of the human potential.

In sum, be aware of the diversity, history, culture, and contemporary problems of Native Americans. Display patience and listen intently. Remaining silent when major points are discussed communicates an understanding of Native American traditions of the time necessary to reason and think through problems (Diller, 2011).

White

White is used here to correspond with the percentage of the dominant population by race reported in Figure 9.1. The term "White" has problems similar to the use of the terms "Asians" and "Hispanics"—these groups of people are not homogenous. There are significant differences within cultural groups as well as differences between groups. White Americans are composed of individuals whose origins may be Western and Eastern European, Arabian, Jewish, South American, and Australian among other nationalities (Brammer, 2012). Other terms used to identify White Americans include Anglo-Saxons, and European Americans. The term "White" usually identifies a group of people who refer to themselves as "Americans" without any prefix. White Americans as a group are thought to be individualistic as opposed to collectivistic.

Throughout this chapter, the terms "individualism" and "collectivism" have been identified in numerous discussions as differences between groups of people that are primarily the result of unique cultural contextual experiences and life course events. Multicultural competency has justifiably focused on preparing counselors to counsel clients who have a different cultural orientation than their own. The focus of multicultural counseling has been directed to White counselors who counsel individuals from different cultural groups. In recent years, however, more professionally trained counselors of different ethnicities are emerging. There appears to be an increased interest in how a counselor who has a strong collectivistic background and may be of a different race is to counsel White clients who are individualistically oriented. The roles have been reversed.

The subtleties of effective counseling are quite extensive and are contained in numerous volumes of research and academic textbooks. Integrating career and personal counseling, however, identifies individual needs including cultural ones that are addressed through tailored interventions. In a whole person or holistic approach, the cultural dimension is a most important factor. Thus counselors must indeed be prepared to understand how cultural orientations can influence development and behavior. In the context of our discussions, the counselor whose cultural origin is collectivism is encouraged to recognize the significance of a client's cultural orientation of individualism. One must also recognize that there is much about the development of behavior that we do not know. We do know, however, that behavior is driven by multidimensional forces that are very inclusive. What I am stressing here is that when an individual is identified as being influenced by a collectivistic or individualistic orientation, there are differences in the degree and strength of the orientation. Again I make the point—there are differences between individuals within groups, which suggest that every client is not exactly of the same ilk in any culture.

The term "individual" has been most important in the history of the United States in that individual rights have been and remain a cornerstone of its development as a nation. In the formative years of this country, the nature of government was to ensure human rights in order for individuals to own property and maximize their freedom. The point here is that the case for the individual has been deeply embedded in individual freedom that includes the option to enhance one's personal and individual achievements; the groundwork for the ideal of personal autonomy was established and for the most part has been nurtured and fostered in American society over time.

I will now focus on European Americans who are generally thought of as representing individualistic characteristics more so than others of a different origin under the category of White reported earlier. For the purpose of clarity, I will refer to the counselor as a minority counselor. What we have here is a European American who is being counseled by a minority counselor whose origin is that of collectivism. Individualism in general terms places the focus on the welfare of the individual as opposed to collectivism that places a greater emphasis on the welfare of the group. Individualistic cultures are thought to value autonomy and independence. One who is individualistic searches for opportunities to achieve, is consumed with the desire to be productive, and strongly desires individual responsibility. Reinforcing one's self-esteem is the approach one uses when faced with a challenge. Self-actualization is another important goal.

In addition, the American dream has many components including the opportunity for an individual to choose an optimal career based on one's self-interests and future aspirations. More on collectivism and individualism can be found in the references cited in this chapter. I now turn to some suggestions for minority counselors who counsel European Americans.

The preparatory stage for entering a counseling relationship is most important. Counselors who counsel individuals from a different culture than their own are to focus on the client's cultural identification, identity development, socioeconomic influences, potential stereotypes of others, and the strengths the client associates with her or his race. This information is obtained before counseling and in the intake interview. One is to focus on cultural contexts of the client that can influence career development and behavior. For example, are the client's contextual experiences for the most part individualistic or collectivistic?

Next, minority counselors are to establish the counseling relationship. One is to structure the relationship in order for the client to be proactive. The recommendation here is one of collaboration in which there is consensus of opinion that determines the direction counseling is to take. More than likely an individualistic-oriented client will prefer a well-structured counseling approach—one must be organized and businesslike. Organization of materials (good organizational skills on the part of the counselor) and a solution-based counseling approach will likely impress a European American client. The availability of assessment instruments and their purpose are to be carefully explained. After all, one is not to waste time but make progress toward solving problems.

The counseling process as you have often heard requires effective communication skills. Minority counselors are to be very direct; explicit verbal communications are common in the European American community. Questions are to be directed at specific topics such as background data, current and past concerns, and expected outcomes. Most European American clients expect to discuss one's lifestyle and other personal matters. One is to focus on acknowledging concerns, and it is most desirable to carefully discuss each concern with the client; European American clients expect the counselor to be very attentive to their personal needs. Acknowledgment and empathy of one's concerns are most desirable.

Time is of the essence for most European Americans, who are considered to be of an individualistic orientation. Punctuality is a sign of respect. It is most important to start and end each session exactly on the time agreed upon. Keep in mind that some clients plan each day with firm time constraints in order to meet goals of accomplishment they have set. Any interruption in their schedule can be most annoying.

The client's perception of the counselor is most important. In most cases, one can expect clients to respect earned credentials and they can be most impressed with the training program counselors have experienced. Prestige of university degrees and internships and residencies are also important to the client. The point here is that almost all clients are interested in their counselor's background, but in the case of European Americans, credentials can be most significant (Slattery, 2004). One's achievements are a significant part of the European American's lifestyle. One who enjoys and endorses personal achievement is more comfortable with another person who demonstrates those traits.

The counselor should keep in mind that some European Americans can be very action oriented. There is a strong need to take control of self and solve problems. In these cases, counselors are to use a variety of homework assignments that could be beneficial to the client. Homework assignments fit in nicely with clients who are driven by the need to work hard to overcome any barriers that diminish their ability to succeed. Periodic reinforcements of individual progress by the counselor can enhance the counseling relationship.

Counselors are to stress the strength of the individual. This does not suggest that we dismiss the value of social support from others, but European Americans strongly endorse independence. There is the feeling that an individual is able to overcome most obstacles through hard work and dedication. One is to bolster their self-efficacy through a series of successes. There is a strong desire to view the future as a challenge to their individualistic views of self. Engaging the client in the counseling process as much as possible reinforces individualistic views. What could *you* do to make it better? Do you think that *you* could achieve these goals? Is it important for *you* to be judged by your individual achievement? These are examples of engaging European Americans who strongly believe that personal effort is the pathway to success.

In this very brief discussion of suggestions for minority counselors who counsel European Americans, I offer only a few. As is often suggested in the counseling literature, one is to locate an ally who can be of assistance in developing counseling skills with clients who have a different worldview than their own. One can also expect to find more relevant research from which one can build their counseling skills in the future. In the meantime, follow the suggestions of how one can become a competent multicultural counselor discussed earlier in this chapter: (1) Learn to understand your assumptions, values, and biases, (2) become familiar with the worldview of culturally different clients, and (3) develop effective and appropriate intervention strategies (Sue, Arredondo, & McDavis, 1992).

Some Mental Health Issues of Cultural Groups

In this section, I address abnormal behavior of culturally different people to determine if their mental health disorders meet universal standards of abnormality or whether abnormality varies across cultures. Not surprisingly a great deal of research has been done to answer these questions. The interest in the answers is quite obvious. If abnormality is universal, then helpers would use universally validated diagnosis procedures and intervention strategies. If the opposite were true, and abnormality does indeed vary across cultures and is considered to be culture specific, counselors would turn to unique aspects of a particular culture for determining counseling procedures including diagnosis and interventions. In the next paragraphs, I will briefly review studies of anxiety disorders, depression, personality disorders, somatoform disorders, and schizophrenia. The symptoms of each disorder were discussed in chapter 5 and will not be emphasized here. I use the term "mental health disorders" instead of "psychological disorders" in this section as used by the World Health Organization.

Anxiety Disorders

Anxiety is expressed in a variety of ways including fear and panic that exist worldwide. Horwath and Weissman (1997) found similar rates of panic among ethnic groups found in the United States, Canada, Puerto Rico, New Zealand, Italy, Korea, and Taiwan. These findings give some support to the position of universality. The opposing argument of this position, however, suggests that there are differences in the way in which a person expresses reactions to an anxiety disorder. Castillo (1997) suggests that anxiety is conceptualized as manifestations of emotional distress that are based on culturally developed cognitive schemas. In addition, he suggests that the key to understanding the emotional process of all clients is to focus on the meaning that person draws from her or his unique experiences. Meaning in this context refers to contextual experiences that are unique aspects of a particular culture. It appears that symptoms of anxiety as a mental health disorder are similar among cultural groups, but the expression of anxious feelings tends to be culture specific.

Depression—A Mood Disorder

In the 1980s the World Health Organization conducted a very thorough study of depression in Canada, India, Iran, Japan, and Switzerland. The researchers found constant symptoms of depression across cultures (World Health Organization, 1983). Thus the conclusions of this research suggest that the way people experience depression is constant across cultures; the position of universality of mood disorders is supported. The opposing view focused on how cultures vary in the way they communicate emotional terminology when expressing symptoms of depression. Three important conclusions were reached: (1) There are only a few words in the respondent's language to convey certain emotions, (2) non-Westerners describe anxiety by focusing on bodily symptoms, and (3) the expression of depression itself may be different in some cultures. Once again it is suggested that the symptoms of depression are similar across cultures, but the expression of depression is culturally determined.

Personality Disorders

Similar personality structures were found in German, Portuguese, Hebrew, Chinese, Korean, and Japanese people (McCrae & Costa, 1997). There have been other studies that have reached similar conclusions, suggesting that personality structures are similar across cultures (Matsumoto & Juang, 2013). The argument here is centered around evidence that personality structures are indeed universal, but other aspects of personality are culturally unique and are considered to be indigenous personality structures. Examples of indigenous personality descriptions include the Korean concept of cheong, which refers to human affection (Choi, Kim, & Choi, 1993); the Mexican concept of simpatica which refers to avoidance of conflict (Triandies, Marin, Lisansky, & Betancourt, 1984); and the Indian concept of kuma karma which refers to detachment. We can expect to learn more about indigenous personality development in the future. In the meantime, Matsumoto and Juang (2013) suggest that we could blend the universal concepts of personality with indigenous personality structure in order to have a more meaningful appreciation of one's personality. Their point is well taken—cultural contexts are a most relevant part of one's personality structure.

Somatoform Disorders

This group of disorders includes psychological concerns with appearance and functions of the body. The major focus of these disorders involves imagined illness, conflicts that are converted into physical systems, and imagined defects of physical appearance. High levels and consistent patterns of anxiety over time are thought to be precursors to the development of somatoform disorders. For a long period of time, somatoform disorders were thought to be more common in developing countries; however, more recent research tells us that these disorders are uniform worldwide (Durand & Barlow, 2013).

Another false assumption was the belief that some cultures tended to camouflage psychological symptoms by reporting physical symptoms. In short, there is evidence to support the existence of symptoms associated with somatoform disorders worldwide, but as with most other mental health disorders, there is evidence of culture-specific meanings and recognition of expression modes used by different cultures (Matsumoto & Juang, 2013).

Schizophrenia

The World Health Organization (1981) sponsored and supervised research concerning the prevalence of schizophrenia in Czechoslovakia, Denmark, England, India, the Soviet Union, Taiwan, and the United States. Symptoms across all cultures were identified as auditory and verbal hallucinations, lack of insight, and references to self, indicating that one is viewed as the center of attention. Another most interesting finding was that the course of illness appeared to be easier and faster for clients in developing countries when compared to clients in highly industrialized countries. Castillo (1997) made a strong case for differences between cultures in the way schizophrenia is viewed. His major point was that people in the United States view schizophrenia as an internal problem, whereas in many other countries the cause of psychotic symptoms is thought to be external to the individual. Furthermore, causation is thought to be from external forces that can be overcome and there is less criticism and hostility directed to the one who is ill. I am not suggesting that schizophrenia does not involve internal problems, but once again there is support for both universal and culture-specific symptoms of a mental health disorder—schizophrenia is no exception (Sue et al., 2014).

In this brief review of five mental disorders, I conclude that the cultural meaning of mental health symptoms provides one with a most important understanding of mental health problems. One should look beyond Western norms and meanings to develop necessary insight as to how mental health problems are perceived by people of different cultures. One can recognize the relevance of what constitutes abnormal behavior and in so doing come to the realization that what is considered abnormal in one culture may be judged quite differently in another. The case for the unique aspects of a culture suggests that beliefs derived from culture-specific contexts are to be included in the counseling process. In essence, cultural relativism is an endorsement of unique individuals whose socialization includes sociocultural events and experiences.

In the next part of this chapter, I address multicultural perspectives of men and women.

Strategies for Dealing with Multicultural Influences

The point has been made that women and men are socialized in a particular culture. By incorporating ethnicity in career development of both sexes, we gain a greater understanding of multiple facets of influence that shape values, beliefs, actions, and worldviews. A most important point to remember is that one's development does not take place in isolation but is greatly influenced by salient messages received within the environment. Hence, ethnic-related messages are integrated with other variables that greatly affect gender-role development. We will briefly examine ethnicity and gender of African Americans, Southeastern Asians, Hispanics, and Native Americans.

Working with African American Women and Men

African American women have a long history of doing menial labor as cooks, housemaids, nannies, and other low-pay-scale jobs (Galliano, 2003). More recently, African American women are found in professions largely as a result of federal legislation and affirmative action policies (Higginbotham, 1994; Matlin, 2004). An increasing number of African American women have been successful in owning their own businesses (Ballard, 1997). Most overall career growth appears to be in the public sector; however, women of color continue to be subjected to discrimination in the private sector.

The collective strengths of African American women are in social networks of other women and relatives such as sisters. Many regularly participate in sororities, church women's groups, and women's social clubs. In essence, female friendship is a strong support system for African American women. Women support each other in difficult times and remain loyal to their churches. African American women have a strong spiritual commitment that is used to counteract the unfairness and hardships of oppression and racism (Pedersen et al., 2008). Some of the challenges facing African American women are health problems associated with poverty and isolation. Teenage pregnancy among African Americans is declining, but the problem remains a challenge.

Career counseling for ethnic women was discussed and illustrated in chapter 3. I cannot overemphasize the point that career counselors must recognize that there is diversity in any subgroup. Thus, African American women are not to be considered as a homogeneous group. Job training and child care are two primary needs of many African American women.

Parham (1996) makes the point that African American men value treating others with respect, kindness, and decency. He infers that African American men have not received reciprocal treatment in this country by the White dominant society. He suggests that counselors become active advocates to change discriminatory practices in communities. Furthermore, he suggests that counselors address the oppressions associated with racism and White supremacy directly with clients. A most important counseling goal is for counselors to assist African American men to develop self-awareness or self-knowledge. Counselors, for example, are to assist African American men in developing a self-identity that underscores their ability to express themselves openly and freely. Strongly suggested here is that we must "help African-American clients more fully understand, appreciate, and express, their Africanness" (Parham, 1996, p. 188). Finally, some developmental strategies to help African Americans include assisting self-concept development, developing more internally directed behavior, becoming more aware of job opportunities, clarifying motivational aspirations, and dealing with ambivalence toward Whites.

Working with Asian Women and Men

Southeastern Asian American women have received little attention in the research literature. This population consists of a variety of groups including women from Vietnam, Laos, and Cambodia. Since 1975, more than 1 million Southeastern Asian refugees have migrated to the United States (Zaharlick, 2000). Of this group, the Vietnamese are thought to be the best educated and most fluent in English and have the most experience in professional and technical occupations. There is much diversity among this subgroup of people, however, although some values are shared. Southeastern Asian women feel a strong devotion to their children and to family continuity, they strive to avoid actions that would bring shame to the family, and they strongly embrace self-control (Goldenberg & Goldenberg, 2013).

A couple I know owned and operated a restaurant and both worked on the midnight shift in a local weaving plant. Their goal was to provide the necessary funds for their son's educational expenses. Their devotion to their child's education is a good example of their values and family commitment. When I expressed this to them, their response was simply that they expected him to spend most of his time studying. They did not seem to feel that what they were doing was anything special and showed great pride in their son's achievement. Obviously, in this case, family and devotion to their child were of major importance.

Southeastern Asian women have difficulty in witnessing current breakdowns in family honor as their children adopt more of the values and lifestyle of the dominant culture. Their children are learning from a new and different peer group that individualism is the contemporary lifestyle. A pervasive problem for Southeastern Asian women is the growing trend of children to disobey family rules. Conflicting information experienced by all family members in a new and different society can result in family discord. Counselors can expect to find that some Asian clients have serious conflicts about their future work and life role.

When the needs of Asian American men are addressed, the tremendous diversity within and between groups should be kept in mind. According to Matsumoto and Juang (2013), however, individualism and collectivism are key variables for understanding differences between Asian Americans and Euro-Americans. This is especially true for Asian Americans who are less acculturated. Asian American men consider family honor more important than personal goals; hence, decisions are based on what is best for the family.

Client–counselor relationships, especially among less acculturated men, must be carefully balanced. Asian Americans, for example, expect a hierarchical relationship with counselors. More specifically, Asian American men expect a professional relationship rather than an egalitarian one. Balancing the roles of counselor and counselee is essential, therefore, for effective interviewing and intervention strategies. Some suggested developmental strategies for Asian American men are learning to understand organization systems and bureaucracies, improving communication skills, and learning to understand the give-and-take of work environments. Counselors may find that using Asian Americans as role models will enhance the effectiveness of counseling goals (Matsumoto & Juang, 2013).

Working with Hispanic Women and Men. Hispanic women, a very diverse group who have migrated from many different countries, have some common background variables such as religion preference. Most are Christian and members of the Catholic Church, although in recent years some have joined Protestant groups. Hispanic women learn from their religion that they are to view their chief roles as mothers and wives. They are the primary caregivers and center their lives around family needs. Career, therefore, may not be a very meaningful term for many Hispanic women who are overseeing several children.

Traditionally, the health needs of some Hispanic women are taken care of by home remedies and other women in the family, and they use indigenous healing systems by referring individuals to a currandismo (Mexican folk healer). Counselors are to approach this subject carefully because some Hispanics strongly support indigenous healing systems. Although more information about the benefits of current medical practices may be needed, all nontraditional methods, remedies, and healers should be recognized (Paniagua, 2005; Sue, Ivey, & Pedersen, 1996).

Ortiz (1996) points out that more Hispanic women are migrating and joining the U.S. labor force. Most have few skills, little education, and end up finding work as maids, factory workers, or in nonskilled jobs. Their major goal is to send their earnings back to their country of origin to support their families. Short-term goals include finding a place to live and a job. Long-term goals usually include becoming legal citizens and bringing their children, if any, and families to join them.

All Latino subgroups, such as Mexican, Cuban, and Puerto Rican, are quite nationalistic. Gender identity for men is associated with the term "machismo," which generally stands for arrogance and sexual aggression in Latino/Latina relationships. Machismo is also associated with men having firm control of their families. This stereotyped portrayal of men suggests that more value is placed on boys than on girls in Latino/a culture. However, the reverence for motherhood has influenced the trend toward equalization of sexes in the Hispanic cultures (Arredondo, 1996; Pedersen et al., 2008; Slattery, 2004).

Because of the great diversity among Hispanics, counselors should spend considerable time learning about specific cultures. Suggested developmental strategies for Hispanic American males include learning about effective communication skills, work environments and organizations, the use of career information, job search strategies, and interpersonal relationships. Other suggestions include learning goal-setting and problem-solving skills, developing working-parent skills, and improving financial management of resources.

Working with Native American Women and Men

Neal (2000) also reminds us that there is great diversity among the customs and cultures of Native Americans. "The roles of women vary from tribe to tribe and geographical region to geographic region" (p. 166). Native American women historically have been influential within their tribes. This tradition continues in many tribes; for instance, Wilma Mankiller was the Chief of the Cherokee Nation of Oklahoma in 1985 (Mankiller & Wallis, 1993). Other Indian nations have also elected women as chairpersons or chiefs. Some tribes have a council of women elders that has control of ceremonial life and businesses operated by the tribe. However, the traditional primary role for Native American women, similar to so many other cultures, is care of the family.

Of most significance to Native American women as homemaker and caregiver is that Native American families are the poorest socioeconomic group (Tischler, 2014). The most impoverished families in this country are Native American families with no husband present. The source of strength among Native Americans, however, is their biological family and the extended community family. They also find spiritual strength from their traditional ancestral homelands.

Native Americans are also a very diverse group of people who have been grossly misunderstood. Native American men have very often been stereotyped as drunkards who sit around the reservation and do little work. This reputation has unfortunately been widespread in this country and in Canada. The most devastating aspect is that the blame for alcoholism has been placed completely on the Native American. One needs to investigate the historical relationship between the U.S. government and Native Americans to understand the full extent of their losses individually and collectively.

LaFromboise and Jackson (1996) suggest that we return the principle of empowerment to the Native Americans so they can control their own lives: "People are capable of taking control but often choose not to do so because of social forces and institutions that hinder their efforts" (LaFromboise & Jackson, p. 196). The following strategies are designed to help Native American men maintain their cultural heritage while introducing concepts of career development of the dominant society:

1. Use parents and relatives as counseling facilitators. The rationale for this approach is embedded in the strong family ties of Native Americans.
2. Use Native American role models. They should assist in helping break down resistance to counseling objectives. Native Americans should react more favorably to other Native Americans.
3. Emphasize individual potential in the context of future goals. Identify conflicts that make it difficult for Native Americans to project themselves into other environments, including work environments.

In sum, counselors must be prepared to meet the needs of clients who have been shaped and influenced by their cultural heritage. This brief review of gender issues from different cultural groups suggests that much is to be learned about diversity issues in career counseling.

In this chapter, we have only touched on what it really means for someone to fully understand their cultural bias, racism, and stereotypical thinking. We have learned that culture is a learned behavior. Within our own ecological system, we have learned and accepted beliefs, traditions, and developed worldviews. Human development theorists inform us that an individual's developmental process is both continuous and discontinuous over the life span. In other word, we make gradual progress to comprehend the world we live in or we stagnate. In this context, there are periods in our lives when we choose to take the time and "back away," so to speak, in order to think through a situation that has emerged as a critical incident—for example, coming face-to-face with cultural differences that are difficult to comprehend. The times we spend during these periods of critical thinking are most important, primarily because we have chosen to not act emotionally, with little thought given to the consequences of our actions. On the contrary, we search for solutions and answers that include different approaches, an enlightened perspective of the past and the future, and in the end a means to live our life more fully.

Matsumoto and Juang (2013) suggest that we recognize that culture is the degree to which a group of people share attitudes, values, beliefs, and behaviors. It is not a race, nationality, or birthplace! From this perspective, we view culture as a psychological construct or a learned worldview and a way of thinking and living. We approach each person, therefore, as a unique individual who has learned customs and traditions from contextual interactions in a unique environment. Differences in behavior and thinking are the result of individual development and not meant as an insult or confrontation to others. Understanding how one's beliefs have been developed is the key to understanding why differences exist between cultures and individuals from different cultures. From this perspective we can move away from negative stereotypes on to a more comprehensive viewpoint that recognizes that cultural differences are legitimate. We are indeed the product of a unique multidimensional developmental process. As a result, we just happen to think and behave differently.

Summary

1. Culture is a very complex concept that can refer to many aspects of life and living. Culture is a learned behavior. Two people from the same race could share some values, attitudes, and so on, but might also be very different in their cultural makeup. Counselors should be alert to value orientation when working among different cultural groups. One is likely to find differences in the way people from different cultures view work and associations. In negotiations, for example, cultural groups have different opinions of how the best results are achieved. One group may be completely business oriented, whereas the other cultural group believes that one is to develop a social relationship to make the process successful.

2. Five major cultural groups are African Americans, Asian Pacific Americans, Hispanic Americans, Native Americans, and Whites. Currently, the largest racial minority group in this country is Hispanics. The Hispanic family is a closely knit group that greatly influences the value system of its members. African Americans continue to make progress in social equality. Some of both sexes have achieved upward mobility to professional occupations as the overall success of African Americans' upward movement increases. Many Asian Americans place a high value on education. Asian Americans tend to inhibit emotional expression and do not actively participate in counseling programs. Native Americans are culturally conditioned to view life from a different perspective than that of the dominant White culture. Native Americans are generally not motivated to achieve status through the accumulation of wealth. The lifestyle of most Native Americans is extremely democratic, and their culture promotes egalitarianism. The White dominant population is made up of people from a variety of nationalities. Their lifestyle, especially European Americans, is influenced by an individualistic orientation.

3. Culture variability of worldviews includes constructs of individualism and collectivism. Examples of other differences in cultures are time orientation, view of human nature, and personal space and privacy. Worldviews should be considered unique for each individual.

4. Culture does have an important role in work-related values. Differences between cultures help us understand employee attitudes, values, behaviors, and interpersonal dynamics.

5. Effective counselors have knowledge of, and are sensitive to, different cultural orientations when establishing rapport in counseling relationships. To be effective with populations of different cultures, counselors must be aware of different worldviews (the psychological orientation of thinking, behavior, and interpretation of events). Counselors must be careful not to impose their values on others. Necessary skill areas include awareness of differences, self-awareness, knowledge of the client's culture, and adaptation of counseling method, materials, and procedures.

6. Counselors must develop a greater sensitivity to culturally diverse clients when conducting an interview. Technique issues include eye contact, touch, probing questions, space and distance, verbal style, restrictive emotions, confrontation, self-disclosure, and focus on self-in-relation and self-in-context.
7. Mental health issues of cultural groups that involved anxiety disorders, depression, personality disorders, somatoform disorders, and schizophrenia were found to have symptoms that are universal as well as culture-specific symptoms.
8. Strategies for dealing with multicultural groups include the recognition of differences between cultural groups as well as differences between gender roles in multicultural groups.

Supplementary Learning Exercises

1. Define your cultural background and that of a classmate. Compare differences and similarities.
2. How would you explain the differences between individualism and collectivism? What socialization variables influenced the differences between them?
3. Take one or more of the five major cultural groups discussed in this chapter and develop culture-specific issues that should be addressed in career counseling.
4. Write an essay about how cultural worldviews are developed. Include differences between other cultures and the White dominant culture.
5. Describe how different cultural work values can be sources of conflict and misunderstanding in the workplace. Develop appropriate interventions.
6. What do you consider to be the most difficult obstacle to becoming culturally competent?
7. What do you consider to be the most difficult culturally competent skill to learn? Explain.
8. Interview a culturally different person. Share your experience with the class.
9. Which of the following two methods do you consider to be the most effective for career counseling? Support your conclusions.
   a. Use of culture-specific information
   b. Use of human universality information
10. Explain how mental health issues of cultural groups are intertwined with career counseling.

10

Gender Issues and Dual Careers

A few short years ago, career counseling programs for women consisted of exploring the traditionally held working roles. The choices were narrowed to such occupations as clerk, teacher, or nurse. One of the first questions asked was, "How will this job fit into your husband's occupational goal?" The message to women was quite clear: You have only a few jobs to choose from, and your career is secondary to your husband's or other family obligations. In the last two decades in which there has been significant unemployment, more women are returning to the workplace out of necessity. Some women, however, have chosen to pursue a career in a wide range of occupations. A career first and marriage maybe now or later is the new order of preference for those who aspire for a career outside the home. In this post–women's movement era, women continue to look beyond the traditional feminine working roles. The women who embark on this career course will find that many barriers still remain. First, the bias associated with gender stereotypes in the working world still exists (Galliano, 2003; Tischler, 2014). Second, the woman who gives her career development equal status with her husband's will find acceptance of her role personally challenging, with little support from many men and women (Andersen & Taylor, 2013; Matlin, 2004). Although there are gender issues that are troublesome and can inhibit a women's career development, the future should present more opportunities for women to advance their careers. The recession of 2009, however, may delay career opportunities for both men and women.

In the first part of this chapter, I will address gender issues and women in the workplace, followed by issues facing dual-career couples. Although these issues are somewhat related, I separate them to focus on gender issues such as gender stereotypes, occupational inequality, and sexual harassment, among others. While addressing issues facing dual-career couples, I will focus on role conflict, child care, and other relational and personal factors. I begin with factors that influence gender development.

Factors That Influence Gender Development

It should not be surprising that most researchers seem to agree that gender development is a continuing process over the life span. Gender development does not stop when you graduate from high school, tech school, or college, or even when and if you get married. It is a continuous process in which behavior is modified and reinforced by contextual and situational factors one experiences. In essence, it is a lifetime event. Counselors should recognize, however, that people modify their behavior and adapt to changes over their lifetime. Second, the sociocultural context of one's environment determines to a large extent the character and uniqueness of each individual's gender development.

Currently, women's psychology has been integrated into mainstream psychology and especially into several academic disciplines, including human development, counseling, and sociology. In the last three decades, gender differences have been the primary focus of research efforts among several academic disciplines. After reviewing significant research findings on gender differences, Galliano (2003; Ferrante, 2013) concluded that researchers should address the position that men and women are more similar than different. They suggest that we should not view men and women as "separate spheres" but observe gender behavior in shared contextual relationships. This does not mean that we do not continue to point out differences between women and men. What is suggested is observing and evaluating contextual interactions between men and women as in a systems approach in order to build a greater understanding of the gender socialization process.

A significant amount of research has focused on interacting influences on gender development. More specifically, do the environmental and relational gender-role influences from early childhood and adolescence carry over to adulthood? The general consensus is that, because of the complexity of factors involved in the gender developmental process, it is difficult to determine the degree and significance of influences from early childhood that are related to the way an adult thinks and behaves.

These factors and others are part of what can influence one's development. In the biopsychosocial model discussed in previous chapters, behavior is influenced by multidimensional forces that include biological, psychological, and social/cultural factors. The major focus of the biopsychosocial model is on individual development that is influenced by a combination of (1) biological factors such as inheritance, brain and central nervous system functions, chemical imbalances among other bodily functions, and nutrition; (2) psychological factors such as internal perceptual, cognitive, and emotional development; and (3) ecological system experiences such as life course events (Kail & Cavanaugh, 2014).

What is most important for counselors to recognize here is the case for individual development. Although we can generalize about some events and experiences we share with others, individual interpretation of situational experiences and events are unique. One's gender development may take an entirely different path than someone who is a close colleague. Thus, the counselor focuses on the client's unique development. In sum, each individual is indeed influenced by a number of specific cultural and situational factors that contribute to the development of preferred gender roles (Brinkerhoff, Weitz, & Ortega, 2014).

Overview of Gender in the Workplace

In early human existence women and men worked side by side and shared home responsibilities. Together they gathered food, worked in fields, hunted, and raised livestock. In the home, both contributed to caring for children, completing household chores, and making and mending household items. Generally, this type of sharing continued for thousands of years and in some remote areas of the world remains the modus operandi today (Galliano, 2003). One contributing factor to the division of labor by gender was the Industrial Revolution.

The rise of industrialism in the late 18th century created vast social changes, including restructuring how we work and live in most industrialized nations today. A most significant change was the relocation of the workplace. As urban areas grew, generating job opportunities in manufacturing, work was divided between those who worked in a factory (mostly men) and those who stayed home for household tasks (mainly females). The division of labor by gender during the Industrial Revolution that placed women in a secondary position in society was a pervasive element that eventually led to calls for equality and set the stage for the first women's movement to gain the right to vote. It should also be mentioned that in some nations at the beginning of the 21st century, women continue to be treated as second-class citizens with few rights.

The division of labor by gender became an accepted way of life in the 20th century and still exists today, as women continue to be viewed as primary caregivers and homemakers. Men, on the other hand, are the breadwinners and head of the household. In effect, women were relegated to a lower status or, as some prefer, a lower position identity. Some women did work in factories and some were employed as secretaries, teachers, and nurses, jobs that met the approval of society as appropriate for women. Men, however, identified more strongly with their work role and forged ahead in leadership roles in industry, government, and civil service. Before World War II, middle-class America endorsed the concept of division of labor by gender (Galliano, 2003).

Shortly after World War II began, however, jobs that were primarily considered men's work were being done by females of all ethnicities. Women worked on the production line in manufacturing plants, helped build ships and aircraft, and held management positions as well. But after the war was over in 1945, most women were sent home to resume their household tasks. The prewar trends of gender ideals had been established and were reinforced by white middle-class families that centered their attention on the success of the father's career. The ideal family of the 1950s was portrayed as the attractive housewife appropriately dressed, wearing a neat apron while joyfully involved in household chores. The father in suit and tie returns triumphantly to the ideal suburban home after a day on the job.

Three influential social movements that culminated in the 1970s brought a large number of women back to the workforce: The civil rights movement, anti–Vietnam War protests, and the second wave of the women's movement all contributed to socioeconomic change. During this period, many families found it necessary to have two paychecks to pay their bills. As a result, women returned to the workforce with career goals of their own. Women workers in other countries also continued to grow. Women can currently be found in a variety of occupations worldwide and next we will reveal the top 10 occupations for women in this country. According to the U.S. Department of Labor, Bureau of Labor Statistics (2010), the top 10 full-time female-dominated jobs were as follows:

Secretaries/administrative assistants

Elementary and middle-school teachers

Registered nurses

Nursing, psychiatric, and home health aides

Bookkeeping, accounting, and auditing clerks

Receptionists and information clerks

Maids and housekeepers

Teacher assistants

Child care workers

Personal and home care aides

During the first decade of the 21st century, women continue to struggle for work identity. Ferrante (2013), for example, suggested that women have lower career aspirations than men and take longer to choose a career path, whereas men advance faster, further, and earn more pay than women. According to Anderson and Vandehey (2012), career-type barriers in the corporate world are perceived differently by men and women. On the one hand, it should not be surprising that women are more concerned about prejudices of colleagues, sexual discrimination and harassment, inflexible work patterns, and difficulty in being accepted in the senior management "club."

On the other hand, women have made progress in pursuing medical degrees. In 2002, 40% of entering medical students in the United States were women, compared to only 5.5% in 1950 (Matlin, 2004). In the corporate world, however, perceptions of effective leadership styles and management approaches have remained solidly masculine.

Matlin (2004) suggests that the number of women entering professional schools for the study of law and veterinary medicine is increasing, but it will be well into the 21st century before they are equally represented. In the meantime, we find that women continue to be employed in traditionally female occupations. In an overwhelming majority, women are employed as secretaries, dental hygienists, registered nurses, elementary-school teachers, and social workers.

In this brief historical summary of gender and work, we can gain a fuller understanding of the significant role of gender in career development of women and men alike. Although we have emphasized the need for research on shared work roles, differences in gender roles between men and women are significant variables to consider in career choice and in work-related behavior. Currently, we have witnessed some progress for women in the work world, but inequality in the workplace has remained a deterrent for many.

Inequality in the Workplace

There appears to be a general agreement among sociologists that general inequality in the workplace continues to exist. The good news, however, is that women now occupy an increased share of high-paying jobs. The downside is that women also dominate low-paying jobs (Tischler, 2014). But more disturbing is the evidence that when women and men occupy the same occupation, men receive higher pay. Examples of the occupations in which men earn more than women are chief executives, lawyers, computer programmers, school teachers, and retail sales persons (Brinkerhoff et al., 2014).

Another study reveals the differences in income between men and women by gender and race. The following conclusions are based on median incomes in 2009 by race and gender for full-time workers.

White men (non-Hispanics) received significantly higher pay than female Whites. The same was true for African Americans, Hispanics, and Asian Americans. The differences between African men and women and between Hispanic men and women, however, was not as large as the differences between White men and women. (Andersen & Taylor, 2013)

Income Differences Between Men and Women. The results of these two studies strongly indicate that women as a group tend to earn less than men. The greatest inequality between men and women takes place between the ages of 45 and 55 and the least inequality between men and women between the ages of 16 and 24 (Ferrante, 2013). Some straightforward explanations for income difference between men and women and the inequality that currently exists are presented in Box 10.1.

Gender Stereotypes. The influence of gender socialization is also a most relevant factor in career choice, as well as in working relationships and interactions. The next society as identified by Drucker (2002) suggests an increase of shared working roles among women and men. It appears that women and men will continue to have different and same status levels in the workplace in contemporary society. In a future knowledge society, however,

---

BOX 10.1

Some Income Differences Between Men and Women

- Women are disproportionately employed in lower-paying, lower-status occupations.
- Women choose or are forced into lower paying positions that are considered sex-appropriate, such as teacher, secretary, and caregiver. Female-dominated occupations such as caregiver are valued less than male-dominated occupations such as auto mechanic and construction worker.
- Women choose or are forced into positions that offer fewer, more flexible hours to meet caregiving responsibilities.
- Women choose or are forced into lower paying subspecialties within higher paying positions; for example, women tend to be divorce lawyers rather than corporate lawyers, and pediatricians rather than heart surgeons.
- Employers underinvest in the careers of childbearing-age women because they assume the women will eventually leave to raise children.
- Women leave the labor market to take care of children and elderly parents and may eventually reenter it.
- Employers continue to view women's salary needs as less important than men's and pay women accordingly. Unfortunately, women's earnings often are considered supplemental to men's—earnings that can be used to buy "extras"—when in reality many women are heads of households.
- When negotiating salaries, women underestimate their worth to employers and ask for less than male counterparts.
- Some employers steer males and females into sex-appropriate assignments and offer them different training opportunities and chances to move into better paying jobs.
- Women encounter the "glass ceiling," a term used to describe a barrier that prevents women from rising past a certain level in an organization, especially when women work in male-dominated workplaces and occupations.

Source: From *Sociology: A Global Perspective*, 8th ed., pp. 261–262, by J. Ferrante, Copyright 2013. Reprinted with permission from Wadsworth Cengage Learning.

more work tasks can be done equally well by both sexes. Gender stereotyping is a significant obstacle in the workplace that needs to be removed to promote shared work roles.

Gender stereotypes are beliefs that one holds about the characteristics and traits of women and men. Gender stereotypes are also what one perceives as appropriate roles for women and men, whether they are accurate or not. It is a belief system that has been largely internalized by sociocultural contextual interactions. The important point here is that one's beliefs about gender stereotypes are a pervasive influence in the everyday give-and-take of human existence. Matlin (2000), who long ago captured the essence of bias associated with gender stereotyping, states:

> We know that stereotypes simplify and bias the way we think about people who belong to the social categories of female and male. Because of gender stereotypes, we exaggerate the contrast between women and men. We also consider the male experience to be "normal" whereas the female experience is the exception that requires an explanation. We also make biased judgments about females and males—for instance, when we judge whether they are feeling emotional or stressed. (p. 67)

Stereotypical thinking can indeed bias one's perception of appropriate work roles for women and men. Because women and men are once again working side by side in jobs that were once considered for men only, more emphasis needs to be placed on shared roles in counseling approaches. One would not expect such work environments to be completely free of discrimination and sexual harassment even though some progress for equality has been made. Much more needs to be done to debunk stereotypical thinking in the workplace. The "glass ceiling" remains in place in corporate America. This so-called glass ceiling is the invisible barrier that blocks women from high-level positions; "sticky floor" is a metaphor for women who are not promoted from low-level assignments. Barriers consist of subtle attitudes and prejudices that have blocked women and minorities from ascending the corporate ladder (Andersen & Taylor, 2013).

In essence, gender stereotyping promotes the belief that women should be traditionally feminine and men are to be traditionally masculine. In contemporary society, there are inconsistent and mixed messages about traditional roles, but a different message seems to be emerging. The facts are that many women are working outside the home to help maintain a family and others are working because they choose to. We have witnessed a dramatic increase in the number of women who are actively pursuing a career and women who are employed in traditionally male-dominated jobs. Organizations and institutions are searching for ways to promote cooperative working relationships between men and women. The question is how to debunk gender typing and move toward building working relationships in which all participants can experience self-fulfillment (Galliano, 2003; Matlin, 2004; Tischler, 2014).

Gender stereotyping beliefs can be addressed through the medium of faulty conceptions. Counselors should focus on the source of thinking scripts of gender typing and try to restructure and modify cognitive beliefs. Some suggestions are Meichenbaum's (1977) cognitive-behavioral modification and cognitive methods used in rational-emotive therapy (Ellis, 1994). Group counseling may include social-skills training, including role play and homework. The primary goal is to have clients examine their beliefs and work through practical problems of gender stereotyping.

Sexual Harassment

The issue of sexual harassment has been well documented in the workplace for several years. For example, in 1980, the Working Women's Institute concluded that sexual harassment was the single most widespread occupational hazard that women face in the workforce (Lott, 1994). The attention given to sexual harassment was dramatically increased by (1) the 1991 Senate hearings involving Supreme Court nominee Clarence Thomas and his accuser, Anita Hill; and (2) the U.S. Navy Tailhook scandal involving the mistreatment of women by U.S. Navy personnel.

What constitutes sexual harassment has been the central issue of several court cases. The "reasonable woman" standard was applied as the appropriate legal criterion for determining whether sexual harassment had occurred: If a reasonable woman would consider behavior offensive even though a man would not, the court would rule that sexual harassment had occurred (Fitzgerald & Ormerod, 1991). Sexual harassment does indeed occur, according to Barnett and Rivers (1996, cited in Peterson & Gonzalez, 2000); more than 50% of working women will experience sexual harassment in their jobs.

In essence, sexual harassment consists of unwelcome sexual overtures or requests for sexual favors. A legal term used in sexual harassment is *quid pro quo*, which indicates that some type of reward is offered for sexual favors. This kind of behavior creates an offensive and hostile work environment and is most demeaning to women. In many organizations today, sexual harassment awareness and prevention are part of incoming training for new staff. In addition, ongoing sensitivity training programs include topics such as how people respond to being touched when engaged in a conversation, what is considered offensive physical contact, cultural differences in physical contact, and inappropriate verbal statements and comments about physical appearance. The major goal here is to promote appropriate interactions between women and men in the workplace (Aamodt, 2013).

In sum, this chapter introduces some sets of problems and concerns associated with gender issues that influence behavior of women and men in multiple life roles. The focus of concerns has been devoted to career development, career choice, and work-related issues. Career counselors, however, recognize that they are to address the needs of the total person, including multiple roles. Gender issues do indeed represent a pervasive influence in the lives of clients who seek counseling. One core element of gender concerns is gender stereotyping. One's beliefs about gender typing greatly influence career identity, interpersonal relationships, how one communicates, and one's worldview in general. The fear of being perceived as feminine is a driving force behind exaggerated masculinity. Men, for example, fear being perceived as being overly emotional and it is not unusual for men of this ilk to have difficulty when interacting with women.

It should not surprise anyone that sexual harassment creates offensive and hostile work environments. Small as well as large companies provide sensitivity training in an attempt to build more cohesive work relationships. In contemporary workplaces, men and women face stressful conditions, including the need to achieve, outdo competition, and be considered successful. Closely related to these issues are stress-related self-destructive behaviors that can lead to health problems. Learning to deal with stress is an essential task in order to manage all life roles in contemporary society. The call is for a counseling approach that is sensitive to gender and recognizes that behavior should be studied in gendered contexts.

Gender-related norms are best evaluated in situational and contextual interactions between women and men; shared work roles are expected to be the focus of research in future workplace environments. Gender development is a complex process that is both multifaceted and multidimensional. See appendix F for group interventions that address issues discussed here and in the next section.

The Workplace and Family Needs

Women and men also share work roles in dual-career marriages, albeit in a different context than the workplace. In recent years, both parents often have to work to fulfill financial responsibilities, but it should also be recognized that many women choose to work and pursue a career. The results of the Cornell and Couples and Career Study, to no one's surprise, found that females assumed more responsibility than males for child care (Clarkberg & Merola, 2003). In greater numbers, women are assuming the dual role of homemaker and worker (Ferrante, 2013). Families in which both parents work are referred to as either dual-career or dual-earner households. Both types share some common goals and issues. The term "dual career" is usually reserved for families in which both spouses hold professional, managerial, or technical jobs.

As more women have changed roles, men also have changed by assuming a larger share of the homemaker role. But sharing responsibilities, particularly in the home, have caused role conflict, among other problems. Next, I discuss some aspects of family dynamics in a changing world and the challenges that face couples in dual-career roles. Issues include expectations and intentions of work and family, role conflict, child care, and relationship factors.

Issues Facing Dual-Career Families

The following issues are representative of current problems found among dual-career families, some of which apply to dual-earner families as well. This relatively new family structure was brought to the attention of researchers by the studies of British university graduates in the 1970s by Rapoport and Rapoport (1978). Following their work, many studies involving dual-career families contained serious methodological limitations, such as focusing on women only and using only academics as samples (Herr, Cramer, & Niles, 2004). Nevertheless, the following issues emerged as potential career counseling concerns and have been refined by a number of studies of dual-career families by Galliano (2003), Goldenberg and Goldenberg (2013), and Matlin (2004), among others.

Expectations and Intentions of Work and Family

In a study of university students in the 1990s, Gilbert (1993) found that young women and men reared in dual-career families were highly committed to a role-sharing marriage. The logical conclusion from the results of this study suggested that children reared in dual-career families were more likely to develop positive views of integrating occupation and family work. Even though this view of married life is in contrast with traditional family structures, it seems plausible to suggest that after years of observing a successful role-sharing marriage, the tendency to want the same in one's marriage is plausible. What is suggested here is that the kind and type of role sharing observed during childhood by both sexes greatly influence their expectations of roles in marriage (Mooney, Knox, & Schacht, 2013).

Goldenberg and Goldenberg (2013) argue that a lack of agreement between expectations of roles in marriage has the potential to create interpersonal tension. The point is that role overload typically occurs between spouses when family roles are not clearly defined. For example, if the husband's occupational role is assumed to be primary, or if a wife views the husband's employment as a less important career, there is a greater potential for minimal sharing of household work. Currently, the good news is that men seem to be more willing to participate in household tasks than in the past. Not surprisingly, partners appear to benefit from relationships of sharing, which are thought to contribute to feelings of equity in multiple roles.

Role Conflict

Role conflict is generally thought of as a system of competing demands from different roles; in the case of the dual-career family, the conflict is between family roles and work roles. Although society generally has viewed the woman as the primary homemaker, the growing trend is for husband and wife to share family roles. The division of family roles between spouses is usually the result of negotiating family roles, which are more complex when the family responsibilities include child care. When a husband neglects household tasks, however, his spouse may experience role overload. What we have here is the necessity of cooperation and, perhaps more important, the willingness and belief that men should share responsibility of child care and household tasks; then the chances of role conflict are decreased. The chances of role conflict increase, however, when the husband or both husband and wife believe that men should continue to fulfill the traditional role of family breadwinner (Matlin, 2004).

Evidence in the 1990s suggests that role conflict and role overload were decreasing somewhat in dual-career families; men seemed to be increasingly willing to share in household tasks and in child care (Dancer & Gilbert, 1993). In the beginning of the 21st century, Goldenberg and Goldenberg (2013) report that men continue to assist in child care and household tasks in dual-career families. Some evidence also supports the position that, in heterosexual marriages, African American and Hispanic American men tend to spend more time doing household tasks than do European American men (Andersen & Taylor, 2013). Although women have been somewhat relieved of household tasks during the past three decades, they continue to do the most work and assume the most responsibility for household tasks (Kail & Cavanaugh, 2014).

In the late 1980s, Klinger (1988) developed a model designed to delegate household tasks based on interests, aptitudes, and time available. This flexible model provides for changes in tasks and in who performs them as the situation or as economic factors change. It also addresses the supposition that some tasks are viewed as more desirable than others, so that the most preferred and least preferred tasks should be rotated between the spouses. The last part of the model provides for a "recycling" that ensures an equitable division of labor. Although this model was developed in the late 1980s, it appears to be relevant for dual-career families today.

Part I—Formulate list of household tasks.

Part II—Agree on the frequency of the tasks (daily, biweekly, weekly, monthly, annually).

Part III—Agree on the person(s) responsible for accomplishing the tasks (considering each person's available time, interest, abilities). Highly desirable or highly undesirable tasks are rotated.

Part IV—Review of the tasks to determine the following:

a. Did the person(s) designated perform the task?

b. Was the task viewed as satisfactorily completed?

For "no" responses to questions (a) or (b), what were the obstacles to completing the task?

What additional resources (time, dollars, people, or other factors) are needed to complete the task successfully?

Part V—Recycle: Add or delete tasks. Change person(s) responsible for completing tasks, if changes are necessary to maintain the perception of both persons that the division of labor is equitable.

This model also can be adapted to include child care. When the couple begins using the model, both partners should go through all the stages on a weekly basis. As they become familiar with the model, and if they are generally satisfied, they can cycle through less frequently. The main determinant in that how frequently the process is reviewed should be the level of dissatisfaction: The greater the level of dissatisfaction, the greater the need for the couple to recycle through the process.

Matlin (2004) also suggests that a major problem of dual-earner families is the division of responsibility for a variety of household tasks. She suggests that couples are to develop a list of tasks, including shopping for food, cooking, washing dishes, doing laundry, and paying bills. When the list is completed, couples are to decide which partner has the primary responsibility for each task. This process not only provides a means of negotiating household tasks but also can build the perception of an equitable relationship of sharing family responsibilities.

Child Care

When both parents work, the care of children becomes a critical issue. Because more than half of the mothers in the United States work outside the home, child care has been an increasing concern. According to Andersen and Taylor (2013), one-half of 3-year-olds and two-thirds of 4-year-olds are in day care facilities. There has been a steady increase in the use of day care since 1965. Other forms of day care include sitters, day care homes, and relatives. Currently, day care facilities continue to be widely used by dual-earner families, although the trend of home-based enterprises, which allows time for providing child care in one's home, also has increased.

Organizations also have recognized the need to provide for child care, and some offer one or more of the following alternatives:

Emergency care: Companies provide temporary care when employees' regular arrangements fail.

Discounts: Organizations arrange for a discount from national day care chains or pay a small portion of the fees.

Vouchers: Some organizations pay subsidies or offer special assistance to some low-paid employees.

Referral services: Organizations may offer employees a list of approved day care centers.

On-site day care: Day care centers are located on the organization's site.

Flexible benefits: Money paid to day care centers is deducted from each employee's salary; thus, it is not considered taxable income.

Some organizations have developed family-oriented work policies that are designed to help dual-career families with child care responsibilities. Most are designed to help parents by offering flexible work policies as follows:

1. Telephone access is an organization's policy that permits parents to make personal calls to their children or receive them.
2. Parental leave also is provided by many organizations. This type of leave is different from maternity leave in that it is primarily for care of children who are seriously ill.
3. Flextime permits parents to choose arrival and departure times within a set range.
   a. Flexible work arrangements permit arranging part-time work, job sharing, flex-place work (part of the day at home and part at the office), or telecommuting (work from home or satellite office).

As reported earlier, home-based enterprises are increasing. One partner or both partners can remain at home to perform certain kinds of work for an organization. Technology has provided the means for home-based work through the use of e-mail, faxing capabilities, and telecommuting (Aamodt, 2013). One of parents' major concerns, however, is the potential negative effects on children who are placed in day care centers. Research in the early 1990s indicated that day care infants were no different from infants who were reared in their homes on measures of cognitive, linguistic, and social development (Clark-Stewart, 1993). Most studies at that time actually suggested that children benefited from their day care experiences (Sigelman & Shaffer, 1995). Because low-quality care was found to be associated with poor outcomes, researchers became more concerned about how to determine quality of care among day care centers. Research focusing on identifying the core elements of high-quality day care centers was reviewed by Shaffer (2002) and has been compiled into characteristics of high-quality infant and toddler day care as reported in Table 10.1.

The information in this table points out that a pleasant, nurturing environment and child care ratio are highly important. Caregivers also must be well trained in child development and should be emotionally able to establish relationships with infants. Licensing groups also provide some assurance of the quality of care. A most interesting additional finding about child care is the importance of the mother's perception of dual-earner families and work per se. In essence, a mother's positive attitudes about work and mothering are most important to how a child will react to day care center activities. Rightfully so—the pressure of positive day care results should not wholly be the mother's responsibility. Fathers can enhance day care outcomes of their children by showing support and appreciation of their spouses' working and parenting role (Tischler, 2014).

Relationship Factors

A pivotal point in dual-career families is a geographical relocation to enhance the husband's or the wife's career. Clearly, a move could represent a sacrifice by one spouse. According to Goldenberg and Goldenberg (2013), the husband usually receives the major benefits from geographical moves; however, more couples are deciding to move to favor the wife's career. In some situations, a decision is made to commute so they can maintain their current residence.

Table 10.1	**Characteristics of High-Quality Infant and Toddler Day Care**
Physical setting	The indoor environment is clean, well lit, and ventilated; outdoor play areas are fenced, spacious, and free of hazards; they include age-appropriate implements (slides, swings, sandbox, etc.).
Child: caregiver ratio	No more than three infants or four to six toddlers per adult caregiver.
Caregiver characteristics/ qualifications	Caregivers should have some training in child development and first aid; they should be warm, emotionally expressive, and responsive to children's bids for attention. Ideally, staffing is consistent so that infants and toddlers can form relationships (even attachment relationships) with their caregivers.
Toys/activities	Toys and activities are age-appropriate; infants and toddlers are always supervised, even during free play indoors.
Family links	Parents are always welcome, and caregivers confer freely with them about their child's progress.
Liscensing	Day care setting is liscenced by the state and ideally accredited by the National Family Day Care Program or by the National Academy of Early Childhood Programs.

SOURCE: From *Developmental Psychology: Childhood and Adolescence*, 6th ed., by D.R. Shaffer © 2002. Reprinted with permission of Wadsworth Thomson Corporation.

Competition between partners in dual-career homes usually is associated with a need to achieve and be recognized. Competition tends to emerge when one spouse develops feelings of insecurity or frustration associated with his or her career (Galliano, 2003). Feelings of competition might not be expressed directly but, instead, could result in debates about a variety of family or career concerns. For example, the tendency to address the issue of competition indirectly might lead to arguments about issues such as work schedules, vacation schedules, and child care commitments. The view that competition is largely inappropriate can cause dual-career partners to deny or avoid the issue.

Another important aspect of dual-career relationships is the decision-making process within the family—more specifically, who is empowered to make decisions. This factor seems to boil down to the question of equity in the decision process. For dual-career families, it is particularly important to reach mutual agreement on both major and minor decisions. Otherwise, one partner may feel treated unjustly.

The sharing of decision making and subsequent agreement of common life goals can serve as a foundation of support for family roles. Likewise, the sharing of perceptions of women's and men's roles in dual-career marriages is considered significantly relevant to how partners combine occupational and family roles (Kail & Cavanaugh 2014; Matlin, 2004). See appendix F for intervention strategies such as Working Climate, Expressiveness Training, Dual-Career Roles, and Lifestyle Skills.

Summary

1. Women continue to reassess their career priorities and are looking beyond the traditional feminine working roles. Even though women are being given greater opportunities to expand their career choices, barriers to the changing role of women in the working world still exist.

2. Counselors must be aware of unique influences that shape gender-role development. Cultural groups have some special needs that must be addressed, and individual differences within groups must be recognized.

3. Each individual is influenced by a number of specific cultural and situational factors that contribute to gender stereotyping. It is not certain how and to what extent gender differences remain stable among adults.

4. The division of labor by gender is attributed to the Industrial Revolution. Men became the primary breadwinner and women, caregivers. In World War II, women took over jobs that traditionally were reserved for men. After the war they were sent home to continue as primary caregivers. The second wave of the women's movement paved the way for women to return to the workforce in large numbers. Currently, women have made great progress, but gender stereotyping has remained a deterrent for many.

5. Inequality in the workplace continues to exist. Men still receive higher pay than women even though they occupy the same job. There are also differences in income between men and women by gender and race.

6. Sexual harassment remains a serious problem in the workplace. As a result of inappropriate interactions between men and women, sexual harassment is being addressed in many organizations.

7. As more women have returned to the workforce, the issues associated with dual-earner and dual-career families have resurfaced.

8. Some of the issues facing dual-career couples are expectations of work and family, role conflict, child care, geographic moves, competition, and relational factors.

9. Implications of career counseling include illuminating underlying issues of gender equity, couple communication, sharing exercises, family and career status, and conflict resolution.

Supplementary Learning Exercises

1. Develop a scenario that demonstrates gender role stereotyping in a work setting. Present it to the class for critique.

2. Interview a woman and a man who currently hold nontraditional jobs. Summarize the problems they have faced and their recommendations to others.

3. While observing several television programs, develop a list of characters who represent dimensions of gender-role appropriate behavior.

4. List your experiences in school and home that influenced appropriate gender-role behavior. Compare and discuss your list with classmates.

5. Develop a counseling component that is designed to help women and men recognize stereotyping in the work environment.

Case 10.1   **Dual-Career Marriage**

Almost everyone viewed Maria's and Jose's relationship as dynamic and exciting because of their prestigious career positions. Although their marriage situation is unusual in a number of ways, Maria was experiencing typical problems associated with a dual-career marriage.

Maria was reared on the West Coast with two siblings. Both parents were professionals. Maria recalls that even though her parents were busy with their careers, they made time for their children. They had a maid who also served as their nanny when their children were young, but both parents shared in household tasks and driving Maria and her playmates to fun places.

Maria is now an internationally known architect employed by a prestigious international firm based in Phoenix. She is pleased with her current position. Her husband Jose is a college professor currently employed at a university in southern California. Jose flies to his job every week, leaving on Monday and returning on Friday. He now has tenure and does not want to give up his current position.

Jose and Maria moved to Phoenix when a position opened in an architectural firm. Jose decided that if someone had to travel on a regular basis, he should be the one to do this. When Jose is asked about this decision, he usually replies, "It's best for the kids to have their mother with them." Maria is not particularly pleased with this response, however, as it indicates that Jose doesn't recognize her achievements and that she had been selected after a highly competitive search by the firm. By his response, Jose seems to ignore the reality that she receives more than three times his pay and that they had agreed that most of her earnings would be set aside for the children's education. Maria doesn't expect Jose to tell every casual acquaintance about all these details, but she does expect more appreciation for a mutual decision that had been discussed thoroughly and agreed upon. Jose, however, thinks that Maria overlooks his traveling time and the hardships associated with it. Maria seems to view his position as just another professor's job that is relatively unimportant.

Maria now was having difficulty with her oldest son, who was losing interest in all his school subjects. At home, he has refused to obey her on a number of occasions. When she discussed this situation with her mother by phone, Maria got the usual response: "Maybe you should give more attention to your children."

Jose grew up in a Midwestern state with three siblings. Jose's father was a successful business owner. His mother was a homemaker who had no intention of working outside the home. Jose recalls the scrumptious meals that his mother prepared and that she always seemed to be there when he needed her. Jose's relationship with his father was one of respect, but there was never much affection expressed between the two, and his father was often too busy to spend time with him and his siblings. Jose describes his family system as a traditional one.

Jose and Maria met in graduate school. After a courtship of two years, they became engaged and were married soon after graduation. They lived in the Northwest and on the Atlantic coast, then moved southern California when a university professor's position opened. Each move was made to improve Jose's career. Maria had taken jobs in nearby cities in each location, and her growing reputation as an outstanding architect finally gave her the opportunity to take "the job of a lifetime," and so the family moved to Phoenix.

It was Friday, and Jose was on his way home for the weekend. He had invited one of his male colleagues, Bob, to join him. They had planned for time to prepare a research project.

BOB: Jose, this is a nice flight, but doesn't it get tiresome to do this every week?

JOSE: I'm used to it by now, but I have to admit that there are times I would much prefer to stay at home. Actually, it's not the flight as much as it is the nights away from home that bother me.

BOB: Well, I hated to see you move. I still don't know why you had to do it.

JOSE: Maria just had to have this job, and I guess I had to cave in just this once. But I hope you understand that I get my way most of the time. Anyway, let's start talking over our plans for this research project. You know, Bob, I think this project could get us an international reputation.

The first year in Phoenix was a relatively happy one as Maria tried her best to take most of the responsibility of managing the household. During the second year, Jose began to argue about household tasks and spending time with the children on weekends, and he often refused to attend business-related events with Maria's firm. The small arguments seemed to get bigger, and Jose was often irritable. Both Jose and Maria felt they had reached a crucial stage in their marriage.

As you answer the following questions, keep in mind that the problems Jose and Maria are experiencing can be similar to those experienced by other couples whose work roles may be quite different but also demanding.

QUESTIONS FOR DISCUSSION

1. What were Maria's expectations of marriage?
2. What were Jose's expectations of marriage?
3. Conceptualize the role conflicts of both Jose and Maria.
4. Develop a list of relational conflicts between Jose and Maria. Compare your list with a classmate's list.
5. Discuss how you could assist Jose and Maria.

11

Career Counseling for Lesbian, Gay, Bisexual, and Transgendered Clients

CHAPTER HIGHLIGHTS

- Sexual orientation as a factor in career counseling

- Forms of discrimination at work: blackmail, ostracism, sexual harassment, exclusion, the lavender ceiling

- Identity issues and a homosexual identity formation model

- Cultural differences in sexual orientation

- Special needs of youth with same-sex orientation

- Six-stage model for career counseling lesbian, gay, and bisexual individuals

As the 21st century progresses, the chances are that an even greater number of groups of individuals with specific needs will emerge. Thus, what began as a humble counseling program in the 20th century to help job seekers match their skills and interests with requirements of work roles should continue to expand its focus to include appropriate counseling models for other groups who present legitimate needs. Lesbian, gay, bisexual, and transgendered (LGBT) persons are not an exception to that position. This grouping of sexual minorities does not imply that their needs are the same and does not suggest a greater priority for any one group. Distinctions between groups and within groups will be highlighted throughout this chapter. The terms "sexual minority" and "LGBT" will be used interchangeably.

First, some general trends and counseling issues of sexual-minority clients will be introduced. The sections that follow will include discrimination in the workplace of sexual minorities, identity issues, cultural differences in sexual orientation, career counseling suggestions for sexual minority clients, and interventions for LGBT clients.

LGBT Clients

There is a growing trend for more open discussion about the effects of sexual orientation on career development. Barrett and Logan (2002) and Slattery (2004) reported that more lesbian women and gay men are becoming open about discussing issues encountered in the workplace. More business organizations are supporting gay and lesbian groups and networks. Many of these organizations have regarded gay men and lesbian women and transgendered individuals as another diverse group in the workforce and are dealing with this group just as they do with multiethnic groups; they have added a sexual-orientation component to diversity training programs. However, the issues surrounding sexual orientation in general and their effects on career development and bias in the workplace are far from being settled.

In the early 1990s, the major objective of LGBT clients was to find acceptance in the workplace by removing barriers that discriminate and inhibit their career development. Career counselors were involved in counseling approaches that would assist clients find solutions to bias and discrimination. Hudson (1992) suggested that counselors should prepare for counseling sexual minority clients by building an extensive body of resources including specific information on organizations and companies that support LGBT employees. In addition, a list of sexual minority workers who are willing to provide support and information should be provided. Other human service providers and researchers suggested that counselors should (1) keep in mind the subtle, insidious nature of heterosexual bias and use this knowledge as a reminder for reflection; (2) use gender-free language; (3) become familiar with models of LGBT identity formation; (4) identify a consultant who can provide helpful information or

BOX 11.1

A Counselor Checklist of Common Myths Regarding Homosexuality

DO YOU BELIEVE THESE STATEMENTS?

- Most gay men are effeminate, and most lesbians are masculine in appearance and behavior.
- Most gay couples adopt male/female (active/passive) roles in their relationships.
- All gay men are sexually promiscuous.
- Gay men believe that they are women in men's bodies, and gay women believe that they are men in women's bodies.
- Most gay people would have a sex-change operation if they could afford it.
- Most gay people are child molesters.
- People choose to become homosexual.
- Most gay people are unhappy with their sexual orientation and seek therapy to convert to heterosexuality.
- Counselors report high success rates in converting homosexuals to heterosexuals.
- Most gay people are easily identifiable by their dress and mannerisms.
- Homosexual behavior is unnatural because it does not occur in other species.
- Homosexuality is the result of a hereditary defect.
- Homosexuals have hormone abnormalities.
- All homosexual males have dominant, overbearing mothers and weak, passive fathers.
- Homosexuality threatens the continuity of the species.
- All male hairdressers, interior decorators, and ballet dancers are homosexuals.
- Homosexuality is an illness that can be cured.

Source: From *Counseling Today's Families*, 4th ed., p. 250, by H. Goldenberg and I. Goldenberg, Belmont, CA: Brooks/ Cole, 2002. Reprinted with the permission of Springer Science and Business Media from "Gay Patients in the Medical Setting," by N. Gartrell, in *Interventions in Human Sexuality*, p. 396, by C.C. Nadelson and D. B. Marcotte (Eds.). Copyright © 1983, Plenum Publishing Group.

feedback from sexual minorities; (5) provide effective coping techniques for different types of oppression, and become familiar with local support networks (Barrett & Logan, 2002; Eldridge, 1987; Jamil, Harper, & Fernandez, 2009). Counselors also may use the accompanying checklist as a starting point when preparing to counsel sexual minority clients.

Goldenberg and Goldenberg (2008) provided a counselor checklist by containing myths regarding sexual minority clients. There are many purposes for this list, but one of the most relevant is the need for counselor preparation for counseling clients who have different sexual orientations. As mentioned several times in this text, stereotypes have to be debunked when dealing with the needs of special groups, and there are many common myths regarding LGBT clients that have led to identity issues and self-criticism. Therefore, counselors have to build an understanding of the unique development, as well as the basic issues that sexual minorities face in contemporary society (Prochaska & Norcross, 2014).

Some General Counseling Issues

I will focus briefly on problems and concerns that sexual minorities face in career counseling and in the workplace. The first issue that generally surfaces is that of stereotyping about the kind of jobs that gay men and lesbian women commonly hold. For example, gay men are thought to occupy traditional female jobs such as interior decorator or hair stylist; lesbians are firefighters, truck drivers, and auto mechanics. As has been emphasized throughout this text, clients should feel free to explore all occupations of interest. Clients who have had their career aspirations limited because of stereotyping—that is, the jobs they consider appropriate because of their sexual orientation—especially need encouragement to consider all career options. Counselors should take an active role in challenging stereotypes in an effort to expand a client's perception of what an appropriate career is, and in this context sexual orientation should be viewed as only one factor to consider in career exploration and decision making.

Homophobia has been described as "an irrational fear, hatred, and intolerance of LGBT persons" (Gelberg & Chojnacki, 1996, p. 21). This feeling of fear, hatred, and intolerance has led to violence, discrimination, and rejection of sexual minorities in society in general and the workplace in particular. Fear and hatred can enhance negative stereotypes and is deeply embedded in our society and in many other societies around the world. Over time, there have been frequent reports of extreme violence resulting in physical and psychological harm to sexual minorities (Mooney et al., 2013; Slattery, 2004). These violent reactions are thought to be driven by a thinking process that is labeled homophobic.

Internalized homophobia is based on beliefs that focus on rejection of sexual minorities and often are expressed by salient messages in one's environment. In early identity development, some sexual minorities who are greatly affected by internalized homophobia reject themselves as appropriate individuals and form a dislike for self and a self-hatred for their feelings of attraction to members of the same sex. This is particularly true during early stages of awareness of their sexual orientation. Adolescents, for instance, might not fully understand the precise meaning of their differences in sexual identity but quickly learn that it is regarded negatively. They may be described as highly anxious, fearful, guilty, and self-loathing (Barrett & Logan, 2002). Gay and lesbian adolescents are particularly vulnerable to internal conflicts when coming to terms with their sexual orientation and challenges and threats from their peers and others in society (Heatherington & Lavner, 2008). Research also tells us that gay and lesbian adolescents often, but not always, experience mental health problems (Williams et al., 2005).

In contemporary society in the United States and in many other countries throughout the world, heterosexism is considered the only viable lifestyle (Carroll, 2013; Galliano, 2003). The point here is that counselors must be aware of their own homophobic and heterosexist bias when counseling sexual minorities. Counselors who want to become sexual-minority affirmative must challenge their own assumptions when trying to understand the complexity of a sexual orientation different than their own. One's sexual orientation has long-term consequences; for example, two same-sex partners who live together may not have the same rights in most states as legally married individuals of the opposite sex do. Sexual minorities are not welcome in some work environments (Prochaska & Norcross, 2014). The stigma associated with being a sexual minority might continue over the life span. What is suggested here is that sexual minorities are likely to view career–life planning much differently than heterosexual individuals do.

In the early 1990s, the American Psychological Association (1991) issued a published set of guidelines for avoiding heterosexual bias in language. Counselors should carefully choose proper words, especially gender-free nouns such as *partner* or *significant other*. Avoid the term "homosexual," which could imply a diagnostic category of mental illness. Use the term "sexual orientation" rather than "sexual preference."

Counselors also should become familiar with the term "transgendered." As the term implies, it designates "someone who identifies with both male and female roles or as a member of an alternative gender" (Barrett & Logan, 2002, p. 121). Thus, a transgendered person lives as a member of the sex opposite from her or his biological sex. The term "gender identity disorder" is used to describe a person who feels trapped in the body that he or she considers to be the wrong sex (Durand & Barlow, 2013). Sexual reassignment surgery is used for genital reconstruction and is accompanied by rigorous psychological preparation. It should not surprise anyone that people who are identified as transgendered are often subjected to intense criticism and disapproval; they often experience rejection and isolation. Individuals who received sexual reassignment surgery have needs that are similar to other sexual minorities, albeit they also have special needs; they face significant oppression (Brinkerhoff et al., 2014).

More recently, support for gay and lesbian relations and marriage in the United States has increased (Tischler, 2014). In 1996, the Defense of Marriage Act was passed by the federal government, defining marriage as the union between one man and one woman. Today, most states have laws that specifically prohibit same-sex marriage, but some states have adopted laws to recognize same-sex marriages. Massachusetts passed laws to recognize same-sex marriage in 2004, and by 2011 five more states had passed similar legislation. Over time a growing number of Americans have come to favor the marriage of same-sex partners (Andersen & Taylor, 2013; Goldenberg & Goldenberg, 2013).

Many states now have legislation that prohibits discrimination on the basis of sexual orientation. In 2003, the Supreme Court ruled that states could no longer criminalize private consensual same-sex activities. In 2011, the U.S. Armed Forces repealed a law that was built around a "don't ask, don't tell" policy. Today, gays and lesbians can openly serve in any of the Armed Forces (Brinkerhoff et al., 2014). The gay and lesbian rights movement has definitely achieved some support from a growing number of Americans and in a number of countries in Europe and South America (Andersen & Taylor, 2013); however, discrimination against LGBT clients still exits.

Discrimination of Sexual Minorities at Work

There are many forms of discrimination of sexual minorities at work. One example is overt discrimination, which can lead to violence directed at LGBT individuals. "Gay bashing," which is not always work related, has been documented in newspaper articles in various geographical regions. Many incidents of gay bashing are not reported, however, primarily because the victim is reluctant to call attention to his or her sexual orientation. In many cases, violence is simply threatened as a means of harassing sexual minorities in the workplace (Mooney et al., 2013).

"Hidden discrimination" is typically involved in hiring, promotion, and compensation (Barrett & Logan, 2002; Brammer, 2012; Slattery, 2004). Known sexual minorities may be treated differently than are their peers and may experience diminished opportunities for advancement. This form of discrimination is subtle but effectively relays the message that this person is not wanted in an organization. Overt and hidden discrimination in a work environment obviously discourages sexual minorities from making their sexual orientation known.

Other forms of discrimination are blackmail, ostracism, sexual harassment, exclusion or avoidance, termination, and the so-called "lavender ceiling." Openly gay managers may not have access to higher level corporate positions because of their sexual orientation and, as a result, plateau early in their careers when they reach the lavender ceiling. The lavender ceiling for sexual minorities, like the "glass ceiling" for women, is a discrimination method that is often hidden (Andersen & Taylor, 2013). One must also recognize that work violence involving harassment of LGBT workers continues to exist. In one poll, 30% of gay, lesbian, and bisexual respondents and 45% of transgendered respondents experienced harassment on a weekly basis (Rosky et al., 2011).

Discrimination at work, especially in a hostile work environment, has the potential of being threatening to sexual minorities, so support groups may be helpful. Clients may find that networking provides relevant information to help determine if one should leave an organization or transfer to another more friendly and amiable division. Counselors should provide a list of company-based sexual-minority employee groups that can provide information about specific organizations. Statewide gay professional organizations online are another valuable resource. Clients also can be directed to resources that provide the names and addresses of sexual-minority-friendly organizations as listed in the final section of this discussion. Finally, a resource file of individuals who have experienced workforce discrimination as a sexual minority and are willing to help others is a valuable referral source.

Model of Homosexual Identity Formation

Cass (1979, 1984) has developed a gay identity model entitled "homosexual identity formation (HIF)." There appears to be empirical evidence to support its constructs (Levine & Evans, 1991). The HIF contains six stages:

Stage I: Identity Confusion

Stage II: Identity Comparison

Stage III: Identity Tolerance

Stage IV: Identity Acceptance

Stage V: Identity Pride

Stage VI: Identity Synthesis

Identity Confusion, Stage I, may be described as an awareness stage in which the individual recognizes that his or her feelings and behaviors indicate a same-sex orientation. This is a period of soul-searching and internal conflicts and a process of clarifying self-concept in adolescence during which coming to terms with sexual identity is an integral part of development. In Stage II, Identity Comparison, the individual acknowledges the possibility of being attracted to the same sex, feels different, and develops a sense of social alienation; the individual has difficulty in identifying with family and peer groups. During Stage III, Identity Tolerance, the individual tolerates rather than accepts an identification of an individual whose sexual orientation is different; however, the individual begins to contact other sexual minorities to counter isolation. Identity Acceptance, Stage IV, is characterized by continued contacts with other LGBT persons to validate a new identity and a new way of life. The individual accepts a sexual-minority orientation as an alternate identity. In Stage V, Identity Pride, the individual takes pride in disclosing his or her identity as a sexual minority and rejects heterosexuality as the only appropriate lifestyle. In the final stage, Stage VI, Identity Synthesis, the individual is able to integrate her or his identity with other aspects of self and develops compatibility with both heterosexual and sexual minority worlds (Jarrett, 2006).

When using this model as a framework for career counseling, the counselor should be aware of the following four points: (1) Some sexual minorities may recycle through the model depending on experiences and encounters within contextual interactions in their environment and particularly in the work environment; their progress might not be continuous; (2) the time it takes to move through the different stages in the identity model can vary enough so there are significant differences and might involve other factors not accounted for in the model; (3) there appear to be developmental differences between LGBT persons that could result in different patterns of identity development; and (4) sexual orientation is only one variation in human development, and other variables might account for individual variation (Durand & Barlow, 2013).

A good characterization of sexual-minority identity development is a gradual process of discovery rather than a sudden awakening during childhood. Children might sense a feeling of being different, and this perception can provide sexual meaning during puberty. Periods of confusion might be followed by anxiety that usually takes years to resolve. Progress from one stage to another is usually not orderly, but individuals move to and from stages of development sporadically as they struggle with self-awareness (Jamil et al., 2009). Thus, counselors who can identify a client's progress in the HIF model have significant information concerning self-awareness and other factors relevant to career decision making.

Cultural Differences in Sexual Orientation

The research on differences in sexual orientation by culture is sparse (Jernewall & Zea, 2004). More than likely, new themes and patterns of cultural differences in sexual orientation will emerge in the 21st century. In the meantime, this discussion of cultural differences in sexual orientation provides a means of discovering some special needs of Asian Americans, African Americans, Latina and Latino Americans, and Native Americans.

Asian Cultures

According to Chung and Katayama (1999), there are significant differences between Asian and American cultures toward acceptance of the different sexual orientation of

LGBT individuals. Chung and Katayama point out that heterosexism and homophobia are more prominent and intense in Asian cultures and suggest three overarching reasons why homosexuality is not accepted in Asian cultures.

First is the philosophy of harmony and complementary parts of the Chinese *yin-yang*, which has counterparts in other Asian cultures such as Korea and Japan. This philosophy represents a natural order of life that prescribes that persons of the opposite sex are to be unified; thus, it is against nature to have a same-sex orientation.

Second, because traditional gender roles and family systems in most Asian cultures are so highly honored, same-sex orientations are unacceptable. As a result, sexual minority activities and relationships are closely censored.

Third is the prominence of agrarian societies in Asian countries, in which farmlands are passed down from one traditional family to the next. Same-sex orientation works against this long-established tradition.

These traditions and the philosophy of a "natural life," according to yin-yang, does not allow for an open same-sex orientation lifestyle. Because the consequences of disclosing a same-sex orientation are so severe, most sexual minorities remain in the closet. As a result, the concept of LGBT identity had not been recognized in many Asian cultures at the beginning of the 21st century (Chung & Katayama, 1999). Later, Jarrett (2006) suggests that in many Asian cultures a gay or lesbian identity is viewed negatively and would indeed interfere with the important continuation of a family lineage.

In some Asia and Pacific countries, there are mixed messages about same-sex behavior. In Bangladesh, India, Malaysia, Pakistan, Singapore, and Sri Lanka, laws against same-sex behavior have been enforced. The Chinese Psychiatric Association, however, eliminated the term "homosexuality" from mental disorders in the early 2000s (Ruan & Lau, 2004). Also, Buddhism does not condemn homosexuality; thus Thailand, for example, does not have laws against homosexuality. In Hong Kong, however, sex between two men is allowed if both partners have reached their 21st birthday (Carroll, 2013).

Asian American sexual minorities have found a somewhat more compatible environment in the United States, especially in certain geographic regions. Counselors who work with sexual minorities should be aware of the mores, traditions, and lifestyles of the sexual minorities' mother country and its society. In addition, counselors are to build a greater understanding of identity development and contextual messages that individuals receive from their environment in the United States. There is some evidence, for example, that Asian lesbians and gays have difficulty in being accepted in White and middle-class-oriented gay communities (Chan, 1989; Newman & Muzzonigro, 1993). Similar to other minority ethnic groups, Asian lesbians and gays have to deal with a double-minority status. As Chung and Katayama (1999) put it, their "efforts involve the parallel psychological processes of developing integrated ethnic and sexual identities" (p. 166).

In a study by Chan (1989), 19 women and 16 men between the ages of 21 and 36 who identified themselves as lesbian, gay, and Asian American were interviewed and filled out a questionnaire. Most of the sample consisted of Asian Americans who were born in Asia. The results suggested that most of these first-generation individuals preferred to identify themselves as lesbian and gay rather than as Asian American, but others in the sample refused to identify as one or the other, preferring instead to identify with both. This latter group believed that it was as difficult to be accepted by the gay and lesbian community as by the Asian community. Chan (1989) concluded that the stage of identity development largely determined whether an individual was identified more closely with being lesbian or gay or Asian American. Disclosure as lesbian or gay in this sample usually occurred by informing a sister rather than parents. It appeared that most thought their parents would not accept their sexual orientation and feared rejection.

In another study, Chan (1997) suggests that modern homosexual identities are Western constructs. East Asian cultures have no comparable sexual identities. In East Asian cultures, discussions about sexuality are taboo and are considered highly embarrassing even among friends. An individual's sexual orientation is considered to be private. Sexuality issues usually are not expressed in public. Moreover, the concept of individual identity is not a priority in Asian cultures; the most important group identification is as a family member. Thus, cultural differences in identity development, especially among Asian Americans, need further exploration and analysis.

African American Culture

In a study of gay issues among African Americans, Loiacano (1989) found results similar to those reported by Asian sexual minorities. African American lesbians are considered largely incompatible with role expectations in the African American community (Greene, 1997; Lorde, 1984; Smith, 1997). Further, gay and lesbian communities do not offer the same level of affirmation to as they do to their White members. Black gay men often have been viewed as inferior members of gay communities and do not receive the same level of affirmation that White members do. Rosario, Schrimshaw, and Hunter (2004) suggest that Black men are less likely to assume the role of an active member in the gay community when compared to White men. What is also suggested is that Black men are likely to feel alienated and rejected by Black as well as the LGBT community.

A study of 20 older African American gay men living in New York City, whose average age was 56, presents some interesting data. The authors of this study conclude that being an African American gay was different from being White and gay, primarily because of the interpretation of race and color in U.S. society (Adams & Kimmel, 1997). In the African American community, gay men are perceived negatively as wanting to be female, as being cross-dressers, and as threatening family child-rearing responsibilities. Gay men also are perceived as traitors to African American families and their race. The lesbian and gay community is viewed as a White establishment that ignores the needs of people of color. These attitudes and stereotypes make it difficult for African American gay men to feel accepted in both the African American community and the gay and lesbian community (Adams & Kimmel, 1997). The results of this study should be interpreted as characteristic of this sample only; however, similar conclusions were reached by Barrett and Logan (2002), Icard (1986), Lorde (1984), and Loiacano (1993).

Finally, a study of the results of an anonymous questionnaire of 1400 African American gay men and lesbian women from various geographic regions in the continental United States was reported by Peplau, Cochran, and Mays (1997). Significant conclusions of relevant information for career counseling include the findings that interracial partners were relatively common among the respondents and that same-sex activities are often more hidden in the African American community than in White gay and lesbian communities. These conclusions suggest that African American gays and lesbians have little support for their sexual orientation within their communities, which makes it more difficult to integrate identities for career development and to focus on traditional career and life planning issues. Currently, homosexuality is illegal in Nigeria, Sudan, Algeria, Morocco, Ethiopia, and other African countries (Carroll, 2013).

Latina/Latino Cultures

Barrett and Logan (2002) and Espin (1987) found similar results among Latina lesbian women. This group of lesbians also feared rejection in the Hispanic community and received marginal support in the gay and lesbian community. Espin found that it was difficult to determine if ethnic identity or sexual orientation identity was considered more important by the women studied. She concluded that her respondents had varying degrees of success in identifying as both lesbian and Latina.

Morales (1992) suggests that the Latino and Latina community is excessively homophobic and thus has little tolerance for gay and lesbian lifestyle. He suggests that Latino gay men and Latina lesbians exist in three worlds: the gay and lesbian community, the Latino and Latina community, and the White heterosexual mainstream society. Choosing which of the three to identify with presents challenges and conflicts that are indeed complex. In the beginning of the choice process, Latino gay men and Latina lesbians might resort to denial of conflicts. Using the unrealistic logic of denial, they might naively choose a gay and lesbian lifestyle with the hope that they will find a utopian lifestyle free of discrimination and conflicts they encounter in their own communities and in the dominant culture.

A second choice might focus on coming out as a bisexual rather than as gay or lesbian. This choice avoids being labeled and categorized as gay, or in Spanish, *maricón* and, thus, might be more acceptable to individuals who have difficulty in identifying with gay and lesbian communities. In a third choice, Latino gay men and lesbian women choose to live independently in all three communities and not "mix" the three. The conflicts in allegiances that soon develop usually lead to high levels of anxiety and fears of betrayal, and most come to the conclusion that some form of unity is desirable (Morales, 1992).

In the final stages of establishing priorities, the integration process becomes the central focus. Being identified within three communities as gay or lesbian, however, can result in fear and anxiety about the future and lead to the recognition that such an identity will be a constant challenge. These circumstances expose Latino gay men and Latina lesbians to risks of losing career opportunities that are already limited because of their minority status (Morales, 1992). Like other minority groups, Latino gay men and Latina lesbians should be helped throughout this entire process by support groups and relevant information about prospective employers and their hiring policies (Barrett & Logan, 2002; Slattery, 2004). According to the International Gay and Lesbian Human Rights Commission (2010), a number of Latin American countries do not view consensual intimacy between same-sex couples as a criminal activity. In some of the Latin American countries, however, the support for same-sex couples has been diminished by the influence of the Catholic church (Carroll, 2013).

Native American Culture

To understand the gay and lesbian world of Native Americans, we must digress in a few sentences to the mid-18th century. French missionaries at that time reported finding Native American men who dressed in women's clothing, assumed female roles, and accepted other men as sexual partners. The French word *berdache,* meaning male homosexual, was given to these men and also to women who assumed the role of warrior and hunter and wore male attire.

Among the Native Americans in whom this behavior was observed, the berdaches were not only tolerated, but also well accepted in some tribes. The berdache phenomenon was evidently widespread in the major cultural groups in North America, in some tribes in Mexico and South America, and among the Alaskan Eskimo (Mondimore, 1996).

According to Tafoya (1997) and Brown (1997), the berdache phenomenon is part of a Native American's worldview of a "Two-Spirited tradition." In this context, Native Americans are not comfortable with identifying themselves as LGBT persons, but, rather, as individuals who possess both male and female spirits. As Tafoya (1997) explains, "Gay can be seen as a noun, but Two-Spirit as a verb...This is meant as a metaphoric statement, meaning that a noun is a person, place, or thing, whereas a verb deals with action and interaction" (p. 5). What is emphasized here is that the Native American tradition stresses transformation and change that is too flexible to fit the categories of gay or straight. Masculine and feminine concepts of Native Americans are quite different from European concepts. There is a greater spectrum of acceptable sexual behavior among Native Americans, and there is less stigma associated with women who assume male roles and men who assume female roles (Brammer, 2012; Brown, 1997; Highwater, 1990).

The berdache phenomenon and the Two-Spirited person might not be well known among many young Native Americans, especially those who have attended federal boarding or missionary schools. However, a visit to the Lakotas and Sioux in the Northern Plains in 1982 found that the berdache tradition was still practiced, although modified from what was described as the "old ways" (Williams, 1993). Contemporary practices are more secretive and are not enthusiastically endorsed by young Native Americans; however, Native Americans in general have great tolerance and respect for personal choice. In this context, the Native American community might be more accepting of individuals who identify as Two-Spirited in Native American terms, or as LGBT in the dominant society. Nevertheless, LGBT individuals also must face a dominant society that is less tolerant and discriminates against individuals who are identified as having a same-sex orientation. Native Americans are also subject to stereotyping, as discussed in chapter 10.

In sum, one could conclude that ethnic-minority gays indeed have a double-minority status. A lesbian ethnic minority could be given a triple-minority status. Ethnic minority gays and lesbians both struggle with parallel psychological processes of identity; ethnic identity and sexual orientation identity development complement or complicate self-awareness and self-concept development. In addition, lesbians must overcome gender-role socialization that can limit career development.

Throughout this text it has been emphasized that we must identify unique individual needs for career counseling direction. Some needs have been identified here that can be generalized to most ethnic minority LGBT groups. Ethnic minority LGBT persons share some general needs, such as protection against discrimination, but each group of ethnic minorities also has special needs. Within these groups, individual needs also must be unearthed. In essence, all the unique needs of individuals who seek career counseling should be addressed.

Counseling LGBT-Oriented Youth

Counselors often have been reminded that adolescents need their services most. In the context of working with LGBT-oriented youth, the complex task of sexual identity can be disruptive. A counselor who is aware of the issues surrounding the development of self-concept in career development also must be alert to the special problems brought about by sexual minority status during adolescence. Many sexual minority adolescents whom Coleman and Remafedi (1989) interviewed had abandoned their friends, were rejected by their families, had failing grades, and were involved in substance abuse. Similar results have been reported by Marshal et al. (2008), who suggest that adolescent sexual minorities are at risk for substance abuse. Further, half of the sample had run away from home, had been arrested, or had a sexually transmitted disease. A smaller minority of the group had attempted suicide, accepted money for sexual favors, or been sexually victimized.

Other studies in the 1970s, by Bell and Weinberg (1978), Saghir and Robins (1973), and Jay and Young (1979), found that sexual orientation was a precipitating factor in suicide attempts among sexual minorities and that most attempts at suicide occurred before the age of 21. More recently, Ashford and Lecroy (2013) suggest that suicide rates are indeed higher for sexual-minority youth.

Counselors also should recognize that overall health is an important component of career counseling and that it is not unusual for many adolescents to take health for granted in a rather cavalier way. Their attitude about HIV infection might be reflected as a gay's problem; however, we now know that the risks of becoming HIV infected among sexually active adolescents have been well publicized. The point here is the need to inform all adolescents, including sexual minorities, of the probability of HIV infection and other sexually transmitted diseases through sexual activity and the sharing of needles. Moreover, the risks appear greater for all adolescents who have not received instruction of risk-reduction guidelines (Kail & Cavanaugh, 2014; Ryan & Futterman, 1998). What one must make clear here is that HIV/AIDS is not solely an LGBT disease.

Winfeld and Spielman (1995) have proposed an HIV/AIDS education program for the workplace that could be modified and used for other groups as well, including adolescents. Some topics that are relevant to our discussion here are the following:

- Theories of the origin of AIDS
- What are HIV and AIDS?
- How are HIV and AIDS transmitted?
- Who is at the greatest risk?
- Risk-reduction guidelines

Counselors who recognize the influence of sexual orientation on career development will create an atmosphere in which sexuality can be discussed openly. Counselors must be prepared to convey full acceptance of sexual minorities. Counselors are not to assume that every client is heterosexually oriented or that certain clients are sexual minorities on the basis of stereotypical suggestions. The adolescent especially needs to feel comfortable in expressing sexual orientation issues. The counselor should convey a nonjudgmental attitude. Uncertainty, ambiguity, cultural stigma, and fears of the future are viable topics to be integrated in preparing adolescents for career decision making. A summary of other suggestions for counseling LGBT youth is adapted from Barrett and Logan (2002) as follows:

1. Allow adolescents to explore their sexuality by avoiding premature labeling. Encourage clients to seek social and recreational opportunities. Be aware that at this age clients are immersed in a period of exploring and searching for answers.
2. Do not assume that all clients are heterosexual. Be prepared to provide accurate information regarding sexual minorities.
3. Ensure respect and confidentiality. Be prepared to discuss private sexual matters with clients. Make it clear that each client's rights to privacy and confidentiality are legally protected.

4. Be willing to mentor a gay/straight support group. Invite other professionals to become a part of the group's activities.
5. Be prepared to counsel gay youth and their families. Be aware that families may react in a hostile manner. Be prepared to help adolescents and their parents with a wide range of feelings and reactions, including shock, denial, anger, and rejection.

Career Counseling for LGBT Clients

The following six stages are designed for sexual minorities and, most important, can be included within contemporary career counseling models.

Stage 1, precounseling preparation, requires the counselor to evaluate his or her awareness of sexual-minority worldviews and cultures. Counselors must challenge their own assumptions about their client's sexual orientation. An LGBT-affirmative counseling approach is the basic core for counseling procedures (Kort, 2008). One is to be deeply empathic and accepting (Clark, 2010; Perez, Debord, & Bieschke, 2006). Counselors may want to use consultants to assist them in the preparation process. The basic assumptions of counselors who are affirmative sexual-minority helpers are characterized by an adaptation of the work of Schwartz and Harstein (1986) and quoted from Gelberg and Chojnacki (1996, p. 17) as follows:

1. Being lesbian, gay, or bisexual is not a pathological condition.
2. The origins of sexual orientation are not completely known.
3. LGBT persons lead fulfilling and satisfying lives.
4. There are a variety of LGBT lifestyles.
5. LGBT persons who attend counseling without a desire to change their sexual orientation should not be forced into change.
6. LGBT-affirmative individual and group counseling should be available.

Individuals who are LGBT ethnic minorities should be perceived as having double- or triple-minority status. Counselors also may want to include steps that are part of the multicultural career counseling model for ethnic minority women discussed in chapter 3. For example, in Stage 1, counselors may want to self-administer the *Multicultural Counseling Checklist* (Ward & Bingham, 1993) and have their client take the *Career Counseling Checklist* (Ward & Tate, 1990), both of which are displayed in appendixes B and C. Gender issues also may be included for female clients who are considered as having a triple-minority status.

Stage 2, establishing an affirmative trusting relationship, may require considerable time and effort beyond one counseling session. Counselors can expect sexual-minority clients to be reluctant to express themselves freely until a trusting relationship has been established and maintained. A collaborative relationship in which the counselor is an ally is recommended as a viable affirmative approach. To be an effective ally, counselors need to become knowledgeable about sexual minority issues, limitations of career choice, and the influence of homophobic attitudes expressed by important others in a sexual minority's career development. Affirmative career counselors not only assist sexual minorities with career decision making but also remain as allies and resources if and when discrimination is encountered in hiring and in the workplace.

Stage 3, identifying client identity issues, involves the client's place of development on the six stages of the Cass (1979) HIF model. This information is to be used with career development issues to evaluate the readiness of the client to make career decisions. It is also a point of reference for counseling interventions of personal counseling or psychotherapy. For instance, some clients may need further assistance with developing their identities before beginning career counseling or in conjunction with it. Client-identity issues also can be related to problems with irrational thinking and emotional instability (Durand & Barlow, 2013). Difficulty with progression through identity stages also can result in a client's indecisive behavior. The case of a female senior high school student illustrates how identity problems interfere with career decision making.

In her senior year in high school, Liz was asked by her parents to see a career counselor. In the initial counseling session, the counselor observed that Liz's speech patterns were stilted and that she was hesitant to express herself openly, seemingly saying only what was absolutely necessary. Recognizing her reluctance to express herself, the counselor changed the subject to her known interest, horseback riding, and spent the major portion of the first counseling session discussing this topic.

On her next visit to the counseling center, Liz was much more relaxed and warmly greeted the counselor. After a few minutes of small talk, the counselor suggested that they begin the interview. This session and the following session were productive as they discussed demographic information and educational attainment. When future plans were introduced, Liz stated that her parents want her to follow a lifestyle pattern that she is not sure she wants. "Go to college and meet a nice boy you can marry," she stated, as she mocked her parents. This was the beginning of a long story that Liz told, focusing on her confusion with sexual identity, rebellion, and general indecision about what the future holds for her. The more she expressed her thoughts, the more certain the counselor became that Liz was greatly confused about her identity as a woman and was far from being ready to make career choices. The counselor proceeded with personal counseling directed at identity development.

Counselors need to create a counseling climate in which the client feels free to express identity-development issues. Counselors should encourage discussion of contextual interactions that may assist the client in understanding sources of confusion and negative feedback from important others and peers. Specific issues that are ethnically/racially related are most appropriate for multicultural groups. Counselors may want to use a mentor who can participate as an ally in helping clients resolve issues. In essence, counselors should offer support and be an affirmative confidant/confidante.

The following case illustrates the use of an ally in the career counseling process with an ethnic minority gay man.

Julio was born in Texas to immigrant parents from Mexico. He often visited Mexico and was fluent in both English and Spanish. His stated need for career counseling went something like this: "I need a steady job so I can go to college for a better one." As Julio discussed his background, he revealed that he was openly gay, which made him the subject of jokes on the job. He sought advice about how to manage his sexual orientation with his family and fellow workers.

Julio had not met many gays in his new community and felt uncomfortable talking to "straight" men about his problem. The counselor took this opportunity to tell Julio of a gay Mexican man who would be willing to act as an ally to help solve Julio's problems.

After several visits with the ally, Julio informed the counselor that he felt much more at ease when talking about his personal problems to an interested gay man. He felt that he had gained a better understanding of what to expect from members of the local Mexican American community when he is identified as a gay person. He also was given the names and addresses of local business places and organizations that were considered gay- and lesbian-friendly.

In this case, the counselor believed that Julio would react most positively to someone who could share his problems realistically and provide him with advice from real-life experiences. The counselor had learned that it is most difficult to convince an ethnic minority who is gay that the counselor understands the minority's problems. Clearly, one who has experienced similar problems as an ethnic minority and who also has a gay sexual orientation can help clients by sharing personal experiences.

Stage 4, identifying variables that may limit career choice, suggests that discrimination, bias, and stereotyping are negative influences that limit career choices for all sexual minorities, including ethnic-minority individuals. A thorough discussion of these three variables should center on how each might have influenced clients to not consider certain careers. The major basis for their decisions to eliminate certain careers could be so flawed that appropriate careers seem to be only those that are stereotyped for gay men, lesbian women, and ethnic minorities. Obviously, clients should conclude that any and all careers can be considered in the choice process. In essence, the client takes back what has been taken away.

Stage 5, tailoring assessment, should be enhanced by a collaborative working consensus relationship; the client should be included in the selection of assessment instruments. In this process, the purpose of each instrument should be thoroughly explained. In this stage, career counseling models typically proceed to problem identification and the establishment of counseling goals. After client concerns are established as sets of needs and appropriate intervention strategies are suggested, personal and career concerns may be addressed simultaneously. Counselor and client also can develop an individual learning plan similar to the one used in the cognitive information processing model (Sampson et al., 2004) discussed in chapter 3. As counseling progresses, resources for sexual minorities should be provided, including a list of websites that include locations of organizations with nondiscrimination policies, addresses for employer policies, gay employee groups, and gay professional organizations, some of which are listed at the end of Stage 6.

Stage 6, job search strategies, prepares clients for developing their résumés, preparing job interviews, and locating sexual minority affirmative organizations. This process for sexual minorities involves more than finding job opportunities. In some respects, the process adds another dimension to the person-environment-fit constructs: Sexual-minority individuals should locate a work environment that is actively LGBT-affirmative. The astute counselor helps clients avoid many problems that they could face in a hostile work environment by providing direction for locating a friendly environment in the job-search process. The key to resolving these issues is having up-to-date resources. Thus, resources should provide the criteria to determine if an organization is sexual-minority-affirmative, has antidiscriminatory policies that include sexual orientation, domestic partner benefit policies, diversity training that includes sexual orientation, and existence of sexual minority employee groups. Clients also should be able to evaluate overall "gay friendliness" of a potential worksite. Finally, an important resource consists of the networks that provide advice for sexual minorities. Counselors would be wise to compile a list of local available networks that offer assistance to sexual minorities. In addition, counselors should recruit and train local gay men and lesbian women to assist other sexual minorities who need help in locating an affirmative workplace.

Web pages. The following list offers helpful resources for sexual minority clients:

For health problems: http://gmhc.org

For families: www.pflag.org

For education and career resources: Gay, Lesbian, Straight Education Network (GLSEN): www.glsen.org

Public Education Regarding Sexual Orientation Naturally: www.personproject.org

National Gay and Lesbian Task force: www.thetaskforce.org

Youth Resource: A Project of Advocates for Youth: www.youthresource.com

Queer Resources Directory: www.qrd.org

National Youth Advocacy Coalition (NYAC): www.nyacyouth.org

Gay and Lesbian Association of Retiring Persons: www.gaylesbianretiring.org

The American Counseling Association

The American Psychological Association

The National Career Development Association

Unique Issues and Needs. The special needs of LGBT individuals underscore the position that some groups of people do indeed share common concerns that are to be addressed in the practice of career development. Counselors also must recognize that there can be significant differences among individuals. Thus, counselors are to focus on individual interpretations and reactions to contextual issues and life events.

Another unique issue for LGBT persons involved in the job-search process is the question of whether the client should reveal his or her sexual orientation. This decision has many implications for sexual-minority clients. Brammer (2012), Winfeld and Spielman (1995), Gelberg and Chojnacki (1996), Friskopp and Silverstein (1995), and Pope, Prince, and Mitchell (2000) suggest that coming out is a multidimensional process involving a number of factors and variables that include the client's identity development; the LGBT-affirmative status of the employing organization; knowledge of the client's sexual orientation by family, friends, and associates; status of the client's partner and what "coming out" would mean to him or her; and the readiness of the client to face the workplace as a known sexual minority.

Keep in mind that identity development is an ongoing, continuous process that is more cyclical than linear as individuals move up and down the parameters of the HIF model. Counselors can assist clients in making this decision through discussions of the implications of many variables that are both external and internal. Clients may be helped by other LGBT persons who have gone through this process. Counselors also may suggest that clients network with LGBT employees in the organizations of interest.

Suggestions for coming out at work include extensive planning. One must lay the foundation for a positive reception, which includes having an outstanding job performance and building credentials that support and enhance job assignment. Supportive allies also have to be identified. Clients who recruit heterosexuals as allies usually will have a stronger support base. Clients also may be instructed to test the waters by dropping clues about their sexual orientation, for example, by suggesting that they support gay people and their rights. Reactions to such statements provide clues about what one might encounter in coming out.

Barrett and Logan (2002) and Mooney et al. (2013) suggest that gay men and lesbian women must be prepared for coming out at work by being fully aware of the reasons why one should take this step. Relevant questions include the client's short-term and long-term goals for coming out and how these goals can be reached. For instance, should one come out to only a few selected workers and gradually inform other key persons? Will coming out enhance the chances of advancement or detract from it? Clients should be encouraged to anticipate problems that might emerge and how these problems can be solved.

Professional gay men and lesbian women who have experienced coming out strongly suggest that being in the closet is a painful and disturbing experience. For instance, Ike felt relieved that he could now be honest and "above board" with his fellow workers. Ann was tired of a double life and felt much better about herself and her relationships at work after coming out. The major personal benefits derived from coming out appear to be self-acceptance and self-actualization (Barrett & Logan, 2002; Friskopp & Silverstein, 1995; Signorile, 1993; Slattery, 2004). However, each individual should be encouraged to thoroughly evaluate his or her work environment for the consequences of coming out, as well as for his or her ability to manage pressure and discrimination that could result from coming out.

Gay-affirmative policies do not stop discrimination and harassment in the workplace. The results of a national probability survey indicate that employees who revealed LGBT sexual orientation found that they were more likely to experience harassment and discrimination, and in some cases lost their jobs. This study makes it clear why some workers are reluctant to reveal their LGBT status (Sears & Mallory, 2011).

Coming out at lower level jobs or nonprofessional work might be even more risky, especially in highly conservative environments. Clients should be encouraged to evaluate each work environment for its openness shown by other gay employees and the advantages and disadvantages of announcing one's sexual orientation in that environment. It appears that there is a growing trend for more sexual minorities to come out at work primarily because of formal policies that protect them from discrimination (Slattery, 2004; Vargo, 1998). Being closeted at work or coming out at work are viable topics for sexual minorities; however, more research is needed with an in-depth analysis of the psychological antecedents and subsequent consequences of this process.

In sum, LGBT persons have special needs that are to be addressed in the career-counseling process. Career counseling can proceed within existing career counseling models for sexual minorities with some adaptations and modifications. Special needs may be included in career-counseling models as additional components that are relevant to the stages and steps of existing models. Counselors also must account for individual differences and subsequent needs of individuals within groups. For instance, an ethnic-minority lesbian should be viewed as an individual with a triple-minority status. All ethnic minority LGBT persons receive an additional minority status that may reflect unique needs of their ethnic-minority identification.

Summary

1. LGBT persons have special needs because of their sexual orientation that should be addressed in career counseling.
2. More organizations and companies are supporting LGBT associations and networks.
3. Many regard gay men and lesbian women as another diverse group in the workplace.
4. Individuals with a sexual orientation of LGBT continue to be stereotyped as to the kinds of jobs they should hold; are threatened by violence often resulting from homophobia; form a dislike for themselves through internalized homophobia; and generally receive negative feedback from a society that views heterosexuality as the only viable lifestyle.
5. Discrimination in the workplace can involve threats, lack of promotions, blackmail, ostracism, sexual harassment, exclusion or avoidance, termination, and the "lavender ceiling."

6. Ethnic-minority gay men have a double-minority status. A lesbian ethnic minority may have a triple-minority status. Ethnic minorities suggest that they are only marginally received in LGBT communities.

7. Adolescents who are LGBT-oriented face a complex task of developing a sexual identity. They might be abandoned by friends and rejected by their families. Among major problems are suicide ideation and HIV infection.

8. Sexual orientation is considered to be an important component of identity development. Identity development may follow a six-stage process that varies by sex and race, sexual orientation, and other developmental factors associated with individual environments. LGBT clients progress through stages at different rates, and the age when LGBT persons reach the final stage in an identity model varies.

9. Unique issues and needs that sexual minorities bring to career counseling can be resolved in current career models with some adaptations and modifications. Six stages that can be included within current career counseling models are precounseling preparation, establishing an affirmative trusting relationship, identifying client identity issues, identifying variables that may limit career choice, and tailoring assessment and job search strategies.

Supplementary Learning Exercises

1. Develop an informative program about HIV/AIDS that could be used in schools at all levels.

2. Choose three special needs of LGBT clients and develop appropriate intervention strategies.

3. Develop a list of topics that could be used with adolescents who are in the process of developing a sexual orientation of lesbian, gay, or bisexual.

4. Develop a list of publications that could be used by LGBT clients in conjunction with career counseling.

5. Develop a career counseling program that would specifically meet the needs of a triple-minority-status woman.

6. Visit an organization that is LGBT-affirmative. Obtain published materials that state the organization's policies. Share these publications with your class.

7. Interview a lesbian, gay, or transgendered person. Make note of his or her workplace experiences.

8. Identify the topics that you would use in an intake interview with LGBT persons. Specify how you would introduce selected topics.

9. Identify some methods that you would use to inform the public that you are an LGBT-affirmative counselor. List some problems you might experience.

10. Debate the following issues as either pro or con:
    a. LGBT persons should have equal rights.
    b. LGBT persons do not choose their sexual orientation.
    c. LGBT persons should be restricted from choosing certain occupations.

12

Career Counseling for Individuals with Disabilities

CHAPTER HIGHLIGHTS

- The Americans with Disabilities Act (ADA)

- ADA Amendments Act of 2008

- Special problems and needs of individuals with disabilities

- Implications for career guidance

- Rehabilitation programs

Career counseling programs for individuals with disabilities have elements in common with traditional career counseling programs; however, the diversity of needs requires specially designed assessment instruments (see Osborn & Zunker, 2012; Whiston, 2013), career counseling techniques, materials, and career-related educational training programs. The overarching counseling goal for persons with disabilities is to maximize each individual's potential for life and work in the 21st century. It will be emphasized throughout this chapter that persons with disabilities are a diverse group that shares some common elements of thinking and behaving and yet have unique special needs. Helpers have to recognize within-group differences to effectively meet the needs of their clients.

The terms used to describe people with disabilities have been changed to negate stereotypes and false ideas. The major objection was labeling individuals with demeaning names. For example, a "spastic" does not describe a person but refers to a muscle with sudden involuntary spasms. It is much more acceptable to think of a disability as a condition that interferes with an individual's ability to do something independent such as walk, see, hear, or learn. Thus, it is preferable to say "people with disabilities" rather than "the disabled"; "Joe is a wheelchair user," rather than "confined to a wheelchair"; "has a hearing impairment," rather than "is deaf-mute"; and "persons with mental retardation," rather than "the mentally retarded." The focus should be on the unique identity of a person rather than on a label that implies that everyone with that label is alike and has a status separate from the general population. A person's identity should be an individual matter that focuses on a unique condition, and the words we use should convey this message (Cormier et al., 2013; Matlin, 2004).

In this chapter, we first focus on the Americans with Disabilities Act (ADA). The second section describes special problems and needs of individuals with disabilities. Implications for career counseling and the role of state rehabilitation agencies then are discussed. An actual counseling case of an individual with a disability who sought services from a state rehabilitation agency is described in the next section. Finally, a career education program for students with disabilities is reviewed briefly, followed by a description of a group counseling program for individuals with disabilities who have been hospitalized.

The Americans with Disabilities Act (ADA)

The ADA, signed into law on July 26, 1990, is a comprehensive law. For example, Title III regulations require public accommodations (including private entities that own, operate, or lease to places of public accommodation), commercial facilities, and private entities to make reasonable modifications of policies, practices, and procedures that deny equal access to individuals with disabilities. Box 12.1 provides an overview of requirements in public accommodations.

The ADA identifies individuals with disabilities as follows (U.S. Department of Justice, 1991, pp. 3–4). An individual with a disability is a person who has a physical or mental impairment that substantially limits one or more "major life activities," or has a record of such impairment, or is regarded as having such an impairment.

BOX 12.1

Americans with Disabilities Act Requirements in Public Accommodations Fact Sheet

GENERAL

- Public accommodations such as restaurants, hotels, theaters, doctors' offices, pharmacies, retail stores, museums, libraries, parks, private schools, and day-care centers may not discriminate on the basis of disability. Private clubs and religious organizations are exempt.
- Reasonable changes in policies, practices, and procedures must be made to avoid discrimination.

AUXILIARY AIDS

- Auxiliary aids and services must be provided to individuals with vision or hearing impairments or other individuals with disabilities, unless an undue burden would result.

PHYSICAL BARRIERS

- Physical barriers in existing facilities must be removed, if removal is readily achievable. If not, alternative methods of providing the services must be offered, if they are readily achievable.
- All new construction in public accommodations, as well as in "commercial facilities" such as office buildings, must be accessible. Elevators are generally not required in buildings under three stories or with fewer than 3000 square feet per floor, unless the building is a shopping center, a mall, or a professional office of a health care provider.
- Alterations must be accessible. When alterations to primary function areas are made, an accessible path of travel to the altered area (and the bathrooms, telephones, and drinking fountains serving that area) must be provided to the extent that the added accessibility costs are not disproportionate to the overall cost of the alterations. Elevators are required, as described above.

SOURCE: From *Americans with Disabilities Act Handbook,* Coordination and Review Section, 1991, U.S. Department of Justice, Civil Rights Division.

Examples of physical or mental impairments include, but are not limited to, contagious and noncontagious diseases and conditions such as orthopedic, visual, speech, and hearing impairments; cerebral palsy; epilepsy; muscular dystrophy; multiple sclerosis; cancer; heart disease; diabetes; mental retardation; emotional illness; specific learning disabilities; HIV disease (whether symptomatic or asymptomatic); tuberculosis; drug addiction; and alcoholism. Homosexuality and bisexuality are not physical or mental impairments under the ADA. "Major life activities" include functions such as caring for oneself, performing manual tasks, walking, seeing, hearing, speaking, breathing, learning, and working. Individuals who engage in the illegal use of drugs are not protected by the ADA when an action is taken on the basis of their current illegal use of drugs.

ADA Amendments Act of 2008

Over time, the definition of disability has been challenged. The focus of change has been on expanding the original definition of disability to include persons with a serious disease such as epilepsy, AIDS, cancer, and mental illness. These changes were a result of Supreme Court rulings that focused on physical and mental impairments that can limit the interpretation of "major life activities." Thus, the ADA Amendments Act of 2008 expanded the list of "major life activities" that qualify individuals for coverage originally intended. The coverage includes conditions that are episodic, such as epilepsy, and those that are in remission, such as cancer. Over time we are likely to see more amendments to the ADA of 1990 (Cormier et al., 2013).

Of interest also to helpers are the ADA's requirements concerning employment of individuals with disabilities and transportation accessibility. Box 12.2 is a fact sheet prepared by the U.S. Department of Justice on employment and transportation requirements and the effective dates of these requirements. One major issue covered in this act is employment discrimination. The ADA prohibits discrimination in all employment practices, including job application, hiring, firing, advancement, compensation, training, and other terms and conditions of employment. Also included are advertising for employment, fringe benefits, and tenure. Employers are free, however, to select the most qualified applicant available and to make decisions based on reasons unrelated to a disability. For example, two individuals apply for a typist job and one is able to accurately type more words per minute. Thus, the employer can hire the better typist even though that person does not have a disability and the other does. The key to such decisions appears to center on job performance needs, and in this case, typing speed is needed for successful performance of the job.

Other subjects covered in the ADA of interest to helpers are job descriptions, job application forms, job application process, interviews, testing and medical examinations, hiring decisions, benefits, working conditions, raises and promotions, and reasonable accommodations. More information about ADA and the Individuals with Disabilities Education Act of 1992 (IDEA), discussed later in this chapter, can be obtained from the following:

Office on the Americans with Disabilities Act
Civil Rights Division, U.S. Department of Justice
P.O. Box 66118
Washington, DC 20035-6118
www.ada.gov

BOX 12.2

Americans with Disabilities Act Requirements Fact Sheet

EMPLOYMENT

- Employers may not discriminate against an individual with a disability in hiring or promotion if the person is otherwise qualified for the job.
- Employers can ask about one's ability to perform a job but cannot inquire if someone has a disability or subject a person to tests that tend to screen out people with disabilities.
- Employers will need to provide "reasonable accommodation" to individuals with disabilities. This includes steps such as job restructuring and modification of equipment.
- Employers do not need to provide accommodations that impose an "undue hardship" on business operations.

WHO NEEDS TO COMPLY

- All employers with 25 or more employees must comply, effective July 26, 1992.
- All employers with 15 to 24 employees must comply, effective July 26, 1994.

TRANSPORTATION

- New public transit buses ordered after August 26, 1990, must be accessible to individuals with disabilities.
- Transit authorities must provide comparable paratransit or other special transportation services to individuals with disabilities who cannot use fixed route bus services, unless an undue burden would result.
- Existing rail systems must have one accessible car per train by July 26, 1995.
- New rail cars ordered after August 26, 1990, must be accessible.
- New bus and train stations must be accessible.
- Key stations in rapid, light, and commuter rail systems must be made accessible by July 26, 1993, with extensions up to 20 years for commuter rail (30 years for rapid and light rail).
- All existing Amtrak stations must be accessible by July 26, 2010.

SOURCE: From *Americans with Disabilities Act Handbook,* Coordination and Review Section, 1991, U.S. Department of Justice, Civil Rights Division.

Special Problems and Needs of Individuals with Disabilities

The problems and needs associated with disability can be inclusive and pervasive. Using a holistic counseling approach, counselors are to address interrelationships of personal and career concerns, as well as adjustment problems associated with disability. Matlin (2004) captures the essence of how counselors should view their role when she states that "disability is an additional factor that creates variability" (p. 366). Implied here is that disability is multifaceted and that diverse strategies are needed to address self-concept, social status, life roles, resiliency, and especially the work role. The severity of functional limitations and the individual's adjustment to his or her limitations are most important factors to consider in counseling. The special problems and needs of individuals with disabilities discussed in this section should be considered to be representative examples from a diverse population.

Adjusting to Physical Trauma

To begin, we recognize that individuals whose disabilities result from physical trauma might have difficulty adjusting to and accepting disability. Adjusting to the label of a person who has a disability can be a long and painful journey. The process of adjustment can interfere with motivation to seek retraining and employment. Some individuals might experience the feeling that what has happened is their fault, that they have done something wrong and even sinful and are being punished. This kind of faulty thinking can result in shock, depression, and denial before they are ready to accept and start the adjustment process. Psychological denial of a disability is discussed frequently in rehabilitation literature. Failure to accept one's limitations can impede counseling assistance; the individual will not be open to retraining or to experiences provided by rehabilitation agencies or educational institutions (Brammer, 2012; Salsgiver, 1995).

Feelings of Inferiority and Negative Stereotypes

People with disabilities also can experience a sense of rejection from others. Some researchers have contended that individuals with physical disabilities are subject to an inferior status position in our society. The frustrations produced from a physical disability can be accompanied by shame and feelings of inferiority. The acceptance of one's physical condition is often linked to all facets of one's self-esteem. Careful consideration should be given to interrelated sources of poor self-concept, ways of reacting to physical disability, and ways of adjusting to it. Counselors need to assist clients in dealing with prejudice and discrimination, and especially how it affects self-image. They are to focus on helping clients develop a sense of well-being through positive thoughts about future opportunities for individuals with disabilities (Brammer, 2012; Cormier et al., 2013).

Individuals who are labeled as having handicaps or disabilities also can face negative stereotypes from work associates and supervisors, as well as from others in their environment. Negative stereotypes can lead to discrimination in employment, housing, schooling, and social interactions. In addition, employers are reluctant to hire individuals with disabilities because of erroneous assumptions such as the following: Increased sick leave will be required, insurance rates will be affected, safety on the job will be endangered, and plant modifications will be mandatory. People with mental retardation especially are considered to need constant supervision and are perceived as incapable of learning. In general, employers have negative stereotyped views of individuals with disabilities, which can result in discrimination (Corrigan et al., 2000; Scheid, 2005). For example, the label "amputee" might conjure up an image of someone who is severely restricted. Another individual who has had successful open-heart surgery might be perceived as sickly and weak. Such generalizations inhibit opportunities for employment, especially for individuals who have minor functional limitations. The point here is to debunk the faulty thinking that links all persons with a disability together into one category of "handicapped" or "disabled" rather than viewing each person as an individual with unique characteristics.

An advocacy role through personal contact with potential employers is one effective method for building positive attitudes about people with disabilities. The importance of the advocacy role is underscored by Ivey et al. (2014), who contended that individuals with disabilities face an array of negative social attitudes, prejudice, and other social barriers. Providing some examples of successful placement of individuals with disabilities is an effective method that may break down an employer's stereotypes. Scheid (2005) suggests that a disability should be viewed as diversity and not a deficiency; thus, clients are seen as individuals rather than as patients. Employers are to base an individual's ability to perform the work required rather than to dismiss an individual's application for a job simply because he or she is "disabled" or "handicapped" (Brammer, 2012). See Box 12.3.

BOX 12.3

A Disabled Person's Story

I am now officially classified as a 44-year-old person with a disability. About 10 years ago I was diagnosed as having multiple sclerosis (MS) but continued with my job as a sales and account representative with a large international company until 2002. Since then, my life has changed dramatically!

I have difficulty visualizing life without a job or a workplace to go to each day. I continue to wrestle with this problem. After all, I am only in my mid-40s, married to a woman I deeply love, and have a strong desire to do what I always thought I would do—develop a career. Work has been a major focus in my life since graduating from a major university in the Midwest with a degree in business administration.

When I look back at my life, I realize that my work ethic was greatly influenced by my parents. My father was employed by the same major organization for 33 years. My mother not only managed household duties, but when she was young, operated a beauty shop in our basement as well. Later she went to work for a bank and spent 23 years on that job. Work in the lives of family members has always been very important!

My first job after college was with a large international firm as a customer sales representative. My primary responsibilities included all aspects of customer service. During a four-year span, I received several promotions and honor awards. Since my first job, I have worked in two other major organizations as a key account manager and market development representative. I considered my career to be going in the right direction. I enjoyed the work and especially the interaction with clients and fellow workers.

Over 10 years ago I suddenly experienced blurred vision in my left eye and pain in my right toe and heel. Little did I know that these were the initial warnings of MS. Later I was told that this neurological disorder turns the immune system against the body's protective nerve coating and disrupts transmission signals to the brain. Eventually, functions such as walking and cognitive abilities are affected. I started using a cane several years ago but now use an electric wheelchair.

Currently I am on disability, unemployed, and daily contend with muscle spasms and a burning sensation in my legs and feet. One positive note: My wife fully supports me in every way she can.

Despite all the above problems, I still would like to be involved in some kind of work. Work was a major part of my life, and without it I feel empty and unsatisfied. I am currently investigating some possibilities of volunteer work. My recommendation to other people who have a disability is to aggressively seek out available help and assistance. Keep a positive outlook and strive toward goals, put your health first, and realize that you are "differently abled."

I advise counselors to stay current with employment laws and regulations concerning people with disabilities. Also develop a list of companies that have a good track record for employing and mentoring people with disabilities. When you counsel persons with a disability, address personal problems as well as career ones. People with disabilities can use all the help they can get!

NOTE: This is a real-life story of an individual who prefers to remain anonymous.

Focusing on School Dropouts

In schools we find a high dropout rate of students in special education classes. Adolescents who are diagnosed as having an attention deficit hyperactive disorder (ADHD) also have a high dropout rate (McWhirter et al., 2013). Students drop out of school for many reasons, and social alienation of students with disabilities is a contributing factor. Individuals with a disability often are excluded from the mainstream of society and, in schools, experience lack of acceptance by fellow students and even teachers. Some students may be openly defiant, whereas others are more subtle in their rejection.

One way to counter rejection from the mainstream is through legitimate role models. Individuals who have overcome their disability and are now considered to be successful, for instance, can be a source of hope and encouragement. Theatrical interventions in schools with children produced some positive results in changing the way 84 children (ages 9 to 13 years) viewed individuals with disabilities (D'Amico et al., 2001). A musical that incorporated individuals with different disabilities was presented to these children. The reaction to this musical was as expected: Children responded more positively to people with a disability, and perceived that they were able to sing, act, work, and be friends. The lesson here is that counselors, teachers, and all school personnel should be united to confront prejudice against students with disabilities.

Goals of Helpers

As mentioned earlier, disabling conditions have the potential to create a poor self-concept. Individuals with disabilities tend to report lower self-esteem and lower self-awareness. A life associated with constant rejection and being labeled as different can potentially create a poor self-image. "Who am I?" may indeed be a difficult question to answer positively. Helpers' goals in this context are to assist individuals in accurately assessing strengths and weaknesses to help them modify their self-perceptions. Programs that include components to help develop positive self-image are important in meeting the needs of these individuals.

Clearly, people with disabilities will likely have personal concerns that are interrelated with career choice and development. For example, individuals can be deficient in assertiveness and in independence if they have experienced the early onset of a disability, which in turn may lead to indecisiveness when attempting to make a career choice. Onset of disability in adulthood often requires that career counselors reintroduce the process of career redevelopment. By assessing the realities of their functional limitations, for example, individuals may be required to change career direction. In sum, later onset of disability has interrelated elements of career and personal adjustment. One not only is required to adjust to a different work role, but to other life roles as well.

Finally, the lack of visibility of individuals with physical disabilities working successfully in a broad spectrum of career fields reinforces low self-esteem and negative attitudes about labor-market potential. Negative attitudes about potential work environments also can be reinforced by employment personnel who exhibit feelings of discomfort when interviewing individuals with a disability (Cormier et al., 2013). In addition, some standardized tests and inventories used for employment selection can result in conflicting or misleading assumptions concerning employment potential (Aamodt, 2013; Osborn & Zunker, 2012).

In sum, people with disabilities face barriers that are developed from negative stereotypes and generalizations that may limit their potential for employment. They also are confronted with social alienation in schools and mainstream society. Onset of disability is a significant factor in determining strategy interventions. Personal concerns of individuals with disabilities often are generated by poor self-concept and the inability to accept and adjust to their disability. Rejection, inferior status, discrimination, and prejudice lead to low self-esteem and negative attitudes. Counselors are to assume an advocacy role and examine each client's individual needs to determine intervention strategies.

Multicultural Issues

In preceding chapters, we have learned about other special populations—that diversity is multifaceted and multidimensional. Hence, females who are African American and have a disability are labeled as having a triple (gender, culture, and disability) minority status. An Asian man who is disabled would be considered to have a double-minority status. What is suggested here is that some individuals likely will have to overcome double- and triple-minority status in most life roles, including the work role. One could be particularly vulnerable in the job-search process; the chance of obtaining employment could be reduced. Clearly, helpers are to develop effective strategies to help minorities overcome all barriers in the work world and in all life roles.

In this context, helpers are to focus on the interrelationships of double- and triple-minority status with other variables that affect career development. For example, onset of disability, severity of disability, self-image, support networks, and so on are variables that interact with cultural and gender factors that are interrelated and interconnected. All variables are unique individual characteristics that provide direction or pathways to intervention strategies and goals of counseling. In a holistic counseling approach, all sets of concerns are addressed. Counselors become effective advocates by uniting community leaders to participate in the development of plans to help all people with disabilities, including minorities, find employment. More about an advocacy role is discussed in the next section.

Finally, it is generally agreed that career counseling of individuals with disabilities is challenging, especially for culturally diverse clients. In the case example presented later in this chapter, a rehabilitation counselor goes through the steps of developing an individualized plan of employment for a Latina female who has a disability. This carefully designed, comprehensive program includes problem identification, psychological and physical evaluations, a comprehensive plan, financial assistance, college enrollment, job search counseling, and follow-up evaluation. Postemployment services also are discussed.

Implications for Career Counseling

The problems associated with the career development of individuals with disabilities exemplify the often expressed need for counselors to adopt proactive roles. In addition to assisting the client with physical disabilities directly, counselors should support community education and training programs to foster acceptance in the work world. Programs that assist educators, families, and employees in working with individuals with disabilities can be invaluable in reducing the existing physical and psychological barriers.

People with disabilities face negative attitudes, prejudice, discrimination, and other social barriers. As a consequence, holistic-oriented counseling programs should provide more positive roles and role models. Developing positive self-images and interpersonal relationship skills are necessary intervention strategies. A proactive role implies that counselors become advocates with considerable dedication to removing social barriers and providing supportive counseling. Above all, counselors are to help persons with disabilities develop self-directed plans, actions, and behaviors and in effect become self-advocates (DePoy & Gilson, 2004; Tower, 1994).

Educating and Counseling Individuals with Disabilities in Public Schools

Public schools have not always been involved in the education of students with disabilities. Following is a brief historical summary, reflecting on how mainstream society has viewed people with disabilities and the changes in thinking of how their needs should be met through public education.

In the early 1800s, some states established residential schools for the education of students with disabilities. In this protective environment, however, some residents spent their entire life in these schools because there were no provisions for educating individuals with disabilities in public schools. Not until the latter part of the 19th century did special classes in public schools become available. The movement that led to public funds for special classes was driven primarily by parents of children with disabilities who banded together and lobbied for legislation. This movement also influenced research aimed at providing better teaching methods and materials for special classes.

In 1975, Congress passed the Education for All Handicapped Children Act. This act required that all children with disabilities between the ages of 3 and 21 receive education in regular classrooms whenever possible. In an effort to serve children from birth to age 3, the 1975 Act was updated to the Individuals with Disabilities Education Act (IDEA) of 1990. This act provides a special category of "developmental delay" for children who are in need of early interventions and special services. Each state is required to develop specific criteria and evaluations for identifying children who need early interventions (Berns, 2004).

One provision of IDEA allows states to use the category "developmental delay" for preschool children. For example, children with special needs who have been diagnosed with cerebral palsy or spina bifida can be provided with special interventions and special services. Other children who have been exposed to environmental variables such as abuse, disease, or poverty also can receive special services under this act.

Goals for children with disabilities are conceptualized via an Individualized Education Program (IEP) written for each child at the beginning of the school year. This written plan is communicated to key school personnel and family. Included in the plan are the child's level of education performance, goals and objectives, related services provided to the child, evaluation procedures, and transition services for school-to-work or continuing education, usually by the age of 14 to 16.

Students with disabilities also are provided with tutors, interpreters, transportation, speech pathology and audiology, occupational and physical therapy, and medical counseling services among others. They also receive hearing aids, wheelchairs, braille dictionaries, and other supplementary aids. Innovative programs continue to be developed across the nation, including integrated classrooms and using peers as socialization agents (Berns, 2004).

What we have here is a movement from no provision of funds for students with disabilities to a growing recognition that those with disabilities have unique needs that can and should be fostered in public education. Although many citizens recognized the need for funds before 1975, not until around this time was general funding was provided. Sadly, before 1975, people with disabilities were isolated and had little interaction with others. This point underscores the importance of viewing each student as a unique individual rather than as someone who has a disability or a handicap—narrow stereotypical view.

Helpers are to take heed: The general public needs a greater understanding of students with disabilities, their potentials, their individual problems, what these students are capable of accomplishing, and what they can contribute to society. Counselors should recognize that we are only in our infancy in educating the general public about people with disabilities. Counselors are in a good position to develop a unified community effort to support and underwrite programs that provide opportunities for students with disabilities to live and work and, more importantly, be accepted in a community.

To serve students with disabilities effectively, counselors should consider the development of a cooperative plan that involves school personnel and members of the community. Ideally, a cooperative effort between teachers and counselors promotes an effective school program that is supported and recognized by the community. Community leaders are to be encouraged to contribute to special classes in a variety of ways including visitations to work sites. School-to-work transitions require a proactive school effort and strong community involvement.

School counselors have a vital role in assisting teachers build career development plans for students with disabilities. A major focus is on career information that provides an understanding of work roles, responsibilities, and realities of the workplace. Counselors should be prepared to offer suggestions for evaluating and teaching information-processing skills and strategies to enable students to comprehend critical information they will need in the work world. One key to helping teachers is a current comprehensive list of materials and teaching aids that are available in a variety of media formats.

Counselors also will want to provide prevocational skills training specifically tailored for students with a disability. Prevocational skills may include learning to accept responsibility, caring for materials, being punctual, and learning to take initiative. In many cases, this information is included in classroom instruction and counselors act as a consultant to teachers. Counselors also should make available appropriate measurement tools for the specific needs of individual students. What is stressed here is the necessity to use standardized tests that are designed and standardized for students with disabilities or alternative forms of testing similar to methods discussed in chapter 6.

Counselors also can lend a hand with life skills training. Such intervention strategies may include a number and variety of topics that deal with everyday living, including purchasing goods, budgeting, banking, health care, home management, and interpersonal relations training. Understandably, the functioning level of each individual will greatly affect the content and level of life skill training. In other words, intervention strategies should be individualized.

Other career development interventions also are affected by the functioning level of each client. In general terms, clients should be taught interviewing skills, how to relate with authority figures and fellow workers, social skills, and experiences in the give-and-take of working and living. Finally, the transition from student to employee provides the counselor with the opportunity to help students learn to effectively change roles. As Ettinger (1991) long ago pointed out, change in environment is sometimes difficult for people with disabilities.

Privately Supported Rehabilitation Agencies

Among the most widely known, privately sponsored, nonprofit rehabilitation agencies are Goodwill Industries, Salvation Army, Jewish Vocational Services, St. Vincent De Paul Society, National Society for Crippled Children and Adults, United Cerebral Palsy Association, Volunteers of America, and Deseret Industries. Although these organizations and other national, state, and local private rehabilitation agencies sponsor a diversity of programs, Goodwill Industries of America serves as a good example of a national network of programs for individuals with disabilities. Goodwill Industries of America is generally recognized as the world's leading privately sponsored agency for training individuals, and with facilities for individuals with disabilities.

Local Goodwill Industries are autonomous, having their own boards of directors, and are affiliated with the national organization Goodwill Industries of America of Bethesda, Maryland. Goodwill Industries conducts a wide range of activities, including classroom instruction, sheltered workshops, encounter sessions, therapy (physical, occupational, or speech), counseling, and placement.

Many local Goodwill Industries collect donated clothing, furniture, household goods and appliances, books, art objects, radios, and televisions for repairing, refurbishing, and rebuilding by individuals with disabilities. These items are sold in a network of bargain retail outlets. Another method that Goodwill Industries uses to provide jobs is to subcontract with private industries and with state and federal government agencies for assembling and manufacturing goods, janitorial services, grounds maintenance, and other services.

Goodwill Industries also offers educational skills training programs. For example, Goodwill Industries of San Antonio provides the following services: psychological testing, vocational evaluation, personal and social adjustment, work adjustment, prevocational training, special academic instruction, therapeutic recreation, skills training, and job placement. The individualized services offered by this agency are funded from service fees charged to referring agencies, such as the Texas Rehabilitation Commission, the Commission for the Blind, local independent school districts, the City of San Antonio Manpower Consortium, the Veteran's Administration, and private insurance firms.

Most age groups can be served by privately supported, nonprofit rehabilitation agencies. Services include provisions for assistive devices such as artificial limbs, braces, wheelchairs, glasses, and hearing aids. Assistance also is given to help individuals develop independent living skills through programs in which individuals share supervised apartments. The Salvation Army and Volunteers of America have emphasized programs for homeless individuals with alcohol or psychological problems.

Career services providers need to be aware of the goals, objectives, and services of private rehabilitation agencies in their community or local area. Programs that help to prepare individuals with disabilities for employment (such as work-adjustment seminars, prevocational classes, personal counseling, medical management, and mobility training) are valuable referral resources for helpers. Sheltered workshops, supported by a number of private rehabilitation agencies, provide a workplace for individuals who are unable to meet work requirements in the competitive job market. Counseling for disabled individuals is greatly enhanced through a wide variety of programs offered by rehabilitation programs supported by the private sector.

State Rehabilitation Programs

The purpose of state rehabilitation agencies is to provide counseling and other services to individuals who have a disability or disabilities. Each individual with a disability is evaluated to determine if he or she meets the general criteria adopted by the agency that determines eligibility for services. Eligibility generally is determined by two criteria: (1) Each person must have a disability that results in a substantial handicap to employment, and (2) vocational rehabilitation services must reasonably be expected to benefit the person relative to employability. Disabling conditions among populations served by state agencies are extensive and inclusive. Rehabilitation services have been extended to individuals with mental illness, orthopedic problems, mental retardation, visual and hearing problems, circulatory problems, amputation of limbs, and other disabling conditions such as alcoholism, cancer, epilepsy, kidney disease, multiple sclerosis, muscular dystrophy, and cerebral palsy. To meet the needs of such a diverse group of individuals, state rehabilitation agencies have developed numerous and varied programs designed to assist individuals reentering the workforce or maintaining their chosen occupations.

In the early 1980s, Parker and Hansen (1981) compiled a list of services provided by state rehabilitation agencies that are generally in vogue today:

1. Counseling and guidance
2. Medical and psychological evaluation
3. Physical and mental restoration services
4. Prevocational evaluation and retraining
5. Vocational and other training services
6. Expense allowances
7. Transportation
8. Interpretive services for the deaf
9. Reader, orientation, and mobility services for the blind
10. Prostheses and other technical aids and devices
11. Work adjustment and placement counseling
12. Job placement services
13. Occupational license, tools, equipment, and so forth
14. Other goods and services to benefit the client in achieving employability

Rehabilitation agency programs are designed to emphasize inclusion of their clients (Berns, 2004). Epps and Jackson (2000) present a broad view of services for individuals with disabilities to include evaluation, special education, financial assistance, counseling, vocational training, recreation, and referrals for addressing various needs. Sciarra (2004) suggests that school counselors are to work with teachers as partners by responding to in-class behaviors, to address concerns of parents of children with disabilities, and to provide solution-based counseling procedures directly to students with disabilities. The case study involves a client named Dora at a state rehabilitation agency.

Case 12.1   **Rehabilitation in a State Agency**

This is an actual case of an individual who received rehabilitation services from a state agency. Names, dates, and other information have been changed to protect the client's confidentiality. This example illustrates rehabilitation services provided by a state agency in a small town of about 25,000 people. The following steps in the rehabilitation process are covered in this case: (1) initial contact, (2) diagnostic workup, (3) evaluation and certification, (4) vocational assessment, (5) service planning, (6) placement, and (7) postemployment services.

Initial Contact

The purposes of the initial contact are to establish a counseling relationship, to provide the client with information about the state agency, and to obtain information from the client to determine eligibility for rehabilitation services. In this case, Sam, the rehabilitation counselor, interviewed the client to obtain personal/ social information, educational background, past work experiences, physical limitations, and financial needs. Excerpts from the case file illustrate examples of information recorded from the initial contact.

Dora was a self-referred high school graduate and had never received rehabilitation services. She was 40 years old, divorced approximately 3 years ago, and had two children. Her older child was married and living nearby, but the younger child had chosen to live with her. Dora had married at age 18 and had lived in several cities and states with her salesman husband. Sam noted in his report that her mood was flat and that she seemed remorseful and lethargic. She became extremely emotional when she referred to her marriage, stating, "I resent that my husband left me because of my arthritis."

She reported that she had suffered serious problems with arthritis for the past 10 years, requiring five surgical procedures on her hands. During the interview, she demonstrated lack of finger flexibility and restricted hand mobility. She was taking two prescribed medications.

Dora's only source of income was $800 monthly child support, and she had no savings. She was unable to insure her 5-year-old car, and her current rent and utility bills totaled $510. Dora's work experience was limited; she had worked as a teacher's aide for approximately 9 months but was unemployed at the present time.

Sam decided that Dora was a good candidate for rehabilitation services and had her fill out an official request form. She then was scheduled for a medical and psychological evaluation. Sam had to verify her reported physical problems, and he wanted a full report on potential psychological disturbances associated with the emotional instability he had observed. Sam also requested reports of previous medical diagnosis and treatment.

Diagnostic Workup

The orthopedist's report indicated that Dora had a severe case of rheumatoid arthritis. After carefully studying the medical report, Sam arrived at the following functional limitations and vocational handicaps.

1. Can stand for short periods of time only (orthopedic report from Dr. Bone)

2. Unable to lift anything over 10 lbs. on a repetitive basis (orthopedic report from Dr. Bone)
3. Unable to push or pull (client's statement)
4. Cannot bend for prolonged periods (client's statement)
5. Has limited finger dexterity (orthopedic report from Dr. Bone)

The psychological report discussed results of intelligence, academic achievement, personality, and several aptitude tests. Sam summarized Dora's assets from the psychological evaluations as follows:

1. Normal intelligence
2. Good clerical skills
3. Ability to learn and retain new information
4. Good reading skills
5. Good oral expressive skills
6. Average academic achievement for her educational level
7. Potential for college-level training

In addition, Sam summarized Dora's limitations:

1. Diagnosed as depressive reaction
2. Poor self-concept
3. Lack of confidence
4. Subject to mood swings
5. Limited work history
6. Poor manual dexterity
7. Easily fatigued

Evaluation and Certification

After reviewing medical and psychological reports, Sam approved Dora's request for rehabilitative services. The results of her disability, as well as the extent of her handicap, were evaluated. In this case, her physical disability was considered severe enough to merit services. Psychological problems associated with the depressive reaction also would be considered in planning services for her. In developing a rehabilitation plan, Sam was required to address all services that would help Dora reach her rehabilitation goal.

Dora was notified of her acceptance, and an appointment was set for the following day. In preparation for the next counseling appointment, Sam carefully reviewed the material that had accumulated in Dora's file. He paid particular attention to medical problems resulting in functional limitations. The psychological report clearly indicated that Dora would need supportive counseling;

however, he decided that his first goal was to establish a vocational objective.

Vocational Assessment

In the counseling sessions that followed, Dora's limitations and assets were thoroughly discussed. Although she had strongly considered teaching as a vocational objective, she agreed that an interest inventory would help to verify her interests and introduce other career considerations. Dora was given a computer-scored inventory, and a date was set for the next counseling session.

The vocational assessment phase of the rehabilitation process continued with an interpretation and discussion of the interest inventory results and the test data contained in the psychological report. Dora decided that she would like to explore a career in either elementary school teaching or social work. With these two careers in mind, Sam directed her to references describing these occupations in detail. Dora spent considerable time reviewing job descriptions and requirements. At Sam's suggestion, she made on-site visits to a school and a social welfare agency. Shortly after these visits, Dora decided that she would prefer a career as an elementary education teacher.

Service Planning

Sam developed a comprehensive vocational plan for Dora. This plan, known as the Individualized Plan of Employment (IPE), contains the following aspects of action (Roessler & Rubin, 1982, p. 132):

1. The rehabilitation goal and immediate rehabilitation objectives
2. Vocational rehabilitation services
3. The projected date of initiating services and the anticipated duration of services
4. Objective criteria, evaluation procedures, and schedules for determining whether the rehabilitation goal and intermediate objectives are being achieved
5. Explanation of availability of a client assistance program.

Sam postulated that Dora would need assistance with medical and emotional problems during the course of her college training. He also recognized that he would have to assist Dora in obtaining grants and other benefits that might be available to her. Excerpts from Sam's service plan suggestions include

(1) enrollment in a local college with financial assistance for tuition, fees, and transportation; (2) other financial assistance through grants and Social Security benefits; (3) physical treatment to be continued as necessary; and (4) regular counseling sessions necessary to address reported psychological problems.

He was especially concerned that arthritis patients often develop depression, so recommended that an assessment be done. He also suggested some prevention options, such as teaching Dora to self-monitor for depression. Sam decided to provide supportive counseling and, if necessary, refer Dora to the university counseling center or local mental health agency.

Clearly, rehabilitation clients often need extensive personal counseling designed to assist them in accepting their disabilities, adjusting to reactions of others to their disabilities, reintegrating their self-concepts, and adjusting to changes in relationships with family and others in their lives. Counselors need to evaluate different counseling theories and techniques in meeting the needs of different types of clients through an integrative counseling approach. In essence, individuals with disabilities may require extensive personal adjustment counseling that focuses on the interrelationships of personal and career concerns and life roles.

During the next 4 years, Dora made remarkable academic progress despite recurring physical and psychological problems. She had three operations on her hands to improve flexibility, and the regular supportive counseling provided by Sam helped her overcome her depressive reactions and pointed out the importance of support systems such as family and close friends.

Sam and Dora would evaluate the possibility of family counseling in the future. Financial assistance provided by the state and other agencies helped Dora maintain subsistence. During her final year in college, Sam directed Dora to attend seminars on résumé preparation and job interview skills.

Placement

In a conference with Sam, Dora decided that she wanted to remain in the area. Sam evaluated the local job market for teachers and found it to be keenly competitive for elementary school teachers; however, he decided that he could improve Dora's chances of obtaining a position by assisting her in job interview preparation. Sam also helped Dora develop a list of alternative school systems to which she could apply.

Postemployment Services

Sam plans to follow Dora's work for at least 60 postemployment days. He will focus on her adjustment to her new job and adaptations she must make in her daily schedule. Finally, Dora will be notified that if services are needed in the future, he can reopen her case.

Dora's case illustrates the comprehensive nature of rehabilitation counseling for individuals with disabilities. The services offered involved considerable client contact and coordination of functions provided through training programs, financial assistance resources, and medical treatment. Although state rehabilitation programs follow a general pattern, there are variations in the services given. Nevertheless, rehabilitation counselors must possess numerous skills and considerable knowledge to foster client career development.

Summary

1. The terms used to describe people with disabilities have changed to negate stereotypes and false ideas.
2. Passage of the Americans with Disabilities Act (ADA) has focused more attention on career counseling programs designed especially to meet the needs of individuals with disabilities. The ADA is a comprehensive document that covers several subjects significant to the rights of individuals with disabilities, including fair employment practices and access to public accommodations and transportation.
3. Several problems and needs of persons with disabilities include difficulty with adjusting to and accepting physical disabilities, attitudinal barriers, being labeled as "disabled," a lack of role models, onset of the disability, social interpersonal skills, self-concept, skill for independent living, and architectural barriers. Educational programs that develop a better understanding of the special problems are needed by employers and families alike.
4. The ADA Amendments Act of 2008 expanded the definition of disability to include more conditions.
5. The Individuals with Disability Education Act (IDEA) of 1994 requires public schools to provide interventions and special programs for children with "developmental delay." Students with disabilities are provided with tutors, interpreters, transportation, speech pathology, occupational and physical therapy, and medical and counseling services, among others.
6. Privately supported rehabilitation agencies provide educational programs, work information, and counseling programs. More specifically, the services offered are psychological testing, vocational evaluation, personal social adjustment counseling, work adjustment counseling, prevocational training, special academic instruction, skills training, job placement, and sheltered workshops.
7. State rehabilitation agencies provide numerous and varied programs for individuals with disabilities. An actual case of an individual who received rehabilitation services from a state agency included the following steps: initial contact, diagnostic workup, evaluation and certification, vocational assessment, service planning, placement, and postemployment services.

Supplementary Learning Exercises

1. Interview a rehabilitation counselor and obtain program descriptions for individuals with disabilities.
2. Make several observations of a special education class. Compile a list of common problems based on your observations. Relate these problems to job placement.
3. Develop a list of rehabilitation journals that publish articles concerning career counseling programs for individuals with disabilities.
4. Visit an industry that employs individuals with disabilities. Compile a list of jobs performed and worker functions.
5. Survey your campus to find physical barriers that restrict individuals with disabilities. Discuss how these barriers and others contribute to psychological barriers.
6. Interview an individual who has a disability and is currently employed. Report your results to the class.
7. Compile a list of audiovisual materials that can be incorporated into career counseling programs for individuals with disabilities. Review and report on at least two.
8. Develop counseling components designed to meet two or more special problems and needs of individuals with a disability.
9. Survey a community to determine programs available for individuals with disabilities. From the survey results, develop plans for using these programs in a high school or community college counseling program.
10. Interview a personnel director of a company that employs individuals with disabilities to determine common problems experienced by these workers. Develop counseling components to help individuals overcome the problems commonly reported.

PART THREE

Career Transitions and Adult Career Development Concerns

13

Job Loss and Transitions

In this chapter I concentrate on the growing need for programs and strategies to assist adults in career transition. In the last three decades, more attention has been focused on the development of counseling programs for individuals who choose to make a career change and for those who are forced into it. Changing work roles appears to be inevitable and most certainly unavoidable for many in the workforce. As Aamodt (2013) and Drucker (1992, 2002), among others, pointed out in the early 2000s, we are in the middle of a transformation that is not yet complete. A major aspect of this transformation includes changing occupational structures and career patterns. This transformation is rapid and highly discontinuous in nature; changes can be quite drastic and pervasive in scope. Change in the world of work has been described as tumultuous, and its fallout certainly will have an effect on who will prosper in the future. Current speculation suggests that individuals who will prosper are those who are intelligent enough to learn new skills and, most important, those who are willing to experience new and different work situations. The flexibility to adjust and adapt to different work environments and the capacity to relate to other people are the qualities that will characterize future workers. Workers probably will no longer experience the luxury of a steady stream of continuous change but, to the contrary, will be required to adapt quickly to new and different ideas, goals, procedures, tools, and requirements. The reality of today's occupational world is that some individuals will be forced to make career transitions, and others will choose to change careers to find satisfying work, suggesting that there can be positive and negative consequences associated with adults in career transition (Andersen & Taylor, 2013).

Adults in Transition

The problems associated with adult career transitions have occupied the attention of counselors for several decades. In the 1970s, for example, Moos and Tsu (1976) suggested that there are at least two phases of the transition process that can be addressed. The first phase, as one would expect, focuses on elevated stress levels that usually accompany transitions. The researchers in this case have suggested that one's initial reaction in the transition process is similar to a crisis reaction in that one has lost control of situation and fear and panic follow. In the second phase, assuming that the client is in a more relaxed state of mind, one is to focus on situational influences, circumstances, and most important, the client's unique interpretations of past events and current circumstances.

In 1984, Schlossberg's well-known types of transition were identified as *anticipated, unanticipated, chronic hassles,* and *events that do not happen.* In brief, anticipated transitions are events such as graduation from high school and college, finding one's first job, and marriage. The most obvious unanticipated transition is that of being fired or transferred to another location. As the name implies, chronic hassles refer to events such as having to deal with a hostile boss, poor working conditions, and long hours. The transition described as events that do not happen includes not getting a promotion, the corner office, or a requested change in work schedule. No doubt, career transitions are likely to include some of the examples of these transitions and more. The astute counselor, however, assists the client in assessing undesirable factors in a work environment as well as the desirable ones.

One is to also recognize that there are numerous reasons and situational conditions why someone may be anticipating job change. A voluntary job change may simply be an expression of job satisfaction and desire to find a different challenge and opportunity; like so many other changes one makes in life, job change can be an individual matter. Job change or loss, however, also can be the result of a recession such as the one in 2009.

Job Loss Concerns

Clients who have lost their jobs due to the impact of the recession and globalization are likely to experience some psychological effects of job loss and the stress that is associated with job search. These individuals often are required to reevaluate their skills and goals, which may result in a completely different career direction. Beneath the surface of immediate career concerns, an individual's self-worth can be threatened by the loss of a regular paycheck and career identity. Moreover, there often are inter-related personal concerns associated with other life roles that need to be addressed. In essence, psychological effects of unemployment can be pervasive. There are, however, differences in the effects of unemployment by age and gender. Middle-age men tend to react more negatively to unemployment than do older and younger men (Kail & Cavanaugh, 2014; Vosler & Page-Adams, 1996). It appears that workers in their 50s tend to experience less stress because many of them had considered early retirement, changing to a different job, or assuming a consultant role (Feldman, 2002). According to Kulik (2001), women who lose their jobs report a greater decline in general health than men.

Loss of Support of One's Psychological Well-Being

The major intended outcome of employment is to earn a living wage; however, there are also important psychological consequences derived from work that are discontinued when one is out of work. More than 30 years ago, Jahoda (1981) captured the unintended consequences of work as follows: (1) a daily time structure that is devoted to working; (2) shared experiences and interactions with cohorts and other individuals outside the nuclear family; (3) the opportunity to express purpose and goals of life; (4) reinforcement of personal status and identity; and (5) participation in activities associated with work that is viewed as a necessity in the give-and-take of daily life. Be aware that work's pervasive nature and complex meaning in one's life are not the arguments here. What is being emphasized is the loss of valuable sources of support for one's psychological well-being (Compton & Hoffman, 2013). Counselors will find that individuals differ in their reactions to loss of support; for example, some may become clinically depressed, some may experience increased difficulty with personal relationships, whereas others will present significant mood swings. Combinations of concerns are often presented.

Inability to Provide for Family. The inability to provide funds for oneself and/or family can be a major source of stress that will be discussed later in this chapter. The loss of adequate housing, ample food, and other essentials can be devastating for families and is a major source of problems in maintaining relationships. As some see it, there is loss of control over one's life when the social contract for work has been broken. Along with the loss of job is the loss of a socially approved role and social contacts. Counselors should not be surprised to find that individuals as well as family members feel isolated, insecure, and experience a poor sense of well-being. In sum, the psychological effects of job loss vary by age and gender; can be the primary source of mental health problems, relationship concerns, and concerns involving multiple life roles; and negatively affect an individual's sense of well-being.

Mental Health Problems. A study of the effects of unemployment suggested that a significant number of unemployed workers have experienced mental health problems, poor life satisfaction, marital and/or family problems, as well as physical health problems (McKee-Ryan et al., 2005). Not surprisingly, when these workers were reemployed, the negative effects of job loss were moderated significantly. Of interest to counselors are key factors of influence that were variables experienced by the individuals in this study. Cognitive appraisal of circumstances of the individuals studied included stress reactions to job loss, as well as reemployment expectations. Coping resources included personal, social, and financial matters, as well as coping with a lengthy time of unemployment. Coping strategies included job search efforts, problem solving, and focusing on emotional control.

Clearly the personal benefit of the work role was the central focus of concerns among individuals who experienced job loss. However, the effects of job loss can be pervasive in that one's psychological and physical well-being are impacted adversely (McKee-Ryan et al., 2005). Job loss has a substantial negative effect on self-esteem, self-efficacy, and total lifestyle, as well as emotional problems resulting in mood disorders. The major point here is that job loss can indeed create severe problems for those who experience it. Some organizations offer outplacement counseling programs to help clients relocate.

Outplacement Counseling

Marks (2003) suggests that the loss of job can be devastating and can lead to the following reactions:

- A feeling that one has lost control of life
- Stress, anxiety, and a lack of trust
- A fear of taking risks and feelings of insecurity
- Ambiguity and role conflict
- Low morale and loss of confidence
- Guilt and shame

Helping the recently unemployed deal with the above reactions will require counseling approaches that address both career and personal concerns. Many, but not all, organizations offer out-placement programs that typically address problems associated with job loss including emotional counseling, financial assistance, career assessment, and job search training (Weinberg, Sutherland, & Cooper, 2010). In the following description of an outplacement counseling program, the employees who have experienced job loss are referred to as clients.

Denial, Anger, Fear, and Acceptance. Emotional counseling addresses a series of stages (usually four): denial, anger, fear, and acceptance. When in the denial stage, the client is unable to fully accept the job loss. The client may want to believe that there has been a mistake and her or his job will be restored. This stage usually changes quickly, but in some cases these thoughts can last for hours.

In the anger stage, the realization that one has indeed lost his or her job can lead to the development of anger directed at a host of people, events, and the organization. Supervisors and coworkers are usually the target. Support groups usually are used to diminish the negative feelings of anger.

The fear stage can lead to worry about paying the bills and food for family. At this point, the realization of the consequences of job loss has the client's full attention. He or she comes to the conclusion that a new or different job is essential. A spirit of understanding and empathy is expressed by the counselor, who becomes a helper appreciating the depth of the client's feelings of despair and fear.

Finally, in the acceptance stage, the client indeed has accepted that she or he has lost a job and is experiencing what many other individuals have had to endure in current economic conditions. The client now is prepared to take the necessary steps to secure the future (Aamodt, 2013).

Financial Counseling. The financial counseling phase of this program includes addressing stress reactions associated with the client's inability to pay bills. At stake here could be the client's home, food, tuition, and medical costs, among other expenses. Topics addressed are severance pay, medical insurance, unemployed insurance, and other special programs that may be available. At this point, most clients are prepared to begin the job-search process.

In the career assessment and guidance program, the counselor will use career counseling programs similar to ones discussed and illustrated in chapters 2 and 3. The counselor also will focus on transferable skills and available retraining programs. Retraining usually addresses the need for workers to prepare for jobs that require high levels of skills. In addition, clients learn to access the changing job market, find job openings, build a résumé, learn how to do well in the job interview, and make decisions (Aamodt, 2013).

Some Causes of Unemployment

The number of unemployed workers has been reported by most media outlets and debated since the recession in 2009. Unemployment is a hot issue that has touched the very core of society in the United States and has affected the lives of others in countries around the globe. There has been no shortage of speculation as to the causes of unemployment and when it will end. My purpose here is to summarize research-based causes of unemployment for the counselor who will counsel those who have experienced it. A summary of some of the causes of unemployment compiled by Mooney et al. (2013) follows.

First, there seems to be a consensus of opinion that globalization has been a major contributing factor to job loss in America. What is at stake here is the lack of available jobs in general, but especially ones that pay well and provide opportunities for advancement. Lohr (2006), for example, makes the point that the process of globalization tends to begin with outsourcing lower-level jobs. There appears to be a bottom-up process. Thus, jobs that require only simple assembly tasks are among the first to be outsourced. Jobs in the manufacturing of goods soon follow. Skilled work such as computer programming is next. Eventually, the highly skilled jobs performed by research-oriented engineers and scientists are outsourced.

According to Dignan (2010), the outsourcing of information technology and high-level jobs in finance and human resources had contributed directly to the loss of 1.1 million jobs in the United States by 2008, with many more jobs predicted to be lost after that time. The problems of unemployment continue. In 2009, there were six unemployed individuals for every job opening. In 2011, there were 4.3 job seekers for every job opening (Shierholz, 2011). One must recognize, however, that these figures can quickly change. We also cannot be certain if there were significant numbers of part-time jobs in this survey.

The following is a synopsis of reasons for job loss:

1. *Job exportation.* Many jobs have been relocated to other countries, where production costs are much lower than in the United States. Workers in many other countries earn far less than those in the United States. Faced with competitive organizations that can sell their goods cheaper primarily due to labor costs, many organizations were forced to relocate jobs to stay in business. Job exportation also suggests that there are highly skilled and well-trained workers in other countries. But, more significant, they will work for much less pay than workers in the United States.

2. *Outsourcing.* American jobs have been relocated to a third party in other countries to reduce production costs. Third-party organizations also are able to take advantage of lower labor costs that can be passed on to the U.S. organization. Outsourced jobs include accounting, web development, telemarketing, and customer services (Mooney et al., 2013). The results of outsourcing manufacturing jobs have been especially devastating for many American workers.

3. *Automation.* The use of machinery and equipment has replaced human labor. Robots continue to replace workers in a variety of jobs. Sophisticated robots can perform complex tasks, taking over large numbers of workers, especially in the automobile industry. Specially designed machinery to do certain targeted tasks is also reducing workers in a number of industries. Self-operating machines, for example, are used in the production of goods. The future development of automation is expected to take the place of an even greater number of workers.

4. *Increased global competition.* In the global marketplace, it should surprise no one that the cost of a product has a great deal to do with its marketability. Thus, there are fewer products sold in the United States and others that have the label, "Made in the USA." Clearly, global competition has forced many American manufacturing organizations to relocate in other countries to take advantage of low-cost labor to keep their products marketable.

The automobile industry is an example of globalization. Automobiles assembled in the United States, as well as in other countries, contain parts that are produced in a number of different countries. The car part that has the lowest price usually gets the majority of the sales, and the lowest price is usually determined by the cost of labor. The future, however, is difficult to predict. Can the increased use of automation and machinery in the workplace reduce the need for cheap labor? This question cannot be answered currently with any certainty.

All of the above have contributed to the closing and/or downsizing of industrial plants and the loss of jobs for Americans. When there is loss of jobs in one sector of the economy, other sectors usually are affected. Workers and their families simply have less money to spend. The entire community can feel the adverse effects of a downturn in the economy. There is also what is referred to as underemployment. Many individuals have accepted part-time jobs when they are unable to find full-time employment. In many cases the part-time jobs available are low-skill and low-pay. Other workers have taken low-skill jobs because they simply could not find a higher level job for which they have been trained. In essence, many part-time and full-time wage earners who have high-level skills and educational training, but are unable to find a better job are indeed the underemployed.

Many recent college graduates who cannot find a job in their field of study are also considered as underemployed. The unemployment rate of adults 24 years old or younger who have a bachelor's degree or higher was 9.4% in 2011 (Isidore, 2011). This rate is the highest recorded for this group since the Department of Labor began keeping records in 1985 (Mooney et al., 2013). The results of these findings should suggest to high school and college counselors that entering college freshmen could benefit from more information about their potential employment upon graduation.

The results of high unemployment are not only devastating for the individual and family but also have far-reaching consequences for communities. Small business establishments could fail. In some communities, property values are lowered significantly during periods of high unemployment. Thus, communities may not have enough funds to meet their obligations for maintaining a safe environment for their residents. Other city services also can be affected. Some cities may be unable to meet their obligations for future and past employees. In this brief review of the consequences of unemployment and underemployment, the focus has been on the effect on individuals, families, and communities. I now turn to predictions of the future job market through 2018.

Changes in the World of Work

Career counselors are to recognize that the job market is ever changing and at a fast pace. By the time you read this chapter, there could be significant changes in the economy as well as in the job market. Figure 13.1 contains estimates of new job openings from 2008 projected to 2018. The predictions reported here have been compiled by the U.S. Bureau of the Census, Bureau of Labor Statistics (2002) and reflect economic trends as well as future needs in the workforce. The 10 top jobs that are predicted to have the most new openings suggest that most new job openings will occur in the service sector. More specifically, most new job openings will be in sales and health care.

Clearly, economic trends and future job openings are driven primarily by the results of globalization. The major causes of unemployment and underemployment are inextricably connected to globalization. American corporations continue to search for low-cost labor in other countries, especially for computer programmers and call center and factory workers (Brinkerhoff et al., 2014). Your current client may be waiting for the phone to ring for a job, but someone in the Philippines or in India, as well as in other countries, may be waiting also.

Although the information of future job openings may be the best information available, there are many variables in the globalization process that are difficult to predict. Nevertheless, the message for the career counselor is that the workforce and workplace are rapidly changing. What seems quite clear is that one's choice of a future career may be limited. The creation of more highly skilled jobs would certainly

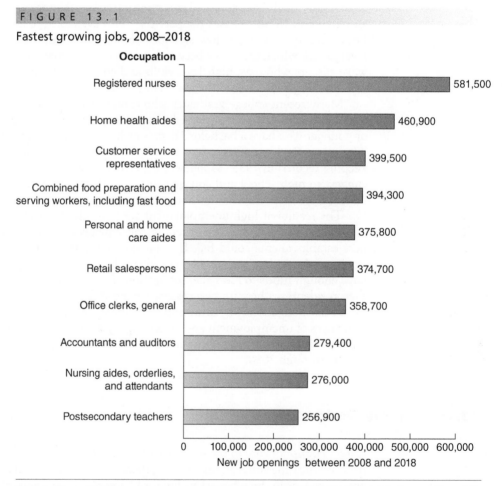

FIGURE 13.1

Fastest growing jobs, 2008–2018

SOURCE: From *Essentials of Sociology*, p. 327, by D. Brinkerhoff, R. Weitz, and S. Ortega, Copyright 2014. Reprinted with permission from Wadsworth Cengage Learning.

be welcomed. Clients who are undecided about a future career, however, may be required to place much more emphasis on the future availability of job opportunities. The underemployed in the current workforce can serve as examples for those who are in the process of making career choices. The counselor's position, however, should remain a collaborative one in which freedom of choice remains a priority. The career counselor and client focus on positive and negative factors of each career under consideration. The alert counselor provides the most current information available for job openings.

One of the major goals of the career counseling movement has been the availability of up-to-date reliable career information. Over time, career information has been available in books, newspapers, a variety of computer programs, and online through a growing number of websites. Clients and counselors have made good use of current information in the decision-making process. Confidence in the ability to predict future trends in the job market has been most helpful. In the not too distant past, clients were encouraged by the opportunities available, but in the current predictions of future job openings, there is despair. The reality of the future job market has been made clear by the number of unemployed and underemployed. Unfortunately, the future job market predictions suggest that most job openings will occur in jobs that do not require a college degree. One must also keep in mind that employers are focused on the cost of labor, especially in an economy that is driven by globalization.

What Has Happened to All the Good Jobs?

The answer to the lack of good jobs provides the counselor with the opportunity to carefully evaluate each client's ability to fully understand the reasons for high unemployment and underemployment. All clients should grasp an understanding of the current economic situation and its fallout. The counselor can make some valid suggestions. The client who has lost her or his job because of downsizing has come face-to-face with the reality of the current job market. Some clients may need personal support in the process of choosing a different career path.

The high school graduate who is going to college should be encouraged to carefully evaluate the selection of a major field of study. Clients can evaluate the requirements that are necessary for high-level jobs in the current job market and use this information to determine a list of possible majors. Likewise, clients who are considering training for specific skills can select appropriate educational and/or training opportunities that provide them with the best chance of finding a job. Manufacturing jobs currently available, for example, are being presented as career pathways in technology-driven occupations. One must be highly trained to make use of sophisticated tools and equipment. Some high schools and community colleges have cooperative programs that offer training for highly skilled technical work opportunities. The importance of evaluating job openings near the beginning of the career-search process suggests to clients that they are to choose training programs that provide them with the best chance of being employed.

Clients should understand that they are competing with determined scholars in this country as well as in many other countries. In China, India, and the Philippines, for example, there are highly efficient workers with impressive backgrounds in the sciences, mathematics, and computer programming. This does not mean that all highly skilled jobs have been exported to other countries. High-skill job openings will likely be competitive. Clients are to recognize the importance of knowledge acquisition and efficiency in their major field of study. Clients also can make use of social networking to find job openings.

Social Networking

Counselors can supplement job information programs with social networks. Websites such as Facebook, LinkedIn, and Twitter are popular social networks. Relationships with others are built over time through online discussion groups, chat rooms, and the use of photographs. Individuals pass on comments to others through network connections that are always present. Social networks have become a platform for millions of users. Information about a job opening, for example, can be passed on to individuals and/or groups through discussions. In the 1980s, Granovetter (1983) published his well-known research about the strength of weak ties or casual relations. He found that 56% of all professional jobs at that time were obtained through personal contacts. The informer was not necessarily a close friend, but more of a casual acquaintance. Thus, the informants and receivers of the information in this research were considered to have weak ties. His research was reinforced by Ibarra (2002).

The power of social networks has to do with what is referred to as *reciprocal power*. The forming of relationships suggests that an almost unlimited number of people pass on information to others in casual conversations on social networks. Counselors should recognize the potential benefits of social networking for clients in search of high-quality jobs (Tischler, 2014). The man or woman your client met online several days ago may provide information about an important job opening that has not been announced publicly. The potential amount of information that is exchanged daily on social networks could be most helpful for clients searching for job openings. In the meantime, clients are to consider the purpose of developing a lifelong learning commitment.

Toward a Lifelong Learning Commitment

The rationale for lifelong learning is based on a continuing need to develop planning strategies to (1) meet technological changes, (2) stay abreast of the information explosion, (3) upgrade skills, and (4) reduce the chances of becoming obsolete. In addition, and perhaps more important, changing individual needs and reformulating goals also create a demand for effective planning. Decision-making exercises should help individuals effectively develop plans and decide on future options. The rationale here is that more adults are to assume a self-directed approach for career development. Learning to effectively process information to clarify future work requirements and identify relevant educational training options should be fostered. Several examples of decision-making strategies are discussed in chapter 3.

Second, the specific task of establishing alternative plans for the future should be emphasized. Skills identification and personal lifestyle preferences are integrated to provide the basis for alternative plans to meet future goals. Clarifying differences between original goals and reformulated goals is a counseling objective of this intervention; effective life-planning strategies help individuals develop options and make effective decisions.

Adults are to be prepared to make the transition to a self-development approach to career development. By identifying attitudes and beliefs that accompany a self-development mind-set, the counselor introduces rich sources of information that can be used in group as well as in individual counseling sessions. Clients must be reminded that they must take full responsibility for their career development, which can start with their willingness to learn new work requirements and relational skills.

Lifelong learning is an ongoing process that should be viewed as cyclic; individual changes and external conditions may require the individual to recycle through one or more counseling intervention strategies. A lifelong learning approach, therefore, should be viewed as continuous, but with intermittent pauses. The message to convey is that one should learn effective methods of how to find and use resource information, how to clarify individual needs, how to make decisions, and how to plan for the future, which may require retraining to meet the needs of the changing workplace.

Industrial organizations have a long history of training workers as a vital part of their career development. Advances in technology have made it necessary to update current workers' skills in many large organizations as well as small businesses. During a severe recession, however, workers who have lost their jobs and are in search of employment may be forced to find training programs through their own initiative, although many organizations have developed effective training and/or retraining platforms for their employees. See chapter 7 for more information about available training programs.

You may recall the case study of Larry in chapter 3, who experienced job loss but found a training program that prepared him for a different type of job that was available. He chose a work role that required skills similar to those he used in his previous job. Many of the unemployed, however, have not been as fortunate as Larry. But learning new skills through a variety of training programs has led some who have experienced the devastation of job loss to find work. What we have here is an approach to helping clients who have lost their job to cope with personal problems associated with job loss and also to take aggressive action through job-search techniques, retraining programs, and technology-driven instruction. Counselors also present interventions designed to deal with the stress, anxiety, and depression accompanying job loss. They address clients' personal as well as career needs.

The case studies feature a client who lost his job because of a severe economic recession and another client who choose to change jobs because of the threat of job loss. The high rate of unemployment during the recession of 2009 and the globalization process are affecting the lives of many Americans as well as the lives of citizens in many other countries across the globe. Many workers have lost their source of income and with it their self-respect. If the past is any indication of the future, we can expect to experience both good and bad economic times accompanied by changing work roles and periods in which there will be job loss. Counselors are to be prepared to address career choice transitions. I address the job loss concerns of Ricardo in the case study.

Case 13.1   Ricardo's Job Loss

A few days prior to Ricardo's visit to a licensed professional counselor, he was told along with a group of other workers that their jobs were being terminated. The foreman announced that due to the sharp decrease of orders for steel products the company was forced to lay off workers. This message was similar to the one that many workers received during the recession in 2009 and when jobs were outsourced to other countries in the 1990s.

Ricardo described his reaction as being completely surprised and then stunned. "I became very frustrated, then angry, and that was followed by a feeling of resentment of being let go. I thought I was one of the best workers—but now I can't help but feel I was a failure—a failure to my family, especially my two children!"

Ricardo continued by stating that at this time he didn't want to talk to anyone and, as he put it, "be left alone." And he added, "I had to do something, so that's why I'm here."

Conceptualization of Ricardo's Concerns in Four Domains

During the initial interview the counselor learned that Ricardo, a 29-year-old married man with two children, was a high school graduate who had lost a well-paying job and was currently experiencing reactions to the stressful situation that accompanies job loss. In addition, he blamed himself for being fired. As is often the case, even when they lose their job due to poor economic circumstances, individuals believe they are the culprit. The severity of the self-referent belief and the loss of self-esteem are often followed by stress-related anger.

The counselor continued interviewing Ricardo, gathering the usual data, including skill and experience identification, and decided that although her observations should be considered only tentative, she conceptualized her client's concerns in four domains in order to begin interventions as soon as possible. Her goal was to modify the severity of Ricardo's concerns and correct faulty thinking and her summation went something like this.

Career: Ricardo's reaction to being fired is accompanied by anxiety, tension, and irritability. These barriers to rational thinking must be removed or moderated before he is able to adequately process information about jobs that may be available. Currently he is very frustrated and is vulnerable to having a complete breakdown. He even rejects positive occupational information that could eventually help him modify his distorted thinking and faulty belief system. Interventions should focus on cognitive restructuring. There were encouraging indications that Ricardo is more than likely a hard worker and can be successful in another work environment. He prefers skilled trades and working with his hands.

Affective: Currently Ricardo is unstable and extremely emotional. He appears to be fragile and gives the impression of someone who can easily lose control of his emotions. The danger here is that he could do irreparable harm to himself and others by overreacting to his false sense of failure. In sum, he is emotionally unstable and he is experiencing feelings of isolation and alienation. His emotional hypersensitivity accompanied by low esteem needs to be addressed.

Cognitive-Behavioral: Ricardo's inappropriate behavior is influenced by faulty thinking and faulty beliefs. His behavior is self-destructive in that he refuses to believe that his job termination was the result of a severe recession; on the contrary, he wrongly believes that he is the culprit. This is a classic example of an overgeneralization of negative experiences associated with job loss and underscores his inability to process information for career decision making.

Culture: Ricardo is a third-generation Mexican American. He holds some traditional values but claims he is more "American" than Mexican, although he does endorse a collectivist view when it comes to his family. His English is more than adequate, and he also claims to speak good Spanish. He suggests that he is an individualist in his approach to work and achievement, but is traditional when it comes to family matters. Conflicts that arise from two different approaches to life and work will need further delineation.

Inventories

To gain a fuller understanding of Ricardo's beliefs, the counselor chose to administer the *Career Thoughts Inventory* (CTI) (Sampson et al., 1996a), which provides three scales—Decision-Making Confusion, Commitment Anxiety, and External Conflict. The *Beck Depression Inventory*-II (BDI-II) (Beck et al., 1996) was also administered to determine the severity of observed symptoms of depression. In addition, he was administered an inventory used to screen clients for substance abuse, the *Substance Abuse Subtle Screening Inventory A2* (Miller, 2001). As one would expect, the results of the inventory measuring career thoughts indicated severe dysfunctional thinking. Ricardo's depression level was considered mild. There were no indications of substance abuse.

Conclusions

Using this information, the counselor and Ricardo agreed that it is most important to address his faulty thinking process. The rationale for this decision was based on the premise that dysfunctional thinking can lead to an increase of depressive reactions and inconsistent behavior patterns. Ricardo agreed that at this time he is not prepared to consider other job opportunities. As he put it, "I have to get hold of myself."

Counselors are to assist clients in understanding how a person integrates data and acts in accordance with their unique interpretations of them. In Ricardo's case, he wrongly believed that being fired from his job was his fault rather than to rationally observe that a severe recession brought about the failure of a number of industrial organizations and subsequent unemployment.

Dysfunctional thinking that was triggered by stressful reactions to job loss can adversely affect all life roles. Job loss is stressful no matter how it happens, but when one wrongly takes the blame,

the chances of developing a psychological disorder increase significantly. One who is full of anger, angry at the world, and lacks self-esteem presents significant deficits that must be addressed.

In Ricardo's case, the counselor suggested cognitive restructuring to help him overcome the effects of dysfunctional thinking. Her major goal was to heighten Ricardo's awareness of his thoughts and self-talk when he experiences anxiety. The point was made that negative thoughts can affect one's ability to work as well as relate effectively to fellow workers. In addition, Ricardo was informed that stress reactivity can trigger faulty thinking as well as physiological responses that are harmful. He learned that the first step is to be aware of and identify faulty thinking and replace it with positive thoughts that can lead to feelings of well-being.

Faulty Cognitions

Helpers are challenged to give more attention to cognitive processes in career counseling from the social-learning and cognitive theory approaches to career development discussed in chapter 2. Somewhat similar approaches to cognitive functioning are irrational beliefs (Ellis, 1994) and faulty reasoning (Beck, 1985). More specifically, the individual's perceptions of self and of people, events, experiences, and environment are seen as potential sources of mistaken and troublesome beliefs. Inaccurate information, inadequate alternatives, and negative constructs derived from life experiences are sources of faulty cognitions.

Faulty cognitions inhibit systematic, logical thinking and can be self-defeating. For example, a client's expectations and assumptions can cause distorted perceptions and unrealistic thinking such as "There's only one career for me." Doyle (1992, p. 185) presented the following examples of faulty cognitions that he suggested can lead to false conclusions and negative feelings:

1. Self-deprecating statements: These expressions reveal poor self-worth, for example, "I'm not a good student" and "No one really likes me."
2. Absolute or perfectionist terms: When an individual sets up overly stringent guidelines for his or her behavior, the individual sets himself or herself up for self-criticism and a negative self-image. Conclusions that are absolute or perfectionist terms often include words such as *must, ought, should, unless,* or *until.* For example: "I should have been the one promoted" and "Unless I get an 'A,' I can't go home."
3. Overgeneralization of negative experiences: These are deductions based on too few examples of situations. Frequently, they are based on negative experiences that make clients think there are many obstacles, making the future hopeless and

bleak. For example: "Since I failed the first exam, I'll fail the course" and "All the children in school hate me."

4. Negative exaggerations: These statements greatly magnify the true meaning of an event or reality. For example: "All professional athletes are greedy" and "You insulted my mother—you hate my family!"

5. Factually inaccurate statements: These remarks are based on inadequate or incorrect information. These erroneous data distort the client's perceptions of reality. For example: "You need an 'A' average to get into college" and "Autistic children are lazy."

Irrational expectations of career counseling, as suggested by Nevo (1987), are other examples of faulty cognitions and irrational thoughts often found in prospective clients:

1. There is only one vocation in the world that is right for me.
2. Until I find my perfect vocational choice, I will not be satisfied.
3. Someone else can discover the vocation suitable for me.
4. Intelligence tests would tell me how much I am worth.
5. I must be an expert or very successful in the field of my work.
6. I can do anything if I try hard; I can't do anything that doesn't fit my talents.
7. My vocation should satisfy the important people in my life.
8. Entering a vocation will solve all my problems.
9. I must sense intuitively that the vocation is right for me.
10. Choosing a vocation is a one-time act.

Although faulty cognitions can lead to a multitude of personal problems, Mitchell and Krumboltz (1996) argued that the career decision-making process is most affected. Looking at it from a positive viewpoint, individuals with accurate, constructive beliefs will have fewer problems reaching their career goals. Moreover, realistic expectations foster positive emotional reactions to self and others.

What we have here are examples of how the thinking process can be adversely affected by cognitive schemas that are developed from one's ecological system in which events and situational experiences influence perceptions and interpretations of current events and situations. The rationale for interventions that address faulty cognitions is designed to debunk thinking that is inconsistent with rational thinking and demeaning self-talk.

One way to reconstruct thinking is to introduce self-enhancing thoughts that can promote the development of self-efficacy by having clients reflect on the long-term consequences of negative and faulty thinking. As one of my clients told me, "It doesn't take a rocket scientist to understand differences between negative and self-enhancing thoughts, but my problem is how to keep from thinking negatively." This statement suggests to counselors that the process of change can take time and requires follow-up and homework assignments that support the development of rational thinking. Two homework assignments are discussed next.

Homework Assignments

Counselors could ask clients to record their thoughts before going to work, during work, and after work. Clients are to construct positive thoughts for those that are considered negative and discuss differences with the counselor.

As another example, clients make a list of goals, such as decreasing doubts about career opportunities, increasing positive thinking through self-talk, and how to be successful in a job that is highly demanding. For each goal, clients are to indicate levels of confidence that can be used as quantitative measures of success.

Goal 1: Decrease doubts about career opportunities from 40% to 80%.

0   10   20   30   40   50   60   70   80   90   100

No confidence a great deal of confidence.

Goal 2: Confidence to increase positive thinking through self-talk from 40% to 70%.

0   10   20   30   40   50   60   70   80   90   100

Goal 3: Confidence in being successful in a job that is very demanding from 50% to 80%.

0   10   20   30   40   50   60   70   80   90   100

These examples can be effective by asking clients to designate their desired level of improvement for more positive thinking. Progress is to be self-monitored (Cormier et al., 2013). Also, commercial workbooks on the market are specifically designed to address dysfunctional thinking.

Another goal the counselor established in the Ricardo case study involved the concept of self-enhancing thoughts in self-talk. The procedure is simply to change negative self-talk to self-enhancing thoughts to boost one's self-efficacy. An example follows:

I'm not very good at explaining procedures.
I know I'll mess up today in that meeting.

Change to:

I'm able to express myself effectively if I put my mind to it.
I believe I can make a contribution by offering my explanations of solutions.

The value of this exercise supports the idea that differences in thinking can make significant differences in one's work role and others' life roles. Another assignment that is effective is for clients to record their negative and positive self-talk for a specified period and discuss their findings with their counselor.

Again with reference to Ricardo, when he began to show evidence of improving his faulty thinking, the counselor introduced career counseling based on cognitive information processing. She chose a counseling program that was consistent with the personal counseling procedures that focused on cognitive processes. Ricardo agreed that he was now prepared to consider job opportunities that were available. He explained that he was fully aware of high unemployment rates and that the recession was responsible for his job loss. He informed the counselor that he was ready to choose the best job available but agreed that assessment instruments the counselor had mentioned would be a good start for exploring job opportunities.

An aptitude test, interest inventory, skills identification exercise, and values inventory results indicated that Ricardo had good basic skills, and a high interest in realistic occupations, and he values creativity, independence, and variety. The results of each inventory were thoroughly discussed and Ricardo appeared to be satisfied with the conclusion that he would search for jobs considered to be skilled trades. He was very open to improving his skills through education or as an apprentice. He recognized that because of a severe downturn in the economy, his choices for finding a job were limited. He also learned that dysfunctional thinking can cause problems in all life roles. He recognized the interrelationship between life roles in that what happens in one's life role can affect what happens in the others.

Ricardo began receiving financial assistance from a government agency to help meet the needs of his family until he would find employment. He continued to see his counselor for support in maintaining a positive approach to his situation, but he admitted that it was difficult to feel encouraged when he failed to land a job.

It is important to point out here that career choice is indeed limited during economic downturns, and when jobs are outsourced to other locations. Clients who wish to remain, or are forced to remain, in their current location are limited to a choice of the best job available. They do not necessarily give up hope for their ideal job of the future but obviously must delay their options in an attempt to secure work that will put food on the table.

Clearly, in certain circumstances the career-choice process must address more than just psychological variables. The opportunities for work and the nature of work are both parts of a changing process that must be addressed in career counseling as well as in personal counseling. In the future, one can expect to experience both good economic times as well as stressful periods when there is a downturn in the economy.

In Ricardo's case he was able to find part-time employment in two different firms. He learned that keeping a positive attitude was most important for his own health and feelings of well-being, as well as being a consistent and dependable worker. His outlook for the future was that of "cautious optimism." He had hopes of landing a full-time job with one of his current employers or finding a full-time job with other employers he contacted.

In the case study of Diane, the stress associated with the possibility of losing her job during economic downtimes illustrates that this threat can dominate a client's lifestyle.

Case 13.2   Diane's Reactions to the Threat of Job Loss

Diane's stress level escalated when workers in a plant near where she worked began to lose their jobs because of poor economic conditions. Her thoughts were focused on what she would do to care for her children if she were to lose her job. She was unable to sleep on most nights, and her days were filled with worrying about the future. Eventually her anxiety level peaked. A depressive episode followed, with the usual symptoms of emotional flatness, poor memory, loss of self-esteem, and exaggerated self-blame and guilt. In essence, her fear of the future and reaction to stress and anxiety triggered biological, psychological, and social influences that led to a depressive reaction.

Diane's clinical social worker, hereafter referred to as counselor, conducted an intake interview. Diane is a 26-year-old African American who is the single mother of two children, a boy age 7 and a girl age 5. She currently lives with her children in an apartment complex that is government-sponsored. When she is at work, her children are cared for by a relative. Diane is a hard worker and is known as being dependable and competent. As a result, she has received pay increases on a regular basis at an assembly plant not far from where she lives. Her commitment to her work has made it difficult for Diane to even think about the prospect of being terminated, and she could not stop worrying.

What we have here is an example of how fear and anxiety can trigger the development of a mood disorder. Diane has not been fired; in fact, no one at the plant where she works has been terminated at this point even though the economy has taken a nosedive. No doubt Diane is not the only person who is worried about the possibility of being terminated, but the difference here is in the severity of her reactions. The counselor wanted more answers as to why Diane has reacted so severely to a potential future event. The counselor realized, however, that even workers whose jobs are not threatened but think they are threatened develop high levels of stress, especially if they are focused on emotional coping strategies (Mantler et al., 2005).

Diane grew up in a neighborhood that was known for its violence and drug-related crimes. She dropped out of high school when she became pregnant, but later finished a high school equivalence program. Diane stated that she liked going back to school and actually would like to continue with her education. In the meantime, her work experience has been rewarding and she is committed to her work. All who know her agree that it would be extremely difficult for her to give up what she has earned for another job.

The counselor decided to approach Diane with the prospect of searching for other work that may be just as rewarding in case her current job is terminated, but the first counseling step is to further evaluate Diane's current concerns. To accomplish this task, the counselor recommended the use of carefully selected assessment instruments. The counselor will ask Diane to join her in selecting all the instruments and will carefully explain their purpose and how they may address her current concerns.

The following assessment instruments were selected:

Adolescent Substance Abuse Subtle Screening Inventory-A2 (SASSI-A2) (Miller, 2001)

Beck Depression Inventory-II (BDI-II) (Beck, Street, & Brown, 1996)

Career Thoughts Inventory (CTI) (Sampson et al., 1996a)

My Vocational Situation (MVS) (Holland, Daiger, & Power, 1980)

Self-Directed Search (SDS) (Holland, 1994a)

The Values Scale (VS) (Nevill & Super, 1989)

The results of an aptitude test Diane recently took also will be used.

A substance abuse inventory, such as the one listed above, is often used as a screening instrument, especially if a client has a history of drug use or has been involved in drug-related activities. In the case of Diane, she informed the counselor that she has used alcohol and drugs recreationally in the past but has stayed away from both since becoming a mother. The counselor decided that because there was a known history of substance abuse, she would make certain that drugs or alcohol were not a part of the current problem. Diane quickly agreed and wanted to prove she was telling the truth.

The BDI-II and the CTI are used to evaluate dysfunctional thinking and the severity of depression observed during the interview. The counselor wanted more specific information to use for interventions that will address a depressive reaction. The CTI is interpreted using three scales: Decision-Making Confusion, Commitment Anxiety, and External Conflict plus a total score. These scores will aid the counselor in determining Diane's readiness for career counseling and, specifically, if she is ready for career decision making. Diane's score on the BDI-II will provide an index of the severity of her depression. The remaining three assessment instruments in the list will be used when Diane is able to begin career counseling.

Diane's Progress

Diane's reaction to counseling assistance was positive. She seemed relieved when she was able to explain why her reaction to recent events was so emotionally charged. She stated, "When I was growing up, we often didn't have enough to eat, and I wanted out of there—anywhere else would do—just let me out!" She explained that similar thoughts stayed with her all these years and provided motivation for self-improvement and her commitment to a job that gave her the means to a better life. She admitted significant mistakes along the way, but now she was heading in the right direction and didn't want anything to get in the way. "I just couldn't handle the threat of losing my source of independence," she stated.

After further discussions, some of the selected assessment instruments were administered. The results indicated that Diane was not likely to be currently involved in using drugs or excessively using alcohol. The counselor was cautious, however, and planned to be on guard for any signs of substance abuse problems. The CTI results indicated that Diane may have some problems in sustaining the decision-making process, more than likely due to her current emotional problems. There were also indications that generalized anxiety may interfere with her ability to commit to an occupational choice. These results support the position that Diane has needs of a personal nature that should be addressed before career counseling.

The following interventions were discussed with Diane, and she agreed to participate to the best of her ability.

Systematic Desensitization

Systematic desensitization involves challenging anxiety-response behaviors through imagery while the client is in a state of physical relaxation. The counselor makes the point that feelings of anxiety have been learned and the goal here is to unlearn anxiety provoking thoughts so they will no longer be stressful. The client is given instructions on relaxation techniques by Wolpe (1958) and is asked to practice them on a regular basis as homework.

In addition, anxiety-provoking situations are developed by the client and counselor. For example, learning that she may lose her job in the future, have to search for another job, and have to move will be used as focal points. The procedure is explained by the following steps: (1) learn relaxation procedures, (2) when completely relaxed, visualize an anxiety-provoking situation without increasing muscle tension, and (3) repeat imagining other anxiety-provoking thoughts, and while staying relaxed, complete the list without feeling muscle tension. To complete the entire list usually requires several sessions.

Cognitive-Behavioral Counseling

Cognitive-behavioral counseling addresses both thinking and behavioral procedures. The rationale here is that thinking must be changed before effective behavior can occur. These procedures consist of learning positive-oriented thinking, homework assignments, and follow-up. Clients need repeated exercises in which they identify thoughts and statements that are negative and are associated with stressful feelings. They are to constantly challenge their thoughts with reality checks.

In the case of Diane, the chances of losing her job are unknown because of changing financial conditions. Thus, she may be worried about an unknown future, but her thoughts went beyond that point as she visualized everything in the future as being negative. The counselor's goal was to address negative-oriented thinking and self-talk and find solutions for future considerations. Other cognitive-behavioral techniques were summarized earlier in this chapter.

Using Data Integration

Diane began career counseling when she was able to relax and make rational decisions. The counselor introduced the strategy component of experience identification and educational training and planning to encourage Diane to openly express her needs. Diane claimed that she was ready to consider other work opportunities realistically without interference from emotional reactions and severe negative thoughts. She was administered the inventory *My Vocational Situation* that identifies difficulties with lack of vocational identity, lack of information and training, and environmental or personal barriers that may affect a person's ability to make career decisions.

Diane had low scores on all three scales, indicating potential problems in making a career choice and processing career information. Her low score on vocational identity, which identifies the clarity of personal goals and self-perceptions, should not be surprising. One of the counselor's major goals is to help Diane discover and, more importantly, become aware of the significance of her interests, values, and aptitudes, as well as to learn more about her occupational choices. There is a definite need for Diane to learn more about occupational information and subsequent training programs.

Environmental barriers have limited her access to occupational information and career opportunities. In Diane's case, life was all about survival rather than considering job opportunities that were desirable and interesting. A different perspective introduced by the counselor will include how to locate and process information about occupations, how to become aware of the importance of self-knowledge, and how to project her abilities and interests into a work environment.

Another relevant point is to assess the future prospects of occupations she is considering. Diane is especially interested in work that has a future. The *Self-Directed Search* yields scores regarding Occupational Daydreams, Preferences for Activities, Competencies, Preferences for Kinds of Occupations, and Abilities in Various Occupations. The scores yield summary codes according to Holland's typology structure, as discussed in chapters 2 and 3. Diane's scores yielded the summary codes of SCR—Social, Conventional, and Realistic. The counselor will use this information to locate specific occupations for consideration. For example, professional nurse is listed as a prospective occupation for someone with a high score in the Social domain. Clients are to compile the list of occupations to consider.

The Values Scale yields scores for the following values:

Ability Utilization	Physical Activity
Achievement	Prestige
Altruism	Risk
Autonomy	Social Interaction
Creativity	Variety
Economic Rewards	Working Conditions
Lifestyle	

Diane's scores indicate that her highest value expectations as measured by this scale are Social Interaction, Working Conditions, Achievement, and Variety. The high score on the Social Interaction scale is a strong indication that she enjoys working with others. Working Conditions, as the name of this scale implies, suggests that it is important for her to have a workplace that is attractive, operational, and pleasant. The feeling that one has produced good results is associated with the value of Achievement. A workplace that provides the opportunity to do different tasks suggests that one values Variety.

Diane's earlier score results were from the *Differential Aptitude Test* (Bennett, Seashore, & Wesman, 1991), which includes the following subtests:

Verbal Reasoning
Numerical Reasoning
Abstract Reasoning
Perceptual Speed and Accuracy
Mechanical Reasoning
Space Relations
Spelling
Language Usage
Scholastic Ability

Diane's highest scores in the above-average range were verbal and numerical reasoning and language usage. These scores are a good index for scholastic aptitude. None of her scores on this test were significantly low.

Conceptualization of Diane's Concerns in Four Domains

The following conceptualization of Diane's concerns incorporates information from the interview and test data as follows.

Career: In the early stages of counseling with Diane, it became obvious that she had personal problems involving depression and dysfunctional thinking that were to be addressed through cognitive-behavioral techniques before career counseling could take place. This assumption was verified with valid assessment instruments that indicated a mild depressive reaction, an inability to sustain the career decision process, and indications of generalized anxiety—all of which interfered with her ability to process information. Following interventions designed to address faulty cognitions and demeaning self-talk, Diane was able to begin career counseling. In a working consensus relationship between client and counselor, several assessment instruments were selected, administered, and scored. These score results were used to assist Diane in the decision process. She will be introduced to available career information in a local community college. The counselor and Diane will continue discussions concerning the processing of information and how to further evaluate potential career choices.

Affective: There is considerable improvement in Diane's emotional control compared to when she first entered counseling. Although there are periods of disruptive thinking, Diane continues to make progress. She will be carefully monitored during career decision making. Diane reacted positively when she was given the opportunity to vent her feelings and connect them with events and situational influences from her environment. Currently she appears to be emotionally stable.

Cognitive-Behavioral: Diane has made progress in addressing automatic reactions to stress that were primarily negative. She has learned that negative thoughts and anxiety can lead to psychological disorders that are domineering. She also is continuing her efforts to improve feelings of well-being through a variety of homework assignments and relaxation techniques. She will continue to be monitored and encouraged to develop self-enhancing thoughts rather than negative ones.

Culture: Diane self-identifies as an African American woman who endorses some traditional values such as support from friends from her church and other groups who are considered as "sisters and brothers." She has been subjected to discrimination and oppression from the White majority as well as other minority groups, but she is appreciative of work opportunities that gave her the opportunity to prove she is indeed capable of achieving a better life. She is making a substantial effort to view the future as positive even though there will be hurdles to overcome along the way.

The counselor reminded Diane that assessment data are used to help individuals in the career choice process and are not the final word to determine a career or careers that she chooses. It is therefore most important to keep in mind that career choice is an individual matter and in effect it will be Diane's call that will decide her future work role. Assessment results are to be considered as only one part of the choice process that presents significant information for career exploration.

The counselor informed Diane that scores and their meaning will be explained for each assessment instrument. Together they will observe any patterns or preferences for work environments that are to be considered as potential choices. As Diane and the counselor discussed the results, Diane recorded information for further exploration. One of the

work environments that was of particular interest was health services. She noted that Social was her highest interest level and she valued social interactions. She was also inspired to consider health services because she had read about the growing need for qualified individuals in health care.

What followed were sessions with her counselor that involved discussions about the possibility of becoming a nurse. For more information, Diane made a visit to a facility that trained licensed vocational nurses. After several more visits with her counselor, she decided to continue with her current work role and also attend classes for licensed vocational nurse training. Her major goal was to become a registered nurse.

This case is a good example of integrating career and personal counseling. In Diane's case, she was successful as well as pleased with her current job, but when the economic downturn happened and her job was threatened, she fell apart when her stress level became unbearable. In many ways, the self-confidence that Diane had created began to fall apart and she once again felt vulnerable to the harsh environment she had experienced as a child. Her thoughts, such as fear and panic, became familiar as her future became even more unpredictable.

The depressive reaction, such as the one Diane experienced, in the case study is depicted in Figure 13.2. It must be addressed before beginning the career counseling process. Counselors are to view depression and other psychological disorders as barriers to the career choice process that must be removed or moderated. This suggestion has been on the books for a considerable time, and no doubt some counseling programs have addressed similar issues in the past. What we need now is a change in the established perception that career counselors are to address only career-related issues that clients bring to counseling; that indeed may be the counselor's intent because of current training programs. I am not suggesting that career counselors take on all clients who have personal problems. They are to refer when they do not have the training to address a client's problem. What I am suggesting is that training programs should recognize the growing awareness of the interrelationships of concerns that clients bring to counseling.

The two cases of Ricardo and Diane are examples of integrating career and personal counseling. The tightly woven connections among career, work, and mental health suggest that counselors are to address all of them and not limit their ability to address an array of personal issues. Job loss is obviously a major problem for many workers during a recession, but job loss also occurs on a fairly regular basis such as during catastrophic events, outsourcing of jobs to other countries, changes in production of goods, new technology, and even when there are indications of a downturn in the economy. One can expect to find stress-related reactions that can lead to emotional instability, as in the case of Ricardo, or depressive reactions, as in the case of Diane. These two case examples make it clear that neither client was prepared for the career-choice process; their personal concerns were barriers to processing information and

FIGURE 13.2

Depression—A mood disorder

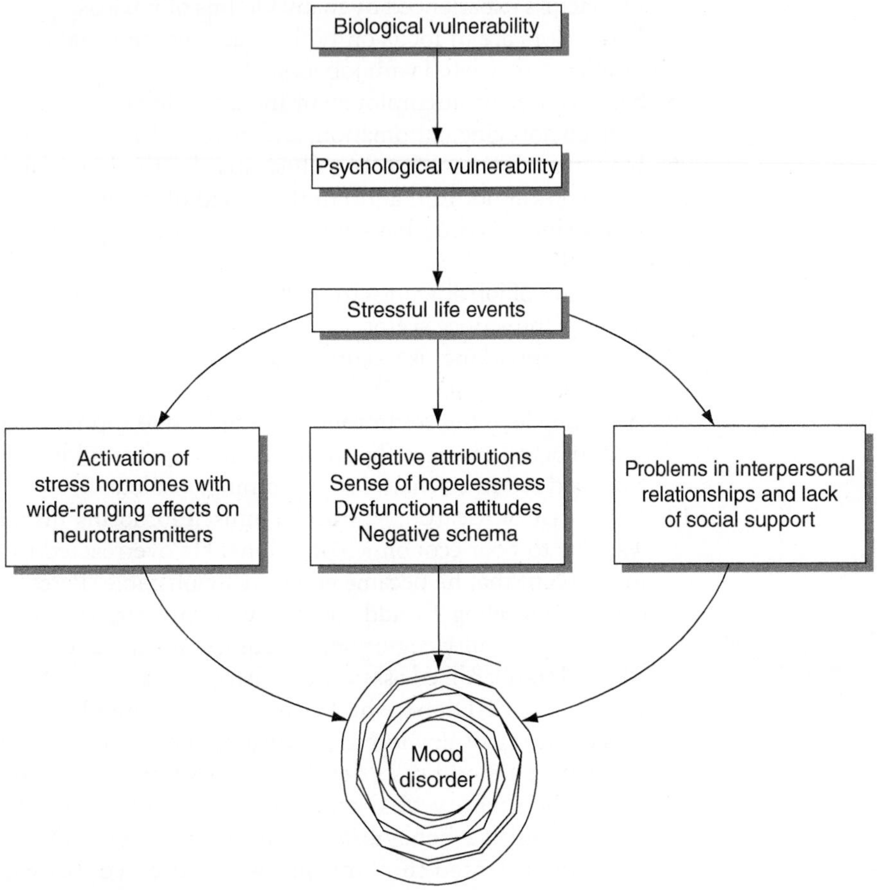

```
                    ┌─────────────────────────┐
                    │ Biological vulnerability │
                    └─────────────────────────┘
                                │
                                ▼
                    ┌──────────────────────────┐
                    │ Psychological vulnerability│
                    └──────────────────────────┘
                                │
                                ▼
                    ┌──────────────────────┐
                    │ Stressful life events │
                    └──────────────────────┘
```

| Activation of stress hormones with wide-ranging effects on neurotransmitters | Negative attributions Sense of hopelessness Dysfunctional attitudes Negative schema | Problems in interpersonal relationships and lack of social support |

Mood disorder

SOURCE: From *Abnormal Psychology: An Integrative Approach*, 5th ed., by D.H. Barlow and V.M. Durand, 2009. Reprinted with permission of Cengage Wadsworth Learning, Belmont, CA.

making optimal decisions. In these two cases and as in others, personal concerns are to be addressed before career counseling.

Summary

1. Changing work roles are unavoidable for many in the workforce. The flexibility to adjust and adapt to different work environments will characterize future workers. Some will choose to change jobs, whereas others will be forced to. The rate of unemployment and underemployment has affected many Americans, families, and communities.

2. Job loss concerns include severe stress and anxiety, especially for middle-aged men and women, which can lead to the development of a psychological disorder. One's sense of well-being and self-worth can be diminished.

3. The negative effects of job loss can lead some clients to mental health problems. Stress reactions are common. Self-esteem and self-efficacy are affected by negative factors experienced by many victims of job loss.

4. Counselors are to focus on both career and personal concerns when addressing problems associated with job loss.

5. Some causes of unemployment include: globalization, recessions, job exportation, outsourcing, automation, and increased global competition.

6. Underemployment is often illustrated by the large number of college graduates who cannot find a job in their field of study. This current situation is the worst since records have been kept on the employment of college graduates after 1985.

7. Estimates of job openings from 2008 to 2018 suggest that most jobs openings will occur in the service sector.

8. Social networking is recommended as good source of information for job openings.

9. A lifelong learning commitment is a pervasive approach for keeping abreast with technological changes, upgrading skills, understanding the information explosion, and reducing chances of becoming obsolete.

10. In the case of Ricardo, he blamed himself for losing his job even though his loss was due to poor economic conditions. He overreacted to a false sense of failure to the point that he became emotionally unstable. Personal counseling preceded career counseling to address faulty cognitions; systematic logical thinking is inhibited by faulty cognitions. Readiness for career counseling was measured by selected standardized assessment instruments.

11. In the case of Diane, she became overwhelmed with the possibility of job loss due to poor economic conditions. Fear and anxiety triggered the development of a mood disorder. Several assessment instruments were chosen to assess the severity of Diane's concerns. Systematic desensitization, among other cognitive-behavioral techniques, helped Diane to control anxiety. Negative-oriented thinking also was addressed. Career counseling included the use of a battery of assessment instruments to enhance self-knowledge and methods of making an optimal career decision. Diane wanted to consider occupations that will be in demand and have the potential for growth in the future.

Supplementary Learning Exercises

1. How would you inform your client of the possibility of changing work roles in the future? Explain causal factors.

2. Compile a list of suggestions your client could use to prepare for the future job market. Share with a classmate.

3. Explain the possible causes of work stress and how to overcome them.

4. Rank-order (starting with most important) the five unintended consequences of work. Defend your rankings.

5. How would you advise a client to overcome stress associated with job insecurity?

Case 13.3   Al's Job Loss

Al drove a truck and delivered food products to local restaurants in the city for 5 years. His job was terminated when a number of his customers closed their businesses because of a severe drop in revenue. Al, a 32-year-old White man, was married and the father of three children. He went to a community mental health center for help, or he had been helped there in the past when he was arrested for fighting. Al told the counselor that he completed high school and one semester in a community college. His previous work experience included being a plumber's helper and working on construction jobs. The mental health counselor read his file and discovered that Al had not been diagnosed with a psychological disorder but had symptoms of poor emotional control, underlying hostility, and low self-esteem. Al told the counselor that he had not been in trouble since the fighting incident but admitted that he was easily provoked and had to struggle to control his emotions.

QUESTIONS AND EXERCISES FOR DISCUSSION

1. What would you do next if you were his counselor?
2. What assessment instruments would you use, if any?
3. What would be your major counseling focus?
4. How would you determine the counseling sequence?
5. Should Al receive career and personal counseling simultaneously?

   Defend your answer.

Case 13.4   Olivia's Job Loss

Olivia told the clinical social worker that she had lost her job as a bookkeeper in a local bank. She had been employed at the bank in the real estate loan division for only a few months. Olivia is a 22-year-old Hispanic who is single and has never married. She attended a local community college for two years and was a business major. Her past work experience was mainly part-time jobs at grocery and clothing stores. When asked about grades she made in college, Olivia explained that she got failing grades in some courses because of ill health. Further explanations revealed that Olivia believes she has a serious illness that her doctors cannot find: "I have pains in my side that move from one side to the other, yet the doctor said I'm in good health." Olivia also stated that she feels fine now and is prepared to take on another job. When the counselor asked if she would be interested in a job that is open with a well-known firm, Olivia told her that she could not take that job because she cannot use an elevator. "I get scared when I'm in enclosed places," she replied.

QUESTIONS AND EXERCISES FOR DISCUSSION

1. What action would you take at this point in the interview?
2. What are your tentative conclusions?
3. What assessment instruments would you use to determine if Olivia is ready for career counseling?
4. How would you conceptualize Olivia's current mental health?
5. Describe how personal and career concerns are intertwined in this case.

14

Career Development and Transitions of Working Adults

There appears to be a growing consensus of opinion that many working Americans will make multiple career choices over their life span. No doubt many in the workforce will be challenged to meet the demands of changing technology as well as changing work roles and rules. The career ladder that was endorsed by many industries in the recent past has almost disappeared. Seniority is no longer the most important factor for obtaining a high-level position. Currently, training for skill and knowledge development is being advanced as self-directed and continuous learning. Current and future workers are being encouraged to sharpen their knowledge and learn new skills.

As discussed in chapter 7, many organizations provide in-house technology-driven instruction, coaching, and mentoring (Aamodt, 2013; London, 2002). Organizational training programs are directed primarily toward current and changing needs of an organization, which suggests that those who successfully complete training programs have enhanced their value as an employee. An important point made here is that workers are to assume more responsibility for being a viable employee. One is to take appropriate steps to develop skills that are marketable in the new work arena that is ever changing. Staying up-to-date in an economy that has been driven by globalization suggests that changes in the workforce could be swift and relatively unpredictable.

Globalization and Job Security

Job security and the promise of a regular paycheck have disappeared for many workers in the last decade. Pay increases are no longer tied completely to longevity. Currently, many workplaces endorse the concept of pay-for-performance. Under these conditions, the employee is challenged to assume the position that career planning will involve circular as well as linear moves. Counselors are to emphasize that learning to adapt and become flexible in the work role are important keys to success in the current job market.

Associated with this shift of responsibility are significant risks and challenges for the individual. What I am emphasizing here is that work in our lives is taking a road less traveled and as a result is introducing unknowns and uncertainties that place greater responsibility on individual initiative and commitment to lifelong learning. Many individuals not only will be required to make a series of career choices, but also will need to muster the personal strength and endurance to compete and learn new skills in multiple job roles and in different worksites. Job fit is to be accomplished through continuous learning that will test the individual's ability to make appropriate decisions while managing their own careers.

Market forces driven by a global economy in the new millennium have been the main impetus behind the shift of risks from employer to individuals in terms of managing employees' careers. Market forces also can determine levels of compensation, advancement, and the nature of work. Individual workers vary in their reaction to the loss of traditional operational procedures that included work stability, advancement opportunities, training, and the possibility of a lifetime job. Some see this as an opportunity to become a free agent and take full control of their work role. Others are threatened by the uncertainties of the future and diminished availability of regular work. Yet others have reacted by being less committed to organizations. Because market forces driven by globalization are the primary determinants of who works and who doesn't, some employees have viewed the organization as being less important and have further reacted by expressing poor attitudes about work, delivering lowered performances, and displaying significantly less motivation about work per se (Leana, 2002).

Pressure on the worker to perform well has long been associated with how well one is compensated and how quickly one advanced up the corporate ladder. In the new workforce, however, the predominant buzzwords are "pay-for-performance" and "pay-for-knowledge" as stated by Drucker (2002). Under these conditions, workers focus more on their career development and have less of a commitment to a particular company. The performance–reward connection in the current work environment is not that different from past work environments. One could argue successfully that workers have been rewarded primarily for demand for their particular skills and their overall contribution to an organization, but many reached this point of competence through a partnership between worker and employer. Developing personnel for organizational purposes is an ongoing practice, but staying abreast of new and different work requirements also requires the employee to remain alert to new and different opportunities that are currently available.

It is not certain what effect the current position of self-development will have on an individual's career choice and development, but the importance of skill development and continuous learning appears to be a reliable predicator of career success for many who are employed and unemployed. Counselors, however, should be in a position to inform clients realistically about the nature of work in the 21st century and how their future may be determined greatly by their own initiative and actions. Box 14.1 suggests that knowledge work and knowledge workers will be driving forces in the future workforce.

BOX 14.1

Knowledge as the Key Resource

Knowledge industries, knowledge work, and knowledge workers are the ingredients that will shape the future workforce. Be aware that the workforce will continue to consist of janitors, clerks, and maids, for example, but a growing number of workers will be known as professional knowledge workers. They will earn their position in the workforce through individual effort and dedication to learning. Collectively, knowledge workers will be the driving force behind the development and production of products. They apply their specialized skills and cooperate with other knowledge workers for product development, advertising, distribution, and training, among other challenging assignments.

Knowledge workers do, and will continue to, occupy positions such as x-ray technicians, paralegals, office technologists, dental technicians, and medical technologists, among many others. What they all have in common is a formal education and participation in continuing education. Knowledge workers prefer to identify themselves as "professionals" rather than as "craftpersons" or "workers." They may work in an organization but will identify themselves by their special skills, such as, "I am an electrical engineer" (Drucker, 2002).

Knowledge work can provide a most important element to the meaning of work in one's life. It provides the individual with a career identity, for instance, and a social position in an ever-changing society. It is not an inherited position, but one that is earned through individual achievement. The potential for upward mobility is a means of hope for workers and an avenue to becoming successful and achieving respect and financial security. As in most other work situations, however, the individual is challenged to maintain a balanced life that addresses all life roles.

Workers can also expect some opportunities for training offered by organizations. On-site training is usually conducted on the job site and involves the totality of the job. On-the-job training is conducted by experienced skilled workers on the job site. Workers observe and imitate the behavior of the instructor. Job rotation is a process in which workers learn a number of skills and work requirements as they rotate through a variety of jobs. Off-site training methods include lectures, seminars, audiovisual material, computer-based training, web-based training, simulation, and role playing (Muchinsky, 2003).

In chapter 13, the focus was on job loss and the uncertainty of job tenure when, indeed, there are few guarantees of lifetime employment in the current work environment, especially when there is a recession. What we have here are life-course events that present significant challenges over the life span; one can be greatly influenced and affected by situations and events such as world wars, economic downturns, and catastrophic events. Counselors also focus on personal and career-related constraints that can become barriers to one's career development.

Biopsychosocial Framework and Life Events

What I am suggesting throughout this text is that counselors are to develop a complete understanding of how personal, career, and life-course experiences are interconnected. The relevance of this position is underscored by the current explanation of *basic forces in human development* referred to as the biopsychosocial framework, discussed earlier, that includes the following by Kail and Cavanaugh (2014, p. 6):

Biological forces include all genetic and health-related factors that affect development.

Psychological forces include all internal perceptual, cognitive, emotional, and personality factors that affect development.

Sociocultural forces include interpersonal, social, cultural, and ethnic factors that affect development.

Life-cycle forces reflect differences in how the same event affects people of different ages.

This inclusive position of what influences human development suggests complex interactive processes—a subject we have discussed in several chapters in this text. The significance of life-course events in the developmental process, however, suggests to the career counselor that one's career choice as well as career development can also be influenced by life-cycle forces—which should not surprise anyone. Take, for example, the person who is required to join the armed services in wartime. The period of time in service exposes one to situational events and experiences that are quite unique and different from what one may experience in their home environments during these formative years. No doubt, some will not waver from preestablished plans, but others who are strongly influenced by life events and other forces may adopt a completely different lifestyle and career. Another example that is most relevant involves a severe recession during which individuals lose their jobs. An individual who had decided to pursue a career that is no longer available is forced to choose another work role or take the best job available.

What is most important to recognize, however, is that there are differences in how the same events can affect future life choices of individuals; perceptions of situational experiences can be very different. I am not suggesting, however, that life-cycle forces alone influence life decisions, but as we have discussed over and over again, human behavior and development are the products of a very complex interaction of biopsychosocial influences. What all this means for counseling is that the adult client should be approached as an individual who has experienced a variety of life-course events that have influenced her or his worldview as well as career development. In the next section I briefly discuss adult career development in early, middle, and late career stages.

Early, Middle, and Late Career Development

Early Career Establishment

The career establishment years, ages 25 to 44, were viewed by Super (1957) as a critical time when one struggles to form a unique identity in the work world. Individuals implement their self-concepts into careers that will provide the most efficient means of self-expression. Erikson (1950) suggested that during this period of time (early career) one is balancing intimacy and isolation while also attempting to maintain a unique identity in the process of developing relationships. What is being stressed here is that early career experiences provide individuals with opportunities to establish themselves in the workplace. There appears to be solid evidence that early encounters in the workplace will significantly influence the outcome of some of the most important socialization processes (Aamodt, 2013; Bauer & Green, 1994; Feldman, 2002; Muchinsky, 2003).

Critical to the individual's career development are supervisor and coworker relationships, especially in the current work environment that stresses teamwork. How individuals respond to authority figures may reflect a low concern for others or a more positive interdependent, cooperative orientation. The implications for counseling are simply that early work experiences may establish enduring positive and negative attitudes about work and relationships at work (Scandura, 2002). Thus, a negative experience in early career with a supervisor and/or peers may make it difficult to establish a working relationship with another supervisor and/or other coworkers. The obvious consequences of an individual who has poor relationships with other workers could be job loss or the desire to make a job change. Clearly, counselors are to evaluate the underlying reasons an individual wants to change careers and/or worksites in early career transitions.

During early career, individuals demonstrate their ability to function effectively on the job. For the beginning worker, it can be an exciting time of entering the workforce. The novice, however, can be naive about the complexities of the work environment and will expend considerable effort in learning how to function within its milieu. Although the pathway to a successful early career has pitfalls and stumbling blocks, there is a relatively well-defined direction. For example, building harmonious relationships in the work environment, becoming oriented to work rules and regulations, and demonstrating satisfactory performance are common concrete tasks of early career. The individual's personal reaction to advancement opportunities and acceptance of the values associated with employer goals and peer affiliates are less tangible. Objective indexes (salary, merit pay, regulations, policies, etc.) and subjective indexes (meeting expectations, goal attainment, match between personal needs and employer needs) are evaluative criteria the individual can use to determine a future direction in the workplace or a change to another work environment.

In the following counseling session, Shanika, who has been with a company for 10 months, stated a need to withdraw and find another work environment:

COUNSELOR: Yes, we do have some information about the supply company you asked about. But first I would like to know about the company you are leaving.

SHANIKA: As you know, it's a well-known organization, and I was excited about the opportunity of working there. But I don't seem to fit in.

COUNSELOR: Could you be more specific?

SHANIKA: Well, the job assignment was not what I expected. The recruiter told me I would have a lot of responsibilities and interact with people at high levels, but in actuality there was little of either.

COUNSELOR: So it really wasn't the kind of job you expected?

SHANIKA: No, I was put off in a side office, and no one seemed to pay much attention to me. I did have a few assignments that seemed more like busywork than anything else.

COUNSELOR: Could this have been a part of the training program?

SHANIKA: Well, partly, but my supervisor hardly ever came around, and when he did, he seemed preoccupied.

In this case, reality shock and unused potential were frustrating experiences for Shanika. She had high expectations on the basis of what she was told about the job and had hoped to be challenged, but she experienced far less. There also appeared to be a communication gap between Shanika and her supervisor. The counselor recognized the potential effect of an early career encounter that could influence this client's future.

Reality shock and lack of appraisal and appropriate feedback while in early career have been major causes of withdrawal from a work environment. In such cases, the career counselor must focus on the individual's perception of workplace situations, and more importantly, his or her level of sophistication in appraising them. Some individuals in early career will have unrealistically high expectations, whereas others may indeed find their jobs to be less than challenging and experience poor feedback from their supervisors.

On the other hand, work environments themselves can be very informative and educational; they provide a variety of learning experiences that are relevant to career development. For example, exposure to unknown jobs could expedite the desire to change career direction. Work experiences and skill development can provide a meaningful sense of direction in career development. Developing harmonious relationships, for example, means learning effective communication skills, interpersonal relationships, and general modes of behavior that are easily transferable to other work environments. Homing in on general and specific skills provides avenues that can lead to a change in career aspirations. Skill development itself can create a desire to change careers in order to find a better fit. When there is congruence between interests, personality traits, and work skills, fewer workers change jobs.

In a study of beginning bank tellers in the 1990s, 45% of them left their job in the first 4 months; however, two-thirds of them took a similar job with another bank (Gottfredson & Holland, 1990). Looking for a better fit appeared to drive beginning bank tellers to search for another work environment rather than completely change careers (Ostroff et al., 2002). The lesson here is that initial career choice and placement are not always right for everyone: Workers want to change careers or worksites for a variety of reasons. Counselors are to revisit the case for the individual that suggests each person is unique (Fouad & Brynner, 2008).

Career Anchors

Schien (1990), who followed the career patterns of alumni from the Massachusetts Institute of Technology (MIT), suggested that career anchors are formed during early career experiences and situations encountered in the workplace. He further suggested that career anchors develop over time and are not easily changed. Career anchors are considered to be core values, interests, and abilities that are developed during early career as follows: (1) technical functional competence—one's commitment to developing skills within a profession; (2) managerial competence—one's desire to assume responsibilities of leading others; (3) autonomy-independence—one's desire to work alone with little or no supervision; (4) security-stability—one's desire for stable employment; (5) service dedication—a predisposition to help and assist others; (6) pure challenge—one's commitment to work that is continually challenging; (7) lifestyle integration—a need to have a balanced lifestyle; and (8) entrepreneurship—one's desire to work in environments that require creativity.

The important and enduring concept of career anchors suggests that the formation of occupational self-concept is driven by talents and abilities developed in real work situations, motives and needs that are illuminated by work experiences, and attitudes and values learned from interactions in the workplace. What we have here are interactive influences from work situations that guide individual career choice in the establishment transitional process. Career anchors are thought to influence career choice and also to restrain it. Individuals therefore seek out work environments in which they have experienced success and avoid those that have the potential of resulting in failure. According to this theory, early work experiences and encounters are very influential in establishing a career direction (Muchinsky, 2003; Scandura, 2002).

Early work experiences also may include a temporary work assignment with a firm, or working in your home using telecommunications. A temporary work assignment could include some of the early experiences cited previously, for example, feedback of work performance from a supervisor and establishing relationships with peers. I mention temporary work assignments here because we may see more temporary workers in the workplace in the future (see Box 14.2). The use of short-term workers and fewer traditional employees is attractive to firms because it reduces worker benefit packages which are expected to be increasingly more expensive. There appears to be a trend among organizations to reduce worker benefits in the very competitive global marketplace. Workers may find that pensions will require more cash from the worker and less, if any, from the employer; workers may have to work longer to meet their retirement needs. More information about retirement will be discussed later.

Midcareer and Maintenance Stage Transitions

Midcareer has been identified as the middle phase of an individual's work life, with its own set of tasks and social-emotional needs. In terms of Super's vocational developmental stages, midcareer may be thought of as the beginning of the maintenance stage, which is characterized by a continual adjustment process to improve working position and situation. Midcareer is also characterized by greater self-understanding and identification within the total system of a career field (Sterns & Subich, 2002). Newman and Newman (2009) labeled the midcareer experience as "settling in," characterized by resolution of conflicts and conflicting demands within the work environment and

BOX 14.2

The Rise of the Temporary Worker

The temporary worker, or "temp," often identified as part of the contingent workforce, is increasingly being used in organizations across the country. In the early 1990s about 100 temporary agencies and around 470,000 temporary employees existed in the United States. By the early 2000s we had 1500 temporary agencies and over 1.6 million temporary workers (Cropanzano & Prehar, 2001). The major reason organizations have adopted the strategy of hiring "temps" is to offset labor costs in response to an unpredictable economy. Many organizations have permanent jobs that are staffed by temporary workers. The irony is that the temporary worker is responsible to the employment agency. They are simply assigned to staff at an organization and perform particular services. The use of temporary workers and contracting for special personnel and/or specialized services is likely to increase as a result of sudden and swiftly changing conditions that organizations are likely to experience.

Temporary workers come from several sources. Some are women who want more flexible work schedules. Workers who have been downsized and are seeking permanent employment are another source. Recent college graduates who could not find permanent jobs are yet another source. Finally, retired individuals who need to supplement their income also search for positions as temporary workers. According to Muchinsky (2003), temporary workers receive less pay than permanent workers and they have little job security or opportunity for growth. Further, many temporary workers are dissatisfied with their employment relationship and feel a sense of powerlessness. The temporary worker is constantly faced with the uncertainty of how long he or she will be employed and the possibility of not having a regular paycheck. Temporary workers may have difficulty in finding work to be an important source of meaning in their lives, and the psychological costs to individuals could be heavy.

in personal life. Midcareer is not necessarily age related; individuals who make career changes may experience several midcareer stages.

The transitional process from early career to midcareer has residual effects, as individuals establish themselves in a work environment or changing work environments. In early career, the major course of change is the socialization process, but in midcareer, changes are from diversified sources, such as new and different technology, product demand, market forces, and changes in the labor market. Developing a perspective of positive growth orientation in work environments and encouraging individuals to adapt to changes are healthy attitudes to promote. Also, finding a meaningful area of contribution is part of the process of establishing a career identity. Individuals must distinguish between real barriers (no growth, slow growth, and organizational decline) and perceived barriers (role confusion, poor career identity, nebulous perceptions of career success and direction) that affect their abilities to reach personal goals (Tischler, 2014). The following dialogue demonstrates some sources of career plateaus:

Counselor: Tell me how you arrived at the decision to change jobs.

Ying: Well, you know, I've been with the company for 12 years, but I don't have the same enthusiasm for the job. I just can't put my finger on it.

Counselor: Is the company doing well financially?

Ying: That's a part of it; no promotion to speak of now.

Counselor: Is this a company policy?

Ying: No. John, a friend of mine, got one the other day. He's a lucky guy. He seems to always be in the right place at the right time.

Counselor: Did you say that John was in your division?

Ying: Yeah, he's always got something going. I don't understand how he does it. He went to this training program and six weeks later there he goes—up to a better job!

Counselor: Tell me more about the training program.

Ying: The company sponsored it. I could have gone, but I don't believe I like that kind of extra work. Besides, it would have interfered with the city golf tournament.

It should surprise no one that the counselor concluded that Ying is not willing to be more assertive in his career development. The source of his plateau appears to be primarily a lack of a strong desire to advance. Perhaps Ying thought that he only needed to put in time for the next advancement. In midcareer, individuals may have difficulty balancing commitment to outside activities with intense competitiveness for promotions.

Mercedes, also in midcareer, tells how she discovered a career path in an organization:

Mercedes: I kept looking in the want ads for a career in management after I finished college. I don't know how many times I was turned down. Finally, I took a temporary job in this company just to tide me over. As I kept looking at the want ads, I also started meeting more people in the company. I began to realize that this wasn't such a bad place after all. But what really did it for me was when I met Linda. When she told what she was doing in the company, I knew I wanted to know more about it. Well, you know the rest of the story. I found out about several jobs I never knew existed, and I landed one I like very much. I have been here for 10 years now, so I guess I'll stick around.

In Mercedes's case, she was exposed to occupations and career opportunities she had never known about before. A temporary job provided the means to discover unknown opportunities, and after a successful socialization period, she discovered a career path that appealed to her.

In a more preconceived manner, Al began his career in a high-tech organization with the goal of reaching the management level.

AL: I started out as a computer salesman. After a few years, the company offered me a retail store management job in the eastern part of the state. My wife didn't want to move. That was a tough decision; the kids didn't want to leave either. We spent 8 years there but made the best of it. Meanwhile, I took advantage of every career development opportunity through a variety of training programs. I got good feedback from my supervisor, which really helped. During that process, I became familiar with many aspects of the company. It finally paid off when I was made regional manager a few years ago. It worked out well. I live near a lake now and in a delightful part of the state.

COUNSELOR: What are your future plans?

AL: I like what I'm doing, but I also have become more interested in civic organizations and church work.

COUNSELOR: Do you have as strong a commitment to the workplace as you once had?

AL: Yes and no. It's different than before. My wife is happy that I devote more time to other things, but I still get excited about the future. I enjoy working with these young kids. They have good management skills, and I enjoy helping them.

As shown in this interview, midcareer is a time when individuals develop an increased awareness of the long-term dimensions of a career and shift their focus from the work world to personal roles. Attention is focused not only on career maintenance, but also on life issues, such as parenting, joining civic organizations, and caring for aging parents. Priorities between work roles and personal roles fluctuate according to circumstances. A healthy attitude to promote is a balance of roles, as career and life changes become increasingly connected.

Midcareer is also a time when individuals become more aware of life stages in terms of time spans and begin to view career in terms of implementing future opportunities. Thus, loss of job is very disturbing to individuals at this point in their career development. The prospect of starting over to reach the point of establishment in career can be a significant problem for many individuals. One would suspect that job loss under these circumstances could involve severe stress reactions that could lead to mental health issues. On the other hand, one who has gone through establishment may be in a position to become an independent consultant; this may be increasingly popular with companies that want to reduce their commitment to traditional employees. There are a number of lessons to be learned here, but of most importance is a satisfying and fulfilling experience for each worker. We do not know at this time if getting from work what really matters will be one of worker's goals of the future, but there could be a change from the struggle to get the best office space or to reach the top of the heap to having a job that allows you to do what you like and have the time to do what you personally want. Predicting the future needs of workers will certainly involve future economic conditions.

▇ Late Career and Transition to Retirement

Studies on aging suggest that the median age of the U.S. workforce reflects an increasing number of older workers (Kail & Cavanaugh, 2014; Newman & Newman, 2009). This growing proportion of older workers has many implications, including ones for counseling. Career issues for older workers include age-related changes in abilities and job performance, changing relationships, age discrimination, health concerns, family factors, and when and if to retire. "Bridge employment" is the term used to describe part-time employment in which the individual typically continues in the same work environment but with reduced responsibilities and time commitment. This arrangement allows workers to keep their career identity until they fully retire (Aamodt, 2013).

A question often considered in the hiring process is as follows: Are aging workers more motivated to do good work than younger workers? Research has shown that age per se is not a good predictor of how well a person will perform in either a blue-collar or a white-collar job. Older workers can be as competent as younger ones and typically have more positive attitudes toward their work. Further, older workers seem to be more satisfied in their jobs, more involved in their work, and less interested in finding a different job (Newman & Newman, 2009; Zastrow & Kirst-Ashman, 2013).

As Sigelman and Rider (2009) point out, job performance of individuals in their 50s and 60s is not very different from that of younger workers. These authors suggest that performance of older workers is not hindered by age-related physical and cognitive declines that usually are significant when one is much older. Also, the American Council on Education (1997) and Kail and Cavanaugh (2014) report that older employees make up the largest percentage of individuals taking courses designed to improve their technical skills.

To meet the challenges of a global economy, organizations and community colleges are offering retraining programs designed to upgrade the skills of older workers. One explanation for these findings is that older workers have found jobs that satisfy them, and they have accepted the downside of the job, realizing that it could be difficult to find a new job. The point here is that workers in their 50s and 60s can make good employees. We also can expect to find retired workers searching for work that will provide them with additional income during economic downturns. Thus, counselors should also expect to see an increase in older workers who return to the workforce to supplement their income. The collapse of financial institutions during the recession in 2009 led to a decline in income from pension plans and saving accounts for many retired workers. Affected also were those workers who were contemplating retirement and came to the conclusion that they must continue to work rather than retire.

In late career, the major focus of an individual's life is on activities outside the workplace. The individual builds outside interests and begins a gradual detachment from the work environment. Activities within the workplace also may shift from a power role to a minor role. Super refers to this stage as decline, characterized by pre-retirement considerations. Within the work environment, the individual is preparing to "let go" of responsibilities and pass them on to others. One major adjustment during late career is learning to accept a reduced work role and changing one's focus away from a highly involved work identity.

Emotional support in late career comes primarily from peers and particularly from old acquaintances. Moving away from the stress and turmoil associated with younger workers who are striving to move upward, late-career employees identify with peers and rekindle closer attachments to spouses. Having resolved many of the uncertainties of midcareer, they tend to focus on broader issues, such as the future of their profession or work. Some will retire and seek a job to supplement their income that also allows them to spend more time with family activities (Kail & Cavanaugh, 2014).

Throughout this book, career development has been presented as a continuous and discontinuous process over the life span. Career development is influenced by many variables: Some are externally generated (e.g., life course events such as economic crisis and job loss), and others are internally generated (e.g., perceptions of retirement), but all are integrated into the career development process. Nevertheless, retirement counseling is often overlooked as part of career development and as a career counseling objective. As we prepare to meet the challenges of individuals in the 21st century, demographic studies suggest that retirement counseling will be a major component in the practice of career development (Ashford & Lecroy, 2013; Sharf, 2013).

To meet this increasing need, some workplaces have developed preretirement programs that offer assistance in projecting pensions and other future benefits when the individual reaches retirement age. Preretirement programs have often been referred to as a "probable inflation" model from which the individual can project his or her financial status at retirement. Other topics often addressed in organizational preretirement programs are optional retirement plans (such as partial retirement, which allows the individual to work part time); time management; financial planning; leisure alternatives; and marital and social relationships (Kail & Cavanaugh, 2014).

Some organizations also offer planning services to individuals nearing retirement age. There are two types: limited and comprehensive. Limited retirement programs typically provide guidance in pension planning, social security and medicare information, health insurance options, and information on retirement benefits at various ages of retirement. Subjects and topics included in comprehensive programs commonly include those covered in the limited programs plus maintaining good health, marital/emotional aspects of retirement, leisure activities, relocation advantages and disadvantages, legal concerns (wills, estate planning, inheritance laws), family relations, employment possibilities, and lifestyle change. Counselors also may find, however, that retirement programs will not be offered to retirees in the future.

Interacting Influences

Throughout this text a holistic or whole-person approach to career counseling has been emphasized. In the adult world of career transitions, the totality of interacting influences of personal and career concerns has significant relevance to career development. This position is especially meaningful if one accepts the proposition that an individual's career transitions over the life span are influenced by both internal and external factors. Earlier in this chapter and in the previous chapter, external factors of organizational context, downsizing, outsourcing, and economic downturns that lead to job loss and job insecurity were emphasized. There are, however, significant concerns that evolve from within the individual as suggested in chapter 4, Table 4.1, including interrelated problems that overlap domains. Individual uniqueness, therefore, is influenced by interacting influences involving each individual's unique traits such as ability, culture, interests, personality, values, and person-in-environment experiences. Hence, career development is an ongoing process during which individuals develop new and different perspectives of life and subsequent short- and long-range goals.

Career development and uniqueness include career maturity fostered through developmental tasks and stages (Super, 1957), experiences and learning in stages of psychosocial development as described by Erikson (1963), and the ability to make consistent generalizations and deal with abstractions through stages of cognitive development (Piaget, 1929). It is therefore likely that individuals will develop new interests, build new and different sets of skills, and explore different lifestyle options. As Feldman (2002) puts it, "The aging process itself creates incentives for individuals to modify their career interests, values, and skills across the life space" (p. 14). The point here is that adults make career transitions for a variety of reasons including ones that are stimulated by the maturation process. Thus, a career change in midcareer may simply be an expression of a different set of interests and values.

The sources of a career change also could be influenced by mental disorders. Potential disruptions of cognitive clarity associated with mental health concerns could interfere with problem solving and the ability to appropriately evaluate experiences in one's ecological system, including the work role (Durand & Barlow, 2013). Counselors play a vital role in these instances by helping clients determine if their reasoning and decision making are rational and realistic. A paranoid client, for example, will more than likely have difficulty with interpersonal relationships. An antisocial client may have difficulty in sustaining productive work, whereas another client's impulsive behavior may interfere with work-role functioning (Schultz & Schultz, 2013). These examples of interacting influences present significant challenges of potential concerns inextricably involved in career transitions.

A holistic or whole-person approach to counseling suggests that the connection of presenting concerns that clients bring to counseling can be deeply rooted. They involve the uniqueness of an individual's personal development, such as the basis from which one interprets events, and situations in environment and numerous external influences, such as organizational context and life-course events (Kail & Cavanaugh, 2014). This is not a simplistic matter. A case in point is a client whose feeling of well-being has been drastically disrupted. The interacting influences in this case may require extensive evaluation to determine its roots. More than likely, concerns overlap domains and will require interventions that address sets of concerns simultaneously.

In sum, the stages of entry in early career are highlighted by the socialization processes that take place in each work environment. The individual evaluates self-in-situation by observing the many facets of environmental working conditions, supervisor–worker relations, opportunities for advancement, and congruence with peer affiliates. During the socialization process, the individual may need support in developing a sense of direction in a workplace's social milieu where he or she is also being observed and evaluated. Early career encounters are to be scrutinized carefully to determine their long-term effects. Helping individuals assess the complexities associated with multiple life roles are counseling goals of this stage. For those who decide to withdraw and try again in a different workplace, the decision process must include a careful analysis of the reasons for the desired change.

Support and keying in on the client's feelings of well-being are important counseling objectives that can help clients manage job loss or job insecurity. Counselors are encouraged to use a holistic counseling approach that integrates personal and career concerns. Loss of income can cause numerous problems including difficulty in maintaining relationships. Uncertainties in the 21st-century work world suggest that clients may make several career changes and find jobs in new and different work environments. Adults should be encouraged to develop their skills through available learning and training programs and to adopt a learning-for-living philosophy.

Learning to deal with competition is one of the major social-emotional needs of middle career, when individuals may need to reevaluate their career direction. As an individual integrates skills and becomes aware of potential career paths, help in establishing a set of new goals is a relevant counseling objective. The hazards associated with obsolescence and "career plateaus," downsizing, and outsourcing suggest that counseling programs encourage continuing education and training.

In late career, the individual is preparing to "phase out" or "let go" of major work responsibilities. Super (1990) used the term "decline" to indicate that a minor work role is imminent. Many people are reluctant to accept the fact that their work lives are almost over. Some may opt for a second career whereas others may choose a bridge employment arrangement that retains career identity but is also considered part-time employment with less responsibility. For others, this stage has been eagerly anticipated as a time of freedom from work and obligations. Counseling strategies that help all workers prepare for this phasing-out should include preretirement and retirement programs. More specifically, career programs should be designed to help individuals assess future needs. In the next section, I discuss the importance of addressing life roles as a most relevant part of one's career development; inter-role conflict and balancing life roles are highlighted.

Discovering the Significance of Life Roles and Potential Conflicts

The impact of decisions on lifestyle, including relationships, is a major part of a more comprehensive view of development. The life roles I discuss in this section include worker, homemaker, leisure, and citizen. It is generally agreed that life roles increase and decrease in importance according to an individual's current status. The student role, for example, is much more dominant in early life, even though career development is continuous and requires lifetime learning involvement. The potential complexity and variety of life roles over the life span can include a multitude of possible scenarios that are important factors in the developmental process. In the following paragraphs, I discuss the significance of life roles and potential conflicts.

An abundance of evidence discussed throughout this book indicates that career counseling is not concerned just with strategies for selecting a career but is much broader in scope and content. Super (1990), among others, has suggested an integrative approach to career counseling that focuses on the development of life roles over the life span, with emphasis on inter-role congruence. A key concept is the effect of the development of one role on others. Has the homemaker role, for instance, inhibited career development of one spouse? Does the work role leave ample time for other life roles? As Super (1980) pointed out, "Success in one facilitates success in others, and difficulties in one role are likely to lead to difficulties in another" (p. 287). What we have here is the position that life roles are a most important factor in career development (Ulrich & Brott, 2005).

Hansen's (1996, 2000) integrative life planning (ILP) model incorporates career development, life transitions, gender-role socialization, and social change. This model involves a "lifelong process of identifying our primary needs, roles, and goals and the consequent integration of these within ourselves, our work, and our family" (Hansen, 1990, p. 10). The ILP model evolved from Hansen's (1978) BORN FREE project, which was designed to expand career options for both men and women. Hansen suggested that fragmented approaches to development place limits on decisions that clients will make in their lifetimes. A more holistic approach recognizes that an individual's total development includes the broad spectrum of domains: social/emotional, physical, sexual, intellectual, vocational, and spiritual. Finally, in the context of our discussion, this model suggests that life roles are to be integrated in our planning and not isolated from the career decision-making process. I begin with the worker role.

Worker Role

Over time, the term "work" has generated many definitions and has meant different things to the individuals who do it. Also, the objectives people have for work can be quite different and might change as they pass through stages of career development. For example, some individuals work for the intrinsic enjoyment of it; for others, the primary objective might be as a way of making a living; and yet others work for social status or for self-identity. For many, a combination of objectives and other factors is equally important. Super (1984) suggested an inclusive perspective of the work role that covers most segments of lifestyle. Recently, the approach has shifted from a focus on work alone as a central life concern to an interest in the quality of life, in which work is one central concern in a constellation of roles such as homemaking, citizenship, and leisure that interact to create life satisfaction. The terms "work motivation" and "job satisfaction" are now perhaps displaced by, and certainly are incorporated into, the terms "quality of life" and "life satisfactions" (p. 29).

The different purposes individuals have for the work role should concern us. Herr, Cramer, and Niles (2004) suggested that the purposes of work can be classified as economic, social, and psychological. For example, a major economic purpose is to provide the individual with assets to satisfy current and future basic needs. This is especially the case for some immigrants who seek work that will provide them with subsistence. In the social realm, friendships and social status are established through peer-group affiliations through which mutual goals are achieved. A work identity, self-efficacy, and a sense of accomplishment are examples of the psychological purposes of work.

The purposes and meanings of work are uniquely individualized. For example, a family-oriented individual who has a strong need to spend ample time with his or her children could be somewhat unhappy in a work role that limits family activities. Men and women alike may opt for flexible work schedules in order to spend quality time with their children. They may want to be there for that first soccer game or a musical performance and for other activities. In this case, the working parent may be taking a more lateral move in the workplace that could delay opportunities for upward movement. In some workplaces this option is indeed available and we could see more working parents choose this path; career–life balance remains a most relevant concept.

Other changes in the work role include use of the Internet in which teams of workers collaborate on plans for starting a new business, for example. This group of workers may live miles apart, in other states, or even in other countries. Skills needed to do team work are essential, but, most important, one must have the knowledge of the subject under discussion to contribute. The competent knowledge worker will be in demand in the current and future workforce. Building a strong knowledge base over time will not only be personally satisfying but also help one to remain a viable employee in a civic or industrial organization. Knowledge workers may also find work tenure and satisfaction as a coach of fellow workers even on a part-time basis as a means of supplementing their income.

We may see a decrease in traditional workers as their jobs are taken over by short-term independent consultants. Work may continue to be accomplished by contractors or temporary workers; firms may want only a few traditional employees. One can visualize the following scenario: A group of leaders of a successful firm have been tossing around ideas for marketing most of the day, and in the late afternoon they contract with another group of workers who live in a different time zone who can have the information they need to proceed right away in the morning. In this case, the old way of using an in-house office staff is too expensive and time-consuming.

I have given only a few examples of how work may be accomplished in the current and future workplace to point out how such changes can affect one's career development. These examples illustrate only a few workplaces, but one can conclude that upward movement in many workplaces will no longer use longevity as the key factor that earns one a promotion. One must be flexible, adapt successfully to workplace changes, learn to work under different management styles, have good interpersonal relationship skills, and learn how to successfully collaborate with team members.

Homemaker Role

The role of homemaker has a wide spectrum of possibilities. For example, a 35-year-old single person might not consider this role a very important one, whereas a married 35-year-old who has children might consider homemaker as a major role. A high school student could consider this role as something to be dealt with in the future, whereas a 50-year-old who has reared several children will place less emphasis on this role when planning a career change. The more recent phenomenon of the househusband and a greater emphasis on the male role as homemaker increase the diversity of possible inter-role conflicts. The number of working mothers has increased dramatically since the 1970s even though the exact percentage of working mothers is fluid. What we do know is that some work part-time as well as full-time (Andersen & Taylor, 2013).

A major concern about maternal employment is its effect on children, the family, and the working women themselves. In a comprehensive review of the literature concerning the effects of maternal employment on children, Herr and Cramer (1996) concluded that in general it does no harm to children (infants, preschoolers, and adolescents). Working mothers also seem to fare well, according to Ferree (1984), who conducted a national research study concerning satisfaction variables. She concluded that there were no significant differences in life satisfaction between working mothers and those who did not work outside the home. In a related study, the results indicated that stress experienced by working women can be offset by spousal support, dependable child care, and shared family responsibilities (Ivey et al., 2014).

The issues surrounding the homemaker role in families where both husband and wife work outside the home (dual-earner and dual-career couples) have major significance. In dual-earner and dual-career families, both husband and wife work outside the home, but dual-career families are characterized as more career-oriented and committed to career development on a continuous basis (Goldenberg & Goldenberg, 2013). Both types of families share some common goals as well as sources of stress, such as role conflict, role overload, and decreased opportunity for leisure. (See chapter 10 for more information on dual-career families.)

Leisure Role

A number of clichés about the relationship of work and leisure have endured for generations. The primary message has been that a quality lifestyle is one in which there is a balance between time spent at work and time devoted to leisure activities. This message still prevails and has received renewed recognition as a means of fostering need satisfaction. Within this frame of reference, quality of life is attained through a more holistic approach (biological, psychological, social/cultural, and life-course events) to human and career development (Kail & Cavanaugh, 2014).

Simply stated, individuals are to recognize that quality of life is associated with all life roles. Central to our concerns as career counselors is a balance of life roles that gives clients the freedom for self-expression to meet their needs (Newman & Newman, 2009). Moreover, when inter-role conflicts are discovered, we have at our disposal a menu of suggestions designed to enhance all life roles.

In the early 1970s, the complementary role that leisure had to the work role was expressed by Kando and Summers (1971) as two-dimensional; that is, it reinforces positive associations that are also expressed in the work role (supplemental compensation) and provides activities to reduce stress associated with unpleasant work experiences (reactive compensation). Brems (2001) took a similar position on the relationship between work and leisure in that both can complement each other for a more balanced and healthier lifestyle. In a discussion of dimensions of leisure, Liptak (2001) makes the point that leisure and work are indeed intertwined. Following this logic, but with a somewhat different twist, Jackson (1988) suggested that individuals can receive psychological benefits from leisure, but only if they learn how to use the time spent in leisure in a purposeful manner. Sources of stress found in work, such as competition, can also become sources of stress in leisure activities. More recently, Gurung (2014) suggested that counselors act in an advocacy role to promote leisure activities in schools, workplaces, homes, and communities.

In sum, the leisure role should be assessed as a prolific means of complementing other life roles. The proportion of time a person allocates to leisure should be judged from the perspective of lifestyle. For example, the ambitious accountant might consider leisure activities as a luxury that has little current relevance, whereas the individual who is working full-time as a bus driver and part-time on two other jobs could view leisure as something that other, more fortunate people have. The involvement in leisure might simply be haphazard and left to chance. Although there is not a plethora of research about the benefits of leisure activities, some research indicates that effective participation in leisure can be therapeutic and can compensate for dissatisfaction found in workplace (Brems, 2001; Gurung, 2014; Kail & Cavanaugh, 2014), which suggests that leisure activities are a most important part of lifestyle. The work–leisure connection may even become more relevant in the future workplace.

Citizen Role

Similar to the leisure role's link to quality of life, the citizen role can serve as an additional or compensating source of satisfaction. It also provides opportunities for fulfilling individual needs in a variety of activities found in most communities. Local civic organizations offer an abundance of opportunities for individuals to express civic responsibility as a way of responding to community needs. Although involvement in volunteerism was on the increase for community, state, national, and international projects in the late 1980s and the early part of the 1990s, downsizing of the

U.S. workforce and the recession in 2009 have created a different atmosphere in many communities. Workers who have lost their jobs and are searching for ways to maintain their lifestyle no longer have the time or inclination to volunteer for civic services. There appears to be general agreement that volunteerism is highly related to general satisfaction with life. Thus, counselors need to observe the citizen role in the context of current conditions within communities.

The concept of balanced life roles implies that there are numerous opportunities to build a quality lifestyle. Individual work situations might not provide outlets to meet client needs associated with, for example, reading to blind students or being a tutor or a hospital aide or working in a dog rescue shelter. Productive opportunities outside the work role, however, are a means of satisfaction that enhance inter-role activities. What we have here is the recognition that some needs that might otherwise be left unmet or that produce stress can be satisfied through civic activities (Newman & Newman, 2009). Bolles (2009), among others, has suggested that skills learned and developed through participation in civic organizations and activities can be used in career decision making. These skills can be matched with work requirements in career exploration. Also, volunteer experiences, along with education and other experiences, can be considered in job placement.

The case study highlights a stay-at-home mother who returns to the workplace. As so many other mothers do during an economic recession, they return to work for the welfare of the family. Many Americans are unemployed, but the actual number has been fluid since the recession in 2009. What we do know is that millions of Americans have been unable to find full-time jobs. In the meantime, dual-earner families have significantly increased. Mothers have returned to work to supplement their family's income, and some mothers are continuing to pursue a career path as their children grow older. The severe unemployment experienced by many families has been pervasive and devastating. Not only is the primary breadwinner challenged as a result of job loss, but also the spillover effect of everyday problems and continuous challenging situations becomes a family matter. This point has been emphasized throughout this text to alert counselors to be aware of individual as well as total-family concerns.

Case 14.1   A Stay-at-Home Mother Returns to the Workplace

The mother in this case study, Lois, has been devoted to child care for almost a decade and now finds it necessary to supplement the family income. Both parents are concerned about the possibility of further layoffs, which could result in the job loss of the primary breadwinner. Clearly the American dream for this family could turn into a nightmare. The mother returning to the workforce has a compelling list of concerns that she will take with her to the workplace each and every day.

Going back to work has been a difficult decision for Lois. Like many other mothers, she was worried about not being there for her two children. She was able, however, to return to the firm she had worked for in the past. She was considered to be a top-notch employee and was respected by her superiors as well as coworkers. Lois and her husband had decided that she would continue to work until the children finished college. This commitment required serious planning for the future that included child care, scheduling time for household needs, participating in events in which the children were involved, balancing the budget, and developing goals and long-term plans.

Lois was welcomed back to work by former friends and colleagues. The first year had its ups and downs, but the family maintained its commitment to make the best of their current situation. Lois and her husband both encouraged their children to do well in school and to participate in family activities. At the beginning of the second year of employment, Lois began to feel the pressure of the obligations she had assumed. Her husband had been very helpful but began to complain about how their lifestyle had changed. His mood changed from happy to sad and then to resentfulness. In addition, the children were not doing well in school. Their teachers complained about their lack of commitment to learning and their being less attentive in class.

The children's problems prompted Lois to take time off from work to make a school visit. The report she received of the children's misbehavior was troubling. It should not be surprising that Lois began to have trouble sleeping, and there were frequent arguments with her husband. She thought completely overwhelmed with personal as well as family problems that were obviously becoming more intense and frequent. Lois asked for a meeting with her supervisor to discuss the possibility of a flexible work schedule. She thought that she could offer her children more support and assume more household tasks to relieve her husband of this obligation. Unfortunately, this relatively small company did not have flexible work schedules. Her supervisor suggested that she see a career counselor for help and gave Lois the name of one she had used in the past.

Lois did make an appointment, but in the meantime noticed that she had difficulty focusing on work tasks. For the first time in her life, she felt inadequate, accompanied by feelings of resentment and a loss of motivation to work. "I don't know what has happened to me," she told the counselor. She also stated that she actually has enjoyed working and appreciated the interrelationships with fellow workers. She stated, "We have great rapport, but now I'm depressed, frustrated, and very unhappy."

As is often necessary when clients express symptoms associated with stress, the counselor assumes an empathic and caring role, addressing anxiety, frustration, and depression, among other symptoms. The counselor immediately recognized symptoms of work stress and decided that Lois was in no position to become involved in searching for other worksites that have flexible work hours. The

counselor decided to address a host of problems usually associated with work stress.

Following several more brief interviews, she conceptualized Lois's concerns as follows:

Career: Lois had a successful work experience over several years. She had excellent ratings from her supervisors and was respected and popular with fellow workers. Currently she is confused, undecided, and frustrated with her work performance and life in general. She is experiencing stress reactions from numerous sources in her environment. Her ability to fulfill job requirements may be at risk.

Affective: Currently Lois is emotionally unstable. Her emotional instability appears to have disrupted all of her life roles. Poor self-esteem and feelings of inferiority appear to be related to reactions to stressful conditions in the home and workplace. Her feelings of helplessness have led to depressive reactions that could affect her ability to make rational decisions concerning the future of her family. Her inability to control her emotions strongly suggests that she could benefit greatly from cognitive restructuring techniques.

Cognitive-behavioral: Lois's view of herself has changed from a positive one to a negative one. Currently she appears to have a negative opinion of herself. Negative views of oneself can lead to depression, anger, and erratic behavior. Currently, Lois may have extreme difficulty in making rational decisions about the give-and-take of daily life. Her negative view of self should be a priority in the counseling process.

Culture: Lois was born into a White working-class home. She characterized her family as caring, warm, and loving. In addition, the family stressed self-reliance and self-discipline. Lois set similar goals for her family and currently blames herself for the problems her children are experiencing. These feelings of failure reflect deeply rooted beliefs in a family structure that encourages a positive sense of well-being.

In the next counseling session, the counselor focused on coping skills that are to be used to counter the effects of stress that Lois is currently experiencing. Topics discussed included self-confidence, self-efficacy, self-esteem, and social support. The counselor began by reminding Lois of their discussion about the importance of well-being they had at the beginning of the interview. She found that Lois completely agreed that feelings of well-being would be more than welcomed at this point in her life. They also agreed that positive thoughts and actions can be revitalizing (Ivey et al., 2014). The counselor pointed out how self-efficacy could be most helpful in that this term represents one's perception of capability and controllability. If one strengthens these characteristics through positive thinking related to feelings of well-being, a strong self-esteem could be revitalized. Positive influences could change the content of Lois's thinking process.

Clearly, the counselor recognized that Lois was indeed a capable employee and could return to her current position if she could learn to control her thinking process that has been filled with negativity. Other topics that were discussed in the subsequent counseling sessions included an explanation of stress and its pervasive nature. The counselor explained that some people inherit tendencies to express certain behaviors. There is a genetic predisposition or vulnerability to mental illness. There is what is labeled a *diathesis stress model*, which suggests that stress triggers one's vulnerability to develop serious personal problems that can be devastating (Durand & Barlow, 2013). Thus, one is to build coping abilities as a defense against stress reactions. The reactions to stressful conditions are considered to be an individual matter and not limited to any one life role.

The counselor was as pleased as Lois concerning her progress. There were sessions with Lois and her husband and with the entire family. In the meantime, the counselor arranged for members of the workplace to offer Lois support and encouragement. The counselor was pleased to find that all workers were willing to help Lois and her family by supporting them whenever needed. They all realized that this mother was a good one who just has been derailed for a period of time but is now back in control and is a vital member of their group.

We continue with a general discussion of how stress at work can be pervasive and destructive. Several suggestions for counseling strategies are presented.

Stress at Work

In the late 1990s, Rice (1999) suggested that job-related stress leads to dissatisfaction, burnout, and obsolescence. He considered psychological systems of work stress to include the following (p. 195):

- Anxiety, tension, confusion, and irritability
- Feelings of frustration, anger, and resentment
- Emotional hypersensitivity and hyperactivity
- Suppression of feelings, withdrawal, and depression
- Reduced effectiveness in communication
- Feelings of isolation and alienation
- Boredom and job dissatisfaction
- Mental fatigue, lower intellectual functioning, and loss of concentration
- Loss of spontaneity and creativity
- Lowered self-esteem

Such symptoms, according to Rice (1999), can lead to several behaviors, including lower performance, procrastination, work avoidance, aggression, depression, and increased alcohol and drug use and abuse. Work-related stress also can be the major source of family problems, poor relationships with other workers and friends, and in severe cases might be one factor that leads to violence in the workplace (Sulsky & Smith, 2005).

Specific job features can pose a threat to the worker. What is being suggested here is that stress involves interactions of work conditions with worker traits that change normal psychological and/or physiological functions. Thus, features of a job exceed the worker's coping abilities. Using this logic suggests that job-related stress is only one factor among others that leads to work stress. Major job stressors, however, are contributing factors to serious consequences for the worker, such as work overload, role ambiguity, technostress, under- and overpromotion, spillover, and electronic performance monitoring (Harrington, 2013). A brief explanation of these factors follows:

1. Work overload is viewed as a compromise between quantity and quality of performance. It can be experienced by white-and blue-collar workers. Health care workers, as well as teachers and social workers, are examples whose job demands may be excessive.
2. Role ambiguity suggests that workers are uncertain as to what management expects in the way of accomplishment. The results are usually high levels of anxiety and tension; one's job performance is usually affected.
3. Technostress involves changing technology in the workplace causing many workers to feel the effects of stress when they are required to learn a new level of skills. Changes in procedures can be threatening to some workers, especially those who have become comfortable with current use of technology. The uncertainty of learning a new skill can be stressful. The need to learn a new skill may cause some workers to experience low esteem, and subsequently their feelings of well-being.
4. Under- and overpromotion suggests that some workers think that their skills and hard work are not appreciated by their superiors and as a result view their work environment as having few prospects for promotion. Being passed over and not noticed can be disheartening and demeaning. Overpromotion suggests that they are not capable of meeting the demands of their job requirements. Workers' perception of being "over promoted" can be devastating. In both cases, lowered productivity and job dissatisfaction are probable.
5. Spillover effect suggests that what happens in one life role affects other life roles. For example, problems in the work role can be the driving force that causes problems in the home or vice versa. Work–family conflict has become a growing concern for individual workers and their families, as well as those who manage workers on the job. Stress is the most pervasive source of conflict in most life roles.
6. Electric performance monitoring (EPM) in contemporary workplaces is a relatively new innovation that management uses to evaluate the productivity and behavior of workers online. Clerical workers have been the major target of this type of monitoring; however, other workers including upper-echelon employees are not exempt from this type of monitoring. As evidence is compiled from research, EPM could be labeled as a major factor in the workplace that is considered to be most stressful for employees.

Gurung (2014) and Newman and Newman (2009), among others, point out that stress is pervasive, and they suggest that workers are to use cognitive, affective, and behavioral strategies to manage stress. Cormier and colleagues (2013) suggest that self-management strategies designed to deal with stress can be effective. These strategies include self-monitoring by recording thoughts, feelings, and behaviors when interacting within the environment. These recordings are to be reviewed for further insights into cognitive processes. Second, prearranged stimulus control that decreases disturbing reactions to certain events is suggested. Individuals learn to control or modify their disturbing reactions to certain stimuli. A third self-management strategy includes self-reward or a positive stimulus following a desirable reaction to target behaviors. Individuals learn to provide their own positive reinforcement for desirable behaviors. A fourth strategy suggests that individuals are to visualize how they could successfully perform a goal behavior. This strategy suggests projecting one's self as a model when performing in a desired manner. The major goal of these strategies is to build self-monitoring, self-directed procedures for managing stressful conditions and situations.

Types of interventions for coping with stress suggested by Sulsky and Smith (2005) and Harrington (2013) include meditation, exercise, and relaxation techniques. In addition, organizations are to evaluate job design, selection and placement programs, and general working conditions. Job placement and demands are to consider a person's style of fit including participation preferences and coworker relationships. Clearly, the individual and the organization share the need to develop an awareness and recognition that stress at work should be systematically addressed (Aamodt, 2013).

There is a growing recognition among employers of the stressful conditions involving the interplay between work and family. The increased number of dual-earner families and the desire to hold on to effective knowledge workers have motivated organizations to become more family role-oriented. Another driving force is the realization that material and socioemotional rewards are not mutually exclusive (Muchinsky, 2003). In other words, family life and the time to become involved in other interests and to be with friends also play an important role in individual happiness and satisfaction.

Progressive organizations have indeed viewed family relationships as inclusive. For example, perceptions of family relationships now include multiple relationships including stepparenting, committed relationships between unmarried couples, and extended family responsibilities such as caring for nieces, nephews, grandchildren, and elderly relatives (Feldman, 2002). The point here is that increasing family responsibilities and subsequent conflicts may have the potential of a meltdown in the workplace as family conflicts can also decrease an individual's ability to tolerate stress derived from the workplace (Harrington, 2013; Stephens & Feldman, 1997; Zunker, 2008). Integrating work and life and finding a life balance are current subjects of interest to employers as well as employees (Fox & Spector, 2005). In response to work–family conflicts, organizations have established on-site or near-site child care centers and exercise facilities, and some have offered elder care assistance, such as arranging for transportation, medical schedules, and personal services. Flexible work schedules also are offered by many organizations.

In this chapter I have discussed adult career development concerns that include early to late career and the importance of life roles in the career development process. I also have called attention to the pervasive nature of work stress as an important factor that can greatly affect one's career development. In the following case study, I provide an example of a young adult who wants to change careers for a completely different reason than those discussed previously. In this case, the client's life story at the age of 26 is a good example of how life-course events can shape one's future goals.

Case 14.2   Alex Wants to Change Careers

Alex, a 26-year-old employee of a company that maintains and installs air conditioning and heating units, told the counselor that he wanted to change jobs. His life story went something like this: "I joined the Army soon after I finished high school because the job market had tanked." During 4 years in the service, Alex learned how to maintain heating and air-conditioning units and decided to leave the service and do this same type of work as a civilian. He was hired by a local firm and quickly became successful at his job and received several pay increases. Alex continued by telling the counselor that he learned much more than maintenance skills while in the service. He was sent to several foreign countries as well as bases in several states.

> Alex said: I grew up in rural Texas on a farm, and there's no way this Texas boy could have traveled to Iraq, Italy, Germany, Greenland, and Labrador if I hadn't been in the service. Besides, I saw some of the great cities in this country, and I even got to see several baseball games at Yankee Stadium, and I went to concerts, art shows, plays, and museums that were fabulous. All these experiences were really an eye-opener— I realize now that I gained a new perspective of life. I thought A/C work would be a hot job, and it was for a while, but now there's something more that I want, and while I'm still single, I want to find something new and different. Can you help me?

There is a growing interest in research that addresses the sources that prompt some adults to change career paths. Career development theorists have suggested that there are some stable human characteristics, such as interests, personality traits, and values, that guide career development over the life span (Brown, 1996; Dawis, 1996; Holland, 1992). Yet, some adults suggest that changes in these internal characteristics and traits have influenced them to consider a career change. Feldman (2002), among others, believes that changes within people over time and person-in-environment interactions can persuade adults to change careers. Clearly, the changing nature of work and life-course events has led many workers to reevaluate their career goals and make subsequent changes in career direction (Zunker, 2008).

Alex is an example of an adult who wants to change careers not because of job insecurity or because he dislikes his current work, but because he has reevaluated his career goals and is in search of something more challenging that he cannot identify at this time. One also should recognize that Alex has enhanced his feeling of self-efficacy from being successful in his current job. His expressed desire to do "something different" perhaps is the result of increased confidence that he can function effectively in other work roles that are more demanding. It appears plausible to suggest that life course events have influenced Alex's worldview and subsequently influenced his desire to learn more about himself and the opportunities he might pursue. Counselors can expect to counsel clients who have similar reactions to life-course events and desire information about career opportunities as they gain a better perspective of self-knowledge and confidence that one can succeed in other life roles.

Alex's counselor began career counseling by using the interview procedures described in chapter 5; she wanted to maintain her focus on unique individual traits in order to assist Alex in his quest for self-knowledge. She also would carefully choose assessment instruments to screen for drug use, faulty cognitions, and symptoms of psychological disorders; she wanted to identify the presence of any barriers to career choice. Her focus was on cognitive processes to make certain that Alex would be able to process career information and assessment results of personal traits such as academic ability, interests, personality, and values. His ability to integrate data would be carefully monitored. His assets and strengths include self-confidence, feelings of self-efficacy, and good interpersonal skills. He also appears to be highly motivated to find other career options. Following is the conceptualization of Alex's concerns.

Career: The driving forces behind Alex's desire to change career goals is a combination of an awareness of self-concept and a changing worldview that has prompted a need to expand his career options to include work roles that offer opportunities to contribute to the welfare of all citizens. In short, Alex desires to help others expand their perceptions and worldviews as he did. The counselor recognized that Alex may be a long way from choosing a specific career goal, but his assessment test scores indicated that he does have the educational background and ability to be successful in college. The interest inventory results indicated that he prefers social interaction and is interested in educational activities. Teacher, social worker, and counselor are preferred occupations. On a personality inventory his score results indicate that he is open to taking part in a variety of experiences, and on a values inventory his highest values were in altruism, social interaction, and social relations. There were no indications of drug abuse or significant symptoms of psychological disorders or dysfunctional thinking.

Affective: Alex gives the impression that he is in complete control of his emotions. There were no indications of emotional instability during the interview or during the time when assessment instruments were administered. His demeanor may be described as calm, friendly, and cooperative.

Cognitive-Behavioral: A test designed to uncover dysfunctional thinking that could affect decision making provided further evidence that Alex was capable of rational decision making but may not be ready to commit to a specific career at this time. All data indicate that Alex prefers to delay career choice until he has had the opportunity to take college courses and gather more occupational information. His ability to process career information does not appear to be hampered.

Culture: Alex is a White male who grew up in rural Texas with a strong religious background and a good work ethic. He strongly believes in individual responsibility and that people succeed in life through hard work and personal commitments. He stated that he is fully committed to getting an education and choosing a career that will provide him with the opportunity to help others. He claims that these characteristics are part of what he learned from his parents and siblings. As he put it, "We all had responsibilities for keeping up our family farm and keeping it productive—I quickly learned that if I didn't do my part, I was in deep trouble."

Alex and the counselor agreed that he would begin college next semester with an undeclared major. Alex will use his GI Bill to fund his education, and he will continue to work part-time. Alex will continue career counseling at the university counseling center.

This case is a good example of how life-course events can influence one's worldview and career goals. Although Alex will make a career choice during his freshmen or sophomore year in college, he will do it with the sophistication that usually accompanies life experiences that have been most enlightening and educational. Those who have been given the opportunity to experience the give-and-take of work and life over several years will more than likely increase their chances of making an optimal career choice.

What counselors can learn from this case is that situational experiences that enhance self-efficacy are significant influences in one's career development. According to Bandura (1986), performance is a result of high and realistic efficacy expectations; that is, an individual's beliefs and convictions can produce certain behaviors. In some work environments, early career experiences that are positive and meaningful promote individual career development; one person may want to continue with the possibility of upward mobility, whereas others may decide to change course and establish a completely different career path. Career development is indeed an individual matter.

Summary

1. Global market forces influence nature of work available to the U.S. worker.
2. Workers who will prosper in the 21st century are those who are intelligent enough to learn new skills. A lifelong commitment to learning will be necessary for most workers.

3. The major causes of career erosion in traditional organizations are changing organizational context. Gone are the promises of traditional organizations including stable employment.

4. Current management has shifted from a worker organization to a work organization that is less willing to assume responsibility for an employee's career development.

5. Career planning in the future will include circular as well as linear moves. Workers are expected to work at multiple sites and to be involved in new and different work requirements.

6. In the current and future workforce, pay-for-performance and pay-for-knowledge will predominate. Workers who have the knowledge to perform well will more than likely get the best jobs. Knowledge work will be in demand.

7. Human development is influenced by biological, psychological, sociocultural, and life-cycle events.

8. Early career is the time when workers establish a career identity and develop relationships. Midcareer is the maintenance stage in which there is a continual adjustment and greater understanding of the work role. Late career is characterized by changing relationships and preparing to let go of responsibilities and retirement.

9. Life roles include worker, homemaker, leisure, and citizen.

10. A lifelong learning commitment is a method of keeping abreast of technological changes, upgrading skills, understanding the information explosion, and reducing chances of becoming obsolete.

11. A case study about a stay-at-home mother returning to the workforce illustrates problems associated with stress.

12. The effects of stress are pervasive. Work performance and interrelationships are often affected. Stress affects all levels of workers from executives to blue collar.

13. A second case study illustrates how situational experiences that enhance self-efficacy can significantly influence career development. Life-course events can influence career development.

Supplementary Learning Exercises

1. What is a knowledge worker? Give examples. How and why will they dominate the workforce of the future?

2. How would you prepare a client for early career? Give examples of potential problems.

3. How has globalization affected working in the 21st century? List the consequences of globalization in the workplace.

4. Why is it important for counselors to understand the basic forces of human development?

5. Will it be necessary for workers to delay retirement in the future? Explain.

Case 14.3   The Perils of Being Downsized

This is the story of a woman named Ethel who lost three jobs because of a weak economy. Ethel worked in a meat-packing plant for a year before it was downsized. Her second job was with a bank as a clerk in the mailroom that paid $2.00 less per hour than the meat-packing plant. After working at a bank for a few months, the workforce in the bank was downsized. Ethel took a third job, loading newspapers for delivery for a publishing company for $1.25 per hour less than her job at the bank. Each time Ethel lost a job as a result of downsizing, the next job paid less per hour. One may find that the unemployed often will take the next job available just to survive. Ethel is 42 years of age, divorced, and has two grown children who are now on their own. She has a high school diploma and took courses in a community college for one year.

After Ethel told the counselor about her work problems, she explained that she was divorced because her husband deserted the family some 10 years ago. She continued by telling the counselor that her older son was killed in a car accident several years ago and that her husband was never the same. He first blamed Ethel for what happened, and then himself, and finally "he just walked away from all of us." She tried to find him for several years but has now given up.

This story exemplifies the difficulty that workers face at the lower end of the economic ladder. In addition to the personal/social problems faced by people in these circumstances, they also need assistance to find resources for training programs to upgrade their skills.

Ethel continued by stating that she would like to find work that pays more and a job she can count on even if the economy is not strong.

QUESTIONS FOR DISCUSSION

1. How would you conceptualize Ethel's career and social problems?
2. Develop a list of assessment instruments that could be useful.
3. Develop a list of educational and personal needs for Ethel.
4. Develop a list of some specific goals for career training and placement in the future?
5. What agencies would you contact for help in this case?

Case 14.4   The Loan Officer

A loan officer, age 50, was told he no longer had a job when he returned from a vacation. The news was certainly devastating, but worse problems were yet to come. His wife divorced him, and his children shunned him because, as they put it, "He embarrassed us by being fired." He told the counselor that he took any job he could find, such as working in a service station and being a tour guide. Soon after he was fired from his job at the bank, the bank failed and was bought by a larger one. Thus, the fallout from a recession can indeed be a life-course event that is significant for many workers. The victims of job loss not only are in search for new jobs, but also may be burdened with serious personal problems as well. The counselor noted that her clients' behavior closely resembled other clients' who were depressed.

QUESTIONS AND EXERCISES FOR DISCUSSION

1. How would you determine this client's level of depression?
2. If you were conducting the interview, what further information do you consider most critical?
3. What are this client's advantages and disadvantages for finding work?
4. How would you address future career development issues?
5. Provide examples of how career and personal concerns are connected to career development in this case study.

PART FOUR
Career Counseling in Educational Settings

15

Career-Related Programs for Career Development in Elementary Schools

CHAPTER HIGHLIGHTS

- Building support for career-related programs

- Strategies for helping children learn

- Influences of family interaction on career development

- Counseling culturally different children

- Types of developmental disorders

- Role of elementary school counselors

- Strategies for integrating career development concepts

Career-related programs in elementary schools have come to be viewed by many as essential ingredients in the educational process of all students (Berns, 2004; Ebert & Culyer, 2011; Sciarra, 2004). Comprehensive career-related programs that are currently in vogue are intentional and sequential. They begin in prekindergarten with the assumption that career development is considered to be a lifelong process; comprehensive career programs are to be age-appropriate and should include experiential activities. Effective career-related programs in schools require a cooperative effort that usually includes planning, oversight, and operational procedures that are a product of a joint efforts by administrators, teachers, counselors, parents, and community volunteers. Comprehensive developmental school guidance programs in vogue today are primarily the result of well-construed national standards developed by counseling professional associations. National guidelines for career-related activities in schools have been successfully used to develop local programs. Thus, we begin this chapter with an overview of career-related programs for schools.

Overview of Career-Related Programs in Schools

Many individuals were involved in the development of comprehensive developmental school guidance programs. Gysbers and Henderson (2001), among others, suggested that counseling programs in schools should focus on developmental domains to make a direct connection to the purpose of life education that have been strongly supported by educators (Compton & Hoffman, 2013; Sciarra, 2004). Thus, comprehensive developmental school guidance programs address the needs of students at all grade levels as they make progress within a competency-based curriculum. Therefore, as schools established learning domains and goals and objectives for each domain, standards for achieving success also were developed. Using this rationale, the American School Counselors Association (ASCA) developed the National Standards for School Counseling Programs and Suggested Student Competencies (ASCA, 2003) known as the ASCA National Model: A Framework for School Counseling Programs (see appendix G).

Meanwhile, the National Career Development Association (NCDA) also established what is known as the National Career Development Guidelines (NCDG), which were updated by the U.S. Department of Education Office of Vocational and Adult Education and published in 2005 (see appendix H). The NCDG also established goals and objectives for three domains and standards for achieving success. The NCDG provides a framework for defining career development competencies or learning stages by (1) knowledge acquisition, stage (K), (2) application, stage (A), and (3) reflection, stage (R). What is suggested here is that the (1) knowledge acquisition stage involves increasing their knowledge concerning a specific goal; they have increased their awareness of what is to be learned and continue to compile information. As the name implies, the (2) application stage is characterized as using or applying the knowledge they have compiled. Finally, when reaching the (3) reflection stage, they are able to assess and evaluate what they have learned and how it may be useful as a tool in the future. In this chapter and in the final two chapters of this book, I refer to the NCDG and the ASCA national models for counseling programs in schools.

Clearly, career-related programs in elementary schools require the development of model programs, resources, and strategies, and most importantly, carefully planned methods of curriculum integration. Obviously, counselors play a significant role as proactive agents in promoting, developing, and evaluating career development programs. In addition to counseling duties, counselors assume multiple roles, such as coach, leader, consultant, coordinator, teacher, team facilitator, career-related information specialist, and promoter of community involvement; the role of the counselor is inclusive.

Public schools are universal in that they are open to all, and they are considered prescriptive by providing standards of achievement primarily based on the needs of an ever-changing society (Berns, 2004; Rathus, 2014). First and foremost are academic goals of mastering basic skills that prepare learners to embark on a lifelong journey of learning. Students are expected to master numerous skills and understand concepts that will equip them with the ability to solve problems, think rationally, and accumulate general knowledge. Social, civic, cultural, and personal goals are to be enhanced and promoted as an important part of interpersonal understanding, social enculturation, and emotional and physical well-being (Berns, 2004; Goodlad, 1984; McWhirter et al., 2013). A most important perspective, however, is that vocational goals are considered to be the product of the total educational experience, which includes career education programs designed to prepare students for career choice and subsequently make a successful transition from school-to-school and/or school-to-work. Although these goals may be listed as separate categories, they are inherently interrelated. A deficiency in basic skill development, for example, could affect one's progress in all educational programs. Hence, the focus in this chapter will be on vocational goals for students in elementary schools that reflect interrelationships of all educational goals.

The Search for Effective Schools

There has been a growing concern among parents as well as educators concerning the effectiveness of school programs. The focus of these concerns has included a need to identify the characteristics of effective schools. Recent research by Slavin (2012) and Woolfolk (2013) provide examples of what they believe are the characteristics of good schools. Rathus (2014, p. 437) reports their results as follows:

- An active, energetic principal
- An atmosphere that is orderly, but not oppressive
- Empowerment of teachers, that is, teachers participating in decision making
- Teachers who have high expectations that children will learn
- A curriculum that emphasizes academics
- Frequent assessment of student performance
- Empowerment of students, that is, students participating in setting goals, making classroom decisions, and engaging in cooperative learning activities with other students

What stands out in schools that are considered effective is active leadership, a focus on academic achievement, and the active participation of teachers, parents, and students. There is order without oppression. Students are encouraged to study on their own but also participate in group learning activities. Academic performance is reinforced through frequent assessment of progress. Finally, small class size is most important for a number of reasons; for example, students are able to express themselves more often and participate in small-group activities. In addition, and of the utmost importance, teachers are able to provide more individual attention when teaching the "basic" subjects (Ebert & Culyer, 2011).

I now focus on building support for career-related programs starting in elementary schools, followed by a discussion of cognitive development and learning. Then I turn to the family as a system, career goals and competencies, and representative examples of specific classroom and/or group activities.

Building Support for Career-Related Programs—Keys to Success

Counseling programs at all school levels usually require counselors to justify program content and materials. Building support for career-related programs in the elementary school requires a sophisticated approach to justify time and effort in an already crowded curriculum. A critical step in establishing elementary school career-related programs, therefore, is to convince teachers, administrators, and parents of the need for career education. Counselors are to base their recommendations on a background of accepted academic findings and research, as well as straightforward information that identifies connections between learned basic skills and work requirements.

Building support and developing career-related programs require an academic foundation and background in a number of disciplines including developmental psychology. Human development in this context usually refers to systematic changes of physical, cognitive, and psychosocial development as interactive influences that shape individuals. How children learn, their ways of responding, and their readiness for learning provide an essential foundation for program planning and counseling children. Thus, the developmental period of early childhood is a relevant concern of the elementary school counselor. Planning strategies and joint activities with teachers and parents that meet the approval of administrators is an awesome task and requires a solid academic background and relevant professional experience. The following example underscores this recommendation.

An elementary school counselor who moved to a different location in a large city discovered that her new school did not have a parent–teacher organization. The school was located in what was considered to be a poor area of the city. It soon became apparent that parents had little understanding of what they could do to help their children learn. The counselor approached the school's principal for permission to solicit the teachers' help in organizing group meetings with parents to inform them of how they could be advocates for helping children learn and understand the significant role that parents play in career development. From these beginnings and with the support of the teaching staff, programs were established to involve parents in their children's education, including career-related projects. Specific goals included the need for parents to collaborate with teachers in program development, to support career-related programs by precept and example in the home, to become involved in developing their children's self-concept, and to encourage their children to explore many career opportunities. A major goal was to encourage family members to provide needed support for career development learning activities and to ensure that their children will come to school to learn. Box 15.1 contains suggestions for involving parents in learning activities.

The lesson here is that counselors are to be prepared to appreciate and understand the ecological system of the community in which they are working. With

BOX 15.1

Strategies for Involving Families in Learning

1. Recognize and show that parents are significant contributors to their child's development. Call on parents for advice, help, support, and critical evaluations.
2. Present a realistic picture of what the child's program is designed to accomplish.
3. Maintain ongoing communication with parents. Provide written information regarding due process procedures and parent or parent–teacher organizations, as well as oral and written information about the child's progress.
4. Show parents that you care about their child. Call, write notes, and spend time listening to parents' concerns.
5. Keep parents informed as to how they can help their child at home. Enable parents to enjoy their children.
6. Use parents' ideas, materials, and activities to work with their child.
7. Be familiar with community services and resources so you can refer parents when necessary.
8. Be yourself. Don't pretend to know all the answers when you don't; don't be afraid to ask for advice or refer parents to other professionals and resources.
9. Recognize that diverse family structures and parenting styles influence parental participation.
10. Help parents grow in confidence and in self-esteem. (Gargiulo & Graves, 1991; Heward, 1999)

SOURCE: From *Child, Family, School, Community: Socialization and Support*, p. 283, by R. M. Berns. © 2004. Reprinted with permission from Wadsworth, a part of the Thomson Corporation.

this knowledge, counselors are in a better position to approach parents, secure their support, and identify community resources. Developing an understanding of contextual issues and the current political climate helped the counselor in our example obtain the endorsement of community members. Cooperative efforts among teachers, counselors, and parents are usually developed through collaborative relationships. In many instances, community resources can be used to support school programs. Counselors can play a helpful advocacy role in gaining community cooperation and support.

Finally, career development involves a series of competencies that are evaluated by indicators of competence to demonstrate their knowledge and skills. One important outcome of this process is the development of a sense of life purpose. This objective may appear to be overwhelming, and indeed it is a pervasive goal; however, children search for a means of connectedness with others and the world around them as they develop a sense of the future. One way to help children begin their lifetime journey is to provide them with the means to become involved in their own development, encouraged and reinforced by collective efforts of family members (McWhirter et al., 2013). The importance of a compassionate, involved caregiver cannot be overemphasized.

Collectively, parents, counselors, and teachers are to unify their efforts to foster the development of a sense of life purpose that is embraced by a significant work role in the future. Be aware that we do not suggest that all educational goals are to be directed to establishing a work role. On the contrary, purpose of life is a pervasive concept that is inclusive. The position here is that the work role is relatively easy for elementary school children to observe and comprehend. They can make connections and identify with the work roles of their parents and other important adults. They can make concrete connections between workers and individuals as they become self-aware and develop self-image and self-concepts. Thus, the broader and more sophisticated conceptualization of career-life perspective and the interrelationships of all life roles have roots that are firmly embedded in observations and experiences in early childhood. Within this environment, the important concept of resiliency has emerged.

Resiliency in Children

The perspective of resilient children has become the centerpiece of research that addresses how family, community, peers, teachers, and schools can foster the development of children. What is being stressed here is that resilient children develop the ability to cope with adversity. Good relationships with family members and friends, for example, can foster protective factors of resilience in children. Children learn to cope effectively with negative factors from positive experiences in their environment. A close supporting friend can bolster one's ability to cope with adversity. Supportive parents can enhance a positive outlook and a positive self-perception. Teachers can promote good problem-solving skills and self-efficacy. Positive self-perceptions and/or self-efficacy are most important concepts for each individual's career development. Box 15.2, from Compton and Hoffman (2013), presents protective factors for promoting resiliency in children. More about resilience is discussed in the next two chapters. Now I turn to cognitive development and learning.

BOX 15.2

Protective Factors for Resilience in Children and Youth

In the Family and Close Relationships
Positive attachment relationships
Authoritative parenting
Organized home environment
Positive family with low discord between parents
Connections to prosocial and rule-abiding peers
Socioeconomic advantage

In the Community
Effective schools
Ties to prosocial organizations
Neighborhoods with high "collective efficiency"
High levels of public safety
Good public health

In the Child
Good problem-solving skills
Self-regulations skills for self-control of attention, arousal, and impulses
Positive self-perception or self-efficacy
Positive outlook on life
Faith and sense of meaning in life
Easy temperament as child, adaptable personality when older

SOURCE: From *Positive Psychology: The Science of Happiness and Flourishing*, 2nd ed., p. 191, by W. Compton and E. Hoffman. Copyright 2013. Reprinted with permission, Wadsworth Cengage Learning, Belmont, CA.

Cognitive Development and Learning

Piaget (1929), noted for his work in cognitive development, has provided a description of how humans think and the characteristics of their thinking at different stages of development. In early development, children cultivate "schemes" through their senses and motor activities. During ages 2 through 5, children begin to develop conceptual levels but do not yet have the ability to think logically or abstractly. By the time children reach elementary school age, they have developed the ability to apply logic to thinking and can understand simple concepts. Through concrete experiences, children learn to make consistent generalizations. Children learn, for example, to classify persons or objects in more than one category (e.g., the Little League coach also can be a police officer).

Encouraging and directing concrete experiences to promote increasingly abstract conceptual operations during this stage of development are a vital part of educational and career guidance programming in elementary schools. A sample exercise to illustrate this process would be asking students to identify one type of skill necessary for good schoolwork and then asking them to identify a job that requires a specific school subject. According to Piaget, the formal operational period begins by the time one has reached the approximate age of 11. The period of time for one to reach this stage can vary. It is during the formal operational period that individuals are able to think hypothetically and reason abstractly (Kail & Cavanuagh, 2014).

Piaget indeed does provide a comprehensive theory of cognitive development (only examples are discussed here) that has endured for a significant period of time. With all due respect to Piaget's major contributions to child development, some elements of his theory have been criticized as follows: His theory (1) underestimates cognitive competence in infants and young children and overestimates cognitive competence of adolescents, (2) does not clearly explain the processes and mechanisms of change, (3) does not take into account variability in some children's performance, and (4) does not account for the influence of sociocultural environmental factors (Siegler & Alibali, 2005). Keeping Piaget's extensive research in mind, we now focus on information-processing strategies for learning.

Information-Processing Strategies for Learning

The general principles of information processing suggest that human thinking is driven by *mental hardware* (mental and neural structures that influence how the mind operates) and *mental software* (mental programs that are the basis for human performance); the combination of the two provides children and adults with the ability to accomplish tasks. As one grows and develops, mental software becomes more complex, efficient, and powerful. Thus, *efficiency* in processing information is the major focus of attention. What is suggested here is that human thought takes place in what is referred to as *working memory* in which a small number of thoughts and ideas can be stored temporarily. To retain thoughts and ideas in the working memory, one has to transfer them to *long-term memory*, the permanent storehouse of knowledge that is thought to have unlimited capacity.

This brings us to an important point in our discussion of how one learns and then retains information: Children learn to use *memory strategies* that will transfer thoughts and ideas from the working memory to long-term memory. Some memory strategies are rehearsal (repetitively naming the information to be stored); organization (structuring information in order to place it with related information); and elaboration (embellishing information to be remembered) (Kail & Cavanaugh, 2014). What is important to grasp here is that parents, teachers, and counselors can prepare learning opportunities for children to develop effective memory strategies. The discussion of information-processing skills continues in the chapters that follow.

The above brief discussions of Piaget's work and the principles of information processing suggest that learning is a complex process that begins in early childhood and continues over the life span. You will recall that in career counseling much emphasis is placed on information processing. Actually, counselors search for barriers that may restrict a client's ability to process information in the career counseling process; it is a major focus of counseling. Learning memory strategies is indeed a necessary skill that is to be nurtured. Children often begin with the basic strategy of rehearsal to store ideas in memory, and progress to more sophisticated processes such as organization and elaboration.

Memory strategies for children can be reinforced in a number of ways. One simple example is the use of an external device such as a simple calendar to remember information about significant dates. From such early beginnings, children learn to use different kinds of strategies to improve the effectiveness of memory strategies. In addition, teachers, counselors, parents, siblings, and peers can offer guided assistance that has proven to be most effective (Berns, 2004 ; Kail & Cavanaugh, 2014; Shaffer & Kipp, 2014).

Learning by Observation

Observation is another contributing element to early cognitive development. Krumboltz's learning theory of career choice and counseling, discussed in chapter 2, emphasizes the importance of observation learning attributed to reactions to consequences, observable results of actions, and reactions to others (Mitchell & Krumboltz, 1996). Children are particularly prone to adopting the behavior models they observe (Bandura, 1986). According to Bandura, there are five stages of observable learning: (1) paying attention; (2) remembering what is observed; (3) reproducing actions; (4) becoming motivated (to reproduce what is observed); and (5) perfecting an imitation according to what was observed. Within this frame of reference, parents, teachers, teachers' aides, and classmates are potential models that elementary school children will imitate. Of course, models may come from other sources, such as television, movies, and books. The potential benefits of observational learning for career development of elementary school children are important. Directed observable learning experiences involving work roles, for example, are a component of early career guidance programs. An important part of early development is self-concept development.

Self-Concept Development

In chapter 2, we briefly mentioned Super's self-concept theory and its pervasive nature (Super et al., 1963). Super (1990) also clarified his position on the nature and scope of self-concept in career development. Individuals, in Super's view, have constellations of self-concepts, or "self-concept systems," that denote sets or constellations of traits. In an elementary school setting, for example, an individual might have a different view of self as a student and as a member of a peer group. An individual might see himself or herself as gregarious, but also as a weak student or not very intelligent. Elementary students formulate sets of self-concepts as they focus on class requirements; interrelationships with peers, teachers, and important adults; and the social structure in which they live and function. Thus, self-concept is defined in many childhood relationships (Shaffer & Kipp, 2014).

In her theory of circumscription and compromise, discussed in chapter 2, Gottfredson focuses on the development of self-images and occupational aspirations in four stages. In the first stage, orientation to size and power (ages 3 to 5), children recognize adult occupational roles and exhibit same-sex preferences for adult activities, including employment. During stage two, orientation to sex roles (ages 6 to 8), children focus on what is appropriate for their sex; they now recognize that adult activities are sex typed. As a result, children tend to dismiss occupations that are considered appropriate for the other sex. In stage three, orientation to social valuation (ages 9 to 13), children rule out low-status occupations as preferences. As Gottfredson (1996) puts it, "They reject occupational alternatives that seem inconsistent with those new elements of self" (p. 193). Stage four is characterized as an orientation to the internal unique self beginning at age 14. Individuals gain self-awareness and project self, sex role, and social class into their perceptions of vocational aspirations.

Self-concept development is not a static phenomenon but, rather, an ongoing process, which changes sometimes gradually and sometimes abruptly as people and situations change. In elementary school, children experience for the first time many aspects of existence in an adult world, such as competition and expectations of productive performance. In play, they interact with peers and also assume roles in supervised and unsupervised situations. Self-esteem for some will be enhanced through academic achievement, whereas others will experience both positive and negative feedback in peer socialization activities. Enhanced self-esteem encourages development of personal ideas and opinions of a positive nature; accurate self-concepts contribute to career maturity (Super, 1990). We observe development by stages and required tasks discussed next.

Development by Stages and Tasks

Stage theorists have concentrated on developmental patterns of accomplishments, events, and physiological and sociological changes in human development. During the transition process from one stage to another, developmental tasks provide a description of requirements or actions that are necessary to pass successfully through a stage of development. This perspective suggests a foundation for building effective career-related programs.

The developmental tasks expected of students before leaving the sixth grade reveal a set of physical and academic skills, social role development, and personalized values. Almost all of these tasks can be related to Super's (1990) concept of career development tasks (see chapter 2). For example, during the growth stage (to age 14), according to Super's scheme of developmental stages and tasks, individuals go through numerous experiential learning activities while developing greater self-awareness. Directed experiences in elementary school that promote physical and academic growth, interpersonal relationships with members of the same and the opposite sexes, and self-concept development are components of career development. Students who fail to achieve the developmental tasks could require special attention and direction.

Erikson (1963) suggested that the stage of development from ages 6 to 11 emphasizes industriousness; that is, children learn that productivity brings recognition and reward. In Erikson's view, children develop a sense of industriousness through their accomplishments, but they also can be intimidated by the requirements of success and develop a sense of inferiority. Expressing success through academic achievement, for example, is a major contributor to establishing industriousness in work-role and self-concept development (self-efficacious thinking). A sense of inferiority at this stage of development, however, calls for individualized intervention strategies.

Differences in growth and physiological changes between girls and boys in elementary school greatly influence social relationships and emerging self-perceptions. Learning appropriate masculine or feminine roles, according to Kail and Cavanaugh (2014), among others, precludes greater equality between sexes, especially in occupational behavior. Particularly important are perceptions of appropriate behavior patterns—that is, patterns regarded as acceptable for a given sex. Sex-role stereotyping is fostered through observation and imitation of male and female models. Other influences come through textbooks, other books, and popular television programs that describe and depict differences in rules for boys and girls. In family, discussed next, relationships are integral in the development process of children.

The Family as a System

The family is conceptualized here as a social system. Any system, whether a corporation, a city government, or a family, comprises interdependent elements that have interrelated functions and share some common goals. From this perspective, we view individuals in families as interconnected elements, each of whom contributes to the functioning of the whole. Thus, we cannot wholly understand the system by focusing on the component parts because each is affected by every other part; the relationships of those parts result in a larger coherent entity. Families are viewed as composites of many factors, such as genetic heritage from parents that are passed on to their children, and members share common experiences and develop common perspectives of the future.

The family system is embedded in larger social systems. The nuclear family, most common in the United States, consists of husband/father, wife/mother, and at least one child. The extended family, the most common form around the world, is one in which parents and their children live with other kin. The sequences of changes in families are referred to as *family life cycles* (Sigelman & Rider, 2009; Zastrow & Kirst-Ashman, 2013).

In this respect, the family itself is also a developing organism of roles and relationships that occur over the family life cycle (Kail & Cavanaugh, 2014; Shaffer & Kipp, 2014). Among others, Rowland (1991) and Shaffer and Kipp (2014) point out that an increasing number of people do not experience the traditional family life cycle; social changes have altered the makeup of the typical family in a changing world. Sigelman and Rider (2009) suggest that the following trends of change in family systems alter the quality of family experience:

1. *More single adults.* Although more adults are staying single, more than 90% of today's young adults are expected to marry eventually.
2. *Postponement of marriage.* More adults are delaying marriage. The average age at first marriage for men is 26 and for women, 24.
3. *Fewer children.* The average number of children in U.S. families is 1.8. Adults are waiting longer to have children, and increasing numbers of young women are choosing to remain childless.
4. *More women working.* About 12% of married women with children under age 6 worked outside the home in 1950; the figure increased by the early 1990s to 57%, and to 62% in 2000.
5. *More divorce.* As many as 4 in 10 newlyweds are expected to divorce.
6. *More single-parent families.* A growing number of children live with only their mothers and a much smaller percentage live only with their fathers.
7. *More children living in poverty.* The increasing number of single-parent families has led to the increase in numbers of impoverished children. Today, nearly 1 in 5 children in the United States live in homes below the poverty level.
8. *More remarriages.* Most divorced individuals are remarrying. About 25% of U.S. children will spend some time in a reconstituted family, usually consisting of a parent, a stepparent, and children from another marriage.
9. *More years without children.* Adults are spending more of their later years without children in their homes for the following reasons: Some who divorce do not remarry, people are living longer, and couples bear children in a shorter time span.
10. *More multigeneration families.* Because people tend to live longer, more children establish relationships with grandparents, and some with great-grandparents. Parent–child relationships last longer, some for 50 years or more.

In addition, McWhirter et al. (2013, p. 6) report the following:

- African American and Latino children are disproportionately poor. Those in poverty were 1 in 10 White (11%), 1 in 3 Black (35%), and 1 in 3 Hispanic (31%).
- In 2008, 27% of children in the United States (20.2 million) lived in families where no parent had full-time, year-round employment. More than a half million were living away from their families in foster care, generally prompted by neglect

or abuse. In 2008, 1.4 million teenagers between the ages 16 and 19 were not in school, working, or enrolled in school; African American, American Indian, and Latino teens were more than likely to be in this situation than were Asian or White young people.

- In 2010, more than a million teenagers were not in school and had not graduated from high school.

These trends of change in family systems and a large increase of children in poverty pose some crucial questions concerning career development. For example, will perceptions of life roles, including the work role, be altered? What impact will family transitions have on career development? Several researchers found that some aspects of men's behaviors in the home appear crucial to a child's developing self-concepts. Moreover, fathers in dual-earner families are likely to model less stereotypic behaviors, thus providing children with a more positive role of being involved in parenting. Also, observing women as economically independent and as having more choices and opportunities influences children's perceptions of what women can do and become. The point is that although these trends likely may have negative effects on images that children form about career and life roles, counselors have to remain aware of potential causal factors that contribute to and influence career development in these rapidly changing times (Galliano, 2003; Zastrow & Kirst-Ashman, 2013).

In their study of parent–child relations, Roe (1956) and Roe and Lunneborg (1990) stand out as pioneers in directing considerable attention to the developmental period of early childhood. Super (1990) projected the homemaker role as a major life role in the life-span, life-space approach to career. In the late 1990s, Gottfredson's (1996) treatise on sex-role orientation emphasized the role of family influence. Mitchell and Krumboltz (1996) suggested that environmental conditions and events are factors that influence career paths.

In sociological perspectives on work and career development, family effects on career development are considered a major variable: "The focus is on how family structure (intact, not intact) and maternal work roles influence development of work-related attitudes and choices of youth" (Hotchkiss & Borow, 1996, p. 284). Goldenberg and Goldenberg (2013), Berns (2004), and Matlin (2004), among others, continue to emphasize the family's influence on career- and life-role development. The factors reported earlier about the serious problems children and teenagers experience suggest that much more attention should focus on the career development of all children, especially children of different cultures.

Many other factors of parental actions and behaviors—such as parents' expectations for their children's success and parents' perceptions of their children's competence, interests, skills, and activities (Eccles, 1993)—are potential causal factors of career development. These examples, among others, suggest that more emphasis should be given to the study of familial variables to determine the extent which these variables affect career development. As we progress in the 21st century, we are encountering a different world in which traditional family systems have been altered, transformed, and reconstituted. Further, determining the extent to which variables such as single parents, dual-worker parents, divorce, and remarriage shape career development is a challenge for professionals from several academic disciplines. Changes in family systems suggest that career development also might be changing its course. To fully delineate career development, the career counseling profession will likely require a closer alliance with other academic disciplines that view the work role as a pervasive variable in the lives of current and future generations.

Culturally Diverse Families

Counselors have to be sensitive to the values and traditions of culturally diverse families. Significant diversity among ethnic groups greatly contributes to attitudes, values, behavior patterns, and acceptable roles of family members. A historical continuity of unique roles by ethnic groups shapes family identities. Ethnicity, therefore, is a powerful driving force in determining the rules, rituals, and esprit de corps of family members. Understanding the family context provides clues for each individual's unique development. The point is made several times in this text that there are significant differences within groups. This position is especially noteworthy when counseling members of culturally diverse groups. Counselors are to remain alert to a client's unique social system of rules and roles of her or his ethnic group. We can expect to find clients who have different levels and degrees of assimilation into dominant middle-class society. Some will maintain their family roles, whereas others may alter their views of traditional roles. In essence, all families are not alike. The roles and rules of family life may differ from culture to culture and family to family (Ashford & Lecroy, 2013).

The work role of culturally diverse individuals is especially shaped by differing worldviews. In collectivist societies of Africans, Asians, and Hispanics, it is expected and accepted that all members of a family contribute to its welfare and survival; individual aspirations are secondary. Consequently, providing career counseling approaches that include family and family needs are often most effective. Therefore, counselors may find it productive to also discuss an individual's career concerns with some family members.

In Asian and Hispanic families, husbands are typically the head of the family and the family usually maintains strong traditional gender roles, including stereotypical male–female relationships. There are more women who are head of the family in African American homes and who assume the role of primary breadwinner. Behavior, conduct, and family roles in most culturally diverse groups are also influenced by religious issues. All of these factors can affect an individual family member's approach to work roles. To put their counseling needs in perspective, some problems that members of culturally diverse families have and will face are listed, adapted from Goldenberg and Goldenberg (2008). These can serve as a checklist when evaluating potential conflicts with members of culturally diverse families.

Effects of poverty (poor housing, lack of transportation, and health care)

Country of origin (language barrier, work-role perceptions, and view of government)

Circumstances of immigration (political oppression and lack of trust for governmental agencies)

Degree of acculturation (worldviews, conflicting messages of appropriate behavior, and perception of work role)

Spiritual beliefs (family roles, health care issues, and social activities)

Skin color (discrimination and exclusion from some work roles)

Feelings of powerlessness (lack of direction and difficulty adjusting to new environment)

Poor self-esteem (depression, restriction of job choice, and interpersonal relationships)

Lack of trust of institutions (resist using agencies for assistance)

English fluency (restricted job choice and limited personal contacts)

Intergenerational family conflicts (conflicts over parents' view of appropriate behavior and contemporary views of the host country)

Lack of support in community (isolation and restricted community involvement)

Discrimination (feelings of oppression, isolation, and restricted career choice)

Socioeconomic status (exclusion of opportunities in life, work, and leisure)

In sum, families in cultural transition may experience stress associated with coping with the demands and mores of the dominant society. On the one hand, for new immigrants the first priority is to find work that will maintain their family. Many individual family members do not view career choice as their own. On the other hand, many culturally diverse families have resided in this country for several generations and have adopted some of the dominant society's rules and roles. They continue to struggle for acceptance and opportunities for career advancement and recognition. Some still face discrimination and rejection from the dominant society. They often need support and direction for finding solutions to real-life problems. In dealing with complex issues of culturally diverse families, counselors may assume the role of teacher, coach, adviser, advocate, problem solver, and even role model (Goldenberg & Goldenberg, 2013; McWhirter et al., 2013).

Counseling Children from Different Cultures

Beginning in chapter 3, various approaches to counseling multicultural groups were illustrated. In chapter 9, which was devoted entirely to multicultural counseling, the point was made repeatedly that individuals from different cultures may share some common beliefs, but the significant differences within groups suggest that each client be treated as an individual. Counselors, however, should be aware of culture-specific traits, beliefs, and customs from which counselors can vary their approaches. For instance, emotional boundaries of closeness of relationships are most difficult to observe. Indo-Chinese, for example, discuss problems only with family members (Matsumoto & Juang, 2013; Thompson, Rudolph, & Henderson, 2004). In this context, counseling relationships might have to be delineated carefully to client and family.

Of utmost importance, counselors must evaluate the client's level of acculturation when determining how counseling will proceed. For instance, a fifth-generation Latina girl might aspire to a professional career, whereas a Latina immigrant female might be conditioned to consider her role as only that of a homemaker. The point here is not to stereotype individuals because of their cultural backgrounds but, rather, to remain alert to modifying counseling to meet individual needs. In essence, counselors often might have to offer nontraditional means of services to some clients. Children who have been affected negatively by racism and oppression, for instance, might react positively to spiritually oriented counseling programs to gain self-respect. Counselors may find that African Americans turn to their church as a resource for helping (Berns, 2004; McWhirter et al., 2013).

People of color can be reluctant to seek counseling because of a lack of understanding of its purpose and perhaps fear of its consequences. Native American children might feel that going to a counselor is a sign of weakness (LaFromboise & Jackson, 1996). Some children from Asian American cultures might view going to a counselor as shameful and embarrassing or as an action indicative of failure (Matsumoto & Juang, 2013; Ponterotto et al., 2010). In general, children from different cultures have different worldviews from which they interpret relationships. Some have a need to avoid loss of face; others prefer subtle forms of communication (Matsumoto & Juang, 2013; Pedersen et al., 2008). Clearly, it is essential that counselors learn about culture-specific variables in the lives of children from different cultures (Shaffer & Kipp, 2014).

In sum, the elementary school counselor is challenged with the responsibility of developing and promoting pervasive career development programs that include specific competencies. These competencies foster self-knowledge and introduce educational and occupational exploration and career planning, among other goals. In the process, students discover the relationship between education and work roles and learn more about themselves and the interrelationships of all life roles. Teachers, counselors, and parents are to foster positive attitudes toward work.

Ideally, students become actively involved in their own career development and learn to involve their families in the process. Family members can serve as representatives of certain occupations, but, more importantly, can support and reinforce student career-related activities. Finally, students learn that educational competencies are necessary to survive in an ever-changing work environment (Herring, 1998; Rathus, 2014). This process is viewed as a joint effort of school personnel, parents, and community. In this context, the elementary school counselor is a teacher, counselor, consultant, planner, and an expert resource person. Some example concepts are discussed next, from the National Standards for School Counseling Programs [(American School Counselors Association) and the National Career Development Guidelines (NCDG)].

Examples of the ASCA National Standards for School Counseling Programs

The American School Counselors Association (2003) national standards are divided into three major developmental areas: Academic Development, Career Development, and Personal–Social Development. Under the major heading of Career Development, we find three subheadings: (1) Students will acquire the skills to investigate the world of work to relation to knowledge of self and to make informed career decisions; (2) students will employ strategies to achieve future career goals with success and satisfaction; and (3) students will understand the relationship between personal qualities, education, and the world of work. Under each of the subheadings, competencies are listed for accomplishing the goals and objectives of each subhead (see appendix G).

The National Career Development Guidelines have similar goals and objectives. Both sets of standards stress educational achievement, personal social development, and similar elements of career development among other factors. What is most important to observe, however, are the career development processes considered to be major goals of educational outcomes in schools. In developing local standards, school systems can make use of both sets of standards when tailoring their career development programs to meet local needs.

National Career Development Association Guidelines (NCDG)

The National Career Development Association Guidelines (NCDG) (2005) is to be used as career development goals for children, youth, and adults. Goals are grouped in three broad domains: Personal Social Development, Educational Achievement, and Career Management. Indicators providing evidence that an individual has reached a specific goal are also included. The major purpose of the guidelines is to assist educators, career professionals, and community leaders develop high-quality career development programs. Under each of the broad-domain goals, indicators describe specific knowledge, skills, and abilities related to one's development. The three stages of learning are as follows: the knowledge stage (K), the application stage (A), and the reflection stage (R). An example of an indicator for the knowledge stage could be K1 or the first level of the knowledge stage for a specific goal. Examples of specific goals are as follows: (1) identify your interests, likes, and dislikes and (2) demonstrate behavior and decisions that reflect your interests, likes, and dislikes.

To fully appreciate the NCDG, one must have a working knowledge of all levels of indicators, such as the knowledge stage (K), the application stage (A), and the reflection stage (R). The complete guidelines and indicators can be found in appendix H.

In the pages that follow, I offer some specific suggestions for enhancing the career development of children in the elementary school, applying group strategies, but first I provide the elementary school counselor with a brief overview of types of developmental disorders.

Types of Developmental Disorders

Developmental disorders usually appear early in a child's development. Thus, parents are usually, but not always, informed about which skills are disrupted by a given disorder. The purpose of this discussion is to inform counselors about attention deficit hyperactivity disorder (ADHD), some learning disorders, and pervasive developmental disorders such as autistic disorder and intellectual disability. Although most of the developmental disorders discussed here are usually addressed in special education programs, counselors may have some involvement with children experiencing symptoms of developmental disorders. This discussion of developmental disorders, however, should be viewed only as an introduction to the disorders discussed here and as a source of information that can be used for referral. Counselors are to be prepared to refer parents to a child development specialist for diagnosis and assistance. Research designed to provide answers to causes and treatment of developmental disorders is ongoing and intense.

Table 15.1 provides an overview of types of developmental disorders. A brief explanation of the disorders in this table should suggest to the counselor that the severity of developmental disorders in early childhood requires the assistance of highly trained professionals, including medical doctors who are specialists in this field. Biological factors including the involvement of genetics in many of the causes of developmental disorders suggest that there is much more to be learned about child development. In the meantime, informed counselors are aware of their limitations but also are prepared to recognize symptoms of disorders suggesting that a referral is necessary. In cases involving children who are mentally challenged, counselors are often involved in establishing training programs that eventually can help children become productive workers.

In sum, children with ADHD have deficits that severely disrupt their academic activities and social interactions. Boys are more likely to be diagnosed with this disorder. Children with this disorder have difficulty in sustaining attention in most activities. They have a tendency to be highly overactive, such as quickly jumping out of their chair or climbing on a table. Children with ADHD have difficulty

Table 15.1	**Types of Developmental Disorders**
Attention deficit hyperactivity disorder (ADHD)	Impulsive behavior that is disruptive. Children are hyperactive, inattentive, and impulsive.
Learning disorders	Reading, writing, and math disorders.
Communication disorders	Stuttering, expressive language disorders. Selective mutism—failure to speak in certain situations. Tic disorders—involuntary movements and vocalization.
Pervasive developmental disorders	Significant impairment in socialization and communications.
Autistic disorder	Restricted patterns of behavior, interests, and activities.
Rett's disorder	Normal early development followed by deteriorating motor skills and constant hand wringing.
Intellectual disability	Intellectual functioning impaired ranging from mild to profound.

SOURCE: *Essentials of Abnormal Psychology*, 6th ed., by V. Durand & D. Barlow (Belmont, CA: Wadsworth Cengage Learning, 2013).

spending more than 5 minutes on a task; they often do not seem to listen when spoken to directly; they do not follow-through on instructions; they are easily distracted, squirm in their seats, and often talk excessively (American Psychiatric Association, 2000; Rathus, 2014). These few examples of behavior, among many others, indicate the disruptive nature of children with ADHD.

Children with learning disorders are most deficient in subjects such as reading, writing, and mathematics. Learning disorders cannot be related to intelligence or other impairments such as poor sight or hearing. What is being suggested here is that children with learning disorders do not have other conditions that could explain their poor performance, such as sensory impairment or inadequate instructions. Children with learning disorders all share genetic, neurobiological, and environmental factors that affect their learning. In 2007 it was believed that approximately 6 million children were diagnosed as having a specific learning disorder (Altarac & Saroha, 2007).

Communication disorders are closely related to learning disorders. Stuttering or a disturbance in speech fluency and other problems with speech can be debilitating. According to Kroll and Bertchman (2005), stuttering may be caused by multiple brain pathways and genetic influences. The causes of limited speech or selective mutism involved in social interactions may be related to unknown psychological factors and perhaps to inner ear infections (Durand & Barlow, 2013).

Tic disorders include head twitching, vocalization, and grunts that occur in rapid succession. The causes of involuntary movements and vocalization are not fully established but are suspected to involve strong genetic components that are unknown.

All of the pervasive developmental disorders include problems with language, socialization, and cognition (Durand, 2005). These problems are pervasive in that they affect individuals over the life span. Significant impairments in social interactions and in communications associated with autistic behavior are among the significant problems of all disorders in this group.

Symptoms of autistic disorder include failure to develop relationships, repetitive language, hand- or finger-flopping or twisting, odd whole-body movements, and preoccupation with objects (American Psychiatric Association, 2000). Complex whole-body movements are often involved in nonfunctional routines and rituals.

Rett's disorder has an unusual development in that it takes place after an apparent normal developmental period. This disorder affects girls primarily. Symptoms include severe intellectual disabilities and impaired motor skills similar to those experienced by individuals who have been diagnosed as autistic. Fortunately, this disorder is rare (Durand & Barlow, 2013).

Intellectual disability includes several levels as follows:

Mild	IQ level	50–55 to approximately 70
Moderate		35–40 to 50–55
Severe		20–25 to 35–40
Profound		below 20 or 25

Fortunately, severe forms of intellectual disability are relatively uncommon; in fact, profound, severe, and moderate forms of intellectual disability total about 10% of all cases. Many individuals who are classified as having a moderate intellectual disability can support themselves by working in sheltered workshops under close supervision. The approximately 90% of individuals who are diagnosed as having a mildly intellectual disability go to school and can learn many academic skills, though at a lower rate than the average student. Many of these students also get jobs after they are given special training to learn vocational and social skills (Kail & Cavanaugh, 2014).

Ideally, career-related objectives and goals should be integrated and infused in classroom instruction. It is, therefore, essential that classroom teachers support the development of career-related competencies as integral in their instructional program. Elementary school counselors should be prepared to assist classroom teachers in creating career-related modules including supplementary materials and to serve as proactive consultants for community resources. What we have here is a need for elementary school counselors who have a good background in curriculum development and teaching methods. An overarching goal is to focus on classroom learning activities that address vocational competencies and foster career development. Within this context, elementary school counselors become a part of curriculum development through consultation. Thus, counselors' ability to work with classroom teachers is essential. To enhance the effectiveness of career-related programs, counselors should have a working knowledge of effective classroom instruction and supplementary materials that address specific career development goals. Some strategies follow.

Representative Strategies for Classroom Activities

The competencies below are designed as strategies to promote self-knowledge, educational and occupational exploration, and career planning. Competencies provide specific objectives that counselors and teachers use as indicators of a student's comprehension of a strategy or tasks that represent mastery and understanding of career development goals. Teachers and counselors alike are to develop strategies to enhance career development. In some cases, community resources also can be used. Representative examples of specific classroom activities follow.

Self-Knowledge Strategies

1. In a group discussion, ask students to use open-ended sentences, such as,
   I'm happy when _____.
   I'm sad when _____.
   I'm afraid when _____.
2. Have students compile a list or draw pictures of people they talked to during the week. In groups, discuss types of relationships that students have with the people they talked to.
3. Ask students to describe a friend and then themselves. Discuss and describe individual differences.
4. Play "Who Am I?" with one student playing a role and others trying to guess the role.
5. Have students select magazine pictures of events, places, and people that interest them. Share interests.
6. Ask students to summarize ways in which individuals may be described. Then, ask students to select and describe self-descriptions.
7. Ask students to answer the following questions in writing or orally: What do I do well? What goals do I have? What do I do poorly? Who am I like? What makes me different from others?
8. Have students make lists of "Things I like" and "Things I don't like." Compile the lists and discuss the variety of interests.
9. Form a "Who Am I?" group and meet once a week, during which each student describes a personal characteristic of an individual who performs a specific job. Compile a list for future discussions.
10. Ask students to list several interests and to describe how they became interested in an activity.

Educational and Occupational Exploration Strategies

1. Arrange a display of workers' hats that represent jobs in the community. Have each student select a hat that indicates a job he or she would like to do someday and explain why the job is appealing.
2. Assign students to develop a list of skills for their favorite jobs and describe how these skills are learned.
3. Ask each student to pretend that a friend wants a certain job, and ask each to describe the kinds of skills the friend would need.
4. Have students develop a list of activities that their parents do at home and have them identify those that require math, reading, and writing.
5. Have students make a list of school subjects and identify jobs that use the skills learned from the subjects.

6. Refer to a list of occupations and have students describe what kind of person might like a given occupation.
7. Have students make a list of occupations involved in producing a loaf of bread.
8. Ask students to find a picture from a magazine or newspaper that depicts a woman and a man in nontraditional jobs.
9. Have students interview their parents about their work roles, and discuss these roles with the group.
10. Ask each student to adopt the identity of a worker and list work roles. Discuss how work has a personal meaning for every individual.

Career Planning Strategies

1. Ask students to make a list of jobs/occupations they would use to describe their neighbors or acquaintances. Share with others.
2. Have students identify the kinds of people who work in a selected list of occupations. Emphasize likenesses and differences.
3. In a self-discovery group, discuss how people have different interests and enjoy different or similar activities.
4. Have students describe how workers in different activities are affected by weather.
5. Ask students to collect newspaper and magazine photos of different people and describe likenesses and differences.
6. Have students identify workers who visit their homes. Identify differences of work and occupations.
7. Assign students to write a short paragraph answering the question, "If you could be anyone in the world, who would it be?" Follow with a discussion.
8. Divide the class into groups of boys and girls, and ask each group to make a list of jobs girls can and cannot do. Compare lists and discuss how women are capable of performing most jobs.
9. Have students describe in writing, orally, or both "someone I would like to work with." Make a list of positive characteristics that each student describes.
10. Discuss how people work together and demonstrate using the example of three people building a doghouse together. What would each person do?

Career Infusion

The idea of integrating career development concepts into existing curricula is referred to as *infusion*. This technique requires that teachers expand their current educational objectives to include career-related activities and subjects. For example, teaching decision-making skills can be infused with traditional academic courses. Planning a class project with a designated time limit involves certain decisions, such as specifying the goals of the project, determining the possible approaches to the project, selecting the best one, and actually following through. Decision-making and planning skills are applicable to many—if not all—subjects and should be consciously taught as skills to be developed and refined. Infusion of career objectives requires that formal attention be given to career-related skills and tasks.

The following career infusion module for elementary schools (Box 15.3), by Healy and Quinn (1977), is designed to improve career awareness. This module was developed in the 1970s during the heyday of the career education movement and remains viable as a learning module today (economic conditions will affect the use of this module).

BOX 15.3

Career Infusion Module

Subject: Math, reading, language

Concept: Career awareness

Answering a Job Advertisement

Rationale: Students should have an understanding of the jobs described in want ads and be able to develop an awareness of various occupations. Students also should learn about the requirements of various occupations and draw conclusions of whether they would like to work in the environment described by a want ad and during follow-up.

Objective: Students will describe in writing how different occupations are described in terms of salary, hours of work, training, and educational requirements.

Description:

1. Discuss various ways people find out about openings in the job market.
2. Present a page from the local newspaper with want ads listed.
3. Have students select three careers in which they are interested and research the requirements, salary, training, and education necessary for the job being advertised.
4. Have the students write a description of the job that appeals to them the most and explain their choices.
5. Have students share their findings with classmates in a 3–5 minute report.

Where activity occurs: Classroom

Personnel required: Teacher

Cost: Cost of newspaper

Time: Discussion, one-quarter period; research and select careers, one and one-quarter periods; share with classmates, one-quarter period

Resources: Newspaper

Evaluation measures: Oral and written report

SOURCE: *Project Cadre: A Cadre Approach to Career Education Infusion,* by C. C. Healy and O. H. Quinn, 1977. Unpublished manuscript. Reprinted by permission.

This module provides rationale, objectives, description, location of activity, personnel required, cost, time, resources, and evaluation measures.

Resources for Classroom Strategies

Another essential part of the elementary school counselor's role is that of keeping up-to-date career resources that effectively address career development goals. Materials that provide interactive programs can be highly effective. For example, an interactive career CD-ROM program for grades three and up combines animation, photography, voice interviews, and music. Included in the package is a simple self-assessment that matches answers by referring students to occupational clusters.

In another resource, students from grades two to six can take a video field trip in their classroom. Topics might include Timber! From Logs to Lumber, The Fire Station, The Airport, The Dairy, and others. For many such activities, complete lesson plans are available along with suggested additional activities. Also, the *Children's Dictionary of Occupations* is available on CD-ROM and in print. Student's activity packages for these publications are opportunities for interactive participation.

These examples suggest that an abundance of relevant materials is available to assist teachers and counselors in meeting the goals of career development in the elementary school. The materials mentioned here are published by

MERIDIAN Educational Corporation

200 American Metro Blvd

Suite 124

Hamilton, NJ 08619

www.cust.sev.film.com

800-727-5507

Another important resource is:

Center on Education and Work

964 Educational Sciences Building

1025 W. Johnson St.

Madison, WI 53706-1796

800-446-0399

Fax 608-262-9197

www.cew.wisc.edu

cewmail@education.wisc.edu

These facilities have numerous resources for teachers, counselors, administrators, and employers which are designed for student programs for K–12, college level, and for adults. They also sponsor an annual series of career conferences designed to assist with implementing career-related programs.

Implications for Career Development Programs in Elementary Schools

The recommended areas of career development for students in elementary school, combined with other research reported, suggest many ideas that can be applied to career guidance programs in elementary schools. A representative list follows.

1. Self-concepts begin to form in early childhood. Because of the influence of self-concept formation on career development, strong evidence supports directed experiences in enhancing self-concept.
2. An important aspect of career development is to build an understanding of strengths and limitations. Learning to identify and express strengths and limitations is a good way to build a foundation for self-understanding.
3. Elementary school children imitate role models in the home and school. Parents and teachers alike can provide children with positive role models through precept and example.
4. Children learn to associate work roles by sexual stereotyping at an early age. Exposure to career information that discourages sex-role stereotyping will broaden the range of occupations considered available by children of both sexes.
5. Community resources provide a rich source of career information, models, and exposure to a wide range of careers. Students from families whose parents did not attend high school have a special need for community opportunities.

6. Self-awareness counseling is a major goal of the growth stage in elementary schools. Methods used to enhance self-awareness encourage development of the ability to process and interpret information about self and others and about differences among people.

7. Learning to assume responsibility for decisions and actions has major implications for future career decisions. Some beginning steps include skill development that enables children to analyze situations, to identify people who can help them, and to seek assistance when needed.

8. Understanding the relationship between education and work is a key concept for enhancing career development. Skills learned in school and during out-of-school activities should be linked to work-related activities.

9. The idea that all work is important builds an understanding of why parents and others work. Reflection on the reasons for working fosters awareness that any productive worker should be respected.

10. Learning about occupations and about people who are actually involved in occupations builds an awareness of differences among people and occupations.

Summary

1. National standards for career development have been developed by the American School Counselors Association and the National Career Development Association.

2. Building support of parents, teachers, administrators, and members of the community is an important key to success.

3. Involving family members in career development activities can be very productive. Parents, teachers, and community leaders are to support career development learning activities. Children develop coping techniques—often referred to as resiliency—from caring parents, teachers, and members of their community.

4. Cognitive development learning activities include concrete experiences that promote the development of abstract conceptual operations. Information-processing strategies for children include the development of memory strategies. Learning by observation includes learning experiences involving work roles.

5. Elementary school students develop self-concepts as they focus on peers, teachers, important adults, and school requirements. Developmental tasks involve social development and personalized values.

6. Understanding one's family context provides clues for each individual's development. Families in cultural transitions are subject to experiencing stress. Changing trends in family systems introduce new and different career developmental tasks.

7. Counselors may be required to modify career-related programs for children from different cultures.

8. Types of developmental disorders among children include attention deficit hyperactivity disorders (ADHDs), learning disorders, autistic disorder, and intellectual disability.

9. Goals for elementary school students include awareness of self, knowledge of the diversity of the world of work, relationships between school performance, career-choice options, and development of a positive attitude toward work.

10. Career-related programs in elementary school require the development of model programs and carefully planned strategies for curriculum integration. Integrating career development concepts into existing curricula is referred to as infusion.

11. Elementary school counselors assume multiple roles such as teacher, coach, consultant, team facilitator, career information specialist, and advocate for community involvement.
12. Career-related programs are considered to be an essential part of elementary school education.

Supplementary Learning Exercises

1. Defend the following statement with examples to prove your point: Individuals have a profound adaptive capacity at various stages of development.
2. Construct at least two activities/strategies in which concrete experiences promote abstract conceptual operations.
3. Construct at least two activities/strategies of observational learning that would promote career development of elementary school-age children.
4. Survey a sample of elementary school students to determine their perception of appropriate career roles for their sex.
5. Describe your development from childhood. Identify significant transitions and their influences on your career.
6. Give as many reasons as you can for the significance of Roe's needs theory of career development for elementary school counseling.
7. Present several examples of how worldviews of children from different cultures affect their career decisions.
8. Explain how human development and career development are interrelated. Give at least five examples.
9. Why is it important to involve parents and other community members in the elementary school career guidance program? Give examples.
10. Using one or more of the implications for career counseling in the elementary school, identify specific career guidance needs and develop activities and strategies to meet them.

16

Career-Related Programs for Career Development in Middle School

CHAPTER HIGHLIGHTS

- The psychological impact of puberty

- The relevance of peer relationships

- Career development goals and competencies

- Learning strategies for career development

- Stages of career development

- Becoming resilient

Middle school has long been associated with the general turmoil surrounding students who are in the process of bridging the gap between childhood and adolescence. No doubt, onset of adolescence creates potential problems for most individuals who go through it, but one should continue to focus on individual reactions to stressful times in the career development process. I am not suggesting that we dismiss the research concerning the struggles associated with stages of life during the middle school years. On the contrary, counselors are to focus on uncovering numerous potential problems that are defined by evidence-based research. I am also suggesting that counselors will likely find different levels and combinations of concerns among individual clients; situational experiences can be interpreted differently. As with most groups, individuals experience reactions to potential problems similar to their cohorts, but one also must be cognizant of different reactions within groups, as well as differences between groups. What I am suggesting here is that dysfunctional thinking, for example, cannot be simply dismissed as something that happens during middle school and most students will get through it. More importantly, one is to find solutions to developing problems that could have serious consequences. The severity of the individual's concerns should be evaluated and addressed.

Counselors should not overestimate or underestimate the severity of concerns that children in middle school bring to counseling. The process of moving from childhood to adolescence is a period of time that heightens one's vulnerability to some forms of psychological disorders. Most in middle school will learn to cope with factors such as, for example, physical maturation, emerging cognitive abilities, social demands, and more complex school settings. One would suspect that some clients will experience anxiety and/or mild depression, as well as threats to their feelings of well-being. But, for the most part, the majority of students will come through this period remarkably well; a minority of students, however, can experience serious psychological problems. What is suggested here is that counselors are to carefully evaluate personal problems in terms of long-term consequences. Students in middle school are not too young to have serious personal problems (Sigelman & Rider, 2009).

Potential Problems for Middle School Students

I limit my discussion of potential problems in this section to the psychological impact of puberty, peer relationships, and identity issues. The important issues of family relationships and types of developmental disorders were discussed in the previous chapter. The three special concerns discussed here are among the many issues that can limit and influence an individual's career development.

Psychological Impact of Puberty

"One of the first signs of puberty is rapid physical growth accompanied by types of physical changes that mark the transition from childhood to young adulthood" (Kail & Cavanaugh, 2010, p. 294). A 10-year-old male, for example, may gain 5 to 7 pounds and can grow 2 to 3 inches over a relatively short period of time. During peak growth periods, a girl may gain up to 14 pounds in a year and a boy up to 17 pounds. Girls typically start their adolescent growth spurt earlier than boys. At around the age of 12, girls are often taller than boys and also appear to be more mature. Body fat also increases during growth spurts, but more rapidly in girls. It should surprise no one that one's appearance becomes a most important factor in the daily lives of both boys and girls in early adolescence (Sigelman & Rider, 2009).

Body images become the center of attention! Girls are particularly affected by their appearance and often compare their appearance with peers. Boys are also concerned about their appearance and they especially idealize a strong muscular body (Carlson-Jones, 2004). Accompanying and/or preceding sexual maturity are dramatic bodily changes, such as increased muscle tissue and body stature, which permit the adolescent to perform adult physical tasks for the first time. In middle school and continuing in high school, concern for appearance reaches its peak as girls compare themselves to movie and television stars, females appearing in commercials, and professional models. Boys use the standards of physical strength and facial and body hair for judging early maturity (Kail & Cavanaugh, 2014; Mendle, Turkheimer, & Emery, 2007). Feeling comfortable within the dominant peer group is highly related to being judged as "grown-up" or mature.

Research studies that followed the development of girls over several years have shown that early maturing girls often lack self-confidence, are less popular, and more than likely will experience depression and/or become involved in antisocial behavior. The research results of early maturing boys have been mixed; that is, for some boys early maturation is desirable in that they tend to date more often and are proud of their physical development. Other studies suggest that some boys would prefer to mature when most other boys do—they are somewhat stressed about early maturity (Mendle et al., 2007; Rathus, 2014).

Reflecting on sexual maturity, Cal related the following incident:

I wanted to do everything I could to be grown up, but I was just a little twerp. I even tried to imitate how men walked. I guess I was 12 or 13 when I smoked my first cigarette. Even though I coughed until I almost choked, I kept on smoking that cigarette! Yes sir, I wanted to be one of those "cool cats" with all the know-how. But the worst of it was P.E. I didn't want to undress in front of anybody. I made up all kinds of excuses until the locker room was clear, and then I went home and showered. You know, it was important then to be accepted by my friends. I guess I ended up being liked by most of them. Now when I look back, it seems we were all trying to fool each other.

Quiang, an early-maturing middle school student, reflected on her experiences:

All of a sudden it seemed I had outgrown everyone—especially the boys. Some of the girls seemed as physically mature as I was, but they usually acted uneasy around me, and I certainly felt awkward around them. It was during this time that I made friends with some older girls. As far as the boys were concerned, there were mixed feelings. The older boys didn't accept me because I was "too young," while the younger ones were too little for me. I just felt out of place for a few years until everybody caught up.

The effects of early and late sexual maturity provide a frame of reference for counseling intervention. Evidence suggests that early-maturing males are more than likely to receive approval and reinforcement for their behavior among male peer groups and adults. Late-maturing girls also enjoy acceptance and popularity (Rathus, 2014; Sigelman & Rider, 2009). Simmons and Blyth (1987) confirm early- and late-maturity differences and their related benefits and costs, and they report some additional special effects:

- Early-maturing boys had more dates and dated more often than did late-maturing boys. Furthermore, early-maturing males were more positive about physical development and athletic abilities.
- Early-maturing girls had poorer grades in school and had more discipline problems. They were also more negative about their physical development.

Sexual maturity may be one basis for differentiating career guidance activities. Late-maturing males and early-maturing girls might experience a greater need for counseling intervention than their peers. It seems that middle school and high school students benefit from guidance programs that inform them of the extent, type, and variation of physiological changes in early adolescence and that specifically address anxieties related to bodily changes (Kail & Cavanaugh, 2014; Sigelman & Rider, 2009; Williams & Currie, 2000).

Peer Relationships

For most people, close friends are easily remembered, especially those with whom one has shared secrets; good friends are to be treasured. It is generally agreed that good friends help one cope with the stresses of daily life even in middle school where understanding is most certainly needed. One can learn coping techniques from friends and find comfort in venting their personal problems. On the other hand, one can be misled by friends who persuade them it is okay, for example, to drink, smoke, or have sex. An overly aggressive friend can influence one to become overly aggressive also; friends can reinforce troubling behavior. Some have labeled such actions as peer pressure that has been a popular subject of influencing behavior during early adolescence; it is often characterized as a harmful force.

The good news is that not all teenagers are susceptible to peer influences. It appears that parenting style has a lot to do with those who resist the temptations of becoming involved in harmful behavior. Interestingly, parenting style that is less authoritative strongly influences teenagers to be less susceptible to peer pressure (Mounts & Steinberg, 1995). More recently, Rathus (2014) suggests that parents and peers exert influence in different ways. For example, adolescents tend to agree with parents on matters involving serious issues, such as moral principles and career goals, but are more likely to conform to peers' standards when it comes to clothing, music, hair styles, and speech patterns.

A most important factor in peer relationships is one's popularity and acceptance. Being rejected or neglected by one's peer group can be most devastating. Research on peer relationships suggests that popular children are liked by their peers, rejected children are not, controversial children are liked and disliked by their peers but without intensity, and neglected children are ignored. Research also suggests that the consequences of rejection by peers may have long-term consequences. Some teenagers who are rejected by peers may drop out of school and/or become involved in antisocial behavior (Cillessen & Rose, 2005; Hymel, Vailliancourt, McDougall, & Renshaw, 2004; McWhirter et al., 2013). The alert counselor will engage rejected peers with social skills training with the use of peer helpers. One's self-esteem is an important component in making optimal choices for the future.

Peer approval is a relevant factor for most students in middle school; in fact, it is reasonable to conclude that peer approval is not only important during middle school but also over the life span. What is also pertinent to development here is that they learn to build relationships with their cohorts and are reinforced for their efforts in numerous ways. They not only gain the support of cohorts but also learn the importance of relationships and how to go about creating them. They have become efficient in another most important role in life and at the same time have built a sense of self-efficacy that will enhance their ability to build relationships in the future.

Identity Issues

Adolescence is often described as a period of turmoil that is partly the result of numerous transitions from childhood. Continuity of development is, for some, sporadic and chaotic. The key characteristic of this stage of development, according to Erikson (1963), is the search for identity. During this transition stage, one subordinates childhood identifications and reaches for a different identity in a more complex set of conditions and circumstances. The major danger of this period is role confusion; thus, this stage is often designated "identity versus confusion." In Erikson's view, this is a critical period of development. As he put it:

> These new identifications are no longer characterized by the playfulness of childhood and the experimental zest of youth: with dire urgency they force the young individual into choices and decisions which will, with increasing immediacy, lead to commitments for life. (p. 155)

A young person unable to avoid role confusion might adopt what is referred to as a "negative identity," assuming forms of behavior that are in direct conflict with family and society. Those who develop a more appropriate sense of direction can find this experience positive, but for others, the negative identity can be maintained into adulthood. Identity diffusion, according to Erikson, often results in lack of commitment to a set of values and, subsequently, to occupations. Thus, many adolescents may react to career development programs as something they will commit to later and simply place a psychological moratorium on decision making until further options are explored. Excerpts from an interview with Ted illustrate this point:

TED: My parents want me here so that I can choose a career. They don't like it that I haven't picked one.

COUNSELOR: As I said, we should be able to help you, but first tell me about jobs or careers you have considered.

TED: I thought about a few, like the guy who takes pictures, but I don't really know what I want.

COUNSELOR: Tell me about your thoughts about photography.

TED: A photographer like Mr. Brown is not what I want to be. I guess I'd like to work for a magazine.

COUNSELOR: You mentioned Mr. Brown. What you don't like about his job?

TED: I don't want to take pictures of weddings and things like that. To tell the truth, I don't really know about what a photographer or any other worker does. I just wish my parents would leave me alone until I get into high school.

A young person unable to avoid role confusion might adopt what is referred to as a negative identity, assuming forms of behavior that could lead to long-lasting consequences. Those who develop a more appropriate sense of direction can find this experience as positive; for others, the negative identity is maintained throughout the school years and perhaps later in adulthood.

Identity development has also been approached by observing stages of development in the 1980s. The often quoted work of James Marcia (1980) includes the following stages:

> *Identity diffusion.* Individuals in this stage have given little thought to resolving identity issues—they have not gotten around to such questions as who am I and what will I do in the future.
>
> *Foreclosure.* Individuals in this stage have made premature commitments but have given little thought to the consequences of an alleged commitment.
>
> *Moratorium.* In this stage individuals are actively searching for answers to future commitments, but many are experiencing anxiety and are somewhat troubled about deciding about their future.
>
> *Identity development.* Individuals in this stage have made insightful considerations of identity issues and have made firm commitments to future goals and values.

What is suggested by Marcia is that the process underlying identity development requires adolescents to be proactive, to self-assess, and to use personal agency to work-through solutions for future commitments. This complex process suggests that one is to make mature decisions and assumptions; therefore, it should not be surprising to find that some adolescents will delay commitments while others will resist making any decisions altogether. In Marcia's scheme of identity development, one can expect to find that many adolescents will recycle through the different stages and in late adolescence shift between the moratorium and identity development stages several times before making a firm commitment to a career. Making a commitment is the result of a multidimensional process that involves the individual's personal traits as well as factors such as economic conditions and changing work rules and roles.

The more recent studies on identity development suggest that identity development is an ongoing process during adolescence and may extend into adulthood. Others have suggested that identity is in many respects a process that continues over the life span. Currently, more individuals are delaying a career commitment until they learn more about their abilities, interests, values, and changing work roles and work environments (Feldman, 2002). What is suggested here is that middle school students are to begin a series of learning interventions that will enhance self-knowledge and awareness, improve their knowledge of occupations, and provide them with assistance in developing strategies for career planning. Awareness of one's current values, interests, attitudes, and aptitudes, for example, can bolster efforts to continue one's development and avoid the crisis associated with stagnation. One may choose to know more about self and the world of work in order to form an identity.

A question that arises in our discussion at this time is: What are the important factors that can influence the development of an identity for students in middle school? This position suggests that we not only bolster awareness of our current traits as mentioned previously, but also must assist clients in developing self-esteem. Research indicates that a child's interests, abilities, and self-concept are what are referred to as *coupled*: Their self-esteem is bolstered when they are involved in activities in which they can excel, such as solving arithmetic problems. Their thoughts may go something like this: "I like to do math problems. Maybe I'll get a job that requires me to do math."

As we learned from our discussion of peer relationships, students seek the approval of their peers; their self-esteem is greatly affected by how their peers view them. Counselors and teachers who help middle school students with social interactions can make a major contribution to a student's self-esteem. Another factor that I discussed in the previous chapter concerns family relationships as an important element of self-esteem development. Not surprisingly, a child's self-worth is bolstered by warm and affectionate parents who are actively involved with them (Compton & Hoffman, 2013). Self-esteem is to be viewed as a significant characteristic in developing one's identity. While in middle school, students are in the process of a journey that may require assistance and guidance along the way. One should be encouraged to learn as much as possible about one's personal traits and characteristics, as well as about future opportunities concerning the fulfillment of all life roles.

Super (1990) and Crites and Savickas (1996) suggest strong relationships between identity and career commitment as variables of *career maturity*. Career maturity implies a stabilized identity that provides individuals with a framework for making career choices, a crystallized formation of self-perceptions, and developed skills. Career maturity is a continuous developmental process and presents specific identifiable characteristics and traits essential to career development. Some characteristics of career maturity are decisiveness and independence, knowledge of occupational information, and acquiring planning and decision-making skills. (Chapter 6 reviews career maturity inventories that provide specific information about other dimensions of career maturity.)

Cognitive Development and Learning

Cognitive development during early adolescence, according to Piaget and Inhelder (1969), is the transition from concrete operational thinking to formal thought—a gradual process beginning at approximately 11 years of age. During early adolescence, patterns of problem solving and planning are quite unsystematic. Near the end of middle school, however, the adolescent has the ability to deal with abstractions, form hypotheses in problem solving, and sort out problems through mental manipulations. Linking observations and emotional responses with a recently developed systematic thinking process, the adolescent reacts to events and experiences with a newly found power of thought. In formal thought, the adolescent can direct emotional responses to abstract ideals as well as to people. Introspective thinking leads to analysis of self-in-situations, including projection of the self into the adult world of work (Elkind, 1968; Kail & Cavanaugh, 2014; Piaget & Inhelder, 1969).

The cognitive development of formal thought introduces sets of ambiguities. On the one hand, the adolescent is developing a systematized thinking process to solve problems appropriately. On the other hand, there is unrestrained theorizing, extreme self-analysis, and more than usual concern about the reactions of others. By virtue of concern for others, the peer-group influence is particularly strong during adolescence. Self-analysis can lead to what Miller-Tiedeman and Tiedeman (1990) referred to as "I-power" as a means of self-development. Increased self-awareness is an essential part of the adolescent's development, particularly in clarifying self-status and individualized belief systems in the career decision-making process.

In the *development of formalized thinking*, adolescents do not simply respond to stimuli but also interpret what they observe (Bandura, 1977, 1986). In this connection, they will perceive stimuli in the environment as having positive and negative associations. An example of a negative association is taken from a middle school student who believes that lawyers "rip you off because they are all crooks." In this sense, perceptions and values associated with occupations are developed through generalizations formed by experience and observations. Newman and Newman (2009) and Rathus (2014) found that parents have the greatest influence on the long-range plans of adolescents, but peers are more likely to influence immediate identity or status. Occupational stereotypes as perceived in career decision making may be generalized from interactions with parents and peers alike, as well as gained through other stimuli, such as films and books.

Information Processing Development During Adolescence

The move from childhood to adolescence also includes changes in one's ability to process information. The working memory and the speed with which one processes information achieve adult-like levels in adolescence (Ashford & Lecroy, 2013; Kail & Cavanaugh, 2014). The working memory of adolescents has about the same capacity

Table 16.1	**Information Processing During Adolescence**
Feature	State in Adolescence
Working memory and processing speed	Adolescents have adult-like working memory capacity and processing enabling them to process information efficiently.
Content knowledge	Adolescents' greater knowledge of the world facilitates understanding and memory of new experiences.
Strategies and metacognitions	Adolescents are better able to identify task-appropriate strategies and to monitor the effectiveness of those strategies.
Problem-solving and reasoning	Adolescents often solve problems analytically by relying on mathematics or logic, and they are able to detect weakness in scientific evidence and logical arguments.

SOURCE: From *Human Development* (p. 313), by Robert V. Kail and John C. Cavanaugh, 5th ed., 2010, Belmont, CA: Wadsworth Cengage Learning.

as adults, which suggests that teenagers are able to process information much faster than children. Also much improved is the adolescents' ability to solve problems and their ability to use reason in search of problem identification and solutions. The ability to find weaknesses and flaws in arguments has significantly improved, compared to childhood days. Table 16.1 provides more specifics concerning an adolescent's improved skills in processing information.

In sum, working memory increases in capacity and reasoning and is becoming more advanced. Content knowledge significantly increases and adolescents can solve problems analytically. They also develop skills in detecting weakness in arguments for and against scientific experiments. In essence, the cognitive sophistication level is in the process of developing adult-like skills; decision making includes different variables that need to be considered. Thus, when solving problems, one recognizes that solutions are not as straightforward and simplistic as once perceived, but on the contrary causes of problems and solutions to them can be multidimensional and require careful thought and analytical skills to solve.

Rebounding from Developmental Issues: Becoming Resilient

Middle school students develop resiliency from family, friends, and community, as outlined in the previous chapter. During the turbulent years of middle school, students use their assets and strengths to overcome numerous challenges associated with this period of one's life. Students are to learn that they can build strengths from a variety of experiences in an ongoing process over the life span. A more sophisticated approach to meeting the challenges of middle school can be of the utmost importance for bridging the gap from childhood to adolescence to becoming an adult.

An innovative model of resilience has been developed by Sue et al. (2014) as depicted in Figure 16.1. This model emphasizes how strengths and assets can

FIGURE 16.1

Model of Resilience

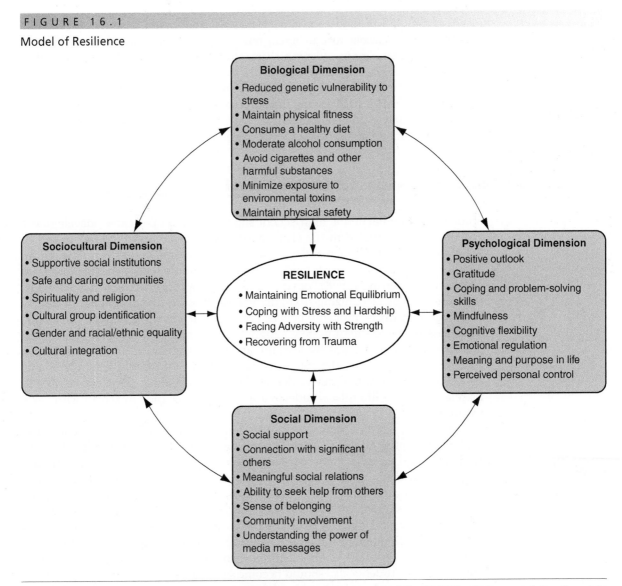

SOURCE: From *Essential of Understanding Abnormal Psychology*, 2nd ed., Foreword, by S. Sue, D. W. Sue, D. Sue, and, S. Sue. Copyright 2014. Reprinted with permission from Wadsworth Cengage Learning.

maximize mental health. To put it simply, one does not give in to stressful conditions or trauma, but one faces adversity with strengths! Recall that assets and strengths come from many sources, such as family relationships, supportive friends, and caring teachers and counselors, plus many supportive community activities. One has a connection to positive events and people who have been supportive. Feelings of well-being can make it much easier to cope successfully when faced with adversity. One strives to maintain emotional equilibrium when faced with difficult decisions. In addition, feelings of belonging, love, and support are used to bolster an inner strength to cope with troubling thoughts and circumstances.

Throughout this book I have recommended a biopsychosocial model for understanding what drives behavior. More recently, some researchers have referred to this model as a multipath model for understanding mental health concerns. Figure 16.1 presents four dimensions that are interacting factors that can build resilience. What is important for counselors to understand here is that mental disorders do not develop only from negative factors, but, most importantly, to recognize that they also develop when there is a lack of individual strengths, positive outlook, social support, coping skills, and other assets. When life has meaning and purpose, it is much easier to cope with stress, to face adversity, and to fulfill one's goals. In this respect, the middle school experience is indeed a most important part of each individual's path to adulthood.

Career Goals and Competencies for Middle School

Students in middle/junior high school should continue the career development goals that were initiated in the elementary school, including the development of self-knowledge, educational and occupational exploration, and career planning. In addition, a summary of career guidance goals for middle school students has been compiled by Herring (1998), paraphrased as follows: (a) decision-making skills, self-awareness by recognizing strengths and weaknesses; (b) educational awareness by recognizing the relationship between educational and work skills; (c) economic awareness by understanding how supply and demand influence job availability; (d) occupational awareness by learning about the content of jobs; and (e) work attitudes by recognizing the role of work in society. In middle school, students are encouraged to gain a greater depth of information about the work world and its relationship to life roles. Students also link skills learned in school with work requirements.

During the middle school years, students are to make tentative plans and explore occupations on their own. The timing of learning modules coincides with student development of more conscious recognition of their self-characteristics and the importance of relationship skills. An increasing awareness of self suggests more focus on personal attributes and how they could fit an occupational environment. Ideally, students also should learn more about the decision-making process and potential career paths and/or work environments. Discussion with students about job requirements should be designed to foster an appreciation of the role of work in their future. As they learn how to interpret information about career opportunities, students also should become aware of skills needed to find a job. In sum, career-related programs should foster more awareness of local occupations, their requirements, and the opportunities they offer (Drummond & Ryan, 1995; Sciarra, 2004).

Examples of the ASCA National Standards for School Counseling Programs

The National Standards for School Counseling Programs, by the American Association of School Counselors, introduced in the previous chapter, suggested student competencies for career development goals including the goal of enhancing career awareness. This goal is a good example for middle school students in their quest for becoming more alert to connecting academic subjects to work requirements. To investigate the world of work in relation to school academic requirements, one should indeed learn how to evaluate and interpret career information and develop an understanding of the importance of planning. Thus, these specific competencies are among others suggested for increasing one's career awareness. Career awareness, for example, also includes knowledge of one's abilities, interests, values, and motivations; one is to make decisions based on a multitude of factors. Students in middle school are to begin to recognize that career development is not a simplistic matter, but indeed there is much to learn about one's personal social development and how that knowledge can help one make connections to the world of work.

These examples to develop career awareness are good illustrations of the goals and competencies for career development suggested by the American Association of School Counselors. Examples of other objectives include learning how to acquire career information, develop employment readiness, and learn how to apply one's skills to achieve career goals. Specific competencies for each of the numerous objectives in this framework for school counseling contain information for developing intervention strategies for middle school students (see appendix G for more information).

National Career Development Guidelines

Competencies for middle school students are carefully delineated in the National Career Development Guidelines (NCDG), described in appendix H. These competencies focus on three broad domains: personal social development, educational achievement, and career management. Counselors and teachers are to plan for strategies that enhance competencies as a part of classroom instruction. What, for example, is an effective intervention strategy for identifying environmental influences that are associated with students' attitudes, behaviors, and aptitudes? And more important, how can career-related skills become part of the academic achievement of basic skills? These examples are only a few of the numerous challenges that teachers, counselors, and parents can address jointly. First and foremost, the focus should be on increasing academic achievement, followed by helping students make sound decisions and developing personal qualities they will need in future life roles. Following are the three NCDG broad-domain goals and subgoals for each domain:

Personal Social Development Domain

Develop understanding of yourself to build and maintain a positive self-concept.
Develop positive interpersonal skills including respect for diversity.
Integrate personal growth and change into your career development.
Balance personal, leisure, community, learner, family, and work roles.

Educational Achievement and Lifelong Learning Domain

Attain educational achievement and performance levels needed to reach your personal and career goals.
Participate in ongoing, lifelong learning experiences to enhance your ability to function effectively in a diverse and changing economy.

Career Management Domain

Create and manage a career plan that meets your career goals.
Use the process of career decision making as one component of career development.
Use accurate, current, and unbiased career information during career planning and management.

Master academic, occupational, and general employability skills in order to obtain, maintain, and/or advance your employment.

Integrate changing employment trends, societal needs, and economic conditions into your career plans.

More information about the NCDG includes specific indicators of goal achievement and more specific information about how each goal is accomplished. In addition, there are 11 goals and a series of indicators under each goal. The three levels of learning include the knowledge stage (K), the application stage (A), and the reflection stage (R).

Group Strategies for Addressing Career Development

The following suggested activities are strategies designed to meet the objectives of self-knowledge, education and occupation information, and career planning for middle school students. Recall that these objectives are a continuation of objectives used for elementary school children. The continuation of what has been learned in the elementary school requires middle school students to explore career information in greater detail, gain greater insight into self-concept and self-knowledge, and apply planning skills. Some representative strategies follow.

Self-Knowledge Strategies

1. Introduce the concepts of self-image, self-worth, and self-esteem. Assign small groups to discuss the relationship of these concepts to educational and occupational planning. Compile a list from these groups.
2. Ask students to complete a standardized or original personality inventory. Using Holland's (1992) classification system, have students relate personality characteristics to work environments.
3. Have students list courses in which they have excelled and those in which they have not. Ask students to relate skills learned to their personality characteristics and traits and interests.
4. Have students construct a lifeline in which they designate places they have lived and visited, experiences in school and with peer groups, and major events. Have them project the lifeline into the future by identifying goals.
5. Have students discuss how different traits are more important for some goals than for others. Compile a list of jobs and corresponding traits.

Educational and Occupational Exploration Strategies

1. Ask students to write a description of the type of person they think they are, their preferences for activities (work and leisure), their strengths and weaknesses, and their desires for a career someday. Discuss.
2. Have students list several occupations that are related to their own interests and abilities. Discuss.
3. Lead a class discussion by identifying relationships of interest and abilities to various occupations. Each student should explore one occupation in depth, including reading a biography, writing a letter to someone, or conducting interviews. The student should research training requirements, working conditions, and personal attributes necessary for the job.

4. Ask each student to visit a place in the community where he or she can observe someone involved in a career of interest. Have students discuss their observations, such as type of work, working conditions, or tools of the trade.
5. Have the students make a list of the school subjects that are necessary for the success of persons whose careers are being investigated. Discuss.
6. Ask students to research preparation requirements for several selected occupations. Have them identify one similarity and one difference in preparation requirements for each of the occupations listed. Discuss.
7. Have students write short narratives explaining why certain jobs have endured and others have disappeared. Discuss.
8. Have students classify 10 occupations by abilities needed, such as physical, mental, mechanical, creative, social, and others. Have students select three occupations that match their abilities and interests.
9. Have students do a mini-internship where they shadow a worker. Discuss and share with other students.
10. Have students write a story about the many jobs involved in producing a hamburger. Discuss.

Career Planning Strategies

1. Present steps in a decision-making model and discuss the importance of each step. Ask students to identify a problem and solve it by applying steps in the model.
2. Organize students into groups and have them construct a list of resources and resource people who could help solve a given problem.
3. In a group discussion, compare a horoscope from a daily newspaper with other ways of solving problems and making decisions.
4. Have students select three occupations and then choose one using a decision model. Share and discuss in groups.
5. Have students prepare an educational plan for high school. Share and discuss in groups.

In sum, counselors should provide the means by which middle school students learn more about career development. Such strategies do indeed foster self-knowledge, exploration of careers, and career planning. Counselors not only conduct individual and group counseling sessions but also teach, mentor, consult, and provide appropriate resources. Infusion opportunities discussed in the previous chapter should continue in middle school. The example in Box 16.1 for a geography class is designed to include planning, decision making, and awareness of career opportunities while completing a lesson in geography.

The geography module in Box 16.1 encourages middle school students to expand their career development competencies as they learn more about self, self-in-situation, and that learning is a lifelong process. More sophisticated and insightful responses are expected, especially in describing changes in physical, psychological, social, and emotional development. Students are to continue relating school subjects to work roles and describing the importance of improving and enhancing their skills in middle school courses. Self-knowledge becomes more individualized as students are able to draw more in-depth conclusions from classroom experiences and standardized test results. There is an increased emphasis on effectively locating and using career information. In general, students are to expand their vision of the future while developing an appreciation of the importance of work in our society.

BOX 16.1

Career Infusion Model

Subject: Social studies, geography
Concept: Planning and decision making
 Career awareness
 Chamber of Commerce exercise
Rationale: Students should be exposed to different ways in which different groups make decisions in order to improve their own decision making.

Objectives:

1. Students will be able to describe their part in the project to accord with teacher observation.
2. Students will list all the republics of South America and at least one feature from a tourist bulletin for each.
3. Students will identify at least two ways in which their project activity corresponds to duties in two specific occupations.

Description: During a unit on South America, divide the class into six groups. Each group will be a Chamber of Commerce for a republic of South America. Each group can plan a tourist bulletin with articles and drawings.

1. Students will tell how their group decided who would research information, write articles, draw pictures, and so on.
2. Students will describe their responsibilities in preparing the tourist bulletin and tell how they think those responsibilities were like some they might have on a job.
3. Students will answer the question, "Can you see how assuming responsibility for something in this project might help you assume responsibilities in an adult occupation?"

Personnel required: Teacher
Cost: None
Time: 3 or 4 periods, estimated
Resources: Maps of and information about South America
Impact on regular offering/curriculum goals: Complement regular unit on South America; help students remember important information about the area.
Evaluation measures: Paper/pencil test

Source: *Project Cadre: A Cadre Approach to Career Education,* by C. C. Healy & O. H. Quinn, 1977. Unpublished manuscript. Reprinted by permission.

Using Assessment Results for Career Development

Flexibility is the key to a successful assessment model. A model should be structured to meet the needs of all students and have the flexibility to blend with traditional career development goals. Standardized and self-assessment techniques both can be used and, in fact, are to complement each other.

The use of an assessment model that is built on a collaborative student–counselor relationship, however, does not decrease counselors' responsibilities; actually, it requires counselors to sharpen their knowledge of assessment standards for instrument selection and use. Counselors should be proficient in effectively relating the purpose of assessment and in interpreting the results in a meaningful manner. Clearly, the effective use of assessment results to promote career development requires a knowledge base of psychometric theory and practice. Counselors should be prepared to evaluate psychometric evidence of validity, reliability, and appropriate norms for each standardized test. Following are some guidelines for effectively using an assessment model for career development:

1. Counselors are to be aware of current references that evaluate standardized instruments. Counselors also can consult with test publishers and consultants for advice on selecting and using assessment instruments.
2. Counselors should use caution when using nonstandardized assessment instruments or exercises that are used to complement or replace standardized instruments. For example, guided fantasy should not be used by counselors who have not been trained or supervised in its administration and use. The rule to follow is that all instruments and exercises require training and supervision.
3. Counselors should be able to explain how assessment is to be used. Students who understand the purpose of each assessment instrument are to become active learners.
4. Counselors need to inform students how to self-assess.
5. Formulating goals is a most important next step in career development.

Self awareness gleaned from assessment results and discussions with a counselor more than likely will create motivation to learn more about oneself and information about occupations. The goal here is not career selection but is directed to increasing one's self-knowledge and self-awareness. Some suggestions for using results from interest, personality, and value inventories follow (Osborn & Zunker, 2012).

Interest Inventories

> Ask students to link their interests with a variety of occupations. Share in groups.
> Ask students to link occupational interests to academic interests.
> Ask students to identify interests as components of uniqueness. Share results with others.
> Ask students to compare interests with their grades in specific subjects. Share their conclusions.

Personality Inventories

> Using identified personality traits, ask students to write a composition describing themselves and/or project their future lifestyle.
> Ask students to share, describe, and discuss how differences among people can influence lifestyle and work-related goals.
> Ask students to develop a list of occupations that match their personality characteristics and traits.

Value Inventories

> Ask students to identify occupations that they believe would meet the needs of individuals who share their values.
> Form discussion groups of students who have the opposite or the same values.
> Have students compare their work values with their parents' occupation. Share conclusions.
> Have students discuss how values can influence people's likes and dislikes for certain occupations and/or lifestyle.

Implications for Career Development

The recommended areas of career development for students in middle school, combined with research, yield numerous implications for career development programs.

1. In many respects, middle school is an educational transition from structured classroom settings to more specialized educational programs. The transition can be problematic for some students who may require intervention strategies.

2. There appears to be a strong need to increase middle school students' abilities to realistically appraise their own abilities, achievements, and interests. Minority students and students from homes where parents' education level is low need special assistance in understanding their strengths and limitations.

3. Students in middle school have difficulty identifying and evaluating their interests in relation to total life experiences. Learning to relate acquired skills to educational and occupational goals promotes exploratory reflection and activities.

4. Limited knowledge of occupations makes it difficult for middle school students to relate in- and out-of-school activities to future jobs. Exposure to jobs and career fields should be expanded to provide a basis for linking various activities to work.

5. Naiveté and limited knowledge of the factors necessary for evaluating future work roles suggest the desirability of introducing informational resources and teaching the necessary skills for their use. Learning about career options, for example, increases awareness of exploration opportunities.

6. Physiological development and sexual maturity during middle school involve individual changes in self-perceptions and social interactions. Opportunities to explore, evaluate, and reflect on values seem to be desirable activities for promoting a better understanding of self during this stage.

7. Middle school students will greatly benefit from hands-on experience with skill activities associated with occupations. Basic and concrete experiences provide a means of learning skills used in work.

8. Because middle school students should begin to assume responsibility for their own behaviors, they would benefit greatly from improved knowledge of planning, decision-making, and problem-solving skills.

9. Increased awareness of sexual differences among junior school students suggests that emphasis be placed on learning how sex-role stereotyping, bias, and discrimination limit occupational and educational choices.

10. Students in middle school who continue the process of awareness initiated in elementary school will recognize the changing nature of career commitment. The skills and knowledge learned to evaluate initial career choices will be used to evaluate multiple choices over the life span.

Summary

1. Potential problems for middle school students include the psychological impact of puberty. Early-maturing girls often lack self-esteem and are less popular. Some early-maturing boys are proud of their physical development, whereas others prefer to mature when their cohorts do. Peer relationships are often the center of attention for boys and girls alike. Popularity and acceptance by their classmates

are most important. Identity development requires them to be proactive and use personal agency to work-through solutions for further commitments.

2. In early adolescence, planning for the future is unsystematic. Near the end of middle school, however, students can deal with abstractions and successfully solve problems. The working memory becomes adult-like and the processing of information is faster than in children. Becoming resilient helps students overcome numerous challenges. Feelings of well-being make it easier to cope with adversity.

3. Stages of career development include the fantasy stage (choices are considered unrealistic); tentative stage (gradual recognition of work requirements); and realistic stage (one is able to make balanced decisions).

4. Career goals for students in middle school developed by the American School Counselors Association include the development of decision-making skills, becoming more aware of educational, occupational, and economic factors, and developing a positive work attitude.

5. National Career Development Guidelines includes the development of competencies in the personal and social domains, educational achievement domain, and career management domain.

6. Classroom and/or group strategies include exercises for developing self-knowledge, occupational exploration, and career planning.

7. Assessment results of interests, personality traits, and values are used to enhance self-knowledge.

Supplementary Learning Exercises

1. Explain how you would build support for career-related programs in a middle school that is located in an affluent neighborhood.

2. Build an intervention that addresses social skills training for middle school students. Defend your program with a rationale for its components.

3. Construct some exercises that could be used by middle school students to enhance their memory skills.

4. Survey the career expectations of middle school students and report results.

5. Survey the neighborhood in which you live or work for the purpose of locating community members who could assist in helping students learn firsthand about occupations.

6. In your opinion, the most resistant group to career-related programs in middle school would be (chose 1) parents, administrators, teachers, or community members. Defend your opinion.

7. Identify worldviews of at least two cultural groups, and explain how worldviews can influence career decisions.

8. Develop a class project that could enhance a student's self-knowledge.

9. Develop a class project that could enhance a student's occupational knowledge.

10. Interview a counselor who is assigned to a middle school. Report your findings.

17

Career-Related Programs for Career Development in High School and Beyond

CHAPTER HIGHLIGHTS

- Career goals and competencies for high school

- Group strategies for career development

- Career-related programs in high school

- College awareness and readiness for low-income students

- Career and technology programs

- Placement services in career centers

- Career counseling programs at community colleges and universities

The high school years are truly a time of learning to prepare for and make decisions about one's future. The rights of passage from adolescence to young adult are a most relevant period of transition. A greater sense of awareness and knowledge of the world of work are guiding principles for the next great step in life. Moreover, students who have come to endorse a lifetime of learning should be prepared to fully recognize that various options await them.

Many of the concerns experienced during the middle school years, however, sometimes remain as obstacles to overcome in high school. Body images, for example, that were so important in middle school remain the center of attention. Girls and boys alike are most sensitive about physical changes and appearance. Peer relationships remain a challenge in that peer approval is of most importance. Learning how to build relationships is indeed an important developmental skill for the transition to future life roles that are enhanced by effective interpersonal skills. Identity development is also an ongoing task as students in high school make insightful observations concerning self-awareness and commitments to future goals. Socially responsible behavior becomes more relevant as individuals are faced with important decisions concerning the consequences of their choices.

In essence, the rights of passage present significant challenges during the high school years. In the pages that follow, I will address some significant challenges that high school students may encounter, but first I continue our discussion of cognitive development and learning that was highlighted in the previous chapter.

Cognitive Development and Learning

In our discussion of cognitive development in middle school, I emphasized the process of transition from concrete operational thinking to formal operational thought according to Piaget (1929). Near the end of middle school, most students have developed the ability to sort out and solve problems. The thinking process is more systematic and introspective. Generalizations are formed by experience and observations. During the high school years, however, skills learned earlier are greatly enhanced as adolescents develop new conceptual skills, as compiled by Newman and Newman (2003) from the work of Neimark (1982) and Gray (1990):

- Ability to manipulate mentally more than two categories of variables simultaneously.
- Ability to think about changes that come with time.
- Ability to hypothesize logical sequences of events.
- Ability to foresee consequences of actions.
- Ability to detect logical consistency or inconsistency in a set of statements.
- Ability to think in relativistic ways about self, others, and the world. (Newman & Newman, 2003, p. 299)

These new enhanced conceptual skills suggest that adolescents have developed the ability to consider different variables when planning future events. One is able to recognize that conditions and colleagues can change in the future. One is able to make predictions about future plans such as going to college or getting a job. One also can anticipate consequences of one's actions. One also is able to judge consistency of actions by others, as well as their own. Finally, adolescents learn to recognize what is the expected behavior of people in their community and culture (Newman & Newman, 2003).

The ability to separate and distinguish between reality and possibility suggests that one is prepared to make important decisions concerning the future. Counselors are to be aware, however, that initial choices by some adolescents may not be mature or realistic decisions but indeed may be motivated by fantasy or unrealistic criteria; there are significant differences within high school groups as well as between groups. The suggestion that adolescents have the ability to do hypothesis testing might foster decisions that distinguish between reality and possibility.

When considering future employment, one's enhanced basic capacities continue to increase the wisdom of choices. Is one capable of doing a certain type of work? Is the pay sufficient? What are the means of transportation to and from work? These are examples of questions to contemplate. What is being stressed here is that when individual students observe flaws in reasoning, they are to use more relevant information to revise problem-solving strategies. I am suggesting that counseling programs designed to assist high school students in decision making are most relevant, as are programs that promote self-knowledge, occupational knowledge, and career planning skills.

Information-Processing Development During Adolescence

As adolescents progress in their ability to process information, they are able to make deliberate use of memory strategies they have learned through experience. They are able to dismiss irrelevant material and focus on what is considered most relevant in solving a problem. Sophistication in processing information is usually accompanied by increased processing speed. The efficiency level of processing information is also enhanced by changes in working memory. Adolescents learn to allocate time for learning difficult material, and they can learn to use a variety of study skills. They learn whether to skim-read or to read for meaning by underlining material in a text-book to improve their ability to remember what was read. The point here is that cog-nitive changes do take place during adolescence, as it is indeed a period of transition or a work in progress. Therefore, it is not considered to be a distinct stage of cognitive development; there is much more to be learned (Kail & Cavanaugh, 2014).

Problem solving and reasoning ability gradually become adult-like as students in high school are exposed to an ever-increasing complex level of knowledge. In the process, they learn strategies appropriate for specific tasks and they learn to moni-tor their progress to be certain their strategy is effective. Some students even turn to making lists of the material they know well and other material they should study more (Ashford & Lecroy, 2013; Kail & Cavanaugh, 2014).

What is suggested here is that information-processing skills used to solve prob-lems involves a series of thought processes that many adolescents in high school are capable of accomplishing. Although the many problems faced during adoles-cence may have significant differences, information-processing skills that have been learned primarily from educational activities can be applied to solve them. However, the numerous problems associated with career choice—such as self-knowledge, the enormous amount of career information available, problems associated with eco-nomic instability, changing job markets, globalization, and the influence of family and friends, among many other factors—can be overwhelming. The point here is that career development should be addressed during the transitional period of adolescence in high schools; one is also to recognize that career development will continue over the life span. Cognitive development and the development of information-processing skills suggest that students can be introduced systematically to career development programs that are indeed a necessary part of their educational program. In the pages that follow, some career development programs for high school students will be intro-duced, but first we discuss goals and standards for high school students.

Goals and Standards

The role and scope of the high school counselor includes a continuation of prepar-ing students for a variety of life roles. In comprehensive career counseling programs, planning for life becomes more relevant for students in high school. Understanding life roles and their interrelationship is good perspective to foster. Competency-based goals that characterize comprehensive career counseling programs provide specific objectives for the high school counselor. As Sciarra (2004) has pointed out, there is less flexibility to infuse career development programs into classroom learning activi-ties in high school than in elementary and middle schools. Counselors, therefore, are more restricted to individual and group counseling in most high schools. Thus, coun-selors are to become familiar with national standards when developing tailored inter-ventions to meet the unique needs of their student body.

The national standards for school counselors developed by the American School Counselors Association (2003) provide counselors with goals and competencies from which they can develop group and individual counseling strategies for high school students.

Examples of ASCA National Standards for School Counseling Programs

Among the many career development goals and objectives for high school students are skills needed to prepare for employment. Even though many students will attend community colleges, universities, and/or tech-prep programs, others will seek full-time employment. Moreover, most students can benefit from career development programs that prepare them for eventual employment. The employment readiness competencies developed by the American School Counselors Association (ASCA) offer many learning opportunities for students who will make the transition from high school to a work role. What seems to be the overriding goal of employment readiness is to prepare students to understand the importance of accepting responsibility for being dependable workers. The message is that the work role requires them to be honest, forthright, and dependable. They are to put forth their best effort. In essence, they are to develop a positive attitude about the work role. A positive attitude also suggests that one is a lifelong learner; thus, the workplace provides an abundance of learning opportunities to enhance career development.

The ASCA national standards also contain many practical and straightforward learning outcomes. One should learn the principles of how to work in teams, solve problems through group interactions, and develop organizational skills. The development of good interpersonal skills is considered to be most important in many workplaces. Other competencies include how to apply for a job, understand the rights of employees, develop knowledge of the changing workplaces, and learn how to prepare a résumé. Students also should be prepared to learn task-management skills and to learn how to utilize time. As in all other periods of transitions in life, there is much to be learned. Counselors should be prepared to offer learning options that require a combination of skills, especially in the personal–social development domain. One learns skills from practical straightforward goals that can be used to master more inclusive goals in life planning—adolescence to young adulthood. Some examples of national career guidelines developed for the National Career Development Association are presented next.

The National Career Development Guidelines (NCDG)

The National Career Development Guidelines is competency-based and focuses on three broad domains: personal social development, educational achievement, and career management. Specific competencies for career development goals from the national career guidelines are included in appendix H. These competencies require a sophisticated understanding of purpose and scope of career development goals. Students are each to evaluate their knowledge stage concerning a specific goal, how they could apply this knowledge, and assess the consequences of using the knowledge. What these steps suggest is that individual goals require them not only to acquire knowledge but also to demonstrate an acceptable level of awareness by applying the knowledge, and, finally, to recognize how this knowledge has enhanced their capacity to deal with other challenges. They are to become lifelong learners.

Examples of goals that focus on self-understanding and building a positive self-concept include the following sequence: (1) identify abilities, skills, and talents; (2) demonstrate the use of these traits; and (3) determine how these traits could impact one's career development. This example, taken from the personal social domain, illustrates how students are to build an understanding of how their personal abilities, skills, and talents are to be important factors in their career development. The knowledge, application, and reflection stages provide a three-dimensional learning approach to career development that should effectively challenge most students in high school.

Group Strategies for Addressing Career Development

The following strategies are designed to meet the goals of self-knowledge, educational and occupational exploration, and career planning in high school. These strategies were developed over time, and especially during the career education movement, but remain viable for addressing career development in high school.

Self-Knowledge Strategies

1. Have students list five roles they currently fill. Discuss in small groups and identify future roles, such as spouse, parent, and citizen.
2. Discuss or show films on sex-role stereotyping. Have students identify how sex-role stereotyping prohibits many individuals from becoming involved in certain events, including work roles.
3. Assign students to select newspaper and magazine pictures and articles that illustrate societal perceptions of appropriate behavior and dress. Discuss.
4. Have students discuss physical differences among their peers. Emphasize how differences could affect individuals.
5. Discuss the value of cooperative efforts in the work environment, and have students develop a project in which cooperation is essential.
6. Have students observe workers performing specific tasks and make notes of skills and time required to complete tasks. Discuss.
7. Have students discuss employer expectations compared with their own. Develop a consensus about how both are justified and can be attained.
8. Have students role-play a supervisor reacting to an employee's work performance. Discuss reactions of supervisors in a variety of situations.
9. Have students research the various causes of tardiness and absenteeism among workers. Discuss.
10. Ask students to interview at least three workers and three supervisors of workers on the subject of good work habits. Discuss.

Educational and Occupational Exploration Strategies

1. Have students identify geographical factors that can affect their career choice (Geary, 1972). Obtain newspapers from urban and rural areas. Compare employment opportunities and contrast differences.
2. Have students identify high school courses required for entry into trade schools, colleges, or jobs (Walz, 1972). Discuss elements of required courses and develop brochures that list jobs and corresponding high school courses required.
3. Help students understand how human values are significant in career decision making (Bottoms, Evans, Hoyt, & Willer, 1972). Develop a list of values that could influence selection of a career. Have each student select two values of importance and locate a career that would be congruent with those values. Discuss.
4. Help students understand the principles and techniques of life planning (Brown, 1980). In small groups, in eight 1-hour meetings, six components are presented

and discussed: "Why People Behave the Way They Do," "Winners and Losers," "Your Fantasy Life," "Your Real Life," "Setting Goals," and "Short- and Long-Term Planning."

5. Help students prepare for entrance into colleges and universities (Hansen, 1970). A college-bound club discusses in weekly meetings topics such as how to read a university catalog, how to visit a campus, and how to evaluate universities and colleges.

6. Discuss the value of leisure activities. Have students report on the benefits involved in five leisure activities of their choice. Discuss.

7. Have students develop a list of leisure activities they enjoy, and estimate the amount of time necessary to participate in each. Form groups to decide which occupations would most likely provide the necessary time and which ones would not.

8. Ask students to debate the pros and cons of selected leisure activities.

9. Ask students to develop a list of leisure activities they enjoy now and project which of these can be enjoyed over the life span. Have students collect and discuss brochures from travel agencies and parks.

10. Have students discuss the concept of lifestyle in terms of work commitment, leisure activities, family involvement, and responsibilities, and share their projections of future life roles and lifestyle.

Career Planning Strategies

1. Ask students to review several job search manuals. Discuss the steps suggested in the manuals, and develop strategies for taking these steps.

2. Assign students to visit a state employment agency and describe its functions. Discuss.

3. Have students research newspaper want ads and select several jobs of interest. Discuss and identify appropriate occupational information resources.

4. Have students demonstrate the steps involved in identifying an appropriate job, filling out an application, and writing a résumé. Discuss.

5. Have students participate in a mock interview. Critique and discuss appropriate dress and grooming.

6. Help students develop planning skills (Hansen, 1970). A one-year course, taught as an elective, covers six major areas of study: (a) relating one's characteristics to occupations; (b) exploring manual and mechanical occupations; (c) exploring professional, technical, and managerial occupations; (d) relating the economic system to occupations and people; (e) exploring clerical and service occupations; and (f) evaluating and planning ahead.

7. Help students evaluate careers relative to standards of living and lifestyle (Sorapuru, Theodore, & Young, 1972a; Steidl, 1972). Students project themselves 10 to 15 years in the future and identify the kind of lifestyles they would like to have. Each student selects four careers and conducts research to determine if the projected lifestyle can be met through these careers.

8. Provide good job search procedures (Sorapuru, Theodore, & Young, 1972b). Students who have had part-time jobs explain how they got them. Groups investigate local organizations that help people find jobs. Students investigate telephone directories, school placement center files, and state employment agencies for leads to jobs. Students write résumés and "walk-through" steps for applying and interviewing.

9. Help students understand the stressors of work responsibility (Bottoms et al., 1972). Students identify individuals who recently attained a position of prominence and compare changes in lifestyle (work, leisure, and family).

10. Involve parents in career planning and decision making in high school (Amatea & Cross, 1980). Students and parents attend six 2-hour sessions per week and discuss the following at school and at home: self-management and goal setting, elements in career planning and decision making, comparing self with occupational data, information-gathering skills, and training paths.

Box 17.1 addresses issues surrounding sex-role stereotyping. This strategy prepares boys and girls for sharing work rules in the future.

Role modeling is another counseling component that can effectively emphasize the occupational potential of girls. Examples of women who have enjoyed successful careers provide girls with concrete evidence that women do have opportunities to develop careers in a working world thought to be dominated by men. Numerous techniques apply to such a component. One method is to have students interview working women and write a summary of their work-related experiences.

Biographies of women also may be reviewed and discussed. These examples should emphasize how women can overcome gender role stereotyping and find equal opportunity in the job market. They also illustrate that women can effectively assume leadership roles in the world of work. Finally, role models provide support for girls who are seriously considering a career-oriented lifestyle and may provide some potential mentors.

Locating a mentor to learn the skills of a given career directly is usually highly productive. Therefore, career education and career counseling programs that instruct

---

BOX 17.1

Overcoming Gender Role Stereotyping

All students need to be prepared for self-sufficiency in the future, and a major challenge is to assist boys and girls alike in overcoming the problems associated with gender-role stereotyping. Counseling component modules for the classroom present one method of accomplishing this objective.

Sari and John are in a high school self-discovery counseling group. The counselor asks each member to study an advertisement that uses a man or a woman on television and also to locate one in a magazine. Each will record the product being advertised and describe the individual in the ad.

Sari and John recorded the information for two ads, which were discussed in the next group session. Sari's notes included the following: "This woman was beautiful on television, in a long flowing dress with gorgeous hair blowing in the wind. She was advertising a soap to be used for the face and hands for keeping them soft and pretty."

John took notes from a magazine ad: "This ad was on a full page in a magazine. It showed a man advertising imported beer who had a tattoo on his hand. He looked like a cowboy with a weather-beaten face."

The counselor asked the group to discuss the characteristics of each character in the two ads. The adjectives used to describe each character were recorded. For the woman in the ad, the list included beautiful, graceful, clean, dainty, sexy. The list for the man included macho, handsome, outdoorsman, self-assured, rugged.

The counselor asked the group to discuss the appropriate roles in life for men and women as implied by these advertisements. The apparent differences in roles then were extended to typical gender-role stereotypes, such as women are to be pampered, dependent, and pretty; men are strong, free to do as they please, and independent. The group discussed how these ads and other types of gender-role stereotyping have influenced their own perceptions of lifestyles for men and women and, subsequently, the careers they find appropriate for men and women. The counselor summarized the influence of gender-role stereotyping found in advertising and elsewhere in society. Finally, the changing role of women in general and in the workforce in particular was emphasized.

girls about the values of mentor relationships are useful. A mentor is usually an older person who is admired and respected and has tremendous influence on the young. The point here is that women who aspire to professional careers have fewer opportunities to find a mentor than do men, primarily because fewer female mentors are available. There is some evidence that cross-gender mentoring can be of value, but because some men have a tendency not to take career women seriously, there is the danger of increasing the chances of gender-role stereotyping.

Career Development Infusion

Developing planning skills for future educational and vocational choices involves a multitude of learning activities and guidance programs. Decision-making skills and knowledge of occupations and job placement are key factors to emphasize in career development infusion. The career infusion module for a high school English class, in Box 17.2, should help students become more aware of the importance of decision making. It could be modified for group use.

BOX 17.2

Career Infusion Module

Subject: English

Concept: Planning and decision making
Decision making exemplified in literature

Rationale: Students should become more aware of the importance of decision making.

Objectives:

1. Students will arrange, in order, the steps in the systematic decision-making model discussed in class.
2. Students will analyze either a personal decision or a decision made by a literary character by listing the steps taken in making the decision; students will write in one page how that decision followed the steps in the model or, if it didn't, how it could.

Description: Read and hold a class discussion on Robert Frost's poem "The Road Not Taken," having students express their thoughts about the importance of decision making and talk about experiences that led them to make an important decision or to change their minds after making one. Bring out the following points in the discussion:

1. It is important that the student make a decision systematically and participate in its formulation.
2. Before making a decision, one must examine the consequences of the decision, both pro and con.
3. To do this, one must try to get accurate information about each decision.
4. Decision making can be thought of as a series of steps: (a) set the goal; (b) figure out alternative ways of reaching the goal; (c) get accurate information to determine which alternative is best; (d) decide on an alternative and carry it out; (e) figure out if the choice was correct and why; and (f) if you did not reach the goal, try another alternative or start the process over again.

Personnel required: Teacher

Cost: None

Time: One period

Resources: Robert Frost's poem "The Road Not Taken"

Source: *Project Cadre: A Cadre Approach to Career Education Infusion*, by C. C. Healy & O. H. Quinn, 1977. Unpublished manuscript. Reprinted by permission.

Other Career-Related Programs in High School

The career infusion module is a good example of how to address career decision making within a learning component in an English class in high school. The goals of this project are most obvious in that the classroom objectives of developing an appreciation of literature are addressed, as well as an important career development objective. As stated earlier in this chapter, there is generally less flexibility in high school classrooms. Counselors have to recognize that all teachers have education goals that must be met and that they are under pressure to fulfill those obligations. Thus, the career infusion module could be modified for smaller counseling groups.

Career-Related Programs

Over time, educators have made significant changes in high school career-related programs that existed in most communities several decades ago. The reasons for changes are numerous, including new and different work requirements, technology advances, and global competition for manufacturing of goods. What has remained is the emphasis for high school students to attend college. The need for continuing education beyond high school has resulted in the current buzzword "lifelong learning."

The current focus on lifelong learning has made it clear to many high school students that education beyond high school is a must. Thus, most high schools have programs that encourage students to include plans for continuing their education beyond high school to build their skills for career development. Most schools focus on preparing students to go to a university or college to obtain a bachelor's degree. Counselors, therefore, accumulate information about college entry requirements and may offer "college nights" for student and parents to discuss and share information. Increasingly students are taking courses in high school that will transfer to some colleges as college credit. Some high schools offer courses that prepare students for advanced placement exams. During economic downturns many students attend community colleges while planning to eventually transfer to a university to finish a bachelor's degree.

The point of this discussion is that college preparation remains a viable counseling objective in many high schools. I will review some current career development programs in high schools: college awareness and readiness for low-income students, tech prep programs, and career and technology programs.

College Awareness and Readiness Programs for Low-Income Students

This U.S. Department of Education has entered into partnerships with state departments of education and local school districts to support programs that stress college awareness and readiness for low-income students. These programs are designed to inform students from low-income families about the benefits of obtaining a college education. The emphasis is on learning to build effective study habits and making good grades. The rationale is that early awareness of the benefits of a college education, beginning in middle school, will encourage students to make good grades in both middle school and high school. Along with the idea of making good grades and having a high attendance rate is an awareness of financial assistance that could make going to college affordable. Students who do well academically in high school by maintaining an outstanding grade average could be awarded a college scholarship.

Students whose parents have agreed to let their child enter this program are also consulted about the benefits of an undergraduate degree and are encouraged to support their child's efforts to do well and attend school regularly. Support from the family is considered to be of utmost importance. During the school year, students have planned visits to nearby colleges and universities that have agreed to be partners in this program. A major part of this program is devoted to helping students learn more about potential careers in the future and use data from a variety of assessment instruments to assist in the career choice process. A goal for students and families is to be fully aware of strengths and assets as well as what is needed for self-improvement.

Partnerships Between High Schools and Community College Districts

During the last decade, we have witnessed the building of an increasing number of community colleges. Community colleges have many missions including offering college courses that can be transferred to four-year institutions of higher education. Students as well as parents learn quickly that the rising costs of four years of college can be overwhelming; thus, attending a community college can become a viable option. Community colleges offer a wide variety of courses. In addition to basic courses during the freshmen and sophomore years in college, these colleges also offer courses in skilled trades for students who want to opt out of a four-year college plan. Courses such as plumbing, welding, auto collision repair, and culinary arts are examples. Some students find that attending a community college to learn a skilled trade may be a plausible alternative for their future work role.

Partnership arrangements between school districts and community college districts are formed to meet the needs of each community. In some community colleges, juniors in high school are given the opportunity to attend a designated community college where they are to finish high school requirements and earn college credit at the same time. College credit may be offered in several career fields, for example: aviation technology, aerospace engineering, home building, culinary arts, diesel technology, drafting, and hotel/restaurant management. Admission to these programs is limited, and students are administered an entrance test and inventories that are used to advise them in course selection. Community college programs of this type vary greatly from state to state, so careful consideration is necessary.

Tech-Prep Programs

Tech-prep is a national strategy designed to ensure that students exit high school or a community/technology college with marketable skills for job placement, have academic credentials to pursue higher education, or both. In this context, tech-prep means integrated academics and technical training for secondary, postsecondary, and apprenticeship students, plus curriculum development to meet the skills requirements of advanced technology jobs. Also included are innovative career counseling programs that provide information about high-demand occupations, a comprehensive assessment program for students in middle school, and an individualized career and educational plan for high school graduates.

To accomplish the goals of tech-prep programs, some school systems and cooperating colleges and universities form consortiums with industry. Through these organizations, educators and industrial representatives can effectively address and coordinate work-site-based training. A major goal of tech-prep programs is to encourage vocational education students to take more advanced, academically oriented courses. Typically, schools devise a variety of two-year technical curricula that include subjects such as applied mathematics, applied biology/chemistry, and principles of technology. They often have a working relationship with cooperating colleges that have agreed, by prior arrangement, to accept these courses for college credit or as entrance requirements.

In sum, tech-prep programs in high school are college-preparatory programs for technical careers; they are considered to be a solid basis for baccalaureate study. In some instances, however, students may find that they have the necessary skills for immediate entry-level employment. Thus, they could choose to work for a period of time before continuing their education.

Career and Technology Programs

More school districts appear to be adopting career and technology education programs to meet the increased demand for training that will lead to job placement. Most career and technology education programs incorporate academic courses with training for a specific career. In most cases, they offer a wide range of technology courses, for example: accounting, advertising design, architectural design, automotive technology, business support systems, cosmetology, criminal justice, and graphic arts. Advanced manufacturing associations also are cooperating with high schools and community colleges by offering college credit for work experiences in high-tech manufacturing workplaces. One can expect to find differences in course offerings in technology in different school districts within a state, as well as differences in courses offered between states.

Some instructional settings for career and technology courses of study include the following:

1. Internships are conducted off campus and students rotate in a variety of work stations.
2. Career preparation, formerly known as cooperative education, now consists of a combination of classroom training and on-the-job training.
3. Job shadowing consists of time spent shadowing and observing an employee who is actively involved in a specific field of work.
4. Laboratory courses are designed to simulate a business or industrial workplace for hands-on experiences.
5. Work-based learning consists of hands-on experiences in the workplace.

Courses that integrate classroom and on-the-job instruction are the hallmark of career and technology education. What is stressed here is that mentoring of students on a job site has distinct advantages. Thus, a work-based learning approach is designed to develop skills in critical thinking, problem solving, communications, and interpersonal relations. These programs are indeed a combination of education and work experience. Students experience work norms of real workers, work habits, and worker relationships that hopefully will lead to effective work behavior. They build technical skills and observe how technical tasks relate to theoretical knowledge. What is suggested here is that students will become more motivated in all academic programs when they are able to experience the connections and links between their schoolwork and what is required on a worksite. In an ever-changing society, quality-of-life and work options will be determined largely by basic skills and commitment to be a lifelong learner.

Placement Services

Here, I cover the role of placement services in secondary schools and also the role of state employment agencies. The integration of career planning and placement services in many educational institutions has evolved gradually during the last three decades. There has been a concerted effort to eliminate the word *placement* as a part of the name of the center where career services are offered (Carter, 1995a). This name change is the result of changing missions in educational institutions. Many career centers, for instance, have focused more on preplacement services, such as general information about educational programs, outreach programs, internships, part-time jobs, and computerized career guidance and information systems.

Placement services should remain the primary service offered by educational institutions, but in institutions where career planning and placement services have been combined into career centers, the services include a wide variety of programs that have received equal and, in many cases, more attention than placement has. Thus, a more appropriate name for locations that provide career-related services, including placement, is the more generic term *career centers*.

The Purpose and Rationale for Career Centers

Career centers, sometimes called "go centers" or "go to centers," have been developed as a major component of career development programs. The management of programs and the use of occupational information material are major responsibilities of the career counselor. The counselor's knowledge of how to use occupational information is reflected in the effectiveness of the career center. Counselors also must be well acquainted with the content of the various sources of career information. What is being stressed here is that program development for individual and group use of the center must be carefully planned.

Presentation of materials will vary according to the differing needs of groups and individuals. For example, a senior high school freshman class may be given an overview demonstration of the various resources in the center, whereas a group of high school juniors is presented with specific resources needed for a class project. Or a group of high school seniors may be given the assignment of researching the various careers in their declared majors.

Individual use of career information is highly personalized, and the counselor must recognize that different learning styles among clients call for flexibility in the use of career information resources. Moreover, Sharf (2013) pointed out that information-seeking behavior will vary from client to client. As counselors help individuals sort and assimilate information, they also must provide direction by generating questions concerning specific information that can be obtained from available resources. Just as career decision making is an individualized process, so, too, is the use and assimilation of career information. In sum, the career center is used by individuals who are in various phases of career decision making; some are seeking information to narrow their choices, whereas others are searching for answers in the beginning phases of decision making. It is also a place where instructors can meet with groups of students or entire classes for a variety of career guidance objectives. Finally, the entire professional staff is encouraged to use the center as a resource for ongoing projects.

Several advantages of career centers are worth considering. First, a centralized location provides the opportunity to systematically organize all career materials

into more efficient and workable units. The centralized facility also allows counselors to monitor materials on hand and simplifies the task of maintaining and
selecting additional materials. Second, students and faculty are attracted to cen-
trally displayed materials that are easily accessed. Thus, a wider use of materials
is usually assured, and in addition, attention is directed to programs offered by
the career center. In essence, the career center brings into focus career-related
programs and career resources offered by an institution. A third consideration
involves the methods of promoting coordination and acceptance of career-related
programs among faculty, staff, administration, students, and community. A well-
organized and well-operated career center will encourage a variety of members
of an institution to participate in development, programming, and evaluation of
career center materials and facilities. A commitment from a cross-section of individuals will greatly enhance the career development efforts that an educational
institution offers.

A final consideration involves programming innovations for the use of career
materials and outreach activities, which usually are generated within the career center
or sponsored by the career center. A well-planned facility can become the focal point
in planning new programs and innovative activities for career development and career
education. In essence, the career center should facilitate a wide variety of program
development opportunities among staff and faculty.

The Role of Placement in High School

A major component of the placement aspect of career planning involves job listings from local, state, regional, national, and international sources. The numerous
federal and state programs that provide job placement for high school graduates and
dropouts are valuable referral sources for secondary schools. A cooperative venture
between the school, the business community, and federal and state agencies is essential in developing local sources of job listings. One of the most effective approaches is
through a community advisory committee (Gysbers & Henderson, 1988, 2001). Local
service clubs, chambers of commerce, federal and state agencies, and professional and
personnel organizations are excellent resources for developing a local career advisory
committee. As demand for hands-on experience increases, local career opportunities
will be essential to the success of these programs. A viable listing of local part-time
and full-time jobs also will enhance the popularity of the career planning and placement office.

Programs that enhance the transition from school to work that are offered in
senior high schools should view placement as a vital function and a continuation of
career development programs (Herr et al., 2004). Some suggested program topics
include how to prepare for an interview, write a résumé, locate job information, apply
for a job, learn if you are qualified for a job, and find the right job.

Finally, computer-assisted career guidance programs (discussed in chapter 7)
provide vital, timely information about the current job market. The ability to generate local job information on available computer programs is extremely helpful to the
job seeker. The fast-changing job market may well require that computer capabilities
be frequently updated.

Placement services also can provide a vital link between academics and the working world. Career planning and placement services offered early in secondary programs should provide the student with knowledge of career skills to be developed in
secondary education. These programs should be established not to discourage future

formal academic training but, rather, to provide relevance and added motivation for learning per se. Career planning and placement in this sense should be an ongoing program for students in various levels of secondary education, with the placement function playing a vital role in student services.

Placement by State Employment Agencies

State employment agencies consist of a network of local offices in cities and rural areas across the nation. This network is based on federal and state partnerships, with the U.S. Employment Service providing broad national guidelines for operational procedures in state and local employment offices. One principal source of job information has been compiled into what is referred to as a job bank. The job bank is a listing of all job orders compiled daily within each state. Offices with computer terminals have direct access to the job bank. This up-to-the-minute job information is available to all job seekers, who are required to fill out an application and be interviewed before they are given access to the job bank.

The functions of state employment agencies, which have active placement programs, are to help the unemployed find work and to provide employers with qualified applicants for job orders. Many state agencies divide their services into two categories: (1) placement for job seekers and (2) services to employers. For job seekers, state agencies offer the following services:

1. Job listings in professional, clerical, skilled, technical, sales, managerial, semi-skilled, service, and labor occupations
2. Personal interviews with professional interviewers
3. Assistance with improving qualifications
4. Referral to training
5. Testing
6. Counseling
7. Service to veterans
8. Unemployment benefits (for those who qualify while they are looking for work)

Services offered to employers are as follows:

1. Screening for qualified applicants
2. Professional interviews
3. On-site recruitment and application taking
4. Computerized job listings in most areas of the state
5. Aptitude and proficiency testing
6. Labor market information on technical assistance
7. Technical assistance with job descriptions, master orders, and turnover studies
8. Unemployment insurance tax information

Job placement is the focus of state employment agencies, but career counseling is available when requested. State employment agencies also administer assessment instruments that typically are used in career counseling, such as aptitude and achievement tests. Individuals are regularly referred to state employment agencies by other state agencies. For example, rehabilitation agencies refer clients who have had extensive career counseling and are in need of job listings. The placement function is enhanced by computerized job banks and lists of qualified job applicants that provide a readily accessible matching system. Employment opportunities are quickly available to job seekers who need immediate placement.

Career Counseling in Educational Institutions Beyond High School

Comprehensive career services are offered at many community colleges and universities. Some offer credit for career-related courses, and many offer seminars presented by counselors, faculty members, paraprofessionals, and/or business leaders. The content of career-related services varies and may include seminars on career options and alternatives, programs for undeclared majors, the connection between college majors and work roles, job search strategies, how to do an interview and prepare a résumé, and making an effective transition from college to work (Morrison, 2002).

Example of Career Prep at a Community College Consortium

In central Nebraska, 38 high schools have formed a consortium known as Central Nebraska Tech-Prep Consortium. This consortium uses the combined expertise of its professional staff to develop materials and counseling strategies that are designed to accomplish their collective career guidance mission. Each spring, career guidance staffs selected from the consortium meet to revise their plans and materials. Counselors bring new ideas and materials that are evaluated and eventually distributed to the consortium members.

Each member of the consortium uses a student career preparation handbook that is designed to be used with all high school students. This handbook can be considered as an extension of a comprehensive career guidance system that students have participated in during elementary, middle/junior high, and high schools. The handbook is designed to continue the development of self-knowledge, educational and occupational exploration, and career planning. For example, a section entitled "Career Prep" is designed to help students make intelligent decisions about acquiring skills needed for careers in the 21st century. Another informative section of the handbook describes the variety of two-year programs that are offered at local community colleges as well as four-year university programs in Nebraska.

Other interesting topics include employability skills, how education enhances employability, and 20 "Hot Track Jobs." As students proceed through the handbook, they self-administer a career path assessment, identify their interests, and self-rate their abilities while reflecting on working conditions. On the basis of these results, students can investigate career clusters in Arts and Communication, Business, Management, Technology, Human Services, Industrial and Engineering Technology, Natural Resources and Agriculture, or a combination of these. Each cluster is divided into specific jobs. For example, the Health Services section contains Laboratory Technology with listings of Pharmacists, Clinical Laboratory Technicians, Medical Laboratory Technicians, Pharmacy Technicians, and Ultrasound Technologists.

Academic expectations in community and technical schools, four-year institutions of higher learning, and a directory of most Nebraska postsecondary educational institutions are also provided. Internet addresses are given for websites that contain related information such as American Job Bank, National Career Search, Peterson's Education Center, Employment Opportunities, and many more. Students also can review high school educational planning suggestions that include samples of curriculum requirements for different tech-prep plans. Also included are postsecondary entrance test requirements, a senior year planning checklist calendar, postsecondary visitation features, application process, financial and scholarship information, budgeting tips, sample student résumés, and an example letter of application.

In sum, this program suggests that students have important decisions to make concerning their futures. What is stressed here is that intelligent educational decisions are going to be necessary now and in the future. Students are informed that they need to be prepared for a lifetime of learning new skills for new and different jobs in a global society. They are encouraged to recognize the relationship between high school courses and the work world. They also are to recognize that they have choices that include a two-year associate degree, vocational/technical training, and attending a four-year university. Moreover, it is pointed out that a planning strategy is essential for meeting individual short- and long-term goals. This handbook supports the principles of what students have learned about themselves thus far in the educational process and suggests that much more is to be learned about the future. Finally, a life-long learning approach is strongly endorsed, and students are encouraged to continue career planning.

Examples of Career-Related Services in Four-Year Institutions of Higher Education

Counselors will find numerous career-related programs in four-year institutions of higher learning. Career-related programs in universities have steadily grown, especially since the 1950s. In the late 1970s, Reardon, Zunker, and Dyal (1979) were able to identify 31 categories of career-related programs in 302 institutions of higher education. Examples of services offered included occupational information via computers, assessment services for career counseling, educational information, and numerous training programs including training for decision making, communications skills, learning to become assertive, career planning, job interviewing, and how to use self-help materials effectively.

Currently, some institutions offer credit for 1- or 3-hour courses that are built around some aspect of career development. An undergraduate career course at Florida State University, for example, has been offered since 1974, and approximately 6200 students have taken it (Reardon et al., 2000). This course covers a variety of topics including career planning, self-knowledge information, decision making, information about the global economy and the work world, career and family roles, job-hunting techniques, and discussions about one's first job and early career moves. In addition to the undergraduate course in career development offered at Florida State University, the counseling staff has developed an inclusive career counseling program for all students discussed next.

Curricular Career Information Service (CCIS): A Module Model

An innovative program for delivering educational and vocational information was initiated at the Florida State University career center in 1975. The program emphasizes an instructional approach to career planning services. It has been updated and modified periodically since its inception, and continues to be a major delivery system of career services and a support network for other career-related programs that the university offers.

The CCIS is self-help-oriented, uses instructional models, and is multimedia-based; the program is delivered by paraprofessionals. The CCIS is an outreach program used in residence halls and the university student center. In addition, the modules have been used as the nucleus of a 3-hour credit course in career planning offered by two academic departments at Florida State University. The instructional modules were conceptualized to meet specific counseling goals and are structured around behavioral objectives.

Modules I through V are shown in Table 17.1. Modules VI through XVI can be found in Sampson et al. (2004) and/or obtained from the following address:

Dr. Robert Reardon
Florida State University
The Career Center
Tallahassee, FL 32306-1035

After a brief interview, a typical student is directed to the first module, which begins with a 10-minute slide presentation outlining the goals and purposes of the CCIS. The second module provides an overview of variables considered desirable in career planning through the use of slides and selected materials. The third module requires self-assessment, primarily accomplished through self-administration and self-interpretation of the SDS (*Self-Directed Search*) interest inventory (Holland, 1987b). The fourth module consists of a slide presentation of career information resources. The fifth module assists the student in locating careers related to academic majors. Other modules include employment outlooks, leisure planning, career planning for African Americans, career decision making for adult women and students with disabilities, and career interest exploration through work and occupational skills.

The instructional approach to career planning used in the CCIS has potential application for many career-related programs. The overall effectiveness of each module is evaluated according to behavioral objectives. Major and minor components of each instructional unit can be effectively evaluated through a systematic review process. Thus, the CCIS provides the opportunity for continuous modification and upgrading of each instructional component. As career-related materials and programs change rapidly in the future, the opportunity to systematically evaluate and subsequently upgrade them will be a major asset. Additional modules also can be developed as needs are identified.

Thus, one major advantage of instructional modules is that they are flexible. Once a system of instructional modules has been established, the building of additional modules is encouraged by a review of needs that are identified by staff members. Also inherent in this process is the identification of additional career materials. What we are stressing here is that instructional modules provide independent learning experiences that are self-paced and can be delivered effectively by paraprofessionals. The diversity of learning activities provided through a series of career planning modules gives individuals a greater variety of options and an effective means of choosing a point of entry for career exploration. In additions, the development of modules for specific groups (such as older adults, females, minority groups) represents a multifaceted approach to career counseling that eliminates the necessity of prescribing the same program for everyone. A diversity of programs also provides an attractive means of creating interest in career exploration activities.

University career centers across the nation also offer seminars or workshops on a variety of career-related subjects including the interrelationship of life roles, benefits of a college education, the connection between majors and work roles, self-help programs, and availability of internships, among many other topics. In some institutions, instructors assign career-related projects that are to be done in the university career center. Individual and group counseling is available at most institutions, and most institutions have a placement office or an employment services office available to students. One can expect to find computerized career guidance

Table 17.1	**Curricular Career Information Services (CCIS) Modules**	
Module Title	**Objectives**	**Activities**
I. Everything You've Always Wanted to Know About CCIS	1. To introduce you to the CCIS. 2. To help you select activities that will assist you in solving your career problem.	a. Examine a Career Center brochure located on the yellow rack near the Career Center entrance to learn more about CCIS services and programs. b. Ask a Career Advisor to explain CCIS and the career advising process to you. c. Attend a Career Center tour. d. Browse the remaining module sheets on the yellow rack to learn more about some of the common concerns addressed through the career advising process.
II. What's Involved in Making a Career Decision?	1. To dispel common misconceptions about career planning. 2. To help you identify areas that are important to consider development. 3. To help you establish some guidelines for the process of career decision making.	a. Review the "What's Involved in Career Choice" sheet to gain a greater awareness of the career decision-making process. b. Review "A Guide to Good Decision Making" sheet to explore more effective ways to make career decisions. c. Review the "Career Choice Resources in CCIS" and/or books catalogued IA in The Career Center Library. d. Review materials in the Module II folder in the Mobile file (File 1). e. Attend a "Choosing a Major/Career" workshop in CCIS. f. With the assistance of a Career Advisor, complete the "Guide to Good Decision Making Exercise." g. Register for Units I and II of the Introduction to Career Development Class. A course syllabus is available for your review in the Module XVI section of the Mobile File (File 1).
III. Looking at You	1. To help you examine some of your interests, values, and skills. 2. To help you identify some occupations or fields of study for further exploration.	**Interests** a. Complete the Self-Directed Search (SDS). b. Complete the "Career Areas" topic in the Explore section of the CHOICES computer program. c. Complete the Internet Inventory in the "Learning About Yourself" module of the DISCOVER computer program. d. Complete the "Self-Assessment" section of SIGI PLUS. **Values** a. Interact with the SIGI PLUS computer program. b. Complete the Values Card Sort. c. Complete the Values inventory in the "Learning About Yourself" module of the DISCOVER program. **Skills** a. Complete the aptitudes section in the CHOICES Guidebook. b. Interact with the Micro Skills computer program.

Table 17.1	**(Continued)**	
Module Title	**Objectives**	**Activities**
		c. Complete the Motivated Skills Card Sort.
		d. Complete the Abilities Assessment in the "Learning About Yourself" module of the DISCOVER computer program.
IV. Information: Where to Find It and How to Use It	1. To help you locate all Career Center information related to your educational and career planning needs.	a. Perform a search using Career Key for the topic of interest to you.
		b. Review the diagram on the back of this sheet to locate various multimedia resources available in The Career Center Library.
V. Matching Majors and Jobs	1. To help you learn how specific job titles relate to college majors or fields of study.	a. Review printed materials in the Module V "Matching Majors and Careers" folders in the Mobile File (File 1), specifically the "Match-Major" sheets.
		b. Read sections in these books or others found in Area IIC of The Career Center Library.
		IIC AA C7 The College Board Guide to 140 Popular College Majors
		IIC AA M3 What Can I Do With a Major in . . . ?
		IIC AA N3 College Knowledge and Jobs
		IIC AA P4 College Majors & Careers
		IIC AA O2 The Occupational Thesaurus (Vols. 1 & 2)
		IIA 025 Occupational Outlook Handbook
		c. Perform a search on Career Key under the topic *Occupations by Major* to get a list of relevant CCIS resources. Ask a Career Advisor for assistance.
		d. Use the *College Majors Card Sort* to find majors and occupational opportunities.
		e. Review employment information in the *Undergraduate Academic Program Guide* for FSU majors.
		f. Use the SDS code assigned to a particular FSU major to search for occupations in the *SDS Occupations Finder* or the *Dictionary of Holland Occupational Codes* (IA G6).
		g. Examine materials on FSU academic programs in File 3.
		h. Review selected Employer Directors that list organizations by major, career, or geographical areas.
		i. Consult with Career Center staff members in Placement Services and Career Experience Opportunities (CEO).
		j. With assistance from a Career Advisor, explore opportunities on Career Key for informational interviews, extern experiences, and networking assistance with participating professionals and FSU alumni.

SOURCE: From *Curricular Career Information Service*, by R. C. Reardon, 1996. Unpublished manuscript, Florida State University. Reprinted by permission.

systems and internships at most institutions of higher learning. (See chapter 7 for more information on career centers.) Finally, some institutions offer career-related services to alumni.

Career Counseling: A Metroplex Model

A large university located in a metropolitan area may have the added responsibility of satisfying heavy alumni demand for career-related services. Not only is the career center faced with a large volume of currently enrolled students choosing from diverse academic programs, but also must respond to a wide variety of alumni requests for career counseling. Alumni contemplating career changes with subsequent reentry into the workforce represent a unique dimension of career counseling.

The following examples of unique client needs exemplify the complexity of programs needed in career centers: (1) individuals (young adults through middle age) anticipating a change of career direction; (2) individuals seeking relocation within their career field; (3) individuals desiring mobility within their career field through further educational training; (4) individuals seeking information about specific current job-market trends; (5) individuals seeking college reentry planning; and (6) individuals seeking second careers after early retirement from a primary career. In addition, many adults residing in the metropolitan area will seek assistance for career education planning before university enrollment. Thus, a career center metroplex model must be able to provide a wide range of services for currently enrolled students, as well as for alumni and others in the community seeking assistance and/or career redirection.

Work- and Experience-Based Programs

A growing trend in all levels of education is to provide students the opportunity for work experience as a vital part of their educational programs. Although student teaching and a variety of intern and extern experiences are not novel ideas in institutions of higher learning, some innovations should interest the career counselor. One such innovation is the extern experience.

The *extern* model provides the student with an opportunity to observe ongoing activities in his or her major field of study and to interact with individuals on the job. The extern model differs from an internship in two ways: (1) the extern experience is of short duration, usually during semester breaks, and (2) students usually do not receive course credit for an extern experience, as most of their experiences involve observation and job shadowing. Generally, at the beginning of or before the senior year, students submit a proposal of their career goals with a statement of how the extern experience would help them meet these goals. Career centers or other administrative entities have agreements with host agencies to offer such experiences. Selected students will spend a specified time with a host agency during midsemester break or during an interim semester.

Intern models, by contrast, provide students with the opportunity to spend more time in a workplace and are more work-experience oriented than extern models. Interns actually do the work they are being trained to do. For example, junior-level students planning to become accountants may be chosen by an accounting firm to intern in one of its offices. Actual accounting work will be done under the supervision of a member of the firm. The time spent in this experience is usually negotiated so it doesn't interfere with the student's progress toward a degree.

Job shadowing also gives college students a window to view future work environments. In this program, college students explore an occupation by observing at a job site. As they observe, they ask questions and practice working with people while making valuable contacts for future use. This program requires colleges and universities to make certain that work observation will be meaningful and constructive. Formal programs include orientation (briefing students on program requirements); matching (students are matched with volunteers who have agreed to serve as a host); shadowing (students spend several hours on the job with the host and may do hands-on work); and after-shadowing (students write thank-you letters and reflect on what they have learned). Job shadowing usually takes place during semester breaks (Mariani, 1998).

The practice of providing college students with actual work experience related to their college majors should proliferate during the 21st century. The duration of the experience also may increase; students will find an expanded timeframe more beneficial than current extern programs allow. As colleges attempt to help students make more realistic career choices, more experience-based models could certainly emerge. In sum, some students may spend a part of their university experience off-campus.

Summary

1. During high school, improved perceptual skills help students make accurate predictions of the future, judge consistency of actions, and recognize expected behavior in their community and culture.

2. High school students have developed enhanced information-processing skills that help them solve problems, process information, and learn to use a variety of study skills.

3. Career goals and competencies for high school suggest more independent actions on the part of high school students, and greater acceptance of more responsibility for their decisions.

4. ASCA National Standards for School Counseling Programs and Suggested Student Competencies include the domains of Academic Development, Career Development, and Personal–Social Development.

5. National career guidelines include a competency focus on three broad domains—personal social development, educational achievement, and career management.

6. Group strategies for addressing career development include enhancing one's self-knowledge, occupational exploration skills, career planning skills, learning how to avoid sex-role stereotyping, and improving decision-making skills.

7. Career-related programs in high school include preparing students for college, addressing college awareness and readiness for low-income students, tech-prep programs, and career and technology programs.

8. Placement services are an important part of career centers in schools and colleges. State employment agencies also offer placement services.

9. A variety of career counseling programs are offered at community colleges and four-year institutions of higher education.

Supplementary Learning Exercises

1. Interview a representative from the business community for suggestions about how to establish collaborative efforts to meet school-to-work objectives. Summarize your recommendations.
2. Interview a school counselor to determine the role and scope of his or her career development program. Evaluate your findings and offer suggestions.
3. Develop a format that could be used annually to evaluate the career planning progress of high school students.
4. Develop objectives and goals for a mini-course on decision making for senior high school students.
5. Visit a local industry to determine the kinds of on-site job experiences available. Write a description of at least five possible on-site jobs.

Case 17.1   A High School Student's Father Loses His Job

Ben grew up in a small town in the midwest. He is now a sophomore in the local high school. He has one older brother and two younger sisters. His father was employed in a local manufacturing plant for 15 years until it closed about 4 months ago. Ben's father now works as a clerk in a local department store. His mother has returned to work as a secretary in a legal firm. She had been a stay-at-home mother for more than a decade but returned to the workforce when the local manufacturing plant was shut down and Ben's father lost his job. The family home has been located in the same neighborhood for 15 years. Like many other families in this small town, Ben's family lives on a tight budget.

Ben and his older brother are very close. Ben often seeks his brother's advice and he has good relationships with his sisters. The family has been united in their efforts to overcome the loss of what was supposed to be the father's lifetime job. All members of the family have taken on assigned household tasks. The family attends church each Sunday and has been active in community organizations.

It was during the early part of the spring semester that Ben's teacher noticed a significant change in his behavior. He had become a loner, was inattentive in class, and ignored his friends. In a meeting after class, Ben told his teacher that he did not like school any longer. Ben also stopped going to baseball practice. Sensing a developing potentially serious problem, the teacher referred Ben to the counseling center.

Ben reported to the career counselor who had previously advised him about the future job market. The counselor quickly recognized that Ben was not the same Ben that she had met with before. He was distant, rather lethargic, and presented other signs of depression, as well as anxiety. Ben was restless and focused on concerns about life circumstances including family matters and changes in family life that he didn't like or accept. The impact of job loss by his father had taken its toll on the entire family. Ben stated, "My father tried to cover up his worries after he lost his job but it's not working anymore."

Use the model of resilience by Sue et al. (2014) as presented in the previous chapter on page 377 to organize your response. How would you explain to Ben how the following intervention components could be helpful now and in the future?

1. Learn coping and problem-solving skills.
2. Use meaningful social relationships.
3. Learn to control emotions.
4. Seek help through connections with others.
5. Learn to face adversity with personal assets and strength.

Discuss with classmates how resiliency is related to career choice and development. Emphasize identity, self-determination, self-esteem, self-efficacy, and values.

Appendix A

Chronology of Counseling Movement

1850–1920

- The rise of industrialism in the late 1800s significantly changed the way people worked and lived. Urban areas grew quickly, attracting many immigrants and people from rural areas. Work and living environments were significantly changed for both men and women. Men worked in factories and women worked at home.

- There was a significant loss of jobs in the agricultural sector.

- Early in the 20th century, George Merrill developed a plan for students to explore industrial arts courses in San Francisco.

- Between 1898 and 1907, Jeff Davis was designated as an educational and vocational counselor at Central High in Detroit. Later, as a school principal in Grand Rapids, Michigan, he provided class time to offer career-related information to students.

- Frank Parson, often referred to as the father of the vocational guidance movement, founded the Vocations Bureau of Boston in 1908. He published *Choosing a Vocation* in 1909, establishing a three-step procedure for career decision making that remains as a significant benchmark. He also lobbied to eliminate child labor.

- By 1910, about 35 cities had some form of vocational guidance in their schools. The first National Conference on Vocational Guidance took place in Boston in 1910. Other conferences followed, and in 1913 the National Vocational Guidance Association (NVGA) was incorporated.

- The first vocational guidance course was taught at Harvard by Meyer Bloomfield in 1911. Hugo Munsterberg of Harvard established industrial psychology as a relevant field of applied psychology.

- His book *Psychological and Industrial Efficiency*, published in 1913, included studies of occupational choice and worker performance. This movement focused attention on work organizations and their employees.

- In 1915, the NVGA began publishing the *Vocational Guidance Bulletin*.

- In 1917, the Smith-Hughes Act was passed to provide funds for vocational guidance services. As a direct result, nationwide vocational guidance programs were launched.

- During the late 1800s, the mental measurement movement also grew and flourished. In 1890, James M. Cattell introduced the concept of mental tests to determine mental abilities as an important factor of human traits. In 1909, the first intelligence test was developed by Binet and Simon in France. In 1916, L. M. Terman of Stanford published the *Stanford-Binet Intelligence Test*.

- During World War I (1914–1918), large numbers of recruits were administered ability tests, known as Army Alpha and Beta tests for classification and placement in the armed services. These tests also served as an example for the development of assessment measures used in career counseling.

- E. K. Strong of Stanford introduced the *Strong Vocational Interest Blank* in 1927. This measure of interest, constructed from the responses of individuals in certain occupations, provided an important tool for linking assessment of interests with certain occupations.

- In 1928, Clark L. Hull published *Aptitude Testing*, suggesting that human traits could be matched with job requirements.

- Achievement testing in schools made rapid progress during the 1920s. Personality testing was used during World War I but was much slower in development.

1930–1950

- The significant events that took place during this time were the Great Depression and World War II (1939–1945) and its aftermath. Unemployment was a major social issue in this country and in many others.

- During the Great Depression in the 1930s, the federal government passed several legislative acts designed to help individuals find work. Two federal agencies that helped create jobs were the Works Progress Administration and the Civilian Conservation Corps.

- In addition, the U.S. Employment Service was established in 1933 by the Wagner-Peyser Act.

- The Occupational Information and Guidance service was established in 1938 under the George-Dean Act.

- The first edition of the *Dictionary of Occupational Titles* was published in 1939 by the U.S. Department of Labor.

- In the private sector, the B'nai B'rith Vocational Service Bureau was established in 1938 and offered vocational guidance programs in metropolitan areas.

- During World War II, the armed services once again needed testing procedures to classify recruits. As a result, the *Army General Classification Test* (AGCT) was developed in 1940.

- In 1944, the Veterans Administration established centers throughout the country for career-related services that were offered to returning veterans.

- The George-Barden Act was passed in 1946, making funds available to establish counselor-training programs in all states.

- *How to Counsel Students* by E. G. Williamson was published in 1939; this work was characterized by some as supporting a directive counseling approach of matching abilities and interests with job requirements.

- Carl Rogers's famous book *Counseling and Psychotherapy* was published in 1942. He and his colleagues joined together to attack directive counseling by suggesting that more attention should be given to clients' needs to gain an understanding of self and to take steps to control their own destiny. More emphasis was directed to the client and his or her ability to solve personal concerns.

- The *Occupational Outlook* was first published in 1948 by the U.S. Department of Labor.
- The measurement movement continued its growth with the establishment of the Educational Testing Service in 1948. This entity published the *Scholastic Aptitude Tests*, designed to measure one's potential of success in college.

1950–1980

- Two events that stand out at the beginning of this period were the Korean War (1950–1953) and the expansion of the "cold war."
- In 1951, an important merger of professional organizations took place. The following organizations merged to form the American Personnel and Guidance Association (APGA): American College Personnel Association, National Association of Guidance Supervisors and College Trainers, National Vocational Guidance Association, and Student Personnel Association for Teacher Education.
- In the early 1950s, Ginzberg, Ginsburg, Axelrad, and Herma (1951); Roe (1956); and Super (1957) developed and published career development and occupational choice theories. These were followed by theories from Blau, Gustad, Jessor, Parnes, and Wilcox (1956) and Tiedeman and O'Hara (1963). Career development theories became landmarks in the career counseling movement. More theories followed, including one by Holland (1966), and others continue to be developed.
- The American College Testing Program (ACT) was founded in 1959. Other commercial test publishers merged into larger companies and corporations.
- Working conditions generally improved after the World War II years. By 1960, the career counseling movement increasingly was supported by federal and local governmental bodies, including schools and universities.
- Manpower legislation designed to create new jobs through occupational training was passed by Congress.
- Civil rights legislation was enacted in 1964. The 1960s were known for major value upheavals in response to the Vietnam War.
- Amendments to the Vocational Educational Act of 1963 provided guidance services for elementary and secondary schools, public community colleges, and technical institutes. Counselor training programs expanded and flourished.
- The career education movement in the 1970s was created to specifically address career development, attitudes, and values infused within traditional learning. Career education focused on career awareness, career exploration, value clarification, decision-making skills, career orientation, and career preparation.
- In 1976, the National Occupational Information Coordinating Committee was established by Congress. Its purpose was to sponsor projects to establish national career counseling and development guidelines at state and local levels.

1980–Present

- During this period of time, the career counseling movement continued to flourish and expanded its services with a greater concentration on the needs of minorities and women. The global economy became a driving force behind changes in how and where people work.

- The Joint Training Partnership Act (JTPA) was enacted in 1982. It provided career services for retraining workers and for disadvantaged youth. The Carl Perkins Vocational Education Act of 1984 expanded career services to address the needs of vocational education students. Other expansions of this act in the 1990s have continued to support career services.

- In 1984, the National Certified Career Counselors organization was founded to offer national certification to counselors.

- The NVGA changed its name to the National Career Development Association (NCDA) in 1985. In 1986, its publication *Vocational Guidance Quarterly* became the *Career Development Quarterly*.

- The Americans with Disabilities Act (ADA) was passed in 1992, which provided that employers are to have reasonable work accommodations for persons with disabilities.

- In the 1990s, the Internet offered career counseling websites that are increasingly being used by job seekers and adults in career transition. Ethical standards continue to be developed concerning the use of websites for job search, assessment, and career counseling.

- The School-to-Work Opportunities Act was passed in 1994. This act provided funds to enhance school-to-school and school-to-work transitions.

- In 1998, the Workforce Investment Act offered career services to disadvantaged youth, adults, and dislocated workers.

- In 1999, the NCDA board of directors endorsed a new Council on Workforce and Career Development Associations, reflecting a broad scope of interests and collaborations with private practice, business, and agency counselors both domestically and internationally (Pope, 2000).

- On September 11, 2001, terrorists attacked the United States and the war on terrorism was launched. Career counseling will continue to focus on the relationship between career issues and other life issues that evolve from these events.

- The economic recession in 2009 led to massive financial problems for major firms as well as small businesses. Unemployment significantly increased in this country and globally. Job loss has affected many American families.

The major sources of this chronology is from Herr (2001), Picchioni and Bonk (1983), and Pope (2000).

Appendix B

Table of Basic Assumptions, Key Terms, and Outcomes

Theories	Basic Assumptions	Key Terms	Outcomes
Trait-Oriented Theories			
Trait-and-Factor	Individuals have unique patterns of ability or traits that can be objectively measured and correlated with requirements of occupations.	*Traits* primarily refer to abilities and interests. Parsons's three-step model includes studying the individual, surveying occupations, and matching the individual with an occupation.	The primary goal of using assessment data was to predict job satisfaction and success. Contemporary practices stress the relationships between human factors and work environments. Test data are used to observe the similarity between client and current workers in a career field.
Person-Environment–Correspondence Counseling	Individuals bring requirements to a work environment, and the work environment makes its requirements of individuals. To survive, individuals and work environments must achieve some degree of congruence.	*Personality structure* is a stable characteristic made up of abilities and values. *Ability dimensions* indicate levels of work skills. *Values* are considered as work needs. *Satisfactoriness* refers to clients who are more achievement-oriented. *Satisfaction* refers to more self-fulfilled oriented clients. *Work adjustment* refers to a worker's attempt to improve fit in a work environment.	Client abilities (work skills) and values (work needs) are criteria used for selecting work environments. Work requirements determine reinforcers available by occupations. Knowledge of clients who are more achievement- (satisfactoriness) or self-fulfilled (satisfaction) oriented enhances career choice.
John Holland: A Typology Approach	Career choice is an expression of or an extension of personality into the world of work. Individuals search for environments that will let them exercise their skills and abilities, express their attitudes and values, and take on agreeable problems and roles. There are six kinds of occupational environments and six matching personal orientations.	The six types of categories for individuals and work environment are *Realistic, Investigative, Artistic, Social, Enterprising,* and *Conventional. Consistency* refers to personality, i.e., those clients who relate strongly to one or more of the categories. *Differentiation* refers to those who have poorly defined personality styles. *Identity* refers to the degree in which one identifies with a work environment. *Congruence* is a good match between individual and work environment.	Individuals are products of their environment. Stability of career choice depends on dominance of personal orientation. Individuals who fit a pure personality type will express little resemblance to other types. Clients who have many occupational goals have low identity. Congruence occurs when client's personality type matches the corresponding work environment.

THEORIES	BASIC ASSUMPTIONS	KEY TERMS	OUTCOMES

Social Learning and Cognitive Theories

THEORIES	BASIC ASSUMPTIONS	KEY TERMS	OUTCOMES
Krumboltz's Learning Theory Approach	Each individual's unique learning experiences over the life span develop primary influences that lead to career choice. Development involves genetic endowments and special abilities, environmental conditions and events, learning experiences and task approach skills.	*Genetic endowments* are inherited qualities that may set limits on career choice. *Environmental conditions* are contextual interactions that influence individual choices. *Instrumental learning experiences* are those acquired through observation, consequences, and reaction of others. *Associative learning experiences* are negative and positive reactions to neutral experiences. *Task approach skills* are work habits, mental sets, emotional responses, and cognitive responses.	Learning experiences should increase the range of occupations in career counseling. Assessment is to be used to create new learning experiences. Clients need to prepare for changing work tasks. Career decision making is a learned skill. Clients need to be empowered as active participants in career search.
Career Development from a Cognitive Information-Processing Perspective	Ten basic assumptions of this theory are outlined and explained in Table 2.2. Two overarching assumptions facilitating the growth of information-processing skills and enhancing the client's ability to solve problems and make career decisions.	CASVE involves the following generic processing skills: *Communication* (identifying a need), *Analysis* (interrelating problem components), *Synthesis* (creating likely alternatives), *Valuing* (prioritizing alternatives), and *Execution* (forming means-end strategies).	Career problem solving is primarily a cognitive process. Information processing can be improved through learning. Effective information-processing skills can empower individuals to determine their own destiny. Making career choices is a problem-solving activity.
Career Development from a Social Cognitive Perspective	This theory is embedded in general social cognitive theory, which blends cognitive, self, regulatory, and motivational processes into a lifelong phenomenon. Personal and physical attributes, external environmental factors, and overt behavior all interact as causal influences on individual development.	*Personal agency* reflects how a person exerts power to achieve a solution. *Triadic reciprocal interactions,* as explained in the basic assumptions, are from Bandura's (1986) social learning theory.	Self-efficacy is strengthened as success is experienced in a performance domain and is weakened with repeated failures; outcome expectations are shaped by similar experiences. Personal goals and/or personal agency act to sustain behavior. Career choice is influenced by environmental factors. Overcoming barriers to choice is a significant goal of this theory.

Developmental Theories

THEORIES	BASIC ASSUMPTIONS	KEY TERMS	OUTCOMES
Life-Span, Life-Space Approach	Career development is multidimensional. There are developmental tasks throughout the life span. Vocational maturity is acquired through successfully accomplishing	Stages of vocational development are Growth, Exploratory, Establishment, Maintenance, and Decline. Developmental tasks are Crystallization, Specification, Implementation, Stabilization,	Career development is a lifelong process occurring in stages. Self-concept is shaped through life experiences. Clients are involved in several life roles of child, student, leisure, citizen, worker, spouse, homemaker, parent,

THEORIES	BASIC ASSUMPTIONS	KEY TERMS	OUTCOMES

Developmental Theories (*Continued*)

| | developmental tasks within a continuous series of life stages. Individuals implement their self-concepts into careers that will provide the most efficient means of self-expressions. Success in one life role facilitates success in another. | and Consolidation. Self-concept is the driving force that establishes a career pattern. Attitudes and competencies are related to career growth and identified as career maturity. | and pensioner. All life roles affect one another. In development, societal factors interact with biological and psychological factors. |
| *Circumscription and Compromise: A Developmental Theory of Occupational Aspirations* | A key factor in career decision is self-concept, determined by one's social class, level of intelligence, and experiences with sex-typing. Individuals progress through four stages and learn to compromise based on generalizations of cognitive maps of occupations. Individuals are less willing to compromise job level and sex-type. | *Self-concept* is one's view of self. *Cognitive maps* of occupations reflect dimensions of prestige level, masculinity/femininity, and field of work. *Social space* refers to a zone or view of where each person fits into society. *Circumscription* is the process of narrowing one's territory of social space or alternative. *Compromise* suggests that individuals will settle for a good choice but not best. | Individual development consists of four stages: Orientation to size and power, orientation to sex roles, orientation to social valuation, and orientation to internal unique self. Socioeconomic background and intellectual level greatly influence self-concept. Occupational choices are determined by social space, intellectual level, and sex-typing. Career choice is a process of eliminating options through cognitive maps. Individuals compromise occupational choices because of accessibility. Circumscription of occupations occurs through self-awareness, sex-type, and social class. |

Person-in-Environment Perspective

| *Career Construction: A Developmental Theory of Vocational Behavior* | This theory focuses attention on contextual interactions over the life span. One's career development is constructed as individuals influence and are influenced within environmental systems. Clients are viewed as products of their environment. Vocational behavior is a core element in career construction theory. | Self-concepts guide and evaluate one's behavior. Career patterns are determined primarily by a combination of parental status, one's educational level, traits, and self-concepts. Vocational maturity as a psychosocial construct is determined by one's level of vocational development. Life roles are interactive and are reciprocally shaped by each other. Developmental tasks in career construction include growth, exploration, crystallization, establishment, maintenance or management, and disengagement. | Career construction theory focuses on assisting individuals with developmental tasks over the life span. It is a counseling process that helps clients construct and manage their careers. One overarching goal is to help individuals to increase their realism in making career choices and transitions. To accomplish this goal, they are to focus on understanding their vocational self-concept and validate their vocational identity. Each client's life story becomes a means of understanding self and subsequent focus for future growth. |

THEORIES	BASIC ASSUMPTIONS	KEY TERMS	OUTCOMES

Person-in-Environment Perspective (*Continued*)

A Contextual Explanation of Career	As people and their environments interact, development can proceed along many different pathways, depending on how one influences the other. A developmental-contextual life span assumes that interacting with a changing environment provides a foundation for individuals to form their own development.	*Contextualism* is a method of describing events or actions in an individual's life and a way in which counselors understand influences in career development from an individual's environmental interactions. *Actions* refer to the whole context in which an action is taken, how events take shape as people engage in them.	The study of actions is the major focus of the contextual viewpoint. Actions manifest behaviors they are internal processes, and they have social meaning. Environmental actions are to be observed from a "wholeness," that is, the influence of events that people engage in. Events take shape as people engage in them, and the totality of the actions and events influences participants.

Other Theories

Ann Roe: A Needs Approach	Early childhood experiences and parental style affect the needs hierarchy and the relationships of those needs to adult lifestyle. Those who choose nonperson-type jobs are meeting lower-level needs for safety and security. Those who choose to work with other people have strong needs.	Examples of person-oriented occupations are service, business contact, managerial, teaching, and entertainment. Nonperson-oriented occupations are technology, outdoors, and science.	Original position was that individuals who enjoy working with people were reared by warm accepting parents and those who avoid contact with others were reared by cold or rejecting parents. Current position is that there are other important factors that determine occupational choice not accounted for in her theory.
Ginzberg and Associates	Occupational choice is a developmental process covering 6 to 10 years beginning at age 11 and ending shortly after age 17. As tentative occupational decisions are made, other choices are eliminated.	Stages of career development are Fantasy, Tentative, and Realistic. In *Fantasy*, play becomes work-oriented. In *Tentative*, there is recognition of work requirements and one's traits. In *Realistic*, one narrows occupational choices.	Career choice is a developed precept of occupations subjectively appraised in sociocultural milieu from childhood to early adult. There are three stages of development from before age 11 to young adult.

Appendix C

Multicultural Career Counseling Checklist for Female Clients

If you have a client of a different ethnicity/race than yours, you may wish to use this checklist as you begin to do the career assessment with your client.

The following statements are designed to help you think more thoroughly about the racially or ethnically different client to whom you are about to provide career counseling. Check all the statements that apply.

My racial/ethnic identity: _____

My client's racial/ethnic identity: _____

I. Counselor Preparation

❑ 1. I am familiar with minimum cross-cultural counseling competencies.

❑ 2. I am aware of my client's cultural identification.

❑ 3. I understand and respect my client's culture.

❑ 4. I am aware of my own worldview and how it was shaped.

❑ 5. I am aware of how my SES influences my ability to empathize with this client.

❑ 6. I am aware of how my political views influence my counseling with a client from this ethnic group.

❑ 7. I have had counseling or other life experiences with different racial/ethnic groups.

❑ 8. I have information about this client's ethnic group's history, local sociopolitical issues, and attitudes toward seeking help.

❑ 9. I know many of the strengths of this client's ethnic group.

❑ 10. I know where I am in my racial identity development.

❑ 11. I know the general stereotypes held about my client's ethnic group.

❑ 12. I am comfortable confronting ethnic minority clients.

❑ 13. I am aware of the importance of the interaction of gender and race/ethnicity in my client's life.

II. Exploration and Assessment

❑ 1. I understand this client's career questions.

❑ 2. I understand how the client's career questions may be complicated with issues of finance, family, and academics.

❑ 3. The client is presenting racial and/or cultural information with the career questions.

❑ 4. I am aware of the career limitations or obstacles the client associates with his/her race or culture.

❑ 5. I understand what the client's perceived limitations are.

❑ 6. I know the client's perception of her/his family's ethnocultural identification.

❑ 7. I am aware of the client's perception of his/her family's support for her career.

❑ 8. I know which career the client believes her/his family wants him/her to pursue.

❑ 9. I know whether the client's family's support is important to him/her.

❑ 10. I believe that familial obligations are dictating the client's career choices.

❑ 11. I know the extent of exposure to career information and role models the client had in high school and beyond.

❑ 12. I understand the impact that high school experiences (positive or negative) have had on the client's confidence.

❑ 13. I am aware of the client's perception of his/her competence, ability, and self-efficacy.

❑ 14. I believe the client avoids certain work environments because of fears of sexism or racism.

❑ 15. I know the client's stage of racial identity development.

III. Negotiation and Working Consensus

❑ 1. I understand the type of career counseling help the client is seeking (career choice, supplement of family income, professional career, etc.).

❑ 2. The client and I have agreed on the goals for career counseling.

❑ 3. I know how this client's role in the family influences her/his career choices.

❑ 4. I am aware of the client's perception of the work role in the family and culture.

❑ 5. I am aware of the client's understanding of the role of children in his/her career plans.

❑ 6. I am aware of the extent of exposure to a variety of career role models the client has had.

❑ 7. I understand the culturally based career conflicts that are generated by exposure to more careers and role models.

❑ 8. I know the client's career aspirations.

❑ 9. I am aware of the level of confidence the client has in the ability to obtain her/his aspirations.

❑ 10. I know the client understands the relationship between type of work and educational level.

❑ 11. I am aware of the negative and/or self-defeating thoughts that are obstacles to the client's aspirations and expectations.

❑ 12. I know if the client and I need to renegotiate her/his goals as appropriate after exploring cultural and family issues.

❑ 13. I know the client understands the career exploration process.

❑ 14. I am aware of the client's expectations about the career counseling process.

❑ 15. I know when it is appropriate to use a traditional career assessment instrument with a client from this ethnic group.

❑ 16. I know which instrument to use with this client.

❑ 17. I am aware of the research support for using the selected instrument with clients of this ethnicity.

❑ 18. I am aware of nontraditional instruments that might be more appropriate for use with clients from this ethnic group.

❑ 19. I am aware of nontraditional approaches to using traditional instruments with clients from this ethnic group.

❑ 20. I am aware of the career strengths the client associates with her race or culture.

Appendix D

Career Counseling Checklist

The following statements are designed to help you think more thoroughly about your career concerns and to help your assessment counselor understand you better. Please try to answer them as honestly as possible. Check all of the items that are true for you.

- ❏ 1. I feel obligated to do what others want me to do, and these expectations conflict with my own desires.
- ❏ 2. I have lots of interests, but I do not know how to narrow them down.
- ❏ 3. I am afraid of making a serious mistake with my career choice.
- ❏ 4. I do not feel confident that I know in which areas my true interests lie.
- ❏ 5. I feel uneasy with the responsibility for making a good career choice.
- ❏ 6. I lack information about my skills, interests, needs, and values with regard to my career choice.
- ❏ 7. My physical ability may greatly influence my career choice.
- ❏ 8. I lack knowledge about the world of work and what it has to offer me.
- ❏ 9. I know what I want my career to be, but it doesn't feel like a realistic goal.
- ❏ 10. I feel I am the only one who does not have a career plan.
- ❏ 11. I lack knowledge about myself and what I have to offer the world of work.
- ❏ 12. I do not really know what is required from a career for me to feel satisfied.
- ❏ 13. I feel that problems in my personal life are hindering me from making a good career decision.
- ❏ 14. My ethnicity may influence my career choice.
- ❏ 15. No matter how much information I have about a career, I keep going back and forth and cannot make up my mind.
- ❏ 16. I tend to be a person who gives up easily.
- ❏ 17. I believe that I am largely to blame for the lack of success I feel in making a career decision.
- ❏ 18. I have great difficulty making most decisions about my life.
- ❏ 19. My age may influence my career choice.
- ❏ 20. I expect my career decision to take care of most of the boredom and emptiness that I feel.
- ❏ 21. I have difficulty making commitments.
- ❏ 22. I don't have any idea of what I want in life, who I am, or what's important to me.
- ❏ 23. I have difficulty completing things.
- ❏ 24. I am afraid of making mistakes.
- ❏ 25. Religious values may greatly influence my career choice.

❑ 26. At this point, I am thinking more about finding a job than about choosing a career.

❑ 27. Family responsibilities will probably limit my career ambitions.

❑ 28. My orientation to career is very different from that of the members of my family.

❑ 29. I have worked on a job that taught me some things about what I want or do not want in a career, but I still feel lost.

❑ 30. Some classes in school are much easier for me than others, but I don't know how to use this information.

❑ 31. My race may greatly influence my career choice.

❑ 32. My long-term goals are more firm than my short-term goals.

❑ 33. I have some career-related daydreams that I do not share with many people.

❑ 34. I have been unable to see a connection between my college work and a possible career.

❑ 35. I have made a career choice with which I am comfortable, but I need specific assistance in finding a job.

❑ 36. My gender may influence my career choice.

❑ 37. I have undergone a change in my life, which necessitates a change in my career plans.

❑ 38. My fantasy is that there is one perfect job for me, if I can find it.

❑ 39. I have been out of the world of work for a period of time and I need to redefine my career choice.

❑ 40. Making a great deal of money is an important career goal for me, but I am unsure as to how I might reach it.

❑ 41. My immigration status may influence my career choice.

Appendix E

The Decision Tree

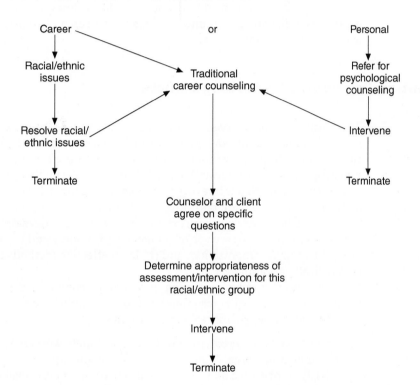

Appendix F

Intervention Strategies

Intervention strategies should focus on multiple factors associated with gender typing and its effect on career development and multiple life roles. A number of cognitive-behavioral techniques can be used to modify gender stereotypes. Group counseling composed of both women and men can include an almost endless number of components. The following group interventions are representative of activities that can be used to address gender issues.

Intervention Component I—Working Climate

The purpose of this intervention strategy is to prepare men and women alike for challenges they may face in work environments. Each individual will face a different set of circumstances, especially those who are required to work in different sites, but some general guidelines are relevant for all: (1) learn effective methods of communicating in work environment that is free of gender-role stereotyping, (2) recognize that positions of authority may include both males and females, (3) be prepared to interact with members of both sexes in decision-making groups, (4) develop skills that contribute to good worker–supervisor relationships, (5) understand the role of the informal group in a typical organization, and (6) learn effective methods of establishing rapport with all peer affiliates.

A combination of role-playing exercises, discussion groups, and effective use of audiovisual material is recommended for accomplishing the specific tasks of this intervention. Some specific tasks are as follows:

1. Identify typical stereotyping of female and male workers in the workplace and illustrate how stereotyping affects work relationships.
2. Clarify competitive nature of working environment especially among knowledge workers of both sexes.
3. Identify and clarify interpersonal skills needed by both men and women in the work environment.
4. Discuss a variety of potential interactions in work settings including shared work roles and power relationships.

Intervention Component II—Expressiveness Training

The two goals of this component are to help clients identify situations in which it is appropriate to express their emotions and to learn that it is acceptable to freely express emotions in those situations. Inexpressiveness can become highly dysfunctional in many relationships, including those with peer affiliates in the work environment, children, spouse, and friends. Self-disclosure may be difficult for some participants who may be especially guarded and do not want to reveal any real or imagined weakness to fellow workers. Men as well as women may resist certain cooperative tasks that could expose their vulnerability.

Counselors should recall that some cultural groups, especially Asian Americans and Native Americans, believe that someone who publicly displays emotional responses is weak or immature. Special consideration should be given to these groups by explaining differences between cultures and American workers who have a European background.

Specific tasks of this intervention strategy follow.

1. Clarify how individual behavior has been shaped through contextual situations and conditions. Explore differences and similarities between men and women.
2. Discuss the advantages of expressive behavior and disadvantage of inexpressive behavior.
3. Identify rigid gender roles that affect one's resistance to disclose followed with examples and illustrations.
4. Clarify potential problems of inexpressive behavior at work, in the home, with colleagues, and with friends.
5. Identify and discuss factors that prohibit expressive behavior.
6. Clarify the differences between self-control and inexpressive behavior.
7. Role-play/rehearse expressive behavior.

Intervention Component III—Dual-Career Roles

In chapter 10, we acknowledged that an increasing number of women are planning lifelong careers in a wide range of occupations. Women are giving career development a higher priority than—or at least equal status to—other priorities, such as marriage and family. Dual-career families are becoming less novel in the 2000s, but the increased prevalence of this lifestyle has not been accompanied by changes in values, beliefs, or behaviors of many of the men or women in these marriages. Men may have difficulty making the transition from traditional attitudes of man-at-work/woman-at-home to that of negotiating dual-career and family roles. These entrenched attitudes and perceptions of appropriate masculine roles will die slowly because of the longstanding socialization process that has stereotyped gender-role models. The process of change requires one to recognize deeply rooted patterns of masculine role behavior and attitudes toward women in general. However, research in the early 1980s and 1990s indicates that when men are challenged to modify their behavior in dual-career families, they change their attitudes and actions (Matlin, 2000).

The recent shift of roles in dual-career families gives this intervention component credibility for helping husbands make adjustments in their attitudes toward their wives' career aspirations, demonstrating advantages of fathers being able to participate in their children's lives more directly, and encouraging men to assume a greater role in household management responsibilities. Women as well as men should learn to understand that modifying gender-role behaviors and the thinking process that drives behavior will require cooperation between both spouses.

The specific tasks in this strategy are designed to clarify the concept of dual-career families and to introduce changes in male role models. Special consideration should be given to the task of identifying and clarifying dual-career family problems. Rapoport and Rapoport (1978) captured the essence of dual-career family problems in the 1970s that continue to be relevant: (1) overload dilemmas (the management of household and child-rearing activities), (2) personal norm dilemmas (conflicts arising from what parents consider proper lifestyle and what other individuals consider proper), (3) identity dilemmas (intrinsic conflicts associated with life roles), (4) social network dilemmas (conflicts associated with relatives, friends, and other associates), and (5) role cycle dilemmas (conflicts associated with family life cycles such as birth of a child, a child leaving home, and other domestic issues that produce stress on career development). Suggested solutions include shared responsibility exercises, time-management techniques, and effective planning between parents who have discussed and established individual and family priorities. Shared responsibility and role-coping exercises also can be used in this component.

Specific tasks include the following:

- Clarify the concept of dual earners and dual careers.
- Clarify how socialization has determined gender roles in the United States.
- Clarify the concept of an egalitarian marriage.
- Identify and discuss methods of sharing household management and tasks.
- Clarify how husband and wife can visualize multiple life roles as a joint family effort.
- Identify and clarify changing styles of interaction between spouses who both support dual-career concepts.
- Identify changing attitudes in relation to work and responsibilities in dual-career families.

Intervention Component IV—Lifestyle Skills

To learn that every person is unique and should be considered as an individual who has certain aptitudes, interests, and aspirations is the primary purpose of this intervention strategy. Women, especially in developed countries, have more control over their lives than ever before. Men also determine their lifestyle orientation and preferences in regard to career, family, leisure, place of residence, work climate, and overall style of life. We have not yet reached the ultimate androgynous society and probably never will, but we have taken giant steps away from gender-role stereotypes. Specific tasks include the following:

- Explore lifestyle factors of financial orientation including independence and social prominence.
- Discuss benefits derived from participation in community activities and community services.
- Clarify work-related needs of achievement, career development, and commitment.
- Clarify orientation toward family life.
- Explore the reasons for a commitment toward self-improvement through lifelong learning.
- Identify how life roles are interrelated and intertwined.

In sum, what should be communicated is that every person is an individual who has certain strengths and weaknesses and, like everyone else, is unique. The challenge is to clarify individual uniqueness (self-image, skills, and aspirations) and to project those characteristics into all life roles. In this intervention component, special attention is directed toward goal-setting from an individualized frame of reference. Clarifying work identity, free of sex-role stereotyping, along with individual strengths and weaknesses, is to be fostered. Learning to be assertive and not overly aggressive is an important lifestyle skill. One's individuality could be explored through discussing background experiences, including contextual interactions involving family, peers, school, and other life events. Finally, gender issues are to be viewed as important constructs to be addressed in one's worldview.

Appendix G

National Standards for School Counseling Programs and Suggested Student Competencies

I. Academic development
  A. Students will acquire the attitudes, knowledge, and skills that contribute to effective learning in school and across the life span.
    1. To improve academic self-concept, students will:
      - articulate feelings of competence and confidence as a learner
      - display a positive interest in learning
      - take pride in work and in achievement
      - accept mistakes as essential to the learning process
      - identify attitudes and behaviors which lead to successful learning
    2. To acquire skills for improving learning, students will:
      - apply time management and task management skills
      - demonstrate how effort and persistence positively affect learning
      - use communication skills to know when and how to ask for help when needed
      - apply knowledge of learning styles to positively influence school performance
    3. To achieve school success, students will:
      - take responsibility for their actions
      - demonstrate the ability to work independently, as well as the ability to work cooperatively with other students
      - develop a broad range of interests and abilities
      - demonstrate dependability, productivity, and initiative
      - share knowledge
  B. Students will complete school with the academic preparation essential to choose from a wide range of substantial postsecondary options, including college.
    1. To improve learning, students will:
      - demonstrate the motivation to achieve individual potential
      - learn and apply critical thinking skills
      - apply the study skills necessary for academic success at each level
      - seek information and support from faculty, staff, family, and peers
      - organize and apply academic information from a variety of sources
      - use knowledge of learning styles to positively influence school performance
      - become self-directed and independent learners
    2. To plan to achieve goals, students will:
      - establish challenging academic goals in elementary, middle/junior high, and high school
      - use assessment results in educational planning

Sharing the Vision: The National Standards for School Counseling Programs (pp. 20–31) by C. A. Campbell and C. A. Dahir. Copyright by the American School Counselor Association. Reprinted with permission.

- develop and implement an annual plan of study to maximize academic ability and achievement
- apply knowledge of aptitudes and interests to goal setting
- use problem-solving and decision-making skills to assess progress toward educational goals
- understand the relationship between classroom performance and success in school
- identify post-secondary options consistent with interests, achievement, aptitudes, and abilities.

C. Students will understand the relationship of academics to the world of work, and to life at home and in the community.
1. To relate school to life experiences, students will:
   - demonstrate the ability to balance school, studies, extracurricular activities, leisure time, and family life
   - seek co-curricular and community experiences to enhance the school experience
   - understand the relationship between learning and work
   - demonstrate an understanding of the value of lifelong learning as essential to seeking, obtaining, and maintaining life goals
   - understand that school success is the preparation to make the transition from student to community member
   - understand how school success and academic achievement enhance future career and avocational opportunities

II. Career development
A. Students will acquire the skills to investigate the world of work in relation to knowledge of self and to make informed career decisions.
1. To develop career awareness, students will:
   - develop skills to locate, evaluate, and interpret career information
   - learn about the variety of traditional and non-traditional occupations
   - develop an awareness of personal abilities, skills, interests, and motivations
   - learn how to interact and work cooperatively in teams
   - learn to make decisions
   - learn how to set goals
   - understand the importance of planning
   - pursue and develop competency in areas of interest
   - develop hobbies and avocational interests
   - balance between work and leisure time
2. To develop employment readiness, students will:
   - acquire employability skills such as working on a team, and problem-solving and organizational skills
   - apply job readiness skills to seek employment opportunities
   - demonstrate knowledge about the changing workplace
   - learn about the rights and responsibilities of employers and employees
   - learn to respect individual uniqueness in the workplace
   - learn how to write a résumé
   - develop a positive attitude toward work and learning
   - understand the importance of responsibility, dependability, punctuality, integrity, and effort in the workplace
   - utilize time- and task-management skills

B. Students will employ strategies to achieve future career goals with success and satisfaction.
1. To acquire career information, students will:

- apply decision-making skills to career planning, course selection, and career transitions
- identify personal skills, interests, and abilities and relate them to current career choices
- demonstrate knowledge of the career planning process
- know the various ways in which occupations can be classified
- use research and information resources to obtain career information
- learn to use the Internet to access career planning information
- describe traditional and non-traditional occupations and how these relate to career choices
- understand how changing economic and societal needs influence employment trends and future training

2. To identify career goals, students will:
- demonstrate awareness of the education and training needed to achieve career goals
- assess and modify their educational plan to support career goals
- use employability and job readiness skills in internship, mentoring, shadowing, and/or other world of work experiences
- select course work that is related to career interests
- maintain a career planning portfolio

C. Students will understand the relationship between personal qualities, education, training, and the world of work.

1. To acquire knowledge to achieve career goals, students will:
- understand the relationship between educational achievement and career success
- explain how work can help to achieve personal success and satisfaction
- identify personal preferences and interests which influence career choices and success
- understand that the changing workplace requires lifelong learning and acquiring new skills
- describe the effect of work on lifestyles
- understand the importance of equity and access in career choice
- understand that work is an important and satisfying means of personal expression

2. To apply skills to achieve career goals, students will:
- demonstrate how interests, abilities, and achievement relate to achieving personal, social, educational, and career goals
- learn how to use conflict management skills with peers and adults
- learn to work cooperatively with others as a team member
- apply academic and employment readiness skills in work-based learning situations such as internships, shadowing, and/or mentoring experiences

III. Personal/social development

A. Students will acquire the knowledge, attitudes, and interpersonal skills to help them understand and respect self and others.

1. To acquire self-knowledge, students will:
- develop a positive attitude toward self as a unique and worthy person
- identify values, attitudes, and beliefs
- learn the goal setting process
- understand change as a part of growth
- identify and express feelings
- distinguish between appropriate and inappropriate behaviors

- recognize personal boundaries, rights, and privacy needs
- understand the need for self-control and how to practice it
- demonstrate cooperative behavior in groups
- identify personal strengths and assets
- identify and discuss changing personal and social roles
- identify and recognize changing family roles

2. To acquire interpersonal skills, students will:
   - recognize that everyone has rights and responsibilities
   - respect alternative points of view
   - recognize, accept, respect, and appreciate individual differences
   - recognize, accept, and appreciate ethnic and cultural diversity
   - recognize and respect differences in various family configurations
   - use effective communication skills
   - know that communication involves speaking, listening, and nonverbal behavior
   - learn how to make and keep friends

B. Students will make decisions, set goals, and take necessary action to achieve goals.
   1. To apply self-knowledge, students will:
      - use a decision-making and problem-solving model
      - understand consequences of decisions and choices
      - identify alternative solutions to a problem
      - develop effective coping skills for dealing with problems
      - demonstrate when, where, and how to seek help for solving problems and making decisions
      - know how to apply conflict resolution skills
      - demonstrate a respect and appreciation for individual and cultural differences
      - know when peer pressure is influencing a decision
      - identify long- and short-term goals
      - identify alternative ways of achieving goals
      - use persistence and perseverance in acquiring knowledge and skills
      - develop an action plan to set and achieve goals

C. Students will understand safety and survival skills.
   1. To acquire personal safety skills, students will:
      - demonstrate knowledge of personal information (i.e., telephone number, home address, emergency contact)
      - learn about the relationship between rules, laws, safety, and the protection of an individual's rights
      - learn the difference between appropriate and inappropriate physical contact
      - demonstrate the ability to assert boundaries, rights, and personal privacy
      - differentiate between situations requiring peer support and situations requiring adult professional help
      - identify resource people in the school and community, and know how to seek their help
      - apply effective problem-solving and decision-making skills to make safe and healthy choices
      - learn about the emotional and physical dangers of substance use and abuse
      - learn how to cope with peer pressure
      - learn techniques for managing stress and conflict
      - learn coping skills for managing life events

Appendix H

National Career Development Guidelines (http://www.ncda.org)

The National Career Development Guidelines (NCDG) initiative is a major nation-wide effort to foster excellence in career development for people of all ages, genders, and cultural backgrounds. The NCDG offers direction by providing a blueprint of career development goals that children, youth, and adults should master. The NCDG also identifies indicators of evidence to show that individuals have reached the goals. These goals and indicators are grouped into three broad domains: Personal Social Development, Educational Achievement, and Career Management. The NCDG helps educators, career professionals, and community leaders develop high-quality career development programs which in turn

- Increase academic achievement;
- Help students make sound decisions related to planning for, preparing for, and financing postsecondary education or training;
- Contribute to safe and drug-free schools;
- Help students develop the positive personal qualities they will need in their future roles as parents, workers, and community members; and
- Help adults manage career transitions smoothly and effectively.

The NCDG goals and indicators describe the outcomes expected of individuals who have participated in career development programs. They can also be the basis for determining program content. The goals are broad competencies, whereas the indicators describe specific knowledge, skills, and abilities related to a person's career development. There are eleven goals and a series of indicators under each goal. All indicators are written at three levels/stages of learning. The first level is the knowledge stage (K); the second is the application stage (A); and the third is the reflection stage (R).

Note that the learner outcomes are the responsibility of each district, school, or job center to determine and are more specific than the indicators in that they describe <u>who</u> will master the indicator, <u>when</u> they will do it, and <u>how</u> the evidence of mastery will be displayed. For example, under the Goal ED 2 (Participate in ongoing, lifelong learning experiences to enhance your ability to function effectively in a diverse and changing economy), one of the indicators (ED2.A5) states: "Show how you are preparing to participate in ongoing learning experiences (e.g., two- and four-year colleges, technical schools, apprenticeships, the military, online courses, and on-the-job training)". The learner outcome for that indicator might read as follows:

All 11th grade students will complete a learning plan that contains a detailed description of where they plan to head after graduation and how they plan to get there.

This plan could include the courses they plan to take, the assessments they plan to complete (SAT or ACT), and the extra-curricular activities that they plan to participate in.

The guidelines and indicators are included on the following pages. They can also be accessed on the website www.acrnetwork.org/ncdg.htm You will note that there is a number/letter sequence identifying each goal and indicator. The goal is identified by the domain and then the number of the goal within that domain (e.g., *PS1* is the first goal in the Personal Social Development Domain: *CM5* is the fifth goal in the Career Management Domain). The indicators come under the goals and the code by the indicator also contains the level of learning (e.g. *PS1.K1* is the first indicator under the first goal in the Personal Social Development Domain and is at the knowledge stage (K) of learning; *ED2.R7* is the seventh indicator under the second goal in the Educational Achievement and Lifelong Learning Domain at the reflection (R) stage of learning).

NATIONAL CAREER DEVELOPMENT GUIDELINES REVISION 09/30/04

PERSONAL SOCIAL DEVELOPMENT DOMAIN

GOAL PS1	**Develop understanding of yourself to build and maintain a positive self-concept.**
PS1.K1	Identify your interests, likes, and dislikes.
PS1.A1	Demonstrate behavior and decisions that reflect your interests, likes, and dislikes.
PS1.R1	Assess how your interests and preferences are reflected in your career goals.
PS1.K2	Identify your abilities, strengths, skills, and talents.
PS1.A2	Demonstrate use of your abilities, strengths, skills, and talents.
PS1.R2	Assess the impact of your abilities, strengths, skills, and talents on your career development.
PS1.K3	Identify your positive personal characteristics (e.g., honesty, dependability, responsibility, integrity, and loyalty).
PS1.A3	Give examples of when you demonstrated positive personal characteristics (e.g., honesty, dependability, responsibility, integrity, and loyalty).
PS1.R3	Assess the impact of your positive personal characteristics (e.g., honesty, dependability, responsibility, integrity, and loyalty) on your career development.
PS1.K4	Identify your work values/needs.
PS1.A4	Demonstrate behavior and decisions that reflect your work values/needs.
PS1.R4	Assess how your work values/needs are reflected in your career goals.
PS1.K5	Describe aspects of your self-concept.
PS1.A5	Demonstrate a positive self-concept through your behaviors and attitudes.
PS1.R5	Analyze the positive and negative aspects of your self-concept.
PS1.K6	Identify behaviors and experiences that help to build and maintain a positive self-concept.
PS1.A6	Show how you have adopted behaviors and sought experiences that build and maintain a positive self-concept.
PS1.R6	Evaluate the affect of your behaviors and experiences on building and maintaining a positive self-concept.
PS1.K7	Recognize that situations, attitudes, and the behaviors of others affect your self-concept.
P51.A7	Give personal examples of specific situations, attitudes, and behaviors of others that affected your self-concept.
PS1.R7	Evaluate the affect of situations, attitudes, and the behaviors of others on your self- concept.

PS1.K8	Recognize that your behaviors and attitudes affect the self-concept of others.
PS1.A8	Show how you have adopted behaviors and attitudes to positively affect the self-concept of others.
PS1.R8	Analyze how your behaviors and attitudes might affect the self-concept of others.
PS1.K9	Recognize that your self-concept can affect educational achievement (i.e., performance) and/or success at work.
PS1.A9	Show how aspects of your self-concept could positively or negatively affect educational achievement (i.e., performance) and/or success at work.
PS1.R9	Assess how your self-concept affects your educational achievement (performance) and/or success at work.
PS1.K10	Recognize that educational achievement (performance) and/or success at work can affect your self-concept.
PS1.A10	Give personal examples of how educational achievement (performance) and/or success at work affected your self-concept.
PS1.R10	Assess how your educational achievement (performance) and/or success at work affect your self-concept.
GOAL PS2	**Develop positive interpersonal skills including respect for diversity.**
PS2.K1	Identify effective communication skills.
PS2.A1	Demonstrate effective communication skills.
PS2.R1	Evaluate your use of effective communication skills.
PS2.K2	Recognize the benefits of interacting with others in a way that is honest, fair, helpful, and respectful.
PS2.A2	Demonstrate that you interact with others in a way that is honest, fair, helpful, and respectful.
PS2.R2	Assess the degree to which you interact with others in a way that is honest, fair, helpful, and respectful.
PS2.K3	Identify positive social skills (e.g., good manners and showing gratitude).
PS2.A3	Demonstrate the ability to use positive social skills (e.g., good manners and showing gratitude).
PS2.R3	Evaluate how your positive social skills (e.g., good manners and showing gratitude) contribute to effective interactions with others.
PS2.K4	Identify ways to get along well with others and work effectively with them in groups.
PS2.A4	Demonstrate the ability to get along well with others and work effectively with them in groups.
PS2.R4	Evaluate your ability to work effectively with others in groups.
PS2.K5	Describe conflict resolution skills.
PS2.A5	Demonstrate the ability to resolve conflicts and to negotiate acceptable solutions.
PS2.R5	Analyze the success of your conflict resolution skills.
PS2.K6	Recognize the difference between appropriate and inappropriate behavior in specific school, social, and work situations.
PS2.A6	Give examples of times when your behavior was appropriate and times when your behavior was inappropriate in specific school, social, and work situations.
PS2.R6	Assess the consequences of appropriate or inappropriate behavior in specific school, social, and work situations.
PS2.K7	Identify sources of outside pressure that affect you.
PS2.A7	Demonstrate the ability to handle outside pressure on you.
PS2.R7	Analyze the impact of outside pressure on your behavior.

PS2.K8	Recognize that you should accept responsibility for your behavior.
PS2.A8	Demonstrate that you accept responsibility for your behavior.
PS2.R8	Assess the degree to which you accept personal responsibility for your behavior.
PS2.K9	Recognize that you should have knowledge about, respect for, be open to, and appreciate all kinds of human diversity.
PS2.A9	Demonstrate knowledge about, respect for, openness to, and appreciation for all kinds of human diversity.
PS2.R9	Assess how you show respect for all kinds of human diversity.
PS2.K10	Recognize that the ability to interact positively with diverse groups of people may contribute to learning and academic achievement.
PS2.A10	Show how the ability to interact positively with diverse groups of people may contribute to learning and academic achievement.
PS2.R10	Analyze the impact of your ability to interact positively with diverse groups of people on your learning and academic achievement.
PS2.K11	Recognize that the ability to interact positively with diverse groups of people is often essential to maintain employment.
PS2.A11	Explain how the ability to interact positively with diverse groups of people is often essential to maintain employment.
PS2.R11	Analyze the impact of your ability to interact positively with diverse groups of people on your employment.
GOAL PS3	**Integrate personal growth and change into your career development.**
PS3.K1	Recognize that you will experience growth and changes in mind and body throughout life that will impact on your career development.
PS3.A1	Give examples of how you have grown and changed (e.g., physically, emotionally, socially, and intellectually).
PS3.R1	Analyze the results of your growth and changes throughout life to determine areas of growth for the future.
PS3.K2	Identify good health habits (e.g., good nutrition and constructive ways to manage stress).
PS3.A2	Demonstrate how you have adopted good health habits.
PS3.R2	Assess the impact of your health habits on your career development.
PS3.K3	Recognize that your motivations and aspirations are likely to change with time and circumstances.
PS3.A3	Give examples of how your personal motivations and aspirations have changed with time and circumstances.
PS3.R3	Assess how changes in your motivations and aspirations over time have affected your career development.
PS3.K4	Recognize that external events often cause life changes.
PS3.A4	Give examples of external events that have caused life changes for you.
PS3.R4	Assess your strategies for managing life changes caused by external events.
PS3.K5	Identify situations (e.g., problems at school or work) in which you might need assistance from people or other resources.
PS3.A5	Demonstrate the ability to seek assistance (e.g., with problems at school or work) from appropriate resources including other people.
PS3.R5	Assess the effectiveness of your strategies for getting assistance (e.g., with problems at school or work) from appropriate resources including other people.
PS3.K6	Recognize the importance of adaptability and flexibility when initiating or responding to change.

PS3.A6	Demonstrate adaptability and flexibility when initiating or responding to change.
PS3.R6	Analyze how effectively you respond to change and/or initiate change.
GOAL PS4	**Balance personal, leisure, community, learner, family, and work roles.**
PS4.K1	Recognize that you have many life roles (e.g., personal, leisure, community, learner, family, and work roles).
PS4.A1	Give examples that demonstrate your life roles including personal, leisure, community, learner, family, and work roles.
PS4.R1	Assess the impact of your life roles on career goals.
PS4.K2	Recognize that you must balance life roles and that there are many ways to do it.
PS4.A2	Show how you are balancing your life roles.
PS4.R2	Analyze how specific life role changes would affect the attainment of your career goals.
PS4.K3	Describe the concept of lifestyle.
PS4.A3	Give examples of decisions, factors, and circumstances that affect your current lifestyle.
PS4.R3	Analyze how specific lifestyle changes would affect the attainment of your career goals.
PS4.K4	Recognize that your life roles and your lifestyle are connected.
PS4.A4	Show how your life roles and your lifestyle are connected.
PS4.R4	Assess how changes in your life roles would affect your lifestyle.

EDUCATIONAL ACHIEVEMENT AND LIFELONG LEARNING DOMAIN

GOAL ED1	**Attain educational achievement and performance levels needed to reach your personal and career goals.**
ED1.K1	Recognize the importance of educational achievement and performance to the attainment of personal and career goals.
ED1.A1	Demonstrate educational achievement and performance levels needed to attain your personal and career goals.
ED1.R1	Evaluate how well you have attained educational achievement and performance levels needed to reach your personal and career goals.
ED1.K2	Identify strategies for improving educational achievement and performance.
ED1.A2	Demonstrate strategies you are using to improve educational achievement and performance.
ED1.R2	Analyze your educational achievement and performance strategies to create a plan for growth and improvement.
ED1.K3	Describe study skills and learning habits that promote educational achievement and performance.
ED1.A3	Demonstrate acquisition of study skills and learning habits that promote educational achievement and performance.
ED1.R3	Evaluate your study skills and learning habits to develop a plan for improving them.
ED1.K4	Identify your learning style.
ED1.A4	Show how you are using learning style information to improve educational achievement and performance.
ED1.R4	Analyze your learning style to develop behaviors to maximize educational achievement and performance.
ED1.K5	Describe the importance of having a plan to improve educational achievement and performance.
ED1.A5	Show that you have a plan to improve educational achievement and performance.

ED1.R5	Evaluate the results of your plan for improving educational achievement and performance.
ED1.K6	Describe how personal attitudes and behaviors can impact educational achievement and performance.
ED1.A6	Exhibit attitudes and behaviors that support educational achievement and performance.
ED1.R6	Assess how well your attitudes and behaviors promote educational achievement and performance.
ED1.K7	Recognize that your educational achievement and performance can lead to many workplace options.
ED1.A7	Show how your educational achievement and performance can expand your workplace options.
ED1.R7	Assess how well your educational achievement and performance will transfer to the workplace.
ED1.K8	Recognize that the ability to acquire and use information contributes to educational achievement and performance.
ED1.A8	Show how the ability to acquire and use information has affected your educational achievement and performance.
ED1.R8	Assess your ability to acquire and use information in order to improve educational achievement and performance.
GOAL ED2	**Participate in ongoing, lifelong learning experiences to enhance your ability to function effectively in a diverse and changing economy.**
ED2.K1	Recognize that changes in the economy require you to acquire and update knowledge and skills throughout life.
ED2.A1	Show how lifelong learning is helping you function effectively in a diverse and changing economy.
ED2.R1	Judge whether or not you have the knowledge and skills necessary to function effectively in a diverse and changing economy.
ED2.K2	Recognize that viewing yourself as a learner affects your identity.
ED2.A2	Show how being a learner affects your identity.
ED2.R2	Analyze how specific learning experiences have affected your identity.
ED2.K3	Recognize the importance of being an independent learner and taking responsibility for your learning.
ED2.A3	Demonstrate that you are an independent learner.
ED2.R3	Assess how well you function as an independent learner.
ED2.K4	Describe the requirements for transition from one learning level to the next (e.g., middle school to high school, high school to postsecondary).
ED2.A4	Demonstrate the knowledge and skills necessary for transition from one learning level to the next (e.g., middle to high school, high school to postsecondary).
ED2.R4	Analyze how your knowledge and skills affect your transition from one learning level to the next (e.g., middle school to high school, high school to postsecondary).
ED2.K5	Identify types of ongoing learning experiences available to you (e.g., two- and four-year colleges, technical schools, apprenticeships, the military online courses, and on-the-job training).
ED2.A5	Show how you are preparing to participate in ongoing learning experiences (e.g., two- and four-year colleges, technical schools, apprenticeships, the military, online courses, and on-the-job training).
ED2.R5	Assess how participation in ongoing learning experiences (e.g., two- and four-year colleges, technical schools, apprenticeships, the military, online courses, and on-the-job training) affects your personal and career goals.

ED2.K6	Identify specific education/training programs (e.g., high school career paths and courses, college majors, and apprenticeship programs).
ED2.A6	Demonstrate participation in specific education/training programs (e.g., high school career paths and courses, college majors, and apprenticeship programs) that help you function effectively in a diverse and changing economy.
ED2.R6	Evaluate how participation in specific education/training programs (e.g., high school career paths and courses, college majors, and apprenticeship programs) affects your ability to function effectively in a diverse and changing economy.
ED2.K7	Describe informal learning experiences that contribute to lifelong learning.
ED2.A7	Demonstrate participation in informal learning experiences.
ED2.R7	Assess, throughout your life, how well you integrate both formal and informal learning experiences.

CAREER MANAGEMENT DOMAIN

GOAL CM1	**Create and manage a career plan that meets your career goals.**
CM1.K1	Recognize that career planning to attain your career goals is a lifelong process.
CM1.A1	Give examples of how you use career-planning strategies to attain your career goals.
CM1.R1	Assess how well your career planning strategies facilitate reaching your career goals.
CM1.K2	Describe how to develop a career plan (e.g., steps and content).
CM1.A2	Develop a career plan to meet your career goals.
CM1.R2	Analyze your career plan and make adjustments to reflect ongoing career management needs.
CM1.K3	Identify your short-term and long-term career goals (e.g., education, employment, and lifestyle goals).
CM1.A3	Demonstrate actions taken to attain your short-term and long-term career goals (e.g., education, employment, and lifestyle goals).
CM1.R3	Re-examine your career goals and adjust as needed.
CM1.K4	Identify skills and personal traits needed to manage your career (e.g., resiliency, self-efficacy, ability to identify trends and changes, and flexibility).
CM1.A4	Demonstrate career management skills and personal traits (e.g., resiliency, self-efficacy, ability to identify trends and changes, and flexibility).
CM1.R4	Evaluate your career management skills and personal traits (e.g., resiliency, self-efficacy, ability to identify trends and changes, and flexibility).
CM1.K5	Recognize that changes in you and the world of work can affect your career plans.
CM1.A5	Give examples of how changes in you and the world of work have caused you to adjust your career plans.
CM1.R5	Evaluate how well you integrate changes in you and the world of work into your career plans.
GOAL CM2	**Use a process of decision-making as one component of career development.**
CM2.K1	Describe your decision-making style (e.g., risk taker, cautious).
CM2.A1	Give examples of past decisions that demonstrate your decision-making style.
CM2.R1	Evaluate the effectiveness of your decision-making style.
CM2.K2	Identify the steps in one model of decision-making.
CM2.A2	Demonstrate the use of a decision-making model.
CM2.R2	Assess what decision-making model(s) work best for you.
CM2.K3	Describe how information (e.g., about you, the economy, and education programs) can improve your decision-making.

CM2.A3	Demonstrate use of information (e.g., about you, the economy, and education programs) in making decisions.
CM2.R3	Assess how well you use information (e.g., about you, the economy, and education programs) to make decisions.
CM2.K4	Identify alternative options and potential consequences for a specific decision.
CM2.A4	Show how exploring options affected a decision you made.
CM2.R4	Assess how well you explore options when making decisions.
CM2.K5	Recognize that your personal priorities, culture, beliefs, and work values can affect your decision-making.
CM2.A5	Show how personal priorities, culture, beliefs, and work values are reflected in your decisions.
CM2.R5	Evaluate the affect of personal priorities, culture, beliefs, and work values in your decision-making.
CM2.K6	Describe how education, work, and family experiences might impact your decisions.
CM2.A6	Give specific examples of how your education, work, and family experiences have influenced your decisions.
CM2.R6	Assess the impact of your education, work, and family experiences on decisions.
CM2.K7	Describe how biases and stereotypes can limit decisions.
CM2.A7	Give specific examples of how biases and stereotypes affected your decisions.
CM2.R7	Analyze the ways you could manage biases and stereotypes when making decisions.
CM2.K8	Recognize that chance can play a role in decision-making.
CM2.A8	Give examples of times when chance played a role in your decision-making.
CM2.R8	Evaluate the impact of chance on past decisions.
CM2.K9	Recognize that decision-making often involves compromise.
CM2.A9	Give examples of compromises you might have to make in career decision-making.
CM2.R9	Analyze the effectiveness of your approach to making compromises.
GOAL CM3	**Use accurate, current, and unbiased career information during career planning and management.**
CM3.K1	Describe the importance of career information to your career planning.
CM3.A1	Show how career information has been important in your plans and how it can be used in future plans.
CM3.R1	Assess the impact of career information on your plans and refine plans so that they reflect accurate, current, and unbiased career information.
CM3.K2	Recognize that career information includes occupational, education and training, employment, and economic information and that there is a range of career information resources available.
CM3.A2	Demonstrate the ability to use different types of career information resources (i.e., occupational, educational, economic, and employment) to support career planning.
CM3.R2	Evaluate how well you integrate occupational, educational, economic, and employment information into the management of your career.
CM3.K3	Recognize that the quality of career information resource content varies (e.g., accuracy, bias, and how up-to-date and complete it is).
CM3.A3	Show how selected examples of career information are biased, out-of-date, incomplete, or inaccurate.
CM3.R3	Judge the quality of the career information resources you plan to use in terms of accuracy, bias, and how up-to-date and complete it is.
CM3.K4	Identify several ways to classify occupations.

CM3.A4	Give examples of how occupational classification systems can be used in career planning.
CM3.R4	Assess which occupational classification system is most helpful to your career planning.
CM3.K5	Identify occupations that you might consider without regard to your gender, race, culture, or ability.
CM3.A5	Demonstrate openness to considering occupations that you might view as non-traditional (i.e., relative to your gender, race, culture, or ability).
CM3.R5	Assess your openness to considering non-traditional occupations in your career management.
CM3.K6	Identify the advantages and disadvantages of being employed in a non-traditional occupation.
CM3.A6	Make decisions for yourself about being employed in a non-traditional occupation.
CM3.R6	Assess the impact of your decisions about being employed in a non-traditional occupation.
GOAL CM4	**Master academic, occupational, and general employability skills in order to obtain, create, maintain, and/or advance your employment.**
CM4.K1	Describe academic, occupational, and general employability skills.
CM4.A1	Demonstrate the ability to use your academic, occupational, and general employability skills to obtain or create, maintain, and advance your employment.
CM4.R1	Assess your academic, occupational, and general employability skills and enhance them as needed for your employment.
CM4.K2	Identify job seeking skills such as the ability to write a résumé and cover letter, complete a job application, interview for a job, and find and pursue employment leads.
CM4.A2	Demonstrate the following job-seeking skills: the ability to write a résumé and cover letter, complete a job application, interview for a job, and find and pursue employment leads.
CM4.R2	Evaluate your ability to write a résumé and cover letter, complete a job application, interview for a job, and find and pursue employment leads.
CM4.K3	Recognize that a variety of general employability skills and personal qualities (e.g., critical thinking, problem solving, resource, information, and technology management, interpersonal skills, honesty, and dependability) are important to success in school and employment.
CM4.A3	Demonstrate attainment of general employability skills and personal qualities needed to be successful in school and employment (e.g., critical thinking, problem solving, resource, information, and technology management, interpersonal skills, honesty, and dependability).
CM4.R3	Evaluate your general employability skills and personal qualities (e.g., critical thinking, problem solving, resource, information, and technology management, interpersonal skills, honesty, and dependability).
CM4.K4	Recognize that many skills are transferable from one occupation to another.
CM4.A4	Show how your skills are transferable from one occupation to another.
CM4.R4	Analyze the impact of your transferable skills on your career options.
CM4.K5	Recognize that your geographic mobility impacts on your employability.
CM4.A5	Make decisions for yourself regarding geographic mobility.
CM4.R5	Analyze the impact of your decisions about geographic mobility on your career goals.
CM4.K6	Identify the advantages and challenges of self-employment.
CM4.A6	Make decisions for yourself about self-employment.
CM4.R6	Assess the impact of your decision regarding self-employment on your career goals.
CM4.K7	Identify ways to be proactive in marketing yourself for a job.
CM4.A7	Demonstrate skills that show how you can market yourself in the workplace.
CM4.R7	Evaluate how well you have marketed yourself in the workplace.

GOAL CM5	**Integrate changing employment trends, societal needs, and economic conditions into your career plans.**
CM5.K1	Identify societal needs that affect your career plans.
CM5.A1	Show how you are prepared to respond to changing societal needs in your career management.
CM5.R1	Evaluate the results of your career management relative to changing societal needs.
CM5.K2	Identify economic conditions that affect your career plans.
CM5.A2	Show how you are prepared to respond to changing economic conditions in your career management.
CM5.R2	Evaluate the results of your career management relative to changing economic conditions.
CM5.K3	Identify employment trends that affect your career plans.
CM5.A3	Show how you are prepared to respond to changing employment trends in your career management.
CM5.R3	Evaluate the results of your career management relative to changes in employment trends.

Appendix I

Counseling Websites

The following professional associations and their websites provide an abundance of information about career counseling including competencies, ethical standards, and guidelines for using assessment.

American Counseling Association

http://www.counseling.org/

American Psychological Association

http://www.apa.org

American Psychological Association Code of Ethics

http://www.apa.org/ethics/code.html

American Psychological Association Healthy Lesbian, Gay, and Bisexual Students Project

http://www.apa.org/pi/lgbt/programs/hlgbsp/index.aspx

Americans with Disabilities Act

http://www.ada.gov/

Association for Assessment and Research in Counseling

http://aarc-counseling.org/

Association for Lesbian, Gay, Bisexual, and Transgender Issues in Counseling

http://www.algbticconference.org/

Guidelines for Use of the Internet for Provision of Career Information and Planning Services

http://ncda.org/aws/NCDA/pt/sp/guidelines_internet

National Career Development Association

http://ncda.org

National Career Development Association Career Software Review Guidelines

http://www.ncda.org/aws/NCDA/pt/sp/guidelines

National Career Development Association Ethical Standards

http://ncda.org/aws/NCDA/asset_manager/get_file/3395/code_of _ethicsmay-2007.pdf

NBCC Policy Regarding the Provision of Distance Professional Services

http://www.nbcc.org/Assets/Ethics/
NBCCPolicyRegardingPracticeofDistanceCounselingBoard.pdf

Services by Telephone, Teleconferencing and Internet: A Statement by the Ethics Committee of the American Psychological Association

http://www.apa.org/ethics/education/telephone-statement.aspx

Appendix J

2009 CACREP Standards Related to Career Development

Career development studies provide an understanding of career development and related life factors including all of the following:

Book Chapter	CACREP Standards
1, 2, 3, 4, 9, 12,13	a. career developmental theories and decision-making models
1, 7, 12, 13, 15, 16, 17	b. career avocational, educational, occupational, and labor market information resources, visual and print media, and career information systems
3, 12, 13, 14, 15, 16, 17	c. career development programing, organization, implementation, administration, and evaluation
1, 5, 9, 10, 13, 14	d. interrelationships among and between work, family, and other life roles and factors including the role of multicultural issues in career development
3, 9, 14, 15, 16, 17	e. career and education planning, placement, follow-up, and evaluation
5, 6, 9, 12, 13, 16	f. assessment instruments and techniques that are relevant to career planning and decision making
2, 3, 9, 10, 11, 12	g. career counseling procedures, techniques, and resources including those applicable to special populations

References

Aamodt, M. G. (1999). *Applied industrial/organizational psychology* (3rd ed.). Pacific Grove, CA: Brooks/Cole-Wadsworth.

Aamodt, M. G. (2004). *Applied industrial/organizational psychology* (4th ed.). Belton, CA: Wadsworth/Thomson Learning.

Aamodt, M. G. (2013). *Industrial organizational psychology: an applied approach* (7th ed.). Belmont, CA: Wadsworth Cengage Learning.

Adams, C. L., & Kimmel, D. C. (1997). Exploring the lives of older African American gay men. In B. Greene (Ed.), *Ethnic and cultural diversity among lesbians and gay men* (pp. 132–152). Thousand Oaks, CA: Sage.

Aguinis, H., & Kraiger, K. (2009). Benefits of training and development for individuals and teams, organizations and society. *Annual Review of Psychology* (2009). 60: 451–474.

Altarac, M., & Saroha, E. (2007). Lifetime prevalence of learning disability among U. S. children. *Pediatrics, 119* (Suppl. 1), 577–583.

Amatea, E. S., & Cross, E. G. (1980). Going places: A career guidance program for high school students and their parents. *Vocational Guidance Quarterly, 28*(3), 274–282.

American College Testing Program. (1984). *DISCOVER: A computer-based career development and counselor support system.* Iowa City, IA: Author.

American College Testing Program. (1987). *DISCOVER.* Iowa City, IA: Author.

American College Testing Program. (1996a, Winter). *Activity, 34*(1). Iowa City, IA: Author.

American Council on Education. (1997). Many college graduates participate in training courses to improve their job skills. *Higher Education and National Affairs, 46*(19), 3.

American Counseling Association. (ACA). (1995). Code of ethics and standards of practice. In *Codes of ethics for the helping professionals,* 1–17. Pacific Grove, CA: Brooks/Cole.

American Counseling Association. (1999). *Ethical standards for Internet on-line counseling.* Alexandria, VA: Author.

American Mental Health Counselors Association. (2000). *Code of ethics for mental health counselors.* Alexandria, VA: Author.

American Psychiatric Association. (2000). *Diagnostic and statistical manual of mental disorders* (4th ed., rev.). Washington, DC: Author.

American Psychiatric Association. (2013). *Diagnostic and statistical manual of mental disorders* (5th ed.). Washington, DC: Author.

American Psychological Association. (1990). Ethical principles of psychologists (amended June 2, 1989). In *American Psychology,* pp. 453–484. New York: Wiley.

American Psychological Association. (1991). Avoiding heterosexual bias in language. *American Psychologist, 46,* 973–974.

American Psychological Association. (1992). *Ethical guidelines of the American Psychological Association.* Washington, DC: Author.

American Psychological Association. (1999). *Standards for educational and psychological testing.* Washington, DC: Author.

American School Counselors Association. (1998). *Ethical standards for school counselors.* Alexandria, VA: Author.

American School Counselors Association. (2003). *The ASCA national model: a framework for school counseling programs.* Alexandria, VA: Author.

Andersen, M. K., & Taylor, H. F. (2013). *Sociology: the essentials* (7th ed.). Belmont, CA: Wadsworth Cengage Learning.

Anderson, P., & Vandehey, M. (2012). *Career counseling and development in a global society* Belmont, CA: Brooks Cole Cengage Learning.

Anderson, D. A. (1994). Lesbian and gay adolescents: Social and developmental considerations. *High School Journal, 77*(1/2), 13–19.

Anderson, J. R. (1985). *Cognitive psychology and its implication* (2nd ed.). San Francisco: Freeman.

Arbona, C. (1995). Theory and research on racial and ethnic minorities: Hispanic Americans. In Frederick T. L. Leong (Ed.), *Career development and vocational behavior of racial and ethnic minorities* (pp. 37–61). Mahwah, NJ: Erlbaum.

Arbona, C. (1996). Career theory and practice in a multicultural context. In M. L. Savickas & W. B. Walsh (Eds.), *Handbook of career counseling theory and practice* (pp. 45–55). Palo Alto, CA: Davies-Black.

Armstrong, P. I., & Crombie, G. (2000). Compromises in adolescents' occupational aspirations and expectations from grades 8 to 10. *Journal of Vocational Behavior, 56,* 82–98.

Arredondo, P. (1996). MCT theory and Latina(o)-American populations. In D. W. Sue, A. E. Ivey, & P. B. Pedersen (Eds.), *A theory of multicultural counseling and therapy* (pp. 217–233). Pacific Grove, CA: Brooks/Cole.

Ashford, J., & Lecroy, C. (2013). *Human behavior in the social environment* (5th ed.). Belmont, CA: Brooks/Cole Cengage Learning.

Ashkenas, R., Ulrich, D., Jick, T., & Kerr, S. (1995). *The boundaryless organization: Breaking the chains of organizational structure.* San Francisco: Jossey-Bass.

Astin, A. W. (1984). Student values: Knowing more about where we are today. *Bulletin of the American Association of Higher Education, 36*(9), 10–13.

Atkinson, D. R., Morten, G., & Sue, D. W. (1993). *Counseling American minorities: A cross-cultural perspective* (4th ed.). Dubuque, IA: William C. Brown.

Axelson, J. A. (1993). *Counseling and development in a multicultural society* (2nd ed.). Pacific Grove, CA: Brooks/Cole.

Axelson, J. A. (1999). *Counseling and development in a multicultural society* (4th ed.). Pacific Grove, CA: Brooks/Cole.

Bailey, L. J., & Stadt, R. W. (1973). *Career education: New approaches to human development.* Bloomington, IL: McKnight.

Baker, L. J., Dearborn, M., Hastings, J. E., & Hamberger, K. (1988). Type A behavior in women: A review. *Health Psychology, 3,* 477–497.

Ballard, D. (1997). *Doing it ourselves: Success stories of African-American women in business.* New York: Berkley.

Bandura, A. (1977). *Social learning theory.* Englewood Cliffs, NJ: Prentice-Hall.

Bandura, A. (1986). *Social foundations of thought and action: A social cognitive theory.* Englewood Cliffs, NJ: Prentice-Hall.

Bandura, A. (1989). Regulation of cognitive processes through perceived self-efficacy. *Developmental Psychology, 25,* 729–735.

Barak, A., & English, N. (2002). Prospects and limitations of psychological testing on the internet. *Journal of Technology in Human Services, 19,* 65–89.

Barlow, D. H., & Durand, V. M. (2009). *Abnormal psychology: An integrative approach* (5th ed.). Belmont, CA: Wadsworth Cengage Learning.

Barnett, R. C., & Rivers, C. (1996). *She works, he works: How two-income families are happier, healthier, and better off.* San Francisco: Harper.

Baron, S. A., Hoffman, S. J., & Merrill, J. G. (2000). *When work equals life: The next stage of workplace violence.* Oxnard, CA: Pathfinder.

Barrett, B., & Logan, C. (2002). *Counseling gays and lesbians.* Pacific Grove, CA: Brooks/Cole.

Barrett, R. C., & Hyde, J. S. (2001). Women, men, work, and family. *American Psychologist, 56,* 781–796.

Basow, S. A. (1992). *Gender: Stereotypes and roles* (3rd ed.). Pacific Grove, CA: Brooks/Cole.

Bauer, T., & Green, S. (1994). Effect of newcomer involvement on work-related activities: A longitudinal study of socialization. *Journal of Applied Psychology, 79,* 211–223.

Beck, A. T. (1976). *Cognitive therapy and the emotional disorders.* New York: International Universities Press.

Beck, A. T. (1985). Cognitive therapy. In H. J. Kaplan & B. J. Sadock (Eds.), *Comprehensive textbook of psychiatry* (pp. 1432–1438). Baltimore: Williams & Wilkins.

Beck, A. T., Street, R. A., & Brown, G. K. (1996). *Beck Depression Inventory II* (BDI-II). San Antonio, TX: Psychological Corporation.

Beehr, T. A., & Bowling, M. A. (2002). Career issues facing older workers. In D. C. Feldman (Ed.), *Work careers: A developmental perspective* (pp. 214–245). San Francisco: Jossey-Bass.

Bell, A., & Weinberg, M. (1978). *Homosexualities: A study of diversity among men and women.* New York: Simon & Schuster.

Bennett, C. E., & DeBarros, K. A. (1995). The Black population. In *U.S. Bureau of the Census, current population reports, series P23-189, population profile of the United States: 1995* (pp. 44–45). Washington, DC: U.S. Government Printing Office.

Bennett, C. E., & Debarros, K. A. (1998). *The Black population.* Washington, DC: U.S. Bureau of Census.

Bennett, G. K., Seashore, H. G., & Wesman, A. G. (1991). *Differential aptitude test.* San Antonio, TX: Psychological Corporation.

Berns, R. M. (2004). *Child family-select community: Socialization and support* (6th ed.). Belmont, CA: Wadsworth/Thomson Learning.

Bernstein, R. (2007). More than 300 counties now "majority-minority. "Retrieved November 25, 2007, from http://www,census.gov/Press-Release/www/rerelease/archives/population/01482.hyml

Betz, N. E. (1992b). Counseling uses of career self-efficacy theory. *Career Development Quarterly, 41,* 22–26.

Betz, N. E., & Corning, A. F. (1993). The inseparability of career and personal counseling. *Career Development Quarterly, 42,* 137–142.

Betz, N. E., & Fitzgerald, L. F. (1987). *The career psychology of women.* Orlando, FL: Academic.

Betz, N. E., & Fitzgerald, L. F. (1995). Career assessment and intervention with racial and ethnic minorities. In Frederick T. L. Leong (Ed.), *Career development and vocational behavior of racial and ethnic minorities* (pp. 263–277). Mahwah, NJ: Erlbaum.

Betz, N. E., & Hackett, G. (1986). Applications of self-efficacy theory to understanding career choice behavior. *Journal of Social and Clinical Psychology, 4,* 279–289.

Biehler, R. F., & Hudson, L. M. (1986). *Developmental psychology.* Boston: Allyn & Bacon.

Biernat, M., & Wortman, C. (1991). Sharing of home responsibilities between professionally employed women and their husbands. *Journal of Personality and Social Psychology, 60,* 844–860.

Bingham, R. P., & Ward, C. M. (1996). Practical applications of career counseling with ethnic minority women. In M. L. Savickas & W. B. Walsh (Eds.), *Handbook of career counseling theory and practice* (pp. 291–315). Palo Alto, CA: Davies-Black.

Blau, P. M., Gustad, J. W., Jessor, R., Parnes, H. S., & Wilcox, R. S. (1956). Occupational choices: A conceptual framework. *Industrial Labor Relations Review, 9,* 531–543.

Bloland, P. A., & Edwards, P. B. (1981). Work and leisure: A counseling synthesis. *Vocational Guidance Quarterly, 30*(2), 101–108.

Blotzer, M. A., & Ruth, R. (1995). *Sometimes you just want to feel like a human being: Case studies of empowering psychotherapy with people with disabilities.* Baltimore: Paul H. Brookes.

Blustein, D. L. (1990). An eclectic definition of psychotherapy: A developmental contextual view. In J. K. Zeig & W. M. Munion (Eds.), *What is psychotherapy? Contemporary perspectives* (pp. 244–248). San Francisco: Jossey-Bass.

Blustein, D. L., & Flum, H. (1999). A self-determination perspective of interests and exploration in career development. In M. L. Savickas & A. R. Spokane (Eds.), *Vocational interests: Meaning, measure, and counseling use.* Palo Alto, CA: Davies-Black.

Blustein, D. L., Phillips, S. D., John-Davis, K., Finkelberg, S. L., & Roarke, A. E. (1997). A theory-building investigation of the school-to-work transition. *Counseling Psychologist, 25,* 364–402.

Blustein, D. L., & Spengler, P. M. (1995). Personal adjustment: Career counseling and psychotherapy. In W. B. Walsh & S. H. Osipow (Eds.), *Handbook of vocational psychology: Theory, research, and practice* (2nd ed., pp. 295–329). Mahwah, NJ: Erlbaum.

Boer, P. M. (2001). *Career counseling over the internet: Am emerging model for trusting and responding to online clients.* Mahwah, NJ: Erlbaum.

Bolles, R. N. (1991). *Job-hunting tips for the so-called handicapped or people who have disabilities.* Berkeley, CA: Ten Speed.

Bolles, R. N. (1993). *A practical manual for job-hunters and career changers: What color is your parachute?* (9th ed.). Berkeley, CA: Ten Speed.

Bolles, R. N. (2000). *A practical manual for job-hunters and career changers: What color is your parachute?* (16th ed.). Berkeley, CA: Ten Speed.

Bolles, R. N. (2009). *A practical manual for job-hunters and career changers: What color is your parachute?* Berkeley, CA: Ten Speed.

Bottoms, J. E., Evans, R. N., Hoyt, K. B., & Willer, J. C. (Eds.). (1972). *Career education resource guide.* Morristown, NJ: General Learning Corporation.

Bowman, S. L. (1995). Career intervention strategies and assessment issues for African Americans. In Frederick T. L. Leong (Ed.), *Career development and vocational behavior of racial and ethnic minorities* (pp. 137–161). Mahwah, NJ: Erlbaum.

Braiker, H. (1986). *The Type E woman.* New York: Dodd, Mead.

Brammer, L. M., Abrego, P. L., & Shostrom, E. L. (1993). *Therapeutic counseling and psychotherapy* (2nd ed.). Englewood Cliffs, NJ: Prentice-Hall.

Brammer, R. (2012). *Diversity in counseling.* Belmont, CA: Brooks/Cole-Thomson Learning.

Brems, C. (2001). *Basic skills in psychotherapy and counseling.* Belmont, CA: Wadsworth/Thomson Learning.

Bretz, R. D., Jr., & Judge, T. A. (1994). Person-organization fit and the theory of work adjustment: Implications for satisfaction, tenure, and career success. *Journal of Vocational Behavior, 44,* 32–54.

Brinkerhoff, D. B., Weitz, R., & Ortega, S.T. (2014). *Essentials of sociology* (9th ed.). Belmont, CA: Wadsworth Cengage Learning.

Brolin, D. E., & Gysbers, N. C. (1989). Career education for students with disabilities. *Journal of Counseling and Development, 68,* 155–159.

Bronfenbrenner, U. (1979). *The ecology of human development.* Cambridge, MA: Harvard University Press.

Brown, B. B., Mounts, N., Lamborn, S. D., & Steinberg, L. (1993). Parenting practices and peer group affiliation in adolescence. *Child Development, 65,* 467–482.

Brown, D. A. (1980). Life-planning workshop for high school students. *School Counselor, 29*(1), 77–83.

Brown, D. (1996). Brown's values-based, holistic model of career and life-role choices and satisfaction. In D. Brown, L. Brooks, & Associates (Eds.), *Career choice and development* (3rd ed., pp. 337–338). San Francisco: Jossey-Bass.

Brown, D. (2007). *Career information, career counseling, and career development* (9th ed.). Boston: Pearson Education, Inc.

Brown, D., & Associates. (2002). *Career choice and development* (4th ed.). San Francisco, CA: Jossey-Bass.

Brown, D., & Brooks, L. (1991). *Career counseling techniques.* Boston: Allyn & Bacon.

Brown, D., Brooks, L., & Associates. (1990). *Career choice and development* (2nd ed.). San Francisco: Jossey-Bass.

Brown, D., Brooks, L., & Associates. (1996). *Career choice and development* (3rd ed.). San Francisco: Jossey-Bass.

Brown, K. G., Milner, K., & Ford, J. K. (1998). The design of asynchronous distance learning courses. *Technical Report for the National Center for Manufacturing Sciences,* Ann Arbor, MI.

Brown, L. E. (1997). *Two-spirit people.* Binghamton, NY: Haworth Press.

Brown, L. S. (1995). Lesbian identities: Concepts and issues. In A. R. D'Augelli & C. J. Patterson (Eds.), *Lesbian, gay, and bisexual identities over the lifespan* (pp. 3–24). New York: Oxford University Press.

Bryan, W. V. (1996). *In search of freedom: How people with disabilities have been disenfranchised from the mainstream of American Society.* Springfield, IL: Charles C. Thomas.

Burgos-Ocasio, H. (2000). Hispanic women. In M. Julia (Ed.), *Constructing gender: Multicultural perspectives in working with women* (pp. 109–139). Pacific Grove, CA: Brooks/Cole.

Bynner, J. (1997). Basic skills in adolescent's occupational preparation. *Career Development Quarterly, 45,* 305–321.

Cabrera, N. J., Tasmis-LeMonda, C. S., Bradley, R. H., Hofferth, S., & Lamb, M. E. (2000). Fatherhood in the twenty-first century. *Child Development, 71,* 127–136.

Camilleri, C., & Malewska-Peyre, H. (1997). Socialization and identity strategies. In J. W. Berry, P. R. Dasen, & T. S. Saraswathi (Eds.), *Handbook of cross-cultural psychology* (Vol. 2, pp. 41–67). Boston: Allyn & Bacon.

Campbell, C. A., & Dahir, C. A. (1997). *The national standards for school counseling programs.* Alexandria, VA: American School Counselor Association.

Campbell, R. E., & Cellini, J. V. (1981). A diagnostic taxonomy of adult career problems. *Journal of Vocational Behavior, 19,* 175–190.

Cappelli, P., Bassi, L., Katz, H., Knoke, D., Osterman, P., & Unseem, M. (1997). *Change at work.* New York: Oxford University Press.

Carnoy, M. (1999). The family, flexible work and social cohesion at risk. *International Labor Review, 138*(4), 411–429.

Carlson-Jones, D. (2004), Body image among adolescent girls and boys: A longitudinal study. *Developmental Psychology, 40,* 823–835.

Carroll, J. (2013). *Sexuality now: Embracing diversity.* Belmont, CA: Wadsworth Cengage Learning.

Carson, A. D., & Mowesian, R. (1993). Moderators of the prediction of job satisfaction from congruence: A test of Holland's theory. *Journal of Career Assessment, 1,* 130–144.

Carter, J. K. (1995a, Winter). Applying customer service strategies to career services. *Journal of Career Development, 22*(2), 85–139.

Carter, R. T. (1995b). *The influence of race and racial identity in psychotherapy: Toward a racially inclusive model.* New York: Wiley.

Carter, R. T., & Qureshi, A. (1995). A typology of philosophical assumptions in multicultural counseling and training. In J. G. Ponterotto, J. M. Casas, L. A. Suzuki, & C. M. Alexander (Eds.), *Handbook of multicultural counseling* (pp. 239–262). Thousand Oaks, CA: Sage.

Castillo, R. J.(1997). *Culture and mental illness: a client-centered approach.* Belmont, CA: Wadsworth Cengage Learning.

Cass, V. C. (1979). Homosexuality identity formation: A theoretical model. *Journal of Homosexuality, 4*(3), 219–235.

Cass, V. C. (1984). Homosexual identity formation: Testing a theoretical model. *Journal of Sex Research, 20*(2), 143–167.

Cattell, R. B., Eber, H. W., & Tatsuoka, M. M. (1970). *Handbook for the sixteen personality factor questionnaire (16PF).* Champaign, IL: Institute for Personality and Ability Testing.

Cautela, J., & Wisock, P. (1977). The thought-stopping procedure: Description, application and learning theory interpretations. *Psychological Record, 2,* 264–266.

Cavanaugh, J. C., & Blanchard-Fields, F. (2002). *Adult development and aging* (4th ed.). Belmont, CA: Wadsworth/Thomson Learning.

Chan, C. S. (1989). Issues of identity formation among Asian-American lesbians and gay men. *Journal of Counseling Development, 68,* 16–20.

Chan, C. S. (1997). Don't ask, don't tell, don't know: The formation of homosexual identity and sexual expression among Asian American lesbians. In B. Greene (Ed.), *Ethnic and cultural diversity among lesbians and gay men* (pp. 240–249). Thousand Oaks, CA: Sage.

Chandler, M., Lalonde, C., Sokol, B., & Hallett, D. (2003). Personal persistence, identity development, and suicide. *Monographs of the Society for Research in Child Development, 68* (2. Serial No. 273).

Choi, S. C., Kim, U., & Choi, S.H. (1993). Indigenous analysis of collective representations: A Korean perspective. In U. Kim & S. J. Berry (Eds.), *Indigenous psychologies: Research and experience in cultural context* (pp. 193–210). Newbury Park, CA: Sage.

Chu, L. (1981, April). *Asian-American women in educational research.* Paper presented at annual conference of the American Educational Research Association, Los Angeles.

Chung, Y. B., & Katayama, M. (1999). Ethnic and sexual identity development of Asian American lesbian and gay adolescents. In K. S. Ng (Ed.), *Counseling Asian families from a systems perspective* (pp. 159–171). Alexandria, VA: American Counseling Association.

Chusmir, L. H. (1983). Characteristics and predictive dimensions of women who make nontraditional vocational choices. *Personnel and Guidance Journal, 62*(1), 43–48.

Cillessen, A. H. N., & Rose, A. (2005). Understanding popularity in the peer system. *Current Directions in Psychological Science, 14,* 102–105.

Clark, A. (2010). Empathy: An integral model in the counseling process. *Journal of Counseling and Development, 88,* 348–356.

Clarkberg, M., & Merola, S. (2003). Competing clocks: Work and leisure. In P. Moen (Ed.), *It's about time: Couples and careers* (pp. 35-48). Ithaca, NY; Cornell University Press.

Clark-Stewart, A. (1993). *Daycare* (rev. ed.). Cambridge, MA: Harvard University Press.

Cochran, L. (1994). What is a career problem? *Career Development Quarterly, 42,* 204–215.

Cohn, D., & Fears, D. (2001, March 7). Hispanics draw even with Blacks in new census. *Washington Post,* A1.

Coleman, E., & Remafedi, G. (1989). Gay, lesbian, and bisexual adolescents: A critical challenge to counselors. *Journal of Counseling and Development, 68,* 36–40.

Colozzi, E. A. (2000). Toward the development of systematic guidance. In D. A. Luzzo (Ed.), *Career counseling of college students* (pp. 285–311). Washington, DC: American Psychological Association.

Coltrane, S. (2000). Research on household labor: Modeling and measuring the social embeddedness of routine family work. *Journal of Marriage and Family, 62*, 1208–1233.

Comas-Diaz, L. (1996). Cultural considerations in diagnosis. In F. W. Kaslow (Ed.), *Handbook on relational diagnosis and dysfunctional family patterns* (pp. 159–160). New York: Wiley.

Comas-Diaz, L., & Grenier, J. R. (1998). Migration and acculturation. In J. Sandoval, C. L. Frisby, K. F. Geisinger, J. D. Scheuneman, & J. R. Grenier, *Test interpretation and diversity* (pp. 213–241). Washington, DC: American Psychological Association.

Compton, W., & Hoffman, E. (2013). *Positive psychology: The science of happiness and flourishing* (2nd ed.). Belmont, CA: Wadsworth Cengage Learning.

Coon-Carty, H. M. (1995). *The relation of work-related abilities, vocational interests, and self-efficacy beliefs: A meta-analytic investigation.* Unpublished master's thesis, Loyola University, Chicago.

Coontz, S. (1997). *The way we really are.* New York: Basic Books.

Copeland, L., & Griggs, L. (1985). *Going international.* New York: Random House.

Corey, G. (1991). *Theory and practice of counseling and psychotherapy* (4th ed.). Pacific Grove, CA: Brooks/Cole.

Corey, G. (1986). *Theory and practice of counseling and psychotherapy* (3rd ed.). Pacific Grove, CA: Brooks/Cole.

Cormier, L. S., & Hackney, H. (1987). *The professional counselor: A process guide to help.* Englewood Cliffs, NJ: Prentice-Hall.

Cormier, W., & Cormier, L. S. (1991). *Interviewing strategies for helpers: Fundamental skills and cognitive behavioral interventions* (3rd ed.). Pacific Grove, CA: Brooks/Cole.

Cormier, S., Nurius, P. S., & Osborn, C. J. (2013). *Interviewing and change strategies for helpers* (7th ed.). Belmont, CA: Brooks/Cole.

Corrigan, P. W., River, L. P., Lundin, R. K., Wasowski, K. U., Campion, J., Mathisen, J., Goldstein, H., Bergman, M., Gagnon, C., & Kubiak, M. A. (2000). Stigmatizing attributions about mental illness. *Journal of Community Psychology, 28*, 91–102.

Costa, P. T., & McCrae, R.R. (1992). *Revised NEO Personality Inventory (NEO-PI-R) professional manual.* Odessa, FL: Psychological Assessment Resources.

Cox, M. J., Owen, M. T., Henderson, V. K., & Margand, N. A. (1992). Prediction of infant–father and infant–mother attachment. *Developmental Psychology, 28*, 474–483.

Crace, R. K., & Brown, D. (1996). *Life values inventory.* Minneapolis: National Computer Systems.

Crites, J. O. (1973). *Theory and research handbook: Career maturity inventory.* Monterey, CA: CTB-MacMillan-McGraw-Hill.

Crites, J. O. (1981). *Career models: Models, methods, and materials.* New York: McGraw-Hill.

Crites, J. O., & Savickas, M. L. (1995). *The career maturity inventory—Revised form.* Clayton, NY: Careerware: ISM.

Crites, J. O., & Savickas, M. L. (1996). Revision of the career maturity inventory. *Journal of Career Assessment, 4*(2), 131–138.

Cronbach, L. J. (1990). *Essentials of psychological testing* (5th ed.). New York: Harper & Row.

Cropanzano, R., & Prehar, C. A. (2001). Progress in organizational justice: Tunneling through the maze. In C. L. Cooper & I. T. Robertson (Eds.), *International review in the workplace and organizational psychology* (Vol. 2). Mahwah, NJ: Erlbaum.

Cross, T. L., Bazron, B. J., Dennis, K. W., & Isaacs, M. R. (1989). *Toward a culturally competent system of care.* Washington, DC: Georgetown University Child Development Center.

D'Amico, M., Barrafato, A., Peterson, L., Snow, S., & Tanguay, D. (2001). Using theatre to examine children's attitudes toward individuals with disabilities. *Developmental Disabilities Bulletin, 29*(1), 231–238.

Dancer, L. S., & Gilbert, L. A. (1993). Spouses' family work participation and its relation to wives' occupational level. *Sex Roles, 28,* 127–145.

D'Augelli, A. R. (1991). Gay men in college: Identity processes and adaptations. *Journal of College Student Development, 32,* 140–146.

Davidson, S. L., & Gilbert, L. A. (1993). Career counseling is a personal matter. *Career Development Quarterly, 42,* 149–153.

Dawis, R. V. (1991). Vocational interests, values, and preferences. In M. D. Dunnette & L. M. Hough (Eds.), *Handbook of industrial and organizational psychology* (Vol. 2, 2nd ed., pp. 833–871). Palo Alto, CA: Consulting Psychologists Press.

Dawis, R. V. (1996). The theory of work adjustment and person-environment-correspondence counseling. In D. Brown, L. Brooks, & Associates (Eds.), *Career choice and development* (3rd ed.), pp. 75–115). San Francisco: Jossey-Bass.

Dawis, R. V. (2002). Person–environment–correspondence theory. In D. Brown & Associates (Ed.), *Career choice and development* (4th ed., pp. 427–465). San Francisco: Jossey-Bass.

Dawis, R. V., Dohm, T. E., Lofquist, L. H., Chartrand, J. M., & Due, A. M. (1987). *Minnesota occupational classification system III.* Minneapolis: Vocational Psychology Research, Department of Psychology, University of Minnesota.

Dawis, R. V., & Lofquist, L. H. (1984). *A psychological theory of work adjustment: An individual differences model and its application.* Minneapolis: University of Minnesota.

De Jong, P., & Berg, I. K. (2002). *Interviewing for solutions* (2nd ed.). Pacific Grove, CA: Brooks/Cole.

Denmark, F. (1994). Engendering psychology. *American Psychologist, 49,* 329–334.

Dent, H. S., Jr. (1998). *The roaring 2000's.* New York: Simon & Schuster.

DePoy, E., & Gilson, S. F. (2004). *Rethinking disability: Principles for professional and social change.* Belmont, CA: Brooks/Cole-Thomson Learning.

Derogates, I. R. (1993). *The brief symptoms inventory (BSI).* Minneapolis: Pearson Assessments

Derogates, I. R. (1994). *The symptoms checklist-90-revised (SCI-90-R).* Minneapolis: Pearson Assessments.

DeRouin, R. E., Parrish, T., & Salas, E. (2005), *On the job training: A review for researchers and practitioners.* Poster session presented at 20th annual conference of the Society for Industrial and Organizational Psychology, Los Angeles.

Diamond, E. E. (1975). Overview. In E. E. Diamond (Ed.), *Issues of sex bias and sex fairness in career interest movement.* Washington, DC: U.S. Government Printing Office.

Dickstein, L. J. (1996). Sexual harassment in medicine. In D. K. Shrier (Ed.), *Sexual harassment in the workplace and academia: Psychiatric issues* (pp. 223–243). Washington, DC: American Psychiatric Press.

Dignan, L. (2010) "Offshore's Toll: IT Departments to Endure Jobless Recovery through 2014" ZDNET, November 18. Available at http:www,znet,com/

Diller, J. V. (2004). *Cultural diversity: A primer for the human services.* Belmont, CA: Brooks/Cole-Thomson Learning.

Diller, J. V. (2007). *Cultural diversity: A primer for the human services* (3rd ed.). Belmont, CA: Wadsworth Cengage Learning.

Diller, J. V. (2011). *Cultural diversity: A primer for the human services* (4th ed.). Belmont, CA: Wadsworth Cengage Learning.

Dix, J. E., & Savickas, M. L. (1995). Establishing a career: Developmental tasks and coping responses. *Journal of Vocational Behavior, 47,* 93–107.

Doyle, R. E. (1992). *Essential skills and strategies in the helping process.* Pacific Grove, CA: Brooks/Cole.

Doyle, R. E. (1998). *Essential skills & strategies in the helping process* (3rd ed.). Pacific Grove, CA: Brooks/Cole.

Drucker, P. F. (1992). *Managing for the future.* New York: Truman Talley Books/Dutton.

Drucker, P. F. (2002). *Managing in the next society.* New York: Truman Talley Books.

Drummond, R. (1992). *Appraisal procedures for counselors and helping professionals* (2nd ed.). New York: Macmillan.

Drummond, R. J., & Ryan, C. W. (1995). *Career counseling: A developmental approach.* Columbus, OH: Merrill.

Dumenci, L. (1995). Construct validity of the *Self-Directed Search* using hierarchically nested structural models. *Journal of Vocational Behavior, 47,* 21–34.

Duran, E., & Duran, B. (1995). *Native American postcolonial psychology.* Albany: State University of New York Press.

Durand, V. M., (2005). Past, present, and emerging directions in education. In D. Zager (Ed.), *Autism spectrum disorders: Identification, education, and treatment* (3rd ed., pp. 89–110). Hillsdale, NJ: Lawrence Erlbaum Associates.

Durand, V., & Barlow, D. (2013). *Essentials of abnormal psychology* (6th ed.). Belmont, CA: Wadsworth Cengage Learning.

Eagly, A. H., Karau, S. J., & Makhijani, M. G. (1995). Gender and the effectiveness of leaders. *Psychological Bulletin, 117,* 125–145.

Ebert, E. S., & Culyer, R. C. (2011). *School: An introduction to education* (2nd ed.). Belmont, CA: Cengage Learning.

Eccles, J. S. (1987). Gender roles and women's achievement-related decisions. *Psychology of Women Quarterly, 11,* 135–172.

Eccles, J. S. (1993). School and family effects on the ontogeny of children's interests, self-perceptions, and activity choices. In J. E. Jacobs (Eds.), *Nebraska Symposium on Motivation: 1992* (Vol. 40, pp. 145–208). Lincoln: University of Nebraska Press.

Eccles, J. S., Barber, B., & Jozefowicz, D. (1999). Linking gender to educational, occupational, and recreational choices: Applying the Eccles et al. model of achievement-related choices. In W. B. Swann, J. H. Langlois, & L. A. Gilbert (Eds.), *Sexism and stereotypes in modern society* (pp. 153–192). Washington, DC: American Psychological Association.

Educational Testing Service. (1996). *SIGI PLUS.* Princeton, NJ: Author.

Eldridge, N. S. (1987). Gender issues in counseling same-sex couples. *Professional Psychology: Research and Practice, 18*(6), 567–572.

Eldridge, N. S., & Barnett, D. C. (1991). Counseling gay and lesbian students. In N. J. Evans & V. A. Wall (Eds.), *Beyond tolerance: Gays, lesbians and bisexuals on campus* (pp. 147–178). Alexandria, VA: American College Personnel Association.

Elkind, D. (1968). Cognitive development in adolescence. In J. F. Adams (Ed.), *Understanding adolescence.* Boston: Allyn & Bacon.

Elliot, J. E. (1993). Career development with lesbian and gay clients. *Career Development Quarterly, 41*(3), 210–226.

Ellis, A. (1962). *Reason and emotion in psychotherapy.* Secaucus, NJ: Lyle Stuart.

Ellis, A. (1971). *Growth through reason.* Hollywood, CA: Wilshire.

Ellis, A. (1991). The philosophical basis of rational-emotive therapy (RET). *Psychotherapy in Private Practice, 8,* 97–106.

Ellis, A. (1994). *Reason and emotion in psychotherapy revisited.* New York: Carol Publishing.

Ellis, A., & Grieger, R. (1977). *Handbook of rational-emotive therapy.* New York: Springer.

Engler, B. (2014). *Personality theories* (9th ed.). Belmont, CA: Wadsworth Cengage Learning.

Engels, D. W. (Ed.). (1994). *The professional practice of career counseling and consultation: A resource document* (2nd ed.). Alexandria, VA: American Counseling Association.

Epps, S., & Jackson, B. J. (2000). *Empowered families, successful children.* Washington DC: American Psychological Association.

Erikson, E. H. (1950). *Childhood and society.* New York: Norton.

Erikson, E. H. (1963). *Childhood and society* (2nd ed.). New York: Norton.

Espin, O. M. (1987). Issues of identity in psychology of Latina lesbians. In Boston Lesbian Psychologies Collective (Eds.), *Lesbian psychologies: Exploration and challenges* (pp. 35–55). Urbana: University of Illinois Press.

Etringer, B. D., Hillerbrand, E., & Hetherington, C. (1990). The influence of sexual orientation on career decision making: A research note. *Journal of Homosexuality, 19*(4), 103–111.

Ettinger, J. M. (Ed.). (1991). *Improved career decision making in a changing world.* Garrett Park, MD: Garrett Park.

Evanoski, P. O., & Tse, F. W. (1989). Career awareness program for Chinese and Korean American parents. *Journal of Counseling and Development, 67,* 472–474.

Eysenck, H. J. (1998). *Intelligence: A new book.* New Brunswick, NJ: Transaction Press.

Fagot, B. I., & Leinbach, M. D. (1989). The young child's gender schema: Environmental input, internal organization. *Child Development, 60,* 663–672.

Farmer, R. L. (2009). *Neuroscience and social work: The missing link.* Thousand Oaks, CA: Sage.

Fassinger, R. E., & Schlossberg, N. K. (1992). Understanding the adult years: Perspectives and implications. In S. D. Brown & R. W. Lent (Eds.), *Handbook of counseling psychology* (2nd ed., pp. 217–249). New York: Wiley.

Feldman, D. C. (1988). *Managing careers in organizations.* Glenview, IL: Scott, Foresman.

Feldman, D. C. (Ed.). (2002). *Work careers: A developmental perspective.* San Francisco: Jossey-Bass.

Feller, R. (1994). *650 career videos: Ratings, reviews and descriptions.* Fort Collins: Colorado State University.

Fernandez, J. P. (1999). *Race, gender, & rhetoric.* New York: McGraw-Hill.

Fernandez, M. S. (1988). Issues in counseling southeast Asian students. *Journal of Multicultural Counseling and Development, 16,* 157–166.

Ferrante, J. (2013). *Sociology: A global perspective* (8th ed.). Belmont, CA: Wadsworth Cengage Learning.

Fitzgerald, L. F., & Betz, N. E. (1994). Career development in cultural context: The role of gender, race, class and sexual orientation. In M. Savickas & R. Lent (Eds.), *Convergence in career development theories: Implications for science and practice* (pp. 103–115). Palo Alto, CA: Consulting Psychologists Press.

Fitzgerald, L. F., & Ormerod, A. J. (1991). Perceptions of sexual harassment: The influence of gender and academic context. *Psychology of Women Quarterly, 15,* 281–294.

Fong, R. (2003). Cultural competence with Asian Americans. In D. Lum (Ed.), *Culturally competent practice* (2nd ed., pp. 261–282). Pacific Grove, CA: Brooks/Cole-Thomson Learning.

Ford, D. H. (1987). *Humans as self-constructing living systems: A developmental perspective personality disorder.* Hillsdale, NJ: Erlbaum.

Ford, M. E., & Ford, D. H. (Eds.). (1987). *Humans as self-constructing living systems: Putting the framework to work.* Hillsdale, NJ: Erlbaum.

Fouad, N. A. (1997). School-to-work transition: Voice from an implementer. *Counseling Psychologist, 25,* 403–412.

Fouad, N. A., & Bingham, R. P. (1995). Career counseling with racial/ethnic minorities. In W. B. Walsh & S. H. Osipow (Eds.), *Handbook of vocational psychology* (2nd ed., pp. 331–366). Hillsdale, NJ: Erlbaum.

Fouad, N. A., & Bynner, J. (2008). Work transitions. *American Psychologist, 63*(4), 241–251.

Fouad, N. A., & Spreda, S. L. (1995). Career behavior of Hispanics: Assessment and career intervention. In F. T. L. Leong (Ed.), *Career development and vocational behavior of racial and ethnic minorities* (pp. 165–187). Mahwah, NJ: Erlbaum.

Fox, A. (1991). Development of a bisexual identity: Understanding the process. In L. Hutchins & L. Kaahumanu (Eds.), *Bi any other name: Bisexual people speak out* (pp. 29–36). Boston: Alyson.

Fox, S., & Spector, P. E. (2005). *Counterproductive work behavior: Investigations of actors and targets.* Washington, DC: American Psychological Association.

French, S. (1996). The attitudes of health professionals towards disabled people. In G. Hales (Ed.), *Beyond disability: Towards an enabling society* (pp. 151–162). London: Sage.

Friedman, M., & Rosenman, R. (1974). *Type A behavior and your heart.* Greenwich, CT: Fawcett.

Friskopp, A., & Silverstein, S. (1995). *Straight jobs, gay lives.* New York: Scribner.

Fullerton, H. N. (1999). Labor force projections to 2008: Steady growth and changing composition. *Monthly Labor Review, 122,* 19–32.

Furnham, A. (2001). Vocational preference and P-O fit: Reflections on Holland's theory of vocational choice. *Applied Psychology: An International Review Special Issue: P-O Fit, 50,* 5–29.

Gajendran, R., & Harrison, D. (2007). The good, the bad, and unknown about telecommuting: Met-analysis of psychological mediators and individual consequences. *Journal of Applied Psychology, 92*(6), 1524–1541.

Galliano, G. (2003). *Gender: Crossing boundaries.* Belmont, CA: Wadsworth/Thomson Learning.

Garcia, E. E. (Ed.). (1995). *Meeting the challenge of linguistic and cultural diversity in early childhood education.* New York: Teachers College Press.

Gargiulo, R. M., & Graves, S. B. (1991). Parental feelings. *Childhood Education, 67*(3), 176–178.

Gartrell, N. (1983). Gay patients in the medical setting. In C. C. Nadelson & D. B. Marcotte (Eds.), *Treatment and interventions in human sexuality.* New York: Plenum.

Geary, J. (1972). Forty newspapers forty. In J. E. Bottoms, R. N. Evans, K. B. Hoyt, & J. C. Willer (Eds.), *Career education resource guide.* Morristown, NJ: General Learning Corporation.

Geisinger, K. F. (1998). Psychometric issues in test interpretation. In J. Sandoval, C. L. Frisby, K. F. Geisinger, J. D. Scheuneman, & J. R. Grenier (Eds.), *Test interpretation and diversity* (pp. 17–31). Washington, DC: American Psychological Association.

Gelberg, S., & Chojnacki, J. T. (1996). *Career and life planning with gay, lesbian, & bisexual persons.* Alexandria, VA: American Counseling Association.

Gelso, C., & Fretz, B. (2001). *Counseling psychology.* Belmont, CA: Wadsworth.

Gilbert, L. A. (1993). *Two careers/one family.* Newbury Park, CA: Sage.

Gillies, P. (1989). A longitudinal study of the hopes and worries of adolescents. *Journal of Adolescence, 12,* 69–81.

Ginzberg, E. (1966). *Lifestyles of educated American women.* New York: Columbia University Press.

Ginzberg, E. (1972). Toward a theory of occupational choice: A restatement. *Vocational Guidance Quarterly, 20,* 169–176.

Ginzberg, E. (1984). Career development. In D. Brown & L. Brooks (Eds.), *Career choice and development.* San Francisco: Jossey-Bass.

Ginzberg, E., Ginsburg, S. W., Axelrad, S., & Herma, J. L. (1951). *Occupational choice: An approach to general theory.* New York: Columbia University Press.

Glasser, N. (Ed.). (1989). *Control theory in the practice of reality therapy: Case studies.* New York: Harper & Row.

Goldenberg, H., & Goldenberg, I. (2002). *Counseling families today.* Pacific Grove, CA: Brooks/Cole.

Goldenberg, H., & Goldenberg, I. (2008). *Family therapy: An overview* (7th ed.). Belmont, CA: Brooks Cole Cengage Learning.

Goldenberg, H., & Goldenberg, I. (2013). *Family therapy: An interview* (8th ed.). Belmont , CA: Brooks Cole Cengage Learning.

Golding, J. M. (1989). Role occupancy and role-specific stress and social support as predictors of depression. *Basic and Applied Social Psychology, 10,* 173–195.

Goldstein, E. B. (2011). *Cognitive psychology: Connecting mind, research, and everyday experience* (3rd ed.). Belmont CA: Wadsworth Cengage Learning.

Goldstein, I. L., & Ford, J. K. (2002). *Training in organizations* (4th ed.). Belmont, CA: Wadsworth.

Goodlad, J. I. (1984). *A place called school: Prospects for the future.* New York: McGraw-Hill.

Goodman, J. (1993, April 29). *Using nonstandardized appraisals, tools and techniques.* Presentation to Michigan Career Development Association Annual Conference, Kalamazoo.

Gordon, L. V. (1967). *Survey of personal values.* Chicago: Science Research Associates.

Gottfredson, G. D., & Holland, J. L. (1989). *Dictionary of Holland occupational codes.* Odessa, FL: Psychological Assessment Resources.

Gottfredson, G. D., & Holland, J. L. (1990). A longitudinal test of the influence of congruence: Job satisfaction, competency utilization, and counterproductive behavior. *Journal of Counseling Psychology, 37,* 389–398.

Gottfredson, G. D., & Holland, J. L. (1991). *The position classification inventory: Professional manual.* Odessa, FL: Psychological Assessment Resources.

Gottfredson, G. D., & Holland, J. L. (1994). *The career attitudes and strategies inventory.* Odessa, FL: Psychological Assessment Resources.

Gottfredson, G. D., Jones, E. M., & Holland, J. L. (1993). Personality and vocational interests: The relation of Holland's six interest dimensions to five robust dimensions of personality. *Journal of Counseling Psychology, 40,* 518–524.

Gottfredson, L. S. (1981). Circumscription and compromise: A developmental theory of occupational aspirations. *Journal of Counseling Psychology, 28*(6), 545–579.

Gottfredson, L. S. (1990). A longitudinal test of the influence of congruence: Job satisfaction competency utilization, and counterproductive behavior. *Journal of Counseling Psychology, 37,* 389–398.

Gottfredson, L. S. (1996). Gottfredson's theory of circumscription and compromise. In D. Brown, L. Brooks, & Associates (Eds.), *Career choice and development* (3rd ed., pp. 179–228). San Francisco: Jossey-Bass.

Gottfredson, L. S. (1997). Why g matters: The complexity of everyday life. *Intelligence, 24*(1), 79–132.

Gottfredson, L. S. (2002). Gottfredson's theory of circumscription, compromise, and self-creation. In D. Brown & Associates (Eds.), *Career choice and development* (4th ed., pp. 85–149). San Francisco: Jossey-Bass.

Graesser, A., Conley, M., & Olney, A. (2012). Intelligent tutoring systems. In K. Harris, G. Steve., T. Urdan, A. Bus, S. Major, & H. Swanson (Eds.), *APA educational psychology handbook, Vol 3: Application to learning and teaching* (pp. 451–473). Washington, DC: American Psychological Association.

Granovetter, M. (1983). The Strength of Weak Ties; A Network Revisited. *Sociological Theory* I, 201–233.

Gray, W. M. (1990). Formal operational thought. In W. F. Overton (Ed.), *Reasoning, necessity, and logic: Developmental perspectives* (pp. 227–253). Hillsdale, NJ: Erlbaum.

Green, L. B., & Parker, H. J. (1965). Parental influence upon adolescents' occupational choice: A test of an aspect of Roe's theory. *Journal of Counseling Psychology, 12,* 379–383.

Greene, B. (1997). Ethnic minority lesbians and gay men: Mental health and treatment issues. In B. Greene (Ed.), *Ethnic and cultural diversity among lesbians and gay men.* New York: Guilford Press.

Greenglass, E. R. (1991). Type A behavior, career aspirations, and role conflict in professional women. In M. J. Strube (Ed.), *Type A behavior* (pp. 277–292). Newbury Park, CA: Sage.

Grossman, G. M., & Drier, H. N. (1988). *Apprenticeship 2000: The status of and recommendations for improved counseling, guidance, and information processes.* Columbus: National Center for Research in Vocational Education, Ohio State University. (ERIC Report No. ED 298 356)

Grubb, W. N., Davis, G., Lum, J., Plihal, J., & Mograine, C. (1991). *The cunning hand, the cultured mind: Models for integrating vocational and academic education.* Berkeley, CA: National Center for Research in Vocational Education. (ERIC Report No. ED 334 421)

Guinn, B. (1999). Leisure behavior motivation and the life satisfaction of retired persons. *Activities, Adapting and Aging, 23,* 13–20.

Gunther-Mohr, C. (1997). Virtual reality training takes off. *Training and Development, 51,* 47–48.

Gurung, R. A. (2014). *Health psychology: A cultural approach* (3rd ed.). Belmont, CA: Wadsworth Cengage Learning.

Gysbers, N. C., & Henderson, P. (1988). *Developing and managing your school guidance program.* Alexandria, VA: American Association for Counseling and Development.

Gysbers, N. C., & Henderson, P. (2001). Comprehensive guidance and counseling programs: A rich history and bright future. *Professional School Counseling, 4,* 246–256.

Gysbers, N. C., & Moore, E. J. (1987). *Career counseling, skills and techniques for practitioners.* Englewood Cliffs, NJ: Prentice-Hall.

Hackett, G. (1993). Career counseling and psychotherapy: False dichotomies and recommended remedies. *Journal of Career Assessment, 1,* 105–117.

Hackett, G. (1995). Self-efficacy in career choice and development. In A. Bandura (Ed.), *Self-efficacy in changing societies* (pp. 232–258). Cambridge, MA: Cambridge University Press.

Hackett, G., & Lent, R. W. (1992). Theoretical advances and current inquiry in career psychology. In S. D. Brown & R. W. Lent (Eds.), *Handbook of counseling psychology* (2nd ed., pp. 419–451). New York: Wiley.

Hackett, G., Lent, R. W., & Greenhaus, J. H. (1991). Advances in vocational theory and research: A 20-year retrospective. *Journal of Vocational Behavior, 38,* 3–38.

Hackett, R. D., & Betz, N. E. (1981). A self-efficacy approach to the career development of women. *Journal of Vocational Behavior, 18,* 326–329.

Hackney, H., & Cormier, L. S. (2001). *The professional counselor.* Boston: Allyn & Bacon.

Halaby, C. N., & Weakliem, D. L. (1989). Worker control and attachment to the firm. *American Journal of Sociology, 95,* 549–591.

Hall, D. T., & Associates (1996). *The career is dead: Long live the career.* San Francisco: Jossey-Bass.

Hall, D. T., & Mirvas, P. H. (1996). The new protean career: Psychological success and the path with a heart. In D. T. Hall & Associates (Eds.), *The career is dead: Long live the career: A relational approach to careers* (pp. 15–45). San Francisco: Jossey-Bass.

Hall, D. T. (1971). *Beyond culture.* New York: Anchor/Doubleday.

Hall, E. S., & Hall, D. T. (1979). *The two-career couple.* Reading, MA: Addison-Wesley.

Hall, E. T. (1982). *The hidden dimension.* New York: Anchor/Doubleday.

Hammer, M., & Champy, J. (1993). *Reengineering the corporation: A manifesto for business revolution.* New York: HarperCollins.

Hansen, J. C., Collins, R. C., Swanson, J. L., & Fouad, N. A. (1993). Gender differences in the structure of interests. *Journal of Vocational Behavior, 42,* 200–211.

Hansen, L. S. (1970). *Career guidance practices in school and community.* Washington, DC: National Vocational Guidance Association.

Hansen, L. S. (1978). *BORN FREE: Training packets to reduce stereotyping in career options.* Minneapolis: University of Minnesota Press.

Hansen, L. S. (1990, July). *Integrative life planning: Work, family and community.* Paper presented at International Round Table for the Advancement of Counseling, Helsinki, Finland.

Hansen, L. S. (1991). Integrative life planning: Work, family, community. [Special Issue from World Future Society Conference on "Creating the Future: Individual Responsibility," Minneapolis: July 25]. *Futurics, 14*(3 & 4), 80–86.

Hansen, L. S. (1996). ILP: Integrating our lives, shaping our society. In R. Feller & G. Walz (Eds.), *Career transitions in turbulent times* (pp. 21–30). Greensboro: ERIC Counseling and Student Services Clearinghouse, University of North Carolina.

Hansen, L. S. (2000). Integrative life planning: A new worldview for career professionals. In J. Kummerow (Ed.), *New directions in career planning and the workplace.* Palo Alto, CA: Consulting Psychologists Press.

Hansson, R. O., DeKoekkoek, P. D., Neece, W. M., & Patterson, D. W. (1997). Successful aging at work: Annual review, 1992–1996: The older worker and transitions to retirement. *Journal of Vocational Behavior, 51,* 202–233.

Harley, S. (1995). When your work is not who you are: The development of a working-class consciousness among Afro-American women. In D. Clark-Hine, W. King, & L. Reed (Eds.), *We specialize in the wholly impossible: A reader in Black women's history* (pp. 25–38). Brooklyn, NY: Carlson.

Harmon, L. W. (1996). A moving target: The widening gap between theory and practice. In M. L. Savickas & W. B. Walsh (Eds.), *Handbook of career counseling theory and practice* (pp. 37–45). Palo Alto, CA: Davies-Black.

Harmon, L., Hansen, J. C., Borgen, F., & Hammer, A. (1994). *Strong interest inventory manual.* Palo Alto, CA: Consulting Psychologists Press.

Harmon, L. W., & Meara, N. M. (1994). Contemporary developments in women's career counseling: Themes of the past, puzzles for the future. In W. B. Walsh & S. H. Osipow (Eds.), *Career counseling for women: Contemporary topics in vocational psychology* (pp. 355–367). Hillsdale, NJ: Erlbaum.

Harrington, R. (2013). *Stress, health and well-being: Thriving in the 21st century.* Belmont, CA: Wadsworth Cengage Learning.

Harrington, T. F., & O'Shea, A. J. (1992). *The Harrington/O'Shea system for career decision making manual.* Circle Pines, MN: American Guidance Service.

Harris-Bowlsbey, J., Dikel, M. R., & Sampson, J. P. (2002). *The Internet: A tool for career planning.* Columbus, OH: National Career Development Association.

Hartung, P. J. (1999). Interest assessment using card sorts. In M. L. Savickas & A. R. Spokane (Eds.), *Vocational interests: Meaning, measurement, and counseling use.* Palo Alto, CA: Davies-Black.

Hartung, P. J., & Niles, S. G. (2000). Established career theories. In D. A. Luzzo. (Ed.), *Career counseling of college students.* (pp. 3–23). Washington, DC: American Psychological Association.

Harway, M. (1980). Sex bias in educational-vocational counseling. *Psychology of Women Quarterly, 4,* 212–214.

Haverkamp, B. E., & Moore, D. (1993). The career-personal dichotomy: Perceptual reality, practical illusion, and workplace integration. *Career Development Quarterly, 42,* 154–160.

Havighurst, R. (1953). *Human development and education.* New York: Longman.

Havighurst, R. (1972). *Developmental tasks and education* (3rd ed.). New York: Longman.

Healy, C. C. (1982). *Career development: Counseling through life stages.* Boston: Allyn & Bacon.

Healy, C. C. (1990). Reforming career appraisals to meet the needs of clients in the 1990s. *Counseling Psychologist, 18,* 214–226.

Healy, C. C., & Quinn, O. H. (1977). *Project Cadre: A cadre approach to career education infusion.* Unpublished manuscript.

Heatherington, L, & Lavner, J. A. (2008). Coming to terms with coming out. Review and recommendations for family systems focused research. *Journal of Family Psychology, 22,* 329–343.

Helms, J. E. (1990). An overview of Black racial identity theory. In J. E. Helms (Ed.), *Black and White racial identity: Theory, research and practice* (pp. 9–32). Westport, CT: Greenwood.

Helwig, A. A. (1992). Book review of career development and services. *Journal of Employment Counseling, 29,* 77–78.

Henderson, A. (1984). Homosexuality in the college years: Developmental differences between men and women. *Journal of American College Health, 32,* 216–219.

Heppner, P., & Kranskopf, C. (1987). An information processing approach to problem solving. *Counseling Psychologist, 15,* 371–447.

Hermans, H. J. M. (1992). Telling and retelling one's self-narrative: A contextual approach to life-span development. *Human Development, 35,* 361–375.

Herr, E. L. (1996). Toward convergence of career theory and practice: Mythology, issues, and possibilities. In M. L. Savickas & W. B. Walsh (Eds.), *Handbook of career counseling theory and practice* (pp. 70–85). Palo Alto, CA: Davies-Black.

Herr, E. L. (2001). Career development and its practice: A historical perspective. *Career Development Quarterly, 49*(3), 196–211.

Herr, E. L., & Cramer, S. H. (1996). *Career guidance and counseling through the life span: Systematic approaches* (5th ed.). New York: HarperCollins.

Herr, E. L., Cramer, S. H., & Niles, S. G. (2004). *Career guidance and counseling through the life span: Systematic approaches* (6th ed.). Boston: Pearson Education, Inc.

Herring, R. D. (1990). Attacking career myths among Native Americans: Implications for counseling. *School Counselor, 38,* 13–18.

Herring, R. D. (1998). *Career counseling in schools.* Alexandria, VA: American Counseling Association.

Heward, W. L. (1999). *Exceptional children: An introduction to special education* (6th ed.). Englewood Cliffs, NJ: Prentice-Hall.

Higginbotham, E. (1994). Black professional women: job ceilings and employment sectors. In M. Zinn & B. Dill (Eds.), *Women of color in the U.S. society* (pp. 113–131). Philadelphia: Temple University Press.

Higginbotham, E. and M. Andersen, Eds. (2012). *Race and ethnicity in society: The changing landscape* (3rd ed.). Belmont, CA: Wadsworth Cengage Learning.

Highwater, J. (1990). *Sex and myth.* Boston: Harper & Row.

Hochschild, A. R. (1997). *The time bind.* New York: Holt.

Hofstede, G. (2001). *Culture's consequences: International differences in work-related values* (2nd ed.). Thousand Oaks, CA: Sage.

Hogan, R., & Blake, R. (1999). John Holland's vocational typology and personality theory. *Journal of Vocational Behavior, 55,* 41–56.

Holland, J. L. (1966). *The psychology of vocational choice.* Waltham, MA: Blaisdell.

Holland, J. L. (1985a). *Making vocational choices: A theory of careers* (2nd ed.). Englewood Cliffs, NJ: Prentice-Hall.

Holland, J. L. (1985b). *Manual for the vocational preference inventory.* Odessa, FL: Psychological Assessment Resources.

Holland, J. L. (1987a). Current status of Holland's theory of careers: Another perspective. *Career Development Quarterly, 36,* 31–34.

Holland, J. L. (1987b). *The self-directed search professional manual.* Odessa, FL: Psychological Assessment Resources.

Holland, J. L. (1987c). *The occupations finder.* Odessa, FL: Psychological Assessment Resources.

Holland, J. L. (1992). *Making vocational choices* (2nd ed.). Odessa, FL: Psychological Assessment Resources.

Holland, J. L. (1994a). *Self-directed search (SDS), Form R.* Odessa, FL: Psychological Assessment Resources.

Holland, J. L. (1994b). *You and your career booklet.* Odessa, FL: Psychological Assessment Resources.

Holland, J. L. (1996). Exploring careers with a typology: What we have learned and some new directions. *American Psychologist, 51,* 397–406.

Holland, J. L., Daiger, D., & Power, P. G. (1980). *My vocational situation.* Odessa, FL: Psychological Assessment Resources.

Holland, J. L., Fritzsche, B. A., & Powell, A. B. (1994). *The SDS technical manual.* Odessa, FL: Psychological Assessment Resources.

Holland, J. L., Johnston, J. H., & Asama, N. (1993). The vocational identity scale: A diagnostic and treatment tool. *Journal of Career Assessment, 1,* 1–12.

Holland, J. L., Powell, A. B., & Fritzsche, B. A. (1994). *The SDS: Professional user's guide.* Odessa, FL: Psychological Assessment Resources.

Holmberg, K., Rosen, D., & Holland, J. L. (1990). *Leisure activities finder.* Odessa, FL: Psychological Assessment Resources.

Hood, A. B., & Johnson, R. W. (2007). *Assessment in counseling: A guide to the use of psychological assessment procedures* (4th ed.), Alexandria, VA: American Counseling Association.

HOPE in Focus (2000, Spring). *CAT emerges as national technology research center.* Detroit, MI: Hope in Focus and Center for Advanced Technology.

Hopkinson, K., Cox, A., & Rutter, M. (1981). Psychiatric interviewing techniques III: Naturalistic study: Eliciting feelings. *British Journal of Psychiatry, 138,* 406–415.

Horwath, E., & Weissman, M. (1997). Epidemiology of anxiety disorders across cultural groups. In S. Friedman (Ed.), *Cultural issues in treatment of anxiety* (pp. 21–39). New York: Guilford Press.

Hotchkiss, L., & Borow, H. (1996). Sociological perspective on work and career development. In D. Brown, L. Brooks, & Associates (Eds.), *Career choice and development* (3rd ed., pp. 281–326). San Francisco: Jossey-Bass.

Houston, B. K., & Kelly, K. E. (1987). Type A behavior in housewives: Relation to work, marital adjustment, stress, tension, health, fear-of-failure and self-esteem. *Journal of Psychosomatic Research, 31,* 55–61.

Hsia, J. (1981, April). *Testing and Asian and Pacific Americans.* Paper presented at National Association for Asian and Pacific American Education, Honolulu.

Hudson, J. S. (1992). *Vocational counseling with dual-career same-sex couples.* Unpublished manuscript, Southwest Texas State University.

Humes, C. W., Szymanski, E. M., & Hohenshil, T. H. (1989, Nov./Dec.). Roles of counseling in enabling persons with disabilities. *Journal of Counseling & Development, 68,* 145–149.

Hunter, J. E., & Hunter, R. F. (1984). Validity and utility of alternative predictors of job performance. *Psychological Bulletin, 96,* 72–98.

Hymel, S., Vailliancourt, T., McDougall, P., & Renshaw, P. D, (2004). Peer acceptance and rejection in childhood. In P. K. Smith and C. H Hart (Eds.), *Blackwell handbook of childhood social development* (pp. 265–284). Malden MA: Blackwell.

Iacarino, G. (2000). Computer-assisted career guidance systems. In D. A. Luzzo (Ed.), *Career counseling of college students* (pp. 173–200). Washington, DC: American Psychological Association.

Ibarra, H. (2002). *Working identity: Unconventional strategies for reinventing your career.* Cambridge, MA: Harvard Business School Press.

Icard, L. (1986). Black gay men and conflicting social identities: Sexual orientation versus racial identity. In J. Gripton & M. Valentich (Eds.), *Special issue of the Journal of Social Work & Human Sexuality, Social work practice in sexual problems,* 4(1/2), 83–93.

International Gay and Lesbian Human Rights Commission. (2010). Middle East and North America. From http://www.iglhr.org/cgi-bin/iowa/region/10.html

Isidore, C. (2011). The great recession's lost generation. *CNNMoney,* May 17. Available at http:II money.cnn.com

Issacson, L. E. (1985). *Basics of career counseling.* Boston: Allyn & Bacon.

Ivancevich, J. J., & Matteson, M. T. (1980). *Stress and work, a managerial perspective.* Dallas: Scott Foresman.

Ivey, A. E. (1986). *Development therapy.* San Francisco: Jossey-Bass.

Ivey, A. E., & Ivey, M. B. (1999). *Intentional interviewing & counseling* (4th ed.). Pacific Grove, CA: Brooks/Cole.

Ivey, A. E., & Ivey, M. B. (2003). *Intentional interviewing & counseling* (5th ed.). Pacific Grove, CA: Brooks/Cole–Thomson Learning.

Ivey, A. E., & Ivey, M. B. (2008). *Essentials of intentional interviewing: Counseling in a multicultural world.* Belmont, CA: Brooks Cole Cengage Learning.

Ivey, A.E., Ivey, M. B., & Zalaquett, C. P. (2014). *Intentional interviewing and counseling* (8th ed.). Belmont, CA: Brooks/Cole.

Jackson, E. L. (1988). Leisure constraints: A survey of past research. *Leisure Sciences, 10,* 203–215.

Jacobson, E. (1938). *Progressive relaxation.* Chicago: University of Chicago Press.

Jahoda, M. (1981). Work, employment and unemployment: Values, theories, and approaches in social research. *American Psychologist, 36,* 184–191.

Jamil, O., Harper, G., & Fernandez, M. (2009). Sexual and ethnic identity development among gay/bisexual/questioning (GBQ) male ethnic minority adolescents. *Cultur Divers Ethnic Minor Psychol.* (2009 July). 15(3): 203–214. Doi: 10.1037/a0014795

Jarrett, K. (2006). The relationship between gay-related stress and ethnicity for homosexual and bisexual males. (2006). *Honors Projects,* p. 5. http://digitalcommons.iwu.edu/psych-honproj/5

Jay, K., & Young, A. (Eds.). (1979). *The gay report: Lesbians and gay men speak out about their sexual experiences and lifestyles.* New York: Simon & Schuster.

Jernewall, N., & Zea, M. (2004). Invisibility of lesbian, gay, and bisexual people of color in psychological research. A content analysis of empirical articles over the last ten years. *Cultural Diversity and Ethnic Minority Psychology, 10,* 120–135.

Jiang, W., Babyak, M., Krantz, D. S., Waugh, R. A., Coleman, R. E., Hanson, M. M., Frid, D. J., McNulty, S., Morris, J. J., O'Connor, C. M., & Blumenthal, J. A. (1996). Mental stress-induced myocardial ischemia and cardiac events. *Journal of the American Medical Association, 275,* 1651–1656.

Johansson, C. B. (1975). *Self-description inventory.* Minneapolis: National Computer Systems.

Johnson, M. J., Swartz, J. L., & Martin, W. E., Jr. (1995). Applications of psychological theories for career development with Native Americans. In F. T. L. Leong (Ed.), *Career development and vocational behavior of racial and ethnic minorities* (pp. 103–129). Mahwah, NJ: Erlbaum.

Johnson, P. R., & Indvik, J. (1994). Workplace violence: An issue of the nineties. *Public Personnel Management, 23,* 515–523.

Johnston, R. (1995, June). *The effectiveness of instructional technology: A review of the research.* Proceedings of the Virtual Reality in Medicine and Developers' Exposition. Cambridge, MA: Virtual Reality Solutions, Inc.

Jurafsky, D., & Martin, J. (2008). *Speech and language processing: An introduction to natural language processing, computational linguistics, and speech recognition.* Upper Saddle River, NJ: Prentice-Hall.

Kail, R. V., & Cavanaugh, J. C. (1996). *Human development.* Pacific Grove, CA: Brooks/Cole.

Kail, R. V., & Cavanaugh, J. C. (2000). *Human development* (2nd ed.). Belmont, CA: Wadsworth.

Kail, R. V., & Cavanaugh, J. C. (2004). *Human development* (3rd ed.). Belmont, CA: Wadsworth.

Kail, R. V., & Cavanaugh, J. C. (2010) *Human development* (5th ed.). Belmont, CA: Wadsworth Cengage Learning.

Kail, R. V., & Cavanaugh, J. C. (2014). *Human development* (6th ed.). Belmont, CA: Wadsworth Cengage Learning.

Kandel, E. R. (1983). From, metapsychology to monocular biology: Explorations into the nature of anxiety. *American Journal of Psychiatry, 140,* 1277–1293.

Kando, T. M., & Summers, W. C. (1971). The impact of work on leisure: Toward a paradigm and research strategy. *Pacific Sociological Review, 14,* 310–327.

Kaneshige, E. (1979). Cultural factors in group counseling and interaction. In G. Henderson (Ed.), *Understanding and counseling ethnic minorities* (pp. 457–467). Springfield, IL: Charles C Thomas.

Kanfer, G. H. (1980). Self-management methods. In F. H. Kanfer & A. P. Goldstein (Eds.), *Helping people change* (pp. 309–355). New York: Pergamon.

Kanter, M. (1989). *When giants learn to dance.* New York: Simon & Schuster.

Kapes, J. T., Borman, C. A., Garcia, G., Jr., & Compton, J. W. (1985, April). *Evaluation of microcomputer-based career guidance systems with college students: SIGI and DISCOVER.* Paper presented at annual meeting of American Educational Research Association, Chicago.

Kapes, J. T., & Whitfeld, E. A. (Eds.) (2001). *A counselors guide for career assessment instruments* (4th ed.). Tulsa, OK: National Career Development Association.

Kaplan, R., & Saccuzzo, D. (2013). *Psychological of testing: Principles, application, and issues* (8th ed.). Belmont, CA: Brooks/Cole Cengage Learning.

Karasek, R., & Theorell, T. (1990). *Healthy work: Stress, productivity, and the reconstruction of working life.* New York: Basic Books.

Kasl, S. V. (1978). Epidemiological contributions to the study of work stress. In C. L. Cooper & R. Payne (Eds.), *Stress at work* (pp. 119–128). New York: Wiley.

Katz, M. R. (1975). *SIGI: A computer-based system of interactive guidance and information.* Princeton, NJ: Educational Testing Service.

Katz, M. R. (1993). *Computer-assisted career decision-making: The guide in the machine.* Hillsdale, NJ: Erlbaum.

Kavruck, S. (1956). Thirty three years of test research. A short history of test development in the U.S. Civil Service Commission. *American Psychologists, 11,* 329–333.

Keating, D. P. (1980). Thinking processes in adolescence. In J. Adelson (Ed.), *Handbook of adolescent psychology.* New York: Wiley.

Kelly, G. A. (1955). *The psychology of personal constructs.* New York: Norton.

Kelly, J. R. (1996). Activities. In J. E. Birden (Ed.), *Encyclopedia of gerontology: Age, aging, and the aged* (Vol. 1, pp. 37–49). San Diego, CA: Academic Press.

Kendall, P. C. (2011). *Child and adolescent therapy: Cognitive-behavioral procedures* (4th ed.). New York: Guilford.

Kendler, K.S., et al. (2011). The impact of environmental influences on symptoms of anxiety and depression across the life span. *Psychological Science, 22* (1), 1343–1352.

Kimmel, P. R. (1994). Cultural perspectives on international negotiations. *Journal of Social Issues, 50* (1), 179–196.

Kinnier, R. T., & Krumboltz, J. D. (1984). Procedures for successful career counseling. In N. C. Gysbers (Ed.), *Designing careers: Counseling to enhance education, work, and leisure* (pp. 307–335). San Francisco: Jossey-Bass.

Kinsey, A. C., Pomeroy, W. B., & Martin, C. E. (1948). *Sexual behavior in the human male.* Philadelphia: Saunders.

Kivlighan, D. J., Jr., Johnston, J. A., Hogan, R. S., & Mauer, E. (1994). Who benefits from computerized career counseling? *Journal of Counseling and Development, 72,* 289–292.

Klinger, G. (1988). *Dual-role model.* Unpublished manuscript, Southwest Texas State University, San Marcos.

Knowdell, R. L. (2009). What is career coaching and how did it get here? *Career Planning and Adult Development Journal, 25,* 204–210.

Kobylarz, L. (1996). *National career development guidelines: K-adult handbook.* Stillwater, OK: National Occupational Coordinating Committee Training and Support Center.

Kohlberg, L. (1973). Continuities in childhood and adult moral development revisited. In P. B. Baltes & K. W. Schase (Eds.), *Lifespan development psychology: Personality and socialization.* New York: Academic Press.

Kolb, B., Gibb, R., & Robinson, T. B. (2003). Brain plasticity and behavior. *Current Directions in Psychological Science, 12,* 1–5.

Kort, J. (2008). *Gay affirmative therapy for the straight clinician: The essential guide.* New York: W. W. Norton.

Kroll, R., & Bertchman, J. H. (2005). Stuttering. In B. J. Sadock & V. A. Sadock (Eds.), *Kaplan and Sadock's comprehensive textbook of psychiatry* (pp. 3154–3159). Philadelphia: Lippincott, Williams, & Wilkins.

Kronenberger, G. K. (1991, June). Out of the closet. *Personnel Journal,* 40–44.

Krumboltz, J. D. (1983). *Private rules in career decision making.* Columbus, OH: National Center for Research in Vocational Education.

Krumboltz, J. D. (1988). *Career beliefs inventory.* Palo Alto, CA: Consulting Psychologists Press.

Krumboltz, J. D. (1991). *Career beliefs inventory.* Palo Alto, CA: Consulting Psychologists Press.

Krumboltz, J. D. (1992). Thinking about careers. *Contemporary Psychology, 37,* 113.

Krumboltz, J. D. (1993). Integrating career and personal counseling. *Career Development Quarterly, 42,* 143–148.

Krumboltz, J. D. (1996). A learning theory of career counseling. In M. L. Savickas & W. B. Walsh (Eds.), *Handbook of career counseling theory and practice* (pp. 55–81). Palo Alto, CA: Davies-Black.

Krumboltz, J., & Coon, D. W. (1995). Current professional issues in vocational psychology. In M. L. Savickas & W. B. Walsh (Eds.), *Handbook of career theory and practice* (pp. 55–80). Palo Alto, CA: Davies-Black.

Krumboltz, J. D., & Hamel, D. A. (1977). *Guide to career decision-making skills.* New York: Educational Testing Service.

Krumboltz, J. D., Mitchell, A., & Gelatt, H. G. (1975). Applications of social learning theory of career selection. *Focus on Guidance, 8,* 1–16.

Krumboltz, J., & Nichols, C. (1990). Integrating the social learning theory of career decision making. In W. B. Walsh & S. H. Osipow (Eds.), *Career counseling: Contemporary topics in vocational psychology* (pp. 159–192). Hillsdale, NJ: Erlbaum.

Krumboltz, J. D., & Sorenson, D. L. (1974). *Career decision making.* Madison, WI: Counseling Films.

Kuder, G. F. (1963). A rationale for evaluating interests. *Educational and Psychological Measurement, 23,* 3–10.

Kuder, G. F. (1964). *Kuder general interest survey: Manual.* Chicago: Science Research Associates.

Kuder, G. F. (1966). *Kuder occupational interest survey: General manual.* Chicago: Science Research Associates.

Kulik, L. (2001). Impact of length of unemployment and age on jobless men and women: A comparative analysis. *Journal of Employment Counseling, 38,* 15–27.

Kumata, R., & Murata, A. (1980, March). *Employment of Asian/Pacific American women in Chicago.* Report of conference sponsored by the Women's Bureau, U.S. Department of Labor, Chicago.

Kurpius, D., Burello, L., & Rozecki, T. (1990). Strategic planning in human service organizations. *Counseling and Human Development, 22*(9), 1–12.

LaFromboise, T. D., & Jackson, M. (1996). MCT theory and Native-American populations. In D. W. Sue, A. E. Ivey, & P. B. Pedersen (Eds.), *A theory of multicultural counseling & therapy* (pp. 192–202). Pacific Grove, CA: Brooks/Cole.

LaFromboise, T. D., Trimble, J. E., & Mohatt, G. V. (1990). Counseling intervention and American Indian tradition: An integrative approach. *Counseling Psychologist, 18*(4), 628–654.

Landauer, T. K., (2007). LSA as a theory of meaning. In T. Landbauer, D. McNamara, D. Simon, & W. Kintsch (Eds.), *Handbook of latent semantic analysis* (pp. 3–34). Mahwah, NJ: Erlbaum.

Lapan, R. T., & Jingeleski, J. (1992). Circumscribing vocational aspirations in junior high school. *Journal of Counseling Psychology, 39,* 81–90.

Lauer, R. H., & Lauer, J. C. (1986). Factors in long-term marriages. *Journal of Family Issues, 7,* 382–390.

Lazarus, A. A. (1989). *The practice of multimodal therapy.* Baltimore: Johns Hopkins University Press.

Lazarus, R. S. (2000). Toward better research on stress and coping. *American Psychologist, 55,* 655–673.

Leana, C. R. (2002). The changing organizational context of careers. In D. C. Feldman (Ed.), *Work careers: A developmental perspective* (pp. 274–294). San Francisco: Jossey-Bass.

Leana, C. R., & Feldman, D. C. (1991). Gender differences in responses to unemployment. *Journal of Vocational Behavior, 38,* 65–77.

Leana, C. R., & Feldman, D. C. (1992). *Coping with job loss: How individuals, institutions and communities deal with layoffs.* San Francisco: New Lexington Press.

Leclair, S. W. (1982). The dignity of leisure. *School Counselor, 29*(4), 289–296.

Lent, R. W., Brown, S. D., & Hackett, G. (1996). Career development from a social cognitive perspective. In D. Brown, L. Brooks, & Associates (Eds.), *Career choice and development* (3rd ed., pp. 373–416). San Francisco: Jossey-Bass.

Lent, R. W., Brown, S. D., & Hackett, G. (2002). Social cognitive career theory. In D. Brown & Associates (Eds.), *Career choice and development* (4th ed., pp. 255–312). San Francisco: Jossey-Bass.

Lenz, J. G. (2000). *Paraprofessionals in career services; The Florida State University model* (Tech. Rep. No. 27). Tallahassee: Florida State University, Center for the Study of Technology in Counseling and Career Development.

Leong, F. T. L. (1993). The career counseling process with racial/ethnic minorities: The case of Asian Americans. *Career Development Quarterly, 42,* 26–40.

Leong, F. T. L. (1996a). Challenges to career counseling: Boundaries, cultures, and complexity. In M. L. Savickas & W. B. Walsh (Eds.), *Handbook of career counseling theory and practice* (pp. 333–347). Palo Alto, CA: Davies-Black.

Leong, F. T. L. (1996b). MCT theory and Asian-American populations. In D. W. Sue, A. E. Ivey, & P. B. Pedersen (Eds.), *A theory of multicultural counseling and therapy* (pp. 204–214). Pacific Grove, CA: Brooks/Cole.

Leong, F. T. L., & Serafica, F. C. (1995). Career development of Asian Americans: A research area in need of a good theory. In F. T. L. Leong (Ed.), *Career development and vocational behavior of racial and ethnic minorities* (pp. 78–99). Mahwah, NJ: Erlbaum.

Leung, P., & Cheung, M. (2001). Competencies in practice evaluations with Asian American individuals and families. In R. Fong & S. B. C. L. Furuto (Eds.), *Culturally competent practice: Skills, interventions, and evaluations* (pp. 426–437). Boston: Allyn & Bacon.

Leung, S. A., Conoley, C. W., & Scheel, M. J. (1994). The career and educational aspirations of gifted high school students: A retrospective study. *Journal of Counseling & Development, 72,* 298–303.

Levi, L. (1984). *Preventing work stress.* Reading, MA: Addison-Wesley.

Levine, H., & Evans, N. J. (1991). The development of gay, lesbian, and bisexual identities. In N. J. Evans & V. A. Walls (Eds.), *Beyond tolerance: Gays, lesbians, and bisexuals on campus* (pp. 1–24). Alexandria, VA: American College Personnel Association.

Levinson, D. J. (1980). The mentor relationship. In M. A. Morgan (Ed.), *Managing career development* (pp. 22–37). New York: Van Nostrand.

Levinson, D. J. (1996). *The seasons of a woman's life.* New York: Knopf.

Levinson, D. J., Darrow, C. N., Klein, E. B., Levinson, M. H., & McKee, B. (1978). *The seasons of a man's life.* New York: Knopf.

Liptak, J. J. (2001). *Treatment planning in career counseling*. Belmont, CA: Wadsworth/ Thomson Learning.

Livson, N., & Peskin, H. (1980). Perspectives on adolescence from longitudinal research. In J. Adelson (Ed.), *Handbook of adolescent psychology* (pp. 47–98). New York: Wiley.

Lofquist, L. H., & Dawis, R. V. (1984). Research on work adjustment and satisfaction: Implications for career counseling. In S. Brown & R. Lent (Eds.), *Handbook of counseling psychology* (pp. 216–237). New York: Wiley.

Lofquist, L. H., & Dawis, R. V. (1991). *Essentials of person-environment-correspondence counseling*. Minneapolis: University of Minnesota Press.

Lohr, S. (2011). Carrots, sticks, and digital health records. *New York Times*, Feb 26. Available at http://www.nytimes

Lohr, S. (2006) Outsourcing is climbing skills ladder. *New York Times*, Feb 16. Available at http // www.nytimes.com

Loiacano, D. K. (1989). Gay identity issues among black Americans: Racism, homophobia, and the need for validation. *Journal of Counseling & Development, 68*, 21–25.

Loiacano, D. K. (1993). Gay identity issues among black Americans: Racism, homophobia, and the need for validation. In L. D. Garnets & D. C. Kimmel (Eds.), *Psychological perspectives on lesbian and gay male experiences* (pp. 364–376). New York: Columbia University Press.

London, M. (2002). Organizational assistance in career development. In D. C. Feldman (Ed.), *Work careers: A developmental perspective* (pp. 323–346). San Francisco: Jossey-Bass.

Lorde, A. (1984). *Sister outsider*. Trumansburg, NY: Crossing.

Lott, B. E. (1994). *Women's lives: Themes and variations in gender* (2nd ed.). Pacific Grove, CA: Brooks/Cole.

Lowman, R. L. (1993). *Counseling and psychotherapy of work dysfunctions*. Washington, DC: American Psychological Association.

Lucas, M. S. (1996). Building cohesiveness between practitioners and researchers: A practitioner-scientist model. In M. L. Savickas & W. B. Walsh (Eds.), *Handbook of career counseling theory and practice* (pp. 81–89). Palo Alto, CA: Davies-Black.

Lum, D. (Ed.) (2007). *Culturally competent practice* (3rd ed.). Belmont, CA: Brooks Cole Cengage Learning.

Mackelprang, R., & Salsgiver, R. (1999). *Disability: A diversity model approach in human service practice*. Pacific Grove, CA: Brooks/Cole.

Magnuson, J. (1990). Stress management. *Journal of Property Management, 55*, 24–28.

Mankiller, W., & Wallis, M. (1993). *Mankiller*. New York: St. Martin's.

Manson, N. M. (Ed.). (1982). *Topics in American Indian mental health prevention*. Portland: Oregon Health Sciences University Press.

Mantler, J., Matejicek, A., Matheson, K., & Anisman, H. (2005). Coping with unemployment uncertainty: A comparison of employed and unemployed workers. *Journal of Health Psychology, 10*, 200–209.

Mariani, M. (1995–96, Winter). Computers and career guidance: Ride the rising ride. *Occupational Outlook Quarterly, 39*, 16–27.

Mariani, M. (1998, Summer). Job shadowing for college students. *Occupational Outlook Quarterly, 40*, 46–49.

Marks, M. (2003). *Charging up the hill. Workplace recovery after mergers, acquisitions, and downsizing*. San Francisco: Jossey Bass.

Marshal, M. P., Friedman, M. S., Stall, R., King, K. M., Miles. J., & Gold M. A. (2008). Sexual orientation and adolescents substance use: A meta analysis and methodological review. *British Journal of Addiction, 103*, 546–556.

Martell, R. F., Parker, C., Emrich, C. G., & Crawford, M. S. (1998). Sex stereotyping in the executive suite: "Much ado about something." *Journal of Social Behavior and Personality, 13,* 127–138.

Martin, C. L., & Ruble, D. N. (1997). A developmental perspective of self-construals and sex differences: Comment on Cross and Madson. *Psychological Bulletin, 122*(1), 45–50.

Martin, J. (1996). *Cybercorp: The new business revolution.* New York: AMACOM.

Martin, W. E., Jr. (1995). Career development assessment and intervention strategies with American Indians. In F. T. L. Leong (Ed.), *Career development and vocational behavior of racial and ethnic minorities* (pp. 227–246). Mahwah, NJ: Erlbaum.

Matlin, M. W. (2000). *The psychology of women* (4th ed.). Belmont, CA: Wadsworth/Thomson Learning.

Matlin, M. W. (2004). *The psychology of women* (5th ed.). Belmont, CA: Wadsworth/Thomson Learning.

Matsumoto, D. (1996). *Culture and psychology.* Pacific Grove, CA: Brooks/Cole.

Matsumoto, D. (2000). *Culture and psychology* (2nd ed.). Belmont, CA: Wadsworth.

Matsumoto, D., & Juang, L. (2004). *Culture and psychology* (3rd ed.). Belmont, CA: Wadsworth/Thomson Learning.

Matsumoto, D., & Juang, L. (2013). Culture and psychology (5th ed.). Belmont, CA: Wadsworth Cengage Learning.

Maze, M., & Cummings, R. (1982). Analysis of DISCOVER. In M. Maze & R. Cummings (Eds.), *How to select a computer-assisted guidance system* (pp. 97–107). Madison: University of Wisconsin, Wisconsin Vocational Studies Center.

McBride, A. B. (1990). Mental health effects of women's multiple roles. *American Psychologist, 45,* 381–384.

McCarn, S. R., & Fassinger, R. E. (1996). Revisioning sexual minority identity formation: A new model of lesbian identity and its implications for counseling and research. *Counseling Psychologist, 24*(3), 508–534.

McCormac, M. E. (1988). Information sources and resources. *Journal of Career Development, 16,* 129–138.

McCrae, R. R., & Costa, P. T. Jr. (1997). Personality trait structure as a human universal. *American Psychologist, 53,* 509–516.

McDaniels, C. (1990). *The changing workplace: Career counseling strategies for the 1990s and beyond.* San Francisco: Jossey-Bass.

McKee-Ryan, F., Song, Z.,Wanberg, C.R., & Knicki, A. J. (2005). Psychological and Physical during unemployment: A meta analytic study. *Journal of Applied* Psychology, *90,* 53–76.

McKinlay, B. (1990). *Developing a career information system.* Eugene, OR: Career Information System.

McLennan, N. A., & Arthur, N. (1999). Applying the cognitive information processing approach to career problem solving and decision making to women's career development. *Journal of Employment Counseling, 36,* 82–96.

McRoy, R. (2003). Cultural competence with African Americans. In D. Lum (Ed.), *Culturally competent practice* (2nd ed., pp. 217–238). Pacific Grove, CA: Brooks/Cole-Thomson Learning.

McWhirter, J. J., McWhirter, B. T., McWhirter, E. H., & McWhirter, R. J. (2004). *At-risk youth* (3rd ed.). Belmont, CA: Brooks/Cole Thomson Learning.

McWhirter, J., McWhirter, B, McWhirter, E., & McWhirter, R. (2013). *At risk youth* (5th ed.). Belmont, CA: Brooks/Cole Cengage Learning.

Meara, N. M. (1996). Prudence and career assessment: Making our implicit assumptions explicit. In M. L. Savickas & W. B. Walsh (Eds.), *Handbook of career counseling theory and practice* (pp. 315–331). Palo Alto, CA: Davies-Black.

Meichenbaum, D. (1977). *Cognitive behavior modification: An integrative approach.* New York: Plenum.

Meir, E. I., Esformes, Y., & Friedland, N. (1994). Congruence and differentiation as predictors of workers' occupational stability and job performance. *Journal of Career Assessment, 2,* 40–54.

Meister, J. C. (1994). *Corporate quality universities: Lessons in building a world-class workforce.* New York: Irwin.

Mendle, J., Turkheimer, E., & Emery R. E. (2007). Detrimental psychological outcomes associated with early pubertal training in adolescent girls. *Developmental Review, 27,* 13–19.

Michael, R. T., Gagnon, J. H., Lauman, E. O., & Kolata, G. (1994). *Sex in America: A definitive survey.* Boston: Little, Brown.

Miller, G. A. (1997). *The Substance Abuse Subtle Screening Inventory 3*(SASSI-3). Springfield, IN: SASSI Institute.

Miller, G. A. (2001). The adolescent substance abuse subtle screening inventory-A2 (SASSI-A2). Springville, IN: SASSI Institute.

Miller, J. M., & Springer, T. P. (1986). Perceived satisfaction of a computerized vocational counseling system as a function of monetary investment. *Journal of College Student Personnel, 27,* 142–146.

Miller, K. L., & McDaniels, R. M. (2001). Cyberspace, the new frontier. *Journal of Career Development, 27*(3), 199–206.

Miller, N. B. (1982). Social work services to urban Indians. In J. W. Green (Ed.), *Cultural awareness in the human services.* Englewood Cliffs, NJ: Prentice-Hall.

Miller-Tiedeman, A. (1988). *Lifecareer: The quantum leap into a process theory of career.* Vista, CA: LIFECAREER Foundation.

Miller-Tiedeman, A. L., & Tiedeman, D. V. (1990). Career decision making: An individualistic perspective. In D. Brown, L. Brooks, & Associates (Eds.), *Career choice and development: Applying contemporary theories to practice* (2nd ed., pp. 308–337). San Francisco: Jossey-Bass.

Mitchell, K. E., Levin, A. S., & Krumboltz, J. D. (1999). Planned happenstance: Constructing unexpected career opportunities. *Journal of Counseling and Development, 77,* 115–124.

Mitchell, L. K., & Krumboltz, J. D. (1987). Cognitive restructuring and decision-making training on career indecision. *Journal of Counseling and Development, 66,* 171–174.

Mitchell, L. K., & Krumboltz, J. D. (1990). Social learning approach to career decision making: Krumboltz's theory. In D. Brown & L. Brooks (Eds.), *Career choice and development: Applying contemporary theories to practice* (2nd ed., pp. 145–196). San Francisco: Jossey-Bass.

Mitchell, L. K., & Krumboltz, J. D. (1996). Krumboltz's learning theory of career choice and counseling. In D. Brown, L. Brooks, & Associates (Eds.), *Career choice and development* (3rd ed., pp. 233–276). San Francisco: Jossey-Bass.

Mondimore, F. M. (1996). *Homosexuality.* Baltimore: Johns Hopkins University Press.

Mooney, L., Knox, D., & Schacht, C. (2013). *Understand social problems* (8th ed.). Belmont, CA; Wadsworth Cengage Learning.

Moos, R. H., & Tsu, V. (1976). Human competence and coping: An overview. In R. H. Moose (Ed.), *Human adaptation: Coping with life crisis* (pp. 3–16). Lexington, MA: Heath.

Morales, E. S. (1992). Counseling Latino gays and Latina lesbians. In S. H. Dworkin & F. J. Gutierrea (Eds.), *Counseling gay men and lesbians: Journey to the end of the rainbow* (pp. 125–141). Alexandria, VA: American Counseling Association.

Morgan, R. B., & Hawkridge, D. G. (1999). Guest editorial—Global distance learning. *Performance Improvement Quarterly, 12*(2), 6–8.

Morrison, W. W. (2002). The school-to-work transition. In D. C. Feldman (Ed.), *Work careers: A developmental response* (pp. 126–159). San Francisco: Jossey-Bass.

Mounts, N. S., & Steinberg, L. (1995). An ecological analysis of peer influence on adolescent grade point average and drug use. *Developmental Psychology, 31,* 915–922.

Muchinsky, P. M. (2003). *Psychology applied to work* (6th ed.). Belmont, CA: Wadsworth/ Thomson Learning.

Multon, K. D., Brown, S. D., & Lent, R. W. (1991). Relation of self-efficacy beliefs to academic outcomes: A meta-analytic investigation. *Journal of Counseling Psychology, 38,* 30–38.

Munk, N. (2000, March 5). The price of freedom. *New York Times Magazine,* pp. 50–54.

Munsterberg, H. (1913). *Psychology and industrial efficiency.* Boston: Houghton Mifflin.

Murphy, B. C., & Dillon. C. (2003). *Interviewing in action relationship, process, and change* (2nd ed.). Pacific Grove, CA: Brooks/Cole.

Myers, L. J., Speight, S. L., Highlen, P. S., Cox, C. I., Reynolds, A. L., Adams, E. M., & Hanley, C. P. (1991). Identity development and worldviews toward an optimal conceptualization. *Journal of Counseling and Development, 70,* 55–63.

National Board for Certified Counselors Inc. and Center for Credentialing and Education, Inc. (2001). *Standards of the ethical practice of Internet counseling.* Greensboro, NC: Author.

National Career Development Association. (1997). *Guidelines for the use of the Internet for provision of career information and planning services.* Alexandria, VA: Author.

National Career Development Association. (2003). National Career Development Association ethical standards. (On-line). Available: http://ncda.org/about/poles.html

National Commission on Children. (1993). *Just the facts: A summary of recent information on America's children and their families.* Washington, DC: Author.

National Consortium of State Career Guidance Supervisors. (1996). *Planning for life: 1995 compendium of recognized career planning programs.* Columbus: Center on Education and Training for Employment, Ohio State University.

Neal, B. E. (2000). Native American women. In M. Julia (Ed.), *Constructing gender: Multicultural perspectives in working women* (pp. 157–174). Pacific Grove, CA: Brooks/Cole.

Neff, W. S. (1985). *Work and human behavior* (2nd ed.). Chicago: Aldine.

Neimark, E. D. (1982). Adolescent thought: Transition to formal operations. In B. B. Wolman (Ed.), *Handbook of developmental psychology* (pp. 486–489). Englewood Cliffs, NJ: Prentice-Hall.

Neimeyer, G. J. (1989). Applications for repertory grid techniques to vocational assessment. *Journal of Counseling and Development, 67,* 585–589.

Neukrug, E. (1999). *The world of the counselor.* Pacific Grove, CA: Brooks/Cole.

Nevill, D. D., & Super, D. E. (1986). *The Salience Inventory manual: Theory, application, and research.* Palo Alto, CA: Consulting Psychologists Press.

Nevill, D. D., & Super, D. E. (1989). *The Values Scale.* Palo Alto, CA: Consulting Psychologists Press.

Nevo, O. (1987). Irrational expectations in career counseling and their confronting arguments. *Career Development Quarterly, 35,* 239–250.

Newman, B. M., & Newman, P. R. (1995). *Development through life: A psychosocial approach.* Pacific Grove, CA: Brooks/Cole.

Newman, B. M., & Newman, P. R. (2003). *Development through life: A psychological approach* (8th ed.). Belmont, CA: Wadsworth.

Newman B. S., & Newman, P. R. (2009) *Development through life: A psychological approach* (9th ed.). Belmont, CA: Wadsworth Cengage Learning.

Newman, B. S., & Muzzonigro, P. G. (1993). The effects of traditional family values on the coming out process of gay male adolescents. *Adolescence, 28,* 213–226.

NICHD Early Child Care Research Network. (2000). The relation of child care to cognitive and language development. *Child Development, 71,* 960–980.

Niles, S.G., & Harris-Bowlsbey, J. (2009). *Career development interventions in the 21st century.* Upper Saddle River, NJ: Pearson Education, Inc.

Niles, S. G., & Hartung, P. J. (2000). Emerging career theories. In D. A. Luzzo (Ed.), *Career counseling of college students* (pp. 23–43). Washington, DC: American Psychological Association.

Noble, M. (1992). *Down is up for Aaron Eagle: A mother's spiritual journey with Down syndrome.* San Francisco: Harper.

Ogbu, J. (1990). Cultural model, identity and literacy. In J. Stigler, R. Shweder, & G. Herdt (Eds.), *Cultural psychology* (pp. 520–541). New York: Cambridge University Press.

Ojanen, T., & Perry, D. G. (2007). Relational schemas and developing self: Perceptions of mother and self as joint predictors of early adolescents' self-esteem. *Developmental Psychology, 43,* 1474–1483.

Okun, B. (2002). *Effective helping* (6th ed.). Pacific Grove, CA: Brooks/Cole.

Okun, B. F., Fried, J., & Okun, M. L. (1999). *Understanding diversity: A learning practice primer.* Pacific Grove, CA: Brooks/Cole.

O'Neil, J. M. (1982). Gender role conflict and strain in men's lives: Implications for psychiatrists, psychologists, and other human-services providers. In K. Solomon & N. B. Levy (Eds.), *Men in transition* (pp. 5–44). New York: Plenum.

O'Neil, J. M. (1990). Assessing men's gender role conflict. In D. Moore & F. Leafgren (Eds.), *Men in conflict* (pp. 23–38). Alexandria, VA: American Association of Counseling and Development.

O'Neil, J. M., Good, G. E., & Holmes, S. (1995). Fifteen years of theory and research on men's gender role conflict: New paradigms for empirical research. In R. Levant & W. Pollack (Eds.), *The new psychology of men* (pp. 164–206). New York: Basic Books.

Ortiz, V. (1996). Migration and marriage among Puerto Rican women. *International Migration Review, 30*(2), 460–484.

Osborn, D., & Zunker, V. (2012). *Using assessment results for career development.* Belmont, CA: Brooks/Cole Cengage Learning.

Osipow, S. H. (1979). Occupational mental health: Another role for counseling psychologists. *Counseling Psychologist, 8*(1), 65–70.

Osipow, S. H. (1983). *Theories of career development* (3rd ed.). New York: Appleton-Century-Crofts.

Osipow, S. H., & Fitzgerald, L. (1996). *Theories of career development* (4th ed.). Needham Heights, MA: Allyn & Bacon.

Ostroff, C., Shin, Y., & Feinberg, B. (2002). Skill acquisition and person-environment fit. In D. C. Feldman (Ed.), *Work career: A developmental perspective* (pp. 63–93). San Francisco: Jossey-Bass.

Paisley, P. O., & Hubbard, G. T. (1994). *Developmental school counseling programs: From theory to practice.* Alexandria, VA: American Counseling Association.

Palkovitz, R. (1984). Parental attitudes and fathers' interactions with their 5-month-old infants. *Developmental Psychology, 20,* 1054–1060.

Paniagua, F. A. (2005). *Assessing and treating culturally diverse clients: A practical guide* (3rd ed.). Thousand Oaks, CA: Sage Publications.

Parcel, T. L., & Menaghan, E. G. (1994). Early parental work, family, social capital, and early childhood outcomes. *American Journal of Sociology, 9,* 972–1009.

Parham, T. (1996). MCT theory and African-American populations. In D. W. Sue, A. E. Ivey, & P. B. Pedersen (Eds.), *A theory of multicultural counseling & therapy* (pp. 177–190). Pacific Grove, CA: Brooks/Cole.

Parker, R. M., & Hansen, C. E. (1981). *Rehabilitation counseling.* Boston: Allyn & Bacon.

Parsons, F. (1909). *Choosing a vocation.* Boston: Houghton Mifflin.

Pascarella, E. T., & Terenzini, P. T. (1991). *How college affects students: Findings and insights from twenty years of research.* San Francisco: Jossey-Bass.

Patton, W., & McMahon, M. (1999). *Career development and systems theory.* Pacific Grove, CA: Brooks/Cole.

Pedersen, P. B., Lonner, W. J., Draguns, J. G., & Trimble, J. E. (2008). *Counseling across cultures* (6th ed.). Thousand Oaks, CA: Sage Publications.

Peplau, L. A., Cochran, S. D., & Mays, V. M. (1997). A national survey of intimate relationships of African American lesbians and gay men: A look at commitment, satisfaction, sexual behavior, and HIV disease. In B. Greene (Ed.), *Ethnic and cultural diversity among lesbians and gay men* (pp. 11–39). Thousand Oaks, CA: Sage.

Pernanen, K. (1991). *Alcohol in human violence.* London: Guilford.

Perez, R. M., DeBord, K. A., & Bieschke, K. (Eds.). (2006). *Handbook of counseling and psychotherapy with lesbian, gay, and bisexual clients* (2nd ed.). Washington, DC: American Psychological Association.

Peterson, G. W., Ryan-Jones, R. E., Sampson, J. P., Jr., Reardon, R. C., & Shahnasarian, M. (1987). *A comparison of the effectiveness of three computer-assisted career guidance systems on college students' career decision-making processes* (Technical Report No. 6). Tallahassee: Florida State University, Center for the Study of Technology in Counseling and Career Development.

Peterson, G. W., Sampson, J. P., & Reardon, R. C. (1991). *Career development and services: A cognitive approach.* Pacific Grove, CA: Brooks/Cole.

Peterson, G. W., Sampson, J. P., Jr., Reardon, R. C., & Lenz, J. G. (1996). A cognitive information processing approach to career problem solving and decision making. In D. Brown, L. Brooks, & Associates (Eds.), *Career choice and development* (3rd ed., pp. 423–467). San Francisco: Jossey-Bass.

Peterson, N., & Gonzalez, R. C. (2000). *The role of work in people's lives: Applied career counseling and vocational psychology.* Pacific Grove, CA: Brooks/Cole-Wadsworth.

Philips, S. D., & Imhoff, A. R. (1997). Women and career development: A decade of research. *Annual Review of Psychology, 48,* 31–59.

Piaget, J. (1929). *The child's conception of the world.* New York: Harcourt Brace.

Piaget, J., & Inhelder, B. (1969). *The psychology of the child.* New York: Basic.

Picchioni, A. P., & Bonk, E. C. (1983). *A comprehensive history of guidance in the United States.* Austin: Texas Personnel and Guidance Association.

Pietrofesa, J. J., & Splete, H. (1975). *Career development: Theory and research.* New York: Grune & Stratton.

Polkinghorne, D. E. (1990). Action theory approaches to career research. In R. A. Young & W. A. Borgen (Eds.), *Methodological approaches to the study of career* (pp. 87–105). New York: Praeger.

Ponterotto, J. G. (1987). Counseling Mexican Americans: A multimodal approach. *Journal of Counseling and Development, 65,* 308–311.

Ponterotto, J. G., Casas, J. M., Suzuiki, L. A., & Alexander, C. M. (2010). *Handbook of Multicultural Counseling* (3rd ed.). Thousand Oaks, CA; Sage Publications.

Ponterotto, J. G., Utsey, S.O., & Pedersen, P. B. (2006). *Preventing prejudice: A guide for counselors, educators, and parents* (2nd ed.). Thousand Oaks, CA: Sage Publications.

Pope, M. (2000). A brief history of career counseling in the United States. *Career Development Quarterly, 48,* 194–211.

Pope, M. S., Prince, J. P., & Mitchell, K. (2000). Responsible career counseling with lesbian and gay students. In D. A. Luzzo (Ed.), *Career counseling of college students* (pp. 267–285). Washington, DC: American Psychology Association.

Pope, R. L., & Reynolds, A. L. (1991). Including bisexuality: It's more than just a label. In N. J. Evans & V. A. Wall (Eds.), *Beyond tolerance: Gays, lesbians, and bisexuals on campus* (pp. 205–212). Alexandria, VA: American College Personnel Association.

Powell, D. H. (1957). Careers and family atmosphere: An empirical test of Roe's theory. *Journal of Counseling Psychology, 4,* 212–217.

Prediger, D. J. (1994). Multicultural assessment standards: A compilation for counselors. *Measurement and Evaluation in Counseling and Development, 27,* 68–73.

Prediger, D. J. (1995). *Assessment in career counseling.* Greensboro: ERIC Counseling and Student Services Clearinghouse, University of North Carolina.

Prochaska, J. O., & Norcross, J. C. (2014). *Systems of psychotherapy: A transitional analysis* (8th ed.). Stamford, CT: Cengage Learning.

Rabinowitz, F. E., & Cochran, S. V. (1994). *Man alive: A primer of men's issues.* Pacific Grove, CA: Brooks/Cole.

Ragheb, M. B., & Griffith, C. A. (1982). The contribution of leisure participation and leisure satisfaction to life satisfaction of older persons. *Journal of Leisure Research, 14,* 295–306.

Ragins, B. R., & Scandura, T. A. (1995). Antecedents and work-related correlates of reported sexual harassment: An empirical investigation of competing hypotheses. *Sex Roles, 32,* 429–455.

Rapoport, R., & Rapoport, R. (1978). The dual career family. In L. S. Hansen & R. S. Rapoza (Eds.), *Career development and the counseling of women.* Springfield, IL: Charles C Thomas.

Rathus, Spencer A. (2014). *Childhood: Voyages in development* (5th ed.). Belmont, CA: Wadsworth.

Rayman, J. (1996). Apples and oranges in the career center: Reaction to R. Reardon. *Journal of Counseling & Development, 74,* 286–287.

Reardon, R. C., & Lenz, J. G. (1998). *The self-directed search and related Holland materials: A practitioner's guide.* Odessa, FL: Psychological Assessment Resources.

Reardon, R. C., Lenz, J. G., Sampson, J. P., & Peterson, G. W. (2000). *Career development and planning: A comprehensive approach.* Pacific Grove, CA: Brooks/Cole.

Reardon, R. C., Petersen, G. W., Sampson, J. P., Ryan-Jones, R. E., & Shahnasarian, M. (1992). A comparative analysis of the impact of SIGI and SIGI PLUS. *Journal of Career Development, 18,* 315–322.

Reardon, R. C., Zunker, V. G., & Dyal, M. A. (1979). The status of career planning programs and career centers in colleges and universities. *Vocational Guidance Quarterly, 28,* 154–159.

Reich, R. B. (1991). *The work of nations.* New York: Knopf.

Remafedi, G. (1999). Sexual orientation and suicide. *Journal of American Medical Association, 282*(13), 1291–1292.

Reskin, B. F. (1993). Sex segregation in the workplace. *Annual Review of Sociology, 19,* 241–270.

Reskin, B. F., & Pakavic, I. (1994). *Women and men at work.* London: Pine Forge.

Reynolds, A. L., & Hanjorgiris, W. F. (2000). Coming out: Lesbian, gay and bisexual identity development. In R. M. Perez, K. A. DeBord, & K. J. Bieschke (Eds.), *Handbook of counseling and therapy with lesbians, gays, and bisexuals.* Washington, DC: American Psychology Association Press.

Reynolds, A. L., & Pope, R. (1991). The complexity of diversity: Exploring multiple oppressions. *Journal of Counseling and Development, 70,* 174–180.

Rice, P. L. (1999). *Stress and health* (3rd ed.). Pacific Grove, CA: Brooks/Cole.

Richards, M. H., & Larson, R. (1993). Pubertal development and the daily subjective states of young adolescents. *Journal of Research on Adolescence, 3,* 145–169.

Richardson, B. (1991). Utilizing the resources of the African American church: Strategies for counseling professionals. In C. Lee & B. Richardson (Eds.), *Multicultural issues in counseling: New approaches to diversity* (pp. 65–75). Alexandria, VA: American Association for Counseling and Development.

Richardson, M. S. (1993). Work in people's lives. *Journal of Counseling and Development, 40,* 425–433.

Richardson, M. S. (1996). From career counseling to counseling/psychotherapy and work, jobs, and career. In M. L. Savickas & W. B. Walsh (Eds.), *Handbook of career counseling theory and practice* (pp. 347–360). Palo Alto, CA: Davies-Black.

Rickel, J., & Johnston, W. L. (1999). Animated agents for procedural training in virtual reality: Perception, cognition, and motor control. *Applied Artificial Intelligence, 12,* 343–382.

Rider, E. A. (2000). *Our voices: Psychology of women.* Pacific Grove, CA: Wadsworth.

Ridley, C. R.(2005). *Overcoming unintentional racism in counseling and therapy* (2nd ed.). Thousand Oaks, CA: Sage Publications.

Rifkin, J. (1995). *The end of work: The decline of the global labor force and the dawn of the post-market era.* New York: Putnam.

Rimer, S. (1996). The fraying of community. In *New York Times, The downsizing of America* (pp. 111–138). New York: Time Books.

Rodriguez, M., & Blocher, D. (1988). A comparison of two approaches to enhancing career maturity in Puerto Rican college women. *Journal of Counseling Psychology, 35,* 275–280.

Roe, A. (1956). *The psychology of occupations.* New York: Wiley.

Roe, A. (1972). Perspectives on vocational development. In J. M. Whiteley & A. Resnikoff (Eds.), *Perspectives on vocational development* (pp. 61–82). Washington, DC: American Personnel and Guidance Association.

Roe, A., & Lunneborg, P. W. (1990). Personality development and career choice. In D. Brown & L. Brooks (Eds.), *Career choice and development: Applying contemporary theories to practice* (pp. 68–101). San Francisco: Jossey-Bass.

Roessler, R., & Rubin, E. (1982). *Case management and rehabilitation counseling: Procedures and techniques.* Baltimore: University Park Press.

Rogers, C. R. (1942). *Counseling and psychotherapy.* Boston: Houghton Mifflin.

Rogler, L. H. (1994). International migrations: A framework for directing research. *American Psychologist, 49,* 701–708.

Roos, P. A., & Jones, K. W. (1993). Women's inroads into academic sociology. *Work and Occupations, 20,* 395–428.

Rosario, M., Schrimshaw, E., & Hunter, J. (2004). Ethnic/racial differences in the coming-out process of lesbian, gay, and bisexual youths: A comparison of sexual identity development over time. *Cultural Diversity and Ethnic Minority Psychology, 10,* 215–228.

Roselle, B., & Hummel, T. (1988). Intellectual development and interaction effectiveness with DISCOVER. *Career Development Journal, 35–36,* 241–251.

Rosen, D., Holmberg, K., & Holland, J. L. (1994a). *Dictionary of educational opportunities.* Odessa, FL: Psychology Assessment Resources.

Rosen, D., Holmberg, K., & Holland, J. L. (1994b). *Educational opportunities finder.* Odessa, FL: Psychological Assessment Resources.

Rosen, J. (2000). *The unwanted gaze: The destruction of privacy in America.* New York: Random House.

Rosky, C., Christy, M., Smith, J., & Badgett, M. (2011, January). Employment discrimination against LBGT Uthans: Executive summary. Williams Institute. Available at http://www3. law.ucla.edu

Rotter, J. B. (1966). Generalized expectancies for internal versus external control of reinforcement. *Psychological Monographs, 80* (Whole No. 609).

Rounds, J. B. (1990). The comparative and combined utility of work value and interest data in career counseling with adults. *Journal of Vocational Behavior, 37,* 32–45.

Rounds, J. B., Henly, G. A., Dawis, R. V., Lofquist, L. H., & Weiss, D. J. (1981). *Manual for the Minnesota Importance Questionnaire.* Minneapolis: University of Minnesota, Psychology Department Work Adjustment Project.

Rounds, J. B., & Tinsley, H. E. A. (1984). Diagnosis and treatment of vocational problems. In S. D. Brown & R. W. Lent (Eds.), *Handbook of counseling psychology* (pp. 137–177). New York: Wiley.

Rounds, J. B., & Tracey, T. J. (1990). From trait-and-factor to person-environment-fit counseling: Theory and process. In W. B. Walsh & S. J. Osipow (Eds.), *Career counseling: Contemporary topics in vocational psychology* (pp. 1–44). Hillsdale, NJ: Erlbaum.

Rounds, J. B., & Tracey, T. J. (1993). Prediger's dimensional representation of Holland's RIASEC circumplex. *Journal of Applied Psychology, 78,* 875–890.

Rounds, J. B., & Tracey, T. J. (1996). Cross-cultural structural equivalence of RISEC models and measures. *Journal of Counseling Psychology, 43,* 310–329.

Rousseau, D. (1995). *Psychological contracts in organizations: Understanding written and unwritten agreements.* Thousand Oaks, CA: Sage.

Rowland, D. T. (1991). Family diversity and the life cycle. *Journal of Comparative Family Studies, 22,* 1–14.

Ruan, E., & Lau, M. (2004). China. In R. T. Francoeur & R. Noonan (Eds.), *The continuum international encyclopedia of sexuality* (pp. 182–209). New York/London: Continuum International.

Russo, N. F., Kelly, R. M., & Deacon, M. (1991). Gender and success-related attributions: Beyond individualistic conceptions of achievement. *Sex Roles, 25,* 331–350.

Rust, P. C. (1996). Managing multiple identities: Diversity among bisexual women and men. In B. A. Firestein (Ed.), *Bisexuality* (pp. 53–84). Thousand Oaks, CA: Sage.

Rutter, M. (2010). Gene environment interplay. *Depression and Anxiety, 27*(1), 1–4.

Ryan, C., & Futterman, D. (1998). *Lesbian and gay youth: Care and counseling.* New York: Columbia University Press.

Ryan, E. S. (2000). Comparing 21st century job-skill acquisition with self-fulfillment for college students. *Education, 119,* 529–536.

Ryan, J. M., Tracey, T. J., & Rounds, J. (1996). Generalizability of Holland's structure of vocational interests across ethnicity, gender, and socioeconomic status. *Journal of Counseling Psychology, 43,* 330–337.

Ryan, L., & Ryan, R. (1982). *Mental health and the urban Indian.* Unpublished manuscript.

Rychlak, J. F. (1993). A suggested principle of complementarity for psychology. *American Psychologist, 48,* 933–942.

Ryckman, R. (2013). *Theories of personality* (10th ed.). Belmont, CA: Wadsworth Cengage Learning.

Rynes, S. L., & Gerhart, B. (2000). *Compensation in organizations.* San Francisco: Jossey-Bass.

Sadker, M., & Sadker, D. (1994). *Failing at fairness: How America's schools cheat girls.* New York: Scribners.

Sadri, G., & Robertson, L. T. (1993). Self-efficacy and work-related behavior: A review and meta-analysis. *Applied Psychology: An Internal Review, 42,* 139–152.

Saghir, M. T., & Robins, E. (1973). *Male and female homosexuality: A comprehensive investigation.* Baltimore: Williams and Wilkins.

Salomone, P. R. (1996, Spring). Tracing Super's theory of vocational development: A 40-year retrospective. *Journal of Career Development, 22*(3), 167–184.

Salsgiver, R. O. (1995, March 4). *Persons with disabilities and empowerment: Building a future of independent living.* Unpublished invitational speech to the Council on Social Work Education Annual Program Meeting, San Diego, CA.

Sampson, J. P. (1983). Computer-assisted testing and assessment: Current status and implications for the future. *Measurement and Evaluation in Guidance, 15*(3), 293–299.

Sampson, J. P. (1994). *Effective computer-assisted career guidance: Occasional paper number 2.* Center for the Study of Technology in Counseling and Career Development, Florida State University.

Sampson, J. P., & Lumsden, J. A. (2000). Ethical issues in the design and use of Internet-based career assessment. *Journal of Career Assessment, 8,* 21–35.

Sampson, J. P., Peterson, G. W., Lenz, J. G., & Reardon, R. C. (1992). A cognitive approach to career services: Translating concepts into practice. *Career Development Quarterly, 41,* 67–73.

Sampson, J. P., Jr., Peterson, G. W., Lenz, J. G., Reardon, R. C., & Saunders, D. E. (1996a). *Career thoughts inventory: Professional manual.* Odessa, FL: Psychological Assessment Resources.

Sampson, J. P., Jr., Peterson, G. W., Lenz, J. G., Reardon, R. C., & Saunders, D. E. (1996b). *Improving your career thoughts: A workbook for the Career Thoughts Inventory.* Odessa, FL: Psychological Assessment Resources.

Sampson, J. P., & Pyle, K. R. (1983). Ethical issues involved with the use of computer-assisted counseling, testing and guidance systems. *Personnel & Guidance Journal, 61*(3), 283–287.

Sampson, J. P., Reardon, R. C., Peterson, G. W., & Lenz, J. G. (2004). *Career counseling & services: A cognitive information processing approach.* Belmont, CA: Brooks/Cole-Thomson Learning.

Sandoval, J. (1998a). Testing in a changing world: An introduction. In J. Sandoval, C. L. Frisby, K. F. Geisinger, J. D. Scheuneman, & J. R. Grenier (Eds.), *Test interpretation and diversity* (pp. 3–17). Washington, DC: American Psychological Association.

Sandoval, J. (1998b). Test interpretation in a diverse future. In J. Sandoval, C. L. Frisby, K. F. Geisinger, J. D. Scheuneman, & J. R. Grenier (Eds.), *Test interpretation and diversity* (pp. 387–403). Washington, DC: American Psychological Association.

Sanguiliano, I. (1978). *In her time.* New York: Morrow.

Sastre, M. T. M., & Mullet, E. (1992). Occupational preferences of Spanish adolescents in relation to Gottfredson's theory. *Journal of Vocational Behavior, 40,* 306–317.

Saunders, L. (1995). Relative earnings of black and white men by region, industry. *Monthly Labor Review, 118*(4), 68–73.

Savickas, M. L. (1989). Career-style assessment and counseling. In T. Sweeney (Ed.), *Adelerian counseling: A practical approach for a new decade* (3rd ed., pp. 289–320). Muncie, IN: Accelerated Development Press.

Savickas, M. L. (1990). The use of career choice measures in counseling practice. In E. Watkins & V. Campbell (Eds.), *Testing in counseling practice* (pp. 373–417). Hillsdale, NJ: Erlbaum.

Savickas, M. L. (1993). Career counseling in the postmodern era. *Journal of Cognitive Psychotherapy: An International Quarterly, 7,* 205–215.

Savickas, M. L. (2002). Career construction: A developmental theory. In D. Brown & Associates (Eds.), *Career choice and development* (4th ed., pp. 149–206). San Francisco: Jossey-Bass.

Savickas, M. L., & Hartung, P. J. (1996). The career development inventory in review: Psychometric and research findings. *Journal of Career Assessment, 4,* 171–188.

Savickas, M. L., & Walsh, W. B. (Eds.). (1996). *Handbook of career counseling theory and practice.* Palo Alto, CA: Davies-Black.

Scandura, T. A. (2002). The establishment years: A dependence perspective. In D. C. Feldman (Ed.), *Work careers: A developmental perspective* (pp. 159–186). San Francisco: Jossey-Bass.

Scarr, S., Phillips, D., & McCartney, K. (1989). Working mothers and their families. *American Psychologist, 44,* 1402–1409.

Schafer, W. (2000). *Stress management for wellness.* Belmont, CA: Wadsworth/Thomson Learning.

Scheid, T. (2005). Stigma as a barrier to employment: Mental disability and the American with Disabilities Act. *International Journal of Laws and Psychiatry, 28,* 670–690.

Schien, E. H. (1990). *Career anchors: Discovering your real values.* San Diego, CA: University Associates.

Schultheiss, D. O. (2000). Emotional-social issues in the provision of career counseling. In D. S. Luzzo (Ed.), *Career counseling of college students* (pp. 43–63). Washington, DC: American Psychological Association.

Schultz, D. P., & Schultz, S.E. (2005). *Theories of personality* (8th ed.). Belmont, CA: Wadsworth Cengage Learning.

Schultz, D., & Schultz, S. (2013). *Theories of personality* (10th ed.). Belmont, CA: Wadsworth Cengage Learning.

Schunk, D. H. (1995). Self-efficacy and education and instruction. In J. E. Maddux (Ed.), *Self-efficacy, adaptation, and adjustment: Theory, research, and application* (pp. 281–303). New York: Plenum.

Schwartz, R. D., & Harstein, N. B. (1986). Group psychotherapy with gay men: Theoretical and clinical considerations. In T. Stein & C. J. Cohen (Eds.), *Perspectives on psychotherapy with lesbian and gay men* (pp. 157–177). New York: Plenum.

Sciarra, D. T. (2004). *School counseling: Foundations and contemporary issues.* Belmont, CA: Brooks/Cole-Thomson Learning.

Sears, T., & Mallory, C. (2011). "Evidence of Employment Discrimination on the Basis of Sexual Orientation in State and Local Government: Complaints filed with the State Enforcement Agencies 2003–2007." Williams Institute. Available at http://www3.law.ucla.edu/

Seligman, M. E. (2011). *Flourish: A visionary new understanding of happiness and well-being.* New York: Free Press.

Sexton, T. L., Whiston, S. C., Bleuer, J. C., & Walz, G. R. (1997). *Integrating outcome research into counseling practice and training.* Alexandria, VA: American Counseling Association.

Shaffer, D. R. (1999). *Developmental psychology: Childhood and adolescence* (5th ed.). Pacific Grove, CA: Brooks/Cole.

Shaffer, D. R. (2002). *Developmental psychology: Childhood & adolescence* (6th ed.). Belmont, CA: Wadsworth/Thomson Learning.

Shaffer, D., & Kipp, K. (2014). *Developmental Psychology: Childhood and adolescence* (9th ed.). Belmont, CA: Wadsworth Cengage Learning.

Sharf, R. S. (2010). *Applying career development theory to counseling* (5th ed.). Belmont, CA: Brooks Cole Cengage Learning.

Sharf, R. S. (2013) *Applying career development theory to counseling* (6th ed.) Belmont, DA: Brooks Cole Cengage Learning.

Shelton, B. A., & John, D. (1993). Ethnicity, race, and difference: A comparison of white, black, and Hispanic men's household labor time. In J. C. Hood (Ed.), *Men, work and family* (pp. 131–150). Newbury Park, CA: Sage.

Shierholz, H. (2011) September 7). "The U.S. Doesn't lack the Right Workers, It Lacks Work." The Economy Policy Blog. Available at http://www.epi.orp.

Shmotkin, D. (2005). Happiness in the face of adversity: Reformulating the dynamic and modular bases of subjective well-being. *Review of General Psychology, 9*(4), 291–325.

Shostak, A. B. (1980). *Blue-collar stress.* Reading, MA: Addison-Wesley.

Shotter, J. (1993). *Conversational realities: Constructing life through language.* Newbury Park, CA: Sage.

Shulman, B. (2003). *The betrayal of work: How low-wage jobs fail 30 million Americans.* New York: New Press.

Shulman, L. (1999). *The skills of helping individuals, families, groups, and communities.* Itasca, IL: F. E. Peacock.

Siegler, R. S., & Alibali, M. W. (2005). *Children's thinking* (4th ed.). Upper Saddle River, NJ: Prentice-Hall.

Sigelman, C. K., & Rider, E. A. (2003). *Life-span human development* (4th ed.). Belmont, CA: Wadsworth/Thomson Learning.

Sigelman, C. K., & Rider, S. E. (2009) *Life-span development* (6th ed.). Belmont, CA: Brooks Cole Cengage Learning.

Sigelman, C. K., & Shaffer, D. R. (1995). *Life-span human development* (2nd ed.). Pacific Grove, CA: Brooks/Cole.

Signorile, M. (1993). *Queer in America: Sex, media, and the closets of power.* New York: Random House.

Silberstein, L. R. (1992). *Dual-career marriage: A system in transition.* Hillsdale, NJ: Erlbaum.

Simmons, R. G., & Blyth, D. A. (1987). *Moving into adolescence: The impact of pubertal change and school context.* New York: Aldine De Gruyter.

Simon, S. B., Howe, L. W., & Kirschenbaum, H. (1972). *Value clarification.* New York: Hart.

Skovholt, T. M. (1990). Career themes in counseling and psychotherapy with men. In D. Moore & F. Leafgren (Eds.), *Men in conflict* (pp. 39–56). Alexandria, VA: American Association for Counseling and Development.

Skovholt, T. M., Morgan, J. I., & Negron-Cunningam, H. (1989). Mental imagery in career counseling and life planning: A review of research and intervention methods. *Journal of Counseling and Development 67,* 287–292.

Slattery, J. M. (2004). *Counseling diverse clients: Bringing context into therapy.* Belmont, CA: Brooks/Cole-Thomson Learning.

Slavin, R. E. (2012). *Educational psychology: Theory and practice* (10th ed.). Upper Saddle River, NJ: Pearson.

Smith, A. (1997). Cultural diversity and the coming-out process: Implications for clinical practice. In B. Greene (Ed.), *Ethnic and cultural diversity among lesbians and gay men.* New York: Guilford Press.

Smith, P. L., & Fouad, N. A. (1999). Subject-matter specificity of self-efficacy, outcomes, expectations, interests, and goals: Implications for the social-cognitive model. *Journal of Counseling Psychology, 44,* 173–183.

Solomon, K. (1982). The masculine gender role: Description. In K. Solomon & N. B. Levy (Eds.), *Men in transition.* New York: Plenum.

Somerville, H. (2014, January 13). Virtual reality changing real-life shopping. San Antonio Express-News, B 1, 5.

Sophie, J. (1986). A critical examination of stage theories of lesbian identity development. *Journal of Homosexuality, 12*(2), 39–51.

Sorapuru, J., Theodore, R., & Young, W. (1972a). Financial facts of life. In J. E. Bottoms, R. N. Evans, K. B. Hoyt, & J. C. Willer (Eds.), *Career education resource guide* (pp. 218–220). Morristown, NJ: General Learning Corporation.

Sorapuru, J., Theodore, R., & Young, W. (1972b). Job hunting. In J. E. Bottoms, R. N. Evans, K. B. Hoyt, & J. C. Willer (Eds.), *Career education resource guide* (pp. 236–237). Morristown, NJ: General Learning Corporation.

Spearman, C. (1927). *The abilities of man.* New York: Macmillan.

Speight, S. L., Myers, L. J., Cox, C. I., & Highlen, P. S. (1991). A redefinition of multicultural counseling. *Journal of Counseling and Development, 70,* 29–35.

Spence, J. T. (1999). Thirty years of gender research: A personal chronicle. In W. B. Swann, J. H. Langlois, & L. A. Gilbert (Eds.), *Sexism and stereotypes in modern society* (pp. 255–290). Washington, DC: American Psychological Association.

Spencer, A. L. (1982). *Seasons.* New York: Paulist.

Splete, H., Elliott, B. J., & Borders, L. D. (1985). *Computer-assisted career guidance systems and career counseling services.* Unpublished manuscript, Oakland University, Adult Career Counseling Center, Rochester, MI.

Spokane, A. R. (1985). A review of research on person-environment congruence in Holland's theory of careers [Monograph]. *Journal of Vocational Behavior, 26,* 306–343.

Spokane, A. R. (1989). Are their psychological and mental health consequences of difficult career decisions? A reaction to Herr. *Journal of Career Counseling, 16,* 19–24.

Spokane, A. R. (1991). *Career intervention.* Englewood Cliffs, NJ: Prentice-Hall.

Spokane, A. R. (1996). Holland's theory. In D. Brown, L. Brooks, & Associates (Eds.), *Career choice and development* (3rd ed., pp. 33–69). San Francisco: Jossey-Bass.

Spokane, A. R., & Holland, J. L. (1995). The self-directed search: A family of self-guided career interventions. *Journal of Career Assessment, 3,* 373–390.

Spokane, A. R., Luchetta, E. J., & Richwine, M. H. (2002). Holland's theory of personalities. In D. Brown & Associates (Eds.), *Career choice and development* (4th ed., pp. 373–427). San Francisco: Jossey-Bass.

Stamps, D. (1999). Enterprise training: This changes everything. *Training, 36,* 40–48.

Steele-Johnson, D., & Hyde, B. G. (1997). Advanced technologies in training: Intelligent tutoring system and virtual reality. In J. K. Ford & Associates (Eds.), *Improving the effectiveness in work organizations.* Mahwah, NJ: LEA.

Steidl, R. (1972). Financial facts of life. In J. E. Bottoms, R. N. Evans, K. B. Hout, & J. C. Willer (Eds.), *Career education resource guide* (pp. 218–220). Morristown, NJ: General Learning Corporation.

Stephens, G. K., & Feldman, D. C. (1997). A motivational approach for understanding work versus personal life investments. *Research in Personnel and Human Resource Management, 15,* 333–378.

Stephenson, W. (1949). *Testing school children.* New York: Longmans, Green.

Sterns, H. L., & Subich, L. M. (2002). Career development in midcareer. In D. C. Feldman (Ed.), *Work career: A developmental perspective* (pp. 186–214). San Francisco: Jossey-Bass.

Stoltz-Loike, M. (1992). *Dual-career couples: New perspectives in counseling.* Alexandria, VA: American Association for Counseling and Development.

Strong, E. K. (1983). *Vocational interest blank for men.* Stanford, CA: Stanford University Press.

Strong, E. K., Hansen, J., & Campbell, D. P. (1994). *Strong interest inventory.* Palo Alto, CA: Consulting Psychologists Press.

Strube, M. J. (Ed.). (1991). *Type A behavior.* Newbury Park, CA: Sage.

Sturdivant, S. (1980). *Therapy and women.* New York: Springer.

Subich, L. M. (1996). Addressing diversity in the process of career assessment. In M. L. Savickas & W. B. Walsh (Eds.), *Handbook of career counseling theory and practice* (pp. 277–291). Palo Alto, CA: Davies-Black.

Substance Abuse and Mental Health Services Administration, Office of Applied Studies. (2007). *The NSDUH report: Worker substance abuse by industry.* Washington, DC: Author.

Suchet, M., & Barling, J. (1985). Employed mothers: Interrole conflict, spouse support, and marital functioning. *Journal of Occupational Behavior, 7,* 167–178.

Sue, D. (1998). The interplay of sociocultural factors on the psychological development of Asians in America. In D. R. Atkinson, G. Morten, & D. W. Sue (Eds.), *Counseling American minorities* (5th ed., pp. 205–213). Boston: McGraw-Hill.

Sue, D. W. (1978). Counseling across cultures. *Personnel and Guidance Journal, 56,* 451.

Sue, D. W. (1981). *Counseling the culturally different.* New York: Wiley.

Sue, D. W. (1994). Asian American mental health and help-seeking behavior: Comment on Solberg et al. (1994), Tata & Leong (1994), and Lin (1994). *Journal of Counseling Psychology, 41,* 292–295.

Sue, D. W., Arredondo, A., & McDavis, R. J. (1992). Multicultural counseling competencies and standards: A call to the profession. *Journal of Counseling and Development, 70,* 477–486.

Sue, D. W., Ivey, A. E., & Pedersen, P. B. (1996). *A theory of multicultural counseling and therapy.* Pacific Grove, CA: Brooks/Cole.

Sue, D. W., & Sue, D. (1990). *Counseling the culturally different: Theory and practice* (2nd ed.). New York: Wiley.

Sue, D. W., & Sue, D. (2003). *Counseling the culturally diverse: Theory and practice* (4th ed.). New York: Wiley.

Sue, D., Sue, D. W., Sue, D., & Sue, S. (2014). *Essentials of understanding abnormal behavior* (2nd ed.). Belmont, CA: Wadsworth Cengage Learning.

Sue, S., & Okazaki, S. (1990). Asian American educational achievements: A phenomenon in search of an explanation. *American Psychologist, 45*(8), 913–920.

Sulsky, L., & Smith, C. (2005). *Work stress.* Belmont, CA: Thomson Wadsworth.

Suomi, S. J. (2000). A behavioral perspective on developmental psychopathology. In A. J. Sameroff, J. Lewis, & S. M. Miller, *Handbook on developmental psychopathology* (pp. 237–256). New York: Kluwer Academic/Plenum.

Super, D. E. (1949). *Appraising vocational fitness.* New York: Harper & Brothers.

Super, D. E. (1957). *The psychology of careers.* New York: Harper & Row.

Super, D. E. (1970). *The work values inventory.* Boston: Houghton Mifflin.

Super, D. E. (1972). Vocational development theory: Persons, positions, and processes. In J. M. Whiteley & A. Resnikoff (Eds.), *Perspectives on vocational development* (pp. 17–31). Washington, DC: American Personnel and Guidance Association.

Super, D. E. (1974). *Measuring vocational maturity for counseling and evaluation.* Washington, DC: National Vocational Guidance Association.

Super, D. E. (1977). Vocational maturity in mid-career. *Vocational Guidance Quarterly, 25,* 297.

Super, D. E. (1980). A life-span, life-space approach to career development. *Journal of Vocational Behavior, 16,* 282–298.

Super, D. E. (1984). Career and life development. In D. Brown & L. Brooks (Eds.), *Career choice and development* (pp. 197–261). San Francisco: Jossey-Bass.

Super, D. E. (1990). A life-span, life-space approach to career development. In D. Brown, L. Brooks, & Associates (Eds.), *Career choice and development: Applying contemporary theories to practice* (2nd ed., pp. 197–261). San Francisco: Jossey-Bass.

Super, D. E. (1993). The two faces of counseling: Or is it three? *Career Development Quarterly, 42,* 132–136.

Super, D. E., Bohn, M. I., Forrest, J. J., Jordaan, J. P., Lindeman, R. H., & Thompson, A. A. (1971). *Career development inventory.* New York: Teachers College, Columbia University.

Super, D. E., & Overstreet, P. L. (1960). *The vocational maturity of ninth-grade boys.* New York: Teachers College, Columbia University.

Super, D. E., Savickas, M. L., & Super, C. M. (1996). The life-span, life-space approach to careers. In D. Brown, L. Brooks, & Associates (Eds.), *Career choice and development* (3rd ed., pp. 121–170). San Francisco: Jossey-Bass.

Super, D. E., Starishesky, R., Matlin, N., & Jordaan, J. P. (1963). *Career development: Self-concept theory.* New York: College Entrance Examination Board.

Super, D. E., Thompson, A. S., & Lindeman, R. H. (1988). *Adult career concerns inventory: Manual for research and exploratory use in counseling.* Palo Alto, CA: Consulting Psychologists Press.

Super, D. E, Thompson, R. H., Lindenman, Jordan, J. P., & Myers, R. A. (1988). *Career development inventory.* Palo Alto, CA: Consulting Psychologists Press.

Suro, R. (1998). *Strangers among us: How Latino immigration is transforming America.* New York: Knopf.

Swanson, J. L. (1992). Vocational behavior, 1989–1991: Life-span career development and reciprocal interaction of work and nonwork. *Journal of Vocational Behavior, 41,* 101–161.

Swanson, J. L. (1996). The theory is the practice: Trait-and-factor/person-environment. In M. L. Savickas & W. B. Walsh (Eds.), *Handbook of career counseling theory and practice* (pp. 93–109). Palo Alto, CA: Davies-Black.

Swanson, J. L., & Fouad, N. A. (2010). *Career theory and practice: Learning through case studies* (2nd ed.). Thousand Oaks, CA: Sage Publications.

Tafoya, T. (1997). Native gay and lesbian issues: The two-spirited. In B. Greene (Ed.), *Ethnic and cultural diversity among lesbians and gay men* (pp. 1–10). Thousand Oaks, CA: Sage.

Tang, M., Fouad, N. A., & Smith, P. L. (1999). Asian Americans' career choices: A path model to examine factors influencing their career choices. *Journal of Vocational Behavior, 54,* 142–157.

Telljohann, S. K., & Price, J. H. (1993). A qualitative examination of adolescents homosexuals' life experiences: Ramifications for secondary school personnel. *Journal of Homosexuality, 26*(1), 41–56.

Thomas, K. R., & Butler, A. J. (1981). Counseling for personal adjustment. In R. M. Parker & C. E. Hansen (Eds.), *Rehabilitation counseling* (pp. 37–56). Boston: Allyn & Bacon.

Thomason, T. C. (1991). Counseling Native Americans: An introduction for non-Native American counselors. *Journal of Counseling & Development, 69,* 321–327.

Thomason, T. C. (2000). Issues in the treatment of Native Americans with alcohol problems. *Journal of Multicultural Counseling and Development, 28*(4), 243–252.

Thompson, A. S., Lindeman, R. H., Super, D. E., Jordaan, J. P., & Myers, R. A. (1984). *Career development inventory: Technical manual.* Palo Alto, CA: Consulting Psychologists Press.

Thompson, C. L., & Rudolph, L. B. (2000). *Counseling children* (5th ed.). Belmont, CA: Wadsworth.

Thompson, C. L., Rudolph, L. B., & Henderson, D. (2004). *Counseling children* (6th ed.). Belmont, CA: Brooks/Cole-Thomson Learning.

Thompson, E. H., Grisanti, C., & Pleck, J. H. (1987). Attitudes toward the male role and their correlates. *Sex Roles, 13,* 413–427.

Tiedeman, D. V., & O'Hara, R. P. (1963). *Career development: Choice and adjustment.* Princeton, NJ: College Entrance Examination Board.

Tinsley, H. E. A. (2000). The myth of congruence. *Journal of Vocational Behavior, 40,* 109–110.

Tischler, H. L.(2014) *Introduction to sociology* (11th ed.) Belmont, CA: Wadsworth Cengage Learning.

Tomasko, R. T. (1987). *Downsizing.* New York: American Management Association.

Tower, K. D. (1994). Consumer-centered social work practice: Restoring client self-determination. *Social Work, 41*(1), 191–196.

Triandis, H. C. (1992, February). *Individualism and collectivism as a cultural syndrome.* Paper presented at the Annual Convention of the Society for Cross-Cultural Researchers, Santa Fe, NM.

Triandis, H. C. (1994). *Culture and social behavior.* New York: McGraw-Hill.

Triandis, H. C., Marin, G., Lisansky, J., & Betancourt, H. (1984). Simpatica as a cultural script of Hispanics. *Journal of Personality and Social Psychology, 47,* 1363–1375.

Trimble, J. E., & LaFromboise, T. (1985). American Indians and the counseling process: Culture, adaptation, and style. In P. Pedersen (Ed.), *Handbook of cross-cultural counseling and therapy* (pp. 125–134). Westport, CT: Greenwood.

Trower, P., Casey, A., & Dryden, W. (1988). *Cognitive-behavioral counseling in action.* Newbury Park, CA: Sage.

Trull, T., & Prinstein, M. (2013). *Clinical psychology* (8th ed.). Belmont, CA: Wadsworth Cengage Learning.

Uchitelle, L., & Kleinfield, N. R. (1996). The price of jobs lost. In *New York Times* (et al.), *The downsizing of America* (pp. 3–36). New York: Time Books.

Ulrich, L. B., & Brott, P. E. (2005). Older workers and bridge employment. Redefining retirement. *Journal of Employment Counseling, 42,* 159–170.

Unger, R. K. (Ed.). (2000). *Handbook of the psychology of women and gender.* San Francisco: Jossey-Bass.

Unger, R., & Crawford, M. (1992). *Women and gender: A feminist psychology.* Philadelphia: Temple University Press.

University of Minnesota. (1984). *Minnesota Importance Questionnaire.* Minneapolis: Author.

Uribe, V., & Harbeck, K. M. (1992). Addressing the needs of lesbian, gay, and bisexual youth: The origins of Project 10 and school-based intervention. *Journal of Homosexuality, 22*(3/4), 9–28.

U.S. Bureau of the Census. (1993). *We the Americans: Pacific Islanders in the United States.* Washington, DC: U.S. Government Printing Office.

U.S. Bureau of the Census. (1997). *Statistical abstract of the United States, 1997.* Washington, DC: U.S. Government Printing Office.

U.S. Bureau of the Census. (1999). *Current population survey, racial statistics branch, population division.* Washington, DC: U.S. Government Printing Office.

U.S. Bureau of the Census. (2000a). *Current population, racial statistics branch, population division.* Washington, DC: U.S. Government Printing Office.

U.S. Bureau of the Census. (2000b). *Poverty rate lowest in 20 years, household income at record high, Census Bureau reports.* Washington, DC: U.S. Government Printing Office.

U.S. Bureau of the Census, Bureau of Labor Statistics. (2002). *Occupational outlook handbook, 1997–1998 Edition.* Washington, DC: U.S. Government Printing Office.

U.S. Bureau of the Census (2011). *Labor Statistics; Abstract of the United States, 2010* (126th ed.). Washington, DC: U.S. Government Printing Office.

U.S. Bureau of the Census (2012). *Current Populations Survey. 1960 to 2011 annual social and income supplements.* Washington, DC: U. S. Government Printing Office.

U.S. Department of Commerce, Bureau of Census (1996). *Percentage of population by race: 1990, 2000, 2025, 2050.* Washington, DC: U.S. Government Printing Office.

U.S. Department of Education and U.S. Department of Labor. (1996). *School-to-work opportunities.* Washington, DC: National School-to-Work Office.

U.S. Department of Justice. (1991). *Americans with disabilities handbook.* Washington, DC: U.S. Government Printing Office.

U.S. Department of Labor. (1970a). *Career thresholds.* Washington, DC: U.S. Government Printing Office.

U.S. Department of Labor. (1970b). *Manual for the general aptitude test battery.* Washington, DC: U.S. Government Printing Office.

U.S. Department of Labor. (1992). *Learning for a living: A blueprint for high performance.* Washington, DC: U.S. Government Printing Office.

U. S. Department of Labor (2010). Leading Occupations of Women in 2009. www.dol.gov /wb/factsheets/20lead2009.htm.

Valach, L. (1990). A theory of goal-directed action in career analysis. In R. A. Young & W. A. Borgen (Eds.), *Methodological approaches to the study of career* (pp. 107–126). New York: Praeger.

Van Willigen, M. (2000). Differential benefits of volunteering across the life course. *Journal of Gerontology, 55,* 5308–5318.

Vargo, M. E. (1998). *Acts of disclosure: The coming-out process of contemporary gay men.* New York: Haworth.

Velasquez, J. S., & Lynch, M. M. (1981). Computerized information systems: A practice orientation. *Administration in Social Work, 5*(3/4), 113–127.

von Cranach, M., & Harre, R. (Eds.). (1982). *The analysis of action: Recent theoretical and empirical advances.* Cambridge, UK: Cambridge University Press.

Vondracek, F. W., Lerner, R. M., & Schulenberg, J. E. (1986). *Career development: A life-span developmental approach.* Hillsdale, NJ: Erlbaum.

Vosler, N. R., & Page-Adams, D. (1996). Predictors of depression among workers at the time of a plant closing. *Journal of Sociology and Social Welfare, 23*(4), 25–42.

Wajcman, J. (1998). *Managing like a man: Women and men in corporate management.* University Park: Pennsylvania State University Press.

Walsh, W. B. (1990). A summary and integration of career counseling approaches. In W. B. Walsh & S. H. Osipow (Eds.), *Career counseling: Contemporary topics in vocational psychology* (pp. 263–283). Hillsdale, NJ: Erlbaum.

Walz, A. (1972). Required courses. In J. E. Bottoms, R. N. Evans, K. B. Hoyt, & J. C. Willer (Eds.), *Career education resource guide* (pp. 186–188). Morristown, NJ: General Learning Corporation.

Wanous, J. P. (1980). *Organizational entry.* Reading, MA: Addison-Wesley.

Ward, C. M., & Bingham, R. P. (1993). Career assessment of ethnic minority women. *Journal of Career Assessment, 1,* 246–257.

Ward, C. M., & Tate, G. (1990). *Career counseling checklist.* Atlanta: Georgia State University Counseling Center.

Warr, P. (1992). Age and occupational well-being. *Psychology and Aging, 7,* 37–45.

Warr, P. B. (1987). *Work, employment, and mental health.* Oxford: Clarendon.

Warr, P. B. (2005). Work, well-being, and mental health. In J. Barling, E. K. Kelloway, & M. R. Frone (Eds.), *Handbook of work stress* (pp 547–573). Thousand Oaks, CA: Sage.

Weaver, H. N. (2003). Cultural competence with First Nations Peoples. In D. Lum (Ed.), *Culturally competent practice* (2nd ed., pp. 197–216). Pacific Grove, CA: Brooks/ Cole-Thomson Learning.

Wehrly, B. (1995). *Pathways to multicultural counseling competence.* Pacific Grove, CA: Brooks/Cole.

Weinberg, A., Sutherland, V., & Cooper, C. (2010). *Organizational stress management: A strategic approach*. New York: Palgrave Macmillan.

Weinrach, S. G., & Srebalus, D. J. (1990). Holland's theory of careers. In D. Brown & L. Brooks (Eds.), *Career choice and development: Applying contemporary theories to practice* (2nd ed., pp. 37–67). San Francisco: Jossey-Bass.

Welfel, E. R. (2002). *Ethics counseling psychotherapy* (2nd ed.). Pacific Grove, CA: Brooks/Cole.

Welfel, E. R. (2013. *Ethics counseling and psychotherapy* (5th ed.). Belmont, CA: Brooks/Cole

Wentling, R. M. (1992, Jan./Feb.). Women in middle management: Their career development and aspirations. *Business Horizons*, pp. 48–54.

Werbel, J. D., & Gilliland, S. W. (1999). Person-environment fit in the selection process. *Research in Personnel and Human Resource Management, 17*, 209–243.

Wessel, D. (2011). Big U.S. firms shift hiring abroad. *Wall Street Journal*. April 19:B1.

Westbrook, B. W. (1995). *Cognitive Maturity Test (CVMT)*. Raleigh, NC: Center for Occupational Education, North Carolina State University:

Westermeyer, J. J. (1993). Cross-cultural psychiatric assessment. In A. Gaw (Ed.), *Culture, ethnicity, and mental illness* (pp. 125–144). Washington, DC: American Psychiatric Press.

Whiston, S. C. (2009). *Principles and applications of assessment in counseling* (3rd ed.). Belmont, CA: Brooks/Cole Cengage Learning.

Whiston, S. C. (2013). *Principles and applications of assessment in counseling* (4th ed.). Belmont, CA: Brooks/Cole Cengage Learning.

Whiston, S. C., & Oliver, l. (2005). Career counseling process and outcome. In W. B. Walsh & M. Savickas (Eds.). *Handbook of vocational psychology* (3rd ed., pp. 155–194). Hillsdale, NJ: Erlbaum.

Widiger, T.A., & Trull. T. J. (2007). Plate tectonics in the classification of personality disorders: Shifting to a dimensional model. *American Psychologist, 62*, 71–83.

Wiederhold, B. K., & Wiederhold, M. D. (2005). *Virtual reality therapy for anxiety disorders: Advances in treatment*. Washington, DC: American Psychological Association.

Wiinamaki, M. K. (1988). *My vocational experience*. Unpublished manuscript, Southwest Texas State University, San Marcos.

Wilcox-Matthew, L., & Minor, C. W. (1989). The dual career couple: Concerns, benefits, and counseling implications. *Journal of Counseling and Development, 68*, 194–198.

Williams, J. M., & Currie, C. (2000). Self-esteem and physical development in early adolescence: Pubertal timing and body image. *Journal of Early Adolescence, 20*, 129–149.

Williams, T., Connolly J., Pepler, D., & Craig, W. (2005). Peer victimization, social support, and psychosocial adjustment of sexual minority adolescents. *Journal of Youth and Adolescence, 34*, 471–482.

Williams, W. L. (1993). Persistence and change in the berdache tradition among contemporary Lakota Indians. In L. D. Garnets & D. C. Kimmel (Eds.), *Psychological perspectives on lesbian and gay male experiences* (pp. 339–348). New York: Columbia University Press.

Williamson, E. G. (1939). *How to counsel students: A manual of techniques for clinical counselors*. New York: McGraw-Hill.

Williamson, E. G. (1949). *Counseling adolescents*. New York: McGraw-Hill.

Williamson, E. G. (1965). *Vocational counseling: Some historical, philosophical, and theoretical perspectives*. New York: McGraw-Hill.

Wilson, J. F. (2003). *Biological foundations of human behavior*. Belmont, CA: Wadsworth Cengage Learning.

Winbush, G. B. (2000). African American women. In M. Julia (Ed.), *Constructing gender: Multicultural perspectives in working with women* (pp. 11–35). Pacific Grove, CA: Brooks/Cole.

Winfeld, L., & Spielman, S. (1995). *Straight talk about gays in workplace.* New York: AMACOM.

Wolpe, J. (1958). *Psychotherapy by reciprocal inhibition.* Palo Alto, CA: Stanford University Press.

Wood, J. T. (1994). *Gendered lives: Communication, gender, and culture.* Belmont, CA: Wadsworth.

Wooden, W. S., Kawasaki, H., & Mayeda, R. (1983). Lifestyles and identity maintenance among gay Japanese-American males. *Alternative Lifestyles, 5*(4), 236–243.

Woods, J. F., & Ollis, H. (1996). *Labor market & job information on the Internet.* Submitted for publication in Winter (March 1996) issue of *Workforce Journal.*

Woody, B. (1992). *Black women in the workplace.* Westport, CT: Greenwood.

Woolfolk, A. (2013). *Educational psychology* (12th ed.). Upper Sadler River, NJ: Pearson.

World Health Organization. (1981). *Current state of diagnosis and classification in the mental health field.* Geneva, Switzerland: Author.

World Health Organization. (1983). *Depression disorders in different cultures: Report of the WHO Collaborative Study of Standardized Assessment of Depression Disorders.* Geneva, Switzerland: Author.

Worthington, R. L., & Juntunen, C. L. (1997). The vocational development of non-college bound youth: Counseling psychology and the school-to-work transition movement. *Counseling Psychologist, 25*, 323–363.

Wrenn, C. G. (1988). The person in career counseling. *Career Development Quarterly, 36*(4), 337–343.

Young, R. A., & Valach, L. (1996). Interpretation and action in career counseling. In M. L. Savickas & W. B. Walsh (Eds.), *Handbook of career counseling theory and practice* (pp. 361–376). Palo Alto, CA: Davies-Black.

Young, R. A., Valach, L., & Collin, A. (1996). A contextual explanation of career. In D. Brown, L. Brooks, & Associates (Eds.), *Career choice and development* (3rd ed., pp. 477–508). San Francisco: Jossey-Bass.

Young, R. A., Valach, L., & Collin, A. (2002). A contextual explanation of career. In D. Brown & Associates (Eds.), *Career choice and development* (4th ed., pp. 206–255). San Francisco: Jossey-Bass.

Zaccaria, J. (1970). *Theories of occupational choice and vocational development.* Boston: Houghton Mifflin.

Zaharlick, A. (2000). South Asian-American women. In M. Julia (Ed.), *Constructing gender: Multicultural perspectives in working with women* (pp. 177–205). Pacific Grove, CA: Brooks/Cole.

Zajonc, R. B. (1980). Feeling and thinking: Preferences need no influence. *American Psychologist, 35*, 151–176.

Zastrow, C., & Kirst-Ashman, K. (2013). *Understanding human behavior and the social environment* (10th ed.). Belmont, CA: Brooks/Cole Cengage Learning.

Zielinski, D. (2010). Training games: Simulations teach employees under real-life conditions-without real-world consequences. *HR magazine, 55*(3), 29–36.

Zimmerman, B. J. (1995). Self-efficacy and educational development. In A. Bandura (Ed.), *Self-efficacy in changing societies* (pp. 72–85). Cambridge: Cambridge University Press.

Zmud, R. W., Sampson, J. P., Reardon, R. C., Lenz, J. G., & Byrd, T. A. (1994). Confounding effects of construct overlap. An example from IS user satisfaction theory. *Information Technology and People, 7,* 29–45.

Zuniga, M. E. (2003). Cultural competence with Latino Americans. In D. Lum (Ed.), *Culturally competent practice* (2nd ed., pp. 238–261). Pacific Grove, CA: Brooks/Cole-Thomson Learning.

Zunker, V. G. (2008), *Career, work and mental health.* Thousand Oaks, CA: Sage Publications.

Zunker, V. G., & Brown, W. F. (1966). Comparative effectiveness of student and professional counselors. *Personnel and Guidance Journal, 44,* 733–743.

Zunker, V. G., & Osborn, D. (2002). *Using assessment results for career development* (6th ed.). Pacific Grove, CA: Brooks/Cole.

Zytowski, D. G. (1969). Toward a theory of career development for women. *Personnel and Guidance Journal, 47,* 660–664.

Zytowski, D. G. (1994). Tests and counseling: We are still married, and living in discriminant analysis. *Measurement and Evaluation in Counseling and Development, 26,* 219–223.

Name Index

Subject Index